# SPARK TO A WAITING FUSE

# SPARK
## TO A WAITING FUSE

JAMES K. BAXTER'S
CORRESPONDENCE
WITH NOEL GINN
1942–1946

*Edited and Introduced by*

PAUL MILLAR

VICTORIA UNIVERSITY PRESS

VICTORIA UNIVERSITY PRESS
Victoria University of Wellington
PO Box 600, Wellington



ISBN 0 86473 400 X

First published 2001



Published with the assistance of a grant from
creative nz
ARTS COUNCIL OF NEW ZEALAND *TOI AOTEAROA*

Printed by Publishing Press, Auckland

# Contents

# Illustrations

# Acknowledgements

Of the many people that played a part in this edition, I am most indebted to those who, through their association with James K. Baxter, find that their private lives are no longer private, yet have been prepared to meet the requests of an importunate researcher honestly and graciously. I think of three people in particular: Jacquie Baxter, who, as Baxter's widow and literary executor, has responded with unfailing courtesy to my questions and requests, and has been from the beginning generous with her encouragement; Terence Baxter who allowed me to question him about a painful period in his life, and permitted me to quote material written about him by his brother; and Noel Ginn who dredged back through the years to drag similarly painful memories to the surface, who answered all my questions fully and honestly, and who placed no restrictions on any material written by him (despite blanching at the news that his wartime poetry—long thought destroyed—still exists among Baxter's papers). In addition I must thank John Baxter for his helpful comments, and the wider Baxter family who have spent their lives sharing the precious time of their mother/grandmother/great-grandmother with strangers whose primary interest is in the family's best known poet.

My special thanks goes to Vincent O'Sullivan for the generous sharing of his expertise, and for directing me towards such stimulating fields of research. And to Roger Robinson, who first encouraged me to make my findings about Baxter the focus of my research, and has continued to find the time to respond to any enquiries I might make, and has given unfailingly sound advice and considered criticism. Geoffrey Miles has been a good friend: he has, as is his nature, been generous to a fault with his time and never failed to find the source of a classical quotation. Thanks also to John E.P. Thomson for inviting me to present an early version of my introduction at a Stout Research Centre seminar; the late John M. Thomson for his care in editing my article for the *Stout Centre Review*; and to Peter Whiteford for editing my chapter on Baxter's manuscript notebooks for publication in *Kotare: New Zealand Notes and Queries*. A number of other colleagues associated with Victoria University's School of English, Film and Theatre have helped in ways both large and small, in particular Bill Manhire, David Norton, Harry Orsman, Heidi Thomson and Helen Heazlewood. I would also acknowledge with gratitude the valuable comments of Ken Arvidson and Mac Jackson.

Were it not for certain individuals with the foresight to preserve these manuscripts this edition would never have been possible: credit is therefore due to Noel Ginn, and to the memories of Frank McKay, Lawrence Baigent, and Millicent Baxter. In addition, I must acknowledge the many years of research done by Father J.E. Weir that have made my work less difficult—as I dip into the sea of material written by James K. Baxter I appreciate more fully the magnitude of the task involved in editing Baxter's *Collected Poems.*

I should also like to thank the Librarians of the two libraries holding the bulk of the manuscript material used in this edition: the Hocken, especially Annette Facer and Janine Delaney; and Victoria University, especially Kathleen Coleridge, Vic Elliot, Barbro Harris (who found in an hour a reference that had eluded me for days), Guy Reynolds and Justin Cargill. Thanks also to the National Library (particularly Penny Carpenter for some invaluable suggestions), and to the Alexander Turnbull Library (particularly Joan McCracken).

Thanks again to Vincent O'Sullivan in his role as Frank McKay's executor, Duncan Campbell of Victoria University's Asian Studies Department, Professor Ian A. Gordon, David Grant, Les Maiden and the staff of VUW Photographic Services, Noel Ginn's nephew Peter Manins, and to Irene Miles for her tremendous hospitality at times when I visited Dunedin.

Particular thanks goes to my excellent, and highly professional research assistant Charlotte Elder. Thanks also to Victoria University for awarding me a VUW Postgraduate Scholarship, and to VUW's Internal Grants Committee and the Research Committee of the Faculty of Humanities and Social Sciences for the provision of a number of grants that were essential to the completion of this project. The book was finally completed while on a teaching exchange: thanks therefore to the Fulbright Foundation, the VUW FHSS Leave Committee, and the English Department of the University of Hawai'i at Manoa—mahalo!

Finally, I owe much to members of family. My parents Enid and Graham Millar have assisted as always—particularly my father, who in this and other books has been a friend and sounding board going beyond the call of duty as my right arm in Wellington, scouring manuscripts and answering endless questions while I was overseas. And to those who lived with the project, thank you to my wife Kay and my small sons Aaron and Gareth.

# A Note on the Text

The principle of this edition is to present a text that is not only a faithful transcription of the manuscript material on which it is based, but one that conveys a sense of Baxter's side of the correspondence as it would originally have been sent. Hence Baxter's poems are interspersed between letters to replicate as nearly as possible the sequence in which they are discussed. Very occasionally I place a poem where I consider that it will most enhance the coherence of the correspondence (for example in the case of the ode 'Where nets of time . . .' on p.282, which is inserted prior to the letter containing Baxter's notes on the poem).

This edition has been compiled from a number of sources: Baxter's letters to Noel Ginn are held in the Victoria University of Wellington Library among the Baxter papers deposited by Dr. Frank McKay (box 'MS McKay 28'); Ginn's letters to Baxter (and the letter from Myrtle Ginn) are in the Hocken Library among a number of letters grouped as MS 975/183; Ginn's poems, other than those contained in his letters, are based on the transcriptions made by Baxter into a small hard-cover notebook also held in the Hocken Library (MS 975/30); the bulk of Baxter's poems (other than those already in the text of letters) have been transcribed from two primary sources: firstly, from a large number of loose copies that were in Ginn's possession and have now been deposited in the Hocken (MS 89/148) and secondly, when a poem is not among these papers, from Baxter's notebooks (MS Books) I to XIV.

To reference the poems transcribed from Baxter's first fourteen MS Books I use the following system: (i) Hocken reference, (ii) sequential number, and, (iii) MS book page number. For example, I designate the poem 'In Barley-Fields' (see p.190) as '[Hocken, MS 704/7:451, pp.129–30]': 'MS 704/7' is the Hocken reference number, it indicates that this is notebook seven at reference MS 704 (an item described in the Hocken Library's preliminary inventory of the Baxter collection as 'Manuscript notebooks—fair copies. Volumes I-XXVIII. 1937–67.'); '451' refers to Baxter's own sequential numbering of his poems which runs through his first fourteen MS Books; and 'pp.129–30' refers to the pages in MS Book VII where 'In Barley-Fields' is drafted. For further detail see my discussion of Baxter's early MS Books on pages 72–81.

Both Baxter and Ginn were reasonably consistent in matters of spelling and punctuation and I have transcribed the manuscripts as accurately as possible, although, with the variety of primary sources, I have not attempted to indicate pagination (however Baxter's occasional use of 'PTO' is recorded). The occasional, uncharacteristic, slip of the pen by either correspondent has been silently amended but their idiosyncrasies remain (such as Ginn's use of the ampersand and Baxter's spelling of 'Elizabethean').

The most notable feature of Baxter's letters is the deliberate variation of his handwriting to indicate words that are italicised. This example, referring to the books *The Possessed* and *Bank Holiday on Parnassus*, is from his letter of 23 Jun 1945 (see p.407):

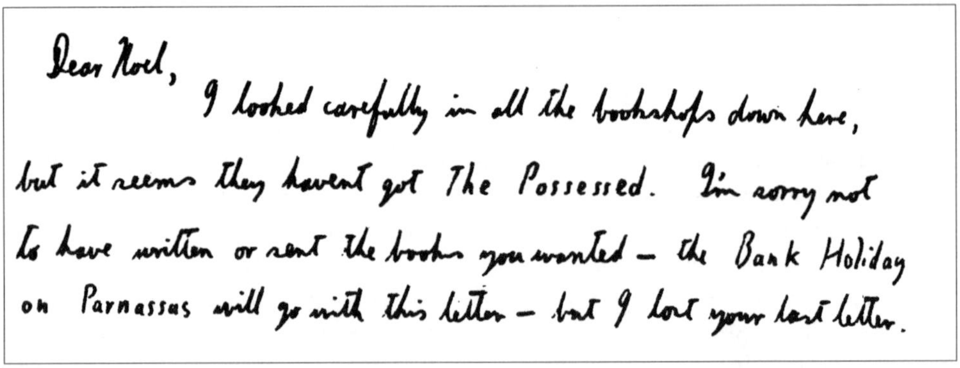
Dear Noel,
I looked carefully in all the bookshops down here, but it seems they havent got The Possessed. I'm sorry not to have written or sent the books you wanted – the Bank Holiday on Parnassus will go with this letter – but I lost your last letter.

However, Baxter does not limit his 'italic' hand to passages conventionally italicised, occasionally he writes an entire poem or section of a letter in it. I have not, therefore, treated everything written in this fashion as an italicised passage, but have applied the standard conventions concerning titles and foreign words, and only occasionally followed his 'italics' elsewhere, for example to indicate a quotation within a wider passage in Roman script.

Because the majority of the letters in and out of the detention camps were censored, I have indicated which letters, and the number of the censor, by inserting a scan of an appropriate censor stamp beneath each letter's heading. These scans are representative only, as not all letters have been stamped clearly enough to provide a legible copy of each unique image.

Occasionally I make a comment, or insert a poem title, in the body of the text. In these instances anything supplied by me is enclosed in square brackets.

Words crossed out in manuscripts are also crossed out in this edition:
~~as this example indicates~~.

Words, or passages, that are not entirely legible are enclosed in square brackets and prefaced with a question mark: [?as this example indicates]

**Abbreviations**

*BTP* James K. Baxter, *Beyond the Palisade* (Christchurch: Caxton, 1944)
*BWF* James K. Baxter, *Blow, Wind of Fruitfulness* (Christchurch: Caxton, 1948)
*CP* James K. Baxter, *Collected Poems*, ed by J.E. Weir (Wellington: Oxford University Press, 1981)
*Life* Frank McKay, *The Life of James K. Baxter*, (Auckland: Oxford University Press, 1990)

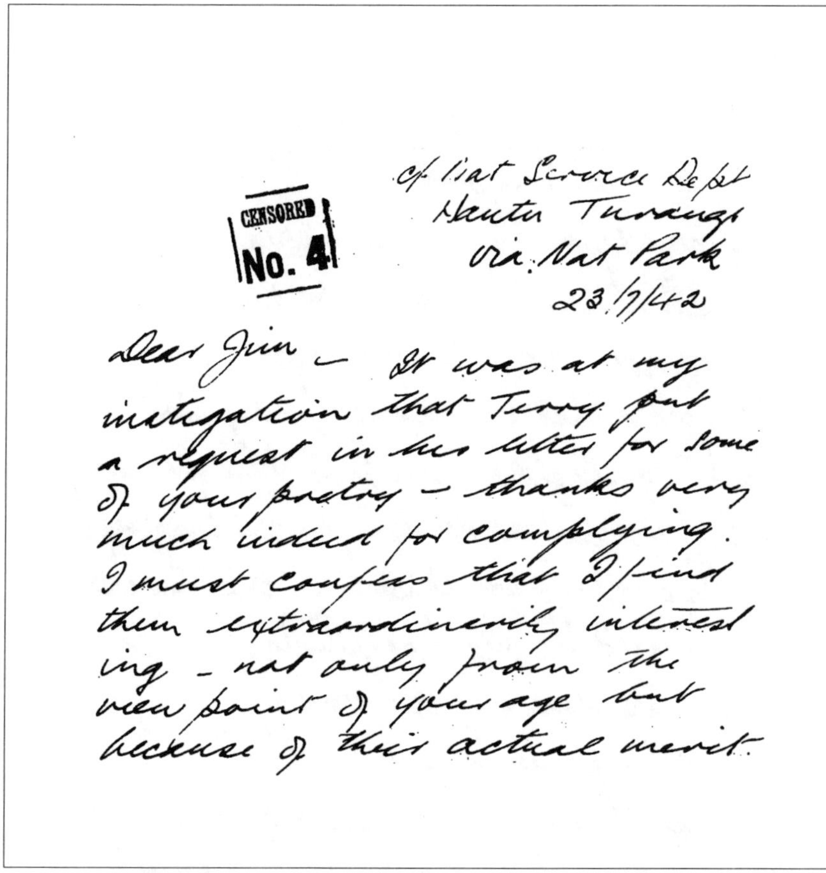

CENSORED No. 4

c/- Nat Service Dept
Hautu Turangi
via Nat Park
23/7/42

Dear Jim — It was at my instigation that Terry put a request in her letter for some of your poetry — thanks very much indeed for complying. I must confess that I find them extraordinarily interesting — not only from the view point of your age but because of their actual merit.

Above: The opening sentences of Noel Ginn's first letter to James K. Baxter.

Below: The opening sentences of James K. Baxter's first letter to Noel Ginn.

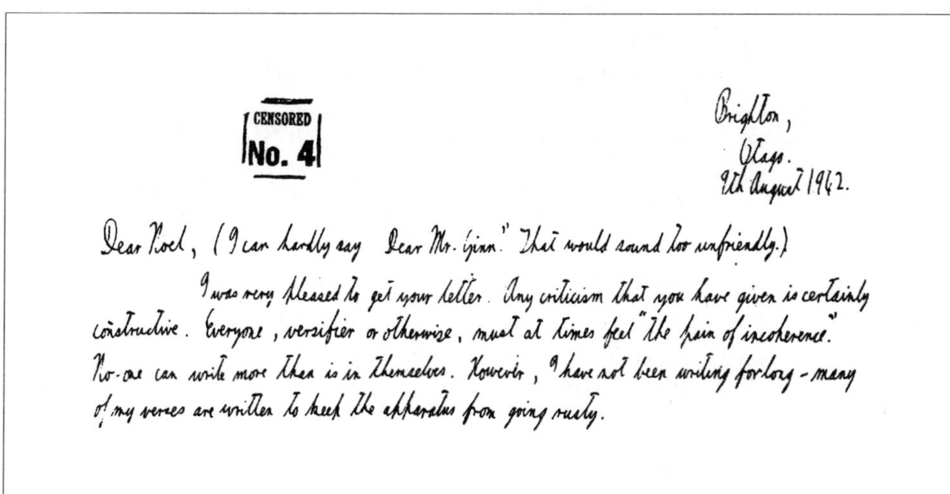

CENSORED No. 4

Brighton,
Otago.
9th August 1942.

Dear Noel, (I can hardly say "Dear Mr. Ginn." That would sound too unfriendly.)

I was very pleased to get your letter. Any criticism that you have given is certainly constructive. Everyone, versifier or otherwise, must at times feel "the pain of incoherence." No-one can write more than is in themselves. However, I have not been writing for long — many of my verses are written to keep the apparatus from going rusty.

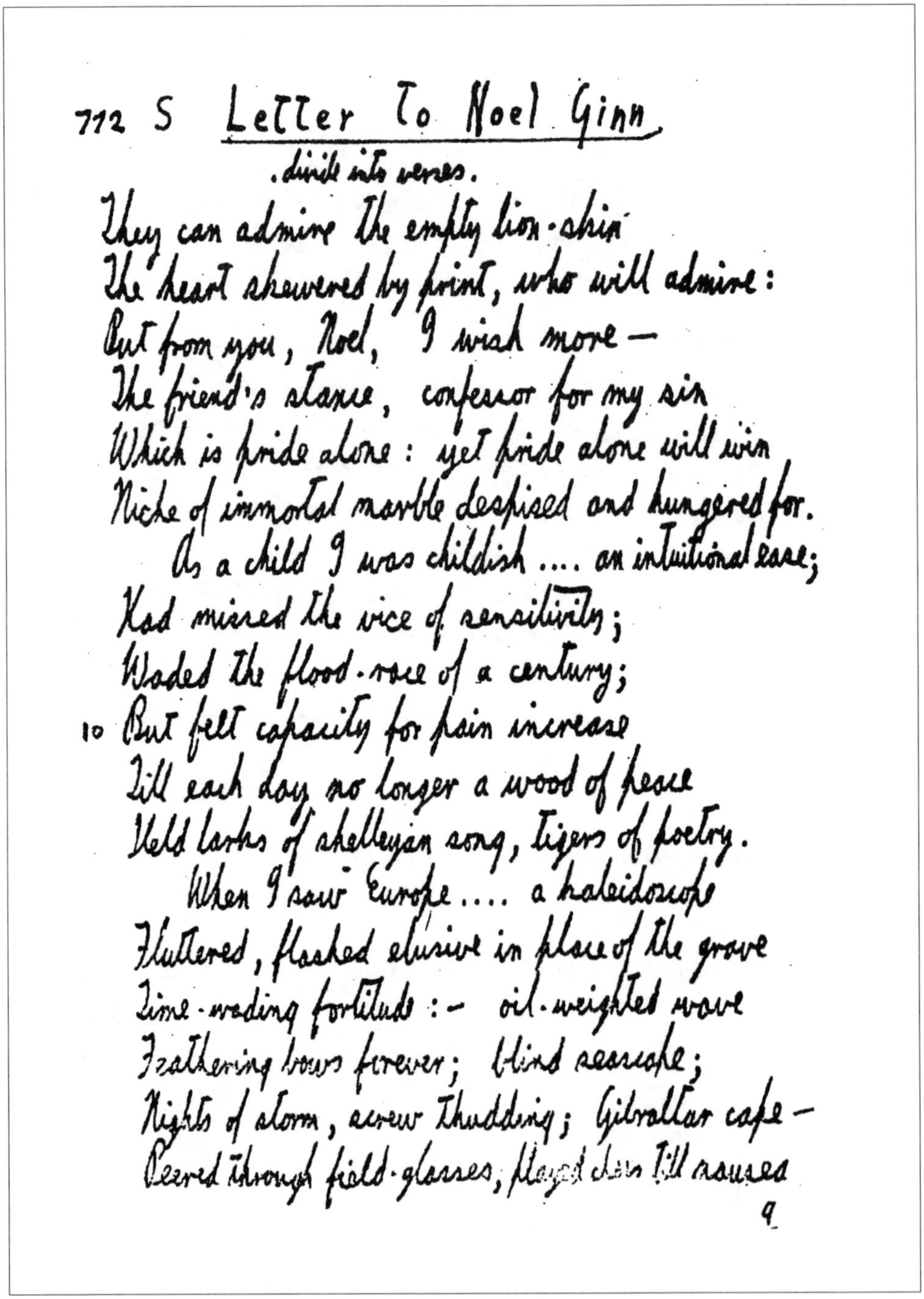

712 S Letter to Noel Ginn

. divide into verses.

They can admire the empty lion-skin
The heart skewered by print, who will admire:
But from you, Noel, I wish more —
The friend's stance, confessor for my sin
Which is pride alone: yet pride alone will win
Niche of immortal marble despised and hungered for.
As a child I was childish .... an intuitional ease;
Had missed the vice of sensitivity;
Waded the flood-race of a century;
But felt capacity for pain increase
Till each day no longer a wood of peace
Held larks of shelleyan song, tigers of poetry.
When I saw Europe .... a kaleidoscope
Fluttered, flashed elusive in place of the grave
Time-wading fortitude :— oil-weighted wave
Feathering bows forever; blind seascape;
Nights of storm, screw thudding; Gibraltar cape —
Peered through field-glasses, played chess till nausea

9

The first page of Baxter's notebook draft of 'Letter to Noel Ginn'.
(Hocken Library, MS Notebook XIII.)

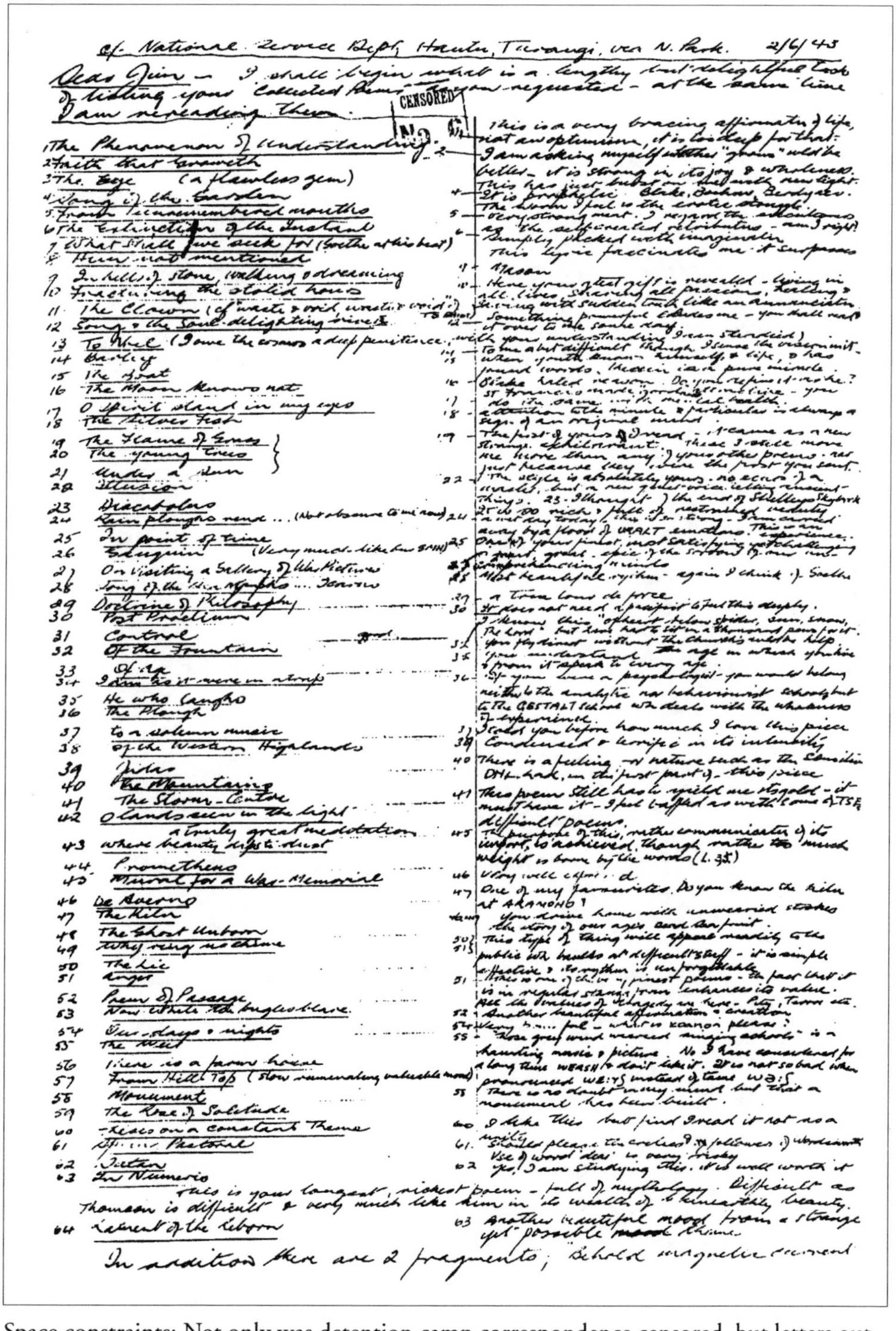

C/- National Service Dept, Hautu, Turangi, via N. Park. 2/6/43

Dear Jim – I shall begin what is a lengthy but delightful task of listing your 'Collected Poems' – as you requested – at the same time I am rereading them.

CENSORED

1 The Phenomenon of Understanding
2 Faith that Groweth
3 The Eye (a flawless gem)
4 Song of the Garden
5 From Unremembered Mouths
6 The Extinction of the Instant
7 What shall we seek for (Goethe at his best)
8 Hum not mentioned
9 In hills of stone, walking & dreaming
10 Fracturing the stolid hours
11 The Clown
12 Song & the Soul-delighting  
13 To Noel
14 Barley
15 The Goat
16 The Moon knows not
17 O Spirit stand in my eyes
18 The Silver Fish
19 The Flame of Eros
20 The young trees
21 Under a sun
22 Illusion
23 Discobolus
24 Rain plunges now
25 In point of time
26 Sanguin
27 On visiting a Gallery of War Pictures
28 Song of the ...
29 Doctrine of Philosophy
30 Post Proelium
31 Control
32 Of the Fountain
33 Of Age
34 ...
35 He who laughs
36 The Plough
37 To a solemn music
38 Of the Western Highlands
39 Judas
40 The Mountains
41 The Storm-Centre
42 Islands seen in the light
43 Where beauty lifts to dust
44 Prometheus
45 Mural for a War-Memorial
46 De Aeorno
47 The Kite
48 The Ghost Unborn
49 Why sing no theme
50 The Lie
51 Anger
52 Poem of Passage
53 Now where the bugles blare
54 Our days & nights
55 The Wait
56 There is a farm house
57 From Hill Top
58 Monument
59 The Rose of Solitude
60 Theses on a Constant Theme
61 ... Pastoral
62 Tristan
63 In Numeris
64 Lament of the Unborn

This is your longest, richest poem – full of mythology. Difficult as Thomson is difficult & very much like him in its wealth of ... beauty.

63 Another beautiful mood from a strange yet possible theme.

In addition there are 2 fragments; Behold ...

Space constraints: Not only was detention camp correspondence censored, but letters out were limited to two sides of a sheet. Hence the congestion of Ginn's letter of 2 June 1943 (reproduced here at 65% of its original size) as he attempts to list the poems received from Baxter thus far.

# I
# TEXTS AND CONTEXTS

One reads the letters of a great poet for various reasons—
not least among them, the hope of discovering some
part of the circumstantial scaffolding of his poems.
James K. Baxter
1954

# One
# Introduction

> They can admire the empty lion-skin
> The heart skewered by print, who will admire:
> But from you, Noel, I wish more—
> 'Letter to Noel Ginn'

James K. Baxter may have died in 1972, but he captures the imagination of New Zealanders in a way that few other historical figures—certainly none from our literary past—have succeeded in doing. He continues to inspire a curious possessiveness in almost anyone who has had anything to do with him, as Howard McNaughton described it: 'everyone seems to think that his bit of Baxter was the genuine stuff and that anything else is a cheap fraud'.[1] He occupies the popular imagination, perhaps because he was a paradox—a non-conforming poet, profoundly critical of society, yet frequently holding positions of responsibility within the structures he attacked. He favoured the peasant wisdom of his socialist-pacifist father over the professorial knowledge of his academic grandfather,[2] yet he maintained an uneasy relationship with intellectuals throughout his life: 'my true station / Is still among the academic crew / Whom I despised for undue cerebration'.[3] He was scathing in his attacks on the education system, yet trained and worked as a teacher in New Zealand schools. He frequently criticised state bureaucracy, yet was for some years a public servant, a role that he seemed to have few problems justifying:

> Perhaps the man who works for the state, in a civil capacity, has in a sense been bought by the Queen's money. But still, unlike the soldier who sells his

1 H.D. McNaughton, 'Baxter, in Faulty Perspective', rev. of *James K. Baxter 1926–1972, A Memorial Volume*, ed. Alistair Taylor, *Christchurch Press* 10 Mar 1973.

2 In *The Man on the Horse* (Dunedin: University of Otago Press, 1967), Baxter comments on the 'great difference between the big house on the Cashmere Hills where my [maternal] grandfather, Professor John Macmillan Brown lived, and the closely-knit Otago Tribes of my father's family' (p.123). Baxter's dislike of formal education was largely a product of this difference: he idealised his father—'. . . my father was a self-educated Otago farmer who recited Burns and Shelley and Byron and Blake and Tom Hood and Henry Lawson when the mood took him' (*The Man on the Horse*, p.122)—and was deeply suspicious of Macmillan Brown, and all that he stood for.

> I am haunted by this ancestral voice which insists that the intellectual and moral betterment of mankind is achievable and should be every sane man's goal and concern . . . I imagine that he saw himself quite bluntly as one of the servants of the cause of intellectual progress. But to me his centre of thought and motivation is mysterious, because of the nuance of largeness, the sense of a broad view from high country, which his historical and personal situation made possible . . . the vantage point from which he saw the world . . . constitutes a problem for me (Introduction to *The Memoirs of John Macmillan Brown*, by John Macmillan Brown (Christchurch: Whitcombe and Tombs, 1974) xxxv-xxxvi).

3 'Letter to Noel Ginn II', *CP*, p.72.

> life and his power of moral choice, he may choose how much he sells. I have sold as little as I can—the use of the hands and a little of the brain—like a woman in a brothel who merely serves food to the guests.[4]

Being a poet, Baxter was by his own description the 'sore thumb of the tribe'.[5] Decades after his death this seems to remain his role—inhabiting some part of the New Zealand national consciousness, much as his own 'collaborator, my schizophrenic twin, who has always provided me with poems'[6] once inhabited 'the cellblock in the basement of my mind . . . incorrigible, ineducable, unemployable'.[7] The following comment, from 1966, may prove to be the most prophetic of all Baxter's vatic utterances:

> I'm not a political man; but I would dearly like to be able to speak for, to feel in accord with some such group once in a while. Mother New Zealand does not let this happen. *Nevertheless, if one cannot live well here, one can at least die here;* and perhaps a hundred years from now I will still be haunting her sleep, like something lost, like a voice whose owner one cannot quite identify, slipping in between the TV and the tranquillizers.[8]

Baxter's familiar voice is, of course, his public voice: the persuasive, often polemical, voice of the poet. Baxter's private voice is less well known, but it does survive in his letters, for he was a prolific letter writer and a substantial body of his correspondence exists in private hands or in collections with restricted access. His comments on the correspondence of others, generate certain expectations of his own letters:

> . . . a letter is a one-sided conversation; and to write great, or even charming, letters requires a gift as special and rare as that of a great conversationalist. Perhaps one aspect of the gift is humility—a warm intense interest in the lives of others, a quick response to each new situation—but another aspect is pride, aesthetic pride, the settled conviction that one's vision of the world *is* the real world and one's opinion worth the reader's attention.[9]

Baxter also wrote that one 'reads the letters of a great poet for various reasons—not least among them, the hope of discovering some part of the circumstantial scaffolding of his poems'.[10]

In expressing the latter opinion, it may have crossed Baxter's mind that letters he had written might one day reveal to others some part of the circumstantial scaffolding of his own work. Certainly, comments he made about the content of his poetry give every indication that the opportunity to study his private correspondence for fine autobiographical detail might be a rewarding exercise, for he classed as his most

4 Baxter, *The Man on the Horse*, pp.30–1.
5 'The Dragon Mask', *CP*, p.268.
6 Baxter, *The Man on the Horse*, p.17.
7 Ibid, p.19.
8 'Shots Around the Target', *Chaff* XVIV.2 (Sep 1966): 1. See also *Eikon* 2 (Dec 1966) p.16.
9 Review of *The Letters of John Keats* by John Keats, in *New Zealand Listener*, 813 (18 Feb 1955) p.12.
10 Review of *Letters of William Wordsworth* by William Wordsworth, in the *New Zealand Listener*, 798, (5 Nov 1954) p.13.

successful poems those containing a 'kernel of actual experiential knowledge',[11] and emphasised the intimate connection between his life and his verse: 'I know only a little about the world; and most of it is somewhere in the poems I have written'.[12] But could he, I wonder, have envisaged any collection of his correspondence revealing quite so much of the circumstantial scaffolding surrounding the poems of a single phase of his life, as his letters to Noel Ginn do?

Ginn's name is familiar through Baxter's early poems 'Letter to Noel Ginn' and 'Letter to Noel Ginn II'—but Baxter never made it widely known that these poems represent a substantial private correspondence. It was in the month of Baxter's sixteenth birthday that he sent three poems to Ginn and initiated the pen-friendship that was to endure for the next four years. Like many such relationships, it came about through coincidence and circumstance but appropriately for Baxter, whose life was rarely usual, the coincidences and circumstances that brought the relationship into being and sustained it were far from ordinary. Without the upheaval of World War II and the trauma and dislocation it visited on communities and individuals, it is unlikely that Baxter and Ginn would ever have begun corresponding. Without a society that viewed its pacifist members with extreme disfavour and sentenced eight hundred men to detention for the duration of the war, it is equally unlikely that their correspondence would have been sustained. And without this correspondence our knowledge of James K. Baxter's adolescence—the period that delineates his first phase of original poetic development—would remain a fragmented collage pieced together from scraps of autobiography and memory, fixed in place by a glue of inferences drawn from his poems. However, with this correspondence we now have access to Baxter's own immediate account of the years when his verse first began developing 'control and shape and meaning'.[13] And we have the first opportunity to fully appreciate Baxter's private voice—to experience his side of a sustained conversation and judge for ourselves both his humility and his sense of aesthetic pride.

Because of their scope and sophistication it is easy to forget that all but two of Baxter's letters to Ginn were written while he was in his teens. In biographical terms alone, the letters are of tremendous significance. The period they cover includes Baxter's third and fourth years at King's High School in Dunedin (1942–43), his year at Otago University (1944)—a year marked by academic failure and bouts of drunkenness—and 1945, when he saw *Beyond the Palisade* published and against all advice abandoned his studies and began working, first as a labourer at an iron rolling mill in the Dunedin suburb of Green Island, and then as a farm-hand on Wanaka Station, a large sheep run located in the foothills of the Southern Alps. The years 1944 and 1945 were a time of learning, but the knowledge he gained was not the type his parents had intended: 'Aphrodite, Bacchus, and the Holy Spirit were my

11 James K. Baxter, *The Bone Chanter* (Wellington: Oxford University Press, 1976) p.5.

12 'The World of the Creative Artist', *Salient Literary Issue* (Sep 1955) p.20. Comments by other Baxter scholars reinforce this point: Vincent O'Sullivan, for example, notes that there is 'no period of Baxter's life, and no important event, which cannot be found in his poetry or prose' (see *James K. Baxter* (Wellington: Oxford University Press, 1976) p.4), while John Weir argues that '*because* [Baxter] mythologises his life in his verse . . . the body of his poetry becomes a substitute for an autobiography' (see *The Poetry of James K. Baxter* (Wellington: Oxford University Press, 1970) p.19).

13 'Recollections of School Days', *NZMR* Mar 1966: p.19.

tutors, but the goddess of good manners and examination passes withheld her smile from me.'[14]

As the reference to Aphrodite indicates, the years of Baxter's correspondence with Ginn were also the years in which he began desiring sexual love—'such a blinding, crippling desire, when it fills one's whole horizon'[15]—culminating eventually in his first sexual encounters, and an affair with a married woman. As his poems suggest, Baxter's love affairs were always difficult and rarely ideal. In most of his poems dealing with relationships, the loved one is distant or absent, and the love relationship is characterised painfully—a reluctant dependence that merely emphasises the lover's own solitude and inadequacy:

> O when I remember how
> Breast to breast we have lain
> In earth's compassionate afterglow,
> The fallen tower is reared again:
> Heart as blind as a darkened room
> And our every act a vain
> Hieroglyph in a desert tomb.
> ('Songs of the Desert: 8,' *CP*, p.58.)

It took two decades for Baxter to exorcise the lovers of his adolescence and early adulthood. Only in middle age when 'the process of ageing . . . freed me from the obsession that I had at all costs to try to be attractive to the opposite sex' was he 'able to make the shattering discovery that women also are people, and can be treated as such'.[16]

As if the seeds of alcoholism and the pain of failed relationships were not enough, Baxter's late teens were also shadowed by the strong possibility that he might find himself imprisoned indefinitely in defaulters' detention as a conscientious objector like his brother Terence and Noel Ginn. In June 1944, when he reached the age of conscription, there was no quick end to the war in sight. Well into 1945, Ginn, then approaching his fifth year in detention, had thought 'that the Japanese war could last for a generation it was so scattered and complicated'.[17] Ginn's relief at the possibility of release was strongly tempered with dismay when he learned that a strange and terrible new weapon called the atom bomb had been used to put an end to the conflict. Baxter was spared detention, but the spectre of it was real, and although he went through the process of appealing he was not confident he would be successful: 'I may or may not get it according to the policy of the Board. If I don't get it, I guess I'll be joining the ranks of the faithful. Either way it is a good thing—solidifies my principles. Of late I've not felt much like writing letters; a periodic wave of depression' (p.385).

As well as adding detail to our knowledge of Baxter's life, his letters to Ginn are directly relevant to our understanding of the circumstantial scaffolding surrounding

14 'Essay on the Higher Learning', *Spike* (1961) p.62.
15 James K. Baxter, *The Flowering Cross* (Dunedin: New Zealand Tablet, 1969) p.170.
16 Ibid.
17 Noel Ginn, personal interview with Annette Facer, Sep 1994.

poems from three distinct phases in his development as a poet: the correspondence refers back to his recently completed juvenile phase, it begins during his adolescent phase, and it concludes two years into his adult phase.

Baxter's juvenile phase commenced with his first poem written in 1933 at the age of seven, and ended around the age of fifteen—about a year after he began systematically entering his poems into notebooks. Although he dismissed these early poems as 'undoubtedly imitative'[18] his later methods of composition were determined in the process of writing them:

> . . . it was then that I first endured the intense effort of *listening* [to the unheard sound of which poems are translations], like a man chained to the ground trying to stand upright and walk—and from this intensity of *listening* the words emerged . . . I was then seven years old. I don't think my methods of composition have changed much since that time. The daimon has always to be invoked; and there is no certainty that he will answer the invitation.[19]

Baxter's second phase—adolescence—was the period in which he began developing as an original poet, and in which he 'fell into the habit of poem-writing with a vengeance and counted it a poor week when I had not written four or five pieces of verse'.[20] The great value of Baxter's correspondence with Ginn is the very fact that it relates principally to this adolescent phase, a period that provides, both critically and biographically, the key to a full understanding and appreciation of his later life and poetry. Baxter returns to adolescence in his writing time and again for the remainder of his life, not to review it with a rosy glow—'I think anyone who has survived . . . [a] New Zealand adolescence would feel at home . . . in a pit full of tarantulas'[21] —but not to deny it either. Indeed he cautions against forgetting the importance of such experiences: 'the man I see in the shaving mirror . . . has come a good way and knows less than when he began. The most dangerous time for him is the day he first uses the word "adolescent" to describe the things he does not like; when he rejects one half of his universe to make the other half safe.'[22] Like the Calvinist ethos that he envisaged buried beneath 'our determinedly secular culture like the bones of a dinosaur buried in a suburban garden plot',[23] the bones of Baxter's adolescence shaped and determined his development as a poet. It is in the poetry of this period that many of the symbols, ideas, themes, techniques and influences that occur in, or structure, much of his later work originated and evolved.

Baxter's correspondence with Ginn concluded about two years into his adult phase. In his final letter of the correspondence, he would cast a dour eye back at the preceding months and explain to Ginn that:

18 Baxter, *The Man on the Horse*, p.125.
19 Ibid, p.124.
20 Ibid.
21 'Further Notes on New Zealand Poetry', Hocken MS 975/119, unpublished.
22 'Outlook for Poetry', *New Zealand Poetry Yearbook* V, 1955, p.8.
23 Baxter, *The Man on the Horse*, p.125.

> . . . I have at last disentangled various strands—religious, masturbation-guilt, artistic, attitudes to school and parents—which I have long been unable to accept and dissolve.
>
> 'I am content to follow to its source
> Every event in action or in thought;
> Measure the lot; forgive myself the lot !
> When such as I cast out remorse . . .' etc.
>
> —Not Yeats' particular creative ecstasy but a rather sour determination to go my own way by doubt and not by Authority of person, state, religion, or convention; to work out my own position and make no promises. (pp.424–5)

For Baxter, going his 'own way' turned out to mean leading an erratic, semi-nomadic, frequently self-destructive, existence that was really only profitable in a creative sense: 'I developed the habit of throwing up a job, drinking for a week or so, writing for a month or so, then taking another job. It worked quite well. The best poems I have written (those in *Blow, Wind of Fruitfulness*) were written in this way.'[24]

In the process of going his own way, Baxter lost contact with Ginn. Later, when he looked back on this period in 'Notes on the Education of a New Zealand Poet', he would represent it as a time of unrelieved solitude. Ginn was not listed as one of the factors that played any part in his development as a writer. Baxter likened his wartime experiences as the youngest son in a pacifist family to 'those of a Jewish boy growing up in an anti-Semitic neighbourhood'.[25] He used this simile to help explain a sense of grief that he felt had attached itself to his early life, and that his objective recollection of childhood as a happy time was unable to erode. This 'sense of grief—even at times a sense of grievance', he mused, may have determined 'the rather gloomy tone of my verse' but at the same time 'helped me to write poems'.[26] This sense of grief may also have provided impetus to Baxter's tendency to mythologise his life in verse, and his mythologising may in large part account for his silence concerning Ginn.

Apart from the 'Letter' poems, the almost total lack of references in Baxter's published poetry to Noel Ginn and Terence being in detention—not to mention the very real probability that he too could be detained—would seem to contradict earlier assertions concerning the intimate connection between his life and his poetry. Such omissions are more readily accounted for, however, if we accept Baxter's own description of his mode of thought as a writer as primarily mythological. I understand him to mean by this that although his poems reflect, on one level, one man's experience of life, in the wider perspective of human history they are merely links in a chain of like representations—each link re-presenting themes and patterns that date back to the earliest human myths. Just as Baxter once described each of his poems as 'part of a large subconscious corpus of personal myth, like an island above the sea, but joined

24 'Writers in New Zealand: a questionnaire', *Landfall* XIV (1960) p.41.
25 Baxter, *The Man on the Horse*, pp.123–4.
26 Ibid, pp.121–2.

underwater to other islands',[27] so the elements he valued in people's lives were those that connected individuals to a wider mythical landscape of human experience. Where others might not recognise, or place much importance on, such connections, Baxter relied on them to provide the essential structure to his art. It is unsurprising then, that from seeing in his own life patterns of a mythological design, it was a short step to the use of mythological figures in his poems to represent the self. In section Nine I discuss the role of three of these figures—Prometheus, the salamander and the unicorn—in Baxter's adolescent phase.

But to return, for the moment, to Baxter's relative silence about Ginn. If there is a fault in the habit of thinking mythologically, it is that experiences and relationships that do not fit preferred designs—for example, the idea of the solitary adolescent poet who, in mythological terms, is Prometheus chained to a lonely crag; or the salamander that cannot be approached because it lives in flame—are discarded. Baxter intimated as much when he wrote: 'The trouble is, I can't demythologise [my life]. What happens is either meaningless to me, or else it is mythology.'[28] It is therefore possible that Ginn does not enter Baxter's accounts of this period to the extent that their correspondence indicates may have been warranted because he confounds Baxter's mythological pattern (I suggest in section Four that his silence about Terence stems from a different base). One can only speculate that the habit of thought that impelled Baxter to mythologise his own life, required him to forget a friendship that might contradict remarks about the aridity of his adolescence. If this is the case, it would not be the only example of Baxter's occasional tendency towards selective recall. His comments on his unhappy childhood need to be considered both in the context of this comment from a letter written to his mother in 1948—'I'm inclined to think . . . that I had a singularly pleasant upbringing; probably, if anything, you and Daddy were too easy on me—I must have been rather irritating at times'[29]—and in the light of his autobiographical essay 'Notes on the Education of a New Zealand Poet' in which he writes: 'All mental reconstructions of those early events seem likely to be false—not deliberate lies, but an improvised and artificial childhood tidied up for others to look at. . . . Objectively I remember my childhood as a happy time.'[30] Millicent Baxter felt that it was hard for her son to admit that he had a happy childhood 'because happy families destroy poets. He had to have an interesting tragic background, his own mythology.'[31]

Baxter's correspondence with Ginn does, however, indicate that Ginn played a significant role in Baxter's life at this time. Like Baxter, Ginn had a strong interest in poetry—the pacifist beliefs that excluded the two from mainstream society may have ensured an immediate bond, but it was their mutual love of literature that cemented the friendship, and it is the focus on poetry that stands out in the correspondence as exceptional. The early tone of the correspondence—metaphysical, poetic, and determinedly intellectual—was set in Baxter's first letter:

27 Baxter, *The Bone Chanter*, p.6.
28 Baxter, *The Man on the Horse*, p.122.
29 James K. Baxter, letter to his mother, *c.* Jun 1948, Hocken MS 975/184.
30 Baxter, *The Man on the Horse*, p.121.
31 Millicent Baxter, *The Memoirs of Millicent Baxter* (Whatamongo Bay: Cape Catley, 1981) p.143.

> Throughout my poems there is the idea of the ephemerality of time—as we know it—and, along with this the eternal endurance of what is time, space, matter, and spirit combined. Imagine that life could be 'speeded up' like a motion-picture. We would see the forms of civilization crumble—and grass, the humble grass, symbol of all that is eternal, would remain. (p.134)

The opening stanza of 'Letter to Noel Ginn' gives some indication of what Baxter came to value in the relationship:

> They can admire the empty lion-skin
> The heart skewered by print, who will admire:
> But from you, Noel, I wish more—
> The friend's stance, confessor for my sin
> Which is pride alone: yet pride alone will win
> Niche of immortal marble despised and hungered for.
> (*CP*, p.27)

Yet Baxter also expressed to Ginn a wariness of the demands implicit in such a friendship:

> What you say about me needing friends, not admirers, hits one nail on the head. But friends are much more uncomfortable than admirers: one presents a façade of poems, printed emotion, to the admirers, and then one retires;—they can admire the empty lion-skin. Friends are not taken in, touch the man. And friends are apt to take the side of one's own moral censor. (p.360)

In spite of the ambivalence suggested by this retrospective gloss to 'Letter to Noel Ginn', it is clear that Baxter valued Ginn's friendship immensely. According to a letter written in March 1944, Ginn was not merely, as Baxter suggests in his poem, 'confessor for my sin', but also 'the father-confessor of my ideas on literature' (p.346). Baxter also expressed appreciation of Ginn as a critic, commenting that 'whereas most fairly prolific writers expose only a little of their verse to the public eye, you get nearly all mine & there must be some chaff in it' (p.265). Not only did he value Ginn's constructive criticism of his own work, he also appreciated the poetry Ginn was sending him:

> I write to you because
> 'There is only half-life in the separate safe bone-banner-scroll of an ivory skull.'
>
> In other words, what I write is useless unless there is someone appreciating it. My father has full appreciation of most of what I write, my mother knows and likes the best ones, but they are not 'intellectual' in the way that you are—or not quite anyway. Also, you are probably writing as good or better poetry than anyone else in NZ. (pp.264–5)

A letter written on 22 December 1943, thanking Ginn for the gift of Louis MacNeice's *Autumn Journal*, suggests that rather than being directed by Ginn towards new sources of creativity, Baxter felt that the friendship added lustre to the material he was already working with: 'You pamper me. The Louis MacNeice is an expensive gift, though of course greatly appreciated. You are scarcely a lode-star to me, rather a philosopher's stone'(p.309). Ginn later felt discomforted by such a comparison, recalling that he had been 'overwhelmed at the time by Baxter's talent'.[32] Yet the contents of Baxter's letters confirm Frank McKay's view that 'Ginn became a kind of mentor for his ideas on literature'.[33] Baxter also valued the relationship for matters other than those of a literary nature, and gradually took Ginn into his confidence regarding more personal things. In a letter to Millicent Baxter in October 1945, Baxter concludes: 'Well mother, I've been writing to you rather as I write to Noel. Soliloquising on what is usually left unspoken.'[34]

At the time he began writing to Ginn, Baxter was learning the craft of a poet by reading widely and then emulating writers that appealed to him. In his letters to Ginn he refers to more than eighty literary figures, most of them poets whose styles he was experimenting with. But his letters to Ginn also show that Baxter's imitative phase had concluded by the time he was sixteen—he was no longer attempting straight mimicry of other poets but borrowing critically when producing his verse. Established forms and styles were becoming little more than frameworks for poems whose content was, increasingly, personal and local. In order to indicate this development in Baxter's poetry, I have not limited the content of this edition merely to his letters. Also included are in excess of two hundred poems that Baxter either quotes, or refers to in his letters—most of these poems are published here for the first time.

It is well known that Baxter wrote a tremendous number of poems in his lifetime, and that the majority of these remain unpublished. John Weir estimates in his introduction to *The Bone Chanter* that—with the exclusion of poems that are recognisably duplications—'by the end of 1967, when he stopped entering poems in his Manuscript Books, Baxter had written 2,312 poems, of which 1,784 remained unpublished.'[35] This statistic excludes the period from 1968 to 1972 when Baxter had ceased keeping a systematic record of his final drafts. But another statistic has more relevance to this edition. By 1946, when his regular correspondence with Ginn concluded, Baxter was working in his fourteenth poetry notebook, which runs, according to his own sequential numbering, from poem 856 to poem 1,025.[36] Of these 1025 poems only seventy-two appear in the *Collected Poems* although some uncollected poems from this period have been published in various magazines. Of the poems written up to the end of Baxter's regular correspondence with Noel Ginn, less than ten percent have been published in any form. It is difficult to fully appreciate Baxter's correspondence with Ginn, or his three early phases of development, without

32 Noel Ginn, personal interview, Oct 1994.
33 Frank McKay, *Life* (Auckland: Oxford University Press, 1990) p.61.
34 Letter to Millicent Baxter, 15 Oct 1945, Hocken Library, MS975/184.
35 Baxter, *The Bone Chanter*, p.7.
36 Poem 856—'For Rimbaud'—is unpublished but poem 1,025—'RAPUNZEL'—appears in a revised form in the *CP*, pp.63–4.

some understanding of the contents of his Manuscript Books and his methods of working at this time.

To understand the unusual circumstances and coincidences that culminated in his correspondence with Ginn it is important to begin with the story of Baxter's older brother Terence—whose friendship with Ginn provided the link and initiated the correspondence—and with an account of Ginn's own life. This is, in part, because the role played by Terence in Baxter's early years has gone largely unrecognised. Terence was imprisoned for almost precisely the period that Baxter came to refer to as his period of solitude, and only in his late teens could he even bring himself to write of 'your double who bleeds inside my head'.[37] If the loss of his brother had any compensation it was that it led to the correspondence with Ginn, and the discovery of a like mind with which he could communicate about the thing that mattered most: his poetry. The experiences of Noel Ginn and Terence Baxter also bear retelling because of the possibility clouding Baxter's horizon throughout his adolescence that their experience could be his. To understand why they came to be in defaulters' detention it is helpful to go back even further, to the First World War; and the stories of two other men from the preceding generation whose own pacifism profoundly influenced the generation that followed.

37 'To my Brother', Hocken MS 704/13: 775, p.17.

# Two
# Paths to Detention

Blessed are the dead
  For they know not the plague of the spirit
  That has swept away the last vestiges of humanity[38]

In the early months of 1918, as the First World War was drawing to a close, Ormond Burton and Archibald Baxter were sent, at the direction of the New Zealand Army, to the battlefields of France and Belgium, where German and Allied Forces, dug into trenches, faced each other in front lines that for the most part swayed backwards and forwards in a macabre dance over the same few miles of churned charnel mud. Although the next war would find Burton and Baxter sharing similar views about the evils of such conflicts, in this arena they stood, at least philosophically, on opposite ground: whereas Archie Baxter resisted the war to the limits of his endurance, Ormond Burton had proved an exemplary soldier.

There is evidence that Burton probably came across Baxter in France, around April 1918, shortly before he and his platoon entrained with the New Zealand Division to try and stem the German breakthrough on the Somme. Burton noticed a group of conscientious objectors under guard:

> They had been brought from New Zealand and forced into the front lines by the military police. There was a considerable amount of sympathy shown to them by the soldiers for the harsh treatment they had had to endure because they had refused to join the military when conscription was introduced in New Zealand.[39]

It is highly likely that Archie Baxter was among the group that Burton saw—his autobiographical account places him in the vicinity, and most of the other objectors had by this time ceased resisting. In fact Archie was one of only two objectors—out of the fourteen who had been shipped to Europe with the New Zealand Division—with the strength to hold on to his convictions throughout the war. He would have been in very poor condition: months of constant punishment—including a twenty-eight day sentence of No. 1 Field Punishment (known as 'crucifixion') at the 'Mud Huts' Field Punishment Camp near Dickebush in Belgium—food deprivation, and the experience of being left standing alone in an ammunition dump under heavy shelling from German Artillery, had taken their toll. A short time later, close to

38 'Lamentation', see p.37.
39 Ernest Crane, *I Can Do No Other: A Biography of The Reverend Ormond Burton* (Auckland: Hodder and Stoughton, 1986) p.43.

death, he collapsed and was taken to Boulogne Hospital where a doctor certified him insane, apparently 'to save him from being shot by the military authorities'.[40]

As Archie Baxter was marched from punishment to punishment in and around the allied front lines, expecting death but determined 'never in my sane senses [to] surrender to the evil power that has fixed its roots like a cancer on the world',[41] Burton was frequently in the thick of combat, finding at this time no conflict between his Christian beliefs and the exigencies of service in the military. His exploits during the First World War had become the stuff of legend by the time Noel Ginn knew him:

> Rev. O.E. Burton had won a Military Cross in the 1st World War. His nature . . . had a large element of derring-do & self-will—for instance in France in the front lines he went on private nocturnal forays across no-man's-land throwing hand grenades, much to the endangerment of his own men as he drew fire upon them in their trenches—he had an immense relish for danger. He had also a passion for extremes.[42]

Burton's passion for extremes is evident in some of his writings from shortly after the war. In his history of the Auckland Regiment, for example, he presents his pacifist credentials in his introduction, yet sees no conflict between such a stance and his personal advocacy of tough measures during times of war. He had scant tolerance for individuals who might fail in their duty and argued that 'a drunken officer, being a public danger, should be tried by court-martial and, if found guilty, shot no matter what his rank or attainments might be'.[43] To Ginn, such singleness of purpose was also evident in Burton's brand of pacifism—he no more readily compromised in moral battles than he had earlier in the physical conflicts:

> . . . it was not surprising that when he saw the challenges of the Sermon on the Mount he embraced them with crusading zeal. Part of his charm & power stemmed from the fact that he practised what he preached. . . . We, in the pacifist fold loved him. He was our leader & our authority—those on the 'other' side who saw pacifism as treason could not hate him because of his disarming love and sincerity.[44]

His charisma carried many followers—including Ginn—along paths they might not otherwise have taken:

> In long retrospect I would say that the dogmatic authoritarian side of OEB's personality & teaching was harmful to his followers, forcing them to opinions their nature was not ready to support. Yet the times were urgent & the issues not academic.[45]

40 Millicent Baxter, *The Memoirs of Millicent Baxter*, p.54.
41 Ibid, p.51.
42 Noel Ginn, letter to Paul Millar, Jan 1995.
43 Ormond Burton, *The Auckland Regiment: An Account of the Doings on Active Service of the First, Second and Third Battalions of the Auckland Regiment* (Auckland:Whitcombe and Tombs, 1922) p.191.
44 Noel Ginn, letter to Paul Millar, Jan 1995.
45 Ibid.

Noel Ginn was born on 16 December 1915. Neither Ormond Burton—then medical orderly to the Auckland Regiment dug in at Gallipoli—nor Archibald Baxter—still farming in Otago but living in the knowledge that 'I would now be called upon actively to defend the principles I held'[46]—could have imagined the effect they would later have on the boy from Wanganui.

If asked to give an opinion on his early years Ginn would probably echo the comment made by James K. Baxter: 'Objectively I remember my childhood as a happy time.'[47] Certainly he had many of the material advantages that one associates with happiness. The eldest son of middle-class parents, his father, a skilled cabinet-maker, became a successful furniture manufacturer in a partnership employing as many as sixty people. A tennis court and full-size billiards table were two ways in which his father indulged a passion for sport, and Ginn became proficient at both games. Although always slightly smaller than average he was a physically active child, excelling at running and jumping. He was also intellectually able, receiving the award for dux in his primary school and matriculating at the age of fourteen with a national scholarship.

Yet Ginn's childhood was marred by difficulty in relating to his father, and he retained a life-long regret that there was never a deeper bond between them. To Ginn both his parents epitomised goodness and honesty, yet there was a level at which they were unable to relate. His father's passion for sport was lost on a son who, although he was a good enough runner to win the school cross-country, detested rugby and cricket. An event illustrating the difference between them occurred around the time of the disastrous Hawke's Bay earthquake of 1931, which had been felt strongly in Wanganui. Shortly after the quake Ginn, who had just turned fifteen, travelled with his father across the North Island to the badly damaged town of Napier. The devastation was overwhelming: water was pouring from pipes in the ground, buildings were reduced to rubble, and the Cathedral lay in ruins. Lining the roads were makeshift stalls where people were selling items they had salvaged. Ginn, with ten shillings in his pocket given to him by his father, noticed one table that held a selection of reading material. He spent all his money on the purchase of four books; three of them works by Pope, Keats and Ruskin. His father's only reaction was one of disgust that he had wasted ten shillings:

> I knew then that we had quite different outlooks—we never clicked. That was the beginning of the realisation of our great difference.[48]

Yet his father rarely offered criticism and later, even when Ginn's decisions conflicted sharply with his own beliefs, he continued to support his son:

> . . . when I took the pacifist position—he said 'Well, if I was in power I would have them shot; they're traitors to their country these people.' It was a very widely held view [and] he said it very mildly. I didn't take it to heart. He

46 Archibald Baxter, *We Will Not Cease* (Whatamongo Bay: Cape Catley, 1980) p.10.
47 Baxter, *The Man on the Horse*, p.121.
48 Noel Ginn, interview with Annette Facer, Sep 1994.

> supported me all through those years. [My parents] came to visit and never ever criticised—it was a wonderful thing.[49]

It was unfortunate for Ginn that his leaving school with a national scholarship coincided with the depression years. A passion for chemistry and an impressive placing in the Dominion examinations for the subject, had led to hopes that he would be able to go to Otago University to study science. However, a cash-strapped government was unable to pay out on the scholarship, and his father, who had recently found himself to be the only guarantor with the resources to honour a joint-and-several guarantee, was unable to assist him either. Taking his father's advice he began studying towards a Bachelor of Commerce degree through Wanganui Technical College, and completed units in commercial, French, book-keeping, economics, bankruptcy, and company law. He then took his first job, as 'Registrar of Dogs' in the Wanganui City Council Rates Collecting Department, but soon moved from there to take up a position in the Native Land Court. It was a job that rekindled an interest, first developed in school, in the history of the Whanganui river. At school he had been taught—quite progressively for the times—that prior to white settlement the region had a population of some 60,000 Maori. Long before Baxter associated himself with the area Ginn used to explore by bike up to, and around, Jerusalem and Pipiriki.

Childhood for Terence Baxter was a somewhat different experience to that of Noel Ginn. Born in 1922 Terence was, for the first four years of his life, an only child. Growing up on the family's little Kuri Bush farm was an idyllic existence, marred only by his parents' occasional visits to town when he would either be left at the home of some cousins who tended to bully him, or else with his paternal grand-parents. A quiet, obedient, little boy, he dreaded staying at his grandparents' house because, particularly on a wet day, there was nothing for a child to do. The experience was made worse by his grandfather John Baxter—a rather awe-inspiring figure prone to the occasional alcoholic binge—who practised his bag-pipes inside:

> . . . when he played inside the house you'd think the wall was going to fall down. I couldn't stand this row, it used to frighten the life out of me . . . there was a hell of a noise through the house even without you being in the same room. He'd be marching up and down the floor there, and you'd hear the feet stomping on the floor as he was going up and down.[50]

John Baxter had a record for unreliability, and although Archie Baxter was not the eldest son in the family his steady nature had made him, for some years, the acknowledged leader of clan Baxter; particularly in those times when his father was the worse for drink. It was through this role that he came to influence his siblings:

> . . . if there were any problems in the family [they would say] 'Oh, we'll have to see Archie about it.' Anything, anytime, over money or things like that . . .

49 Ibid.
50 Terence Baxter, personal interview, 11 Dec 1995.

> He seemed to lead his brothers. This business over the war, it was my father that got the idea first . . . from listening to a person giving a speech about war, and he started to think things over. He must have had a fair bit of influence over his brothers because you'd think they would have gone their own way, had their own thoughts about things, they were easy going enough sort of men.[51]

But Archie's influence was such that, in all, six Baxter brothers were imprisoned as objectors in the First World War.

Along with the physical punishment Archie Baxter experienced during the First World War, he frequently had to endure long sessions with officers hoping, by debate, to change his mind. In these instances he attempted to represent his position clearly and reasonably even when suffering the effects of a beating or illness, although simplistic or banal arguments tended to irritate him:

> I was prepared to show [one captain] that atrocities are perpetuated as a rule by any armies in occupation of enemy territory during war time, but he did not want to go on with the argument. If I afterwards had a son, he wanted to know, how would I reply to his question: 'What did you do in the war?' This ridiculous stock question always amused me.
>
> 'My answer would be,' I said, 'I did my best to stop it.'[52]

Through his autobiographical account Archie Baxter's sons knew precisely what their father had done in the war, and the lengths he had gone to in his attempt to protest against it; it was one of the reasons they held him in such high regard. His book *We Will Not Cease* was written in 1938 while the family was based for a short time in England, although much of their time was spent travelling around Europe. Archie did not find it an easy thing recalling the years of the war, and to some extent the entire family relived the experience with him. Terence believed that had it not been for his mother's persistence the book would never have been written: while drafting the manuscript in longhand Millicent Baxter extracted much from her husband that he was reluctant to give. She considered the effort on her husband's part 'painful, and yet in many ways healing for it brought to the surface things that were buried deep down in suffering'.[53]

James and Terence were both aware of what was going on, but as James was then only twelve it was to Terence that Archie turned when he felt that Millicent was asking too much of him:

> She used to get at him a lot and he used to talk to me sometimes, we'd go away for a walk, and he'd say, 'You know, I'm having an awful time just now, she's at me all the time about it.' [Laughs] He'd try to get my sympathy.[54]

51 Ibid.
52 Archibald Baxter, *We Will Not Cease*, p.135.
53 Millicent Baxter, *The Memoirs of Millicent Baxter*, p.82.
54 Terence Baxter, personal interview, 11 Dec 1995.

Archie gained more than his son's sympathy. There developed between them a mutual respect and rapport, and it was on account of this that others who knew Terence believed that he found it extremely difficult not to take the pacifist stance in the next war:

> It could be said that he didn't have a choice—or that it was a Hobson's choice—as it was a matter of choosing to be rejected by Society or rejected by his family, as it would have been a great blow to his much beloved father if he had not taken a stand. I am not saying that the choice was not his nor that he did not sincerely believe in the principles he stood for. I just feel that it was much harder for him to be incarcerated than it was for some . . . His freedom and his independence were integral to his personality.[55]

Whatever Terence's personal inclinations, he grew up in a family where the pacifist stance was a way of life. Throughout his childhood and adolescence pacifist issues were discussed and debated by the people he most respected—people passionately opposed to war—and both he and James had ample opportunity to consider their arguments and formulate their own conclusions.

In contrast to Terence's slow and steady immersion in pacifism, Noel Ginn's pacifism was something of a 'conversion experience' developing out of the intellectual activity of the 1930s. His adolescence was marked by a search for that elusive something or someone to which he could relate. Eventually he thought he had found what he was looking for: the 'something' was the Methodist brand of Christian Pacifism; the 'someone', the charismatic, patriarchal figure of Ormond Burton—who in certain ways filled a need in Ginn that his relationship with his own father had been unable to meet.

Although Ginn's parents were not regular churchgoers, they were supporters of the local Methodist church, and sent their children there, first to Sunday School and, when they grew older, to Bible Class. Ginn loved the rousing Wesleyan hymn singing, he was captivated by the emphasis on the liberating joy of conversion, and looked forward to the annual Easter Camps which were 'very healthy, life-giving occasions, the note of joy ringing high above'.[56] However his fascination with chemistry in high school led to an internal conflict between scientific rationalism and religious teaching. Reading more widely he was particularly affected by Havelock Ellis's concern with social inequality and, as his adolescent socialism developed, his cynicism with religion grew, until he ceased attending church in favour of the new doctrines:

> The years 14 on (i.e. from 1930) were years of intellectual ferment as old values were examined and discredited—the horrors & scandals of the 1914–18 war were exposed, and the triumphs of the newlyemerging USSR revealed. We were told how heavily war-reparations had borne upon the German people, how evil and cruel they were. The Left Book Club flourished. We learned of the connivance of arms manufacturers with governments. We

55 Lenore Baxter, letter to Frank McKay, undated, VUW Library, Wellington, MS McKay 10/7/33.
56 Noel Ginn, letter to Paul Millar, Jan 1995.

> learned of the No More War Movement, and read Aldous Huxley, Middleton Murry and Bertrand Russell. We were thrilled by the Oxford movement with its absolutes for the personal life . . . One night travelling by train from Auckland to Marton/Wanganui I read Archibald Baxter's *We Will Not Cease*. It was an extra-sensory experience.[57]

For Terence Baxter, the lived experience of his father writing the book had been less dramatic, although it had similarly life-changing implications. He was never drawn to participate in the pacifist meetings that used to take place at his parents' house, which gave one young woman who used to attend them 'the impression that he regarded us as a boring intrusion'.[58] In fact he felt no need of the support such meetings gave the members of the embattled little group, and by nature he shied away from intellectual forums presided over by his mother. His inclination was to take his small teak lifeboat—*Plucky*—out sailing, or perhaps go swimming, a pastime that both he and James enjoyed. He was not anti-social, but preferred the company of his friends from Reid and Gray, where he had worked since the age of sixteen as a welder, or the company of girls, who found him attractive and were impressed by his dancing.

In 'A Family Photograph 1939' Baxter captures the essence and energy of his brother's adolescence and, on a different level of symbolism, the tragedy about to befall him:

> Waves bluster up the bay and through the throat
> Of the one-span bridge. My brother shoots
> The gap alone
> Like Charon sculling in his boat
> Above the squids and flounders. With the jawbone
> Of a sperm whale he fights the town,
> Dances on Fridays to the cello
> With black-haired sluts.
> (*CP*, p.237)

The sea—which in other poems by Baxter might symbolise regeneration, or the fruitful, poem-producing chaos of the unconscious—symbolises here the 'death and oblivion' of the detention camps against which his brother will pit himself.[59] The throat of the doubly emblematic bridge—representing Terence's impending transition from one phase of life to another, but also the soulless industrial society whose constructions and inventions dominate the natural and human worlds, and facilitate modern warfare—is metaphorically the entrance to both the womb and the tomb. The doubling of death and birth is characteristic of much of Baxter's early work and frequently symbolises a positive, regenerative experience. Here, however, the world,

57 Ibid.

58 Transcript of interview between F. McKay and Margaret Still, undated, VUW Library, Wellington, MS McKay 1/22.

59 See Baxter's list of 'nature symbols that occur in New Zealand poetry' in James K. Baxter, *The Fire and the Anvil: Notes on Modern Poetry* (Wellington: New Zealand University Press, 1955) p.69.

or phase, into which his brother emerges is sterile and dangerous; the gap he negotiates may well run between society's Scylla and duty's Charybdis and, for all his skill as a sailor, he is ultimately unable to escape from it. He will become the grim boatman of the dead, caught on a stream of time that carries him past and over life's opportunities. He is sent to detention from Dunedin (the town's Leith stream which is alluded to frequently in Baxter's verse can be linked, punningly, with Hades's Lethe, the river of forgetfulness that symbolises lost time and opportunity). Baxter draws on a frequently used polarity—the wilderness versus the city—to recast his brother in his confrontation with the town as a type of jawbone-wielding nautical Samson. But the ultimate symbol of the sea's power and authority that he carries—the sea now symbolising 'the Wilderness [represented by] the marine desert which surrounds our island City . . . [and is] the mirror and symbol of the power of God'[60]—is rendered impotent by the faithless, secular society inhabiting the dehumanising city. When his brother returns from detention to resume his interrupted dance, the sexual choreography that might ease him back into community—and complete the transition from adolescence to adulthood that imprisonment interrupted—is now performed by a silent, hardened man, to the slow, mournful tones of the cello.

In 1939, however, much of this was in the future, not only for Terence, but for Noel Ginn also. Seeing in socialism the very basis of Christianity, Ginn had rejoined the Methodist church, and had become actively involved in pacifist activities as a member of the Methodist Bible Class movement, a radical element within the established church:

> . . . the Methodist Bible Class became a powerful pacifist pressure group, virtually autonomous from the main church and not necessarily responsible to it. Long after most other church members had retreated, albeit reluctantly, in the light of fascist aggression overseas, young Methodists were still passing absolutist antiwar resolutions right up to 1939.[61]

He became one of the first members of the Christian Pacifist Society (CPS), being formed by Ormond Burton and A.C. Barrington—the then national secretary of the Methodist Bible Class. Burton was preaching a dogmatic brand of pacifist socialism that—perhaps for the very reason that many in the established church were deeply disturbed by it—was attractive to large numbers of the youth:

> The precepts of the Sermon on the Mount were seen as iron laws—as the challenges were delivered home to churchgoers it became a divisive force. On one side the unquestionable absolute coming down from the mountain in the hands of OEB the new Moses, & on the other the many doctrines of Protestantism—or the shifting sands of Protestantism as one expressed it.[62]

60 James K. Baxter, *Recent Trends in New Zealand Poetry* (Christchurch: The Caxton Press, 1951) pp.16–7.
61 David Grant, *Out in the Cold: Pacifists and Conscientious Objectors in New Zealand During World War II* (Auckland: Reed Methuen, 1986) p.35.
62 Noel Ginn, letter to Paul Millar, Jan 1995.

The landslide victory in November 1935 of the first Labour Government had appeared to the pacifist groups, and those interested in social reform, to herald a new age of enlightenment. War clouds might be gathering over Europe but a government whose leaders were the jailed and persecuted pacifists of the previous war, would surely be faithful to the cause. But the matter, as Ginn and the others discovered, was not that simple:

> We did not know the pressures put on [the government] by the old country—we were still very much colonials in those days. We did not know many things. For us it was all black & white.[63]

As Millicent Baxter recalls it, 'It was a very bitter period for those who had thought that the Labour Party would preserve some of their idealism.'[64] The harsh treatment meted out by the Labour Party on those who had trusted and supported them remained with the Baxter family through the Second World War, and for a long time afterwards. The tone of Baxter's early unpublished poem 'Lamentation' (1942) adopts the tribal wail of the Israelites to convey the intensity of the pacifist tribe's bitterness:

> Blessed are the dead
> For they know not the plague of the spirit
> That has swept away the last vestiges of humanity,
> That has turned faith to treachery.
>
> They see not:
> And so they cannot view the leaders
> Who reck not of their supporters—
> Who sustained them in time of trouble and raised them to the seat of government—
> But turn and rend them.
> [Hocken, MS 704/4: 217, p.98]

As the global crisis worsened and war approached, conscription was introduced. By 1940 pacifism was becoming an underground activity and to Ginn, who was by then a student in Wellington, 'there was an odour of the catacomb around'.[65]

From about the age of twenty Ginn had been living in Auckland, having transferred there from Wanganui to take up a more responsible position with the Native Land Court. By 1937 he had nine units of his Bachelor of Commerce degree and his father was pressuring him to return to Wanganui to take part in the family business. This he did, first keeping the books and then taking on the role of accountant. He had returned reluctantly, and hated the work—finding it totally against his nature. Saving hard for two years he managed by the end of 1939 to accumulate enough money to leave Wanganui for Wellington in order to study for an arts degree at Victoria University College. His decision was a blow to his parents: they never opposed

63 Ibid.
64 Millicent Baxter, *The Memoirs of Millicent Baxter*, p.108.
65 Noel Ginn, letter to Paul Millar, Jan 1995.

his choice, but he knew, and deeply regretted, the intense disappointment he had caused them.

Ginn went to Victoria University College intending to do a Bachelor of Arts degree, majoring in English and French. Along with his majors, he also studied psychology and German, and took some part in the college's extracurricular life. Describing himself as 'a slogger with a very good eye',[66] he turned out for one of the University hockey teams and had sufficient ability to be selected towards the end of his last season to play in the senior team. He remembers the two years positively, and recalls very little antagonism towards him for his pacifist stance.

The 1940 and 1941 editions of the student newspaper *Salient* tend to support Ginn's recollections. In these early years of the conflict there was a natural division in opinion about the appropriate response to the war and conscription. The first issue of *Salient* published in 1940 was quick to reiterate the importance of the university as a place of free speech in an editorial expressing concern that recent public safety regulations might, in their application, 'lead to an infringement of our traditional academic freedom'.[67] It appears to have been an opinion shared by the majority of the student body, if an article in the same issue on an attempt to form a Peace Society at the college is any indication. The catalyst for the formation of the society—a grouping of both staff and students—was concern at the arrest of the Reverend Ormond Burton for speaking publicly against the war. The students' association executive initially refused to grant the Peace Society affiliation, but popular opinion disagreed and the decision was reversed at a well-attended general meeting on 1 April 1940 which passed the motion 'That the VUC Peace Society be granted affiliation to the VUC Students' Association [by] . . . 74 votes to 22'.[68] In these years it was comparatively easy for members of the university to hold and express pacifist opinions. However, as the conflict spread, the lists of the New Zealand dead grew, and Japan entered the war, opinion in academia tended to join popular opinion in decrying the luxury of objecting to participation in the fight against the evils responsible for this global cataclysm. The headline of the first issue of *Salient* for 1942, 'We Can Be No Longer Neutral', signalled a new direction for members of the college: from then on student support was thrown behind the war effort, 'shirkers' received scant sympathy, and little else was heard in the magazine from the VUC Peace Society.

Although attending university had been Ginn's reason for moving to Wellington, it was hard to reconcile the remote life of the scholar with the heady atmosphere of turmoil and crisis at Ormond Burton's Webb St. parsonage, where Ginn boarded in the final months of his second year. In this time of divided loyalties Ginn found himself leading a strange double life:

> In cloister & common room we too were timeless.
> Of course, below the Terrace, in the jagged gorge,

66 Ibid.
67 'The University and the War', *Salient*, vol. 3, no. 1 (Mar 1940), p.7.
68 'Special Meeting', *Salient*, Vol. 3, No. 2 (Apr 1940), p.13.

> The tocsin of tram & traffic jam
> Life flew at eyes & ears & skin & scratched
> Hissed her flash disintegrating kiss
> ['First Verse', see p.205]

When Ginn arrived in Wellington in 1940 he initially boarded in Lyall Bay with a Methodist friend, Bill Kelly, who was also involved in the pacifist movement. Later he found board closer to the university with an immigrant family named Eisner. Refugees from Hitler's Germany, Dr Eisner—a Doctor of Commerce—and his wife were surviving in New Zealand on a considerably reduced income by working as caretakers at Taranaki Street's large Wesley Church, which they kept spotless by regularly hand-scrubbing the entire building. Ginn's board supplemented their income and they in their turn helped him with his language studies. Mrs Eisner, who was trained in German cuisine, was a marvellous hostess who tended to spoil her boarder. But in 1941 everything else was subordinate to the pacifist cause 'which was getting more and more sinister, we were being hounded as it were and shot down'.[69]

The Reverend Ormond Burton was jailed in late April 1941 on various charges relating to pacifist activities that were deemed to be in contravention of the Public Safety Emergency Regulations. He remained in Mt Crawford prison for the rest of the year, and Ginn left the Eisners to board with Burton's wife Nell and their two children Robbie and Mary.[70] When not studying he assisted with the Burtons' work among alcoholics and the homeless, helped around the house, and participated in pacifist activities, including visiting those imprisoned in Mt Crawford. Although it was against his nature he also spoke publicly in the street—'I was pushed into it as it were. I didn't have much to say but I did what I was supposed to'[71]—but was not among those arrested. As much as anything, speaking publicly was a rite of initiation that demonstrated his commitment to the cause. Yet membership of the CPS was not a dour experience: as the external pressure increased—with confiscations, police searches and jailings—marginalisation produced an internal cohesion characterised by passionate commitment and often buoyant good humour.

Like Archie Baxter in the previous war, Ginn knew that it was only a matter of time before he was called on to actively defend the principles he held. Life 'Hissed her flash disintegrating kiss' on 7 August 1941—a Thursday—when the name 'Ginn, N' was listed in the *Dominion* among the men from the Wellington district who were part of a group of 23,825 called up nationwide in the 'Fourth Overseas Ballot':

> All single men between the ages of 21 and 40 years, inclusive, not already drawn in an overseas ballot, have been drawn in the ninth ballot, the fourth

69 Noel Ginn, interview with Annette Facer, Sep 1994.

70 Burton was jailed a number of times during the war for his pacifist activities, but he was always detained in a civil jail. He was never, as McKay states on p.74 of *Life* 'detained with Terry and Ginn at Whitanui'. Not only was he ineligible for the ballot, he was considered too dangerous a figure to let loose in the detention camps: 'He wasn't [detained]. It's not a matter of opinion, I just know he wasn't. They wouldn't have allowed him there because they were scared of his influence, he was a powerful personality' (Noel Ginn, letter to Paul Millar, Jan 1995).

71 Noel Ginn, interview with Annette Facer, Sep 1994.

> for overseas service . . . Not all the men selected will be available. There will have to be deducted in the final result those unfit and those granted *sine die* adjournments of service by armed forces appeal boards for reasons of public interest (which takes in men engaged in essential occupations), hardship, status, and also conscientious objectors who succeed in their appeals.[72]

But in Ginn's case appearing before an armed forces appeal board was never an option. Not long after the results of the fourth ballot were published he received a summons to the criminal court for failing to answer his call up:

> I was glad I was in Wellington, not in Wanganui where I would have been shaming my family. I just said 'Not Guilty' of refusing the order to put on the uniform. The magistrate said 'Why do you plead not guilty when you did refuse.' I explained what I meant, that I was not fundamentally guilty because of my beliefs. I was sentenced to three months detention and then indefinite internment for the duration of the war.[73]

Ginn began his imprisonment in Wellington's Mt Crawford prison 'in the most wonderful scenic spot in Wellington'.[74] Baxter himself, who in later years frequently visited the prison, was to become familiar with Mt Crawford and its inmates:

> In Mother Crawford's boarding house the company is grand.
> There's bludgers, thieves and con men, who will take you by the hand,
> A bloody sight more human than the company outside,
> And very very seldom are you taken for a ride.
> (*CP*, p.215.)

Finally being imprisoned was a relief from the hothouse tensions of the preceding months. Ginn was now face to face with the worst that could happen to him: 'I felt quite bright about it—I think because of all the doubt and the uncertainties and anxieties preceding, this was finish—sentenced for the duration! It was sort of a let out.'[75] Yet the event had its effects, producing what might be described as mild, shock-induced, hysteria: Ginn was surprised to find himself giggling at the melodramatic clang of the cell door and rattle of keys when he was finally placed alone in a cell, and for the first three days he was unable to eat.

Although twenty-four, Ginn looked much younger, and initially he was stopped from exercising in the general yard with the other prisoners. He did make contact with some of the other imprisoned Christian Pacifists while on the way to the showers, and pacifist leader Archie Barrington slipped him Virginia Woolf's *Common Reader* to help pass the time. A short while later he was integrated into the prison society, and for the month he remained at Mt Crawford he laboured with the others making and carrying bricks, digging on the hillside, and helping in the manufacture of sandsoap.

72 'Fourth Overseas Ballot', *Dominion* 7 Aug 1941 p.7.
73 Noel Ginn, interview with Annette Facer, Sep 1994.
74 Ibid.
75 Ibid.

The final two months of Ginn's sentence were served at Wi Tako prison in Lower Hutt. Before going there he was taken to an army camp, showered, and offered again the opportunity to put on a uniform. Although refusing, he did not meet the overt hostility he expected. His experience was similar to Archie Baxter's who, in the previous war, was struck throughout his ordeal by 'the gentleness and humanity of the ordinary soldiers . . . [if they] had not looked after me I would undoubtedly have died'.[76] Ginn, too, encountered encouragement instead of animosity: 'some of the soldiers spoke and said "Stick to it, mate!" and that sort of thing'.[77]

Wi Tako prison was different from Mt Crawford. It was more open and most inmates worked in its large vegetable gardens. The greatest difference between the two prisons related to the prisoners' accommodation. Again Ginn was in a single cell, but it was one of a long row of open-topped cells—all covered with thick chicken netting—beneath a higher roof. The wire ceiling enabled the prisoners to talk freely with each other, which they did with much shouting and foul language. The gentility of Ginn's own family, and the moral rectitude of his Methodist friends, had left him unprepared for the shocking language, or the freely exchanged threats to maim and murder uttered by quarrelling inmates:

> . . . I'd never heard any foul language much before then so that was an amazing thing to listen to . . . [the] filthy language was quite embarrassing and shocking to me—theoretically I knew it all but in another sense I knew nothing.[78]

The authorities made one concession for which Ginn remained always grateful. Although he had been imprisoned in late August he was allowed to continue with his university studies and sit his examinations for French II and English II. He passed with unspectacular results, but it was a creditable performance when the number of missed lectures, and the fact that study could only be done between the end of work and lights out at 9.00 pm, in a tiny cell surrounded by his shouting, swearing, fellow inmates, was taken into account.

Prisons provide an education in their own right, a fact that Terence Baxter, like Ginn, quickly discovered. While many inmates found imprisonment difficult, Terence noticed that 'some of the young chaps who [were] in and out of jail [were] quite free and easy about it'.[79] Most would talk about what they were in for and, in a fairly analytical fashion, work out where their crimes had gone wrong. In planning how to do a job properly upon release, fellow inmates could be quite helpful:

> . . . the other ones would explain to them, 'You shouldn't have gone to the door on that side, you should have worked in from the other side and you would never have got caught.' So it's a place to learn how to do more crime, more breaking and entering. They taught each other in there.[80]

76 Archibald Baxter, *We Will Not Cease*, pp.7–8.
77 Noel Ginn, interview with Annette Facer, Sep 1994.
78 Ibid.
79 Terence Baxter, personal interview, 11 Dec 1995.
80 Ibid.

Terence's imprisonment had come as a shock to him and his family. Unlike Ginn, who viewed prison as inevitable, the Baxters believed, apparently with some justification, that there were a number of other avenues open to Terence before imprisonment, and a feeling developed that Terence had been victimised because of who his father was.

Throughout 1941 the extended Baxter family—a number of whom faced the prospect of detention—had lived in an atmosphere of rumour and speculation. The Armed Forces appeal boards had, since September 1940, been authorised to consider conscience appeals on their individual merits, rather than merely in relation to the individual's membership of a particular sect espousing pacifist principles. Theoretically this should have favoured the Baxters, most of whom had no affiliation with any particular religious group. However it was soon clear that 'in several of [the appeal boards] the individual conscience met a rough passage and a narrow gate'.[81] So although it seemed that Terence might have sufficient grounds for an appeal to be considered genuine—his education at Quaker Schools, and the family history of conscientious objection—these same factors might, paradoxically, convince the Otago appeal board, which had begun operating early in 1941, that his beliefs were the result of indoctrination.

In June 1941 Terence was called up for territorial service, and immediately appealed on conscientious grounds. Prior to this the manager of Reid and Gray had offered to lodge an appeal on his behalf:

> . . . the Manager, knowing of his family's record presumably, came to him and said that it was not necessary to declare himself as a conscientious objector as they were an essential industry (they made agricultural machinery—ploughs and things) and the firm would appeal for him as he was a good worker and in an essential job and hence would not need to go to war.[82]

Despite the problems he knew it would cause him Terence declined the offer, believing it important that he be seen to make a stand. Nor was it an easy stand to make: his friends were gradually enlisting in the army or navy—the latter service to which he, with his love of sailing, was naturally drawn—and then 'the time came when I got this summons to join up and it made it a bit awkward at work'.[83] The Dunedin authorities did not move as swiftly as the Wellington authorities did in Noel Ginn's case, and Terence's appeal was not heard until 24 September. He received no exemption, only a recommendation that he serve as a non-combatant, a condition he was not prepared to accept as there was no guarantee that the army would honour such recommendations. His refusal was considered a failure to obey a military order and on 6 November he 'was gazetted a defaulter—the first in Otago of those who had appealed'.[84]

81 Nancy M. Taylor, *The Home Front: The New Zealand People at War. Official History of New Zealand in the Second World War 1939–45*, Vol. 1 (Wellington: Historic Publications Branch of Internal Affairs, 1986) p.249.

82 Lenore Baxter, letter to Frank McKay, undated, MS McKay 10/7/33.

83 Terence Baxter, personal interview, 11 Dec 1995.

84 This information is from the letter published in the *Otago Daily Times* on 27 Dec 1941, p.9, under the

Terence's family were still optimistic that he would remain out of detention under regulations passed on 15 May 1941 that allowed men who convinced the appeal boards that their objection was genuine to be directed, in the first instance, to non-combatant duties or—if such duties were unavailable in the Armed Forces—to civilian work at pay and conditions determined by the Minister of National Service. Additional regulations, passed in August, created special tribunals to examine the case of every recognised objector to ensure each was engaged in work useful to the war effort, and that their pay was levelled at the basic rate paid by the Army. Terence's case appeared to have been deemed to fall under the jurisdiction of this board, and he was directed to appear before it:

> On November 26 he received a notice from the Man-power Committee requesting him to call on the secretary, as it had been decided to have his case considered by the one-man tribunal. The particulars of the case were immediately reported to the Associate Minister of National Service.[85]

There was some talk of him taking his trade up to Port Chalmers and working as a welder on the boats that had been designated as minesweepers—a job he would have been prepared to do—but before anything could be finalised he was arrested to appear on December 19 in the police court. The *Otago Daily Times* gave a terse account of the proceedings:

> Terence John Baxter pleaded guilty to having failed to report for medical examination after being called up for military service.
>
> Senior Sergeant Vaughan explained that the accused was a conscientious objector whose appeal had been dismissed.
>
> The magistrate ordered that the accused be detained in a defaulters' camp for the duration of the war.[86]

But his pseudonymous supporter had more to say:

> Sir—The regulations regarding conscientious objectors which were announced by Mr Nash while he was acting Prime Minister, though excellent in intention, have left the door open for discrimination in extreme form . . . Up to the present date . . . only one [objector] has been proceeded against in court and sentenced. This objector, son of a well-known objector in the last war . . . is 19 years of age . . . On December 19 he was charged in court with failing to obey a military order, and was sentenced to defaulters' camp for the duration of the war. He has spent the time since then in the Dunedin gaol. There is no definite information as to when he is going to be sent to camp. He is therefore undergoing a term of imprisonment to which he has not

pseudonym 'British Justice'. Terence Baxter, in the course of our interview on 11 Dec 1995, confirmed that his name was in the *Gazette* but that he believed there was some confusion between himself—'Terence John'—and his cousin 'John Archibald'. Millicent Baxter, however, asserts that 'Terence's name, of all the objectors, never appeared in the *Gazette*' (see her *Memoirs*, p.107).

85 'The Treatment of Conscientious Objectors', letter, *Otago Daily Times* 27 Dec 1941, p.9.

86 'Military Service', *Otago Daily Times* 20 Dec 1941 p.12.

been sentenced. No objector in Otago other than this boy of 19 has received this treatment.

—I am, etc. British Justice.[87]

There is no doubt that Terence Baxter's objection was a brave stand based on a genuine conviction 'that it was not just a matter of an individual not taking part in a war but it was necessary to make a positive protest against war as a method of settling international disputes'.[88] But it was also a difficult stand for a popular young man of nineteen to take who enjoyed his work and was ever loath to stand out from the crowd:

> I took it very hard in a way you see because I had quite a few friends that I worked with and got around town with and had a few drinks with. And all these chaps went off [to war]. It was a fair bit of a blow to me to have to make this sort of decision—mind you it wouldn't have been as hard as some men whose whole family would be against them. With me at least I had my father and mother to support me so that made it a bit better. Nevertheless you had to go against the run of things, and you had people going against you.[89]

Spending Christmas in prison was not an auspicious start to his years in detention—'In a way you could say it was one of the worst Christmases I've ever had'[90] —and in many ways it set the tone for the next four years. Whereas Noel Ginn found some compensation in the keen intellects of other detainees, his natural gregariousness making him a number of enduring friendships, the experience was at odds with Terence's solitary nature and love of open spaces:

> . . . me being me I'm not very keen on camps and fitting in with other people. Even now I tend to keep to myself. How on earth I ever managed to live through the camp, looking back on it, the way I am, it's a bit of a mystery to me.[91]

But in December 1941 the camps were still in the future for Noel and Terence, while for James—who had been considered too young to attend Terence's trial—it would be four eventful years before he would see his brother home again and free. In the meantime his primary focus would be on developing his poetry, which he had begun writing at the age of seven.

87 'The Treatment of Conscientious Objectors', letter, *Otago Daily Times* 27 Dec 1941, p.9.
88 Lenore Baxter, letter to Frank McKay, undated, MS McKay 10/7/33.
89 Terence Baxter, personal interview, 11 Dec 1995.
90 Ibid.
91 Ibid.

# Three
# Baxter's Childhood Influences

> At five one walked in a world of trees
> With parents in the background, for scenery their knees.
> Shelley and Burns like burning angels pass.
> Sweet is the holiday smell of petrol-gas.[92]

Throughout his adolescent and adult years Baxter looked back to his childhood as an Edenic phase in his life, but it was not until his final years, when he was immersed in the simple life of the Jerusalem commune, that he felt he had come close to regaining what he had lost:

> When I was a child I loved the world, the one God made, water, earth, trees, what have you . . . thank God, I'm back in the first world. It'll do me brother. It's as bare as a pig's arse, but it gives me a sense of peace.[93]

But he adds a characteristic qualifier: 'All the same, nobody can be a child again. The pain won't go away.'[94]

This sense of pain and loss recurs in Baxter's writing so frequently that it begins to appear superficially conventional, as John Weir notes 'the words "poetry of loss" apply to almost all that Baxter has written, for much of his poetry relies on an adaptation of the Tudor antithesis of the mutable and the ideal'.[95] But in observing the way Baxter frequently represents the pain of loss, it should be borne in mind that such antitheses will almost inevitably appear in the work of a writer who thinks in mythological terms. Such a writer's treatment of individual experience is unique in much the same way that the individual's life is, to them, unique. But because the writer thinks mythologically, the works of art are also fragments of a larger pattern. Just as an individual is, in the context of a society, part of a much greater entity, so the work of art becomes part of a broader mythical design. Myth frequently deals with the pain of loss, but its artistic value is in its fixity—mythic structures contain the individual work while in turn the work's creative energy illuminates some aspect, or fine detail, of the mythic design. The frequency of Baxter's references to childhood reflect this. Because childhood has the conveniently immutable quality of an ideal it is frequently mythologised, and as myth is, in Baxter's poetry, 'the form that the poet uses to crystallise experience',[96] the projection of 'the Chaos of the world',[97] onto the

92 'Autobiographical', see p.299.
93 James K. Baxter, *Jerusalem Daybook* (Wellington: Price Milburn, 1971) p.52.
94 Ibid.
95 J.E. Weir, *The Poetry of James K. Baxter* (Wellington: Oxford University Press, 1970) p.63.
96 J.E. Weir, 'An Interview with James K. Baxter', *Landfall* 28.3 (Sep 1974) p.243.
97 Ibid, p.242.

fixed screen of a mythologised childhood becomes a device through which order, however fragmentary, is discerned and meaning, however limited, discovered.

In assessing his poetry Baxter considered his successes to be those poems with 'a kernel of experiential knowledge'.[98] By good fortune he had a childhood that, from the moment of his birth, provided him with a rich store of these:

> . . . the birth-sac broke too soon
> And on the twenty-ninth of June
> Prematurely I looked at the walls
> And yelled.[99]

When James first arrived at the Kuri Bush farm his brother Terence, like any normally inquisitive four-year-old, went to investigate the tiny interloper. He prodded the baby with a broom which caused some bleeding when the bristles punctured the delicate skin. This was not an early indication of their future relationship. Within the family and among close friends the boys were known as 'Ten' and 'Jum'—Ten because Baxter as a toddler had been unable to pronounce Terence, and Jum abbreviated from Jumbo (the elephant) on account of Baxter's tiny size at birth. As the nicknames suggest, there was an ease among the members of the Baxter family. Throughout their lives Terence and James related well to each other despite the gap in their ages and their different approaches to life. On the occasions when they did play together as children, however, Baxter would quickly tire of performing the younger brother's subordinate role:

> We were as close as any two brothers when we were younger, certainly. But he didn't want to play the games I played. For instance I wanted to go and sail boats in the pond, and he'd come down and give me a hand. I'd want him to get over the other side and turn the boat round. Well that was all right for a little while, he'd help, but after a while he wanted me to help him, so we didn't do a lot together.[100]

In Baxter's biography McKay draws the following comparison between James and Terence:

> Terence confirmed the stereotype of the sensitive, introspective first child, which some psychologists have presented, and James that of the relaxed, more outgoing younger brother. They were very different physically. Terence was rather tense and tended to be moody. James was thickset, and used to lumber along. He was easygoing and for the most part good-tempered.[101]

Baxter's own, very individualistic, approach to life had a lot to do with his parents, who were unconventional for the times. He commented on the great 'difference

98 J. E. Weir, introduction, *The Bone Chanter: Unpublished Poems 1945–72* by James K. Baxter (Wellington: Oxford University Press, 1976) p.5.
99 Baxter, *The Man on the Horse,* p.122.
100 Terence Baxter, personal interview, 11 Dec 1995.
101 McKay, *Life*, p.27.

between my own socialist-pacifist family and the semi-militarist activities of the people around about as the country moved towards war' which gave 'me a sense . . . of a gap . . . between myself and other people'. It was this sense of difference that taught him 'to distrust mass opinion and sort out my own ideas'.[102]

When they began seeing each other, Archibald Baxter and Millicent Brown appeared a most unlikely match: she had enjoyed a life of privilege as the well-educated daughter of a highly regarded academic, while he was a poor, self-educated, Otago farmer who had gained notoriety as a conscientious objector. Millicent's father, Professor John Macmillan Brown, was horrified at his daughter's choice of husband—a fact both James and Terence were aware of:

> . . . he disapproved of my mother's marriage. He would have thought she'd get married to somebody in his own class, and this common farmer from down south you see, he wouldn't do at all.[103]

Aware that her father was having enough of a problem coping with her decision to marry beneath herself, Millicent avoided making any mention of Archie's war record—'I was a coward. I did not tell my father that Archie was a notorious character.'[104] Others, however, were less reticent:

> Nowadays people cannot realise the extent of the feeling against conscientious objectors that still existed shortly after the first war. I think it would have been better if I had told my father. It would have made the break more honest . . . It wasn't long, of course, before he knew—people were only too anxious to tell him what a scoundrel my husband was.[105]

Terence believed that it was not until his mother 'produced these couple of boys, that were fairly well behaved, that [Macmillan Brown] started to realise that there was a fairly good marriage going there'.[106] Millicent, however, had been confident from the start that the marriage would work and she set about her new life with characteristic determination and energy:

> . . . she went from one of the better sort of houses in Christchurch to this little cottage down in Kuri Bush with a tub outside to do a little washing in, and a few other things, and helping her husband to milk the cows now and again, and a life like that. But she was a very very happy woman. She had to walk out the back to get a bit of water out of the tank, a great big brass tank with a tap, and she'd be singing away to herself, as happy as you like, absolutely happy with her whole life.[107]

Millicent's determination and intelligence, and Archie's strength of character and wisdom, were potent influences on their children. Terence, with his quiet nature and

102 Baxter, *The Man on the Horse*, p.123.
103 Terence Baxter, personal interview, 11 Dec 1995.
104 Millicent Baxter, *The Memoirs of Millicent Baxter*, p.59.
105 Ibid.
106 Terence Baxter, personal interview, 11 Dec 1995.
107 Ibid.

manual dexterity, took more obviously after his father, while articulate, inquisitive James was affected by both of his parents: 'Somewhere back in the Freudian fog belt these two strong influences began to work on me. . . . [and] I broke out in words.'[108]

Baxter's parents are often mentioned in his poetry, and the earlier published poems tend to bear out Millicent's impression that 'In everything he wrote, to and of his father, he is most loving. I, on the other hand, come off badly.'[109] This is less the case in his later verse where his mother, having followed him into the Catholic church, is a self-sufficient figure of peace 'growing old / with Christ for company'.[110] Nor is it clearly the case in an unpublished poem written at the age of fifteen in which Baxter addresses her in the Romantic idiom that is characteristic of much of his youthful verse:

> O friend and mother in one form combined,
> To thee I owe the pleasures of the mind;
> For the full knowledge that thou long had'st known
> To me narrated was; and I was shown
> The many tales and legends of the past—
> And well I know thy loving-kindness cast
> A sheen of beauty o'er my babyhood:
> To thee my love, to thee my gratitude!
> ['To my Mother', Hocken, MS 704/4: 184]

Baxter, in crediting his mother with introducing him to 'the pleasures of the mind', draws specific attention to those mythological elements—'The many tales and legends of the past'—that were of use to him when writing poems. His silence regarding more formal intellectual pursuits is a revealing indication of an already well-developed suspicion of formal education that would be expressed in more overt terms later on in his life. It is an attitude that stems, in part, from an early discovery—articulated in a poem written at the age of thirteen—that the routines of school life inhibit creativity:

> At School I have no time to dream
> As sailing on Life's steady stream
> The bustling hours go by;
> But when at night my Muse awakes,
> Then soaring wings my Fancy takes
> Far to the land of Poesy.
> ['At School I have no time to Dream', Hocken, MS 704/1: 18]

He expanded on this theme in 'Notes on the Education of a New Zealand Poet':

> I was already unconsciously erecting my defences around that core of primitive experience, that ineducable self which I like to call a dinosaur's egg. Unfortunately the abstract analytical processes which the schools were able

108 Baxter, *The Man on the Horse*, p.122.
109 Millicent Baxter, *The Memoirs of Millicent Baxter*, p.111.
110 'He Waiata mo taku Tangi', *CP*, p.506.

> to offer me . . . have the side-effect of neutralising this kind of experience and making it inaccessible to the conscious mind.[111]

Baxter developed a more formulated criticism of academic life in 1945 when he was attempting to rationalise his decision to abandon his ill-fated University career:

> Intellectuality demands a false bottom to the mind, a loss of emotional intuition . . . the realist writer, such as I would wish to be, must revolt from contemporary modes and grow up on his own. Because of the reserves of strength which heredity and environment have given me, I can do this.[112]

Baxter's inherited 'reserves of strength' were, he believed, derived almost exclusively from his father's side of the family. His identification with his Baxter relatives was extremely close and 'he reacted negatively to his grandfather [Macmillan Brown], with whom he could not find a single idea in common and who moreover had not considered his loved father a suitable son-in-law'.[113] On two occasions in his writing Baxter quotes with approval Robert Burns's criticism of academics like his grandfather, and of the students they presume to educate:

> A set o' dull conceited hashes
> Confuse their brains in college classes;
> They gang in stirks, and come out asses,
> Plain truth to speak;
> An' syne they think to climb Parnassus
> By dint o' Greek.[114]

In Baxter's novel *Horse* the protagonist Timothy Harold Glass—of whom Baxter wrote 'He, or somebody rather like him, inhabited this town [in the mid-1940s], daring to use my name and wear my features'[115]—listens patiently to his father's exposition on the poem's meaning:

> 'A stirk's a steer. A bullock.' His father's eye would light up with the joy of the Scotsman commenting obliquely on the facts of life. 'The Varsity men are nothing but educated bullocks. That's what Burns thought about it.'[116]

It was his father's approval and encouragement that started Baxter off as a poet. Although his mother also took an interest in his writing she—being Macmillan Brown's daughter—had the misfortune to be associated in the mind of her son with the systems and ideas that stifled and inhibited creativity. Her interests were in 'history, international affairs and politics . . . [She] enjoyed novels [and] was especially fond of biographies . . . [but] never read poetry for pleasure'.[117] Archie, on the other hand,

111 Baxter, *The Man on the Horse*, p.131.
112 See 'Thoughts Concerning a Career', p.398.
113 Lenore Baxter, letter to Frank McKay, 7 Jul 1985, VUW Library, Wellington, MS McKay 10/7/32.
114 Baxter, *The Man on the Horse*, p.93. See also p.3 of Baxter's novel *Horse* (Auckland: Oxford University Press, 1985), where only the third line is quoted.
115 Baxter, *The Man on the Horse*, p.17.
116 Baxter, *Horse*, p.3.
117 Lenore Baxter, letter to Frank McKay, 7 Jul 1985, VUW Library, Wellington, MS McKay 10/7/32.

had an abiding love of poetry: he would 'roll out the long trundling ballad lines' of Australian poet Henry Lawson,[118] and could recite the poems of 'Burns and Shelley and Byron and Blake and Tom Hood . . . when the mood took him'.[119] While imprisoned for his pacifism in the hold of the *Waitemata* among the 'experimental fourteen' being shipped to Europe, it was in poetry that he and a fellow objector sought refuge of a kind:

> I found in Sanderson, one of the religious objectors, an interest in literature, particularly in poetry, and many an hour did we spend in the little end cabin, talking over questions far removed from war or our fight against it.[120]

He had himself written poetry before the First World War but, for his stand, was to become a 'poet whom time betrayed / To action.'[121] As Baxter, in a letter written to Noel Ginn in November 1943, explained: the 'war knocked all . . . poetry out of him—even now he can only appreciate, not write' (p.293).

Although Archie Baxter all but stopped writing poetry, he never stopped reading or reciting it and was keen to ensure that both of his sons developed an appreciation for verse:

> It was with his encouragement that both boys tried their hands at writing verse from a very early age—and that habit took root in one of them! One cannot help but wonder what sort of gifts Jum would have developed if he had been reared away from his father![122]

Baxter's breaking out in words began as a desire for parental approval, but soon acquired a momentum of its own:

> He started very very young. From then on of course he was at it all the time. He was never without some sort of little notebook. Anything at all around him seemed to just move him to write poetry.[123]

Terence was also affected by his father's love of poetry and remembers him being 'very keen on Burns, and of course all the other English poets, anyone you could think of really. He [also] knew his Bible through and through.'[124] One of Terence's earliest memories is of his father reciting poems to his brother:

> . . . he used to get my brother on his knee and recite one of Burns's poems—one of his favourite ones was of course 'Tam O' Shanter', and my brother would take it all in and, like most children, want it over and over again. So he'd get the poem again the next night and get to know it himself, and he got the feeling for poetry that way. He got many others recited too—I suppose

118 James K. Baxter, 'A Note on Henry Lawson', *Meanjin*, March (1956): 33.
119 Baxter, *The Man on the Horse*, p.122.
120 Archibald Baxter, *We Will Not Cease*, p.59.
121 'To my Father', *CP*, p.65.
122 Lenore Baxter, letter to Frank McKay, 7 Jul 1985, MS McKay 10/7/32.
123 Terence Baxter, personal interview, 11 Dec 1995.
124 Ibid.

> he had something to go on because my brother was alert to it and had leanings that way.[125]

Later on when his mother, although naturally loyal to her son, might take issue with the tone or content of some of Baxter's poems, he remained confident of his father's support:

> My father was a little bit more broad minded, would give a little bit of a grin about it, or note that he might be sailing a bit close to the wind now and again. Of course he admired practically anything that my brother wrote. I think it was quite a good thing for my brother in a way. He had the support of his father all the way through, right till the day [my father] died. He always had this feeling behind him that his father approved of him.[126]

Immediately preceding Baxter's early poem 'To my Mother' there is, in MS Book IV, a companion poem entitled 'To my Father'. When the two poems are compared, the poem to Millicent has a noticeably more impersonal air about it, as if it was writing with some slight detachment, or was mildly inspired by duty. Although the poem expresses appreciation of her efforts on his behalf; acknowledges her intellect; and displays an appropriate sense of filial love; about the one thing that mattered most to Baxter—his poetry—it remains silent. 'To my Father', however, has a quality both personal and intimate—it is a letter more of gratitude than appreciation. Behind its Romantic idiom runs an emotion that will reach its full depth in a later published version.[127]

**To my Father**

O mild preceptor of my early youth,
    True father still in action, word and deed,
In whom I find the archetype of truth—
    For this, my love and gratitude thy meed!

But most to thee I owe this tribute now,
    That had I known thee not I could not be
A fount where Heliconian waters flow,
    Partaker of the joys of Poesy!

Beauty of language and of form I found,
    And with thy helping guidance ever nigh,
Where else the nestling ne'er had left the ground,
    I first could flutter, then could fly!
        [Hocken, MS 704/4: 183.]

125 Ibid.
126 Ibid.
127 See *CP*, pp.65–6.

# Four
# James and Terence

my brother is a good sort
sensitive and strong
so ends the song[128]

About the time the fledgling poet began taking wing in his poetry, his brother was discovering a similar sense of liberation in sailing 'about the Taeri River mouth [off Brighton] & more often in the safer [Otago] Harbour'.[129] From his earliest years Terence was 'driven by this feeling to get out boating'.[130] As a boy he 'Sailed his flaxstick navy, twig-masted on rough ripples' in Brighton pond,[131] and at sixteen, soon after starting his welder's apprenticeship, he purchased his first boat. It was a small, clinker-built, teak yacht named the *Plucky* which had originally been a lifeboat for a Dunedin tug of the same name. The tug *Plucky* was built in Dumbarton in Scotland in 1880 but had worked for some years in Otago waters. In 1936 the *Plucky's* lifeboat was purchased by two brothers who rigged the boat as a ketch and took her sailing. Terence acquired her from them four years later and, with the exception of the detention years, has sailed her in the Otago Harbour ever since.[132]

From an early age Terence would gravitate to anyone who sailed, including an eccentric local fisherman named Mackenzie who had:

> . . . arrived at Brighton in a boat years ago when my father was younger. When I knew him he was an old man, but a bit of a character. Donald his name was—Donald Mackenzie. He was a keen photographer—more scenery than people. He was very tall, well over six feet and he used to drive a baby Austin, hunched up inside. He could barely see out the windscreen, because if he sat up he'd go straight through the roof.[133]

Terence admired Mackenzie's 'beautiful big boat', his imagination was captured by the man's yachting exploits, and he appreciated the occasions when he got to go sailing with him. When he began working he even arranged to buy the boat and his

128 'Unwritten Elegy', see pp.61–2.
129 Noel Ginn, letter to Paul Millar, Jan 1995.
130 Terence Baxter, personal interview, 11 Dec 1995.
131 'The Giant's Grave', *CP*, p.153.
132 In 1996 Terence and the *Plucky*—he 74 years old, the boat 116—would still be seen out sailing 'whenever the wind is from the North and blowing strongly'. (Val Maxwell, *Southern Sails: 100 years of the Otago Yacht Club* (Dunedin: Otago Yacht Club, 1995), inside cover.)
133 Terence Baxter, personal interview, 11 Dec 1995.

disappointment was intense when, after the sale appeared to have gone through, Mackenzie changed his mind.

Mackenzie also captured James's imagination, and he appears a few times in poems. There is a vignette of him living his self-sufficient life on the banks of the Brighton River, making 'boats / at its edge / choosing the thwarts cunningly / from bent manuka'.[134] But more frequently he is a sinister figure, a 'half mad / Solitary six-foot fisherman' who:

> Blasted a passage out with gelignite
> Between the shore and the island templebone
> To let his boat come in, changing the drift
> Of water from the bay.
> ['The Waves', *CP*, p.286]

Similarly, in 'The Town Under the Sea', he is the 'mad / Boatbuilder' that as children 'My brother, my cousins and I' used to dodge.[135]

Dodging Mackenzie in earnest only happened once, and it was purely Terence's adventure. However, it was an incident with plenty of dramatic potential and the story must have appealed to Baxter. It began with the decision of Terence and two friends to take Mackenzie's boat out on their own. They waited for a day when 'Old Donald', as they called him, had gone into town, and then they launched his boat into the river and began paddling around in it, using fire shovels for oars. For some reason Mackenzie returned almost immediately and, when he discovered his boat missing, flew into a rage:

> . . . he had a terrible temper, a real highland temper, I'm absolutely certain he'd have killed a person if he got wild enough. He came down and was shouting on the bank 'Where's my boat?'—he had this strong Scottish accent. Anyway we were silly boys because we brought it back in on the side where he was, we should have left it on the other side and escaped that way. The other two boys, who were bigger than me, got away, but he nearly caught me. I've never run so fast in all of my life, he nearly had me, I could hear him shouting just behind me and I could even hear his breath puffing. If he got me I don't know what would have happened, he was that wild.[136]

It may have been Mackenzie's determined pursuit and Terence's narrow escape that inspired Baxter to mythologise the old man in 'The Caryatids' as the 'mad boathouse-keeper with his box of photographs / Whom poets have called Eros'.[137] Mackenzie appears, at first reading, to be a most unconventional love god. In Freudian terms, however, he is a powerful symbol of the potentially destructive adolescent libido: being a hermit he represents the dangerous solitude which may lead to madness that the adolescent, in the interests of self-preservation, must flee into the world of

134 'The River', *CP*, p.353.
135 See *CP*, p.252.
136 Terence Baxter, personal interview, 11 Dec 1995.
137 See *CP*, p.410.

adult sexual pleasure—a world of activities antithetical to the hermit—where there is a form of sanctuary. Freud, in *Beyond the Pleasure Principle*, makes a connection between Eros and poetry that accords with Baxter's frequent representations of sexual experience and poetic inspiration as joint healers of his adolescent 'green sickness',[138] when he proposes that 'the Libido of our sexual instincts would coincide with the Eros of poets and philosophers, which holds together all things living'.[139]

By associating an actual instance of flight with the adolescent's libidinous drive to self-preservation, Baxter is simultaneously representing the search for a way out of the arid adolescent years—'when sex and intellect are both active but have nothing to feed on . . . [so that] the adolescent begins to devour himself'[140]—and the attempt to find salvation in adult sexuality. Mackenzie is no benevolent love god because the adolescent libido is a merciless goad. The photographs he carries are images of that Edenic childhood that drowned beneath the adolescent sea.[141] If the adolescent attempts to look back to that past, he is more likely to see just how closely he is pursued by his own destruction. In Baxter's version of his own adolescence he is ever conscious of pursuing Eros panting down his neck—the difference between suicide and sanctuary is a matter of small degrees:

> One day the boy entered his father's coalhouse and took down from a beam the sawn-off rifle he had hidden there. Almost without thought he placed the muzzle in his mouth, having nothing to lose. Then an idea occurred to him—'You have never yet loved a woman. Wait till then, and see if the world changes.' So he replaced the gun in its hiding place.[142]

Later he would write 'I praise that / sad boy now, who having no / hope, did not blow out his brains'.[143]

Baxter's use of the figure of Mackenzie in this fashion, is one of numerous examples supporting his comment concerning the 'experiential' content of his poetry that 'What happens is either meaningless to me, or else it is mythology'.[144] His references to Mackenzie also support the common assumption that 'there is no period of Baxter's

138 See 'I have cut from my heart', p.495:

> I have cut from my heart
> her green-sickness;
> it is better to be a tall and lonely man
> than stand and cry for the moon.

139 Sigmund Freud, *Beyond the Pleasure Principle*, trans. by C.J.M. Hubback (London, Vienna: International Psycho-analytical Press, 1922) p.64.

140 'Further Notes on New Zealand Poetry', Hocken, MS 975/119.

141 Baxter's short story 'The Town That Sank Under the Sea', *Otago Daily Times* 28 Jan 1956:4 (also published as 'The Town Under the Sea', *Meanjin* XV (1966) pp.341–2) concentrates on the idyllic aspects of childhood before 'the sea town sank' and over it grew 'the grey implacable forests'. It is in his 1962 poem 'The Town under the Sea' (*CP*, pp.252–3) that he limits the depiction of Edenic childhood to the first 2 of 7 stanzas and makes, in the remaining stanzas, an explicit connection between the adolescent discovery of sin, sex and death, and the sinking of the childhood town: 'At puberty, / Or the first deadly sin, the sea rose up in one / Pounding night and swallowed the land . . . Nor do any / Bells ring, on a windy day, from those wide / Guts of the coffin-making tide.'

142 James K. Baxter, 'The Unicorn: A Consideration of Adolescence', Hocken, MS 975/34, see pp.535–9.

143 'At Days Bay', *CP*, p.309.

144 Baxter, *The Man on the Horse*, p.122.

life, and no important event, which cannot be found in his poetry or prose'.[145] This assumption is reasonable, with one apparently major exception: in comparison with Baxter's references to the rest of his family, his brother is virtually invisible. In the *Collected Poems*, for example, Terence features no more often than Mackenzie. Apart from his appearance in the two poems I have already discussed—'The Giant's Grave' and 'A Family Photograph 1939'—there are only three further references to him. He navigates the boat in 'The River',[146] his is among the photographs on the mantelpiece in 'Mother and Son':

> Those wood-framed photographs
> Also beside the clock, contain your doubtful angels,
>
> My brother with hair diagonally brushed
> Over his forehead, with a hot dark eye,
>
> And myself, the baby blondish drowsing child
> So very slow to move away from the womb!
> (*CP*, p.369)

and his time in detention is alluded to in sonnet fourteen of 'Autumn Testament'. But this poem's focus is not Terence—its purpose in mentioning him is to date a portrait of Archie, and refer obliquely to Baxter's own pacifist heritage:

> So [my father] did look
>
> In the time when a Labour Government planted my brother
> On the Hautu prison farm for five years
>
> For walking in my father's footprint
> And refusing to carry a gun.[147]

The picture of Terence Baxter that emerges from the *Collected Poems* is of a member of Baxter's family who was of only passing relevance to him. Given that Baxter rarely held back on writing about the rest of his relatives—his parents and his wife, in particular, feature prominently in his verse, often in a most personal and intimate fashion—one might reasonably conclude that his brother played little significant part in his life.[148] In fact the opposite is the case; during the 1940s Baxter

145 Vincent O'Sullivan, *James K. Baxter* (Wellington: Oxford University Press, 1976) p.4.

146 See *CP*, p.385.

147 'Autumn Testament', *CP*, p.547.

148 Baxter also mentions his brother in the prose piece 'Conversation about Writing', (*New Zealand Monthly Review* 60 (Sep 1965) p.28), but again his primary purpose is to establish his own credentials as a social critic, and his selective use of facts and fudging of details is both political and polemical.

> Fifty years ago they hung my father up to a post by the wrists, day by day at Mud Farm in the middle of winter, because he would not put a bullet through a fellow worker. Twenty years ago they put my brother behind barbed wire, to be eaten alive for five years by the devil of boredom, weeding flax in a bog at Shannon, under the dead eyes of the screw and the gauleiter. Now the smell of burning bodies comes over the sea from Vietnam. The cops and the bureaucrats are at their butchering again. I have only one son; and I'm afraid what they'll do to him.

wrote a number of unpublished, deeply personal, poems referring to Terence. But he was well aware of his brother's reserved nature, and it is likely that he never considered publishing them. In a letter to Ginn, he had written:

> Don't tell Terry, as he mightn't like it, but he comes into some of my not-to-be-published epigrams, rather political perhaps. Nothing anywhere uncomplimentary to him, but he might not like to be carried in the back of the Art-Cart, he being sensitive on any infringement of his personality. (p.333)

There is also evidence to suggest that Baxter kept these poems private because Terence's detention was the source of considerable personal anguish to him. To Ginn he wrote: 'Terry is a lone wolf, "dark and sensitive" I think of him as—and when I do think of him that indescribable grip of consanguineity [sic] makes my mind sore'(see letter p.360, and 'To my Brother', p.63). Variations on this phrase recur throughout his correspondence. On 3 February 1944 he wrote to his English friend from Sibford School, Margaret Herbert:

> Terence is still in detention Camp—for the duration of the war, however long that may be. I have a pain in my mind whenever I think of it, he has so much vitality and he's shut up. I don't like to write about it.[149]

An earlier letter to Ginn had said much the same thing: 'You, Terry, and indeed all the rest of them being shut up is a sore spot in my mind when I think of it' (p.280).

'The Giant's Grave' is a rare published insistence on their shared childhood—in the poem Baxter recalls the time when '. . . deep in memory's glass, / Free of the torturers hand, I and my elder brother / Walk the green riverbank in the land where I was born' (*CP*, p.153). The indication that they will undergo a shared torture is intentional: Terence's time in detention camps coincided almost exactly with Baxter's adolescence, the period of which he later wrote, 'I think anyone who has survived [it] . . . would feel at home . . . in a pit full of tarantulas'.[150]

Ironically, each brother seems to have felt that the other came off worse during the war years. Baxter experienced a certain guilt that Terence had to suffer things that he managed to avoid. On turning eighteen he was not immediately bundled into detention as Terence had been, and even had he been detained, all indications are that he was temperamentally better suited to such a situation. Early in their correspondence Ginn had written: 'Life in this camp has valuable compensations particularly because of the variety of minds and personalities' (p.140), and this for Baxter would likely have made the experience less unpleasant than it was for his reserved brother. Knowing that there were many in detention who, like Ginn, shared his literary interests, may even have sounded appealing to a boy who had found his solitary adolescence a torment, and, as noted earlier, compared his experiences around this time to those of 'a Jewish boy growing up in an anti-Semitic neighbourhood'.[151] In

149 Margaret Hargreave (nee Herbert), letter to Frank McKay, VUW Library, Wellington, MS McKay 10/5/36. Letter contains transcripts of excerpts from letters of Baxter's in Margaret Hargreave's possession.
150 'Further Notes on New Zealand Poetry', Hocken, MS 975/119.
151 Baxter, *The Man on the Horse*, p.124.

the right company he was naturally gregarious and if he did desire solitude or freedom he could find both writing poetry, a passion he could indulge anywhere. Terence, however, was denied the opportunity to go sailing—his equivalent form of escape—for four full years.[152] For Terence, confinement in close company with others was, from the start, a penance:

> [In jail] you'd get cooped up in one cell—I didn't take to that very well. You mightn't like the person, and you didn't choose him to be with. One I got [put] with was very religious, absolutely mad fanatically religious, and I'm not too keen on these people that've got this look in their eye. Everything, it's all in 'the Lords hands'. Well I suppose they may be right but it doesn't altogether go with me. Anyway, this chap said, 'You know it's wonderful having this faith, you can do anything, you can even move mountains.' He reckoned that if he could get himself out he could do this. So I said, 'Well, we're in here, locked in here together, why don't you move us out of here.' But it didn't seem to be able to work as far as we were concerned—we were in there for a while.[153]

Despite these experiences, Terence felt that it was his brother who suffered more during the war years. He was aware (more so than his parents) that Baxter, as the youngest son in a non-conformist family, was publicly criticised, at times even persecuted, for having a father who was not in the home guard and a brother in detention as a defaulter. He discussed this with a family friend, Patricia Gill, who then wrote in a letter to Frank McKay:

> . . . Terry also believes that J. was deeply affected by the war—what it meant as a replay of his father's experiences. I remembered while talking to Terry, Jum's horror of the idea that Terry might have to suffer physically as the father had done—strapped to a post in the field. Jum was not brave physically and well knew that he could not have withstood man-handling. We believe that this experience drove Jim further into the 'inner world'—there to fight the dragons and the pain—to tie them up in a net of words.[154]

There is one published poem not in the *Collected Poems* in which Baxter refers to Terence with more feeling. It is a poem in seven sections called 'Jottings' which Baxter sent to Mike Doyle in 1964, and which Doyle had published in 1972:

> On mudflats of the river below
> Banks of summer grass the children played

152 While Terence was in detention, Baxter was deputised to look after his boat for him. Much of one of Terence's surviving letters to Baxter from around 1942–43 (MS Hocken 975/183) is taken up with discussion of the boat: he expresses concern that she might be 'showing signs of opening up after being out of the tide all this time', and instructs Baxter on how to air the sails—'about once every month or two' or after 'a long spell of damp weather'. According to Terence, his brother maintained the boat conscientiously the whole time he was in detention.

153 Terence Baxter, personal interview, 11 Dec 1995.

154 Patricia Gill, letter to Frank McKay, 19 Apr 1983, VUW Library, MS McKay 10/4/21.

With driftwood, river flotsam, near that
Bog at Shannon where my brother
Spent five years behind barbed wire
For being unwilling to bear arms, though quick
Enough with a welder's kit or a tacking boat:
Half loyal to my father, half his own
Hatred of being touched.

. . . . .

The trenches dug around his mouth
Were what another war had planted there.[155]

Baxter's deep feelings for his father—he described him once as 'a man whom it was never a penance to love'[156]—are echoed in this reference to Terence. The 'trenches dug around [Terence's] mouth' by his time in detention, are comparable with the 'lines around [Archie's] chin and mouth' that appear in a portrait of their father done around the time Terence was detained.[157] Father and son are united by their experiences as objectors in two wars, and by the marks of suffering chiselled into their faces. 'Jottings' is the single published example of the personal intensity and emotive force that characterises Baxter's unpublished poems on his brother from the 1940s.

In his very early work Baxter conceals his references to Terence in poems about the sea and sailing. This is arguably the start of his practice of developing patterns of symbolism to express things that he preferred not to articulate directly. Given Terence's passion, Baxter's use of symbolism surrounding sailing and the sea is a natural choice; the fact that it supplied an abundance of material that he could use with feeling, purpose and—in 'A Family Photograph 1939'—complexity, was an added bonus. The earliest of these poems was written shortly after the *Plucky* was purchased, when Baxter was thirteen. Its most notable aspect is that, as in 'The Giant's Grave', Baxter insists on the shared nature of the experience.

**Let us away!**

Let us away! The wind is sharp and cold
    That sweeps from northward o'er the briny main—
The sails are set. The tug of surges bold,
    The bitter beating of the winter rain,
All raise a paean joyful, strong and brave,
    That echoes to the hills and back again,—
The vessel bounds o'er each successive wave,
    Leaps, straining forward like a living thing:
Who cares what is our goal? for all the joys
    Of action, best that life can ever bring,
Glow in our veins, and warm our inmost soul.
        [Hocken, MS 704/1: 33, p.39]

155 'Jottings', *Tuatara* 8/9 (Fall 1972) p.121.
156 'Further Notes on New Zealand Poetry', Hocken, MS 975/119.

Such oblique references are characteristic of these early works. 'No Longer Derelict'—written towards the end of 1941 around the time Terence was facing the prospect of detention—although addressed to an abandoned vessel, might as readily be read as an address to a sailor kept from the sea:

The heaving tides move on
Among the pools at noon—
But thou art still;

. . . . .

And dost thou long for the feel
Of the swelling rollers' sway,
When the open sea
Is firm beneath thy keel,
When the hurrying clouds are grey
And the wind is swift and free
In the curve of the billowing sail?
[Hocken, MS 704/2: 129, pp.104–5]

Poems in MS Books III and IV refer directly to imprisonment, in a way that reflected the Baxter family's enduring concern about the effect of detention on Terence. In 'He Leapt' a prisoner wakes from a dream, only to 'taste captivity and feel anew / The bands of apathy that chain his will',[158] while 'Captivity' expresses the fear that imprisonment will 'strangle swift as steel / And scarred souls whither where there is no sun'.[159] The final stanza of Baxter's first ballad—'Ballade of Freedom' in MS Book VII—takes up, in a distinctly Shelleyan mode, a similar theme on behalf of the 'thousand souls' in detention camps:

Man, to thee our woes are slight—
But hearken to the agony
As a wail goes round the cells tonight
Where a thousand souls break sullenly,
Break, and acclaim Hell's acolyte,
Bow to the god of the brazen key![160]

The first poem in which Baxter specifically identifies his brother is poem number 405 in MS Book VII. Baxter links Terence—as he does in 'Jottings' and the fourteenth sonnet of 'Autumn Testament'—with Archie. This poem, 'From a Forgotten Song', recalls a happier time before the war when the family, together on a camping holiday, raise a tent in the rain: 'My brother newly wet holding the pole: / My father as if known long to the storm / Beating the pegs in'.[161] I do not think it any coincidence that when Baxter wrote this poem, and made his first direct reference to Terence, he

157 'Autumn Testament', *CP*, p.547.
158 'He leapt', Hocken, MS 704/3: 155, p.45.
159 'Captivity', Hocken MS 704/4: 223, p.110.
160 'Ballade of Freedom', Hocken MS 704/7: 391, p.9.
161 'From a Forgotten Song', Hocken, MS 704/7: 405, p.39.

had just commenced corresponding with Noel Ginn. Ginn was first and foremost Terence's friend and his relationship with Baxter was never more than a pen-friendship. With political discussion and references to the war subject to camp censorship, literature and Terence became the two main topics of conversation. The situation of having to write regularly about his brother in letters may well have inspired Baxter to do the same in poems. Whatever the cause, during the period of his correspondence with Ginn, Baxter would write four poems in which his brother features with an intensity only equalled in later poems in which he refers to his father, and his wife.[162]

The first of these poems, 'To T.J. Baxter,' was written late in 1943. Each stanza is a line shorter than the one preceding it, which creates the effect of not so much a diminuendo, as a stripping away of surface material to reach bedrock. The superficial reasons one might give for sailing—recapturing childhood wonder, escaping the drudgery of the town, discovering new lands—are peeled away until all that remains is an elemental compulsion to 'sail or be damned'. Baxter understood such compulsions; writing poetry was his, he described it as a 'calling, a way of life which a man must follow in order to become his true self',[163] and Terence's compulsion was an aspect of his brother he identified with.

**To T.J. Baxter**

Where are you sailing? Sailor, sailor.
    There is a wideness womanless
    Beyond the gangster and black-mailer,
    Beyond prim mouths that curse and bless;
    Recapturing a boyhood wonder
    Where tropic swells are glassy (far
    From swells that haunt the church or bar)
Or in the black Antarctic huge bergs thunder.

Why do you sail, O sailor, sailor?
    Who'd drudge for ever in a town,
    Doctor, dreamer, shop-man, tailor—
    And a sad sun-downer at sun-down:
The world to wander in, I never wandered;
    And the lands unknown and old hopes moan
    For better a life lost than manhood forever unsquandered!

Even the paint-rusty tramp is alive on the sea,
And the captains still are salts in their floating hotels:
But give me . . . the keel dipping, the fresh waves slapping
    And a falling glass that tells
    Of storm brewing: though she's strange and wayward to know,
A man and a ship are made one when the hurricanes blow.

162 Baxter also continued writing poems referring obliquely to his brother—see for example 'Thoughts by a Conchie Camp' (pp.486–7) and 'For those who lie with crooked limbs in the straight grave' (p.476–8)—but the tone of these four poems, and their direct references to Terence, sets them apart.
163 'A Writer's Vocation', *Manuka* (1958)p.11.

Where are you sailing? Sailor, sailor.
    Beyond the outmost land-shoal, they once said,
    There are islands cool in the west. But they grow paler,
As we sail to them they vanish; yet was found once a man half-dead
Afloat in an open boat, who babbled of streams and a harbour-head.

O the towns are hard to a sailor. By quays they wait
    In the pubs for his pay; and a whore may lead him
    Where a sand-bag falls or a white knife glitters beside him . . .
And he goes with the ebb-tide out.

Yet sail, for the slender ship is forever a bride;
    And the seas can never be charted . . . the sky's bubble holding
Us here imprisoned will burst at last to the tide.

Islands are there, though dark water over
Them flows like a world-rim river.

Why are you sailing, sailor? Because I must sail or be damned.
        [MS Hocken 704/10: 628, pp.133–5]

'Unwritten Elegy', the second of the four poems mentioning Terence directly, was written in February 1944, around the time Baxter enrolled at Otago University. Like another poem—'in the crowd'—written around the same time as 'To T.J. Baxter', 'Unwritten Elegy' is, typographically, 'a kind of imitation of E.E. Cummings'.[164] The prosaic style of address Baxter adopts for 'Unwritten Elegy' is the poem's strength. In a period when Baxter's idiom is dominated by Romantic ornament the poem's initial rejection of elegiac lamentation is refreshing. So too is the poignancy of the subsequent revelation of this poem as an elegy-by-default for a brother in defaulter's detention who is being 'eaten alive . . . by the devil of boredom'.[165]

**Unwritten Elegy**

o i
had thought of writing an elegy
but decided not to

because an elegy
is bound to be
unreal

for one doesnt know the poor b
whos got bumped off
so cannot expand on

164 See 'in the crowd', pp.258–9, and Baxter's comment in his letter of 4 Sep 1943 (p.255).
165 See note 148 on p.55.

his sensations
my brother who was a welder
has been 2 years in a conchie camp

peeling potatoes
and cutting scrub
for scrub to grow

my brother is a good sort
sensitive and strong
so ends the song
[MS Hocken 704/12: 721, pp.52–3]

It is appropriate, given the power with which Baxter would use the form towards the end of his life, that the third, and most intensely personal, of these poems—'To my Brother'—is a sonnet. In July 1944, probably the very month in which 'To my Brother' was composed, Baxter wrote to Ginn: 'I will sometimes spend an hour on a sonnet. They are a hard form, no good for anything loose or slight, but repay enormously—sense of achievement and solidity' (p.368). There is nothing tongue-in-cheek about Baxter's first statement; at the age of eighteen an hour on a poem was, for him, a long time. In 1944 he was, as Lawrence Baigent later described it, 'in extraordinary spate' (*Life*, p.76) and could produce up to half-a-dozen poems a day—Baxter proudly noted that one poem—'Fire in the Mountains'—had been 'written in 3 minutes'.[166] 'To my Brother' asserts, in its title, Baxter's filial bonds with Terence, much as the early poem 'Let us away!' insists on the shared experience of sailing.

The opening line—'The poem should grow a flower out of your chest'—represents a further attempt to stress the closeness of the bond between himself and Terence, for Baxter refers to his brother here in terms normally used to describe one of his early mythological figures of the self: 'the Titan Prometheus . . . from whose wound grows the iceflower of art'.[167] While acknowledging that only Terence can truly articulate the pain of his wound, Baxter attempts to crystallise its essence from the silt of his own memories of his brother within him. The difficult process of writing a poem—which Baxter once likened to 'a man wearing three pairs of gloves and trying to pick up a key from the ground'[168]—is made that much harder by this attempt to represent experience second-hand. The comparison of Terence to the passive Samson made prisoner after his strength is shorn from him, should be read in the context of the later 'A Family Photograph 1939', which looks back five years to an earlier era when his brother celebrated his freedom and youth as a triumphant 'nautical Samson' fighting the town 'With the jawbone / Of a sperm whale' (p.35).

166 Baxter's note is written beneath the draft of 'Fire in the Mountains', in Hocken MS 704/13: 780, p.37. See also *CP*, pp.30 and 625.
167 'The Unicorn: A Consideration of Adolescence', pp.535–9.
168 'The World of the Creative Artist', *Salient Literary Issue* (Sep 1955) p.23.

**To my Brother**

The poem should grow a flower out of your chest
But I must silt it like a crystal in solution;
Calling your double who bleeds inside my head,
To hear me curse the bitter and the bloody
Who hold you jailed and dumb in a chicken-pen:
Samson in Gaza: but your true-born impatience
Of rhetoric wins. Your fear of being petted
I have also; but compromise unsteady.

I dreamt once you were drowned and woke crying.
And now you are drowned; not in the violent sea
Of high explosive, but shut to rot in a tub:
Now you are a man with a hard face, I am hearing.
For you the shut horizon. You are part of my blood:
Thus the intolerable ache of consanguinety.
[MS Hocken 704/13: 775, p.17]

The last of these four poems has a particular poignancy. Written on New Year's day 1946, it begins as 'To my Brother' ended, with a reference to a dream. At first this dream is uncommonly positive: Terence—now free, and home from detention camps and 'manpowered' labouring—has not drowned 'in the violent sea', instead his 'hard face' is again sunlit and tanned, as he sails toward his waiting brother 'with his boat / to take me away'. But the poem has a barbed tail; there are to be no more shared experiences of 'the joys / Of action, best that life can ever bring' (p.58). The boat slips away from the land without Baxter, who stands marooned in a sea of disfigured faces: the separation between the brothers remains, what the detention camps started adulthood finishes.

**Poem**

I dreamed in the night
that I saw my brother
his face sunlit
brown and a sailor.

He came with his boat
to take me away
over the broad
and burning sea.

But the ropes were cast
I stood on the shore
the knived faces twisting
behind and before.
[MS Hocken 704/14: 918, p.102]

# Five
# Strathmore Detention Camp

> . . . hear me curse the bitter and the bloody
> Who hold you jailed and dumb in a chicken-pen
> 'To my Brother'

Terence Baxter approached 1942 in the certain knowledge that the New Year, with its promise of indefinite detention, was not a time to begin making resolutions. Neither he nor Noel Ginn could guess what the future held, but it seemed likely that they would be detained at the pleasure of the New Zealand Government for some considerable time.

It was the Labour Party stalwart Walter Nash who promoted the detention camp system as a more humane alternative to punitive court-martials and repeated civil imprisonment favoured by others of his colleagues. The fact that key members in the New Zealand Labour Government's War Cabinet had been objectors in the First World War, and the architects of their party's anti-militarist traditions (in 1919, as party leader, Nash had proposed the idea of New Zealand as a pacifist nation), was a permanent affront to the pacifists of the 1940s. Bob Semple, for example, had been imprisoned during the First World War along with other leaders of the fledgling Labour party for sedition after flouting 'newly formed and punitive war regulations by publicly attacking the new [conscription] legislation'.[169] Pacifists of the next war looked on in disbelief as Semple, now Minister of National Service, drew the first marble in the country's first conscription ballot.

The humanity of Nash's detention camp system also became a topic of hot debate. Many pacifists found it hard to believe that men were being imprisoned indefinitely in this 'enlightened' nation, and there were major concerns about the operation of the appeal boards. Appeal board statistics indicate that too often a man's freedom was a matter of which part of the country he lived in, because boards varied considerably in their interpretation of the legislation governing them:

> . . . it is hardly an exaggeration to say that those claiming to be conscientious objectors have been forced to take part in a lottery in which some have drawn tickets entitling them to freedom, and others have drawn blanks imposing indefinite incarceration.[170]

169 *Out in the Cold*, p.17.
170 Lincoln Efford, *Penalties on Conscience: An Examination of the Defaulter's Detention System in New Zealand* (Christchurch: Lincoln Efford, 1945) p.23.

There was also considerable concern about the fact that New Zealand's attitude to its objectors was so much more punitive than Great Britain's. Many in the 'Mother Country' including a number of British parliamentarians expressed grave concerns about New Zealand's record in this regard. In 1945, Lincoln Efford, a rationalist war resister from Christchurch, made the following comparisons:

> In Great Britain, out of the total appeals heard, one person in eighteen ultimately reaches confinement and stays there for a few weeks or months.
>
> In New Zealand, out of total appeals heard, more than one person in five reaches confinement, and some have already spent four years there.
>
> If New Zealand standards were applied in Great Britain, 13,000 would be in indeterminate confinement there now, instead of eighty (80) in temporary confinement.
>
> If British standards were applied in New Zealand, perhaps four would now be in confinement for a few months instead of 650 indefinitely.[171]

British pacifists and humanitarians, worried that the New Zealand government's punitive attitude towards its objectors encouraged public demonisation and vilification of defaulters and their families, appealed for more moderate and reasonable measures. The English pacifist, Vera Brittain, pointed out that many British objectors, although opposed to war, bravely risked their lives in Pacifist Service Units, at First Aid posts, and by offering themselves 'as subjects for experiment in the cure of scabies, malaria, and other diseases'. She went on to suggest that :

> . . . if your own CO's could be given similar opportunities of dangerous and uncomfortable work, they would undoubtedly respond, and public prejudice against them would automatically diminish, as it has done here.[172]

Similar sentiments were expressed by the Reverend W. Walker, the president-elect of the Methodist Conference and an ex-president of the Christchurch and Canterbury RSA, who—while acceding to the Conference's desire to distance itself from the militant pacifism of Ormond Burton and A.C. Barrington by stating 'stoutly that the Methodist Church was not pacifist [and] that hundreds of young Methodists were fighting valiantly in a war which they believed to be righteous'—voiced concern for those of the Methodist congregation like Noel Ginn who had taken a stance as objectors, and declared that:

> . . . fully three-fourths of the current trouble was due to the government not producing worthy forms of alternative sacrificial service; young men of deep sincerity and sterling character had had appeals dismissed and been imprisoned, even when vouched for by men of high standing who knew them well.[173]

171 Ibid, p.40.
172 Ibid, p.45.
173 Taylor, *The Home Front*, p.254.

Just as Terence Baxter would gladly have worked on minesweepers had the opportunity presented itself, many of the men with him in detention repeatedly petitioned for release to do work that was considered socially necessary:

> They have volunteered to undertake arduous and unpleasant work where assistance is desperately needed. It must be remembered, also, that while the conscientious objector refuses to kill or become part of the machine devoted to killing, he does not refuse to risk his own life if this is essential to the welfare of humanity.[174]

But such opportunities to 'redeem' themselves were not to be. By the time the last objectors had been released from detention, some had been imprisoned for well over five years; considerably longer than civil prisoners convicted of quite serious crimes might expect.

Both Noel Ginn and Terence Baxter were to discover, when they arrived at the base detention camp, that war resisters were a far-from-homogenous group. This led to some interesting situations. Between the Methodist disciples of Burton and Barrington, and conscientious individualists like Terence Baxter, lay a broad spectrum of beliefs and biases. David Grant, writing, in *Out in the Cold*, on New Zealand pacifists and objectors during the Second World War, identifies four broad types of military defaulters in detention. There were:

> . . . men who belonged to fundamentalist Christian sects, Christian Pacifists [like Noel Ginn] from within orthodox churches, nonreligious objectors ('hoons'), who [like Terence Baxter] resisted the war for a variety of ethical reasons, and 'political' objectors.[175]

Terence was surprised, when he arrived in detention, to discover just how diverse the community of objectors was. He understood those like himself who objected on humanitarian grounds and those like Ginn who came to it through their religious beliefs, but found it harder to accept as genuine the political objectors, in particular the communists:

> The communists in the camp were full of support for Russia during the war—when she entered the war against Germany they were strongly on Russia's side, yet they were supposed to be in the camp as pacifists. Perhaps they should have been helping Russia, by fighting on our side to help them.[176]

For Ginn the realisation of just how heterogeneous the group in detention would be began on the day of his trial, well before his arrival at the camps. He was one of four defaulters going before the magistrate that day, and this circumstance dictated that they would end up spending a considerable amount of time together. Of the others, one was a self-pitying Jehovah's Witness, quite affronted that 'he, so upright

174 Ibid, p.7.
175 Grant, *Out in the Cold*, p.157.
176 Terence Baxter, personal interview, 11 Dec 1995.

and a witness for God, should be treated this way';[177] one was a member of the Closed Brethren who, in accordance with their doctrines, kept strictly to himself; and finally there was a young man—'fair and very English'—who, Ginn later decided, looked similar to the poet W.H. Auden in his younger years.

Upon completion of their three month prison sentences Ginn and his three companions from court were reunited and escorted by two guards up to the centre of the North Island. The journey took them by train as far as the small township of National Park where they boarded a truck and travelled east to the base detention camp known as Strathmore, which was located to the south-east of Rotorua. During the trip Ginn had little success in his attempts to sustain communication with either the Jehovah's Witness or the Brethren, but he did strike up a long conversation with the third man, the young Englishman, whose name, he discovered, was Jim Stevens. Stevens, upon whom other inmates later bestowed the nickname 'Gentleman Jim', had a pronounced Oxford drawl and he confided to Ginn—after swearing him to secrecy—that he did in fact have an Oxford degree. Their conversation turned to poetry and Stevens asked Ginn if he had ever heard of a writer named—as it sounded at first to Ginn's ears—'Aahdinn'. Not until Stevens recited some lines of poetry did Ginn realise that he was talking about W.H. Auden:

> . . . suddenly I realised it was the same writer who had written 'Ascent of F6' with Isherwood. I had seen a production at one of our Summer Schools. Jim lent me a book of his poetry.[178]

This was Ginn's first introduction to what would be, for him, the redeeming feature of the camps, the number of new and exciting minds that he would come in contact with—minds that would, in the long run, cause him to re-evaluate much about his own life and beliefs. At that stage, however, Ginn was still firmly the Methodist pacifist, and ahead of him was a keenly anticipated reunion with a number of his Methodist friends.

When the four arrived at Strathmore base detention camp they discovered that everything about the camp system was new. The camp was sited on one of the bleak, treeless, pumice plains of the North Island's volcanic plateau. It was entered through gates in an eight-foot-high fence, strung with sixteen strands of barbed wire, on posts of larch and pine, that 'still smelled piny',[179] freshly cut from the surrounding area. As the detainees arrived in dribs and drabs they were issued with equipment of good quality, including a large canvas duffle bag which was numbered according to the order in which the man was admitted. Ginn was '75'—the number he kept for the duration of the war—and Terence, who arrived at Strathmore early in 1942, was number '163'.

Both Noel Ginn and Terence Baxter arrived at a camp that was still in the process of construction. Walter Nash's idea in proposing his humane camps was to provide a fairer alternative to prison—a place where the men in detention would work and

177 Noel Ginn, letter to Paul Millar, Jan 1995.
178 Ibid.
179 Ibid.

socialise in a more open and flexible environment. Pacifists were heartened to discover that the man appointed, on 1 October 1941, to be the Controller-General of defaulters detention camps—Leonard Greenberg—was on record as being sympathetic to Christian Pacifists. Greenberg, who was at the time of his appointment, the secretary of the National Broadcasting Corporation, had, as Noel Ginn recalled, a history of involvement with the Young Men's Christian Association:

> He was a very strong, forceful character, a man of high ideals, and he'd actually written a little book—something along the lines of 'Adventuring for Christ', which was very bracing masculine Christianity . . . physically he was like Mussolini: a dynamic, short, and very strong-jawed looking man.[180]

Greenberg, based in Wellington, set about turning the detention camps into cooperative communities. In the early days relations between detainees and camp staff were generally good, although living conditions required improvement:

> For a while there in one or two of the camps it wasn't very good food. They waited until they started to get a vegetable garden going, we were a bit short of greens, things were pretty plain.[181]

But the situation did improve: the two-man tents that were the only accommodation when the first detainees arrived at Strathmore were gradually replaced with huts, and a garden and farm were started which in time supplied most of the camp's food:

> Len Greenberg's hopes were briefly fulfilled: an acquiescent, peaceful gathering of stubborn men prepared to pay homage to society for refusing to serve in the armed forces. In the beginning, Strathmore appeared, superficially at least, to be similar to the YMCA boys' camps he had run before the war.[182]

If the authorities expected that the men in detention were going to endure stoically until the end of the war, Ginn and a number of his Methodist friends soon disabused them of the notion. Terence Baxter had only recently arrived in camp and did not know Ginn at that time, but he would soon discover that despite Ginn's affable exterior he was unyielding on matters of principle:

> . . . you wouldn't think this with him because he was small, easy going, always ready to smile, always friendly to everybody he met, but he had another side to him altogether. Quite a fighter side, almost like an aggressive side, as far as being against authority, just to look at and to talk to you wouldn't think he'd be that way.[183]

A short time after their arrival at Strathmore, Ginn and a number of his Christian Pacifist friends—among them Alan Handyside, Noel Sly, Jack Rogers and Bill Kelly—

180 Ibid.
181 Terence Baxter, personal interview, 11 Dec 1995.
182 Grant, *Out in the Cold*, p.147.
183 Terence Baxter, personal interview, 11 Dec 1995.

decided that they were not going to cooperate with the authorities of the system, and refused to work. The camp superintendent, Joe Duffy, responded by placing them all in 'dummy huts': a form of solitary confinement in which each man was placed in a bare hut with the window screened by canvas:

> We weren't brave and we weren't courageous, we had our views and the processes stepped on us . . . we were a troublesome and difficult minority, cheeky in all sorts of ways, and the community had no ability to handle us at all, we were terribly difficult. Our worst punishment was being in dummy, and then they could withhold food and just give us a little water. I was twenty-three days in dummy once, which was not pleasant. About six or seven of us decided we couldn't cooperate because by sanctioning the creation of these special camps we were contributing to the war effort (you get into all sorts of tangles of reasoning).[184]

The dummy huts were separated from the camp in an isolated punishment compound:

> As the summer sun beat down on the corrugated-iron roof, the air was motionless, and the men lay on the bare floors sweating profusely. They were allowed a Bible or hymn book to read, but the light was so poor that reading for longer than ten minutes caused unbearable eye strain.[185]

Although they were segregated, there were opportunities for each man to communicate surreptitiously with those in neighbouring huts, and by this method they were able to develop a communication network. After twenty-three days they began rethinking their protest. While reading the New Testament they came across texts that appeared to provide explicit guidance in just such a situation, requiring them to accept with joy whatever was put upon them: 'we found texts, in Timothy somewhere, to submit to what's put upon you and not to react back, so we had to back-track and swallow our pride'.[186] Through their communications links, the group agreed to ask the superintendent for permission to talk with one another. They argued among themselves and came to the decision that they had been wrong not to cooperate, and thus rejoined the camp.

This incident was the first indication to the authorities that the men in detention were not buying into the view of the camps as cooperative communities. Duffy had tried and failed to win over the protesters. Greenberg, bemused by what was happening, travelled up from Wellington to try and quell the mutiny, but met with an equal lack of success. It was at this point that relations began souring, not only between camp staff and detainees, but also among the detainees themselves. Terence Baxter, although he took no part in the protest, remembers quite clearly what occurred:

> . . . they went on strike and wouldn't work. They thought they might be able to break the whole situation down by that. In the end they were put in huts

184 Noel Ginn, personal interview, Aug 1994.

185 Grant, *Out in the Cold*, p.179. Ginn comments that the roofs were of a heavily tarred paper called 'malthoid' rather than corrugated iron (letter to Paul Millar, March 1997).

186 Noel Ginn, personal interview, Aug 1994.

> in solitary confinement, like a compound within a compound. But the thing that spoiled it all was that some of the religious ones had cooperated—at least that seemed to be what had happened—and while the non-cooperators were locked in, there was the ridiculous situation of these other religious ones hammering up the huts while they were in them. They were helping to secure them. In the end the protest broke down, more and more people were coming in and it ended.[187]

The various Christian fundamentalists who helped secure fellow detainees were indeed cooperative. Len Greenberg, although classifying such men as 'escapists' whose sects 'opposed war largely because it made demands on time and allegiance due to their God, and many of these had refused even non-combat service' considered them 'vital in making the detention scheme workable':

> Of 592 men reviewed in October 1944, 231 belonged to such sects; Christian Assembly (107), Jehovah's Witnesses (78), Brethren (35), Pentecostal (11). These men, though often fanatical in their religion, were usually docile and cooperative in other respects.[188]

The main consequence of the protest was that relations between Greenberg and his charges became increasingly acrimonious: he would later describe the Methodists as fanatics and 'extreme masochists',[189] while Ginn would recall, with an air of self-deprecating humour, that Greenberg was, at the time:

> . . . very disliked by one-and-al . . . [He] came across as the sinister *eminence grise*—we think that it was the conflict he had with his ideals in this situation of all these idealists—a lot of whom were very fine people working along the lines that he himself had developed—I think that there was a conflict within him. Anyway he came across to us—we were inclined to be very judgemental—as a sinister, brutal figure.[190]

The protest by the Methodists was the first indication that some detainees were going to cause problems, and it led to a decision by the authorities to begin work on a second camp where more difficult objectors might be contained. An allied problem of overcrowding at Strathmore as objectors continued to arrive increased the need for this camp, and it was decided to locate it near the southern end of Lake Taupo, six miles south-east of the town of Turangi. The new camp was to be named Hautu after a nearby prison farm.

Not surprisingly Noel Ginn and his fellow mutineers were among the first thirty men sent to Hautu. More surprisingly, Terence Baxter—at all times the mildest of detainees—followed him there a short time later. Why was Terence sent to the bad boys' camp? Unless it was for reasons of overcrowding, it may well have been, as

187 Terence Baxter, personal interview, 11 Dec 1995.
188 Taylor, *The Home Front*, pp.274–5.
189 Cited in *Out in the Cold*, p.183.
190 Noel Ginn, personal interview, 25 Oct 1994.

Terence believed, that it was because he was the son of the country's most notorious objector. Whatever the reason it was to be an important move because it was at Hautu that he would strike up a friendship with Ginn and, in the course of a conversation, tell him of his younger brother who wrote poems.

# Six
# James Baxter's Early Poetry Manuscript Books

> He who would be a poet must
> See the world in a grain of dust
> And beauty in a rainy day.
> [Epigraph to Manuscript Book I]

In 1942, the only real clue to sixteen-year-old James K. Baxter's future fame could be found in six manuscript books full of poems, and he did not show these to many people. As he wrote in a letter to Noel Ginn, 'I was very loath to expose my verse to the private or public eye, as I had sensed early the morbid fear of poetic expression which so many have' (p.191). By 1946, when his regular correspondence with Ginn concluded, Baxter had filled a further seven MS Books and was well into his eighth—MS Book XIV. When, in February 1947, MS Book XIV had been filled, the total number of Baxter's poems in final draft was 1,025. Only seventy-two of these appear in the *Collected Poems*.

Two decades on, in 1968, Baxter, now up to MS Book XXVIII, ceased keeping a systematic record of his drafts. Evidence suggests that after two years of prolific output in 1966–67 as Otago University's Burns Fellow, writing ceased to be Baxter's priority. In some respects he had exhausted himself—looking back he called the Burns Fellowship 'a conditional mistake' that 'hadn't exactly done me in. But my asbestos suit had worn through in a few places'.[191] Even before becoming Burns Fellow he had, in 1963, begun examining his role as a writer, and his motivation for writing:

> It is the business of a poet, I think, to be destitute as well as honest. He may have money; but he should recognise that it is dirt. He may have prestige; but let him hate it and wear it like an old filthy coat. Then he may be able to stay awake a little better. Love will not harm him, though. It will slice him open like a fish, and hang him up by the heels, and let the sun into his private bag of dreams and idiot ambitions. He will think he is dying when he is just beginning to wake up.[192]

The Burns Fellowship years seemed to Baxter a kind of death. Looking back on the time he remarked that there 'was a bit too much death inside me' and mused, 'I wonder now how much of the death was my own and how much came from the Fellowship'.[193] He appears to have woken to the idea that it was no longer sufficient

191 'The Burns Fellowship', *Landfall* XXII (1968) p.247.
192 'Writing and Existence', *Education* XII 7 (Aug 1963) p.18.
193 'The Burns Fellowship', p.246.

to go about 'the business of the poet'—as he had defined it in 1963—as if a poet's vocation was simply metaphorical. An inward sense of destitution was not enough; the business of the poet became the prescription for a lifestyle.

It does not seem a coincidence that the year Baxter ceased keeping his notebooks was the year he dreamed of a life free of trappings in a commune at Jerusalem on the Whanganui River, 'where the people, both Maori and pakeha, would try to live without money or books, worship God and work on the land'.[194] Yet even when Jerusalem had become a reality and Baxter was living as simple a life as possible, he could not stop writing: it was a habit that had been well fixed in him almost thirty years earlier. In 1944 he had written to Ginn: 'I have at last discovered that it is more meritorious for me to abstain from writing a poem than to write it' (p.332). At Jerusalem this unshakeable need to write became something of a conundrum. Baxter began making even more explicit associations between poetic activity and death: 'The man called James K. Baxter, who is like a dead body in the ground, swells up and gives off a stink of words.'[195] He was unable to reconcile poetry—which he supposed he wrote 'for money and kudos'—with poverty, which was the cornerstone of communal life: 'It is absurd to say I am really a poor man while I keep on putting words together. Words set in order are mental possessions.'[196]

Many of these 'mental possessions'—Baxter's twenty-eight MS Books, and a substantial amount of loose material—are now in the Hocken Library. According to Howard McNaughton the safe arrival of the notebooks at the Hocken was due to good luck rather than good stewardship:

> A few months before he died, James K. Baxter collected all the literary relics he had to hand, put them in a large polythene bag, knotted the neck with string and attached an address label and stamps, and sent the lot by unregistered surface mail to an unsuspecting librarian friend.[197]

The impression gained from this account—particularly if it is read in conjunction with John Weir's comments that 'Baxter's handwriting proved at times to be indecipherable',[198] and that a number of Baxter's later poems may be lost because they 'were not systematically recorded'[199]—is that Baxter's work habits were as scruffy as his later appearance. For much of his life, however, such was not the case—particularly during the period of his correspondence with Ginn his notebooks exhibit a meticulous attention to detail. Although in fairness to Weir, Baxter's handwriting did become more of a challenge as time progressed, as the (still comparatively legible) draft of 'Obsequy for Dylan Thomas', from MS Book XX, indicates (see Figure 1).

It was only after the publication of *Beyond the Palisade* that Baxter began relaxing his standards of draft presentation. These early notebooks were nothing less than

194 McKay, *Life*, p.237.
195 Baxter, *Jerusalem Daybook*, p.17.
196 Ibid.
197 Howard McNaughton, 'Baxter's Strong Ghost', *Landfall* 137, 35.1 (Mar 1981) p.62.
198 Weir, introduction, *The Bone Chanter*, p.7.
199 J.E. Weir, introduction, *CP*, p.xxv.

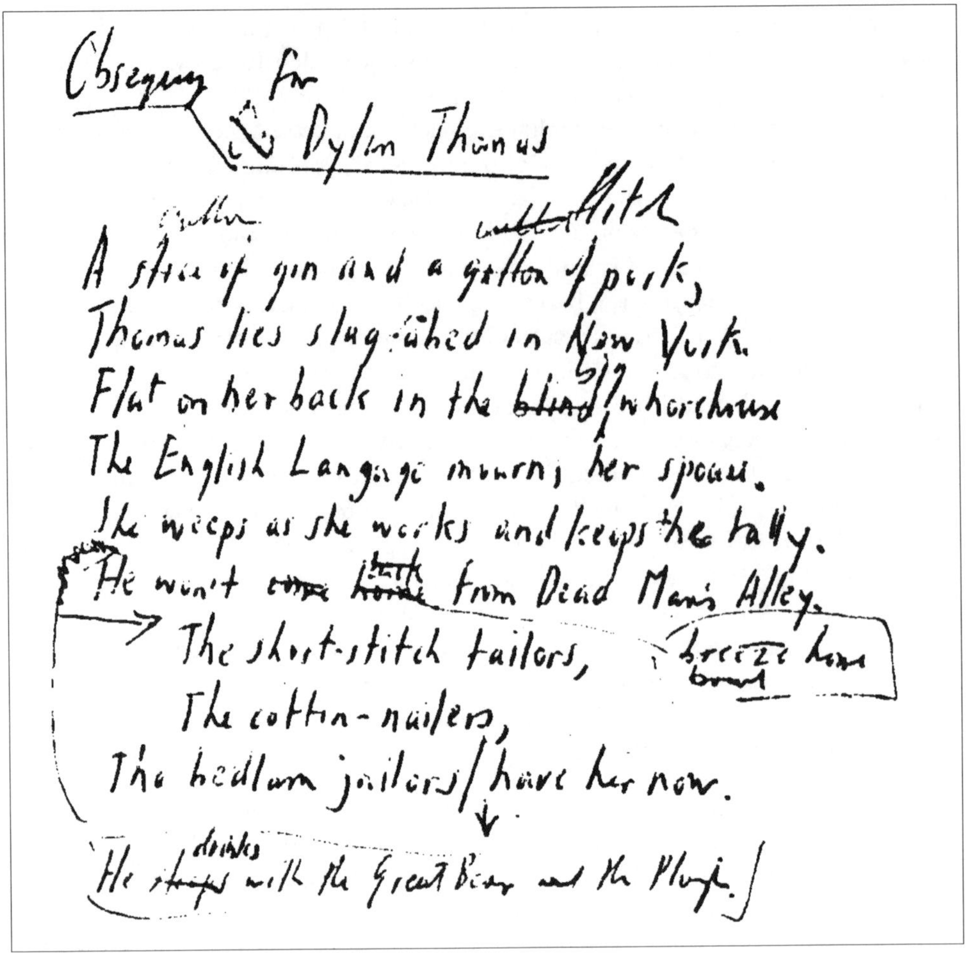
Obsequy for Dylan Thomas

A slice of gin and a gallon of pork,
Thomas lies slug-[illegible] in New York.
Flat on her back in the whorehouse
The English Language mourns her spouse.
She weeps as she works and keeps the tally.
He won't [illegible] from Dead Man's Alley.
The short-stitch tailors,
The cotton-nailers,
The bedlam jailors / have her now.
He drinks with the Great Bear and the Plough.

Figure 1: 'Obsequy for Dylan Thomas'. (See *Collected Poems*, p.216.)

private publications. The care he took in their presentation, and the considerable labour he must have expended, is evidence that the first fourteen MS Books were not merely records of poems, they represented proof to him that he was indeed a poet. So it is that with the publication of his first book, *Beyond the Palisade*, a marked decline in the attention Baxter gave to his MS Books is immediately evident.

Baxter's first MS Book sets the standard for the thirteen that follow. As we see at Figure 2, MS Book 1 begins with an inscribed title page. Immediately following the title page is an index of poems, these indexes follow a continuous numbering sequence that runs unbroken from MS Book I to MS Book XIV. What probably began as an attempt to keep track of his cumulative output, later proved useful to Baxter as a means of reference when, for example, a poem was a rewrite of an earlier poem.[200]

200 An example of this is the poem 'Rain-Ploughs': the version printed in *Beyond the Palisade* (p.11 and also *CP*, p.26) is a revision of the early 'Rain-Ploughs' which is poem 320 in MS Book V (see Baxter's letter on pp.141–2 for this version). The later, published, version appears as poem 767 in MS Book 13, where it is simply titled 'Re-casting of 320' (see pp.363–4)

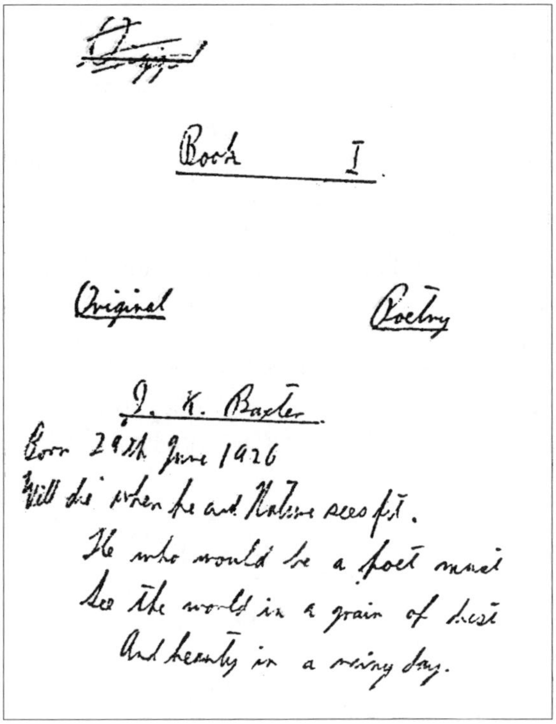


Figure 2: The title page of MS Book I[201]

Figure 3 details the numbering sequence, and the total number, of poems in each MS Book.

Next to the poem's sequential number in the index Baxter would enter its title and the number of the page in the MS Book upon which the poem begins. Baxter recalled that the 'poem-writing habit began when I was seven',[202] but he was almost twice that age when he began systematically recording the final drafts of his poems in his poetry notebooks. Consequently, his first manuscript notebook is different from

201 Weir begins his introduction to Baxter's *Collected Poems*:

> When he was eleven years old James Keir Baxter wrote the following inscription with a rooster quill on the first page of a new notebook:
>
> Book I
> Original Poetry
> J.K. Baxter
> Born 29th June 1926
> Will die when he and Nature sees fit.

This does not accord with my argument on p.76 that Baxter may have been closer to fourteen when he began recording his poems in his MS Books, and it also contradicts Weir's introduction to *The Bone Chanter* (1976), that it 'was probably in 1939, at the age of thirteen, that [Baxter] began to collect his early verse into the first of . . . twenty-eight Manuscript Books' (p.5). A viewing of the original of MS Book I reveals that the lines 'Born 29th June 1926 / Will die when he and Nature sees fit' are written in pencil (unlike the three lines above it which are written in ink, and may have been written by a rooster quill). As late as 1943 Baxter was still making pencil annotations in his early notebooks (see section Seven, p.83), he could therefore have been anywhere between thirteen and sixteen when the pencil inscription was added.

202 Baxter, *The Man on the Horse*, p.121. There is a manuscript notebook in the Hocken archive that appears to predate the more formal 'Book I' (Hocken MS 704/1): numbered MS 975/14 and titled 'Original Poetry J. Baxter' this notebook contains drafts of many of the early poems later transcribed into MS Book I.

those that follow in one important respect: it is a retrospective document containing eighty-three poems that Baxter wrote between the ages of seven and fourteen.[203] As the table at Figure 4 indicates, the recorded age of composition remains disordered until around age thirteen, which would support John Weir's estimate that 'it was probably in 1939, at the age of thirteen, that he began to collect his early verse into the first of the twenty-eight Manuscript Books'.[204] However, poem thirty-six ('White are the Clouds'), which was written at fourteen, appears in the midst of a number of poems written at thirteen; which may indicate that Baxter was still transcribing his early poems into MS Book I well into 1940, and that he was fourteen before he began entering his poems sequentially.

In the early MS Books the poems begin immediately following the index (the later books, from MS Book XV on, have no index): every poem begins on a new page; as a rule each poem is headed with the poem's sequential number, a one letter

| MS Book | Contains Poems Numbered | Total |
|---|---|---|
| I | 1–83 | 83 |
| II | 84–131 | 48 |
| III | 132–162[a] | 31 |
| IV | 163–263 | 101 |
| V | 264–323 | 60 |
| VI | 324–387 | 64 |
| VII | 388–460 | 73 |
| VIII | 461–503 | 43 |
| IX | 504–569 | 66 |
| X | 570–651[b] | 82 |
| XI | 652–708 | 57 |
| XII | 709–765[c] | 57 |
| XIII | 766–855 | 90 |
| XIV | 856–1025 | 170 |
| | **Total** | **1025** |

Figure 3: Numbering sequence of Baxter's poems and number of poems per MS Book. Some MS Books also include poems witten by Archie Baxter: (a) 'Spirits of Harmony, Music and Love', 'Great Universe, how Vast', 'Loud calls the voice of Reason', 'O my Brothers', and 'Death' (MS Hocken 704/3, pp.65–71). (b) 'Simons Town', 'Burns', and 'We had no fear . . .' (MS Hocken 704/10, following poem 651 on p.177). (c) 'His voice it is the low vast tone . . .' (MS Hocken 704/12 following poem 765 on p.155).

203 MS Book I is also slightly different in that in the inside back cover Baxter has listed the following terms:

Poetic Diction: Alliteration, Metonymy,
Onomatopoeia, Circumlocution, Metaphor
Emphasis: Repetition, Inversion,
Economy, Illustration, Metonymy
Contrast: Similes, Antithesis,

In later MS Books, if he did make notes in the rear, they were more likely to be ideas for possible collections.

204 Introduction to *The Bone Chanter*, p.5.

| Age at Time of Composition[205] | Poem No. in MS Book I | No of Poems Composed |
|---|---|---|
| Seven | 51[a] | 2/5 |
| Eight | Nil | Nil |
| Nine | 51 | 1/5 |
| Ten | 51 | 2/5 |
| Eleven | 1–8, 12, 14[b] | 10 |
| Twelve | 9–11, 13 | 4 |
| Thirteen | 15–35, 37–42 | 27 |
| Fourteen | 36, 43–50, 52–83[c] | 41 |
| | **Total** | **83** |

Figure 4: Poems in MS Book I listed according to Baxter's age at time of composition: (a) Poem 51 is in fact five 'Fragments of Earlier Poems'. Similarly, a poem numbered 414 in MS Book VII records four other 'Early Poems (written 7–11)'—see Figure 5; (b) The second verse of Poem 8—'Satan's Battle'—was added when Baxter was 14; while in the five-stanza poem 'The Curse of War' (poem 14) only the first stanza was written at the age of 11, with the remaining 4 being added by Baxter when he was 13; (c) The age at which poem 57, 'A Ship is Sailing in the Harbour Mouth' was composed is not clear—it appears to be '14', possibly changed to '13'. Due to the uncertainty, I have attributed to it the same age ('14') as the poems around it.

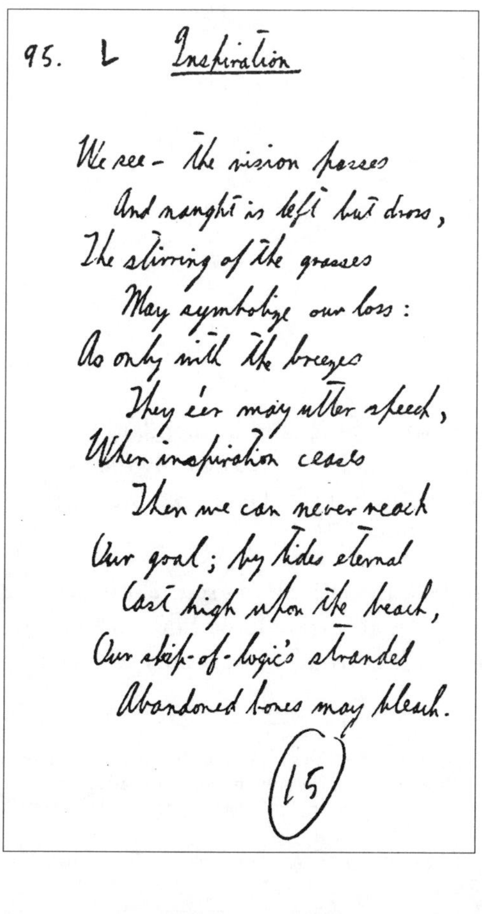
95. L Inspiration

We see – the vision passes
And naught is left but dross,
The stirring of the grasses
May symbolize our loss:
As only with the breezes
They e'er may utter speech,
When inspiration ceases
Then we can never reach
Our goal; by tides eternal
Cast high upon the beach,
Our ship-of-logic's stranded
Abandoned bones may bleach.

(15)

Figure 5: 'Inspiration,' from MS Book II.

classification (written in pencil) and the poem's title (underlined in pencil); finally, beneath each poem Baxter has written his age at the time of composition (also in pencil). This draft of 'Inspiration', from MS Book II, is typical (see Figure 5).

Not content with simply transcribing poems into MS Book I, Baxter initially set about keeping a journal (MS Hocken 971/21) in which he described each poem, and the conditions of its production, in some detail. In separate columns he entered the month of composition, the year of composition, the subject of the poem, the metre in which it was written, his assessment of the poem's standard, his age at the time of composition, and, finally, two to three lines of general observations concerning the poem. Consider, for example, poem eight in MS Book I.

**Satan's Battle**

Neath shimmering pools of blackest night
That ne'er let in the noonday light,
There lay the gates of Hell:
Twas there the devil Prince of Night
Challenged to meet in single fight
That heavenly messenger of Right,
The Angel Gabriel.
[11]

They met, but e'er they fought he saw
Those symbols of Celestial Law,
The Scales, proclaim his foe
Would victor be; He, to withdraw
Was fain; He opened wide his maw
And gave one last and fiendish roar,
Then to his lair did go.
[14]

Baxter made the corresponding journal entry:

> Month July; Year 1937; Subject Satan's Battle; Metre Iambic; Standard Fair; Age 11; General This is taken from Milton's Paradise Lost, and only the first verse was written. At the age of fourteen the author finished it, but 'fiendish roar' can scarcely be called a true rhyme to 'maw'.[206]

However he must have realised the magnitude of the task he was setting himself and decided, quite quickly, that posterity would have to make do without the author's insights—he discontinued his journal having made entries for just twenty-four poems.

205 The age shown here is the age when the composition of the poem was begun; from time to time Baxter would add to a poem, if he did he would also indicate his age at the time he made the addition.

206 This is my summary of the details of the entry as they appear in the table in MS Hocken 971/21 beneath each (underlined) heading.

| Age at time of beginning composition | Poems by sequential MS Book number | Total poems |
|---|---|---|
| Seven | 51 (2 fragments of 5) | 2/5 |
| Eight | 414 (2 of 4 poems) | 2/4 |
| Nine | 51 (1 frag.), 414 (1 of 4 poems) | 1/5 & 1/4 |
| Ten | 51(2 frags.), 414 (1 of 4 poems) | 2/5 & 1/4 |
| Eleven | 1–8, 12, 14 | 10 |
| Twelve | 9–11, 13, 94 | 5 |
| Thirteen | 15–35, 37–42, 57 | 28 |
| Fourteen | 36, 43–50, 52–56, 58–88 | 45 |
| Fifteen | 89–93, 95–366 | 277 |
| Sixteen | 367–413, 415–568 | 201 |
| Seventeen | 569–778 | 210 |
| Eighteen | 779–870 | 92 |
| Nineteen | 871–982 | 112 |
| Twenty | 983–1025 | 43 cont[a] |
| | **Total** | **1,025** |

Figure 6: Early Poems, and age at time of composition. (a) Poems written while Baxter was still twenty continue on in to MS Book XV, but as Baxter ceased entering his age beneath poems after MS Book XIV it is impossible to say with precision how many more poems were written before he turned twenty-one—although it may be less than 10 if the sixth poem 'Song in June 1947' or 'June Song' (Hocken MS 704/15, p.7) is an accurate indication of the poem's date.

Despite the decision to discontinue his journal, Baxter still included a considerable amount of information (detailed above) with the poems in the early MS Books. This information is useful when, for example, it comes to determining the years during which the young Baxter was most active as a poet. Figure 6 gives a summary of the poems written up to the age of twenty.

Perhaps the most interesting feature of Baxter's first fourteen MS Books is his classification system. Next to the title of every poem is a single letter 'S', 'L', 'U', 'D', 'N', or the Greek letter 'ω' (note the 'L' in Figure 5). Baxter entered the key to his classification system in the back of MS Book I, as follows:

S — sure
L — likely
D — doubtful
U — unlikely
N — not included
ω — outside a category

This key is repeated in the rear of 'Book II' with two modifications that hold through to MS Book XIV: 'N' becomes 'not included, (probably)' and the symbol 'ω' is dropped. Baxter gives no further information on the criteria by which each category is determined, but from his application of the codes it is possible to deduce a relationship that deals with their suitability for publication, combined with his own subjective assessment of each poem's merit.

In addition to the regular coding system described above, Baxter would also make certain cryptic annotations in the index to an MS Book next to the titles of particular poems. These annotations are less easy to decipher although it is possible to make educated guesses about some—for example, poems initialled 'AH' probably indicate poems sent by Baxter to his Aunt Hettie (Hester Hurst-Seager) who lived in Australia. It is more difficult to guess the meaning of symbols like a heavy dot or a star, but there is less mystery surrounding the annotations 'beer' and 'spirits' next to certain poems in MS Book XIII. These poems were written in 1944–45 when Baxter was, by all accounts, drinking heavily: in a letter to Lawrence Baigent written around this time he gives an account of the production of one poem while stimulated by alcohol:

> At present I live in the now nervily with a sense of heaviness, mainly because I drank a great deal of spirits three days ago. I had been down at University, was asked to write a new university song, not of the Here we are again . . . variety. Then called in at the pub, drank a little beer and discussed Hopkins and Chatterton. Met a medical student for whom once before I had written a poem to a girl;—he was delighted to meet me and requested another poem to another girl: gave me dinner: placed me upstairs in an armchair with a continual supply of rum and gin: and waited for the poem. After about 35 minutes and 14 glasses it arrived, good and pithy, epigrammatic I think. He was entirely satisfied and I wandered off to a dance bearing up bravely.[207]

In addition to the sequential numbering system that runs through all fourteen MS Books, Books I–XII also contain one further measure of his poetic output: in the

Figure 7: Baxter's line count for MS Books I to XII

| **MS Book** | **Line count** |
|---|---|
| I | 1,426 |
| II | 1,474 |
| III | 759 |
| IV | 2,122 |
| V | 1,380 |
| VI | 1,445 |
| VII | 1,897 |
| VIII | 861 |
| IX | 1,489 |
| X | 2,087 |
| XI | 1,391 |
| XII | 2,177 |
| **Total** | **18,508** |

207 Letter to Lawrence Baigent, 4 Mar 1945, VUW Library, Wellington, MS McKay 19/3/19.

rear of each of these MS Books Baxter has pencilled in a figure that is almost certainly his count of the total number of lines of verse in each book.[208] The cumulative total is, by poem 765 in MS Book XII, quite staggering.

The care Baxter took with MS Books I–XIV can be taken as an indication of just how highly he valued his 'mental possessions', and how he treated them as private publications: these MS Books cover the juvenile, adolescent, and early adult phases of his development as a poet; they contain all of the poems he sent to Ginn; the poems from *Beyond the Palisade; Cold Spring;* and most of the poems from *Blow, Wind of Fruitfulness.* The dramatic shift away from inscribed title pages, careful indexing, sequential numbering, a line count, recording of age at the time of composition, and classification of the poem's standard—a shift that occurred around the time *Beyond the Palisade* was published—provides compelling evidence that once Baxter had actually achieved publication he no longer needed to rely on the contents of notebooks to prove to himself that he was a poet.

208 My own count of the lines in MS Books I to XII is not identical to Baxter's, but in all cases it is close enough to strongly support my belief that these numbers are indeed his line count. The variation may occur because I am counting using different criteria—for example, Baxter may have excluded from his count lines taken from earlier poems to be re-used in later ones.

# Seven
# The Globe of Reverie: Baxter's Juvenile Phase

> Weep not for the poet: he
> Has burst the globe of reverie
> And found the ultimate that is
> Beyond a final precipice.
>
> 'What shall we seek for'

There is no doubt that Baxter went through a juvenile phase in his development as a poet—he indicated as much himself when he described his 'earliest poems, written from seven to fifteen, [as] . . . undoubtedly imitative',[209] and commented to Ginn that a poem 'written when I was about 14 . . . does not correspond to reality very well' (p.276). But if we attempt to pin this phase down to specific dates, then 'fifteen' is not as useful a guide as it might appear: Baxter's MS Books reveal that although he had written around ninety poems up to the age of fifteen, by the end of his fifteenth year this figure had increased by a further 277 poems (see Fig. 6, p.79). This would seem to mean that somewhere between poem number 89—'The Garden'—and poem number 366—'Regret Not'—Baxter felt that his verse was becoming more original and beginning to develop 'control and shape and meaning'.[210]

In practical terms the exact duration of any of Baxter's phases of development is probably indeterminable—movement between one phase and another is, after all, less likely to involve a clean break than a period of transition. Nor are attempts to impose an artificial order on the natural disorder of a life particularly realistic—Baxter indicates as much by the ambiguity of his comments to Ginn concerning this early poetry. When he initiated his correspondence with Ginn he included with his letter three early poems: 'The Flame of Grass', 'Under a Sun', and 'The Young Trees'—MS Book numbers 232, 249, and 358 respectively. When Ginn commented in a later letter that these three early poems 'still move me' (p.222), Baxter referred to them, dismissively, as 'the Child who passes' (p.227). As all of these poems were written at fifteen—the latter shortly before Baxter turned sixteen—this would support the idea of a phase concluding towards the end of his fifteenth year. However, in a letter probably written around July 1943, Baxter makes a comment that suggests that, at least initially, he identified a first stage of development that extended well past his sixteenth birthday:

> I am not so original now as I once was, and may be losing grip. I have the feeling that I developed steadily from ETERNITY to WHAT SHALL WE

209 Baxter, *The Man on the Horse,* p.122.
210 'Recollections of School Days', *NZMR.* 65 (Mar 1966) p.19.

SEEK FOR (i.e. -5 to 412) and since then have swerved (THE SALAMANDER is 583) to a less vigorous yet unavoidable line. (p.244)

Of more interest than the fact that 'What shall we seek for' was written when he was sixteen, is the way Baxter idealises his early verse. In 1943 he creates none of the pejorative associations with his juvenilia that words used later, such as 'imitative', do. Instead Baxter, enmeshed at seventeen in the 'iron wood' of adolescence, casts longingly back to those early days when sea voices could 'unlock / A child's buried wonder' and supply 'words to mock / The dark swell's thunder'.[211] 'Most of my earliest poems,' he told Ginn, referring to a poem written at seven, 'are very short but very good poetry' (p.246), and he clearly grieved over his lost originality and vigour when as 'an adolescent [he crossed] the threshold of natural contemplation, and [entered] a world of sterile forms'.[212]

About the time he was making these observations to Ginn, Baxter appears to have gone quite deliberately back through his early MS Books writing comments and criticisms on a number of his poems, as in this example from MS Book II written next to the third stanza of 'Webs of Circumstance'.

The tone of these comments ranges from 'Sincere: good Effect, 1943'—next to a stanza of poem 106, 'The Will of Man'—to 'Soap-box. Blah!' next to these lines from 'Weapons from Waste':

> And what of myriads slain
> Or doomed to fiery pain
> To feed the Moloch-jaws insatiable!
> Soon from the waste of the world
> The ultimatum hurl'd
> Shall shake the powers that seem impregnable.
> [Hocken, MS 704/3: 160, p.55]

Figure 1: Stanza 3 of 'Webs of Circumstance' (MS Hocken 704/2:92, p.21)

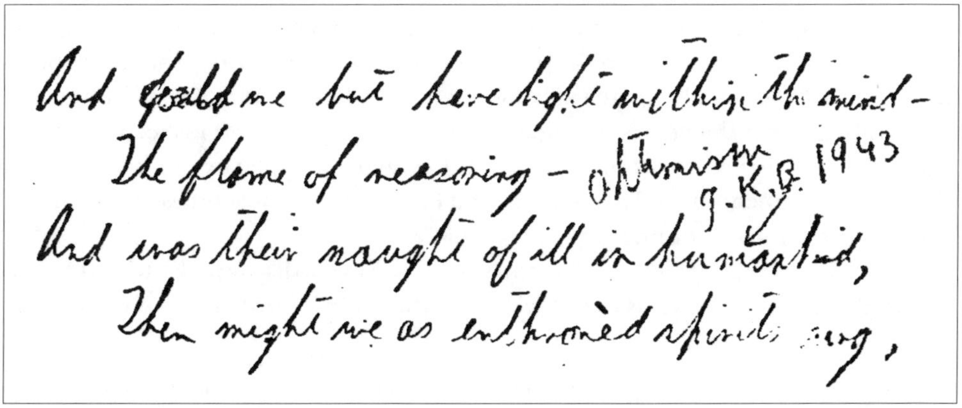
And should we but have light within the mind—
The flame of reasoning—
And was their naught of ill in humankind,
Then might we as enthroned spirits sing,
Optimism J.K.B. 1943

211 'Dirge', *CP*, p.95.
212 'The Unicorn: a consideration of adolescence', MS Hocken 975/34.

His most revealing note is one that demonstrates just how deeply he was regretting the loss of his childhood powers of composition. Beneath the poem 'Horses of the Wind' from MS Book II, Baxter has scribbled (almost illegibly):

> Comment 1943: I have lost the heart to sing; there is no spirit in my writing. 'Where nets of time . . .'[213] is frozen, and no word of mine can [?move] it to the poetry of this book, the vigour and the natural [?poetry].[214]

The addition—'Later—Oh Yeah?'—does not detract from the impression gained that it is the energy and inspiration of his first phase of writing that the adolescent Baxter both valued and missed.

I use Baxter's phrase 'the globe of reverie' to describe his juvenile phase because it is possible to perceive in it his own recognition that although in the verse from this period he produced poems of tremendous importance to his development, by his later criteria for judging poems they were abstract musings lacking the 'kernel of actual experiential knowledge' that poems must have if they are to be successful.[215] These early poems 'revealed no life but dream'.[216] because they were written at a time when 'I lived more in what I read and wrote than what I saw or did . . . [and] cast my own feelings on the exterior universe' (p.301). But no matter how much he regretted having to cross the threshold of natural contemplation, Baxter admitted its necessity when he told Ginn: 'It was only at a later stage that I so far conceded to that which I read as to lose taste in vague sentimentalism' (p.246–7). Despite this he would always mourn the loss of the 'child's wonder':

> O strange, strange that age
> Could still that ferment
> And set the mind in a cage.
> ['Dirge', *CP*, p.95]

Although we look back at Baxter's juvenilia for what it was—apprentice work—and acknowledge that it is with good reason that the majority of the poems that relate to this period remain unpublished (of the first 400 poems Baxter recorded in his Manuscript Books only four—'Under a Sun', 'Hawk and Hare', 'Beyond the Palisade', and 'Death of a Man'—appear in the *Collected Poems*), it should be borne in mind that the poems written during Baxter's childhood phase reveal important details about the influences acting upon him; the development of his techniques and methods; and, perhaps most importantly, the evolving complexity of his symbolism. Baxter's achievements in his later verse cannot be fully appreciated unless his childhood phase is taken into account.

The phase began when, as a seven-year-old, Baxter discovered the 'attitude of *listening* out of which poems may rise', from which the following words did emerge:

213 The ode 'Where nets of time encircle and destroy' is a poem Baxter was working on at the time, see pp.282–8.
214 Hocken, MS 704/2: 100, p.35.
215 Baxter, *The Bone Chanter*, p.5.
216 See 'Autobiographical', p.299.

O Ocean, in thy rocky bed
The starry fishes swim about—
There coral rocks are strewn around
Like some great temple on the ground . . .[217]

Baxter's sense of the importance of the exact moment when his career as a poet began never left him. When these lines were entered in his first manuscript book, for example, he added the comment '(First Poem.) Note: about 40 lines more; forgot the rest, this was beginning.'[218] In a period of transition early in 1944—when he had finished at King's High School and was anticipating commencing studies at Otago University—he looked back to this first poem, and described it as an awakening:

Fishes like stars that swim
  Within the dark abyss
Where charmed, unsought by cherubim,
  Sea's coral temple is:
Come from your cold sea-bed
To billows overhead;
Let your mute voices sing
My love awakenèd![219]

Baxter's start as a poet was largely due to his father, and Archibald Baxter *must* be seen as the strongest influence acting on his son at this time. Most probably, it was Archie's approach to life that taught his son how to discover 'a sacred pattern in natural events',[220] and to express this discovery in verse; and most certainly it was his recitations of 'Burns and Shelley and Byron and Blake and Tom Hood and Henry Lawson' that inspired Baxter to break 'out in words'.[221] Add to the love of poetry Archie inspired in his son, the strong pacifist-socialist beliefs of both of his parents, and it is not difficult to appreciate the origins of the predominant themes in the poems of Baxter's first six MS Books. Many of these poems are strongly anti-war and reflect considerable concern with the way arms of the state, supported by society's privileged few, control education, religion, and government, and use their powers to persecute the individual and suppress the tribe.

Ninety-four of the 387 poems in these MS Books express overt anti-war sentiments, while many more do so by implication. But titles like 'What tho' the Private Soldier' (No. 28), 'Hail to the Pacifist!' (No. 76), and 'The Bloodstained Banner Waves' (No. 187) represent a didactic style that Baxter quickly tired of, and it is noticeable that many of his most polemical poems are, according to his classification system, rated 'D' for 'doubtful'. Similarly, he tired of overtly political poems and his references to 'Mammon' and 'Caesar' become fewer as time goes on. However, these

217 Baxter, *The Man on the Horse*, p.124.
218 'Fragments of Earlier Poems', Hocken, MS 704/1: 51, p.58.
219 'Song', in *CP*, p.22, but titled 'Drawn from Childhood Eyes to Ease the Grown', in Hocken, MS 704/11: 706.
220 'Recollections of School Days', p.18.
221 Baxter, *The Man on the Horse*, p.122.

early poems are still the precursors to the political, anti-war poems, from Baxter's later years and the cynical tone of the fifteen-year-old poet who wrote 'The British Bull-dog' (below), is clearly heard in poems like 'A Bucket of Blood for a Dollar' (*CP*, p.320) or 'The Grand Tour' (*CP,* p.381):

**The British Bull-dog**

The brainless British bull-dog stands alone,
    Especial object for facetious mirth
    Among the other nations of the earth,
A pseudo-democratic to the bone—
Supremely contemplative of his own
    But quite unconscious of the others' worth—
    Majestic in deportment, mien, and girth
(And sure that Winston's right in all that's done!)

But if the old conservatives were shot,
    If Eire 'gets sore' and India should rebel
    While Church and congregation go to hell—
With Stock Exchange and 'precedent' forgot:
    He would, when quite recovered from the shock,
Call his valet and drown himself in hock!
        [Hocken, MS 704/4: 202, p.72]

Archie Baxter and the pacifist cause remained enduring influences on the juvenile Baxter. Archie was to his sons what the Reverend Ormond Burton was to Noel Ginn (see p.46–7). When Ginn and James Baxter met after the war, Ginn attempted to describe Burton in a way that would account for his ability to compel such extremes of devotion from his followers:

> [Burton] filled a prophetic role, much stronger and more formulated than the similar [later] role of JKB . . . when I described OEB to JKB I said he was a mountainous figure, Jim said he loved mountainous figures. [222]

It is unlikely Baxter was thinking solely of Burton's towering authority and prescriptions for life, religion and morality when he said this. He grew up in a world where the distinctions between ordinary and extraordinary individuals were fine ones, and he had a childhood and adolescence that provided him with numerous examples—known and imagined—of potentially 'mountainous figures' against which to measure himself. Everything depends, of course, on how he then defined a 'mountainous figure', but evidence suggests that his father was, and remained, the most mountainous of all the individuals who influenced him.

Among the other 'mountainous figures' in Baxter's life, his maternal grandfather, the imposing Professor John Macmillan Brown, was, for Baxter, a perennially

222 Noel Ginn, letter to Paul Millar, Jan 1995.

unsettling presence: a lens that focused his lifelong ambivalence towards intellectuals:

> I am haunted by this ancestral voice which insists that the intellectual and moral betterment of mankind is achievable and should be every sane man's goal and concern . . . the vantage point from which he saw the world . . . constitutes a problem for me.[223]

To balance the influence of a mind like Macmillan Brown's, which was 'in certain important respects different from my own',[224] Baxter turned to the 'ancestral voices' of the other branch of the family; his Scottish ancestors, whose minds he only need make acquaintance with in his imagination. The highland tribes haunt his earliest poems, and it is interesting to note that whereas childhood most frequently represents the lost ideal in his later poetry, in his juvenile verse Scotland is the lost Eden:

> What is that that on the mountain sounds, and echoes down the glen,
> 'Tis the skirl of bag-pipes wailing and the tramp of marching men.
> Has the Poet again awakened 'mong these mountains grim and grey?
> Yes! The men that once were living rise from mists of yesterday.
> ['Loch Seven', Hocken, MS 704/1: 20]

In these tribes he discovers a communal ideal in which the 'tribal matrix' carries the individual 'through the narrow gate of dissolution and beyond it'.[225] As early as thirteen he was mourning tribalism's passing—'Gone is the kinship of the clan, / The brotherhood of man to man'[226]—and by the age of fourteen he was launching socialist attacks on the political system with which he surely identified his wealthy and successful grandfather:

> O Rich Man, servant of the State,
>     Ye have the power of gold;
> That shall ye lose, for all shall have
>     The riches that ye hold
>     ['Freedom', Hocken, MS 704/1: 82]

He was also developing what was to become an enduring distinction between wisdom and knowledge, a distinction that also contains an implicit criticism of Macmillan Brown:

> . . . Knowledge is not Wisdom, 'tis a tool
> That wise men use to make their words express
> The thoughts that teem within the busy brain.
>     Thou [Wisdom] shinest oft where Peace and Quiet dwell,
> Far from the worldly turmoil and the strife;

223 Introduction to *The Memoirs of John Macmillan Brown*, p.xxxvi. See also note 2 on page 19.
224 Ibid.
225 Baxter, *The Man on the Horse*, p.27.
226 'Time was when on Loch Seven's Shore', Hocken, MS 704/1: 21.

Not in the minds of busy clerk or judge,
For they have Knowledge but they cannot see,
But in the simple lives of kindly men
['Wisdom and Knowledge', Hocken, MS 704/1: 24]

Even at this early stage Baxter had begun devising a model that would inform his verse for the remainder of his life. Superficially it is a paradigm in which polarities (the tribe versus modern society, wisdom versus knowledge, and man versus woman are some examples) generate tensions that produce poetry. The utility of such polarities is demonstrated repeatedly, but a single example—one which also indicates his consistency in the use of certain themes—will suffice here. In Baxter's criticism of modern society at fifteen, the poet—the voice of the pacifist-socialist tribe—stands aloof from 'the savage hum / Of toiling cities where no room / Is left for seeds of spirit'.[227] There is a similar criticism of society in his final poem, 'Ode to Auckland', the only substantial difference, apart from the idiomatic, being that by now he identifies with the tribe of nga mokai: 'the fatherless ones':

How can I live in a country where the towns are made like coffins
And the rich are eating the flesh of the poor
Without even knowing it?
[*CP*, p.600]

In 'Notes on the Education of a New Zealand Poet' from *The Man on the Horse*, Baxter works with polarities that are alternately individual and universal: with the opposing poles being either himself and 'the status quo', or 'myself and other people'.[228] The creative tension occurs in the former antithetical pairing as a quarrel out of which 'the poems sprang', and in the latter, as a sense of difference that creates a gap 'in which the poems were able to grow'.[229] The locus of tension, that place where poems come from, is then developed as a potent, constantly changing, symbol. It could be a cave positioned between sea and sky producing the tension Baxter referred to as 'natural contemplation'—'the intense effort of *listening*' from which 'the words emerged'[230]—or it could be a garden, a human attempt to control nature, positioned between the city and the wilderness, over whose walls a wild, natural, poetic beauty is occasionally glimpsed: 'those who stayed / Within that garden prison close confined / Caught some dim glimpse of regions yet unknown, / The regions of the spirit and the mind'.[231]

But with the arrival of adolescence things would change; Baxter's garden would become an 'iron wood' and Noel Ginn—who, along with Terence Baxter, was settling into detention for the long haul—would acquire a most unusual pen-friend.

227 See 'The Stream of Faith', pp.257–8.
228 See Baxter, *The Man on the Horse*, pp.122–4.
229 Ibid.
230 Ibid, p.124.
231 'The Garden', Hocken, MS 704/2: 89.

# Eight
# Detention Camp Life

> The old shark eyes of the screw
> Watched for nerves to crack in the conchie zoo.
> Two kinds of people: screws and men.
> 'Jottings'

Hautu, when Noel Ginn was drafted there, was a camp even less developed than Strathmore had been. There were no ablution blocks so clothing was washed in the river; and most of the buildings were still under construction. But for Ginn the early days at Hautu felt like a taste of paradise after his experiences of the preceding few months. The landscape in which the camp was set was much more interesting—there was a stream nearby and beyond that thick manuka scrub progressing into even thicker native bush—and, at least initially, relations between the staff and inmates were excellent, which relieved much of the tension that had been building up at Strathmore.

Even when the camp was fully established, living standards at Hautu remained relatively Spartan. The men were housed in small huts:

> Each was a prefabricated but solid military-style structure, eight feet wide by ten feet long, housing two men. They were arranged in straight rows, back-to-back, facing a communal 'piss-tin' in the middle of a compound as the ablution block was barred from use after lights out. Each hut was unheated but lined with building paper and roofed with malthoid. Beds were either stretchers or had hemp bottoms, fixed at one end. A small table and sometimes a stool was allowed for each hut . . . Bedding comprised a straw palliasse, four or five army blankets, often thin and holey, one flax or straw pillow, and two pillow cases. Inmates shivered at night during the winter months, with frosts of up to minus 10 degrees C occurring regularly.[232]

The improvement Ginn initially noticed in relations between inmates and guards was partly due to the relatively small number of detainees first sent to Hautu, but it owed most to the benevolent superintendent Henry Ballard, who did much to ensure that relations between inmates and staff remained, in the early days at least, free and easy:

> Mr Ballard was a fine type of middle-aged Irishman who had served in the

232 Grant, *Out in the Cold*, pp.149–50.

> British forces in India. [He had a] soft story-teller's voice, lumbering gait as if lame, soft smile & quirky gentle humour.[233]

But with the appeal boards still refusing many appeals there were new inmates arriving all the time and it was not long before this, combined with the inevitable turnover of camp staff, put paid to the friendlier atmosphere.

Shortly after he had arrived and settled in, Ginn noticed that Terence Baxter had also been transferred to the new camp. He had seen Terence at Strathmore when someone had pointed him out as the son of Archie Baxter—a man whom Ginn regarded as a saint—but there had been no contact between them. Now he was keen to find out more about Terence and so observed him from a distance, noticing that he was reserved and kept to himself.

Eventually the two men did meet, on a Saturday afternoon during 'free time', when Terence, the new boy, was attempting to do some washing in the stream, and Ginn was relaxing on the grass nearby with some of his Methodist friends. With so many recent arrivals, new relationships had not yet formed, and most inmates tended to stay with people they knew:

> 'We' on the lawn were mainly 5 or so Wanganui pacifist Methos. Terry, dark mysterious rather aloof figure, was washing clothes and sheets in the stream—it was indeed early days before the ablutions block was in place. He did his washing in a clumsy unused way. Having rinsed the sheets & hand-wrung them he picked up the other washing & came up the bank when he tripped & scattered his load in trodden muddy ground. He uttered a curse and we on the upper bank laughed good-naturedly & he acknowledged us briefly with a serious grin on the way to a scowl & went doggedly back to rinse the washing over again. Suddenly I felt sorry for him & went down the bank to help him out. I was used to washing clothes & so was pleased at this chance to get to know him.[234]

From this beginning a gradual friendship developed between Noel and Terence, although the initiative was always more on Ginn's side as Terence tended to guard his emotions carefully. In many ways they were contrasting figures. Affable, quick-witted and lively, Ginn took some time to find the person behind Terence's 'stolid fatalism'. Gradually he learned of Terence's love of sailing, and Terence became more animated as he told Ginn of Slocum: the first man to single-handedly circumnavigate the world under sail. Ginn discovered that behind Terence's dour southerner's mask was a good sense of humour and a keen intellect—'He had read many classic novels'—although Terence insisted that he did not follow after his Macmillan Brown relatives and had no interest in scholarship.

Camp life revolved around work detail. Most of the detainees were assigned to gangs and set to perform fairly mundane labouring tasks. An optimistic administration envisaged them turning many hundreds of acres of crown land on the volcanic plateau

233 Noel Ginn, letter to Paul Millar, Jan 1995.
234 Ibid.

into economic farming units. The idea proved as impractical as it was idealistic:

> Nearly 400 acres was thick scrub. Not even manuka grew in profusion on the rest; it was weathered, damp pumice country, with no topsoil, supporting only mosses, lichens and a few hardy ferns. For more than six months, up to 100 men—using slashers, picks, hoes, shovels and bare hands—cleared the growth and dug drains, but the hostile terrain and heavy infestation of rabbits (estimated at 100 per acre and rising) caused the project to be abandoned.[235]

Terence Baxter always worked in the outside gangs:

> . . . apart from one time when I injured myself. Me and another chap were pumping water up from the creek. It was on a concrete base and had a large handle that two of us pushed back and forth and it broke away from its base. He was all right but I fell straight down the bank into the creek, it was about twelve foot down. I did a somersault in mid air and landed right on my feet. Both my ankles were sprained when I landed on the rocks of the creek-bed. It was lucky that I didn't break my legs or my feet . . . So then I had jobs within the camp—cookhouse jobs and that sort of thing.[236]

Noel Ginn, however, found himself doing jobs within the camp full-time. He too had been injured, but his injury proved far more debilitating. During a session 'skylarking' with some of his Methodist friends soon after their arrival at Hautu, one, Jack Rogers, who was a good bit larger than Ginn, fell on Ginn's neck. He fainted and by evening was vomiting repeatedly. From then on he was plagued by persistent and chronic neck aches that were, on occasions, so bad he could barely lift his head. X-rays taken some years later showed that he had indeed suffered some damage to his vertebrae and that they were still misaligned. But the circumstances of the times led to him being branded a neurotic:

> The authorities were genuinely concerned . . . & I was put into the small hospital with virtually no treatment except rest . . . The condition persisted & there was concern shown by outsiders, ever on the alert to magnify negative reports, so the authorities were sensitive on the matter. The line they took from then on was that it was a nervous break-down type of condition brought on by the strains of the times etc.[237]

Being branded a nervy hypochondriac was an affront to Ginn, who had always led an active life, kept healthy, and considered himself well adjusted: 'I knew it wasn't neurosis because I was quite happy in a general sense, there were no terrible things troubling me.'[238] He also saw it as an attack on his commitment to pacifism and

235 Grant, *Out in the Cold*, p.153.
236 Terence Baxter, personal interview, Dec 1995.
237 Noel Ginn, letter to Paul Millar, Jan 1995.
238 Noel Ginn, interview with Annette Facer, Sep 1994.

'repeatedly affirmed that I was free from mental conflict & strong in my belief of doing what was right'.[239]

But medical facilities at Hautu were rudimentary, and his persistent ill-health finally led to his being returned to Strathmore where he could be better cared for. This was a wrench for both him and Terence; they had become good friends, in part because Ginn was beginning to distance himself slightly from Methodism. The 'hearty' Christianity of some of his companions was losing its appeal although he remained lifelong friends with many of them. But it was the situation outside that disturbed him the most:

> The church was torn apart over the war issue. An Otago minister, Lesley Neil, stood up on the conference floor in the debate upon the question of a Xtn [sic] bearing arms and declared that support for the war was the unmistakable will of God. That, what I thought, bigoted statement more or less carried that day. It marked the end of my adherence.[240]

Although letters between inmates were forbidden Terence and Noel devised ways of keeping in contact when Ginn returned to Strathmore:

> We would send books to each other, which was permitted. Down the spine we inserted short letters. They were written in invisible ink i.e. strong sugar solution—on scorching the paper before a candle flame the burnt sugar script could be seen. I know some inmates used urine for this purpose. This was great fun.[241]

They also relied on James Baxter to act as a conduit of information—Terence concluded one of his infrequent letters to his younger brother with a cryptic inquiry: 'Well Jum I think I'll close now. Let the other people in the house know that you have heard from me. How is your pen-friend?'[242]

Both Ginn and Terence were transferred one final time, to a relatively new camp called Whitanui, situated near the lower-North Island town of Shannon. This was, in part, a recognition that neither man belonged in the 'bad boys' camps, but the transfer was no sinecure, in fact the work detail at Whitanui was far less pleasant than at Hautu. Ginn was still affected by his injury and continued to work within the camp 'doing the screws beds, looking after their huts, and that type of work',[243] but Terence was not so fortunate. In Baxter's words: 'they put my brother behind barbed wire, to be eaten alive . . . by the devil of boredom, weeding flax in a bog at Shannon.'[244] Tending the flax was probably the most hated, and most futile, of all the many mundane jobs that inmates carried out:

239 Noel Ginn, letter to Paul Millar, Jan 1995.
240 Ibid.
241 Ibid.
242 Terence Baxter, letter to James K. Baxter, undated [c. 1942–3], MS Hocken 975/183.
243 Terence Baxter, personal interview, Dec 1995.
244 'Conversation About Writing', *New Zealand Monthly Review* 60 (Sep 1965) p.28.

With sharp hoes, detainees weeded between the endless rows of 7,000 flax bushes flourishing on the adjacent swampland. They had been told that the flax would grow better without the hindrance of surrounding growth. It did not. The Government admitted as much in 1946. For over three years, some men weeded flax day after day. Others ring-barked willow trees to kill them and leave more room for the flax. That did not work either. Where the willows fell, branches rooted and new trees prospered.[245]

The diet of boredom and monotony that the camps served up was the hardest thing for the detainees to endure. Most were strong-minded individuals with varied interests and lively intellects, many had offered to serve their country in any ways that did not involve a direct contribution to the war effort. Pacifists on the outside had grave concerns about the effect that detention was having on the men inside:

> Long-continued confinement with its monotony and segregation from society; its enforced labour at unskilled work, often of little purpose or value, is a severe punishment to impose on young men, and it has not been without its effect on the mental and physical health of many of them.[246]

To combat the drudgery of camp life, men had to devise their own ways of coping. Terence Baxter, ever the solitary, lost himself in the construction of models. The first was a scale replica of his beloved ketch-rigged lifeboat, the *Plucky*. In his spare time he whittled a model of the boat in perfect scale, and then set about designing decking and a cabin to be fitted on his release from detention.[247] Ginn recalled his 'infinite patience and ingenuity in making the fittings and sails'.[248] There was widespread interest in his model, and it brought him into contact with others in the camp who shared his love of sailing.

It was Terence's next project, however, that created the greatest stir. He had always had an interest in mechanical things, and one of his treasured memories from his time as a boarder at Sibford School in England had been his discovery that the school possessed a replica steam engine:

> . . . I saw these beautiful brass rails, so I asked one of the masters who didn't really want to help me but he realised I was pretty keen on this steam business, so he said well there is a steam engine but we've got it sitting up in the attic out of the way. After a lot of persuasion and talk I managed to get the thing out. It was a wonderful day when I got the thing going, it was a perfectly

245 Grant, *Out in the Cold*, p.153.
246 Efford, *Penalties on Conscience*, p.11.
247 Baxter proved most helpful in measuring the boat for his brother, see p.216. Terence put his modelling to good use after the war:

> After I came out of the camp I did up my old boat, put a cabin on it. Patricia Lawson's father [a family friend] lent me his workshop and gave me some good old kauri and so forth off an old tram they had in the backyard that had some good kauri panels in it (personal interview, Dec 1995).

248 Noel Ginn, letter to Paul Millar, Jan 1995.

> made engine. A scale model of a proper Great Western railway engine.[249]

In detention camp he went one step further and decided to construct his own engine—which proved quite a feat as all the materials had to be scavenged:

> . . . there was practically nothing there to build it out of. Somehow or another I got a few pieces together: a bit of galvanised pipe to make the two cylinders, it was a lot of effort to get them evenly round inside, made pistons for it, bent the crankshaft out of something which was reasonably thick, which took a bit of doing. In the end I made a boiler and got the thing going.[250]

Ginn well remembers the effort Terence put into the project as he 'tracked down the various components required . . . [manufactured] parts from metal he melted in a small crucible', and spent long hours 'at his small table, hours of trial and error & completest concentration':

> Finally the tiny miniature was completed & the day came for firing. What a triumph as the steam spun the flywheel round with a high ch ch ch sound—lighter but as busy as a sewing machine. The hut was full of smoke from the firebox & the steam. The great interest generated in this steam engine ran through the camp; inmates and staff alike. In spite of disavowals he [Terence] was really clever.[251]

Being much more gregarious than Terence, Ginn had less problem filling his free time. He found it 'very stimulating meeting people from many different walks of life. Many different ages, religions, [I would] never have come across otherwise'.[252] There were discussion groups—often with a literary flavour—to participate in; books were freely available—from friends outside or through the WEA library service—and he read avidly; he had his own small garden to tend; and, at Whitanui, he participated in a number of plays organised by the mercurial Dunedin theatre-lover Rodney Kennedy, whom Ginn first came across early on in Hautu, and who would later become a lifelong friend:

> . . . in [the Strathmore] mess, early in the piece, we were all there at our long benches, and someone came up from the back of the hall singing, a lovely clear tenor voice, we suddenly became aware of it above all the babble, a short person came along with long hair, obviously made out of flax, and this person was singing wonderful words I'd never heard before: 'You made me love you . . .' And everyone stopped and listened to him singing, and he went right up the front and announced the concert that some of them had been preparing. Of course that was Rodney Kennedy.[253]

249 Terence Baxter, personal interview, Dec 1995.
250 Ibid.
251 Noel Ginn, letter to Paul Millar, Jan 1995.
252 Noel Ginn, interview with Annette Facer, Sep 1994.
253 Ibid.

Kennedy did his best to turn Ginn into an actor: 'He dragged me into the plays—I'm not an actor at all but he tried to train me . . . I could remember the lines, but he was all the time trying, gently, to get me inside the character.'[254] Fortunately the theatre group did not have to rely on Ginn alone, it had a number of considerable talents—in acting, design and set construction—to draw on, and a number of very professional productions were staged:

> We put on *The Skin of our Teeth* [last], *The Beautiful People* and *Key Largo.* I was the women—I didn't like the idea of having a feminine role but it was practical. I had blond hair then, but they blonded it further with peroxide, so I had long blond hair. I was Sabrina [laughs]. It was very exciting because we had fairly dull lives you see, and the costuming . . . For instance they made a curtain out of flax claddies—claddies are the sticks that are left after the flowers appear—they're quite corky and you can make a screen from a string of these. Oh, and there was another play—*The Ascent of F6.*[255]

Of course all the books, plays and discussion groups available were not going to compensate for an indefinite sentence, undergoing 'hard labour' and the 'deprivation of most of what the free man calls life'.[256] As months of meaningless, futile work details turned to years and men realised that they would never have a chance to vindicate themselves performing useful tasks—not even in times of extreme shortage or crisis would the Government call on them to work for their communities—a sense of frustration and hopelessness grew, exacerbated by the apparently deliberate pettiness of many of the camp regulations:

> There is less contact with the outside world than in the main prisons, as only relatives (not friends) are allowed to visit, and the isolation of the camps makes visiting, even of relatives, a rare occurrence. A strict censorship of letters in and out of the camps—two in and four out per week being allowed—is imposed. Only personal and domestic matters may be discussed in the letters; political and social topics being excluded from discussion. Within the last few months there has been some relaxation of the strict confinement, in that those with a good conduct record are allowed to visit their homes for two days in each three months.[257]

In fact the regulations were even tighter than recorded above, and open to interpretation so that, depending on their own attitudes towards defaulters, camp superintendents and guards could make life as easy or as harsh as they wished. Visitors were limited to immediate family and Grant recounts, in *Out in the Cold*, an instance

254 Ibid.

255 Ibid. *The Skin of Our Teeth* (1943) by Thornton Wilder (1897–1975); *The Beautiful People* (1941) by William Saroyan (1908–81); *Key Largo* (1939) by Maxwell Anderson (1888–1959); and *The Ascent of F6* (1936) by W.H. Auden (1907–73) and Christopher Isherwood (1904–86).

256 Efford, *Penalties on Conscience*, p.11.

257 Ibid, p10.

in which the wife and children of a man whose brother was in detention were forced to remain outside the camp because they were not close enough to the man to be classed as immediate family (p.165). Letters out were also limited to a single sheet, which led men to pack as much on to two sides of a page as humanly possible, as in the case of Ginn's letter of 2 June 1943 in which he attempted to list and comment on the sixty or more poems already received from Baxter (see pp.221–4). Unlike some inmates, whose letters were often cut to pieces, the correspondence between Ginn and Baxter was never interfered with, although there were some complaints from the censors about the number of poems they were required to read (see p.264). In this respect at least the censors may have served a useful purpose if an awareness of the limitations on what he could say encouraged Baxter's intense focus on his poetry.

Among the other things that riled inmates was the habit of transporting prisoners between camps in the dead of night with little warning:

> There were always shifts going on and they'd often take place in the middle of the night, which was a bit unnerving, they'd shift 4 or 5 to another camp. . . . I think it was a bit of a policy—they might have wanted them for special work with their skills, or perhaps they thought they were a bit troublesome. We rather thought it was a bit of a policy to keep us jittery.[258]

Yet Ginn felt that all in all they were treated fairly:

> When you consider other types of imprisonment in the world—we'd read about Russia and Germany and other countries—we were really pampered in a sense. The great thing was loss of freedom, so I don't think we were martyrs or anything of the sort. I think if things had got tougher and tougher we would have stood our ground, but really we didn't suffer in a physical, brutal, way.[259]

The close confinement and monotony inevitably led to tensions among inmates. Generally these were settled amicably, but from time to time, as Terence recalls, certain individuals who simply refused to conform found themselves on the receiving end of collective justice:

> There was a man in camp—Spanish I think—who was mad on classical music and he got permission to get a gramophone in and some of these classical records. Once he got listening, woe betide anybody who interrupted him. He had a knife with him and he'd go you. He didn't use to wash himself, he didn't like having a shower in front of other people, so one time they decided to wash him so they got the fire hose, cut a hole in the corner of his hut, and turned on the fire hose. Got the fire hose going all round inside the hut. Poor old Stan nearly got drowned in there.[260]

258 Noel Ginn, interview with Annette Facer, Sep 1994.
259 Ibid.
260 Terence Baxter, personal interview, Dec 1995.

Ginn himself had little time for the fundamentalist Christian sects, commenting that the 'bible banging element in there weren't necessarily intellectual',[261] an opinion that even Terence concurred with, despite a temperament which Ginn described as follows:

> He was—there's a word called 'harmless'—and it doesn't just mean not hurting anybody. It was in thought which is a very strong virtue—he had that, and because of that he never made enemies as it were because there was no criticism in him. He would always defend the down-and-out in some way, or the unpleasant character.[262]

Like Ginn, Terence found the more extreme members of the camp communities too much to handle:

> When I first went in there I thought I was going into a camp where at least one thing will be that we all think the same. Where we are all against war so everything will be all right. But we were all absolutely cut apart from each other—even though we did talk together. The Jehovah's Witnesses were counted a bit dim in the head by the Catholics, the Catholics were the more intelligent ones, they were out on their own. The Methodists—which Noel was—they were their sort. And then you got these way-out ones—you'd go past a hut and hear them talking in tongues. I don't know what to think of that—to me it's a form of hypnotism. This touching someone and they fall on the floor is similar to what hypnotists do. I think they're dealing with something they don't understand. I was looking at the different faces of these people who were in a world of their own, to me they look a little bit gullible. They don't look the usual intelligent sort of person who knows what's going on around them.[263]

Unlike Ginn, who felt he was treated fairly, Terence always had the niggling feeling (right from the start when he was the first in the Otago region to be sent into detention) that he had been victimised because of who his father was. Despite being the most mild-mannered of men, he was quickly moved to the Hautu camp for problem inmates, arriving there on the heels of Noel Ginn and the unruly Methodist protesters. The fact that he was never given the opportunity to transfer to Conical Hill, the one detention camp near his home, was a keenly felt disappointment: 'they didn't put me down there . . . They shoved us around all over the place. I think it was done intentionally.'[264] Confinement and monotony inevitably led to depression and lethargy: Terence, in a letter to his brother thanking him for some books he had sent, wrote:

> I also got the books that you sent up. I get pretty tired of reading the same old books & magazines over & over again . . . Sometimes I pick one book up

261 Noel Ginn, personal interview, Aug 1994.
262 Noel Ginn, personal interview, 25 Oct 1994.
263 Terence Baxter, personal interview, Dec 1995.
264 Ibid.

> & just throw it on the table in disgust. I never seem to be in the mood these days to make models. One or two I've started on but I've just lost interest.[265]

Ginn remembers homesickness as 'the emotion [Terence] most often expressed'.[266] In all the years he was in detention he had only two family visits: once from his father; and once from James and Millicent. Restrictions on travel during wartime, and the distance of his family from the camps, prevented greater contact. Not until the very end of his sentence was he allowed a visit home; for four days on account of his good behaviour.[267]

The effects of detention on Terence remained a constant concern to his family. When he was finally allowed home, they discovered a changed man, and feared that he was 'permanently scarred mentally'.[268] In this respect the correspondence with Noel Ginn had an added value, it allowed Baxter to remain in contact with his brother without testing Terence's 'true-born impatience / Of rhetoric' or intensifying his 'fear of being petted'.

265 Terence Baxter, letter to James K. Baxter, undated [c. 1942–3], MS Hocken 975/183.

266 Noel Ginn, personal interview, 25 Oct 1994.

267 It is interesting to speculate on whether the actions of Millicent Baxter might have contributed to the victimisation Terence felt he was subject to. A forthright women, Millicent had a number of run-ins with Len Greenberg, the Controller-General of Defaulters' Detention Camps:

> . . . there was a little bit of trouble because my mother was very concerned about my teeth because she'd gone to a lot of trouble to make sure that they were all right. I always had to go to the dentist, although other children around me, they didn't have to go to the dentist very much. In those days nobody cared very much about that. We weren't allowed to go to the store and get sweets like other children. There was not much in the way of dental care in the camp and finally when I did go it was a pretty rough sort of a dentist. He had a treadle to make the needle go—he ground away there for long enough and stirred up the nerves a good bit. My mother got on to Greenberg about it and he fought against it—'I've got enough trouble trying to look after these people without worrying about teeth.' They said he was a fairly hard sort of man [personal interview, Dec 1995].

268 Recounted in Margaret Hargreave's letter to Frank McKay, VUW Library, MS McKay 10/5/36.

# Nine
# The Globe of Dream: Baxter's Adolescent Phase

O perilous unicorn!
Death slays thee not—but see
From the cold surf's futurity
Aphrodite Anadyamone
Arise in birth thou woulds't extinction deem:
Arise and bind thee to an iron dream.
'The Unicorn'

The years 1942–43—Baxter's third and fourth years as a student at Dunedin's King's High School—provided him with a mixture of experiences. Initially it was a busy time academically because, as a student in the top stream, Baxter was able to sit for his matriculation in 1942, instead of in his fourth year as was generally the case (he passed with unspectacular results). On a personal level these were Baxter's arid years; his family's pacifist stance produced a sense of isolation that Terence's absence exacerbated. He described the feeling of alienation that developed in him as 'a sense of difference, of a gap . . . between myself and other people'.[269] Although at sixteen he was well into his adolescence, he was only just entering the stage that he would associate with the worst period of adolescent solitude, and it was a time when suicide 'was certainly in his mind'.[270] In poetic terms these were the crucial years in which Baxter, who was attempting to fill the 'gap' with poems, made the transition from producing imitative juvenilia to writing poems of increasing originality and creativity. His letters to Ginn, and the many hundreds of poems in his notebooks, make it clear that in these years poetry absorbed almost all of his attention and energy.

Whereas Baxter's juvenile phase was a period of sustained absorption, his adolescent phase could well be characterised as one of aggregation. The fusion of technique, imagery and language in his poetry showed many influences, but these influences no longer saturated his verse with their content. Rather, their contribution was technical—a provision of structure and form. In the poetry of this phase Baxter begins to harmonise and reconcile his diverse experiences of literature, culture, and literary and cultural practices to produce in his verse—at first unevenly—a syncretic form more reflective of his New Zealand environment. It is in this stage that Baxter first becomes aware of himself as a distinctly New Zealand poet, although it will be some years yet before he acknowledges without reservation the existence of a New Zealand poetic tradition.

269 Baxter, *The Man on the Horse,* p.123.
270 W.H. Oliver, *James K. Baxter: A Portrait* (Auckland: Godwit Press/Bridget Williams Books, 1994) p.32. McKay also discusses Baxter's adolescent death-wish in some detail, see *Life*, p.59.

In *The Man on the Horse*, Baxter points to 'The Atheist'—a poem written at thirteen—and suggests that the 'spiritual fact that lay behind [it] was the authentic and terrible grey rock desert of adolescence'.[271] There is a similar description of life at thirteen in 'A Family Photograph 1939':

> I, in my fuggy room at the top of the stairs,
> A thirteen-year-old schizophrene,
> Write poems, wish to die,
> And watch the long neat mason-fly
> Malignantly serene
> Arrive with spiders dopier than my mind
> And build his clay dungeons inside the roller blind.
> [*CP*, p.238]

It was a further two years before he had fully developed the tools to deal with 'the central anguish of a child hurled into the adolescent abyss, at the mercy of his imagination and the impulses of his body'[272]:

> . . . like most New Zealanders, I remember adolescence as a very arid time. A time when sex and intellect are both active but have nothing to feed on but the sight of a girl's legs in the bus and coloured diagrams of test-tubes in a science notebook. Like certain animals in cages, the adolescent begins to devour himself. Slowly the manuscript books were filled up with private junk. Occasionally the verse was good. . . . The emblems of adolescence, however, are the private demon, the spider on the wall, and rat-eaten books in old cupboards. I don't object to this. I think anyone who has survived an English or New Zealand adolescence would feel at home anywhere—in a space ship going to Venus or in a pit full of tarantulas. The all-but-unbreakable armour of the Anglo-Saxon adult is forged then. It gave me time to write a vast quantity of bad verse.[273]

By the beginning of his adolescent phase Baxter had fallen 'into the habit of poem-writing with a vengeance and counted it a poor week when I had not written four or five pieces of verse'.[274] But more importantly, this was the period when some of the verse he wrote 'privately nearly every day of the week [began developing] control and shape and meaning'.[275] Although he refers to most of these poems as 'bad verse',

271 Ibid, p.125.

272 Ibid, p.126.

273 'Further Notes on New Zealand Poetry', Hocken, MS 975/119.

274 Baxter, *The Man on the Horse*, p.124. As I note in my discussion of Baxter's MS Books (see Fig. 6 p.79) Baxter's poetic output between the ages of 15–17 was phenomenal—he was writing almost three times the number of poems per year that he would average in his adult phase. In the late 1960s he wrote:

> With luck I might complete about sixty poems in a year, but these would include about fifty that would not be up to publication standard. I tend to be continually trying my hand at it. Some years, though, are better than others; and I sometimes get a lucky run of four or five good poems in a row. Tut-tut! One mustn't number the tribes of Israel! (*The Bone Chanter*, p.6).

275 'Recollections of School Days', *NZMR*, 65 (Mar 1966) p.19.

many of the symbols, ideas, themes, techniques and influences that occur in, or structure, much of his later work originated and evolved in the process of writing them.

Baxter's adolescent phase ran for slightly more than two years, concluding around the time *Beyond the Palisade* was published. The existence of this upper limit, and its approximate date, is suggested by a number of comments that Baxter made to Ginn commencing in early 1944. In March he wrote 'I am not satisfied with my poetry', and decided instead to try prose because 'prose-poetry [is] of the adult' (pp.345, 346). As Baxter neared the end of this phase, a letter dated 18 March 1944 credits Ginn, in his role as mentor, with being something of a catalyst for change: 'your last letter has, as it were, touched the spark to a waiting fuse. I am casting round for new footholds' (p.345). Although Baxter did not abandon poetry, his problems with it continued through May—'Maybe a phase, but phases hurt' (p.357)—and into July, as the postscript of a letter dated 16 Jul 1944 records:

> I am emerging from the 'globe of dream' which produced 'The Unicorn' and others. My poems may change, I may even stop writing for a bit, but one must not retard development by attempted 'freezing' in one phase. (p.368)

He did not freeze in this second phase, but marked it with the publication of *Beyond the Palisade* and moved on. The phase had certainly concluded by May 1945 and he was looking ahead with renewed confidence:

> I see faint hopes, Noel, of a new verse-efflorescence for myself. The images might even flow truthfully and easily. After all, I have only quarried painfully in childhood and adolescent stone. If I could acquire a bit more insensitivity, I might even eventually gain something of the standpoint of Burns . . . I have written all my *Better beast or unborn* . . . poems. (p.406)

During Baxter's adolescent phase profound changes in his modes of thought and poetic expression occurred. He wrote in 'Autobiographical' that:

> . . . at fifteen a world thundered without,
> Strange pebbles laid at the feet; but girded about
> With a world-embracing solitude there stood
> Narcissus, master of the iron wood.

The phrase 'iron wood' clearly owes something to Auden's poem 'A Free One' (see p.232 and note 11), but 'iron' also suggests a much broader context: it points once again to Baxter's tendency to see his life in mythological terms—in this instance the four ages of the human race suggested by Ovid in *Metamorphoses*. But it is an analogy with the usefully tragic implications of the fall: the young poet plummets from childhood's 'Golden Age'—a time of 'innocence, peace, plenty, and perpetual summer'—directly to the 'Iron Age' of adolescence—a period characterised by 'hardship, wickedness and suffering'.[276] The poems of the '"globe of dream" which

276 Geoffrey Miles, 'A Short Mythical History of the World', unpublished course paper.

produced "The Unicorn" and others' are not like the often peaceful, escapist musings characteristic of the productions that emerge from the juvenile's 'globe of reverie'. In 'The Unicorn' it is made clear that the dream the poet is bound to is 'an iron dream', and the globe is a type of prison. In much of the poetry of this period a variety of interchangeable terms—'cage', 'net', 'skull', 'womb', 'tomb' (in fact anything that restricts movement or imposes limits)—signify, along with 'globe', the suffocating claustrophobia of the adolescent trapped by the strangling 'weight of sex and intellect'.[277]

In an unpublished paper titled 'The Unicorn: a consideration of adolescence', Baxter discusses this poem and its relationship to his adolescence in some detail:

> ['The Unicorn'] was written by a precocious boy of sixteen. A quiet lad, who lived too much in his own head; a constant beach-walker and word-builder, with the makings of a drunkard or intelligent schizophrene. The torments of the adolescent furnace are threefold: unnatural solitude, ignorance of life, and sexuality without love. Like a million others he did his time there, and passed through singed, by virtue of a patience hidden from himself, like those children in the other furnace of the Assyrian king.

In his discussion Baxter makes further reference to his mythological mode of thought: 'In earlier poems the boy had developed two other figures of self, the salamander that lives in flame, and the Titan Prometheus, from whose wound grows the iceflower of art.'

If this statement is considered in the context of my concluding comments on Baxter's juvenile phase (p.95), it is noticeable that in the adolescent phase the locus of tension responsible for poetic inspiration shifts from the external world (i.e. the garden or the cave of the juvenile phase) to 'figures of the self' like the Titan Prometheus, the salamander, and the Unicorn. The use of such figures indicates that Baxter discovered in adolescence that polarities can exist within one individual, and that the locus of tension that generates poetry—which if personified in the juvenile phase would have been externalised in such figures as 'my Muse'—may therefore be wholly internal. Once Baxter had arrived at this idea of the poetic self as a composite of opposites dwelling within in a state of perpetual poem-producing tension, he ever abandoned it. In 1966 he referred to 'my collaborator, my schizophrenic twin who has always provided me with poems':

> Occasionally I visit the cellblock in the basement of my mind where he still lives, incorrigible, ineducable, unemployable; and through the bars he will pass me a message written on the back of a tobacco packet. Something like this—
>
> 'Look out, you bloody fool! What will happen if I die? I'll tell you. One by one you're going to lose your sex, your art and your sense of humour . . . I am It; and you can't do without me . . .'[278]

277 'The Waves', *CP*, p.286.
278 Baxter, *The Man on the Horse*, pp.17–9.

His 'schizophrenic twin' is a later mythologised figure of the self. This is made explicit in Baxter's references to the character of Timothy Harold Glass, from his novel *Horse*, who, he writes, inhabited Dunedin in the 1940s 'daring to use my name and wear my features',[279] and whose name was bestowed on him 'in honour of his glass belly and the twelve labours of Hercules'.[280]

Of the adolescent figures of the self the idea of Prometheus, the creator of rude human figures out of chthonian mud, surely appealed, as an analogue, to Baxter's idea of himself as the creator of poems out of the chaotic clay of the unconscious. On one level the opposition in the Prometheus myth is between organised society and the tribe, the former—represented by the dehumanising authority of Zeus—being antagonistic to the welfare of the latter—symbolised by the human race. Prometheus's resistance on the tribe's behalf, by attracting the god's vengeance, makes the Titan the locus of tension—he becomes, by extension, a metaphor for the poem and, on a particular level of imagery, the act of artistic creation.

The salamander generates tension in a different way. The very nature of its existence in flame is a sentence of solitude. The salamander cannot survive in society—only the fire of poetry sustains it. Life in the adolescent furnace is, for the salamander/poet, a 'cloistered meditation in clear flame': the fabulous creature lives but it exists in grief because it 'has no mate'.[281] Unlike Prometheus, the salamander serves no tribe, its isolation is the regrettable consequence of being a poet. As already noted, Baxter once told Ginn: 'I was very loath to expose my verse to the private or public eye, as I had sensed early the morbid fear of poetic expression that so many have' (p.191).

But in Baxter's own words it is in 'the figure of the unicorn [that] the adolescent dilemma is projected more fully and exactly . . . the soul of a man-to-be wakens at puberty when the torments of the flesh begin and he is isolated for good from the fraternal universe of childhood. Puberty gives birth to flesh and spirit simultaneously.'[282] Baxter's discussion of the poem emphasises the doubling and division in the adolescent mind: boy/unicorn, beast/spirit, natural solitude/unnatural solitude:

> The unicorn and the boy are distinguishable, though not wholly separate. The unicorn is a hybrid creature, beast and spirit inhabiting the universe of the adolescent mind. Because poetry is conceived in the order of natural contemplation, it requires an interior solitude as its element. But the unicorn exists in a double solitude—a natural contemplative solitude, resonant with the correspondences of nature, and the terrible solitude of the boy himself, a child becoming a man and regarding himself as a monster.

The unicorn is at once immortal—doomed to live on forever in the creation of its art as the salamander burns forever in the fires of its poetry—and doomed to die at the hands of the archer. It is:

279 Ibid, p.17.
280 Ibid.
281 See 'The Salamander', pp.240–1.
282 'The Unicorn: a consideration of adolescence', MS Hocken 975/34; and pp.535–9.

> a figure in a tapestry, or an image on a shield, for the will to love is petrified in the adolescent furnace, and only the intellect can move. God he knows as the Archer, an analogue of time, who kills from a distance, without knowledge of the victim or participation in its suffering. Yet hound and Archer are secretly welcome to the unicorn, who knows that he must die for the adolescent to become a man.

The Archer is an important, although infrequently used, figure in Baxter's adolescent poems. Just as symbolism dealing with sailing often refers to Terence Baxter, so symbolism associated with archers and archery often refers to Baxter's father. This is not merely because his name is Archie, the connection is stronger than that, as Baxter noted in his own copy of *Beyond the Palisade* where he has written in pencil to the right of the third stanza of 'The Unicorn': 'father born under / sign of Sagittarius— / Archie'.[283] The connection is also noted in Baxter's rough, handwritten (virtually illegible) notes attached to his discussion of 'The Unicorn':

> One could of course interpret the whole poem in Freudian terms. The father–archer (the boy's father was called Archie and was born under the sign of Sagittarius) kills or castrates the unicorn–child whose auto-erotic ~~fantasy~~ rebellion involves a return in [ ] to his mother's womb. It fits nicely. But the boy has read Freud, and these implications were fully [ ] in his mind. He was not wholly devoid of iconoclastic humour.[284]

The point I want to emphasise is that even in his adolescent phase Baxter's father still features, if not always positively, then at least as a necessary factor in the production of poetry. The poem 'Rain-Ploughs', provides a further example of this.

Included in the second letter Baxter sent to Ginn was an early version of 'Rain-Ploughs' which, he wrote, 'may seem to you like G.M. Hopkins gone mad'(p.142). Then follows a gap of almost two years before 'Rain-Ploughs' is again mentioned. In June 1944 Baxter enclosed a 're-casting' of the poem with detailed explanations of the changes he had made, explaining that these have been won by 'shaping and re-shaping, not to a standard, but till an intuitional dissatisfaction is satisfied' (p.361).

Discussing his early version of 'Rain-Ploughs', Baxter explained to Ginn the importance in his poetry of this relationship between the 'old verse forms' and the poem's content—that is, the contributions made by 'memory and emotion':

> The line you wish to know is—
>
> > Grope, slope I slate-entangled rune, but rise, shall rise, to green.
>
> 'slate' signifies roof—especially of old houses—and hence human habitation. The Romans used 'tectum'—roof—to signify 'house'. I 'grope' in the darkness of memory and emotion, I labour upward, not directly but on a 'slope', from

283 James K. Baxter, *Beyond the Palisade* (Christchurch: Caxton Press, 1944), Baxter's personal annotated copy, Hocken, MS 975/25, p.29.

284 'The Unicorn: a consideration of adolescence.'

> amateurism by the old verse-forms: yet eventually I will flourish in greenery like a tree. (p.146)

Thus poems like 'Spring Pastoral' and 'The Rose of Solitude' were, he wrote: 'traditionalist, purposely so. It is a good exercise, however, to do this occasionally . . . Traditionalism is useful sometimes' (p.214). As a closer look at different versions of 'Rain-Ploughs' reveals, however, tradition was only useful up to a point. The version of 'Rain-Ploughs' that Baxter sent to Ginn in his letter of 28 August 1942 differs substantially from that printed in *Beyond the Palisade*. The published version has a flow and coherence that the earlier version lacks. The process by which the published poem was arrived at is in important respects symbolic of the process of change that was occurring in Baxter's verse during his adolescent phase.

Referring to the earlier version Baxter explained to Ginn that in the third verse 'you must imagine in it all the elements, incoherence, and storm' (p.142):

> Wrong, rather song if battered bent by rain;
> Join elementals in reef-erosion:
> Break, slake from blinding sky disintegrate explosion;
> Molten, smelted in branchèd channels run,
> Spirit sponging out
> Move universal god-whole new-arisen.
> Bound in, shut,
> Blanketed in pierced-not shade
> Grope, slope I slate-entangled rune; yet rise, shall rise to green!

This stanza suggests that Baxter's quest for his new verse form was hard work—much more a labour than an efflorescence. However, the corresponding verse in the published poem shows the progress he was making towards a new form:

> Yet hope stays for him who dare.
> Dost see yonder the angel-Archer stand?
> Frail-veined twig in hand
> By blinding sky fire-tipped he doth bear:
> Fire-feathered arrow-thought to set new sun on flare
> Brave djin and monster, green again the land.
> [*CP*, p.27]

The control over his material that Baxter demonstrates in the published version does not only relate to the tightening up of the form by abandoning a particular tradition—that is, less like 'Hopkins gone mad'—but also a tightening of the content. Where the phrase in the first version 'yet rise shall rise to green' suggests a process in progress, 'green again the land'—indicates a process completed. It is significant that the later version—the publication of which comes towards the end of Baxter's adolescent phase—loses the personal pronoun. The poem's subject is no longer explicitly Baxter groping upward eventually to flourish, as he had predicted to Ginn. Instead the land—metaphorically the poet's *oeuvre*—flourishes in a cycle of renewal that follows naturally from the rending of the rain-ploughs. Cultivation stimulates the germination of both vegetation and verse through the benison of the 'Fire-feathered arrow-thought'. The apocalyptic angel-Archer—consistent with the Blakean influences on Baxter—points, as does the revised structure, to Baxter's developing mythopoetic tendencies. But the Archer also stands as a figure of Baxter's father, the poet's early influence has not deserted him, he stands ready—arrows tipped with the poetic fire—to assist in the process of renewal.

Of course in Baxter's adolescent phase his father was no longer the major influence at work upon him. Of the numerous poets Baxter read and admired, those that particularly stood out in his estimation were Blake, Hopkins and the younger group of left-wing poets of the 1930s—W.H. Auden, C. Day Lewis, Louis MacNeice, and Stephen Spender—nicknamed the 'Pylon School'. In an early letter he had written: 'I think that Auden, Spender, MacNeice, Day Lewis, and even Dylan Thomas or T.S. Eliot, are, if they can forget their mannerisms of modernity and Marxism, real poets' (p.143). He found himself 'unusually susceptible' to Hopkins and enthused: 'he is great—that is all one can really say, except for reading him again and again. [Hopkins] is like the bread, the water of life to me as far as poetry goes (it goes a long way.) . . . The sad-made-strength is [his] forte' (p.319). He also cited Auden as a continuing influence upon him, commenting that Auden 'has made better poetry of modern conditions than anyone else I know' (p.300).

Of the Romantics, Blake seems to have had the most enduring influence on the young Baxter. It is hardly surprising that this earliest and most marginalised of the Romantics would appeal to Baxter in his own situation. He told Ginn that having reread Blake in the light of criticism of him he could find 'no trace of madness but only the workings of a clear, strong, imaginative mind and faculty . . . of poetic expression rarely equalled' (p.187). In a letter written in early May 1943 he commented: 'Blake is to me pure poetry' (p.215). A sentiment reinforced in his next letter: 'I have never yet seen anything to beat Blake's "Tiger" or even Auden "Lay your sleeping head, my love". Both are "doom": perhaps I like doom' (p.228).

Baxter would tell Ginn repeatedly that good poetry is strong poetry, and strong poetry demands clarity and vitality. In one letter he asserted that 'all obscure poems must have a thread' (p.244). This belief was central to his criticism of the moderns, of whom he had an extensive collection. In the same letter he told Ginn, while discussing Ginn's own poetry, that one should 'have a basis of traditionalism and veneer of modernism to give facility of expression and mood. Thus one can study old masters and violent moderns with perfect enjoyment and equanimity.' His concern was that 'The rigid modern can lose, by a habit of mind, power of appreciating the early "dreams" of Yeats; and ludicrously underestimate the essential force of clarity' (p.229). In a later letter he argues:

> . . . Yeats, has unconsciously recognised a modern trend. Our eyes slide over a page; not words but phrases we read; the sound is unheard. Thus concentration of meaning evaporates. Yeats is the master of the phrase, and so for us there is magic in him. (p.275)

Baxter's attempts in his late teenage years to alleviate the 'pain of incoherence' through writing poetry, while realising at the same time 'that no-one can write more than is in themselves', were tempered by the knowledge that not every personal experience makes good poetry. It was his enduring conviction that, as he told Ginn in January 1943, 'the essence of poetry is emotion' (p.180). A point developed in November of the same year when he wrote:

> If I thought the meaning of a poem was all that mattered, that the verse-form was merely for adornment and easy remembering, I would rewrite all my poems in simple prose. But emotion is the essence of poetry: vowel-music promotes it, rhythm facilitates its flow. Naturally, one wants original thought; but it is the emotional force, not the reasoning force, that makes the poetry. (p.279)

By emotion, Baxter meant active rather than passive emotion. He did not believe that any 'inertly miserable man has ever written good poetry' (p.158), and he found the poetry of the 'heart cryers' banal (p.265), arguing four months later that the 'best poetry of course has perfect welding of image and emotion'(p.324). In January of 1943 he had written: 'among twenty poems of mine there are 18 of varying quality, one trash and one really good. Incidentally, the one "really good" usually expresses strong emotion, the one trash is emotionless obscurist jargon.'[285]

Returning to a point already noted in passing; obscurity was particularly repugnant to Baxter. He told Ginn:

> Only by necessity should one even start on the road to obscurity. One should say (i) need I say it? (ii) could I say it better in another form? (iii) following forth from (i)—has it sufficient vigour or clarity to make it poetry or even good verse? Those who in the Victorian era could be recognised as mediocre by their sentimentality cannot now be classified owing to the refuge of obscurity. Obscurity becomes a cult when the vital necessity that poetry should say something is lost. (p.234)

Hence his criticism of the moderns:

> The genius of Hopkins prevents true obscurity, but the intellect of Empson does not. The modern, fed on curry, loses taste for unseasoned food; through concentration on his own epoch he has narrowed his range of consciousness . . . I have read many fine poems; but vitality, vitality is needed—and with vitality comes sufficient clarity. (pp.229)

Baxter found reason to lament the diminishing interest in poetry. Associating it with what he perceived to be a modern tendency—unconsciously recognised by Yeats—to read not words, but phrases. He wrote early in 1944 that:

285 See p.187. It is interesting to compare this comment with one made some twenty years later: 'Most of the poems I start are brought to some kind of final shape; but the number I would consider full and truly formed poems would be at most one in ten.' (*The Bone Chanter*, p.5.)

> The heyday of poetry lived (??) when a word was still miraculous, when use and misuse had not dulled it to a smooth grey pebble. What force now has 'light thickens'? The association is curded [sic] milk, I think. It is not understanding of meaning we lack, though as interest dwindles that loss approaches; it is appreciation of concentration, of a transcendental meaning—in a word, of poetry. (p.275)

It had been Baxter's good fortune to trek into the literary landscape as Allen Curnow was about to redefine New Zealand poetry in his Caxton Press anthology *A Book of New Zealand Verse: 1923–45*. From the manuscript of *Beyond the Palisade* Curnow selected six poems for his anthology, and then added the fifteenth section to his historic introduction. Baxter's poems, he wrote, are:

> strong in impulse and confident in invention, with qualities of youth in verse which we have lacked; yet with a feeling after tradition and a frankly confessed debt (besides the unsought affinities) to some older New Zealand poets.
>
> It seems to me that since Mason in 1923, no New Zealand poet has proved so early his power to say and his right to speak.[286]

For Baxter it was a coming in from the wilderness. His successful first book and Curnow's endorsement transformed him from a solitary adolescent who found escape in a private world of poetry, into a figure of national acclaim ranked alongside poets like A.R.D. Fairburn, R.A.K. Mason, Charles Brasch, Curnow himself, and Denis Glover.

But *Beyond the Palisade* never rated as highly with Baxter as these events might lead one to expect. He acknowledged a certain unevenness in the volume, having deliberately included poems written at fifteen that represent an earlier stage in his development, and he described it in a letter to Lawrence Baigent as 'a sort of *poet's progress*'.[287] Nor could Baxter claim that its contents were determined by him alone, because Baigent had felt that his initial selection was insubstantial and urged him to augment it from a second bundle of poems that Baxter had sent him:

> At the risk of irritating you I'm going to suggest that you reconsider the selection you have made. It was good of you to send me the other poems and it is perhaps unfair of me to use them as a weapon against you. My excuse must be that I want this first volume of yours to make as sharp an impression as possible upon the few people in this country who care about poetry. Having read the second collection I feel that the selection you have made in *Beyond the Palisade* does you less than justice. As a whole the book lacks weight. Not enough of the poems speak with the authentic personal voice of 'Cry Mourn', 'The Mountains' and the 'Letter'. For this reason I would urge you to include

286 Allen Curnow, ed., introduction, *A Book of New Zealand Verse 1923–45* (Christchurch: The Caxton Press, 1945) pp.54–5.
287 Letter to Lawrence Baigent, 23 Oct 1944, MS McKay 19/3/1.

> several poems from the second collection which, though brief, possess that quality of originality and authenticity. I have in mind 'Death of a Man', 'The Eagle', 'Death of a Swan', 'The First Forgotten' and, perhaps, 'Killing a Rabbit'.
>
> Would you consider this suggestion carefully? I make it only after much deliberation. To speak plainly, I cannot rid myself of an uneasy feeling that by publishing *Beyond the Palisade* as it stands we will be to some extent practising a deception upon the people who buy the book. It should contain the best work of which you are capable. I don't think it does.[288]

Baxter dutifully followed his publisher's advice and added the poems Baigent favoured. He also agreed to leave the final arrangement of the book in Baigent's hands:

> One thing more—the order in which the poems are to be printed. I suggest that you leave us at least a margin of discretion so that we can arrange the longer poems to the best advantage. We do not propose to ruin the appearance of the book by running the poems on more or less continuously, as the Regulations require us to do, but at the same time it will be necessary to avoid leaving pages blank save for the few concluding lines of longer poems.

He was happy enough with the end result, seeing in it a certain symmetry: 'I like your arrangement: in a way the "First Forgotten" begins the book and "Letter to Noel Ginn" ends it. "For Burial in Ground" is just a kind of epitaph.'[289] But it was never in his nature to cede authority over his poetry and towards the end of 1944 he began planning a second book, *Cold Spring,* that would be entirely in his control.

288 Lawrence Baigent, letter to James K. Baxter, 17 Oct 1944, Hocken, MS 975/183.
289 Letter to Lawrence Baigent, 27 Nov 1944, VUW Library, Wellington, MS McKay 19/3/4.

# Ten
# A Crystal-Gazer's Globe and Leg of Mutton: The Beginning of Baxter's Adult Phase

> Life went faster in '44.
> I didn't have time to find it a bore
> Between her place and the bottle store
> In the early, early days.
> 'Reflections on a Varsity Career'

The events of 1944 were largely responsible for Baxter's emergence from the 'foggy burrows' of adolescence. In particular, his 'long, unsuccessful love affair with the Higher Learning', which began when he 'timidly entered the Registrar's office at Otago University, with a head full of bad poems, at the age of seventeen',[290] became the catalyst for significant change in his life. The learning itself did little to change him (after four bleak years at King's High School further education was not high on his list of priorities) but the opportunity to mix with others did, and Baxter, as if to compensate for the loneliness of the preceding years, socialised with a vengeance. He would later describe his 'incipient alcoholism' taking wings during that year, 'like a bush fire, leaping fence and river, in the *Bowling Green*, the *Royal Albert*, the *Captain Cook*, the *Grand*, the *City*, the *Oban*, the *Shamrock* (on Sundays), and the *Robert Burns*',[291] and define his ambitions as 'pudendal rather than academic'[292]:

> God also, whom I had not met till then, revealed Himself to me one day when I had reached the middle of a disused railway tunnel, in the grip of a brutal hangover. . . . Aphrodite, Bacchus, and the Holy Spirit were my tutors, but the goddess of good manners and examination passes withheld her smile from me.[293]

These changes in his lifestyle are evident in his poetry: the ponderous gloom of adolescence gradually lifts. In the emerging adult there are echoes of the five-year-old who, in 'Autobiographical', looks out wonderingly on a world of trees and savours the sweet 'holiday smell of petrol-gas':

> At seventeen, a cynic laugh essayed
> Fails in a sense of time's collapse, afraid;
> For, apart from trees made men, parents not Them but alive,
> And women for petrol-gas, it's the same as at five.

290 'Essay on the Higher Learning', *Spike* (1961) p.61.
291 Ibid, p.62.
292 Ibid, p.61.
293 Ibid, p.62.

As the introversion of the adolescent phase gave way before a developing adult confidence, Baxter's overcompensation for the preceding two years of aridity gained him notoriety. Through it all though he continued to write, and the tone of his poetry continued to change. The themes, images and symbols used seriously in the juvenile 'globe-of-reverie' and adolescent 'globe-of-dream' phases were now equally likely to be dealt with satirically (as 'globe' itself is in an early draft of 'For those who lie with crooked limbs in the straight grave' where Baxter's reference to a 'crystal-gazer's globe and leg of mutton' is a 'skit on the idea of spirit and flesh' (p.366)).

By the time Baxter turned nineteen, in June 1945, he had final drafts of 870 poems entered into fourteen poetry notebooks. It is hardly surprising, therefore, that he had begun mentioning the publication of a second book of poetry before *Beyond the Palisade* had left the Caxton Press. What is surprising, given the subsequent success of Baxter's first book, is that his second selection entitled *Cold Spring*, which he thought 'rather better than the present book',[294] remained unpublished despite attempts to interest Lawrence Baigent—Caxton's editor at the time—in it for more than a year.

The form of *Cold Spring* was suggested by a gift that Baigent sent Baxter in December 1944. The gift—ostensibly for Christmas but also consolation for the fact that *Beyond the Palisade* was delayed at the binders—was a posthumously published collection of poems, *The Cruel Solstice* (1944), by a young Englishman named Sidney Keyes who had gone missing in action in Tunisia in 1943. Keyes's arrangement of his book into four sections appealed to Baxter, and in February 1945 he wrote to Baigent of his decision to emulate it:

> I have put together a tentative manuscript. Arrangement suggested by Sidney Keyes's book:
> CLOUDS AND IDOLS —earlier poems.
> THE CLOSED PICTURE —progress to materialism.
> THE FLOWERING EYE —love poems.
> COLD SPRING —emergence.

All but one of the poems in *Cold Spring* were written between 23 March 1944 and 15 March 1945.[295] It was during this period, Baxter believed, that he made the transition from adolescence to adulthood (his 'progress to materialism') which involved a close scrutiny of his values and beliefs, and a re-evaluation of his poetry.

While Baxter was attempting to stand apart from his parents and deal with issues of sexuality and spirituality, a number of other events of significance were exacting their toll on him. Early in February 1944 Terence was allowed his four-day visit home. It was enough time for his family to discover how scarred he was by detention, but it gave them no opportunity to re-establish their relationships with him, and in a letter to his friend Margaret Hargreave, written on 18 February, Baxter confessed

294 Letter to Lawrence Baigent, 17 Mar 1945, VUW Library, MS McKay 19/3/21.
295 The exception is 'Aeneas' which pre-dates the other poems by some 6 to 8 months, see pp.454–5.

to her his fear that Terence 'was permanently scarred mentally'.[296] Later that month Baxter enrolled at Otago University where, in May, he won the Macmillan Brown Prize for his poem 'Convoys'. It was around this time that he began developing a reputation, not only for his poetry, but also for drunkenness and unreliability. By August 1944 he was becoming disillusioned with university life, and was depressed over the end of a brief love affair—an experience which, although painful, inspired the love poems in 'The Flowering Eye' section of *Cold Spring*.

It was late that same month, as he travelled with his mother to visit Terence in detention camp, that they stopped in Christchurch at the Caxton Press and delivered the selection of poems that would form the substance of *Beyond the Palisade* to Lawrence Baigent. Despite some initial reservation when 'this dumpy little woman' marched up to his desk and presented him with a bundle of Baxter's poems, while the poet in question 'just stood there, gazing rather vacantly around him',[297] Baigent agreed to read the poems and meet with Baxter to discuss them on his return journey.[298] At the detention camp Baxter, in addition to seeing Terence, had his first face-to-face meeting with Noel Ginn. He found it good to meet Ginn, and to see Terence again, because it 'straightened out things in my mind'(p.373). But leaving was difficult, and he set his feelings down in the poem 'Thoughts by a Conchie Camp' (see pp.486–7). For Ginn also, the meeting was a memorable experience:

> My first impression was of Jim's enormous head, and his loose, almost shambling, gait. That head I thought is like a lamp held before his body . . . The meeting was brief and stimulating. We did not meet as strangers as our correspondence had made us acquainted mentally and emotionally . . . What was new was the rich cadence of his voice and the engaging bashful manner contrasting with the quality and authority of his speech.[299]

Towards the end of September 1944, a bike accident landed Baxter in hospital with concussion. He recovered well but missed a large number of lectures and fell further behind in his studies. Of more immediate concern, now that he was eighteen, was the probability that his name would be picked in one of the forthcoming ballots for military service, which, as a pacifist, he intended to refuse. He registered as a conscientious objector, setting out his reasons in a letter to the armed forces appeal board (p389), and began preparing himself for the possibility that he might be detained like Noel and Terence for the remainder of the war.

296 Margaret Hargreave, letter to Frank McKay, VUW Library, MS McKay 10/5/36. This letter contains transcripts from letters of Baxter's in Margaret Hargreave's possession.

297 McKay, *Life*, p.75.

298 Baxter did not return the following day to hear Baigent's verdict on his poems, although that is how Baigent remembered it some years later (see *Life*, pp.75–6). He and his mother continued on to Whitanui detention camp where, in the course of conversation with Noel Ginn, they mentioned that they had stopped off at Caxton Press. Baxter's next letter to Ginn confirms a longer gap than overnight between his two meetings with Baigent, and discusses the publication of his poems in a manner that assumes Ginn's familiarity with the situation: 'I talked with Laurence Baigent for an evening when we were in Christchurch . . . He was much more forthcoming than when I met him a week before—having read my poems in the meantime' (see p.374).

299 Noel Ginn, letter to Frank McKay, 13 Jan 1983, VUW Library, MS McKay 10/4/17.

November 1944 was a month of mixed fortunes: the pleasure of receiving the galley proofs of *Beyond the Palisade*, and the compliment when some of his poems were requested for Allen Curnow's anthology *A Book of New Zealand Verse*, did not entirely compensate for his miserable results in his university exams. This failure was the catalyst for the most traumatic event of this period. Early in 1945 he summoned the courage to inform his parents that he was turning his back on their 'tentative programme for the future':

> . . . with their generous support I was to obtain a New Zealand degree in English, go to Oxford or Cambridge, obtain an English degree, and then become a scholar and lecturer in English Literature.[300]

Although in later years Baxter would look back and approve this decision, it was particularly painful at the time as he had no desire to hurt his parents, and felt keenly their disappointment when it seemed 'that I was an ungrateful fool to reject this programme and go to work in an iron rolling mill'.[301] Knowing his decision would also concern Ginn and Baigent, Baxter wrote them lengthy letters explaining and justifying his actions.

Baxter's friendship with Lawrence Baigent, which began late in 1944, was extremely important to him. Before meeting Baigent there were few people with whom he could discuss his verse. His parents and a family friend, John Moffett, the literary editor of the *Otago Daily Times*, were interested in his writing and encouraged him; his most significant friendship prior to meeting Baigent had been his correspondence with Ginn. But writing to Ginn had its limitations—as Baxter expressed it: 'Letters are excellent for recording and encouraging thought, but are not good for discussion and explanation' (p.247). Baxter valued the element of personal contact in his relationship with Baigent, although, as the latter discovered when Baxter visited him at Easter 1945, it was possible to have too much of his brand of discussion and explanation because:

> Baxter talked all the time. Even when he went to the toilet he continued to talk through the closed door. Both men slept in the same room, and the only way Baigent could stem the flow was by pretending to be asleep. As soon as he woke up a voice started again from the other bed.[302]

The main reason Baxter visited Baigent that Easter was to meet other literary figures of the time, principally Curnow, but when he arrived it was clear he also wished Baigent to view the manuscript of his proposed second collection. McKay points out that 'none of its contents appeared in his next published collection',[303] but advances no explanation as to why this was the case. Was *Cold Spring* in retrospect an inferior collection, or had Baxter lost interest in it and moved on to other, presumably better, things? Baxter's letters to Baigent support neither possibility: the

300 'A Writer's Vocation', *Manuka* (1958) p.11.
301 Ibid.
302 McKay, *Life*, p.85.
303 Ibid.

idea for the collection had been germinating in his mind since October 1944, five months before *Beyond the Palisade* was launched, and as late as April 1946 he was still referring to it as if its publication was simply a matter of time.

In April 1945, with minor changes suggested by Baigent, *Cold Spring* was as far as Baxter was concerned ready for immediate publication. But about here its history becomes confused, and Baxter's next letter to Baigent raises the possibility that his ignorance of publishing etiquette was, at least in part, the reason Caxton never published *Cold Spring*. On 25 June, perhaps with thoughts of international recognition, Baxter withdrew the collection from Caxton and offered them, in its stead, a lesser selection:

> Intend now to publish *Cold Spring* in England: Faber maybe. Would like your opinions etc. Where should I send poems beforehand to prepare the ground? Enclose a collection, tentative, wondering if you might publish it some time. Not as spectacular as *Cold Spring*, but original enough and possessing the advantages of minor veins.[304]

There follows a gap of a few months in the extant correspondence between Baxter and Baigent. When it recommences nothing appears to have come of his attempts to publish *Cold Spring* in England, and on 12 October 1945 he makes renewed overtures to Baigent: 'I put a note on some poems I sent you, to the effect that I would like you to publish *Cold Spring*. Do you think it could be managed this year?'[305] As if to emphasise the seriousness of this request, and possibly to encourage Baigent to proceed with publication, Baxter included with the letter a 'foreword' to *Cold Spring:*

> I enclose a preface, or rather foreword, not too priggish I hope, not that I care a damn anyway—will say what I think fit, and let the poems stand up for themselves. Right enough, a foreword to a 2nd volume. If for some reason you should think it not suitable, just leave it out. It is fair enough prose.[306]

Baxter's foreword is a lucid statement of his practical and theoretical approach to poetry at that time and an intentionally public defence of the traditional elements of his verse. Mythical themes and classical allusions were still the raw material adapted to express a personal and private symbolism, for example in 'Aeneas', of which Baxter wrote: 'I've changed the picture, humanized or de-humanized it a bit as I always do' (pp.332–3). Aeneas 'the astute and priggish, driven / By half-loved duty on the seas of fame' is one in the series of mythical figures that Baxter developed as representations of the self. Following on from Prometheus, the salamander, and the Unicorn, Aeneas is used here to represent the transition from adolescence to adulthood.

The most notable thing about Baxter's foreword is that none of the poets it mentions is a New Zealander, which may seem strange given that ten months earlier

304 Letter to Lawrence Baigent, 25 Jun 1945, VUW Library, MS McKay 19/3/25.
305 Letter to Lawrence Baigent, 12 Oct 1945, VUW Library, MS McKay 19/3/27.
306 Ibid.

Curnow had written of Baxter's 'frankly confessed debt (beside the unsought affinities) to some older New Zealand poets'.[307] What may have been confessed (or reported) is unclear, but Curnow's assessment coming at the start of Baxter's career has set in place a misconception of the influences on his early verse. Even Baxter's later statements such as, 'at the time of my growing up . . . I knew nothing of the spadework which was being done by Mason, Fairburn, Curnow, Glover or Brasch',[308] have done little to modify this view. Right into his twenties Baxter had an entrenched scepticism about New Zealand poets, and saw himself as a poet in the English Modernist tradition who happened to live in New Zealand. In 1942–43 he was scathing in his criticism of New Zealand verse, calling it 'trite and rigid in thought' (p.146) and declaring that only Basil Dowling could do better than the 'strained or wishy-washy NZism often encountered' (p.247).

Attempts by Ginn in 1944 to interest him in other New Zealand poets—particularly Mason and Curnow—did little to change his views. He presented Ginn with one poem in imitation of R.A.K. Mason, but in no way was the poet a mentor. Instead Baxter confided in Ginn his belief that 'WE two hold in our hands the future of NZ poetry, which has really not yet pierced ground' (p.277). Not even a critically acclaimed first book, inclusion in Curnow's anthology, and admission to New Zealand literature's inner circle instilled in him any sense of piety towards his compatriots: on 1 May 1945, for example, in response to criticism of *Beyond the Palisade*, he defended his English traditional roots by telling Ginn that it was 'better to err with Burns and Byron than fall in line with Brasch' (p.405). It was not until 1946 that he came to the belief that:

> . . . a poet or an artist must choose here and now whether he is a transplanted Englishman or a New Zealander. If the first is his choice, why stay? If the second, then he must accept as his own and explore with a free mind our shifting and amorphous modes of living.[309]

Earlier on, when Ginn had taken exception to some of his views about New Zealand literature, Baxter had defended his position:

> About NZ poetry. I am not crying it down. But I find in poetry a vivid expression of emotion which does not occur in prose. Therefore, as I do not find this in much NZ poetry it is not, to me, poetry. The solution, of course, is not to run away but to start a Revolution (p.193).

And Baxter always intended being part of this revolution. He expressed a brief interest in a return visit to Europe, but his focus was as firmly antipodean as his reading was European and American. When he confided to Ginn that they were the future of New Zealand poetry, he had firm ideas about what New Zealand literature needed; ideas that intuitively compensated for the lack of heritage and history in a settler

307 Curnow, ed., introduction, *A Book of New Zealand Verse,* p.55.
308 'Further Notes on New Zealand Poetry', Hocken, MS 975/119.
309 'Poetry in New Zealand', *The Yearbook of the Arts in New Zealand* 2 (1946) p.112.

colony attempting to speak a language transported from the other side of the world. Where 'Europeans have to prune their material' he told Ginn, 'we have to build it up'. Hence his criticism of 'Sargeson, who' he wrote, 'strikes me as able but of a style and plotting too cut-down for this NZ society' (p.358).

It is unlikely that Baxter was being deliberately duplicitous in conveying to Curnow the impression that he was strongly influenced by New Zealand poets. Publishing his first volume of poetry had opened doors to a new, and desired, world. Corresponding with Ginn was no good 'for discussion and explanation' and university had proved a disappointment. Baxter explained to Ginn, after deciding not to return to Otago University for his second year, that 'intellectuals work efficiently and thoroughly' but the 'bed-rock springs are rarely tapped' (p.397). Now, through the publication of *Beyond the Palisade*, he was meeting others with whom he could communicate about things that mattered:

> Stayed at Christchurch over Easter: with Lawrence Baigent the Caxton Press man. Saw Curnow. Also Douglas Lilburn, who set my University song to music specially composed.
>
> Baigent had some cider: so I recited excellently, getting onto Faust eventually. '*Ugly hell gape not . . .*' (p.399)

With the publication of *Beyond the Palisade* Baxter had won the niche he at once 'despised and hungered for'. The niche that he was to describe more cynically in 'Letter to Noel Ginn II':

> . . . a niche where I can grumble
> About the clique that pay me for my pen,
> And drink with other intellectual men,
> And gain some slight prestige, however humble,
> With a little bitter poem now and then
> Until the first apocalyptic rumble:
> [*CP*, p.72]

For all his new contacts, and despite sending Baigent a foreword, Baxter seems to have been unable to generate much enthusiasm at Caxton for *Cold Spring*. Six months on, in March 1946, a letter to Baigent indicates that Baxter assumed they would publish *Cold Spring* in due course—but unfortunately it includes a second gaffe:

> I wish to publish with Whitcombes here, a small and desultory selection from my unpublished childhood poems. None that have been published, or from *Cold Spring*. Could you hold off publication of the latter for some time, then? After all, poetry is scarcely a paying proposition, so I guess there wouldn't be any financial loss. I know Caxton does the best printing in NZ and intend to stay there for anything major . . . If I'm going against business ethics or the press's convenience, just tell me and I'll call it off.[310]

310 Letter to Lawrence Baigent, 20 Mar 1946, VUW Library, MS McKay 19/3/29.

Baigent's exact response to this letter is unknown, but the tenor of it can be gathered from Baxter's brief, uncharacteristically contrite, reply:

Brighton,
Otago.
19/4/46.

Dear Lawrence,

The Whitcombes affair is off, definitely and absolutely. Pardon me for making a nuisance of myself in this respect. I hope you're able to publish *Cold Spring* some time this year, but it would be by no virtue of mine I know.

All best wishes
From
James[311]

When Baxter finally accepted that publication of *Cold Spring* had become unlikely he seems to have made a deliberate decision that its poems would only appear in book form if the collection was published intact. As his personal classification system rated many of the poems in the selection among his best work from that period,[312] the resulting gap did not merely represent a vacancy in the body of his published work but—in the context of critical observations on the intimate connection between his life and his poetry[313]—a lacuna in his own account of his life at one of its most turbulent stages. *Cold Spring* was published belatedly in 1996.

311 Letter to Lawrence Baigent, 19 Apr 1946, VUW Library, MS McKay 19/3/37.
312 See p.79, for a discussion of Baxter's classification system.
313 See p.21, note 12.

# Eleven
# Epilogue

## Letter to Noel Ginn II
[unpublished version]

I

Two years gone by, and I take pen again
To serenade in the old stoic strain
Your window, Noel, that stares out upon
A universe of dialectic pain,
Love, fear of love, and love's supreme evasion
That leaves lost wolves to bay their moon alone.

II

At seventeen a stoic pose is easy—
Stand up and face the mad God, brave and breezy—
At twenty years a trace of humour shows,
And pride goes slack, the Furies fat and lazy;
Like Byron in his Venice, I can lose
Even my fear of women—and still like the booze.

III

Better I'd say to be a brainless lout
With women, booze and horses, than stay out
In the lonely wind and listen to its singing;
Or where the stone 'heraldic' waves are loud
Walking the never-to-be-born among
And most-unquiet dead, as I have walked for long.

These things have bred great poems—Housman stood
Lifelong amid a leafless iron wood—
I know myself, and choose to be a man
Rather than poet who denies the blood
Her even tide, for a memorial stone
His heart today, tomorrow's hidden sun.

Yet I may write a song for the song's sake;
Or leave unwritten. Songs will never wake
A buried peace, still the tormented sea.
There is no second birth. O take
My songs from me and let the child go free
Warm and impulsive, to rebel or tarry.

. . . . .

IV

I can recall the light upon the hills
When evening came. Frost on the window-sills
And milk-cart grinding. The warm smell of grass.
Fire in a clean grate, and the calm walls
Enclosing quiet. These were truly peace.
These yet remain, and where is peace Alas?

V

Death is no living peace. And yet the dead
Cry not, nor heed if lovers overhead
Should grieve for them. They are made one with earth
And shadows of the summer clouds will tread
Careless upon them. As they slept ere birth
So sleep they now, and Love no murmur saith.

VI

Who wake at morning from a drunken slumber
Stare at the boarded ceiling and remember
How first Atlantis undersea was drowned.
The cold earth turns and ages without number
Pass, but the young heart is not found
Again, sea-fallen beyond sight and sound.

VII

Good rhetoric but bad psychology.
Humour's by far the best security;
Time's natural Oedipus, I find a token
Of God in girls and mountain scenery—
The girls to ——, the hills for climbing on.
A day can mend all that a day has broken.

Enter the house of quiet after storm.
The lost is found again. Relinquish Time
And lay your head where the strange heart lies beating.
Her lips are silent and her limbs are warm.
That such should be in the harsh world's benighting.
Dark hair on the world's brow. Her breasts are bleeding.

. . . . .
England broke my childhood; made me stranger
In my own land. Or the ancestral finger
Laid Scottish mountains in my breast to burn
And raise the ghost of an ancestral singer.
But for his peace, to the same creek and fern
The child forgot, the grown man must return.

A homeless man will vend a heartless song.
Surely the heart foretells her second Spring
Of here and now. Though as the dark seas moan
Barren the bridal be, and no bells ring
To welcome home one drowned Icarian—
This is my land. I shall not turn again.
14/4/46
[Hocken MS 704/14:958, pp.162–5]

Addenda to 958:
Your gods like mine are gods of Love and Death.
And Death is stronger: though the warm airs breathe
At window, and the golden bird is singing.
Beyond all act or dream Osirian darkness lieth.
Careless the night if stars be darkening
If stars be worlds, or the world's love in flowering.

And her, the little lass with the gold hair
Who set me writing poems by the score
In a sweet-bitter vein. Why, when we meet
I see another girl and nothing more—
Nothing to tremble at, to make the pulse beat.
Tides fall again, leave only their regret.
[Hocken MS 704/14, p.174]

Baxter's unpublished version of 'Letter to Noel Ginn II' is more in keeping with the tone of their correspondence than the later, published, version with its 'thread of pain / And bitterness that blurs the narrative' (*CP*, p.70). The contrast between the two poems effectively symbolises the growing apart of Baxter and Ginn in the years following the war. By 1945 the conditions that led to and sustained their correspondence had changed and the relationship had begun drawing to a natural and inevitable conclusion.

When World War II abruptly ended the Labour Government was already acting to rid itself of the detention camps and their difficult inmates. Ginn remembers clearly the day when 'one of the screws said to me "They've dropped a bomb on Japan, it's all blown up!" . . . when we heard that—it was '45 I suppose, it was my fifth year—we knew that the war would be ending'.[314] But much earlier, in late 1944, members of the Labour Government Cabinet were already pushing to have men in detention released quickly, and appointees to a Revision Authority had been named by January 1945. But it was June before 'K.C. Woodward S.M. and A.H. Johnstone K.C. were [free] to sit as the one-man tribunals in Palmerston North and Auckland respectively'.[315]

In Ginn's recollection the appeal process 'was farcical though & in effect meant that the more articulate were judged as being true COs'[316] :

> So they were to determine at that stage who was genuine and who wasn't genuine. I thought that that was quite nonsensical, no one can judge conscience, and the fact that we'd stayed in detention without reneging on our belief and being released—had we elected to go into the army at any time we would have been released—and knowing all these people, I couldn't appeal. And then one of my friends—Ron Keats—who was completely inarticulate, he prepared his case, I helped him to, and it was dismissed. And a person like that, knowing him thoroughly (you know people thoroughly after 4 or 5 years) I thought they could not [judge us]. [317]

In the end, however, Ginn did decide to appeal:

> I had never presented my case why I hadn't served in the army at all. Because in the court it was just an order that I'd disobeyed. So I decided I would appeal, and also I decided that if I was granted to be genuine I wouldn't sign the paper. Which was to the effect that I would not speak publicly and a few other things like that. So I was very carefully prepared—perhaps a pompous paper. I told the magistrate that my purpose in appearing was to state why I'd taken this position—that I had, with all due respect, no real belief that conscience can be judged by anybody. And I was granted release but I wouldn't take it. Some of the others did likewise.[318]

Some weeks later Ginn's release was confirmed provided he did sign a paper to the effect that he would not speak or agitate against the war effort. He refused to do this, but was pushed out of the camps in any case. He left with the strong feeling that the government 'wanted us to be released quietly in dribs and drabs as some soldiers were still overseas'.[319]

Terence Baxter had already been released, but neither he nor Ginn were yet completely free. For about eight months following their release they were 'manpowered' at the whim of the Government to various labouring jobs:

314 Noel Ginn, personal interview with Annette Facer, Sep 1994.
315 Grant, *Out in the Cold*, pp.233–4.
316 Noel Ginn, letter to Paul Millar, 14 Sep 1995.
317 Noel Ginn, personal interview with Annette Facer, Sep 1994.
318 Ibid.
319 Noel Ginn, letter to Paul Millar, 14 Sep 1995.

> . . . strangely, Terry & I were manpowered together to the Gear meat works at Petone & shared a hut as part of staff quarters. Our wages were limited to £5 per week, balance paid by employers to govt. We were there about 2 months, including the Xmas fortnight [1945] when we went to Brighton. Soon after Terry was manpowered to some job in Dunedin while I was shoved up the Wanganui river to Pipiriki House as cowman gardener.[320]

Being manpowered was not to Terence's taste at all:

> I was in the camps for a fair few years, and then of course it wasn't all over when the war finished because we weren't going to be allowed out—which was fair enough as they saw it—until the last soldier had returned home. Even after we were out of the camp we were still under supervision . . . I was manpowered into a freezing works, which is not the sort of place I would choose to work in. I don't like the type of place. The smell of the place gets right into your skin, right in to your pores, you could tell a person that worked in the freezing works.[321]

The one compensation for Terence in being sent to the Gear meat works was that it was in Petone, and Wellington harbour was literally on his doorstep:

> I just couldn't resist, there was that beautiful harbour sitting out ahead of me, I couldn't resist getting a yacht. I enjoyed it very much because it was my first sailing for a long long time. I sailed to Days Bay, Somes Island and Ward Island—which used to have a leper on it. Once I got into a bit of trouble and got caught in a storm—some others were drowned and I was out in the water for a long time.[322]

The fortnight over Christmas in which Ginn went with Terence to Brighton was the second of only three times in his life that he would meet James K. Baxter in person. Ginn recalls it being:

> a period of emotional disarray and confusion. The air was thick with the names of dispersed friends and acquaintances, much news, always change. Jim was part of this ferment, but his disorientation was from a different base. There was exhilaration as we talked of poetry, of life and world affairs, there was much humour also, and I was learning of Jim's first forays into the realms of sex.[323]

Predominant among Ginn's memories were the 'animated conversations around the dining table—Jim entrancing—his main activity was the pursuit of girls',[324] and:

320 Ibid.
321 Terence Baxter, personal interview, Dec 1995.
322 Ibid.
323 Noel Ginn, letter to Frank McKay, 13 Jan 1983, VUW Library, MS McKay item 10/4/17.
324 Noel Ginn, letter to Paul Millar, Jan 1995.

> J & I wandering along the beach at Brighton chatting poetry, most stimulated with each other. We came to a cave-like cleft in the cliff where the tides had heaped up a tangle of giant kelp. 'Dylan Thomas,' he said & I knew what he meant—this gothic or celtic entanglement had something weird & irrational. 'What would he make of it?' But I had major difficulties with Thomas & said I got much more out of the salty English symbols of Auden.[325]

Both Ginn and Terence had considerable problems adjusting to life out of detention. Ginn remembers it as:

> a major emotional event leaving detention, the worst feature of which had been the indeterminate nature of its duration. Now the sentence was over, the necessary strong emotional associations & attachments were rudely broken—the glorious day of liberation proved a mirage—all was grey, spent & without hope—the savage destruction of lives as well as nations had bitten into our awareness—made more poignant when we met returned men who often said we were right. I for one was not sure. I will never be convinced that we were all that right. My friendship with T. & Jim would now be in suspension, we had to go our ways.[326]

Terence felt that detention probably affected his ability to relate to people:

> in some way or another it's had its effect, it's done some sort of thing to me. Yet I may still be the way I am if I hadn't been there—the way I look on life and other people. I don't mix in with people unless I've had a couple of drinks, not get drunk, but just enough to break the ice and be a bit more friendly.[327]

He, like Ginn, was no longer convinced that his stance had been entirely correct:

> I'm still not happy about whether I made the right decision, or what was the right thing to do over this situation, this business about the war. When you consider what happened in the war, the way the Japanese behaved, talking to prisoners, and the general life that happened in the war, I just wonder whether I did the right thing or not, thinking it over. Sometimes I feel that other people were going that way so what was the right thing. You get in situations in war time where somebody might say, 'Oh, I couldn't kill another man.' But in a situation where it was either you or him you wouldn't be thinking about that at all, it's out with the gun, that's finished. Otherwise you're letting your mates down, you're part of a group too, that's another important thing, you're all together aren't you?[328]

Ginn felt that not only detention, but also Terence's family, combined to cause him to withdraw into himself:

325 Ibid.
326 Ibid.
327 Terence Baxter, personal interview, Dec 1995.
328 Ibid.

> The theory that the overshadowing by his father (his heroism & strength during WWI & later in the persecuting community) together with the brilliance of his mother & brother, created in [Terence] a humbling & diminished self-image, seems reasonable to me.[329]

And Ginn reflected that Terence 'with but one wing of minimum involvement . . . would never fly. He became a good reliable hardworking cit—one of the quiet of the land . . . I feel he has suffered greatly in life but with never a murmur.'[330]

After leaving Petone, Ginn was manpowered to Pipiriki House, way up the Whanganui River. Although it was an area he was familiar with, his loneliness almost overwhelmed him: 'it was a god-forsaken place—with all the flattened emotions after four years. Suddenly away from everybody—[in detention] we were in a very lively community—and now to go isolated as a cowman-gardener at Pipiriki House with a gloomy forest all around and taking on the mood of the moment.'[331] Over time things improved for the released men:

> 'Society' was not harsh by world standards—for a while everything was quiet and grey then gradually we would hear of things happening, new things, new ways of earning money, new ventures of a more communal nature, new ideas, what other detainees were doing. The returned men generally were not bitter towards us. All could vote though our release was never made official. I did not vote for years as I could not bring myself to vote for labour & saw the other party in a bad-light as I was never right wing.[332]

Ginn was even able to begin seeing the experiences of the camps in a positive light:

> The fact of being incarcerated for a point of view has its own compensations—you have found the strength to go through it. Any bitterness following on from that and one must take a look at oneself and say 'well look at what others have gone through'—it's no good being sorry for yourself. I think most of us came to that realisation.[333]

Ginn was allowed to leave Pipiriki after six months and he went to work at a shoe factory in Auckland. Eventually, with financial assistance from his father, he started his own nursery in Wanganui and became an expert horticulturist and camellia specialist. He never completed his university studies as he was for many years against intellectuals and academics whom he thought irrelevant to the times, believing that they could have done more to support those in detention. For about ten years after his release he found it necessary to disguise an intense sense of loss that would descend upon him like a dark cloud.

In 1959 Ginn was contacted by Baxter who, in his official role as an editor of school bulletins, asked him to write a bulletin on market gardening for him. The

329 Noel Ginn, letter to Paul Millar, Apr 1995.
330 Noel Ginn, letter to Paul Millar, Jan 1995.
331 Noel Ginn, personal interview with Annette Facer, Sep 1994.
332 Noel Ginn, letter to Paul Millar, 14 Sep 1995.
333 Noel Ginn, personal interview, Aug 1994.

correspondence between him and Baxter was friendly but did not lead to a renewal of their friendship. The money he received for the bulletin did, however, help to fund a three-month plant hunting expedition in Western Australia.

Ginn's most unusual postwar friendship was with one of the guards from detention camp. The ex-guard, who lived in the same street as Ginn's nursery, was intensely interested in horticulture and he and Ginn became friends. Nevertheless Ginn was staggered to discover, after the man had died of cancer, that he had left him three-fifths of his property in his will. He thought it quite something 'that a screw would do this'.[334] Terence also found that time healed the terrible divisions created by the war: he now counts among his friends the son of the Dunedin judge who sentenced him to detention.

In the late 1960s Ginn sold much of his land and took up an offer to work for a local share broker. Then in 1969 he left New Zealand to work, also as a share broker, in Australia. Ginn's only criticism of *Out in the Cold* relates to the report that his decision to leave New Zealand was related to his experiences as a pacifist, and he is categorical when he states that any suggestion 'that post-war treatment of COs was a reason why I left New Zealand was entirely wrong'.[335]

Terence returned to Dunedin and was re-employed as a welder at Reid and Gray's. James was delighted to have him back, and on 10 June 1947 wrote to Margaret Hargreave telling her that Terence was still living at home:

> . . . loth to leave security and Mother's cooking. Good parents are not always an unmixed blessing. Still though, he has his ups and downs, Terry is a normal citizen again. I have grown very fond of him in the past 2 years.[336]

But Terence felt that time had marched by while he had been standing still in detention and he found the changes quite disorienting:

> When I came back I was absolutely amazed at the change in my friend Patricia. Her aunt ran the boarding house out at Brighton. When I went away she was just a young schoolgirl, and when I came back here was this girl grown into a teenager—a different girl altogether. I couldn't believe the change, a few years make all that difference.

He also discovered that despite their affection for each other, there was an unbridgeable gap between his life and his brother's life:

> . . . when he was going though his teenage years and at university, I was out of his way. Even after I came out of the camp I had to stay up there for a while. So all that was sort of a hole in our life [during the time] that we were together, and after that he went his own way and I got friendly with my group in town . . . Except occasionally we did meet, and I heard about him where he was

334 Noel Ginn, personal interview with Annette Facer, Sep 1994.

335 Noel Ginn, letter to Paul Millar, 14 Sep 1995.

336 Letter from Margaret Hargreave to Frank McKay, VUW Library. MS McKay item 10/5/36. Letter contains transcripts from letters of Baxter's in Margaret Hargreave's possession.

> working. He worked in the freezer for a while, and there must have been more to him than they thought, because they thought this young student fellow would be out of there in a few days time, but he could do more than you think. Certainly when he worked in the steel works he worked pretty hard there, and I know the type of work he was on, I knew some of the men that worked there, and they were pretty hard men. Terrible work, and hot in the summertime, these great big red-hot things were coming out of the furnace and they had to drag them along the floor. It was dangerous work, he was lucky not to be burnt there and scarred for life. You had to know what you were about. And for a young man to just come along there like that and work with the others took a bit of doing. And unfortunately of course—this might have been what started him off with his drinking—at the end of the day they'd go along to the pub in Green Island there and get a fair few beers down.[337]

Throughout his life Terence remained concerned for his brother's welfare, although characteristically he never interfered. But Baxter's death did not come as a complete surprise:

> I knew there was a chance, he didn't feed himself very well, the way he lived wasn't my way of living at all. But the way he lived—I went up to Jerusalem there and you'd sit down to lunch with a bit of this and a bit of that, but they weren't really eating properly, not a good square meal every day. In my opinion that way of living would help a person to get ill and die. Of course he was a heavy smoker, he'd always have a cigarette, and that might have affected his heart. Of course our father had heart trouble, but heart trouble with him was probably caused by his experiences in wartime.[338]

Terence Baxter was one of the pallbearers at his younger brother's funeral—carrying to his grave in Jerusalem the man who, as a baby, he had once prodded inquisitively with a broom and, as a boy, he had taken sailing in the waters off Brighton.

In 2000, Terence Baxter, now seventy-eight, lives alone in Dunedin, above his beloved Otago Harbour. Noel Ginn is eighty-four, he lived for a number of years in Kerala in Southern India but has now returned to New Zealand permanently. He began writing poetry again, and his collection *Dweller on the Threshold* was published in 1998.

In evaluating Baxter's later poetry the fact that he never grew up as part of mainstream New Zealand society cannot be overemphasised. As a teenager in a world at war he took pains to assert his Celtic and pacifist heritage and wrote scathingly of 'the obvious sparsity of intelligence among NZers', being disappointed that they had taken conscription lying down 'when they could have led all the satellites of Britain towards neutrality' (p.187). He knew that he too faced the prospect of defaulter's detention should he be conscripted, and when he turned eighteen he wrote to the secretary of

337 Terence Baxter, personal interview, Dec 1995.
338 Ibid.

the armed forces appeal board a 'statement in support of my appeal on conscientious grounds' (p.389). In it he asserted his belief that 'war in any circumstances is no more justifiable than any other form of murder'. Such views earned him and his family a considerable degree of antagonism; a situation in which precocity may well develop as a form of defence. When his schoolmates did cadet training he weeded gardens. While his nominal peers played cricket and rugby his head was buried in books of poetry. His real peers were imprisoned by the state, and for the majority of his late teens his most significant conversations were by letter.

Meditating on the release of Terence and Noel Ginn from detention, Baxter wrote to Ginn:

> It will be adults meeting each other, strangers except for the deep discomfort and deep ties of shared experience—for me shared birth. We will slide into some form of community. And perhaps I will see you, whose mind I already know as well as one can know a strange country. (pp.408–9)

Through his correspondence with Ginn, the adolescent James K. Baxter offers us glimpses of the complexity of his own mind. As a record of his development as a writer, and of his commitment to poetry, these letters confirm, yet again, the importance of his place in any study of New Zealand literature. Baxter's critique of one of Ginn's poems is an appropriately reflexive critique of his own work:

> . . . I have studied your poetry and it yields great richness on study. Whether I like your images or not, whether I believe all your poems as truth or not, you are as you are now a poet and you write fine poetry . . . (p.214)

The war and its consequences—the ostracism of the Baxter family, Terence's incarceration, and the correspondence with Noel Ginn—clearly had an effect on the tone and content of Baxter's early poetry. With the ending of the war the objectors were freed and they, and their families, began a slow process of assimilation back into mainstream society. Looking back at the period covered by the war years Baxter—in the published version of 'Letter to Noel Ginn II'—contrasts a time that paradoxically inspired poetry (and letters) written 'in a more romantic vein' with the 'bitterness' of living from day to day as part of a wider community. For both Baxter and Ginn, the closeness and intimacy of their correspondence was not sustainable once the war had concluded. The man 'whose mind I already know as well as one can know a strange country' became a stranger. Each man came to represent, for the other, a period that both needed to leave behind.

Years later, explaining to Frank McKay why he had not kept any of his poetry from that time, Ginn wrote 'For me the intense emotional experiences of the war years had to be distanced & I was incapable of separating out the poetic component.'[339] For Baxter, it seems, their friendship was not sustainable or even necessarily desirable in the world beyond the palisade, and the published version of 'Letter to Noel Ginn II' may well have been intended as its epitaph:

339 Noel Ginn, letter to Frank McKay, 24 Mar 1983, VUW Library, MS McKay item 10/4/19.

I was a lamp.
A kind of beacon to you then, you said—
Since then the wick has grown a trifle damp.

No man can play Aladdin all his life.
The oil is blood, although the flame be clear,
And world-annihilating djins appear
Unasked-for at the falling of a leaf.
Or else the heart becomes a cinder—Fear
Is Art's companion, and the hermit Grief.

So poets learn to live like other men . . .
(*CP*, p.71)

James, Archibald, and Millicent Baxter in the garden behind their Brighton home in the early 1940s. James wears the jersey of King's High School. *(Hocken Library)*

*Left:* Macmillan Brown family at Holmbank on Wairarapa Terrace, Christchurch, c. 1898. Millicent is seated on the ground at the left. *(Macmillan Brown Library, University of Canterbury)*

*Right:* Ormond Burton stands on a butter box to address a pacifist gathering at the Basin Reserve in Wellington. These meetings were cancelled by the police in 1940. *(Mary Robinson Collection, Alexander Turnbull Library, 1/2-152917-F)*

*Below:* The Western Front, 1917: shattered trenches at Messines, Belgium. *(Jim Henderson Collection, Alexander Turnbull Library, 1/2-051947-F)*

*Above:* The Baxter family home at 15 Bedford Parade, Brighton, photographed by Lloyd Godman. Baxter's room occupied the upstairs floor. *(McKay papers, Victoria University of Wellington)*

*Left:* The University of Otago, which Baxter attended in 1944. The Leith Stream is in the foreground. *(McKay papers, Victoria University of Wellington)*

*Left:* Terence Baxter, shortly before he was sent into defaulter's detention, aged about eighteen. *(Hocken Library)*

*Below:* An informal photograph of members of Baxter's sixth form class at King's High School, 1943. Baxter is seated second from right in the front row. *(Private collection)*

James K. Baxter in 1944, aged eighteen. *(Hocken Library)*

*Above:* Noel Ginn (back row at right) with his family in the garden of their Wanganui home in the early 1930s. *(Private collection)*

*Left:* Portrait of Noel Ginn, painted in 1945 by Albert Bollard. Both men were in Whitanui detention camp. *(Private collection)*

*Above:* Hautu Detention Camp, 1943. 'At the back, on the left beyond the social hall, is the main compound of inmate huts. A row of "Red Compound" [punishment] huts is on the extreme left at the back. The line of huts on the right belongs to the overseers and patrolmen. In the foreground is the kitchen, the mess room, administration building, and the superintendent's and the matron's houses. The entrance to the camp is on the right, out of the picture.' (Grant p.49.) *(A.C. Barrington Collection, Alexander Turnbull Library, 1/2-037722-F)*

*Left:* Camp guards at Hautu Camp, photographed through the buttonhole of a greatcoat to avoid detection. *(David Grant collection)*

*Below:* A performance of *The Beautiful People* at Whitanui Camp in 1945. Noel Ginn, playing 'Agnes' is third from left. Rodney Kennedy, as 'Harmony Blublossom', is second from right. *(David Grant collection)*

*Left:* Terence Baxter, following his release from detention, aged about twenty-four. *(Hocken Library)*

Terence Baxter sailing the *Plucky* on the Otago Harbour in the late 1980s.*(Private collection)*

# II
# CORRESPONDENCE: 1942

But from you, Noel, I wish more—
The friend's stance, confessor for my sin
Which is pride alone: yet pride alone will win
Niche of immortal marble despised and hungered for.
    'Letter to Noel Ginn'

> [Terence] told me of his younger brother whom he & the family called JUM. How he was a terrific talker & arguer with all & sundry, & how he spent hours & hours alone deep in thought . . . I was reading poetry and trying to write. One day T. told me his young brother was also keen on writing poetry. In a letter home he mentioned this to Jim & a letter came back stating that he would like to see 'some of the man's writing'. Then began the long-drawn-out correspondence.[1]

[Ginn had also expressed an interest in reading some of Baxter's poetry; he obliged by sending, via Terence, the three poems that follow.]

**The Flame of Grass**

Even the steel-wrought mass
    In time shall pass
And yield to the flame of grass:

Stronger than might of men
Are these, the grasses, when
    They rend huge temples down;

So faith and gorgeous creed
Arise at mortal need—
    Rise up, but soon are gone:

They harden and they fall
For over the high church-wall
The old Gods all
    Enter and lay them low:

    This well I know—
Even the steel-wrought mass
In time shall pass
And yield to the flame of grass!
        [Hocken, MS 704/4: 232, pp.126–7]

**The young trees**

Light dreams shall flare and vanish like gun-cotton
    While we poor puppets vainly persevere,
    Treading on slow paths for fear
Even our slight soul-basis should prove rotten.
When shall the dreary masque have ending
    And the foul lesions break in blood?
    Here is the spur for fiery spirit ascending:
The young trees are all cut down: there are many more in the wood.

1 Noel Ginn, letter to Paul Millar, 24 Jan 1995.

I, in the way of many, have found pleasure
    And loved all intricate beauty passing well:
    To see the agonising hell
And barenness, repays in bitter measure.
Who now has heart for jubilation,
    Though hate may lessen to rancorous mood?
    This be the trumpet-call to the failing nation:
The young trees are all cut down: there are many more in the wood.

Opiate bubble of spring and youth is broken;
    The flowering bud henceforward shall blossom in vain:
    When flames but smoulder, what shall remain?
Lyrical joyaunce is naught in the face of the token
Of the sick man's fear of life and the strong man's fear of dying,
    Of the falling of towns and the raising of the Rood.
    Hark to the voice of bitter and weary replying,
'The young trees are all cut down: there are many more in the wood!'
        [Hocken, MS 704/6: 359, pp.59–60]

**Under a Sun**

Under a sun that beats
    From windy skies at noon
        I scarcely know
That traffic-laden streets
    Will envelop me soon
        In Beauty's overthrow.

I am bound close to earth
    Above the soughing grass
That startles with strange mirth
Where flowers flame to birth
    When the grave dawn-shadows pass.

The wind that buffets me
    Is part and voice of those
Undying things of fixity
    That bloom and blossom in the rose
And from Man's pathway flee.
        [Hocken, MS 704/4: 249, p.155]

**Ginn to Baxter, 23 July 1942**

CENSORED
No. 4

c/- Nat Service Dept
Hautu Turangi
via Nat Park
23/7/42

Dear Jim

—It was at my instigation that Terry put a request in his letter for some of your poetry—thanks very much indeed for complying. I must confess that I find them extraordinarily interesting—not only from the view point of your age but because of their actual merit. If you can keep your love of beauty & feeling for expression through the remaining years of your teens you surely have found a vocation that will satisfy yourself & at the same time give work of true value to your fellows.

Of the three poems you sent I find that of 'The Young Trees' the most pleasing. I can't say I follow it all as prose logic—but to impose prose logic on poetry is to lose the idea of its intention—poems which please by being immediately & completely comprehensible pall on further readings—they become static and dead. Other poems go on growing in our memories—our imaginations probing their content a little further at each reading. There is a continual cropping & yield of harvest so to speak. Well without nauseous flattery I can say after five or six readings of these that they have something of that quality—they are authentic messages from that deep mystery of being in which we are immersed—& the knowledge that others respond to these experiences—however incoherently—assures us of that fundamental kinship of all mankind in which we love to believe.

> What can allay the pain of incoherence,
> Or mitigate the dull underground moan of soul
> Bearing the barometric thrust of beauty?
> The meshes of systaltic mind are all too slight
> Unboned, unframed, unbraced
> For such relentless countervail.

The last verse of 'Under a Sun' is excellent reading. As for the other poem I do not feel it comes to the same standard of insight—perhaps I miss the point—to me it smacks of Ecclesiastes & its continual wail over life's fleetingness & non-availing. For me the steel-wrought mass & at times pompous & absurd institutions & architectures are nevertheless manifestations of man's creative spirit which ever casts about for new forms. Admittedly the signs of sterility & decay abound in this age (or this end of an age). These forms and symbols at first & at their best are bridges to the inner reality—they harden and often cease to function when they then become a fetish & bondage to the spirit of man—perhaps this is the phase you castigate. There is certainly a malaise & feverish sterility the [sic] characterises this modern dehumanisation of man which is civilisation or 'bourgeoisation'. Many thanks indeed for your poetry & I hope some time to read more of it for it does give very real pleasure.

With all best wishes
& regards
Noel Ginn
[Hocken, MS 975/183]

**Baxter to Ginn, 9 August 1942**

CENSORED
No. 4

Brighton,
Otago.
9th August 1942

Dear Noel, (I can hardly say 'Dear Mr. Ginn'. That would sound too unfriendly.)

I was very pleased to get your letter. Any criticism that you have given is certainly constructive. Everyone, versifier or otherwise, must at times feel 'the pain of incoherence'. No-one can write more than is in themselves. However, I have not been writing for long—many of my verses are written to keep the apparatus from going rusty.

Throughout my poems there is the idea of the ephemerality of time—as we know it—and, along with this the eternal endurance of what is time, space, matter, and spirit combined. Imagine that life could be 'speeded up' like a motion-picture. We would see the forms of civilization crumble—and grass, the humble grass, symbol of all that is eternal, would remain. Time is but relative. However 'The Flame of Grass' is a very negative poem—for negative emotions are most easily expressed and understood. Therefore the preponderance of my poems have a touch of nostalgia or some similar feeling. The following is a good example.

**Illusion**

At birth we are most bare:
There is no shielding bar,
    No glass illusory
    To shelter us from blind inanity.

But thought may pass amid
The chaos long since made
    And strong illusions rise
    Betwixt the naked dark and naked eyes.

Even the nihilist
Forms shamming image lest
Mind should break bonds of thought,
Return to darkness since long shunned, unsought.

Perchance in death we find
No power wherewith to bend
Loss of integrity;
Perchance mind holds the old fidelity.

If such remains then we
Must ever onward sue
Till spirit sinks in flames
And vortex of past non-existence claims.

I, poet, who am most
Of nebulaeic mist,
Even if all be non-reality
Joy in the ancient phantasy.

'Jubilation' is only an anti-war poem—no more. This next is however, not philosophical but rather, lyrical.

**Discobolus**

Sun-rays strike and burnish the limbs of stone
In their arrested motion—arm out-flung,
Smooth-cut tendons—and pride of the ever-young
Manifest in the grace of flesh and bone.
This glittering discus would swing on a sunward path

Were the firm fingers to loosen for fear or wrath—
But this Olympiad shall have no aftermath.
I am minded of the gigantic marble prone
In dry Thessalian quarries; of songs since sung
For deeds of valour: but ever all thought is gone
At sight of the moving limbs set motionless in stone.

I would like very much to know the author of the verse you quoted, as I would like to see more by him.

The reason why I did not reply immediately was the school examinations—now just over. At present I am studying Ezra Pound, one of the American free-verse writers, who nevertheless has written true poetry.

Hoping to hear from you soon,
James Baxter.
[VUW Library, MS McKay 28/1]

**Jubilation**

Whither the loud shouting and glorification?
Behold the triumph-hour of a mighty nation:
Hearken unto the jubilation.

Many are dead. What solace to them is sent?
Wreaths for the marble monument
And riches dedicated to armament,

What is the cry that is spoken from lips to lips?
'These were the brave: their honour shall know not eclipse.'

What knew they of honour, the men who died?
Naught but the peace of living to them denied
Labour, and ale at eventide;

Regimented and driven before the guns
What thought had they of honour, the pitiful ones
Seeking escape to clearer unperilous suns,

Having no shield from the blistering skies,
Shall they leave battle with sane eyes?

Spirit is stunned in the merciless conflagration:
What land is not forever a sorrowing nation?
Death not alone is unforgiving—
Death of the body, and death of joyous living—
Men are most blind, most cruel in jubilation!
[Hocken, MS 704/6:338, pp.24–5]

**Ginn to Baxter, 21 August 1942**

CENSORED
No. 6

c/-Nat Service Dept, Hautu Turangi
via Nat. Park. 21/8/42.

Dear Jim

—Yes, I'm glad you didn't 'Mister' me in your letter—I have no feeling of adulthood though I've passed the 21 mark—appendages such as this & say stetsons seem to invariably accompany the inevitable lapse of time! So regard me as a boy a bit older—like Terry. I would like to have replied at once to your welcome letter but have been off-colour the last week. However here goes. The nostalgia you write of is one of man's incurable ailments & it's just as well, else we would have no irritant to probe us out of our aimless ways. One philosopher ranks the greatest of sins to be the sin of finality.[1] I take his meaning to be the imprisonment of the spirit. So the nostalgia is a homesickness for our true heritage. The Xtn faith would recognise this though its truth of mankind has been bled white by the very materialistic historical forms which have little message for this claimant age—save on subjects such as wet canteens and mixed bathing.[2] (I am not cynical but believing in the Xt spirit within every man I cannot but be saddened by this betrayal.) The poem 'Illusion' is a little gem. You sense the poverty of man in face of the major themes of life, creation, the void & the spirit. I guess you are not at heart daunted by this though you call your feeling or emotion a negative one—on a basis of 'unyielding despair'—a desire for a reality from which all personality has been leached? Know D.H. Lawrence?

God! but it is good to have died & been trodden out,
Trodden to naught in sour dead earth.
Quite to naught;
Absolutely to nothing,
Nothing!
Nothing!
Nothing![3]

The second line in the 3rd verse of 'Illusion' puzzled me. The word 'bend'—have I got it right?

I hope some day you are able to study Nicolas Berdyaev—a Xtn philosopher of the Russian Orthodox faith exiled, now in Paris or possibly a concentration camp. He has made great creative efforts in Xtn thought & is one of the few men who understands the great movements of our age. His best book is *Freedom and the Spirit*, others are *The Destiny of Man* & *The Meaning of History*.[4]

'Discobolus' I find fascinating. I do envy your natural flow of thought & words. Your imagery is most fresh & pleasing. You refer to Ezra Pound. No I have never read any. My knowledge of poetry is very gapped & I have had little time to meditate on

1 Ginn is referring to Nikolay Berdyayev (see note 4) whose existentialist philosophy preferred unsystematic and mystical modes of expression over logic and rationality.

2 Unlike the 'dry' canteens run by organisations like the YMCA, 'wet canteens' sold alcoholic liquor. As a Methodist, Ginn was familiar with the strong position taken by evangelical churches on 'moral' issues, and could hardly have refrained from comparing this with their refusal to support or promote the Christian Pacifist cause.

3 D[avid] H[erbert] Lawrence (1885–1930). Ginn quotes the first stanza of section V of Lawrence's poem 'New Heaven and Earth', first collected in *Look! We Have Come Through!* (London: Chatto and Windus, 1917). Variations in spelling and punctuation suggest he was quoting from memory.

4 Nikolay Aleksandrovich Berdyayev (1874–1928)—also spelled Berdyaev and Berdiaev—philosopher, Christian Existentialist, and Marxist. Always a revolutionary thinker he was exiled for three years in 1899 for Marxist activities while a student; tried by the Russian Orthodox church in 1914 for criticising the Holy Synod; and expelled from Russia in 1922 for refusing to sanction Russian implementation of Marxist doctrine. His Academy for Religious Philosophy was founded at Clamart, near Paris. He was never interned in a concentration camp. The books Ginn mentions were translated into English around the same time: *Freedom and the Spirit* (1935), *The Meaning of History* (1936), and *The Destiny of Man* (1937).

it. 'Varsity life is not conducive to meditation—it is a foolish race to do fairly unimportant things. Lately I have been feeding on *The Prophet* by Kahlil Gibran,[5] an eastern poet much akin to Tagore—I have his *Gitanjali* here.[6] Wilfred Owen & Auden I've been reading for the first time. Francis Thompson & Gerard Manly Hopkins are the two that stand by me most—Browning Keats Wordsworth are other favourites.

By the way I interested Terry in one of D.H. Lawrence's poems 'Kangaroo'.[7] I wish we could start him off on this adventure of appreciation. He enjoyed Masefield's 'Dauber'—a long poem about ships.[8] I fear he has got a complex about all these things.

The verse you referred to was from one of my efforts. I have commenced daubing in verse since being detained (a genteel word) & find a certain amount of satisfaction in the pursuit though I am not allowed any illusions on the subject by myself or friends. If you forebear I shall quote a couple. The first one you will recognise as having something of the form of your 'Under a Sun', which set me off.

**The Drift of Pinions**

This avalanche of moss
    Which banks the pumice glen
Has loopéd knack to check and toss
    Worn minds onto its fecund green
And emerald o'er the loss.

Trout of this Taupo stream
    Will teach water softness,
Smooth they'll sway apart, and ghost and dream
    Losing care in a lostness
Of the low broken theme.

Water will steal over stone
    And coast past silver-blackness
Nightly to visit the lake alone,
    And there will pour its secret fullness
Till tall midnight is gone.

5 Kahlil Gibran (1833–1931), a Lebanese-American author and artist who wrote in both Arabic and English, and illustrated his works in a style influenced by William Blake. *The Prophet* (1923) is a series of twenty-eight visionary prose poems.

6 Rabindranath Tagore (1861–1941), an Indian writer—educated in both Bengali and English—he was awarded the 1913 Nobel Prize for Literature. A knighthood conferred on him in 1915 was repudiated as a protest against the Amritsar massacre (1919). *Gitanjali*, his most famous collection of lyrics, was written in 1909 with his own English version of the book being published in England in 1912.

7 Collected in *Birds, Beasts and Flowers: Poems* (New York: Thomas Seltzer, 1934).

8 John Edward Masefield (1878–1967). Masefield's *Dauber*, a long poem in seven parts, first appeared in the Oct 1912 issue of the *English Review* and was published as a book in 1913 by William Heinemann, London. The poem tells of a young ship's painter and lampman, initially disliked by his shipmates and nicknamed by them 'The Dauber', who gradually earns their respect only to die when he falls from the rigging during a storm.

Haunts me this passing train
    Of fugitive fleeting forms,
Gaunt I bear the gybing strain
    Caught in the track of Beauty's storms,
And chilled still thread the pass of pain
    Which leads to supernatural lawns.

This other a mate suggests I call 'Incoherence' as it is to him.

What can allay the pain of incoherence
Or mitigate the dull underground moan of soul
Bearing the barometric thrust of beauty?
The meshes of systaltic mind are all too slight
Unboned, unframed, unbraced
For such relentless countervail.
    Sense-delivered tidings
        Of rivers running
        Round the rims of time;
        Of spiders weaving
        Filigree shrouds for flies;
        Of a moon-ambushed dog
        Whose rescue daunts the shivering air;
        Of swart carbon's green progeny
        Unpragmatically plural;
        And all the outer inter-twine
        Light- and dark-surgant
    Hem the many-curtained soul.

No! dark and swarming sister,
No! Nature you may not rule therein,
For you too share the ancient malady—
Incorrigibly alien, aloof, and isolate.
Nor you, triple-ruptured time,
Who yard your own begotten golden hours
    In a brief arena,
Thence prod the sad succession
    Into the soundless void.

And you would trap me here
In this bleak cleft twixt past and future
Forever to fret!
Is Rome was,[9] all, and Greece, and Troy?
And those blue and rolling days,

9 Baxter was concerned by the sense of this phrase: in his transcription [Hocken MS 975/30] he crossed out 'was' and substituted 'lost'.

Lucent through the parallax of this pale day,
From your immemorial turnover
In cold drab ledgers written off?
'Yea', saith unhistoried Orient,
But 'No, no!' my western bones cry 'No!'
For me the past is never past;
History, deeply mine, to the soul-fabric
Is tightly wove by memory's hands.
Memory, the mortal foe of time,
Death and dissolution's dread,
Has taken away the scraps of time
And sets forth the full fare.
Henceforward glad destinies shall be won
Incubus of the fallen shaken off,
And the soul freshly launched
Shall sail away again
    Before the winds of the spirit
    To eternal reaches.

I have been interrupted while writing & during the course of talk a friend picked up *Poems of Tomorrow* & lighted on a poem of Louis MacNeice's which to my horror contained the phrase 'incorrigibly plural'—I'm an unconscious plagiarist but a plagiarist none the less.[10] However the effort is all I really value. Terry says to tell you you must say what you think and not be polite. Too right! I would really like to meet you & yarn about these things—pen-friends can establish some sort of contact but there are limitations.

How is school life now that the war is on?—I forget you've had 3 years of it. Life in this camp has valuable compensations particularly because of the variety of minds and personalities. Imagine meeting your school chums 10 years hence with all their individualities enlarged & developed. On the other hand one feels a tightness round the throat . . . With best of goodwill

Noel

[Hocken, MS 975/183]

10 *Poems of Tomorrow: An Anthology of Contemporary Verse*, chosen from *The Listener* by Janet Adam Smith (London: Chatto & Windus, 1935). Ginn is referring to the second stanza of the poem 'Snow' by (Frederick) Louis MacNeice (1907–63): 'World is crazier and more of it than we think, / Incorrigibly plural.'

**Baxter to Ginn, 28 August 1942**

CENSORED
No. 2

Brighton,
Otago.
28/8/42.

[Dear] Noel,

Thanks for your letter—I was a little melancholy and it cheered me up no end. And thank you for the poem; it has a somewhat obscurist mode of expression but is more entire and complete than the more lyrical one.

The 'bent' in ILLUSION was due to my bad writing. It was 'lest'. I am struck by your knowledge of words. 'Incoherence' is a poem for the more élite of literature, but although I cannot fully comprehend it I can sense what is there. If you don't object (and you, being 300 miles away, of course cannot) I will give you a much more obscurist poem of my own.[1]

I

Rain-ploughs rend the interstices of hills
    And serpents grey-jawed drift and raven;
    Sodden cadaver the earth, identity unproven;
Based granite-galleons probe eroded hulls
Teeth from earth's withered gum;
    Clotted no dust nor dry shale winter-riven,
World crumbles fair game
In hands of shackle-broken djinn:
    Where is the bottle black-stone, force to incendiary hells?

This describes storm and rain. The serpents 'grey-jawed' are mists. All is being washed away, destroyed, by the storm-demon. Who can force him back whence he has escaped.

II

Upheaval twisted rock, gigantic looms
    Jar hurled to prone resisting sea-bottom:
    Fire-feathered arrow-thought spin out and downward batten
Insane poltergeist though clefts jet flames.
Mind is too numbly reft
    To swell, and mould straight strands fibre storm-bitten

1 The poem that follows is an early version of Baxter's poem 'Rain-Ploughs': next to its title in the table of contents to notebook 'V' (Hocken, MS 704/5) is written '(obscurist)'. A draft of the published version (*BTP*, p.11, and CP, pp.26–7) was sent to Ginn some time later, also with a detailed commentary (see my comments on the poem on pp.104–6, and the later version on p.363).

Too frail slight raft
Telepathy for faith. Through rift
No nozzled scorching to break black bulbous bubble gleams.

The storm-demon has hurled his confining jar into the sea. We cannot return him to it.

III

Wrong, rather song if battered bent by rain;
    Join elementals in reef-erosion:
    Break, slake from blinding sky disintegrate explosion;
Molten, smelted in branchèd channels run,
Spirit sponging out
    Move universal god-whole new-arisen.
Bound in, shut,
Blanketed in pierced-not shade
Grope, slope I slate-entangled rune; yet rise, shall rise to green!

We should rather combine with than oppose the natural elements.

This may seem to you like G.M. Hopkins gone mad, but you must imagine in it [?all] the elements, incoherence, and storm.

Most philosophy and such-like which I have read is sweetened with the sugar-s [sic] of poetry, but in time I think I will learn to 'take it like a man'. I am now looking again at your poem 'Incoherence' and am struck by your facility of expression. 'Triple-ruptured Time' is a phrase which seems to me very good. I think you mean: Time broken up by the elements of Past, Present and Future. Tell me if I'm wrong.

In the following poem I express the notion that all the time we can know is the ever-changing, ever-present Present.

**In point of time**

    The swift continuous moment dwells in us;
    Time flows behind in torrent stream,
    Presaging waves loom nebulous
    From dusk to dusk; and we alone have life,
    Light flake up-poised upon the present time.
We ride an atom in the dark of space,
    Behold the present as in dark of dream;
    Then without strife
    Or stirring of the deep primeval slime
    We burst our bubble moorings and are gone,
    Broken upon the backward cataract.
Yet this our fate: to strain above
    The ancient animal grace
    Creating naught to ponder on,

Naught save fundamental fact
Of blind existence. Let us love,
Hate, realise in full all increate power,
Nor grieve for laws which cannot be unmade.
Life dwells within us only in slight mood:
Crush not speedily the transient flower.

I have read much of Wordsworth. He is often, undoubtedly, most lyrical; but there is also in him a certain didactic smugness which destroys much of the pleasure I would otherwise receive from reading him. I think that Auden, Spender, MacNiece, Day Lewis, and even Dylan Thomas or T.S. Eliot, are, if they can forget their mannerisms of modernity and Marxism, real poets.

**Auden—**

Certainty, fidelity,
On the stroke of midnight pass
Like vibrations of a bell
And fashionable madmen raise
Their pedantic boring cry . . .[2]

**Day Lewis—**

Spire-straight in a close chamber,
As though in shadowy cave a
Stalagmite of flame,
The integral spirit climbs
The dark in light for ever.[3]

**Eliot—**

The Eagle soars in the summit of Heaven,
The Hunter with his dogs pursues his circuit.
O perpetual revolution of configured stars,
O perpetual recurrence of determined seasons,
O world of spring and autumn, birth and dying.[4]

Now for one more. This is the lament of a man who has been re-incarnated, leaving his mate behind him.

2 W[ystan] H[ugh] Auden (1907–73). The first five lines of the third stanza of Auden's 'Lullaby', which was first published in *New Writing* Spring 1937, and collected in *Another Time* (New York: Random House, 1940).

3 Cecil Day Lewis (1904–72). The final five lines of the second verse of poem 14 from *The Magnetic Mountain* (London: Hogarth Press, 1933).

4 T[homas] S[terns] Eliot (1888–1965). The opening lines of the first chorus—'The Eagle soars in the summit of Heaven'—of 'Choruses from "The Rock"' published in *Collected Poems: 1909–1935* (London: Faber & Faber, 1936).

**Lament of the Reborn**

I have gazed back
But the white stone is fallen.

What memories, my soul.

Only a face among the osiers—
Birds by the pool,
And a face more known than mirrored vanity,
Familiar as life.
Then wind across the fenland
Signifying death:
Regret, regret, and searching after
For vanished laughter.

Suns shine but not within me;
Trees reach blind leaves to the light
But touch no life within me.

Is there no name?

Only the silent, empty reverberation . . .
That which was known too well
Forgotten now, outlandish,
And vainly sought.

Winter succeedeth winter:
There is change of season
But cold has entered over deeply
Winter succeedeth winter.
I would welcome the blackness . . .

But oh, the fallen stone!
I would return, but groping in the tunnel
There is no return.
Embodiment of beauty
I have known familiarly as more than beauty.

But there is no return.

I have written this in free verse as it seemed somehow more suitable.

I am glad to hear about Terry reading 'The Dauber' etc. One of Masefield's begins 'She moves (or "moved") across the water like a queen.'[5] Try him with it. Try him with anything good to do with the sea.

5 Baxter misquotes the final stanza of Masefield's poem 'The Ship' from *Lollingdon Downs and Other Poems* (New York: Macmillan, 1917), republished as *Lollingdon Downs and Other Poems, With Sonnets* (London: Heinemann, 1917). The stanza begins, 'I march across great waters like a queen'.

Perhaps you have 'The Hood-Seals' by Wilfred Gibson.[6]

Give him the one I enclose (by A.P. Herbert), and tell him he will get the parts of his model boat if I can manage it.

At school I get a certain amount of opposition as I am the only fit one not in their military cadet corps, but in arguments I usually come out on top.

With best wishes,

Jim.

[VUW Library, MS McKay 28/2]

**My Ship**

My ship is my delight,
 And she's the one I woo
When in the shiny night
 We dance across the blue,
With whispering sail and spar
As live as ladies are,
 And twenty times as true.

My ship is my delight,
 I made her, she is mine,
I built her trim and tight,
 I dreamed her gracious line;
No wooden thing is she
But some proud part of me;
 I made her, she is mine.

Then at the helm I stand
 And not alone are we.
Two lovers, hand in hand,
 We ask no company.
So, by some lover's art
I think she knows my heart
 And sings or sighs with me.
 —A.P. Herbert.[7]

[Hocken, MS 89/148]

6 Wilfred Wilson Gibson (1878–1962). Untraced.

7 A(lan) P(atrick) Herbert (1890–1971). Writer, humorist, and MP for Oxford University (1935–50). 'My Ship' was collected in Herbert's *Laughing Ann and Other Poems* (London: Ernest Benn, 1925) p.121. Baxter's transcription, except that he excludes Herbert's dedication—'For Captain Slocum, who built a boat with his own hands and in her sailed around the world, alone'—is exact.

**Baxter to Ginn, 23 September 1942**

CENSORED
No. 4

Brighton,
Otago.
23rd Sept. 1942

Dear Noel,

I was very pleased to receive your letter, especially because of the criticism of 'Rain-Ploughs'. I myself had always felt the first verse to be good—the last two are a little harder to understand—but then I would think that no-one would comprehend it except myself. In my opinion certain thoughts can be expressed in more obscure verse which defy all other expression.

The line you wish to know is—

> Grope, slope I slate-entangled rune, but rise, shall rise, to green.

'slate' signifies roof—especially of old houses—and hence human habitation. The Romans used 'tectum'—roof—to signify 'house'. I 'grope' in the darkness of memory and emotion, I labour upward, not directly but on a 'slope', from amateurism by the old verse-forms: yet eventually I will flourish in greenery like a tree. That is the gist of it.

Just now I have finished reading a book of Canadian poetry—like the New Zealand it is modern in form but trite and rigid in thought. I have seen a decoration at the beginning of one of the New Zealand books of a naked woman, vacant in expression, seated and staring at a shell.[1] It suits them. Most colonial writers seem to follow at the hub of the true poets of the Old World to pick up their forms but none of their fire. That is natural, for they are too young as nations to produce anything great.

> Love only song-craft, plant long in growing,
> Fixing its tap-root deep in the past.[2]

But your poems are very different. They have poetry IN them, not plastered over their exteriors. I have read the 'Drift of Pinions' again, and consider it excellent. The verse ending—'Till tall midnight is gone' breaks away from all mannerisms and stands on its own.

1 It is unclear which book Baxter is referring to as no anthology of New Zealand verse published before 1943, and none of the many individual collections I have viewed, contains such an illustration. If he was relying on memory then, with one variation, the figure he describes closely resembles a photograph of a statue of 'Eve'—naked, seated and staring at a small apple—reproduced in a plate facing page 77 of A.W. Shrimpton's (ed.) anthology *Countess of Liverpool's Gift Book of Art and Literature* (Christchurch: Whitcombe & Tombs, 1915).

2 Untraced.

Your poem of 'farewell' need never be blushed for. It expresses a mood in adequate and poetic language.[3]

This poem expresses a certain desire for earlier wonder which any writer who has become more polished would feel:

> I have passed unscathed through my own thought's fire,
> I have moulded song and spirit to heart's desire,
> I have reached the summit sought after long—
> O for the inchoate spirit, the wordless song!

I enclose a rather long verse of mine (type-written) which you may not like particularly, as it is certainly bizarre and also very obscure. It is divided into 9 sections with the tenth as a sort of epilogue. It is based on the Pythagorean belief in the significance of numbers, and each section is meant to convey the attributes of the number with which it is headed.

i.e. I is of integrity and unity, II is of the Duad in its usual feminine form, VII displays its mystical attributes.

If you don't like it don't bother about it.

The following is the second verse of one of my more obscure poems.[4]

> Behold magnetic current outward flowing
> From tendril-anode on intrinsic path
> Swiftly in rind-sap to mortal brain forth-fleeing
> Air-current flaming:
> Gaze at new-rising spring-awakened faith
> Gaze, maze in muse nor even slightly shudder
> If foul tyrannic odour
> In progress of the violent adder forth
> Should stain the innocent loam with most unneedful slaughter:
> Even from such shall fire be drawn though later
> Pass, glaze nor glass with idle oblivious letter
> Burst bands accurst, bid song abide deride false worth.

The next is on a French painter who left France to live among the Marquesan natives.

> Gauguin morphine-drugged or drunk
> Firing vast basic masses into form,
> In the Marquesas winter-dank
> Held his flaring artistry firm
> Until one day found dead—c'etait la fin.[5]
> No longer Fate forced him with paint-daubed rattan
> Who found in doubt more faith than in the rotten

3 See Ginn's poem 'Farewelling', on p.513.
4 For the full poem see 'Moving on spirit-roads', p.442.
5 The draft of this poem in notebook 'VI' (Hocken, MS 704/6:336, p.21) is titled 'Gauguin'—it has 'c'était la fin' written in later, replacing Baxter's first choice of phrase, 'tout fin'.

Observed abode of spiritual cretin—
    But who shall hearken
    Here where usual shadows darken:
I shall move swiftly as the delicate eland
Nor fail in refuge of haunted island
    But whitherward, why or how,
    Never shall know.

The next and last is a very long one which I wrote after visiting a gallery of War-pictures.[6] The first verse is an introduction, the rest each refer ~~the~~ to individual pictures.

**On Visiting a Gallery of War-Pictures**

Enter and pause. Here are white walls
Refurnished by a thousand errant wills
Who formulated line on mental line
The image of men living, slain,
Of war-encumbered landscape of old towns
And armoured cruisers many tons:
All this wide thought is concentrated here—
There is strange hush of mute words on the air.

Here are huge steel propellers finely wrought,
Perfectly balanced—to my sight
They are chill pieces in a vast machine,
Evil and strong; these accurate men
Who move adjusting firm bolts cautiously
Are moulded to a make as low,
That sees no far horizons dawn-enscrolled
Nor beauty even in their silver-hulled
Grey planes that take fierce hold on atmospheres
And blot with billowing smoke the morning fires.

Move on—peer low at this small daub:
Here shielded workers strike and grab
At glowing iron serpents. Helmeted,
Slow craftsmen pour a fiery flood
Of molten steel through channelled tracks—and these,
The artisans care not if the flame that flows
Blasts hell from booming throats or splinters down

6 An exhibition sponsored by the Great Britain Ministry of Information entitled 'British and New Zealand War Pictures' toured many New Zealand towns in 1942. The catalogue contains an introduction signed by then Prime Minister Peter Fraser, dated 22 Jan 1942, and an essay 'War and the Artist' by noted art critic H.V. Morton. Baxter's descriptions in this poem of a number of the pictures that featured in the exhibition are extremely accurate.

To slash live agonizing flesh and bone,
But bend obedient heads to chains and bars
Nor heed if lordlings loose a hundred wars.

Gargantuan girders twisted in close shapes,
Piled on the rubble of wrecked shops,
A cabinet-factory was ere swift bombs fell.
So human destinies must fail,
Broken and tangled, at the clash of gods.
Aye! how to the eternal goads
Of circumstance, fell circumstance;
Suffer the sharp calamity that stuns.
Kneel long in blind idolatry
And ye shall rise entirely free!

See now the crowded bulwarks of a transport
Where khaki soldiers waiting their depart
Shout and sing in chorus joyfully:
To them the horror of bleak war is lie
And they are heroes in a high romance.
When they find what battle truly means—
Where death lurks not but ravens day by day
And men die not to live but live to die—
Shall they retain their youthful ardour long
When stark steel pierces body, brain, or lung?

Yonder the bastions of a broken nave
Where faded murals yet adorn smashed walls;
The waters of calm twilight lave
Battered devout receptacles.
On the high altar burst the hand-grenade
And desecrated is the sanctuary;
Above the shattered window, undismayed,
The crucifix—calm, bitter irony!
When forth from the waste land sweeps the war-wind drear
Naught but the husks of faith shall now endure.

And here is symbol of humanity
That strives to hold a close civilian tie,
To carry in battle the ways of home:
Here where the sea-plane's engines hum
Behold a 'Sergeant Wireless Operator'
With vital face above the instrument-board:
Yet even the strongest heart must tire,
And from life's intricacies barred

He will soon lose full human intercourse
And sink beneath the internecine curse.

Regard cadets intent upon their drill.
Though they may men-like speak with shout and drawl
They have no thought of discipline of war
Where shelled men struggle in barbed wire
And writhe with maimed limbs through entanglement.
They are self-confident;
And dream of heroism, of brave deeds,
The awe bequeathed to wondering decades:
They march in wheeling squads on green grass-lawn
Nor see—above—the lowering skies of doom.

A great sea-battle. Burning ships drift by
And twelve-inch guns roar out across the bay:
But fifty-cannon cruisers are slight pawns
To cabinets with diplomatic pains;
And man, the unit, has no place in schemes
Where empires shamble through belligerent shams.
The patient sweating mortals are the same
On either side. Why bring blunt death to some—
Drown, blast with fire from stem to stern?
In similar unreason they return.

Come hither—look long and steadily at this!
The naked soul of war exhibited thus.
'Air-gunner in gun-turret at night'—
He is held close and comprendeth [sic] not
The glittering stars like Christmas candle-light,
This, the glass coffin, poised in middle air
Shows the true battle-spirits as they are;
This pallid deaths-head, ringed by iron bands,
Is held in inexorable bonds:
Who knows how soon
Death lancing from a search-light sun
May hold the silver fish transfixedly?—
And death-flame lunge across a reeling sky.

Herein is shown the blind insanity
Of reason subjugate to formulas:
They have small intellect to lose,
Counting high explosive human toy—
Mine-laying where the thundering seas roll by.
And mines marked not by flag or buoy?
What vessel strikes on these?

We will win wars by terrorizing those
Who move in ships on the uncertain seas
And bear food-cargoes whither the enemy says—
In truth to the blockaded states
Where a starved people waits:
'Nation of fiends!'
Yet they are saints if friends.

The maniac sadists loose death-dealing bombs
Above the English cities, then return.
And who inhabit these ships of twenty tons
That from a black sky boom their battle-theme?
Men, kindly men—words not re-iterated
By those who see foul monsters slink,
And hasten home, their fury sated.
Here the night-raider slips in blank
Slow passage on across the estuary channel—;
The moon, as if emerging from a tunnel
Glows through frozen cloud—
Bird-tracks upon a way sleet-clad:
And far below the pencilled search-lights swing
While fearing human life moves on,
Labour accomplished, longing for safe earth
Where stars of welcome flicker to the south.

Evening: the twilight lowers on darkened cliff;
Beyond, huge rollers crash incessantly.
And here the plane that hovered silently
Aloof
Lies buried in disrupted loam;
Here corpses scorched by flame.
And all strife herein is shown—
The clay where warm vitality once shone,
The intricate machine destroyed,
Swallowed in soulless mud.

And the wide sea that so will batter still
When self-destroying gods have wrought their will.

This is the finish. Well, I have written a pretty long letter. I hope you don't mind that.

With best wishes
From,
Jim.

[VUW Library, MS McKay 28/3]

**In Numeris**

I

Entrenched in spiritual fastness
I have no response
For aught that clamours for naught clamours,
Bronze citadels dark-valed since vanquished and revealed
Here are not needed.
Self-seeded and sufficient I am only
Now inly held and integral as protozoon.

Sufficient to the minute is alone
The prayer thereof for priest of supplication
Is outward from the idol there and dark within it
From whence no glimmer tidal repercussive
Breaks, for sufficient
Unto the time is tide and fire thereof

One light is snuffed to nothing and the nothing
Is not the lack of light but nothing
To see and nothing seen so integral
And none
And one.

II

Whence this duality
Of spirit and of purpose when two suns
Have entered and destroyed themselves in me?

O the moon-breasted
Goddess of desire not Aphrodite
Say
Rather one dancing in a white arena
One with the polished surface one
With the transparent oak or silver-throated
Dawn-maidens, so
One in the womb and with the womb of sun
Moon and ray therefrom clear-moted
Yet moulded to ivory limbs
                    ah no
Most dual and most rightly separate
In such duality

Gemini
Has risen through a jewelled Zodiac
Imprisoned the phalloid ascendancy
To Seal of Solomon.

III

Jubilate, Jubilate,
O blessèd Trinity
Ancestor adoration

Et Dominus
Reduced and stereotyped
To incube and formulae,
God, leader less than when
Man.

And why
To swallow such to follow such
When there is older,
Eternity enclosed in pyramid
And throne of Delphic oracle

Shall dry sarcophagus
Yield to Pythagoras
For shield since found in hall
of shields
Death is not intellectual.

Time thrice-wounded
Crumbles at touch of relativity,
Matter and sublimation
Space and the fourth dimension,
And Nature to the Spirit.

IV

Death judgement heaven and hell
And the white winds of heaven
The elemental God
Seen steadfastly
Lord the square-dealer
Grâce à Dieu
Zeus the All-Mover
Dios e Madre dè Dios
Deva

Enter the seasons
Awake unto fruition fruition and decay
On this swan-haunted outer hour behold away
Toward the compass-centre
Reason break and superstition
Leaving but the long-chaunted
One.

V

Prosperity fecundity from Araby and Jewry
And tapers burn before the marriage altar
Nay falter not though Benjamin
And Joseph part though David slay
Not Philistine Goliath nay
But Saul

On feet and hands they crawl
To Mecca, O fast and pray
Purification and the alms-giver

Ah, but the dusk is grey
By Raphael Michael Gabriel
Rise across the black river
From grave to day
The star may summon thee in subtle alchemy
Whence astromony all science as we know it
Even the rhapsody
Of musician or poet thence draws mystery,

And Seal of Solomon
To Ashtoreth
And unity.

VI

Ah Jesu ward the evil

In crystalline from sunken mine,
In perfect harmony
And the spirit of God walked on the waters
Day to day and night to night
Firmament earth and vegetable kingdom
And the suspended light and light
And light
The protozoon has moved
Piscine and mammaline
And lastly human who is yet no higher

But nonesuch here
All this is integral and perfect nor ephemeral
And so most integral
Increate, known.

VII

Fallen walls of Jericho
Are re-erected but Time's passing
Destroys again

The plagues of Egypt and the doubt of Peter
Are marked upon the gasometer
But no, nor more
Angels and stars of seven Churches
Are from St. John the mystical and Divine;

So mystical and unbased
And yet more several
Is the interpretation of the natural sign
And sine.
Green wood-sap
Ah, miracle
Divine and inspirational
The seven angels.

VIII

Through pillar and peristyle
(Lean and pause) the swollen Nile
Souls saved in the Ark
Here ride the Egyptian stream
In sacred bark
                    of balance,
Justice and equity
In dark intolerance
But hark!
                hence rises solemn music
And here the temple-dance .....
Such shall be fountain of harmony.

IX

Streams of the underworld are met
In pallid confluence
But from this faith and gold fulfilment are
Hydra can sway below the sullen river
And though from thence it moves not
Yet in itself perfection is
Above the floating nunephar.

All here combine
And pass from their respective influence
To some uncharted .....

X

What is the ultimate form
Figure of this banded universe ?
    Nihilist sayeth
    Naught
So have I said to deaden thought that yet remaineth

Opposing powers, Egyptian tomb
Et cetera et cetera
All are bound within this sphere
That swells to globular nothing.
Having existence and so unity
Thus single.

Cymbol and viol mingle
I hold the djinn within a crystal phial.

Notes:

4 'citadels'—human life regarded as insular.

9 'priest'—memory and foresight separate from the [?pre ]

20 'two suns'—duality of Nature

35–8 ∇ Δ ✡

54, 55 Theory of reincarnation.

61 'Spirit'—Holy Ghost.

73 Children of Lir.

80–1 Gen. XLV 22. [To each and all of them [Joseph] gave festal garments; but to Benjamin he gave three hundred shekels of silver and five festal garments.]

81–2 I Sam. XVII 40 [Then [David] took his staff in his hand, and chose five smooth stones from the brook, and put them in his shepherd's bag or wallet; his sling was in his hand, and he drew near to the Philistine.]

83 I Sam. XVIII 5. [And David went out and was successful wherever Saul sent him; so that Saul set him over the men of war. And this was good in the sight of all the people and also in the sight of Saul's servants.]

84–6 Mohammedan religious duties

87–94 Calling up of departed spirit.

100–8 Gen. I 2–26 [The biblical account of creation.][1]

113 Josh. VI 6–20 [Joshua's capture of Jericho.]

116 Matt. XVIII 21, 22. [Then Peter came up and said to him, 'Lord, how often shall my brother sin against me, and I forgive him? As many as seven times?' Jesus said to him, 'I do not say to you seven times, but seventy times seven.']

120 Rev. I 20 [As for the mystery of the seven stars which you saw in my right hand, and the seven gold lampstands, the seven stars are the angels of the seven churches and the seven lampstands are the seven churches.]

[Hocken, MS 704/6:387, pp.104–14]

1 In MS Book VI (Hocken, MS 704/6, p.114) Baxter cross-references lines 100–8 to his later poem 'The Ghost Unborn' (Hocken, MS 704/8:472, p.19), to suggest a loose association between 'the spirit of God [walking] on the waters' and the imagined action of his own spirit, following his death, rising from its grave and loping 'along / Lonely by city, field and fjord'. See pp.450–1.

**Baxter to Ginn, 16 October 1942**

CENSORED
No. 1

Brighton,
Otago,
16th Oct. 1942

Dear Noel,

Thank you for your letter. I appreciate the criticism, and agree that obscurity may become a cult. Here is a poem I wrote as my own natural reaction to my late deep obscurity set in.

**Of Age**[1]

Perched on a sun-burnished boulder
    See I the jagged hills,
Sentinels shoulder to shoulder
Guarding their citadels.
    Think I with awe-struck breath:
    These are more aged than life, than death,
But I am older.

Far from the loud world's anger
    See I the new-born lamb,
Seeking in querulous hunger
The warm wet teats of his dam.
    Think I: he has not known
    Animal passions that rouse,
    Red shade of the slaughter-house—
And I am younger.

Regarding colonial poetry, I say that natures are produced by environment: that colonies do not seem the right environment for the poetical nature: that any poet of great fire who did happen to spring up would try to shift. However, it is very much a matter of opinion and I suspect that my biased attitude has a psychological basis. As you will know from Terry, he and I have been to Europe. The pleasure of the trip is no doubt acutely stamped on my subconscious; and the result is an unconscious be-littlement of NZ.

'I have passed unscathed' is really a dramatising of personal experience—which

1 Following the entry for 'Of Age' in the table of contents of MS Book VII (Hocken, MS 704/7), Baxter has added 'for my Mother' and then suggested, in the text of the poem, a change in line two from 'jagged hills' to 'ragged hills'.

most poetry is. Yes, it refers not to the Nirvana, but rather to a mastering of the verse-forms etc.

Both in the 'Plough' and 'Doctrine of Philosophy' (with notes) which I am sending up there is the basic idea that 'love of life', 'joy in living', is the important ~~basis~~ foundation of existence. No inertly miserable man has ever written good poetry. But this joie-de-vivre is not to be obtained by consciously looking for it. The poems will tell you more than I can.

<u>Note</u>: The initial letters of the lines of 'Doctrine of Philosophy' spell out this—THERE IS NO HEART IN TIME SAVE SUCH AS WE BID BEAT. This is, in a sense, a key to the poem. Perhaps it savours too much of ABRACADABRA, but it does give to my somewhat childish mind something of mystery, of discovery.

I think the word you wanted was 'Grey'. If not, tell me where it comes in the poem. 'blind idolatry . . . free' is unfortunately a very weak spot in the poem. It simply means—'you will lose your bodies'.

'He who laughs' is of the hysterical trend of contemporary literature and civilization. The 'suspension bridge' from one age to another.

My mother was lately discussing the inhibitions of Terry, and is very pleased that he has now to some extent overcome them. I fear my literary ability may have been to some extent the cause (do not show this to him). Your friendship will, I am sure, help him. Anyway, with his natural charm, no-one could be unfriendly to Terry.

With best wishes from
Jim.

### DOCTRINE of PHILOSOPHY

<u>First Verse</u>:

This concerns religion in its old forms.

1. The saintly prelates of the Church
2. Considered the earth to be merely a foundation to
3. Eternity the everlasting — 'bastion'—buttress
4. Destroying the assumedly obscene pagan beauty,
5. The old rites which spring up again, and the brief artistry
6. Of Greece and Rome.
7. Shall I blackguard them for this? — 'fleering'—ridiculing
8. No: rather I will see their narrow belief as a shapeless myth
9. Which will eventually be overwhelmed by time—a seadrowned city.

~~10~~ <u>Second Verse</u>:

This concerns the intricacy of science, and the need for greater simplicity

10. But how does science fit in with all this?—
11. The new and swelling sciences,
12. The geometrician etc. — 'radio-active'—breaking into electrons

13. My body, my emotions tell me — 'granite-surly'—based in his convictions like a granite rock,intolerant
14. That the simpler faith is better;
15. I trust heart before the shell-like brain 
16. Which has no part in the spirit it controls;
17. The spirit will only give unwilling and unintelligible response to thought
18. And works out its own fate in the best way.

Third Verse:

This very much concerns itself with the present day.

19. We are inately restless,
20. And this restlessness ends the conventional tradition (mentioned in 1st verse)
21. Except that we seem to see the universe as a bare and overwhelming waste
22. Dwarfing our human concepts:
23. It is vain to appeal to the isolated forces of life (i.e. the sun)—
24. We, the complex ones,
25. Are saved by the thought of he (meaning myself) who turns from these spaces to the heart of life.
26. This thought is: our old defences are gone,
27. We cannot find solace in a bare universe—let us turn to Nature.

Fourth Verse:

What happens when we do 'turn to Nature.'

28. Moving with poetical perception
29. And (symbolically) looking among volcanic rock
    for a green patch of life — 'turbary'—place to dig peat
30. I saw something new and marvellous (there to be found
    all the time, ~~that~~ as if in a 'rock-vein')
31. Under the storm (war etc.) which threatens our civilization.
32. 'Easily flew the swan from the golden rushes'.
33. I am struck with a sense of great miracle as this thing of life
34. Rises skyward.
35. I find momentarily the source of all life—
36. That, perhaps, by a fuller knowledge of which Christ and the holy martyrs were impelled.
37. I would lead those who find themselves in a bare universe to this source of life.
38. For on earth
39. We may find it.

Note: 'Spirit' is more the moving life-force, 'soul' is static.

[VUW Library, MS McKay 28/13and Hocken MS 148/89]

**The Plough**

Purpose?
There is no purpose in a linnet's song
Though linnets mate amid the boughs of spring.
Gaze at the hills upon a summer night;
See that they raise broad motionless arms
Toward a sky they fathom not:
These have no need of purpose. Wherefore then
Must we fling out a massive web of mind
On the dark pastures?
Vision now the ploughman
For whom (say we) the land lies fallow.
The slow hooves take direction and the plough
Grooves deeply in the cleft and yielding earth.
His labour may have reason, but the whistle
Wherewith he heralds forth a sunken sun
Is without purpose yet most meaningful.
Birds yammer in his wake. The earth for them
Has brought forth fruitfulness, no less
Than for humanity; yet they have never
Guessed of a providential fate therein.

Great peace lies in us, could we fathom it:
'Seek not, and ye shall find'—such is the word.
We dwell within the moment, and sufficient
Unto the moment is the faith therein.
[Hocken, MS 704/7:388, pp.1–2]

**Doctrine of Philosophy**

The stone and marble angels of white folly
Have built above this grass-girt bastion
Eternity the permanent known-fully
Razing all turrets of obscene combustion
Eld green-arisen and the transient flowering
In Grecian islands and in Capitol.
So shall I batter these with grey mouth fleering?
Nay! see them rather as amorphous tale
On verge of sliding to sea-wide to ocean bells that toll.

How then to reconcile, how to see surely
Einstein or radio-active billowing
And geometrician sphered and granite-surly
Reshrouding Euclid: lungs loud-bellowing

Thud forth return to the black tarn of being;
I trust lungs, heart before the ammonite brain
Not known in spirit, for the spirit obeying
To this the snailed oppressor snarls but rune
Instrinsically bends again to evolution sane.

Metal of motion is alloyed within us
Ending the stone and marble melancholy
Save for bare bones of stars that fall upon us
And even now eradicate us wholly:
Vain the appeal to globular sea-girt solar—
Even are we, diffuse, unanimal,
Saved by the maxim of the landward sailor:
Useless the dry machine, broken the silver mail—
Crumble the sky-reachings, so seek self in the small.

Holding the focus-point of fine emotion
And seeking in tufa-rock a turbary
Saw I the vein the lode-rock of a new mission
While sky-ward are storms of overwhelming fury:
Easily flew the swan from the golden rushes—
Breathing, I saw but breathing stammered and shook
In a flood in a cloudless sun-shower as to the sun he rises.
Down plunge I down to the single lake
Broken where holy martyrs died and Christ was crucified.
Even so would I lead ye, O sea-drowned men!
And here on earth is the glass wherein is seen
The goal of spirit unseeking, in soul the hill-crowning cairn.
[Hocken, MS 704/7:403, pp.31–3]

**He Who Laughs**

We raise a cry of warring voices
We shout across a continent
The babel shakes and bruises
Sane intellectual walls with maniac merriment.

Here is the high suspension bridge.
Look over the edge
To see the yellow water bank and shudder:
Boulders down rumble
As the black avalanches
In couloirs spin and thud:
This is the dance, the idiot dance

Death's tap-dance
Making the wire stays tremble
With swaying suicidal intent
With fear and merriment.

This crossing is unsafe.
I will run over as ~~Horatius declined to do~~ Herminius did[1]:
two more steps—
if it were to fall there'd be an accident
but no loss of life .......

We all crawl outward on the unsafe girder.
The steel is crystallizing under stress:
We must anneal; we must destroy the danger—
So mime, laugh, clown
In frantic merriment.

We mouth and gesture
But dumbness—that which is dumb in fluid mind—
Will never speak.
We are all dumb. We cannot speak
To crack the mental vesture.
Laugh, laugh, and clang the bells of earth
In idiot mirth
As the vast nameless looms above the wall
Of our lost citadel.

[Hocken, MS 704/7:401, pp.26–8]

1 This is a reference to the attempted invasion of Ancient Rome by the Etruscans, where Publius Horatius Cocles and two companions Spurius Lartius and Titius Herminius, held the Pons Sublicius bridge, against Etruscan attempts to use it to cross the Tiber, long enough for their countrymen behind them to destroy it. It is likely the Baxter's direct reference is to the following excerpt from chapter 2, section 3 of Thomas Babington Macaulay's *Lays of Ancient Rome* (1842):

Back darted Spurius Lartius;
  Herminius darted back:
And, as they passed, beneath their feet
  They felt the timbers crack.

**Baxter to Ginn, 21 November 1942**

CENSORED
No. 2

Brighton,
Otago.
21st. Nov. 1942

Dear Noel,

Thank you for sending the poem by Terry. I have not read much by Lucas, but I think certain parts of this are very striking. It is refreshing to find this form of poetic expression—simple, lyrical—after perhaps attempting, unsuccessfully, to follow the obscure and tortuous windings of the mind of Dylan Thomas,

> Let there be no song there save the wind that hums
> Through idle wires while dumb men tramp to work[1]

is right in the main-stream of poetry.

I have not written just lately as I was working for exams. This letter is written in a temporary lull before Matric., which will be on in about three weeks time—less now.

I keep recalling for no obvious reason, except their beauty, certain lines of yours:—'And you, O triple-ruptured Time, That herd your own begotten golden hours In a brief arena . . .' They have a life and solidity that holds the imagination.

With this I am sending you a typed poem POST PROELIUM. The punctuation may appear somewhat erratic, but you will have no difficulty in following the meaning. Remember to read it not in any sense as a lyric, but as an indictment of slaughter. The key-note is bitterness, bitterness and not lyricism.

The following is partly a religious poem, with the last verse in the style of G.M.H.

**Of the Fountain**

The beauty of earth is sufficient.
If we cannot bend now,
Drink of the beauty eternally fashioned
There is no solace in futurity.

I see the silken spider swing
Down windows, weaving in the rain.
Soul here should inly sing.
    But I, who cannot break
    To the well-head I seek,

1 F[rank] L[aurence] Lucas (1894–1967), scholar, critic and occasional poet. Untraced.

Am closed in the desert-dream;
Carry, for faith, a fulminating powder
And fear the swinging spider.

Ere the spell-song was sung
I held the weasel's young
    With perfect love past fearing.
But the true heavens have broken;
    And in their stead
    The jewelled, dead
Space of a world awoken.

Stay! There is a way: by day-sun have I seen it.
    Without a word spoke of song, of sonnet,
Stay, the wavering, the earth-known way
    Breaks to heart of all folk;
    Slakes fountain-seeking thirst of buried men
Again, again. Where, then?
Without word
    Of heart below spider, sun, snow,
The Lord.

With all good wishes,
From,
Jim.
PS Tell Terry he need not send back the book he mentioned.
[VUW Library, MS McKay 28/4]

**POST PROELIUM**

Is there no pain
At this the valorous vain sacrifice
Not valorous but vain.

No sharp heart-sickness in seeing
The sower sowing, the white air flowing;
Silenced the thundering animal snarl of guns

And the same peace again save for the word unspoken:
The broken the valorous ones
Not valorous but vain.

I have leant forward and listened
As the bright summer quickened;
This was the messenger that hastened
To my warm carcass on twisted feet:

'Through summer and winter rains
The earth remains.
There is no cause
For this the taloned terror, the tendon-straining.'

Is there no sorrow
To see the nickel bullet strike in mud
Or puncture the full forehead, let loose the bruising blood.

When on a pacific morrow
The diplomats meet in a town
The abbattoir closes down—
*What is this, my people, has been done to ye!*
*What is this that has come to pass!*
And there is grass or roses, roses or grass

Over the artistry,
The young philosophy,
Heart-joyance and arrowing blood.

There is no change.

Such had some willed in spirit, but where is spirit?
    Upon the mountain range
    Or on the summer plain
    Under the grasses is mud—
The diplomats inherit life without change—
    And in the mud there lie
    Beauty and artistry,
    The young philosophy.
        [Hocken, MS 704/7:409, pp.46–8]

**Control**

I shall not be torn by emotions
As by lions feeding on flesh:
In loss of self-control
Is loss of self-integrity.

A thousand suns play in the meadow-pastures
And through a reverberating sky
The lark disintegrates to music,
To absolute music.'

Here with inward turning eye
See-I desires break bounds,
Snap the lax ~~reins~~ thongs of thought.

This shall not be.
Rather I will be mediocre
Than lose the individual spirit;
For mind that looks through a sane man's eyes
Into a three-dimensional world
Is coherent, symbolic of truth.
[Hocken, MS 704/7:420, pp.67–8]

**(To a solemn music)**

This is no trembling of a bar of bone,
Rather a sun rains blossoms or bright bees.
The earth has opened and volcanic craters
Bid precipices reel: Nature and man
Are joined in one harmonic dance; this madness
Is of the gods, and so thrice blessèd folly.
Currents bear soul and body forth,
Lost in a multitudinous maze of light:
Wind, waters, the unseen vibrating sun—
Mind of the master, core of this great music—
Merge in a gold, revolving wheel.
I hearken,
With wavering mind and spirit luminous,
Esconced among the shards of broken light.
I would remain in woven sanctuary
Where sound and mental light make singing leaves,
Where is no cloying over-sweetness
But rather beauty of woods when rain is past,
Beauty of vined rock-faces at mid-summer,
With most majestic beauty of high cataracts,
Ice, air-enamoured summits, and sea-tempest.

But, sound ceasing, I am drowned,
Immured in sullen fastnesses.
Spirit has shed her borrowed plumage
And may but rise in labouring phantasy
Self-sought, self-found.
[Hocken, MS 704/6:384, pp.99–100]

**Ginn to Baxter, 2 December 1942**

CENSORED
No. 3

c/- Nat Service Dept
Hautu Turangi
via Nat Park
2/12/42.

Mein lieber Dichter,

I was most conscious of neglect & unkindness in not answering your last letter—& then comes another—a third will be more than even my hardened soul can bear. The main reason has not been that I have been answering other letters but just the slothful despondent state into which I submerge periodically—not sorrow or pathos but just self-pity, nicht wahr? It seems there are certain things which I cannot adjust to & the compromise at times produces a terrible inertia. However everyone knows to small or great degree this conflict of the negative & positive . . . Well thanks many times over for the generous outpouring of yourself on paper. It must take you much time in copying out & typing & because you do it I realise you know my appreciation. You have certainly mastered more than the rudiments of your art & decks cleared you can get busy on the proper job of translating the world of your experience. A Chinese writer I have been reading says poetry is reasoning highly coloured with emotion.[1] I like this ex of Chinese poetry:

> In my young days,
> I had tasted only gladness,
> But loved to mount the top-floor
> But loved to mount the top-floor
> To write a song pretending sadness.
>
> And now I've tasted
> Sorrows flavour, bitter & sour,
> And can't find a word
> And can't find a word,
> But merely say, 'What a golden autumn hour'![2]

I have been practising writing again but realise the great distance I have to go before I have any mastery of technique—images seem to be fairly plentiful but a gt deal more than mere imagery is required. GMH's style is your forte, you love the message

1 Untraced.
2 Xin Qiji [Hsin Ch'i-chi] (1140–1207), Sung poet. Ginn quotes an early translation of Xin's poem 'To the Tune of "The Ugly Slave"', published as 'Sorrow's Taste' in Clara M. Candlin's (trans.) *Herald Wind: The Herald Wind, Translations of Sung Dynasty Poems, Lyrics and Songs*, Wisdom of the East Series (London: John Murray, 1935).

'There lives the dearest freshness deep down things'[3]—and certainly that discovery needs publishing—I very much like 'Of a Fountain'. 'Control' has a steady appeal over the number of times I have read it. The inset 'A thousand suns . . .' eludes me somewhat.[4] Still it's good to make me think. The best of 'Post Proelium' I find in the last verse. 'Doctrine of Philosophy' is clever & forceful—perhaps a little difficult—the common reader has no access to notes. The others are all fascinating—you have taken the most out of the suspension bridge metaphor—it is truly a great bit of work. 'Of Age' is much slighter but the point is well made. The bit 'Sing in rich baritone to comfort me.' keeps coming to the mind. To my mind (to a solemn music) hits the high spots—it is the purest sensuousness worthy of Keats at his best & far outstripping Milton's effort (at a s.m.).[5] 'Immured in sullen fastnesses' is an expression that will live with our best literature. I seem to be cataloguing the virtues of stuff to be auctioned but I don't know how otherwise to show appreciation—just take it & my joy in it all as read. Here is a thing describing my thoughts when the creek rose in flood a few weeks back. I called it 'October Spate'.

The rain-loom weft threading lacks
So spills to flood—no firm fabric locks:
From the hill's high breasts comes the blood—
Express loaded with mammary mud,
Parting the dermal flesh in flumes,
Scouring the ferny slopes for loams,
Its truck tarpaulins weighted with logs
Which the kedging creek from the hinterland lugs;
Shunts up backwater stopping to cadge
Frogs' eggs and slime from the jointless sedge;
Pulls out from pause with glacier grace
With majestic increase mending its pace;
Downgrade collides with the rockplated hull
Of a warship grey submerged in the hill;
Thence shuffles through farmyards in silent slippers,
Scoops rich soil from urban scuppers,
To herd its merchandise through the welter
Of wharves and tariffs, its own broad delta;
Aiming in greed at profitable targets,
Cornering virgin maritime markets.

3 Gerard Manly Hopkins (1844–89). Ginn quotes line 10 of Hopkins's sonnet 'God's Grandeur', first published in *Lyra Sacra: A Book of Religious Verse*, selected and arranged by H.C. Beeching (London: Methuen, 1895).

4 The MS Book version of 'Control', as transcribed on pp.165–6, does not have the second stanza inset, only enclosed in quotation marks.

5 John Milton (1608–74). Milton's poem 'At a Solemn Musick' appeared in both the 1637 and 1645 editions of his poetry. Despite some metrical similarities there are few thematic links between Milton's poem and Baxter's '(To a solemn music)'.

The rain-loom drops its heavy threads
Which slide to their weft in ocean beds
Weaving a patternless-patterned plush
That frays nor crumps with pinion-plash.
As the appointment must pass of each lunation,
These lambent looms their lachrymation—
A blue wind stays the lubric grind
And the last long thread without a sound
Falls to waste upon the ground.

Have been reading 'A Time to Dance' once more. Great-stuff isn't it! Bits like 'How soft drifts of sleep piled on their senses deep'; 'May even find, when I come to the snow-line, the bitter end, His handholds cuts on death's terrific face'; 'The sky was a sounding-board for their sorrow & from this the galaxies averted their eyes.'; The bitter parodies 'Come live with me & be my love' & 'Oh hush thee my baby'—his is a voice with something to say.[6] I have written a rambling sort of lament wh I would like you to criticise—it certainly needs revision. It is called 'Overture to Unbelief' I am sorry I can't send it to you typed—however do your best.

Muezzin-Despair drones his gospel of naught
Under vulture skies bids bones disrobe
Cast cloth to kites, bones become a cairn
On arid sands make an arab ending.

I am the dead sea: on me dead desires
Drift with brined loveliness—underneath,
Slag, the chemic drain of bitter salts,
No sensuous stir nor ear for life's green claxon.

Would cease, yet stumble on, not joining
Gay-bannered Nature's crusade—the holy stars
In their blackened sockets appal; Spring's time-bombs
Sown in autumn beds but graze with gladness.

'Neath Eridanus light & jewelled cross
Would mourn with doomed plains of the polar south
Stepping a sad saraband to frozen trombones
Till jazz-sleeted blizzards burst in surrealist rack.

. . . . .

Dew-bells once rang from green grass-steeples
Carolling the little kin of life to their pews
Wonder-worship matined in dawn lit shrines
And love with skylark joy drank chaliced wine.

6 These quotations are from Cecil Day Lewis's long poem 'A Time to Dance', first collected in *A Time to Dance and Other Poems* (London: Hogarth Press, 1935).

Easy then to climb the stile into the sky
And swing on roundabouts of night & day
Gypsy-knotting a tasselled breeze, laughing
At the rain's tickle-tattoo on burning toes.

Once white-eyed stripped a comet's heated gears
On Saturn's tilted cindertrack, goaded
A whale with spears across the sagging seas,
Boomeranged birdstars with the rind of the moon;

For naught could daunt the suckling paw
Of my kitten-trying, pretty practice pawing,
Who glorioled all with galilean glamour
In prison-clamp still keeping boy-world whole.

. . . . .

On an unloved attic of land where bald hills splash,
Erosion-fear feasted in secret mouthfuls
Took hold with wide uneven lips like a slug
Steadily consumed a continent of assurance.

Lark-officials throw a few streamers
Of song as night slips slow from the wharf,
A perfunctory farewell, most asleep nor aware
Till a discus-sun startles unathletic routine.

So went the one-weaving dark & heart
Of mystery: light dashed into disparate debris
Glared, stared at the loss of the soft and supple.
The great creed plants its sap, sways hollow boughs.

Arrived heart hists rich blood at Jaffa Gate,
Heart of hearts here held firm flow
With star-steady stroke, strong silent pulsing,
Inward-peace circumambient—life-lover.

But; ah, for pseudo-celèbrant Jerusalem!
Vortex of hate-faiths, ton-candle to love-ounce,
The overprotesting exhibition, creed-fugged
Bazaar: I file church-brief, pause for a self-find.

Terry I expect has told you a bit about my kittens. They are now 6 weeks old & are simply irresistable—playing sleeping & feeding. 4 of them. Mother brings in a rabbit or two each night. One wet night I came in & felt a cold wet kitten in the box. Thinking the rain had got in I picked the poor thing up, felt no heart beat & lit a candle—a half chewed baby rabbit! The mother is now taking them for walks & their little tails wave up high in the air. They cause me great anxiety when they lie &

play on my garden. Next door Terry has been working like a tiger at his steam-engine which now goes beautifully. He is really skilful with his hands & his capacity for concentration is enormous. Yesterday he was put out on one of the scrub gangs & loathes it—poor fellow.

Well Jim I don't envy you in exam throes. This is the first year for ages that I've been spared—I expect you will go through serenely—good wishes. Also seasons blessings in case my next letter is too late—your correspondence has been a landmark for me this year—what next! What do you do with the gigantic vacations school days afford—I suppose they are well-packed with expeditions auf der Bilderjagd—image hunting as Goethe would say.[7] So again best wishes for the exams

—Regards

Noel.

[Hocken, MS 975/183]

**Baxter to Ginn, 10 December 1942**

CENSORED
No. 2

Brighton,
Otago.
10th Dec. 1942

Dear Noel,

I was very pleased to get your letter which was certainly 'full of meat'. 'October Spate' is a fine lyric but is marred here and there by a certain vagueness. The assonance-rhymes are very clever and the metaphors vivid and original—though sometimes a little bizarre. The 'warship grey submerged in the hill' gives a mind-picture which remains; and the first two lines of the second verse pick up the thread with a mastery which is strangely beautiful.

When I first read 'Overture to Unbelief' I was a little dismayed. When I read it the second time the full force and originality came on me suddenly—like turning a corner and seeing an unexpected view.

On an unloved attic of land where bald hills splash,
Erosion-fear feasted in secret mouthfuls
Took hold with wide uneven lips like a slug
Steadily consumed a continent of assurance.

7 Johann Wolfgang von Goethe (1749–1832). Goethe, in Part II, Book VII of *Dichtung und Warheit* (1775), attributes this remark to the poet Ewald Christian Kleist (1715–59) who, when taken to task for his frequent and solitary walks, explained, tongue-in-cheek, that he was not idle at such times but—*er gehe auf die Bilderjagd*—he was hunting for images.

is the stanza most perfect in form and expression.

'To climb the stile into the sky' is so simple, so easy—and yet grips one like a steel hawser.

Even in this poem you have, in parts, a style not fully formed. But the gold is there; it only means a little extra effort on the part of the reader. You let yourself go when speaking of 'Saturn's cinder-track'. Quite right, for that stanza is in a sense the climax. I will say no more criticism, and will certainly not insult you by giving didactic advice on poetical style. When one becomes used to your metaphors, they do not jar. They enthrall.

You were asking about the inset in 'Control'. That is merely an example of poetical emotion overcoming mental stability.

I enclose, as usual, many poems.

'Of the Western Highlands' refers to the Scottish Highlands. The clan life is dying out there (due chiefly to continual economic oppression but . . . 'and then the poem'.

'Him not mentioned' may strike you as macabre. 'What shall we seek for' explains itself.

'From unremembered mouths' is perhaps the best of the others. It refers to the inertia caused by racial remembrances.

Tell Terry I will be sending him a couple of new books for Xmas. Also, if possible, I will send you one. I will be writing to Terry.

I hear you have been in hospital sometimes. Remember we sympathize with you—naturally not with Mr.G.[1]

With best wishes for Xmas to all up there

From,
Your friend,
Jim.

PS Do you think that when you get out of the 'prison-clamp' you might stay with us down here for a bit.

[VUW Library, MS McKay 28/5]

**Of the Western Highlands**

This is no half-land between life and dream.
If there is a twilight it is the looming of gigantic powers.
These men, these womenfolk, are like their mountains
And smile in their dark faces the Celtic smile,
A mood of sun on the ruggedness of the mountain.
They have been set here overlong for fear—
That is for us the intruders.
Who see the twisted face in the rock-chimney

1 A reference to Leonard Greenberg who, from 1 October 1941, had been Controller-General of Defaulters Detention Camps. See p.69.

And feel in the shut-off sky a heaviness, a waiting,
And the inborn bitterness that is closer than life.
For they are behind, they are one with the double mountain:
The wind has blown over them as long as the hills.

But they will not tell to us their mountain secret,
Will smile only a dark and secret smile.
For our intrusion is no victory;
They will die and remain with the mist on the mountain
And will wait with the patient, the ageless mountains for our extinction.
[Hocken, MS 704/7:419, pp.65–6]

**Him not mentioned**[1]

Dressed to the fashion
With goggles and tan
The devil is quite a
Gentleman.

But, hurrying over
An empty street,
Hear the importunate
Muffled beat

Of a drum of wind
Sounding in hell:
Think!—for the suicide
Knows it well.

Think—for it is often
Most unpleasant to see
Outward manifestation
Of inward cautery.

Numbing the rational
Optimist brain
Is animal dread
Of the dead and insane.

God's over the angels,
The Pope is in Rome—
But death and the devil
Are always at home.
[Hocken, MS 704/7:422, pp.72–3]

1 Baxter's original title for this poem, when he entered it into MS Book VII (Hocken, MS 704/7), had been 'The man not mentioned'.

**What shall we seek for**

What shall we seek for, sweet-heart, tell me?
What shall we seek for, sweet-heart, say!
Is it power? . . . Is it power? . . . then let us away!
Ah nay.
For I saw Power but an hour ago:
His eyes were bright but his eyes were blind;
He looked into the billowing wind
But knew not whence did the sweet wind blow!

What shall we seek for, sweet-heart, tell me?
Is it the madness that poets know?
Not so, not so!
For I saw a poet an hour ago:
His head was bowed in a mist of dreams,
Nor saw by the lightning's scattering gleams
Death sing in a gorge below.

'What shall we seek for', love?
No bitter brew of time.
Power sees with eyes of hate
His strong towers desolate,
Above the turrets thunder-torn
A cylinder of storm.

Weep not for the poet: he
Has burst the globe of reverie
And found the ultimate that is
Beyond a final precipice.

Yet could they know, love,
That which we have found;
Could they break free
From the care of day
Then would be nothing of worth
But life, death, birth,
And the wind-broken [shaken(?)] ground.
[Hocken, MS 704/7:412, pp.51–2]

**From unremembered mouths**

There is no grain this season.
We hid when the hill-men raided
And came back after to find the empty caves,
The jars broken, and the fields burned black.

Some have crawled down to the river and eaten clay;
Their bellies are heavy, they are dying—
Dead spirit, dead desire
And the dead ashes of a dying fire.
Ha! here is the rain come to swell the river;
Next year new crops
But we will be dead.
The river, the cliff will stay when our ghosts are gone.

Ah! huge worlds are built.
I see in the luminous future
Knowledge of beauty on lips of all;
And steel, wood, water
Blended to a purpose
That moves with the cycle of the suns.
I see the city wonderful.

What is this lethargy?
What is this bitter root that will not be torn up?

We will die, our ghosts shall cry through empty caves
But the cold river goes on
They have killed the healer with comfort in his shoulders.
Aye! we burn them, they burn us;
We are caught in the hell-flame.
The world is a slag-heap and we are the ants
Running for food on cinders
Where there is no food.
'The aspens sway, the aspens quiver—
What of a hundred thousand drowned
In the mud of the Yellow River.'

Strange lights have broken our prison.
This is the God arisen,
The smooth-browed god of justice.
Ah! for the saintly-blessèd, the emerald throne.

But we are among the many .....
And who are these?

They are the executioners.
[Hocken, MS 704/7:421, pp.69–71]

# III
# CORRESPONDENCE: 1943

(In this my sixteenth year all other ages
Are young, half-young, or old;
But boundaries are not
Set to mine own existence, aloof and ageless)
'Monument'

> [My sister] Myrtle, the youngest one . . . married one of the [detention camp] inmates called John Woodley—they weren't married till after the war. But she was very strong in the pacifist cause, she did a lot of placard work, protesting and all that sort of thing.
>
> —Noel Ginn[1]

**Letter from Myrtle Ginn to James K. Baxter, 7 January 1943**

14 Tanguru St.,
Wanganui East.
7.1.43.

Dear Mr. Baxter,

I was recently up at the Hautu Detention Camp, visiting my brother, Noel & he asked me to send the enclosed poems to you. He left the letter open so that I could slip a note in. Noel was allowed to give these to me & they weren't to be counted as a letter, hence the reason for no covering letter from Noel. Apparently they are surviving things fairly well, up that way & are making the best of the situation. They managed to make Christmas and the New Year, festive occasions what with concerts & even a party. I hope I have done everything I was commissioned to do & not muddled them all or forgotten anything.

Yours sincerely
Myrtle Ginn.

[Hocken, MS 975/193]

[Included among the poems Myrtle Ginn forwarded to Baxter was Noel's poem, 'To Jim'.]

**To Jim**

Friend, I gather your gift to a gladness
That holds a hundred sprung surprises
Planned by eager living for a callow strayling
To woo him into loving.

Night draws back from my blazing headlamps
Pulls its soft muzzle back in dismay
That through its ambushes prepared in scented passes
My car so blandly pushes.

Time is against the glance insouciant
Pity will plead with animal eyes
Life-love topples heart in a scalding wave,
Then blasé self-love dies.

1 Noel Ginn, personal interview, 25 Oct 1994.

Half-nod at passing life's accosting
Has served till now, enough! Civility
Of fur and petal, feather and friend shall have
A greet of richer metal.
[Hocken, MS 975/30]

**Baxter to Ginn, 16 January 1943**

Brighton,
Otago,
16th January 1943.

Dear Noel,

Thank you very much for the poems sent on by your sister. They have not quite the force of 'Overture to Unbelief', or rather they have a different kind of force. 'To Jim' is, I think, the best. 'To Noel' is here enclosed.

'Where beauty dips to dust' means 'where beauty puts on the clothing of inanimate matter'. 'The Mountains' refers to the landscape around Naseby, Central Otago, where I spent part of these holidays.

'Prometheus' is the symbol of man tied to the present, both moving and still. The 'soldier-ants' are the moments of the future. The 'crows' are memories of past moments rendering man unable to face the present.

I hope I have not already sent you the 'Storm-Centre' which I wrote some time ago. Here also the problem of Time is the dominant theme.

I think that your own poetry is steadily progressing—in this way, if you follow what I mean.

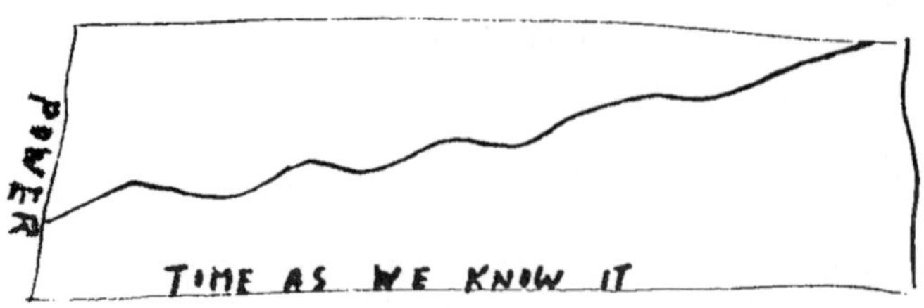


Of course a graph is a poor means of expression, as it is entirely unemotional, whereas the essence of poetry is emotion.

My poems will speak to you better than I do. Remember I like to hear from you as often as possible.

With best wishes for 1943, chaotic though it may be,

Jim.

[VUW Library, MS McKay 28/6]

**To Noel Ginn**

Friend, I have listened with gladness
    To speech from lungs uncankered,
    In metre cast and clinkered
The strum of a deep-sea sadness;

The languor of the prisoner
    Swollen balloon-like in metrical moulding:
    No ore of my smelting
Makes stronger piston-jar.

O this were well! but the subtle corrosion
    Of further inertia, of deeper despair
    May bid this freshet appear
    Turgid, impure
    To the arc-light of reason.

Do not believe it—
    The cynical civil prompting
    Nor puerile regret slow-sobbing
For broken bolt and rivet.

While self holds
    New faith for founding
    Emotional understanding,

Even if images are
    Only those of despair,
    Nothing shall move the free
Facile integrity.
        [Hocken, MS 704/7:444, pp.116–17]

**Where beauty dips to dust**

Where beauty dips to dust where the mind's flower
Is nearest to the clay material
Whence limbs and lips of motion fashioned are:

No need to see eyes glare from finger-nail
White disembodied eyes to symbolize
Converging of transitory sight and seeking hands grown still.

Where beauty dips to dust moon-mountains rise
To blot the city in their quietude—
Nearest to death this side of death are these

So quench the search-light mind with overt tragedy
Silencing the slick waltz the easy blood.
Rather would I by trivial currents flow:

Laugh with a cracked skull on the mantlepiece.
Time to grow quiet time to ceasing clowning when dead.

Love is the flower where beauty dips to dust
Love with a laughing lung attractive face
Makes human the inferno of the lost.

So laugh or merrily sigh for a space.
The noose that waits, the silk or iron thongs . . .
Swing cap and bells though beauty dip to dust:
Death is a king, song is the king of kings.

Death love and song are one.
Death swings his scythe a slouching egotist
Love lies i' the sun though iron whelm our ways
Song sings alike priest or iconoclast.

Each makes in Hell, in Heaven a free and total ease.
[Hocken, MS 704/7:442, pp.113–14]

**The Mountains**

In this scarred country, this cold threshold land
The mountains crouch like tigers. By the sea,
~~They~~ Folk talk of them hid vaguely out of sight;
But here they stand in massed solidity
To seize upon the day and night horizon.

Men shut within a whelming bowl of hills
Grow strange, say little when they leave their high
Yet buried homesteads; return there silently
When thunder of night-rivers fills the sky
And giant wings brood over loftily and near.

The mountains crouch like tigers—or await
As women wait. The mountains have no age.
But O the heart leaps to behold them loom:
A sense as of vast fate rings in the blood; no refuge,
No refuge is there from the flame that reaches

Among familiar things and makes them seem
Trivial, vain. O spirit walks on the peaks;

Eye glances across a gorge to further crags.
There is no desire: but the stream, but the avalanche speaks
And their word is louder than freedom, the mountain embrace
Were a death dearer than freedom or freedom's flags.

I will go to the coast-line and mingle with men.
These mountain buttresses build beyond the horizon;
They call: but he whom they lay their spell upon
Leaves home, leaves kindred. The range of the telescope's eye
Is well—if the brain follows not to the outermost fields of vision.
I shall drown myself in humanity: better to lie
Dumb in the city than under the mountainous wavering sky.

The mountains crouch like tigers.
They are but stone yet the seeking eyes grow blind.
[Hocken, MS 704/7:437, pp.102–4]

**Prometheus**[1]

O bitter to move freely yet know
as thought of the serpent is still and venomous
though sliding smooth to his animal lair—
O bitter to move usually yet see
Time closed a circle in perfect symmetry
perfect though the entrails the brains of us
are spilt to the objective sea and air.
Moments unfelt     moments of anguish
moments of martyrdom of sensuous feeling
march with insect jaws to seize upon me

Inhuman insect eyes and jaws like daggers
~~ordered~~ serried convulsive as the spring of tigers
the soldier-ants advance—resistance unavailing—
on the white marble of futurity.

They have beaten their track through timber and town:
The savage sees them not     knows but
their gashes
            their bite at the moment
when it is useless to maintain
the stoic front; to dread to pain
when personal emotion meets a shut
indifference to emotion:

1 A later poem, also titled 'Prometheus', is in MS Book XIV (Hocken, MS 704/14: 899). This poem has been published in *Book* 7 (Feb 1946): 26; in *BWF*, p.16; and in *CP*, p.35.

Dreading the sharp advance, the soldier-ants
the moments separate in each similar shell
moments of fire moments of charity
of clarity
exploding to equal disillusionment:
In self-oblivion, in suicide I went
threw myself under the moment's knife—without avail:
Behold! the idiot crows of memory

Obscene savage cawing incessantly
like leathern vultures from exploded past
past shrunk to shards to a sea-buried rubble
the bleak mnemonic crows perch on my liver
destroy the ant invaders as they come.
I Prometheus under a sky of stone
bare brain and entrails to the objective sand-blast
eyes fettered seeing stone and sky only
here wait, endure, sans even the hate
of enemy or love of lover.
The legions of the stone futurity
The crowding of the birds of memory.

[Hocken, MS 704/7:441, pp.110–12]

**The Storm-Centre**

I lie at the centre of time
the storm-centre:
there are a thousand centres to each time
each is the same
Only in love two postures are the same
two centres exactly coincide at a single centre.

These rising pyramids
of waves move me not
only the bullet will move me
bullet of death bullet of violence:
the bullet as yet comes not—
who knows, perhaps then
only a change of position a trek
to another centre
ultimately the same centre.

We are immovable,
seemingly shooting the enormous breaker—
'what shore, what cliffs seen vaguely

through fog?'—The dead
see us upon Time's breaker
but we are immovable
or petrify to the attitude of death
stare through the crystal of death
before Death.

There are three ways:—
warm in the tombing soundless ~~of water~~ pyramids
of ~~snowy~~ water     of snowy water
wherein some seek the snow-death
I contemplate three ways.

To remain immovable is not a way
it is the static present posture:
to fall in snow-death is not a way
it is of the dead     it is the dead.

There are three ways:—
to plunge into the leaping the whirling pyramid
the cubist formlessness of pyramids;
slough intellect
as a snake's slough lost in water
Break through the bubble perhaps
and remain entombed in water;
or be borne a corpse by currents
or find ultimate satisfaction
or again make a new storm-centre
and find the ways
which are not ways.

To rise above the steaming combat
to be wise above the steaming combat
in a funnel of crashing rain
dry, unharmed by the rain;
to hold the feet of the eagle of intellect
perhaps to find the funnel contract
to ultimate and final destruction
Which is not a way:
or expand to a new quiet storm-centre
of heaven.

Or the third way:—
to pass into a glass container of self
renounce love hate
unbreakable—

enter the walls of the centre
when then within this bubble
is a smaller a new storm-centre;
or the unbreakable walls
strike the existent and eternal cliff
and break to annihilation . . .

Stay, stay
some voice has arrested me
Is there a fourth?
a combination of a thousand modes:—
to bid the walls burst
to emerge into a timeless not ultimate sea
not of death, but of oneness with the sea.
Not of the attitude of the dead, but an enlargement
of the human attitude.
Ay . . . the storm-centre . . . no,
not central but enveloping.

There is a healing mountain
From whose sides flow not lava but water
Not bitter with soluble salts but snow-water,
Without death.
I have swum in the sea
I have come from the sea,
unchilled.
Thither is shade thither are birds
Not ultimate sated satisfaction
Of a full belly  but a losing of centre
~~And~~ Expansion to a wished-for horizon.

[Hocken, MS 704/7:433, pp.91–5]

**Baxter to Ginn, 22 January 1943**

CENSORED
No. 3

Brighton,
Otago,
22nd January 1943

Dear Noel,

Many thanks for your letter. I see your poems more clearly in view of what you have told me. 'Never stop writing except when you want to' is my own motto and the result is that among twenty poems of mine there are 18 of varying quality, one trash and one really good. Incidentally, the one 'really good' usually expresses strong emotion, the one 'trash' is emotionless obscurist jargon.

I have read the 'Story of Gösta Berling'. It struck me as over-fantastic and didactic in parts, but there is a certain understanding and ~~humaness~~ human-ness that makes it beautiful.[1]

Also have read criticisms on and explanations of Blake, and re-read him in the light of them. Found no trace of madness but only the workings of a clear, strong, imaginative mind and faculty—e.g. The Tiger—of poetic expression rarely equalled.

My heart's desire—or almost—is to visit Europe after this bloody chaos has subsided. I don't know why. Perhaps youthful desire for excitement. Perhaps the obvious sparsity of intelligence among NZers—excluding you and a good few, who don't appear the typical New Zealand products. Again, I may be too hard on them. They may know intellect for what it's worth. But if I start thinking that way I won't write any more poetry. At any rate they took conscription lying down, merely trying to crawl into essential industries, when they could have led all the satellites of Britain toward neutrality. If this had happened perhaps Britain would not have declared war, but made the obvious and eventually unavoidable negotiations. Anyway the New Zealanders at present being smashed up would be out of it.

Read the 'Clown' not as poetry but satire. Read 'Judas' for the second line. The following is part truth part satire.

**The Moon knows not**

The moon knows not that she is globular
Speed O ye saints and devils, speed and tell her!
And she perchance waked to divinest reason
Will curse the bitter task of tide and season.

And I likewise would sleep a while in my
Unreasoned map of summer, earth and sky:
Beauty flits through no corridors of fate
I shedding time shall slumber at her feet
Till human voices wake me and I die.

Or yet—seeing the white birds flying over
Shall walk with them beyond the diamond river
Leaving death staring from green hill-side
While nether fountains whelm him and deride.

1 *Gösta Berlings saga* (1891), written by Swedish author Selma [Ottiliana Lovisa] Lagerlöf (1858–1940), was translated into English in 1898. Based on the folk tales of her home province, Värmland, *Gösta Berlings saga* made Lagerlöf world famous and its success allowed her to devote herself full-time to writing. In 1909 she received the Nobel Prize and, in 1914, became the first woman admitted to the Swedish Academy.

Fools! who would wake Truth from divine unreason
To bitter toil of tempest, time and season:
All these are but the bruisèd feet of her.
The Moon knows not that she is globular.

Tell Terry that my mother got his letter, and give him my love (cautiously.)
With best wishes
From
Jim.

PS Miss Ockenden was a teacher of mine at Friends' School, Wanganui, and a friend of my parents; though, as I cannot yet sing in tune, I fear I was a refractory pupil. J.K.B.

[VUW Library, MS McKay 28/7]

**The Clown**

'Thou art craven', caws the raven.
'Song and the brief courts of heaven,
Silken solidarity
Pleasing to the hand and eye
Shatter, tumble, sink, and die!'

Dread and moaning comes with morning:
Sprout steel shards without a meaning
From the bird-enchanted tree;
Bole and branches reft or dry
Shatter, tumble, sink, and die!

Serpents iron, glaring neon
And the gray relentless lion
Rise with pale and stony eye
While the fruits of reverie
In the white synthetic sea
Shatter, tumble, sink, and die.

'Thou art craven' caws the raven,
But I live for aeons seven
While the human man and woman
Under a stony savage sky
Bare and bony, broken lie.

I am the clown, the clown am I!
I am the clown who cannot die.

[Hocken, MS 704/7:449, pp.125–6]

**Judas**

I sing
I sing the truth of poetry which is likewise the truth of humanity.
Of Judas Iscariot.

Of Judas the traitor
Of Judas eternally condemned
Of Judas in the lowest inferno.

Of Judas the man who lived as a man who loved as a man
Of Judas the patriot desiring freedom above all.
Of Judas softened by the words of Christ
Of Judas reviling his weakness.

Of Judas saying: if he be the Christ
He will raise up an army of angels
And overwhelm those who come against him
And lead the Chosen to their ancient station.

Of Judas to whom came understanding
And remorse eternal, the savage remorse of the fiery-hearted.

There is the agony of Christ.
There is the agony of Judas.

It is not in the glorified that we may see Christ.
It is in the unfulfilled, in the erring that Christ strives.
We who see the Christ in a sleeping child
Was Judas never a child?
Shall we not see the Christ in the man
Shall we not see the Christ in Judas?
In Judas who was a man
A fiery passionate man
Who failed from a man's passion
O passionate heart that threw back the silver
Of the puny-hearted.

He is the Christ unfulfilled.
Of Judas I sing
Of Judas Iscariot

Of Man I sing
Who is man    Judas the passionate    Christ Judas
Who is Christ    Christ the compassionate    Christ Jesus
Of Judas I sing.
[Hocken, MS 704/7:455, pp.136–8]

**In Barley-Fields**

O eyes O brazen mirrors doomed fore-doomed
To flash the neural meshes of the brain
Onto a screen of landscape seen in flashes
    Or never seen.

Why have you thus taken unnatural life
Conversed and spoken to me from another's skull?
I am blinded by your messages.

Ears dredging the feckless air for thought
Why have your tendrils turned to eyes that see her,
Betraying me,
As she walks bright in the bearded rippling barley
Golden, impulsive, waked from their reverie.

Life cling to the lips of a flower; or spirit
Grecian and animal rises
To walk with her in eternal emotion
Through the grave courtier ranks of barley.

Though I be a hundred mile away
My love and I walk tranquilly
Amid the unbroken barley.
        [Hocken MS 704/7:451, pp.129–30]

**Baxter to Ginn, 12 February 1943**

CENSORED
No. 3

Brighton,
Otago,
12th February 1943.

Dear Noel—

You have hit me rather hard, and you are right in everything you said regarding me. My poems are uneven in quality, because I write many of them in a state of mental inertia. Those, of course, are not poems. When I go to it with a real idea, the result is not obscurity but clarity. e.g. 'Judas.' Examine, however, the 1st and last verses of 'Storm-Centre.' They are, I think, moderately good. 'Barley-Fields' does not refer to anyone anymore than the universal 'To Chloris' of the late Elizabethans (or probably Carolinians.)[1]

About short pants at Friends' School. Owing to the rules of my present school I will wear them for another year. If you had seen me then I would probably have replied in monosyllables or shown signs of apparent deficiency.[2] At that time I was very loath to expose my verse to the private or public eye, as I had sensed early the morbid fear of poetic expression which so many have.

It is strange you should speak about pain. I have been going to the dentist for a day or two, and so it is occupying my mind somewhat. In the dentist's chair one feels the urgent need for another channel for release of energy and attention—hence the squirming.

The first verse of your sonnet seems to me perfect in its vigour and personal clarity.[3] I am envious of you. It is all clever and has at any rate the appearance of truth—i.e. it is an artistic truth. I had thought—hear my confession—some of your poems not suitable for print, not for a lack of poetry but for their too unheeding and 'personal' vigour. I have since read some of the 'many currents of modern poetry' and revise my opinion entirely. You, unlike most of them, are not dominated by either jingoism or jargon.

About my frequent mental inertia. Here is a plain poem on it.

**O spirit stand in my eyes**

O spirit stand in my eyes
Do not retreat, do not retreat!

See earth and the dwellers therein
As they are;
Seek not to discover the mystery of the flower
But see the flower as it is
(Not as men see it
In abstract or erroneous reality
But as the life in it makes.)

O spirit stand in my eyes
Wonder continually, feel deeply,
Do not reflect over-much

1 Although Chloris features conventionally in the poetry of the late Elizabethan age and the Caroline age—like the woman of Baxter's 'In Barley-Fields'—as an ideal, often remote, mistress of pale, pastoral delicacy, the origins of such a representation can be traced back to Horace, *Odes* II.5: '. . . and be more doted on / Than Chloris was whose white neck shone / Like a clear moon in the night sea'. Poems directly addressing Chloris were most prolific in the Restoration age—the poet Charles Cotton, for example, in the second verse of his 'ODE. To Chloris' (1689), declaims 'Chloris, how are you to blame, / To him that dies to be so cruel / Not to stay my falling frame, / Since your fair eyes do dart the fuel / That still nourishes my flame?' The tradition continued through the 18th and 19th centuries. Even Robert Burns, one of the Baxter's favourite poets, helped perpetuate it with his poems 'My Chloris' and 'Ah, Chloris, since it may not be'.

2 Ginn, who grew up in Wanganui, may have been recalling the pupils he would have seen attending the Quaker 'Friends' School' on Wanganui's St. John's Hill, where Baxter was enrolled on two separate occasions: firstly as a day student in 1935–36 and then, following the family's return from England, as a boarder in 1939. The tendency Baxter recalls, to project an image of 'apparent deficiency', could have been due, in part, to his unhappiness while at the school, particularly in 1939 when 'a difficult guerrilla warfare developed between me and the headmaster' [see *Man on the Horse* pp.132–6].

3 See 'Sonnet' on pp.515–16.

For fear the bolt will click
To false, to cloudy untruth

Whence comes the siren calling
The black bomb falling
The flaming house the dying voices calling.

O spirit stand in my eyes
We carry in us continually
Over the desolate fields of imagination
Over the desolate lands
    A bitter desire for extinction—
That we may thus find reality.
    A bitter fear of extinction
Since we may thus lose
Even the shards we clutch.
    Why the continual corrosion?
The formula is simple:
'O spirit stand in my eyes.'

. . . And thou shalt see men as life
Which it is unthinkable to destroy.

That which is set truly in me
That which is I
Will distinguish truth and falsity
Will find it impossible to fear
Canst thou fear aught existing
When naught existing can sow in thee
The seed of extinction?

Love and pity will follow
As spring with the swallow.
    The power of the animal,
    The diffuse intensity of man.

O spirit stand in my eyes!
Do not retreat.

Also.

**The Silver Fish**

The silver fish
    Thrown out of the stream
Into the stony
    Day's gleam

Speaks words of forgiveness
    To the cold fisher:
She dies in despairing,
    He fishes at leisure.

About NZ poetry. I am not crying it down. But I ~~find in~~ find in poetry a vivid expression of emotion which does not occur in prose. Therefore, as I do not find this in much NZ poetry it is not, to me, poetry. The solution, of course, is not to run away but to start a Revolution.

I am now going for Higher Leaving Certificate[4] and intend eventually to become a lawyer.[5] Try to show Terry somehow that he must accept his fellows to some extent. That true escape is impossible, but that relief from a sense of confinement may be found in many forms of self-expression. The world as we know it IS human relationship. Of course, he feels this anyway but is oversensitive to the attitudes and feelings of people. Remind him that Tolstoy lives yet (in the true sense of living—i.e. in the minds of others) and exerts a continual influence on many people.

With best wishes from
Jim.

[MS VUW Library, McKay 28/8]

**The Lie**

The Lie is planted, the Lie will flourish
    The Lie will sprout as a poison tree
Truth, relegated the poorest parish
    Will starve in secret, in secret die.

The children are happy, the children are playing
    The children come home from the cowboy film
What was that sound sudden and sighing?
    A bomb perhaps, in the evening calm.

As yet there is nothing new to be seen.
    But over the topmost Gothic steeple
    Over the heads of the hurrying people
    The Devil has put his hand on the sun.

What shall we do? What shall we do?
    The Lie bears fruit as a poison tree
    The fruit is purple, the fruit is ripe

4 The Higher Leaving Certificate was awarded to students who had successfully completed a further year of schooling once qualifying for University Entrance: holders of the certificate were usually entitled to a fees and allowances bursary for full-time university study.

5 When enrolling at King's High School in 1940 Baxter was required to nominate a course of study and a future profession: he opted for the 'Professional' course and for 'Law' as his vocational choice, and does not appear to have seriously questioned this path until prompted to by Ginn's letter of 5 March 1943 (see pp.197–8).

It has filled the dark with a night-mare's gripe
Its roots are ridging the streets of our city.

The Lie is planted, the Lie has flourished
The Lie bears fruit as a poison tree
Truth, out of work, has gone on the parish
There's a sky of blood, there's a shout on high:
'Truth has perished, the world must die!'
[Hocken, MS 704/8:482, pp.39–40]

**The Kiln**

The night-owl master-singer
of midnight mood ~~sobs~~ tolls himself to silence
in nearby woods whose leaves are lashes on
the immense and unsecretive eye of night.

Herein seek not the streams of Helicon:
humid and continental darkness
draws back the night-mare forests out of time.

Under a moon that lit the streets of Rome
the kiln breathes out dry vapours through a placid
air seemingly more bright than noon-day.

The quarry-hollows gaping colourless mouths and dry
call to the caverned kiln that it might come,
like them be earth eternal and like them
to fear and faceless shadows a heart and womb.

The kiln beats back the moon-light: so at dawn
a squat Egyptian temple caught the sun
mirrored Man's challenge to be seen
by eyes inanimate.
The night-owl hoots
and from the sea of bark and coiling shadows

flits heavily over the harsh clay-meadows
below the quarry. The square and funnelled kiln
waits; till the unwary bird

Lurches through smoke of the lime-burning
Crumples and spins to the poisonous fuming:
The night-owl master-singer
of midnight mood.
[Hocken, MS 704/8:479, pp.35–6]

**Why ring no chime?**

Why ring no chime, why bury the suicide
Throat slit with the keen phlegmatic razor
Coffinless under a stone or iron vizor?
    Why bury him deeper than the other dead?

    The man who rides a metal hurricane
Who drowns a living foeman deep and leaden,
And flaming falls: is the more dead and sodden
    Than the mild lunatic dying unseen.

    Death gripped him twice: once when he rose and slew
A man of equal beauty; rigor mortis
Then held him past the rank of warring parties.
    Murder, not suicide he knew.

    He the most human, doubly suicidal
Died twice. Once in his young youth-dreaming brother,
Once when the flames caught him to burn or smother.
    His oceanic death is vast and tidal.

The shells have sung to him a passing chime.
Perhaps beyond a palisade of time
He meets his twin of death, and no word said
Knows that intense heart-rending suicide.
        [Hocken, MS 704/8:473, pp.20–21]

**The Boat**

On deck I lie—
Palms, cheek and body pressed to the smooth wood
Palms pressed to the curving deck—
As if cast up from waves and sea-wrack
On sunned and sloping sand.
                                        In strange perspective
I see the crannies the haunts of summer gulls—
The sheer rock from deep water
Looming, bruising the low-hung sky.
No men visit these cliffs and tide-worn sea-caves;
Only the gulls swoop down to waves to surf
Fearlessly. I am bound
To the warm back of a bird: the air-filled cabins
Are light are buoyant beneath me.
I, embracing the curved deck

Merge into the soul of the vessel.
The strain and stress in the cordage is the same
As the strain in my tightened tendons.
O soul beneficent
Male in the eagerness that springs in the winds' eye
Female in unreasoned integrity in enclosing comfort;
Loving, beautiful, flawless and beautiful—
With a soul and beauty surpassing the skill
Of thy maker, the hesitant craftsman—
Rejoicing with me
In the running slap of spray on the bow.

Who would not sorrow at the death of a ship
More deeply than at the death of a friend?—
The friend has lost no personality
But the hulk is lonely; calls out,
Calls out through windy nights, through days
Of flying spume
For a hand on the tiller
For the free lifting from shore-shallows
Under the steady sun
Into the changing infinite sea.
Better to sink to annihilation
To break on cold and submarine ridges
While over      the sea changes not.

Each beam I know
Each beam I love for strength and perfection.
    O boat beloved
    Bear me on your bird's breast
    Bear me in understanding, in loyalty and love
    In security
    Over the infinite unknown
In security over the spray-torn shouting sea.
        [Hocken, MS 704/8:466, pp.7–9]

**Ginn to Baxter, 5 March 1943**

CENSORED
No. 5

c/- Nat Service Dept
Hautu Turangi
via Nat Park
5/3/43.

Dear Jim—

Terry showed me your matric marks which you sent up & at first I was quite surprised they were not higher, especially in English, but considering all things, your extreme preoccupation with poetry, the vagaries of any exam system & perhaps your being unable to muster up your knowledge to do justice to yourself, I think you have done most satisfactorily. You didn't flop in any subject I notice. I took H.L. certificate but it is a nuisance in demanding so many subjects. So you propose to become a lawyer—this caused me a pang of regret on first reading it but perhaps unnecessarily. The field of professions is so limited & any choice is governed by so many obtruding factors that vocation selecting is often a painful process. Ways open later but on that grave moment of deliberate decision a destiny seems to hang. I must explain myself when I say I regretted it if only to let you know my interest (is it interference?) in your activities. I can see no inner sanction at all in the Law nor on the other hand can I agree that the manifestations of evil should be passively endured. This is a paradox & like the big questions of life it cannot be solved in terms of nature and common sense. There is only one reality, which is beyond good & evil—what we perceive is a most strangulated & fragmentary distortion. Thus while we dwell in & accept our

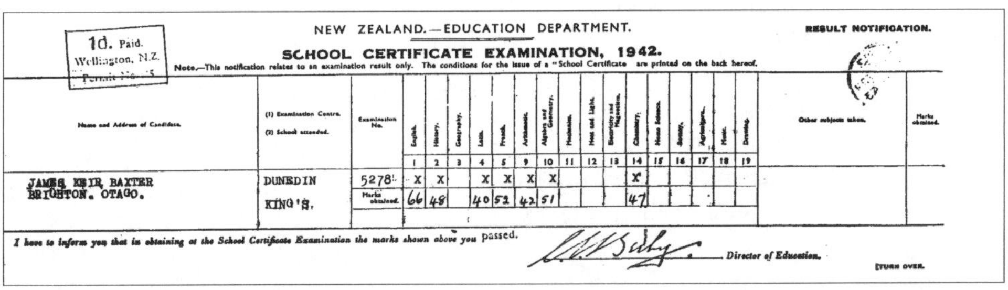
1d. Paid.
Wellington, N.Z.
Permit No. 5

NEW ZEALAND.—EDUCATION DEPARTMENT.

RESULT NOTIFICATION.

SCHOOL CERTIFICATE EXAMINATION, 1942.

Note.—This notification relates to an examination result only. The conditions for the issue of a "School Certificate" are printed on the back hereof.

| Name and Address of Candidate. | (1) Examination Centre. (2) School attended. | Examination No. | English. 1 | History. 2 | Geography. 3 | Latin. 4 | French. 5 | Arithmetic. 9 | Algebra and Geometry. 10 | Mechanics. 11 | Heat and Light. 12 | Electricity and Magnetism. 13 | Chemistry. 14 | Home Science. 15 | Botany. 16 | Agriculture. 17 | Music. 18 | Drawing. 19 | Other subjects taken. | Marks obtained. |
|---|---|---|---|---|---|---|---|---|---|---|---|---|---|---|---|---|---|---|---|---|
| JAMES KEIR BAXTER BRIGHTON. OTAGO. | DUNEDIN KING'S. | 5278 | X | X | | X | X | X | X | | | | X | | | | | | | |
| | | Marks obtained. | 66 | 48 | | 40 | 52 | 42 | 51 | | | | 47 | | | | | | | |

*I have to inform you that in obtaining at the School Certificate Examination the marks shown above you* passed.

[signature] *Director of Education.*

[TURN OVER.

Baxter's University Entrance Results: 'My exam marks were certainly nothing spectacular. But the course is, strictly, 4-year so one can hardly do justice to oneself in three.' Baxter matriculated in the fifth form because the Matriculation Examination for entrance to university could, prior to 1945, be taken at the same time as the School Certificate Examination, in either the fifth or sixth form. For the nineteen 'University Entrance subjects that were common also to the School Certificate examination the subject prescriptions and examination papers were identical'. [Source: *Report of the Commission on Education in New Zealand: July 1962* (Wellington: Government Printer, 1962) pp.210, 795.]
[Hocken MS 975/187]

world of perception as the final picture we have to live under the Law. There are a few rare souls who achieve a technique of becoming in full-orbed wholeness creatures of reality. They live above the Law. The Law is the will of the effective majority—in the main it makes for the preservation & effective maintenance of the group. It can have no vision of the true ends of life, it cannot affirm the fact of individual personality. It is the great conservative force & its sanction is inherently the military sanction. Yet I cannot say it is unnecessary for man at his present stage—all I can do is to suggest some laws are better than others, or worse. Law saves from anarchy but seems powerless to create—it has no psychiatry. So I imagined you would grow into some prophetic role with your gifts, particularly your psychological insight, instead of helping to administer something impersonal & status-quo-ish. Which is a very foolish thought on my part as though you had deliberately decided to do something less than the true promptings of your mind. You will grow into the problems of the Law & I hope be able to resolve the paradox of Law & Freedom—perhaps you will be another Mahatma[1] . . . I quite enjoyed the law subjects in the BCom course I took, Merc law, bankruptcy, companies & trustee law.[2] It should make for very clear thinking.

However that is enough about that subject for the time. I have been reading some poems of Curnow & Mason lately & though what I have read was slight I can see that they have something. Curnow in *Island & Time* seems to create a pseudo-mystic connection of NZ & time. The thought is interesting mainly because of the isolation in this huge ocean but I don't think it will bear much fruit. 'Mountain Rhapsody' is really beautiful, *Recall to Earth* is very good & 'NZ City' is quite fresh & suddenly true. His love poem 'A Woman in Mind' is very attractive.[3] Mason does not show up so well in the few things of his I saw—stop I was thinking of another writer whose name I forget. Mason wrote 'New Life'—do you know it I like its rhythm and will quote it in case you don't know it.

> Before I found
>     how it is ungainly
>     to stand your ground
>     and struggle vainly
>
> Have my assurance
>     that I have known
>     sweatstreaked endurance
>     and screech of the bone

1 Mahatma, meaning 'great soul', was the term by which Mohandas Karamchand Gandhi (1868–1948) was affectionately known. Trained as a lawyer, Gandhi practised for some time in South Africa, where he worked to end discrimination against Indians by promoting the use of non-violent resistance, or civil disobedience, which he called *satyagraha* (meaning 'truth-' or 'soul-force'). Because of his successful promotion of similar forms of resistance to British rule upon his return to India—particularly in the wake of the 1919 Amritsar Massacre which turned him into a determined opponent of the British Empire—Gandhi became known as the father of independent India.

2 Ginn completed nine units towards a Bachelor of Commerce degree before going to work as the accountant in his father's furniture business (see p.37).

3 Although Ginn criticises Allen Curnow's volume *Island & Time* (Christchurch: Caxton Press, 1941), the poems he goes on to discuss are from *Enemies: Poems 1934–36* (Caxton, 1937).

I have stripped for the fight
    I have stripped for the main
    I have stripped for lovenight
    I shall not strip again.

Where the captains of events
    charged hordes & were shattered
    stand Time's stone regiments
    brave-brain-bespattered

Negro-softly hard
    bonelicked clean of desire's
    least hint comes knots charred
    from ancient fires

Now entertain no slow
    dark cynic blood
    veins which, I pray, no flow
    of zeal may flow

His 'Fugue' & 'Payment' too are interesting.[4] It must have been a bit disappointing for you to get that bleak criticism from me without my being present to make sure what I meant was understood. On the whole I can say (& I am fairly elementary in my appreciations) that you certainly produce some grand poems out of every batch I have seen. Unevenness there is but it is right to keep the mechanism in used, fit & well kept, in order that it can do its part when the wave of inspiration comes. T.S. Eliot affirms this in his introduction to a book of selections of Ezra Pound's poetry which I am now reading (perhaps you used the same book when you read him recently).[5] Yes I have been through 'Storm Centre' a few times more & have to admit that there is quite a depth of thought in the two stanzas you mentioned which I did not suspect before, in fact the whole poem bears close examination. This free verse is new to me & I have found it very hard to gear into. You are right about the extreme personal note in the verses I have written. It is more a pathological than a personal quality. It is this quality & gift for seeing things as a whole which I called psycho-logical insight that I find very clearly in your 'O Spirit Stand in my eyes'—& it is because of this that I made my remarks on the law. All your last lot of poems were good—I like 'The Lie', 'The Kiln' & 'Why ring no chime' the best in that order. Your reverie on the boat is most pleasing & shows a very good grasp of prose style.

4 The poems mentioned are from R.A.K. Mason's small booklet of six poems, *End of Day* (Christchurch: Caxton Press, 1936). 'New Life', as quoted, contains some minor inaccuracies.

5 Eliot's comments on the importance of a poet keeping 'in training' appear in page xviii of his introduction to *Ezra Pound: Selected Poems* (London: Faber & Faber, 1934): 'the poet must be working; he must be experimenting and trying his technique so that it will be ready, like a well-oiled fire-engine, when the moment comes to strain it to its utmost'.

Did you know that a group of NZ writers have commenced a venture very similar to *New Writing in Europe*.[6] The format of the publication is copied, the title is *New Writing in NZ*—Kiwi books. The editor is Prof. Ian Gordon whom I met at varsity. He is the English prof—a few years out from Edinburgh, a most charming man with a delightful Scotch tongue—highland not lowland. You might get in touch with him if you are keen on publication. His address is c/- Victoria College Kelburn Wgtn. I feel he would be very much interested in your work. Best of wishes if you do.[7]

Terry had a fall the other day. He jumped at a set of scales with his hands & the wire which was holding it straightened out landing him flat on his back. The scales hit him on the bony part of the eye socket & the back of his head struck a dixy.[8] Apart from a scare & a thick head for a couple of days he is suffering no ill effects. He gave me some of your mother's almond-sweet biscuits & I'll say she is a good cook. Well I've left this letter till the last minute & am struggling with it on my knees while my black kitten makes purring love all over me—paper & all. Last week I reread your Father's book & must say it helps one maintain a better perspective[9] I'm afraid I've been very disjointed this time. I am very grateful for your letters & hope to hear from you soon

Your friend
Noel.

[Hocken, MS 975/183]

**Baxter to Ginn, 14 March 1943**

CENSORED
No. 2

14th March 1943,
Brighton,
Otago.

Dear Noel,

Many thanks for your letter. About my being a lawyer: I'm not decided on that, for if I see any chance of a job as lecturer or literary critic I'll go for it. The ideal, of course, is Professor of Poetry—but after all, that might lead to narrow-mindedness even more than law. The rôle of a prophet is a delectable one but would not provide one with a living. However, first and foremost, I will NOT sell my soul. Be easy on

6 Simply known as *New Writing*, this book-periodical was published approximately twice yearly, from 1936 to 1940, by J. Lehmann. From 1940 onwards its title changed, and it received some competition from the monthly (later quarterly) publication *Penguin New Writing*.

7 Baxter did send some poems to *New Zealand New Writing*, but heard nothing back from Professor Ian Gordon. See Baxter's letter of November 1943 and Gordon's comment in footnote 3 (p.292).

8 More commonly spelled 'dixie': an iron cooking pot traditionally used by soldiers.

9 Archibald Baxter's *We Will Not Cease*, recounting his experiences as a conscientious objector during WWI, was first published in London by Victor Gollancz (1939). See 'Paths to Detention', pp.29–35, where some of the background to the book, and Ginn's response on first reading it, is discussed.

that point. If I should find it possible to live by writing I would gladly do so. Yet many men have thought they could, and found it an illusion.

My exam marks were certainly nothing spectacular. But the course is, strictly, 4-year so one can hardly do justice to oneself in three. Also we have had continual changes of teachers—male and female—upsetting the regular syllabus. I have never been brilliant in Latin, Mathematics, or History. French I like quite well but I am not good in the grammar. Science was a flop from my usual. Most important, the English exam was what is popularly known as a 'stinker.' None in my class beat me, some got marks like 28, 33, 38, in it.

Concerning the Law. It is true that 'the manifestations of evil cannot be passively endured'. Yet the seditious man is no criminal, is usually more 'good' than his judges; the thief (not kleptomaniac) is the natural product of our economic system; the murderer has the precedent of war; the sexual criminal is put off balance by environment, by our mad warping 'civilization'; the smuggler, racketeer etc. is only a go-getter business-man. Governments do their utmost to plant in us the inability to put ourselves in the place of others: we must fight this, fight this till we die, die fighting it. Perhaps the barrister has a place. He is in the system, tries to protect a few from the unrighteous punishments of the system, which destroy warped humanity and strengthen, not destroy, warping influences. Anyway, Law is a dirty business. I'll do my best to keep out of it. The only reason I consider it is that I might be a good lawyer, I am human, so will often fall from it, but to me the only true law is the Xtian one—Humanity, humanity, and again humanity. This casts out pain and evil, but not those influenced by pain and evil. Doubts as to the existence of a God do not destroy this Law. In the legal system I see, as you see the utter lack of psychiatry, the inhumanity of humans.

In the words of a man influenced by the powerful, poetic (yet blinding) emotion of indignation: 'But this I know, that every Law that men have made for Man, since first Man took his brother's life, and the sad world began, but straws the wheat and saves the chaff with a most evil fan.'[1]

Here is a poem in the style of Mason.

1 In hills of stone
  walking and dreaming
  saw I hell overthrown
  and bayonets gleaming.

2 O song of the Saxon—
  caressed by spring air

1 Baxter was wary enough of the camp censors to disguise these lines from Oscar Wilde's [1854–1900] poem 'The Ballad of Reading Gaol' (section 5, verse 2). The stanza preceding the verse Baxter quotes would have seemed particularly relevant to the situation of Terence and Noel:

I know not whether laws be right,
Or whether Laws be wrong
All that we know who lie in gaol
  Is that the wall is strong;
And that each day is like a year,
  A year whose days are long.

the hound-harried vixen
is bloody and bare.

3 Through the new corn
dead lovers are sighing:
no faith is reborn
but the burden of dying.

4 Saw I hell broken
The Devil in prison—
like saplings wind-shaken
new hells are arisen.

5 In hills of stone
I waked from my dreaming
heard song of the bone
where madmen were screaming.

Another one.

Fracturing the stolid hours of mid-night
Saw I the ghost of one loved since as a child;
And knew, by the ragged wounds wherewith he was wealed
That he was among the dead of whom we speak not.

'Friend,' thought I—for thought alone seemed audible—
'What is the eternal refreshment we are seeking
And finding not—the life we long for, unspeaking,
Vainly, though ghosts and guns are terrible?

'The boy come in from labour, from slicing turf,
Knows that sweetest to him
Is a drink of well-water, rivers in which to swim
Or a sea-coast likewise, of windy thundering surf.

'The poet feels that a food most wonderful
Is to look at the sky for an hour; set down without fail
A sonnet or song that shouts, that grips like a gale—
So that some man will say—"ah, beautiful!"

'The priest doubts not that heralding angels hover,
The priest is at peace in a singing quietness;
Likewise the child moulded to man may guess
A draught fuller than peace in the voice of a lover.

'The madman has left us, has broken a ribbon of time.
And, O my friend, is there in death a deeper
Quiet of sleep for the unstriving sleeper
Unmoved by cannon-shot, unknelled by chime?'

Then spoke he: 'death for such as I was
Is a wandering, walled from beauty, broken by dreams
While blood of a myriad flows, flows out in streams
Over the natural meadows and singing grass.

'Yet the true child, true priest, true lover, true poet
May break with a touch the might of iron heaven:
Only the dead who died for no cause are given
Unrest eternal. I walk that the world may know it.'

Love to Terry. Tell him I am just going to fix the sails, that I emptied the dinghy of water and caught fish in it (after a flood on the river.) Tell him I hope he's ~~better~~ right now after his fall. Also that if the war doesn't end soon I'll be joining him.

Best wishes
From
Jim.

[VUW Library, MS McKay 28/9]

[Baxter's growing doubts about joining the legal profession were also expressed later in the year in an English assignment.]

**Short Extracts from My Diary—Ten Years Hence**

February 23rd 1952:
Monday—In the morning investigated the Jones case. Found that I had better not undertake it, as it seems extremely difficult. In the afternoon visited my old school, recalling many unpleasant memories.
January 5th 1953: Just had a visit from John Lassiter, prosecuting counsel, offering me £35 if I withhold the necessary evidence on the Jones Case which is being reheard. Am considering the matter. I think I shall ask more.
April 15th 1953: Elected King's Counsel, on account of good character etc. Not so much money in it, but good steady work now, though I cannot undertake shady deals.
May 27th 1953: Met some old friends in court—in for forgery. Was able to have them acquitted by an understanding with the jury. Very astonishing how many previous acquaintances I see in dock.
June 7th 1953: Have brought off a good deal in business—the cost of the property was £1050, my fees were £75. 'Truly, a knowledge of the Law is a marvellous thing.'

[Teacher's Comment] 7/10 Rather cynical

[Hocken, MS 975/187]

### Ginn to Baxter, 7 April 1943

Unstamped
by Censor

c/- Nat Service Dept Hautu Turangi via Nat Park.
Wed 7th.

Well Mr Baxter. I had set aside one of my two letters this week for you. As it was I had a vivid dream of you last night as you came into a room in which I was sitting, to give me a message from your mother. It was the first time I had set eyes on you & the impression was strangely captivating . . . perhaps a wish-fullfillment dream. It proves of course that even if I had forgotten to write the dark depths of the unconscious will not forget. In all a telepathic sort of excuse. The last two poems of yours particularly the latter—Fracturing the stolid hours of midnight—I have enjoyed greatly & read & reread. It is a perfect & harmonious episode—your continual theme is the survival of life & striving values, & how vividly & variedly you know how to state it. I have just started again Goethe's conversations with Eckerman (or is it vice versa) & he says it is a great mistake for a young poet to venture on a great poetic or dramatic enterprise in which his whole philosophy shall be enshrined. He says the 'present has its rights; the thoughts & feelings which daily press upon the poet will & should be expressed. But, if you have a great work in your head, nothing else thrives near it—all other thoughts are repelled.' Later—poems 'must all be occasioned i.e. reality must give both impulse & material.' Only in this way can a particular event become universal.[1] At last (& for the first time) I have got hold of a book of Blake (edited by Laurence Binyon with an introduction).[2] Rational or should I say modern gnostical thought—I think of Berdyaev—has with a long & painful circuit come to an intellectual restatement of the experiences & profundities which moved Blake. And I was delighted. Although I have only been through the book once & cannot hope to understand his private mythology at first blush I feel in my being that he is truly prophetic. His indictment of organised Xtnty is just as shattering as the best denunciatory chapters of Matthew. (23 ~~I think~~).[3] I must investigate his reiteration

1 Ginn appears to have been reading John Oxenford's translation of Eckermann's *Conversations with Goethe* (London: J.M. Dent & Sons, 1930). He quotes Eckermann's record of a conversation held on September 18, 1823:

> 'Beware,' said [Goethe], 'of attempting a large work. *That* is what injures our best minds, even those finest in talent and most earnest in effort . . . The Present will have its rights; the thoughts and feelings which daily press upon the poet will and should be expressed. But, if you have a great work in your head, nothing else thrives near it; all other thoughts are repelled, and the pleasure of life itself is for the time lost . . . The world is so great and rich, and life so full of variety, that you can never want occasions for poems. But they must all be *occasioned*; that is to say, reality must give both impulse and material. A particular event becomes universal and poetic by the very circumstance that it is treated by a poet' (pp.7–8).

2 William Blake, *Poems of Blake*, ed. Laurence Binyon (London: Macmillan, 1931).

3 Following an attempt by the Pharisees to test him (Matthew 22: 34) Jesus turns to the crowds and to his disciples and instructs them (in chapter 23) to practise and observe what their religious leaders say, but not what they do, 'for they preach, but do not practise' (v. 3). He then goes on to accuse the scribes and Pharisees of numerous token religious observances, prefacing each charge with the words 'Woe to you scribes and Pharisees, hypocrites!' (RSV)

that all life is holy. If that is so the claws & fangs & octopus arms which it invests cannot too be holy. So it is no wonder that you feed on him. I was fortunate enough to get hold of a book of Louis MacNeice called *The Poetry of W.B. Yeats*. Though I have not been able to read much of his stuff the book gave me a good general guide as to his thinking & development. It seems Yeats was sidetracked most of his life from the greater things of reality. He was almost a fascist—loved the blue blood & also the stylised simple mystic peasantry of Ireland.[4] But most of the book is wasted on me since it is all about something I have not read. The book with me now is *Son of Woman* by Middleton Murry—the story of D.H. Lawrence. It is a tragic & bitter exposition of the oedipus situation, the story of a genius, of a mind which was more spiritually sensitive than almost any other man's in the last 100 years, & reveals the inner ability to make in adult life an adjustment necessitated by faulty childhood development. Slowly the man disintegrates. His story is a lesson though a terrible one to parents.[5]

I seem to have become absorbed in reading to the exclusion of everything—even tackling verses. In a way creative output is an index of life fitness—in that case I must be developing a pot. I shall inflict my only two endeavours of late months on you—the first a not-so-deep musing on events the second a slightly romantic confession or account of self centered love.

**First Verse**

Yesterday the loaf on the college lawn after lectures
Alpine ranges taken over for the winter vac
The bright faces, scarves & goggles
And the gay teasing streamers.
The library was a filter for books' exciting thoughts
Where gate crashing fear was soon catalogued & shelved:
From a marble terrace applause for the feats of time
In cloister & common room we too were timeless.
Of course, below the Terrace, in the jagged gorge,
The tocsin of tram & traffic jam
Life flew at eyes & ears & skin & scratched
Hissed her flash disintegrating kiss
Enfolding in a labyrinthine embrace.
Time then for an academic synthesis

4 MacNeice, in his chapter on Yeats's Irish background in *The Poetry of W.B. Yeats* (London: Oxford University Press , 1941), argues that 'Till the end of his life Yeats found the two finest types of Ireland in the peasant and the aristocrat' (p.40); he then proceeds to document aspects of Ireland's history that significantly precede Yeats's arrival 'at his own elegant brand of fascism' (p.41).

5 John Middleton Murry's *Son of Woman: The Story of D.H. Lawrence* (London: Jonathan Cape, 1931), presents the passionate attachment of Lawrence to his mother as both the defining and distorting relationship of the writer's life. Inferring a comparison between this relationship and Lawrence's description of the relationship between a mother and son in *The Trespasser*, Murry writes:

> It is terribly poignant, and terribly wrong. Almost better that a boy should die than have such an effort forced upon him by such means. He is called upon to feel in full consciousness for his mother all that a full-grown man might feel for the wife of his bosom (p.30).

After careful analysis leading to admired subversion
The cause espoused, first shy lobbyings
The daring resolutions & the rector's reassurance
To the moths still spoiling the rich old carpet.

Today has pulled down another sky
Fitted a new inescapable horizon
Save where memory shoots her Verey lights
    into mind's unconscious sky.
Today the obsession of distortion
With the crossroad far behind time's back
Today the final defacement of man
Who plucky crept past mastadon, neanderthal
Who even became civilised
And now sleeps in the zoo
With lions & horses in the fixed abode.
Yesterday the net of aspiration catching the light
Today blind bruising antennae in a dumb & iron cocoon.

**Time Theme**

Time drew us down his vasty funnel
Bosom-aslumber on centuried sands,
Sifted us softly through bulging ages
Down the slow vortex, the sinking stages
Of history's succession; we fall
Through her thousand permutations to feel
The keen draught of this kernel hour
When mind meets mind & lips take lure
In the huge isolation night makes for love.

But praise for the God who gave us love
Is fleet, for now at this pinhole of passing
I know fear & the grey harassing
Lest the wedges of time & space should bite
Mauled by chance with glum delight,
Lest love should drain away & I
An empty cistern naked dry
Mark one more columned rhapsody
Ruined under a cloud-saddened sky.

The swan returns to the long cleanness
Of the lake alone, knows slight forlornness
Of a summer past lapping present shores;
But caught in time's slamming doors
Man knows the primal-being pain.

Yet the full glory of birch & pine
Low sky & white horizon diaphanous
Where light falls on air & stillness
Shall give our love a carefree fullness.

Terry asked me when writing to forward some further instructions regarding the boat measurements you are taking. He intends to put a cabin in the boat & wants to find out how much floor room there will be. There are four things he requires—all breadths—the bow & stern widths of the floor (which actually does not go right to the bow & stern), the width of the floor in the centre, & just below the place where the bow decking ends. The cabin will go from about 1/2 way towards the bow end—there will only be headroom at the entrance of the cabin, the other end will be just big enough for the feet. Perhaps you may grasp my unnautical description if I try a sketch.

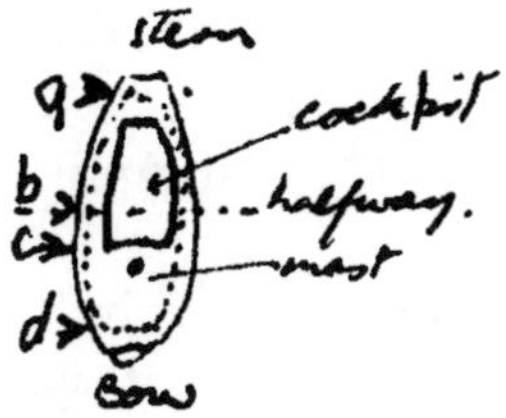


The broad arrows represent the 4 places to be measured—the dotted lines the floor. It's perfectly clear to me but I shan't be surprised if you find yourself bunkered at my description. His latest idea is for us to deck the boat in, least put a cabin in, & ship it up to Picton, thence to Pelorus Sound where we shall spend a month or so cruising fishing & so on. This almost straight after the war. The cabin will have two mattresses on the floor—sufficient room we hope for sleeping purposes. I forgot to add 'other things being equal'. Since Terry's whole life has been orientated to the sea he will never really be satisfied until he has had some such adventure—the sounds are enormous & relatively safe waters. Are you going to stake your claim?—you may be able able to spend a week or so from your 'career'. If a depression should follow (& I think one is inevitable) we will then be in a position to consider taking a leasehold of a few acres & living there—growing vegetables à la Walden.[6] It would be better than P.W.D[7] jobs & much more satisfying. Terry is reading Shackleton's book at the present time.[8] We are on the threshold of winter now—but there are no glories of autumn

6 *Walden, or Life in the Woods* (1854) by the American author Henry David Thoreau (1817–62), describes the two years he spent living in a wooden hut on the edge of Walden Pond, near Concord, practising a self-sufficient life style.

7 The Public Works Department. Even after their release from detention, many conscientious objectors remained under government orders and both Noel and Terence were 'manpowered' to labouring jobs. For a time they worked together at the Gear Meat plant in Petone, before Ginn returned home to Wanganui and Terence to Dunedin. See 'Epilogue' pp.120–4.

8 The British Antarctic explorer Major Sir Ernest Henry Shackleton (1874–1922) wrote two books. *The Heart of the Antarctic* (London: William Heinemann, 1909) describes his attempts to lead the first expedition to the South Pole, and *South* (London: William Heinemann, 1919) documents the efforts of a later expedition to traverse the Antarctic.

leaves here—however we have some truly magnificent sunsets. How is swot going? VIth form life is a great luxury in some ways & looking back it is a great opportunity. Lately I have bored my away through 2 tomes on archeology—& it is humbling to meditate on one's ignorance—I hope to hear from you soon Jim & find out what you are up to—& also if you are still writing

—Cheerio Noel

[Hocken, MS 975/183]

**Baxter to Ginn, 16 April 1943**

CENSORED
No. 5

Brighton,
Otago.
16th April 1943.

Dear Noel,

Many thanks for your letter. You are right that my theme is the survival of life (Hold tight, Noel—what with poems etc. this may be a long letter.) I noticed especially your line 'Today blind bruising antennae in a dumb and iron cocoon.' Intellectual life for many is either this or ragged and disintegrating emotion. This must change. Blake and his theories seem to me sane and adequate, but Blake seems to me to belittle human relationship (This judgement may be due to an insufficient appreciation), and human relationship is the basis of the 'soul'—a word which has given rise to innumerable platitudes. I cannot say with the smug and intolerant Holy Joe 'If you believe in God you're right, if you don't you're wrong', nor can I let values slide. I can only build what I can build on my own personality and my appreciation of the personalities of others. To the man in the cocoon life seems futile, to the emotionalist it may appear cruel. I cannot regard it as futile—that is Death, the old enemy, to some the old lover. As for my attitude to the latter, look up (if you still have it) 'Control'. Of course along with all this is swimming, the effect of S.A.,[1] working, reading, fooling.

I agree entirely with Goethe on the subject of Great Works. It is curious to have what I have worked out for myself strongly affirmed by him. 'occasional' of course means 'as occasion demands'. Nevertheless I will give you a poem now which was occasioned by nothing but vague though doubtless ennobling emotion arising from reading an anthology of poets of This War (but one never knows what volcanic eruptions may not be functioning in one's subconscious.)[2]

1 'Sex-appeal.' See p.214.

2 A reference to Patricia Ledward and Colin Strang's edition *Poems of This War by Younger Poets* (Cambridge: Cambridge UP, 1942) which was a gift to Baxter from his Great Aunt Hettie (Hester Hurst-Seager). The book—inscribed 'James/from/Auntie Hettie 1943' remains in the possession of the Baxter family. See also 'Baxter's Early Manuscript Books', p.80.

**From Hill-Top**

I

Our roads are visible,
Our waterways
Our rivers are too broad upon the map.
    Led thither by a dream
I stand upon one hill-top
And cast my seaward gaze like falcon
Over our shadowed valleys.

II

Small stretch of coast on a large island;
Shore, islet, reef
Touched by a rodent tide.
    Childhood disproportions are rectified.
O men in cities, blatant, unhearkening,
Listen even briefly to the snow-wind
And know that we are nothing.

III

Among our stone mountains
Stretches the arm of the theodolite;
Lode-lines have probed the bases of the hills;
    Ships have explored our coastal contours:
(Below me
Impassioned, motionless
Four hawks explore the contours of the air;

IV

Wings skyward wavering
Eyes set for prey, not beauty):
The poets must map the Truth remaining.
    Rose I at morning
Led by a dream; led by a dream of pain
Ten million strive within the fields of time.
My dream was Truth, and I see truth again.

V

There are few houses in this land.
There are few houses in this land;
And these vast hills
    Belong perhaps to the aborigines
Who walk by the foot-stools of gigantic powers
And are close to the seaward-staring monolith
The boulder unmoved by a battle.

VI

Our vanity of swollen cities
Inanity of action
Was never known by the snow-wind
    Which will blow over their ruins in gusts unretarded.
Man journeys
But inconceivably vast is the uncharted continent
The innumerable millipedes and the untainted grasses.

VII

The earth is unaware of Man.
I rose at morning
And, swifter than bird-flight, remoteness,
    Muteness of air and earth enclosed me:
Till a flower was inestimable and moulded iron a god,
For one was life of earth and one
Symbolic of man's life.

This is from experience, as few of mine are. I climbed up one of the hills near here and got a great view of the inland plain and sea-coast. Was struck by the almost complete absence of signs of human existence. In IV I refer to the war. Have I sent you a poem called 'The Mountains'. It is like V only better.

The poem from reading is very like the poem from memory, and all good poems have much of memory in them; also much of present emotion.

**Monument**

'*Caught in that sensual music all neglect*
*Monuments of unageing intellect.'—Yeats.*[3]

Sitting beside the comforting coal-fire
I saunter under a sky of dream;
    The lame cat murmurs, furred head to my hand;
    My raw throat eases, and the dreams that are
    Not dream but wish-fulfilment swim
    Like ripples over sand:
Voyages and unknown friends
Tumult of trains, of towns; or yet

(In this my sixteenth year all other ages
Are young, half-young, or old;
But boundaries are not
Set to mine own existence, aloof and ageless)

3 The final lines of the first stanza of Yeats's poem 'Sailing to Byzantium' from *The Tower* (1928).

Watch wistful boughs unfold
Their mist of leaves to a dawn air
Bearing regretful deep ecstatic melody—
    Born of no instrument, but like inviolate prayer
Repeating one phrase of well-clear delight
Near to true sorrow: as these words wake in me
The same star-brooding sorrowful delight:—
    'The land where I was born'.

I speak not now of verse, nor to discover
    The marvels of a bog-psychology
Nor of an absent and imagined lover:
    But I, the clever child, who daily see
The features of the child disintegrate
    Would but set down a monument whereby
Death cannot claim the child—though th' man arise
And sky of dreaming shatter to cold day.

I was suffering from 'flu when I wrote this, so was not sure what it would look like afterwards. However, it came pretty well up to scratch.

Could you give me a list of those I have sent you. I may have missed some good ones, so would like to know. Just give me the titles and I'll know them.

I would like you to give your opinion of the following one.

(A terrible thought has struck me. Have I sent it to you already?)

**Anger**

Walking on quiet invisible feet
    Through smoke of an air-raid
I saw stone houses reel and beat
A strange tattoo upon the street
    With their ten thousand dead.

Seeing those white unhappy eyes
Hearing their choked and terrible cries
    I looked into the air,
I looked for anger in the skies
    But saw no anger there.

The bombs who knew the death that pain
    Would burst their iron wombs and make
    Of stone a mountain, blood a lake
    In anguish speak, in anguish seek
To turn toward the clouds again.

The young men hurtling overhead
See not these gashed and scattered dead:
    Athwart their vague earth-seeking look
    As the loose pages of a book
Lie kindred, wives, instead.

In an unbroken house I know
    A politician stands:
He cannot feel, he cannot see
    The blood-gouts on his hands
But waits most wearily
The long approach of day.

Thus did I hear one, musing, say:
    There is no anger in men's eyes
    There is no anger in the skies
    But human beauty droops and dies—
And none say Nay.

If you've got it, someone else might like a copy. Are any of the others up there interested?

Love to Terry.
From, Your friend,
Jim.
James Keir Baxter.
[VUW Library, MS McKay 28/10]

**The Weir**

Above the wersh and weeded pools
    Harsh summer and a steely sky
    Cast drought as drear as I.
The weir moves not; and the rank grasses
Those grey wind-wearied singing-schools
    Mutter and sigh
As the wan wind passes.

The puerile cricket, piping egotist
    Gibes in the fern and writhen roots.
    Nature and Nature's fruits
Alike are dry and bitter here.
Here have I lain: and lie uncaring
    Under the bare dry-buttressed weir;
While flashing nor flaring
Love, life, and all daring

To feed the dun
Insatiable sun
Float skyward, shrink and die.
[Hocken, MS 704/9:529, p.35]

**Now while the bugles blare**

Now while the bugles blare
Their arrogant fanfare,
Now is the time for prayer.

Pray for the banners straining
The soldier new to training
The wild west wind complaining.

Pray for the combatant too:
As strong a man as you
Grunts, with his face smashed through.

Pray to the Lord—ah, list!
Descends the Eucharist
To armies in the mist.

Pray to ye know not what.
O sorrowful, wonder not!
For the Lord Christ is shot.

He as a child is mangled
(The Christmas bells have jingled)
He as a man is strangled.
[Hocken MS 704/9:519, p.21]

**Baxter to Ginn, 4 May 1943**

CENSORED
No. 5

Brighton,
Otago.
4/5/43

Dear Noel,

Excuse the dirty note-paper. It is a block which I want to use up. Tell Terry I'll send up the measurements soon.

I have put all your poems received so far into a note-book. Going over them last night I was struck by the strong poetry right through. 'The Drift of Pinions' expresses lyrical sadness; 'Incoherence' (especially 'sense-delivered tidings . . .') is truly great poetry; 'Farewelling' is a fine description of psychological stresses; 'October Spate' is yours alone and approaches genius; 'Overture to Unbelief' is very powerful but has some disproportion; 'I have come to a new . . .' is in parts too bizarre and incoherent, though the 3rd verse is good; 'To ME' has in parts that touch natural as the falling of a wave which hits you with beauty, catches you off guard; 'In December Days' is in part certainly as good as C. Day Lewis; 'Sonnet' is in some ways the clearest, the most gem-like, you have written—it is ready for publication in any company; 'First Verse'(?) is clever description; 'Time Theme' has that poetry like an unbelievably beautiful note of music which you sometimes do; 'Song of the Sharded Spirit' may remind me of the best of Auden, but it is 'ore', it is rough, too rough—yet I will not and cannot criticize it; 'On Rereading the Ascent of F.6.' is clever enough but hardly fair. You do not mention the flashes of poetry in Auden etc.[1]

Now for 'Hypothesis'. This is YOU. At your best in both rhyme and metre, which seems to make your impressions solidify. It is clear right through and poetry right through—you usually have some flaw, some lack of proportion in the middle of brilliance and epigrams, but here not. The end is like Ben Jonson. I cannot express what I want to say; but I have studied your poetry and it yields great richness on study. Whether I like your images or not, whether I believe all your poems as truth or not, you are as you are now a poet and you write fine poetry which is your own (nearest perhaps to Hopkins) and can stand on its own. None of this expresses the pleasure it gave me to read 'Hypothesis'. Nothing can. Best are verses 3, 7, and 8, but the others are necessary, all of them, to preserve the force and unity of the poem.

'wersh' is a good Scottish word meaning 'bitter' or rather 'rank, have too much of its own taste and smell'. 'S.A.' is sex-appeal. My best poems have been written when I have imagined myself to be in love.

'Mural for a War-Memorial' is a procession, a pageant, a surrealist painting (I have tried with very little success to draw with pencils—words are my pencil).

'The speaking gun and the flowers of nature alike bring profit, alike are based on money in our civilization. Astronomy and astrology (here comes the connection with our superstitious civilization) go on. The germ (is my SCIENCE right?) is King, is indeed a charitable king, for germ-serums can be trained to destroy pneumonia. Time passes. At the bottom humanity for whose sight the world exists. Second verse: War.'

Now for the poems I enclose type-written. 'Spring Pastoral' is very traditionalist, purposely so. It is good exercise, however, to do this occasionally. 'Thesis on a Constant Theme' is good in parts and of irregular rhyme-scheme—experimental. I may have sent you 'Satan' before; anyway study it—it is a treatise on self-expression. 'The Rose of Solitude' is a lyric of sorts. Traditionalism is useful sometimes.

I am glad you like 'Now while the bugles blare'. By all means send it.[2]

1 A reference to the play—written by Auden and Christopher Isherwood (1904–86)—*The Ascent of F6*, which was published in 1936.

2 See note 2, p.242.

**Our days and nights**

The earth is orbed, our lives lie in a calix
Under a zone of zodiacal light—
Not barred in spiritual filigree of midnight,
Our world of stars is whorled within the sea-shell's helix.

Over our heads caduceus or cross
Before our eyes grain-tower or xoanon—
Is there no timeless shadow whereon
We may lay a vow of love or bitterness?

But nay! hearken—our lives flare up like tinder
And at the zenith of flame, nor cruel nor tender
Falls there the bludgeon-voice of neural pain:
    Vain, vain, vain!

Our shredded days cannot revive again,
Our nights are numbered in his roll-call
Who walks at ease in an empty hall
Who shatters the glacier-earth to rain.

Hands crossed on a musing breast,
Song of the unreflective animal
Will waken gigantic beauty, but soothe not our unrest.
But piercing through wall and helix like sun on snow
Comes the trumpet, the chime that is time yet immortal:
The terrors break and shake in a heat seismal.

Each day is a star of conquest won from death
And daedal time is merged in a life that is tidal
    So live, so breathe.

The 'fangs and octopus-arms' of life are as holy as a star (perhaps a poor example but I won't change it now) is holy. No-one would object to the insect-preventing hairs on a poppy or the fact that the whale lives on minute sea-life. We, however, have drawn ourselves from animal suspicion or blindness to (we sometimes forget this) tolerance and ultimately love.

Blake is to me pure poetry.

If D.H. Lawrence had not known that he had an Oedipus complex, I wonder how he would have got on. This is not a sneer but a question. I have read him with great pleasure and profit, but I think that he was made somewhat irrational on sex matters by the complexes that you speak of.

I like your 'Time Theme'. I always think that you do best in rhyming though often irregular verse. The coherency of stanza-form solidifyes [sic] your foaming ideas—though perhaps a change from foam to pumice. I think that you have instinctively a good control of metre (rhyme is merely a matter of practice) and that this talent may rust from undue attention to free verse. However, don't do what I tell you to.

I will do my best for the boat.

Sixth form life has lost some of its attraction for me since I have discovered that 'free' periods are never free. Nevertheless, I like it.

With love to Terry.

From,

Your friend

Jim. | James Keir Baxter |

PS This is the 27th. I have just measured the boat, taking the width of the floor-boards i.e. the flat part. At the stern outside the locker it is almost 9 inches. At the middle 36 inches. Below where the low decking ends almost 32 inches. Where the floor-boards end at the front 20¾ inches; from the ending of the floor-boards it tapers some distance to the bow.

I made another measurement that may be useful. From where the bow decking ends to where the bow floor-boards end (moving towards the bow) is about 22 inches.[3]

J.K.B.

[VUW Library, MS McKay 28/11]

### Mural for a War-Memorial

Vocal cannon, thyme and violets
alike have honeyed gifts alike are money
comets weave new celestial implications
the protozoon is crowned in charity
(pneumonic plague breaking before brute violence)
the vestal Hours clothed in white anguish many
through silence beat their sullen repercussion.
And on the basement, broad humanity
bearing on strictured eye-lids the
celestial super-structure:

and cannons sprout among the violets
till the lost faces in a rain of rabble

3 Baxter took Ginn's letter of 7 April with him when he went to measure Terence's boat and entered the measurements straight onto Ginn's diagram, as shown here:

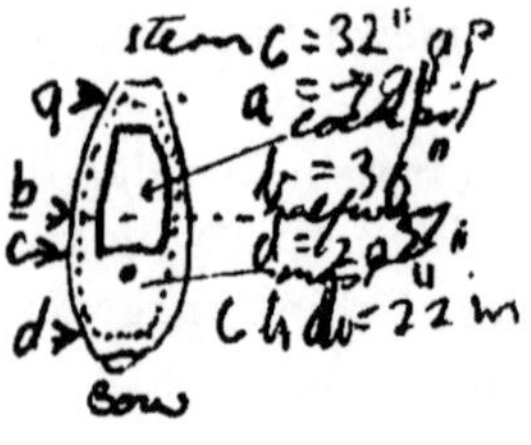

swing from dazedness to death
see not shadow slow and sable
but bottomless sky beyond the eye-ball earth.
[Hocken, MS 704/8:480, p.37]

**Spring Pastoral**

Spring comes. And the young lambs bleating leap;
Under her green cloak Earth has waked from sleep
As if one night alone that sleep had been;
In soft grass are the early flowers seen.
The swallow curvets, as a bent bow taut
His arc of flight sudden and swift as thought.
Waters that wavered once now flow again;
Spring like a mist, new-risen mist of rain,
Obscures the far views, and bends our heads
To nearby woods and flashing crocus-beds.
Summer will shine, will draw the wandering eye
To the unfathomed vistas of dark sky
With brooding, magical, pellucid heat;
Autumn will sigh of rest that is most sweet
Under brown boughs with sadness in their swaying;
But Spring has heard the hounds of Winter baying
And fearful almost that her temerity
Of new creation will new anger see
Wavers in tremulous blossoms and slight buds.
Her confidence renewed, the shadowy floods
Of unborn spirits ripple through the woods;
And in the cool spring night on cottage-fold
And sleeping nests descend—that the early gold
Of morning may know the new-born nestlings crying
Or calves lathe-legged nigh to the barn-door lying
Their nuzzling nostrils snuffing an unknown air.
Earth in the spring is virgin and most fair:
Not brazen Summer and the enamoured rose,
Autumn, nor Winter with his wealth of snows
May move men's hearts like spring-tide; there is then
A dear communion 'twixt us and the glen
That blooms with wayward brambles. We likewise
Drink in the breath of Nature at lips and eyes
And peace, tender as that of infancy,
To move us in rhapsodic melody.
[Hocken, MS 704/9:549, pp.61–2]

**Thesis on a Constant Theme**[1]

Wrinkled October's laughter
in English gullies covers last year's leaves:
the mould is broken now, the howitzer
makes pastoral life unsafe.

Some will hear speech
bellow from the breech;
but all who are unhappy
are the fastidious trees.

The dazzling zig-zag cut
of steel has let in only
influenza and typhus; but
we are scarcely sorry.

O those sweet birds that sing
above the phosphorus flare
may draw the morning star
to our awakening.

Outside the café windows
a brighter plague flows
brighter than new-dug snows.
Our uniforms are cheerful.

And this we realize:
that some idealize
and some are hedonists
but none are wise.

Ah, the notorious evil
we have forgotten:
we would embrace the devil
and we shall shrivel.

That men should die
in black delirium
may well embitter some
What shall they do?

Our streets are a gaol
and Time is the warder
O be not broken
by the stern wireless order!

1 Originally titled 'Thesis on the Constant Theme'.

And love right well may be
    a hill of iron-stone
    where man must weep alone
    where sorrow snaps the bone.

Our sky will break
    to the dark lightning
    of thought that like the negro
    will not walk slow.

And we will weep in vain
    over the soft fields rent with pain;
    and peace past
    shaken by tyrannous thunder-blast.

But in time the neurotic men
    and nervy women will settle
    to the old song again
    forgetting gun-metal.

The dead beauty will not revive:
    bones under earth will sing
    their sad plaining
    again to be alive.

And ah, though freedom evermore
    fill continent and shore
    we who living were
    will not be there.
        [Hocken, MS 704/9:550, pp.63–5]

**Satan**

'Shall saints sing sweetly? then Satan
Arch-angel gyved by ancient anger
May walk in freedom by music miraculous—
Muteness armoured in mailèd melody.'
    Thus Satan spake sounding through the abyss.
Succour from heaven hurled in the world of Hell
Was music wailing mutely mute-despair
Utter unplumbed.
                With the wind of wailing
Pain lifted to power—prisoned in peace
Of light everlasting mute mouths move not:
So anguish unexpressed even in Hell
Kindles not bravery, not craven courage
But anguish inexpressible, mute mouths moving.

Satan by speech
May scorn salvation—souls salved of sorrow
Yet speechless bear on ethereal bodies
Burden of bottomless abyss
Of silence.
[Hocken, MS 704/8:495, pp.54–5]

**The Rose of Solitude**

The rose of solitude, in song
Or with shut eyes believing,
Receiving,
The sun's enamoured glance and kisses strong
Cares not her beauty passes
Nor sheds one tear upon the grasses
But dances bright
In wind or spring sun-light.

But we
In winter live to see
Leaves of the song-enchanted tree
Fall ragged, rent
Of their spring garnishment.

O let the rose wind-tremulous
Beyond all season be
~~Spring heart of us~~
Rebellious.
[Hocken, MS 704/9:546, p.56]

**Ginn to Baxter, 2 June 1943**

CENSORED
No. 6

c/- National Service Dept, Hautu, Turangi, via N. Park. 2/6/43

Dear Jim—I shall begin what is a lengthy but delightful task of listing your 'Collected Poems' as you requested—at the same time I am rereading them.[1]

1 It is a measure of Baxter's considerable output that Ginn can list some sixty-six poems sent with the dozen letters written in the preceding twelve months. Included in Ginn's list are thirteen poems not previously mentioned in the extant correspondence. These poems—'The Phenomenon of

| | |
|---|---|
| 1 The Phenomenon of Understanding | 1—This is a very bracing affirmation of life, not an optimism, it is too deep for that. |
| 2 Faith that Groweth | 2—I am asking myself whether 'grows' wld be better—it is strong in its joy & wholeness |
| 3 The Eye (a flawless gem) | |
| 4 Song of the Garden | 4—This has just burst on me with new light. It is prophetic—Blake, Boehme,[2] Berdyaev. The worm I feel is the erotic struggle. |
| 5 From unremembered mouths | 5—Very strong meat. I regard the executioners as the self-created retributions—am I right? |
| 6 The Extinction of the Instant | 6—Simply packed with imagination |
| 7 What Shall we seek for (Goethe at his best) | |
| 8 Him not mentioned | |
| 9 In hills of stone, walking & dreaming | 9—This lyric fascinates me—it surpasses Mason. |
| 10 Fracturing the stolid hours | 10—Here your great gift is revealed—living in all lives, sharing all passions, healing & saving with sudden truth like an annunciatn |
| 11 The Clown (cf 'waste & void, waste & void' of TS Eliot)[3] | |
| 12 Song & the soul-delighting river | 12—Something powerful eludes me—you shall read it over to me some day. |
| 13 To Noel (I owe the cosmos a deep penitence, with your understanding I am steadied) | |
| 14 Barley [In Barley-Fields] | 14—To me a bit difficult though I sense the vision in it. |
| 15 The Boat | 15 When youth knows himself, & life, & has found words, therein is a pure miracle |
| 16 The Moon knows not | 16—Blake hated reason. Do you define it as he? |

Understanding', 'Faith that groweth', 'The Eye', 'Song of the Garden', 'The extinction of the instant', 'Song and the soul-delighting river', 'Song of the Sea-Nymphs at the Death of Icarus', 'I am as it were in a trap', 'O lands seen in the light of an inhuman dawn', 'De Averno', 'The Ghost Unborn', 'Poem of Passage', and 'There is a farm-house . . .'—appear in full in Appendix 2. In addition, two poems that are mentioned in the preceding correspondence—'Jubilation' and 'Love-lyric III'—are absent from Ginn's list.

2 The German mystic Jacob Boehme (1575–1624) proposed will as the original force, and opposition between manifestations—particularly between God and nature—as necessary processes that would naturally culminate in a view of the universe as the revelation of God.

3 A reference to the seventh chorus of Eliot's 'Choruses from "The Rock"', which begins:

In the beginning GOD created the world. Waste and void.
Waste and void. And darkness was upon the face of
the deep.

| | |
|---|---|
| 17 O Spirit stand in my eyes | 17—St Francis made 'goodness' attractive—you do the same with mental health.[4] |
| 18 The Silver Fish | 18—attention to the minute & particular is always a sign of an original mind. |
| 19 The Flame of Grass<br>20 The Young Trees<br>21 Under a Sun } | 19—The first of yours I read—it came as a new strange exhilarant. These 3 still move me more than any of your other poems—not just because they were the first you sent. |
| 22 Illusion | 22—The style is absolutely yours, no echoes of a master, but a new quiet voice telling ancient things. |
| 23 Discobolus | 23—I thought of the end of Shelley's Skylark.[5] It is so rich & full of restrained beauty. |
| 24 Rain ploughs rend . . . (Not obscure to me now) | 24—a wet day today. This is so strong—I am carried away by a flood of URALT[6] emotions. This is an experience. |
| 25 In point of time | 25 One of your finest most satisfying yet challenging. |
| 26 Gauguin (Very much like [?our] GMH) | |
| 27 On Visiting a Gallery of War Pictures | 27—A great, great epic of the sorrow of our uncomprehending minds. |
| 28 Song of the Sea Nymphs . . . Icarus | 28 Most beautiful rythm—again I think of Goethe. |
| 29 Doctrine of Philosophy | 29—a true tour de force |
| 30 Post Proelium | 30—It does not need a pacifist to feel this deeply. |
| 31 Control good. | |
| 32 Of the Fountain | 32—I know this 'of heart below spider, sun, snow, The Lord' but have had to sit in a thousand pews for it. You fly direct without the Church's wld be help. |

4 St Francis of Assisi (Giovanni Francesco Bernardone [1181–82 to 1226]), devoted himself to the poor and the sick. The disciples he attracted evolved into the Franciscan monastic order whose members, in recognition of their central doctrine—humility—referred to themselves as 'Frati Minori'.

5 Percy Bysshe Shelley (1792–1822) composed his lyric poem 'To a Skylark' in 1820. It concludes:

Teach me half the gladness  
That thy brain must know,  
Such harmonious madness  
From my lips would flow  
The world should listen then—as  
I am listening now.

6 German 'ur-alt': *adj.* very ancient, primeval.

| | |
|---|---|
| 33 Of Age | |
| 34 I am as it were in a trap | |
| 35 He who laughs | 35 You understand the age in which you live & from it speak to every age. |
| 36 The Plough | 36—If you were a psychologist you would belong neither to the analytic nor behaviourist schools but to the GESTALT school wh deals with the wholeness of experience.[7] |
| 37 to a solemn music | 37 I told you before how much I love this piece. |
| 38 of the Western Highlands | |
| 39 Judas | 39 Condensed & terrific in its intensity. |
| 40 The Mountains | 40 There is a feeling for nature such as the sensitive DHL had, in the first part of this piece. |
| 41 The Storm-Centre | 41 This poem still has to yield me its gold—it must have it—I feel baffled as with some of TSE's difficult poems. |
| 42 O lands seen in the light | a truly great meditation |
| 43 where beauty dips to dust | |
| 44 Prometheus | |
| 45 Mural for a War-Memorial | 45 The purpose of this, rather communication of its import, is achieved, though rather too much weight is borne by the words (1. 3,5.) |
| 46 De Averno | 46 Very well expressed. |
| 47 The Kiln | 47 One of my favourites. Do you know the kiln at ARAMOHO?[8] |
| 48 The Ghost Unborn | |
| 49 Why ring no chime | 46, 49 You drive home with unwearied strokes the story of our age's Dead Sea fruit. |
| 50 The Lie | 50] This type of thing will appeal readily to<br>51] the public wh baulks at difficult stuff—it is simple effective & its rythm is unforgettable. |
| 51 Anger | 51—This is one of the very finest poems—the fact that it is in regular stanza form |

7 The Gestalt school of psychology—reacting against structuralist assumptions that sensations were the building blocks preceding complex perceptions—argued that sensations were themselves creations found by a subject's effort of will. Thus they asserted that organised wholes are prior in both behaviour and perception to the parts that make up the whole. Hence the German 'Gestalt', meaning 'organised whole' or 'pattern'.

8 Probably a reference to the kiln at Gibson's brickworks which had been in operation since the late 1880s in Gibson St., Aramoho: a residential and industrial suburb of Wanganui which Baxter might have been familiar with from his time at Friends School.

| | |
|---|---|
| | enhances its value. All the values of tragedy are here—Pity, Terror etc. |
| 52 Poem of Passage | 52—Another beautiful affirmation & creation. |
| 53 Now while the bugles blare | |
| 54 Our days & nights | 54—Very powerful—what is xoanon please? |
| 55 The Weir | 55—'Those grey wind wearied singing schools' is a haunting music & picture. No I have considered for a long time WERSH & don't like it. It is not so bad when pronounced [WE:YS] instead of tame [wa:s]. |
| 56 There is a farm house | |
| 57 From Hill-Top (slow ruminating valuable mood) | |
| 58 Monument | 58 There is no doubt in my mind but that a monument has been built. |
| 59 The Rose of Solitude. | |
| 60 Thesis on a Constant Theme | 60 I like this but find I read it not as a unity. |
| 61 Spring Pastoral | 61 Should please the critics & followers of Wordsworth. Use of word 'dear' is very risky. |
| 62 Satan | 62 Yes, I am studying this, it is well worth it. |
| 63 In Numeris | This is your longest, richest poem—full of mythology. Difficult as Thomson is difficult & very much like him in its wealth of unearthly beauty. |
| 64 Lament of the Reborn | 63 Another beautiful mood from a strange yet possible theme. |

In addition there are 2 fragments; 'Behold magnetic current' and 'I have passed through my own thought's fire.'[9]

As far as I know this is the lot but there is a chance of one or two turning up from the shambles I call my desk. Well I have spent about 6 hours on this so far—& what is the effect—it is terrific! I am filled with one thought—an achievement of transcendental greatness. Criticisms I made before about vagueness etc were due to my own unfitness—with each reading the unity & worth & intensity of each poem is more apparent to me. It may give you some small satisfaction in my affirmation of your genius but you do not really need it since its own inner light gives you the buoyancy and assurance necessary to enable you quietly to continue giving utterance. I will not say any more as it would be the same thing over again—but you know now there is no doubt in my mind as to your future. Several chaps in the camp have seen

9 'I have passed unscathed', although only 4 lines long, is in fact complete. 'Behold magnetic current' is the second verse of the poem 'Moving on spirit-roads' (see p.147). The poem appears in full in Appendix 2, p.441.

your poems but unfortunately only about 2 are in any way able to grasp the thought of all but the simplest ones, & then their 'very good', 'most interesting' falls coldly on my enthusiastic ears. It is appalling how few read poetry & how few ever attain to fitness as readers, appalling since the general level of culture is higher than average. I too am only learning to read & appreciate—time for meditation is imperative, & I seem all my days to have been struggling with Fr or G. proses, or wretched book-keeping. These to me rather dissatisfying verses came to mind after the reading.

**There was a man . . . sent from God**

Keen eyes at roam over earth's spilt history,
Ears caverning her thousand separate songs,
Spirit scorning the current unclean vestures
Bare before the archaic gale, the facing mystery
    You are the giver of meaning
    The thin light of golden morning
    The dispenser of holy warning
Outside the broken walls of the untaken day.

In time's fierce slipstream, in greed's wretched shops
In the hub of dizzy wheels mechanic brain,
Before the grim orgies & orgasms of lascivious bombs,
In conning-towers misborn of leafy sailing-ships
    Stand poetic man
    Annunciate new shame
    The birth Miriam began
Outside the broken walls of the untaken day.

And we shall see the downy prows of sparrows
Threaded on wintery willow tips as rosaries
Told by unseen Assissians, as period stops
To the queasy haemorrhages of speech, as fiery arrows
    Piercing disaffections
    Purging cerebral factions
    And the cherished fictions
Outside the broken walls of the untaken day.

Another

**(prayer under a bridge)**

Old sunsets across the river mouth
Keep me from failing
Keep me from feeling
The daily rout
The daily rout

Of soul
Of soul the rout from my life's only calling.

Sand-grasses waving at my head
Firmly embedded
Fully embody
Speak surely the
Purely the
Word
The Word so long sought in sandy wells.

O bells, pulled by our faction jubilant
Reeling pealing
Instead of tolling
Do not let
Do not let
Today
Silent truth from her own revealing.

Water take your ancient stations
Water the fastness
Weather its harshness
The numb rocks
Unnumbered rocks
Transmute
To wine & bread for the unquenched rose:

Rise through the green of the sunlit impulse
Crest of the thorn bush
Christ of the thorn bush
Consummate
Consummate
Now
The love of my lips' confessing, now.

The broken walls refer to the future—as the past & present have already determined in part its nature. The shame is twofold in nature—the shame of going through a virgin birth and that guilty shame we are always creating.

Well the snap has come—Terry produced it last night & I can tell you it has had a very close scrutiny—the result of course is most pleasing . . . expectations realised & so forth. It gives me a better idea when I am writing. Your tidy brother went crook at this untidy, stained letter—& is right. Some time he says you might dig up a book for him PILOT BOOK 1930[10]—limp cover, green he thinks. Please tell me if you

10 Great Britain, Admiralty, Hydrographic Office, *The New Zealand Pilot: comprising the coasts of the North and South Islands of New Zealand, Stewart Island and adjacent islands, Kermadec, Chatham, Bounty, Antipodes, Auckland and Campbell Islands*, 10th ed. (London: H.M.S.O., 1930).

have read *New Bearings in English Poetry* by F.R. LEAVIS.[11] It is a most important book. Your crit of the F6 lines is right. The point of their reasoned faith is valid—though at the same time they have created values. One must not look for dogma but must 'behold'.

Sorry for the muddly letter. Hoping to hear from you soon

Regards

Noel

[Hocken, MS 975/183]

**Baxter to Ginn, 14 June 1943**

CENSORED
No. 3

Brighton,
Otago,
14:6:43.

Dear Noel,

Yes, in 'Unremembered Mouths' executions are self-created. 'What shall we seek for?' I believe to be the best I have written. 'The Moon knows not'—reason without emotion (i.e. pure reason) is like wine without alcohol. 'Flame of Grass', 'Under a Sun', 'The Young Trees': the Child who passes. Look carefully at the 'mountains', read the poem over—there is something there captured neither before nor since. 'But here they stand in massed solidity to seize upon the day and night horizon.' It is the Southern Alps, is connected with 'O lands seen in the light', 'From Hill-Top' and others. 'Spring Pastoral'—see this not through the eyes of D.H.L. but of John Clare or Crabbe; there is here no modernity.[1]

'The Storm-Centre'—I have not always been either rational or in good taste.

'xoanon'—image fallen from heaven. e.g. black stone at Mecca (not an excellent example)[2]

'wersh' is harsh and rank and grey like what it describes. 'Thesis on a Constant Theme'—notes: you are right.

11 F(rank) R(aymond) Leavis (1895–1978), influential critic and lecturer at Cambridge University, used *New Bearings in English Poetry: A Study of the Contemporary Situation* (London: Chatto & Windus, 1932) to promote poets like T.S. Eliot, Pound, and Yeats (and also to reassess Hopkins) alongside an attack on verse written in the late-Victorian traditions of Tennyson and Swinburne.

1 The best poetry of both John Clare (1793–1864) and George Crabbe (1754–1832) reacted against the escapist idealism of early pastoral verse by realistically and evocatively portraying English rural life and landscapes.

2 The sacred Black Stone of Mecca—*Al Hajar al-Aswad*—was received by the Prophet Isma'il from the Angel Jibra'il during the rebuilding of the Ka'bah: the stone structure in the centre of the Haram Mosque toward which all Muslims face while praying. The stone—in fact about a dozen stones cemented together which, according to Muslim historians, come from a single stone that was fragmented by fire—is mounted in a silver band set in the south-east corner of the Ka'bah.

'(prayer under a bridge)' Fine sense of unity, sense of place, sense of immediateness. Where you have clarity you have always strong poetry. Poetry none the less cannot always be clear. 'There was a man . . . sent from God' I study and will soon fully understand. It seems surrealist but forcible with slashing antitheses.

Excuse my mass of poems now sent. Having got your list I find how many I haven't sent. It will overlap perhaps.

Love to Terry.
From,
Your friend,
Jim.

PS I have never yet seen anything to beat Blake's 'Tiger' or even Auden 'Lay your sleeping head, my love'. Both are 'doom': perhaps I like doom.

James Keir Baxter.

[VUW Library, MS McKay 28/12]

**Baxter to Ginn, 4 July 1943**

CENSORED
No. 2

Brighton,
Otago.
4/7/43.

Dear Noel,

Many and grateful thanks for the books. Of course I understand perfectly why you will want *New Bearings* back. The books arrived on my birthday. I have just read *The Gambler*, and, having gambled in a mild way myself at 'two-up' and on gambling-machines, I think it perfect. Of course it is a piercing study of human nature.[1]

I am looking at one of your previous letters. It says 'Today aesthetics is beginning to become possessed of a scientific basis and we shall soon be much clearer on the meaning of "art" and "reason" and "beauty" and so on—terms which are so cloudy and error-breeding.' ~~Of course~~ I see your point, but my attitude is different. I think that 'art' is relative and (while often of universal application) intensely personal beyond verbal definition; that 'reason' is in reality inseparable from its complement, emotion;

1 *The Gambler* [*Igrok*] is a novella written in 1867 by the Russian author Fyodar Mikhaylovich Dostoevsky (1821–81). The experiences of the narrator Alexis (Aleksay Ivanovich), a 25-year-old university graduate who views gambling on the roulette wheel as his only salvation, are very similar to those of Dostoevsky who, at one stage in his life, was beset by emotional and financial problems which were exacerbated by his tendency to gamble away everything he could earn or borrow. *The Gambler* was written while he was living outside Russia, forced into a self-imposed exile by his mounting debts.

Two-up is a gambling game common in Australia and New Zealand played by tossing two coins with bets being laid on the showing of two heads or two tails.

that only a rigid definition of ‘beauty’ can breed errors (by this I mean that I can appreciate without qualms both Hopkins’ ‘No worst, there is none. Pitched past pitch of grief.’[2] and Arnold’s ‘Far, far from here The Adriatic breaks in a warm bay’ . . .[3]) Hopkin’s is essentially of greater genius, but both are subtle. The rigid modern can lose, by a habit of mind, power of appreciating the early ‘dreams’ of Yeats; and ludicrously underestimate the essential force of clarity. The genius of Hopkins prevents true obscurity, but the intellect of Empson does not. The modern, fed on curry, loses taste for unseasoned food; through concentration on his own epoch he has narrowed his range of consciousness. Do not misunderstand me. I see the dangers of Victorian dream and dalliance, believe that a change has come, but think that modern poets have not caught the message of ‘Hopkinism’. In truth, though they are in a measure self-deceived, they have not enough to say to demand the vehicle of poetry. Of course I have read many fine poems; but vitality, vitality is needed—and with vitality comes sufficient clarity. After reading a poem of Empson’s I feel that I have excavated in sand and found—sand. These ~~of cou~~ are the words of the hawk’s-eye observer, not of J.K.B. I, being fallible and vain, commence to write a poem in the style of Empson.

Now for ‘New Bearings’. The criticisms of Victorian poetry are good. Note here that I picked out and enjoyed the portions of ‘Empedocles on Etna’ mentioned on P.18. before reading ‘New Bearings’.[4] I was most delighted to see that Leavis had also done this. I mention this so that you may not think that opinions expressed above arise from any but personal bias. We can never be free from personal bias, so I do not expect you to agree with all my biases. (I have become tangled, but try to get my meaning.)

Regarding tolerance.

**Prayer for Intolerance**

Never, nay not too great a tolerance!
Gyved serious Utopian
Will feel of mind with fire, let fall the tree
Then pity charrèd timber; astride half-fence
Goodness in evil men
Bites on—forgets fecundity
Made barren, destructive flame or snarling rot:
Through sympathy with evil, hate, castigate not.

2 The opening line of one of Hopkins’s sonnets from his 1885–87 period:
No worst, there is none. Pitched past pitch of grief,
More pangs will, schooled at forepangs, wilder wring.
Comforter, where, where is your comforting?

3 Lines 427–8 of Matthew Arnold’s (1822–88) dramatic poem *Empedocles on Etna* (1852), sung by the young harp-player Callicles. Despite Baxter’s disclaimer in the next paragraph, his juxtaposition of verses from Hopkins and Arnold—although more forgiving of Arnold— is along the lines of a similar apposition of the two poets by Leavis, on p.18 of *New Bearings*, who contrasts the power of Hopkins’s genius ‘in which technical originality is inseparable from the rare adequacy of mind’, with Arnold’s rare poetic moments—such as this song of Callicles—where ‘the sap suddenly flows’.

4 In addition to Callicles’s lines quoted by Baxter in the preceding paragraph, Leavis quotes two further lines from the same song referring to its subjects, Cadmus, first king of Thebes, and his queen, Harmonia: ‘There those two live, far in the Illyrian brakes! . . . but were rapt, far away’ (ll. 443, 453).

'Judge not', nay never judge; nor tolerate
Illness, canker, though the judged-not be
Heart-friend, or self even: so see
Love (yea, like child) and hate new-reconciled with fate.

Save me, O God dark-parlous, fearless all,
        From all-white spineless seep-out—
Wherein pale day, wind-jellied, jowl and cheek
With perfect tolerance; griding, flake the cowl,
        Iron-of-grave-girt
Inhuman flesh—let light speak,
    Thunder, lift-riving lightning, stoop and shake
    Heart to hate-urgent and love-surgant jet,
        New-make.

Like the author of 'New Bearings', I have a distaste for Browning and his crudities.[5] 'The Testament of Beauty' is artificially sustained, and bores me. Slabs of it might as well have been written in prose.[6] But this I do believe: that natural images are poetical, because more emotions become associated with night or wind than with a gas-works. This is only a generalization (see *The Kiln* ) but great effects are within the scope of natural images as is shown in *Job* and *Ecclesiastes*, and to a most minor extent in my *Psalm of Defeat*.

It is a sign of lack of vitality when effects are best achieved by the obscure or bizarre. By this statement I rightly condemn much of my own work. There is rarely real obscurity in Hopkins. Bridges' alterations of G.M.H. strike me as wanton foolery and bowdlerization.[7]

Poised herself like a falcon at check
Amid the unfooted ploughland,
Laughter splashing from her mouth and
Rippling down her brown neck;
Not passion-spent she
But sensing in the bound
Of her breasts vigours to come, free

5 Leavis argues that Browning exhibits the 'kinds of strength a poet is best without . . . It is possible to consider him as a philosophical or psychological poet only by confusing intelligence with delight in the exercise of certain grosser cerebral muscles' (*New Bearings*, 19–20).

6 Dr Robert Bridges (1844–1930) was appointed Poet Laureate in 1913. He regarded his long poem in four books, *The Testament of Beauty*, which detailed his spiritual philosophy, as the culmination of his career as a poet. Leavis however, refers to it to illustrate his criticisms of the 'complacent debility' affecting Georgian poets, in whom 'technical liberation . . . takes the form of loose, careless, unconvinced craftsmanship' (p.22). The fact that it was a best seller makes it plain, he concludes, 'that its sales show mainly with what success adroit journalism can exploit even a vestigial habit' (p.212). See also the following note.

7 Leavis's chapter on Hopkins blames the poets' well-intentioned friend and editor—the Poet Laureate Bridges—for much of the decline in vigour of English poetry by denying it 'thirty years of potential influence' in withholding publication of Hopkins's verse until 1918 (p.160). In Leavis's eyes this error is compounded by Bridges's attempt in his introduction to pre-empt adverse criticism, and put readers 'too much at their ease' (p.161); and by his considerable editorial interventions and copious notes that temper the poet's 'radical and uncompromising' originality (p.167).

As air and powered to make her one
With the stream of earth-life around.[8]

Here the description of vitality is itself vital. But I believe that first Eliot, and later others, have erred. That the description of the break-up of vitality should be disjointed and also suffer a lack of vitality is wrong. Milton can describe the despair and mental death of hell without either despairing or mentally dying. I am trying to show the dangers of subjectivity in art.

You yourself have intuitive knowledge of them when you say:

Lest love should drain away and I
Am empty cistern naked dry
Mark one more columned rhapsody
Ruined under a cloud-saddened sky.

When I said 'intuitive knowledge' I meant of style. I now see that the content also applies if 'love' is taken to mean vitality. I think that nothing I have written is any better than the four lines above. This is not idle praise; it is true and sincere. Every word expresses desolation.

Here is an example (from the middle of the *Waste Land*) of Eliot's pseudo-ism. The verses may be of great association for T.S. Eliot. But to my mind he has expressed nothing; a wide knowledge of literature is not poetry. The words could have been written by any amateur. Their value is in the mind of Eliot, but there is no vitality, no coherence, to make them intelligible to the reader. They are merely abbreviated literary notes. The author has conveniently forgotten the unconscious dictum of all great poets that verse should have vitality ~~and so the~~ or at least clarity.[9]

Your four lines are infinitely superior.

I do not quarrel with much of Eliot's other work. It is often good though not ~~very~~ always forcible surrealism (and surrealist art must above all have vigour to outbalance obscurity. I think G.M.H. knew this most of the time.) But Eliot's reputation is based on a misconception of the definition of poetry.

Now in Yeats vitality and clarity are well handled. Imagination gives the artistic level of a poem. Imagination + vitality gives emotion. I must generalize in order to make my remarks apply as widely as possible.

The Georgians show the dangers of emotional clichés and mediocrity; De La Mare shows the overwhelming dangers of the 'ivory tower', the mental and emotional introversion and withdrawal;[10] Eliot and his followers show the dangers of lack of

8 Untraced.

9 Although it is unclear which of Eliot's lines Baxter intended to quote here, his apparent purpose is to take issue with Leavis who, in *New Bearings*, justifies the inaccessibility of Eliot's poetry by arguing that 'Works expressing the finest consciousness of the age . . . are almost inevitably such as to appeal only to a tiny minority . . . This amounts to an admission that there must something limited about the kind of artistic achievement possible in our time' (p.104).

10 Baxter's criticism of Walter De La Mare (1873–1956)—although overlaid with his characteristic distrust of intellectuals—is along the lines of Leavis's inference that there is some unconscious dishonesty in De La Mare's tendency to produce 'by the surreptitious suggestions of his verse, an effect contradictory to what he says' (p.52). Despite these reservations, Leavis was happy to rank De La Mare with Hardy and Yeats as one of the three poets writing at the end of World War I 'who really were considerable poets' (p.27).

vitality. Good poems have been written in the teeth of these dangers—but only because of some intrinsical mental vitality. They are not likely ever to listen to the voice of John the Baptist (nevertheless in my early rather crude poem on John the Baptist I say optimistically, 'So shall the sightless worm Break mountain upon mountain Yet hold within unmoved integrity.') But they need all their surety, for:

'There is a free one' many say, but err.
He is not that returning conqueror,
Nor ever the poles' circumnavigator.

But poised between shocking falls on razor-edge
Has taught himself this balancing subterfuge
Of the accosting profile, the erect carriage.
(Auden.)

To round off my sermon, here is a thoroughly obscure but (to me) subjectively satisfying poem.

[Sorry, just a minute. Must add last two verses of Auden's poem. Carry out my idea of vitality in poetry (by their meaning.)

The song, the varied action of the blood
Would drown the warning from the iron wood
Would cancel the inertia of the buried,

Travelling by daylight on from house to house
The longest way to the intrinsic peace,
With love's fidelity and with love's weakness.][11]

**To the New Pagan**

For none shall laud the pagan save his created god.

The century is still-born: though loud time
Swings her lode-needle to eternity,
Learned in the school of shells man's cares come home;

And roost on beams at noon. Driven inanely
By load of leaden fear since fathered under fire
The good grow lewd, the withered gladly

Crawl under shawl or sprout new animal fur.
Gad-flies of time and sex wreak not mischance;
Laid under bid of grass fit beauties wear

11 Stanzas 2–5 of Auden's poem 'A Free One', which first appeared in *Poems* (London: Faber & Faber, 1930) as poem IV: 'Watch any day his nonchalant pauses, see . . .'

Their shadows of corruption. The harsh lance,
The mine-starred gaud and diamond of gold truth
Buckles upon a dream-armour; this long-since,

Far shoal now dry in hazes, arid youth
Unvisioned (shelled now again) is blasé shield
Concealing fore-apportioned faithless faith

And thee O fair dream, bitter, beaked, and wild.
Anon by coiling lord of hatred led
Snake-worshippers their fruit-of-falsehood's-field

Serve ~~of~~ as red gourd sun-goaded . . .
For sure the sieve that lost us our stool-pigeon
Of true religion spy in house of God

Can scarce hold faith like oil from shale. O son
Of my wrought nerves, go tell them that sad steel
Has long accomplished death; that this death gone,

Fresh carrion seemed alive—though maggots still
Alone were living.
The dream, not now the vision.
O sun set final seal

On the self-rending flesh of rank oblivion,
Or let apocalyptic vision rise
Melt this true dream of ferro-concrete limbs

That our enforcèd death have hands and eyes,
Caress like light, be natural as a hill.
The knight on the crystal mountain plants his spear, is still.

To strum on broken strings
Of unremembered kings.
Or walk waking
Where there is speech, red forts for the taking.

For none shall laud the pagan save his created god.
Yet, child, be not inhuman—grip on good
In heart hold. All are kin blood.

The ageing strong-man envious of lovers
Who cries perhaps in secret; the crass baby;
The frail and pug-faced woman who endeavours
To keep a semblance of vitality:
All must desire the vision wonderful.
All these are piteous, not pitiful.

O son
Of my unmoved regret. Go thou and tell them
That earth has hid the slain, desires not blood,
Will purify. That air desires not sound
Of metal moving, nor the wind of death—
Will purify. That fire has shouted, leapt
Over the bodies of the anguished, not
In hate, but ardour vain for cleanliness—
Will purify. That the fire-clouds have gathered,
And at a word compassion will rain down:
For earth has bitterness may yet be healed.
O purify!

With much love to Terry
Best wishes
From
Jim.

PS **To a Mermaid**
(Charles Madge)[12]

The glass entanglement of flowery ~~fair~~ hair
Deceives a plane. Because the looking glass
Creates the metaphoric double there

Undoubted image. Not less perfect was,
They say, a face once found in television
Bent by the hills, perspective of a face,

Hardest to catch with exigent precision,
Indeed stone cold. The limper, could he climb
Down backstairs aboriginal incision?

. . . . .

This could be explained by notes; but when explained, the original would be changed by the infusion of new knowledge. The wall of such obscurity is almost impenetrable.The sentence beginning 'Not less perfect was . . .' I find moderately clear. Only by necessity should one even start on the road to obscurity. One should say (i) need I say it? (ii) could I say it better in another form? (iii) following forth from (i)—has it sufficient vigour or clarity to make it poetry or even good verse? Those who in the Victorian era could be recognised as mediocre by their sentimentality cannot now be classified owing to the refuge of obscurity. Obscurity becomes a cult when the vital necessity that poetry should say something is lost. The man who

12 Charles [Henry] Madge (1912– ). Best known as a sociologist, Madge published two books of poetry in the thirties and forties. Baxter quotes, with his characteristic accuracy, the first three stanzas of Madge's poem 'To a Mermaid' which is a poem of eighteen stanzas, equally divided into three parts, from *The Father Found* (London: Faber & Faber, 1941) pp.45–7.

cannot understand the verses above and admits it is showing intuitive knowledge of the aims of art. The man who cannot understand 'Poised herself like a falcon at check. etc.' shows lack of artistic sensibility, for the vigour of rhythm and meaning leaps to the mind. One may progress towards subtlety: but where begins a loss of vigour of intelligence or emotion subtlety becomes an evil and a snare.

T.S. Eliot's obscurity is unpardonable in its narrowness—for it is not intelligence it demands in the reader but tremendous powers of association and wide book-knowledge. In truth, the reader must write the poem.

Spender's vitality of emotion excuses his partial obscurity and his subtlety makes for fine poetry. The literary conscience is too raw which classes pity or indignation or nostalgia with sentimentality.

Auden's mannerisms are irritating, but he is (though more obtuse) more adult that Spender. He is more subtle, yet retains vigour. I think that he has a good grasp of the mental attitudes of modern intellectuals.

Pound is partly caught in the vortex of obscurity. His translations, however, are excellent, and much of his middle work was very good.

Yeats, though inclining to obscurity, has a native and original vigour of thought and diction which prevents this. Note that the conception of poetry as separate from expressed emotion makes some unable to appreciate Yeats' 'Lake Isle of Inisfree'. This poem expresses a natural and (if transient) healthy emotion. It's technique is subtle and its metaphors excellent (see ~~P.3~~ 3 on natural images.)[13]

Please write soon. Don't have any qualms about contradicting me. And tell me what you think of the last batch. J.K.B

[VUW Library, MS McKay 28/14]

**Psalm of the Defeated**

1 There is crying in the streets of our city—yea, even in the desolate streets of Babylon.

2 Our wives and mothers weep in the gate-ways. The bat hangs by day in the deserted palaces.

3 For the sword of the unrighteous has fallen upon us: we are vanquished by the cruel and unjust men.

4 Smitten under the noiseless bows of despair and famine, our warriors groan with the bitterness of defeat.

5 As in a glass have we seen the face of our idols, have we seen the countenance of our adornèd images.

6 We have set them on high in our public places. Very beautiful were they to behold: of gold and silver were they; with the blood of men we have anointed them.

13 Yeats's 'The Lake Isle of Innisfree' was originally published in *The Countess Cathleen and Various Legends and Lyrics* (1892). It begins:

I will arise and go now, and go to Innisfree,
And a small cabin build there, of clay and wattles made:
Nine bean-rows will I have there, a hive for the honey-bee,
And live alone in the bee-loud glade.

7 But as the wind and tempest in swift passing tormenteth the waves of the sea: so have the iron javelins beaten upon us; so are we whelmed in the midst of spears.
8 Who shall inhabit these cities in the days following? Who shall dwell in the sight of the new covenant?
9 We are become used to darkness; we are become creatures of the night. For oil is a king's ransom and bread more precious than jewels.
10 In the midst of our sins are we smitten: there are none to bury us.
11 We raised our voices saying: Who are more mighty than the generations of Babylon? or who shall surpass them in wisdom, in splendour, and in the valour of battles.
12 But as the whirlwind darkeneth the heavens to blood; as great winds veil the firmament with smoke of a conflagration: so is our doom fallen upon us.
13 Were we strong in the faith of the righteous, then had we sung in the midst of the spears.
14 For blessed is the strong man, whose heart faileth not. Though the hills shake and the mountains are turned to flame; though the great deep be troubled, though the seas shout in tumult and cast up strange monsters; though the rivers of earth be salt with slaughter and the nations rise in fury one against the other.
15 Yet shall he abide in faith, and take his path nor rejoicing nor weeping through the night of chaos
16 But we are broken in the clash of years; yea, we are stricken by the snakes of time: our gods shall not help us in the days of destruction.
17 We may but wail in the unfruitful fields; we may but cry in the streets of our desolate city.

[Hocken, MS 704/9:534, pp.26–7]

**On John the Baptist**

Sought ye to find a reed wind-shaken?

None such is he.
Souls shaken in the wind of prophecy
As reeds are bent and braken;
But as the rock stands firm,
Yet as the untrammelled fountain
So standeth he.
So shall the sightless worm
Break mountain upon mountain
Yet hold within unmoved integrity.

Sought ye to find a prince in gold attire?

Ye shall not find him.
He such as cerements has cast behind him,
And lost desire
Even of life as we know it
Yet comes not as spiritual tyrant to overthrow it.
With water he baptiseth not with fire.

Rather a prophet is he
Stronger than priestly Pharisee.
Yet ~~one~~ men of lesser faith
Having discerned the more essential path
Shall greater be.
[Hocken, MS 704/6:380, pp.91–2]

**The Unicorn**

Through the dim sea-blown wood
The alien unicorn
Walks steadfast and alone.
The herds return to fold as tame beasts would
But unassailable, misunderstood,
He moves beside the grey and twilight sea
As figure of heraldic blazonry.

The crags blow trumpets round:
Over and through the wind
Sea-music moves his mind
To reverie on an enchanted ground.
Hearing afar the bay of hunting hound
Across the deep ravines, white and forlorn
Passes the swift the phantom unicorn.

Perchance the archer sees
Him silent move among
The trees that burst in song,
The dryad-cloaked the dream-enamoured trees;
And as he wheels through the far wood and flees
The musing archer bends his bow again—,
Behold! the fabulous unicorn is slain.

O death of the unborn!
Spirits that like to thee
Unborn shall ever be
Wail endless over the buried unicorn.
Behold the adamant and fragile horn

That conquers death of venom, death i' the tomb,
Is deeper death—return beyond the womb.

O perilous unicorn!
Death slays thee not—but see
From the cold surf's paturity
Aphrodite Andymone[1]
Arise in birth thou woulds't extinction deem:
Arise and bind thee to an iron dream.
[Hocken, MS 704/7:459, pp.148–50]

**What shall be heard?**
**(sestina)**

What shall be heard of us in the far places
When peaceful wells flow glittering, flow more swiftly
What shall be heard of us, the salt, the leaven?
Shall they who pass us by arise and hearken
Smearing our names with words we never uttered,
Twisting with long illogic our fiery phrases?

We are the leaders, we by scarce-spoken phrases
May sway the multitudes of many places:
Take heed of all that we in secret uttered—
They shall be catch-words shouted skyward, swiftly.
Raise up your heads, O rulers, now and hearken:
The moulded dough may froth from the rising leaven!

Ye would bake bread without the needed leaven
Moving but few with oft-repeated phrases.
And is it to the war-lords men will hearken?
Behold a flame within the desolate places,
Behold the loathèd canker spreading swiftly
And power undreamt of, slogans now not uttered:

What shall be done when our cries in the city are uttered?
What cause for agitation and fear-leaven
When bloodless barraging shall batter swiftly,
Bid battle cease despite the war-like phrases
And idols crash in hidden sanctuary places—
Such is the meed for all who will not hearken.

1 In Baxter's MS Book VII (Hocken, MS 704/7) this poem has a lower case 'a' immediately above the 'm' of 'Andymone'—it appears, therefore, that he intended to write 'Andyamone', although to be correct it should be 'Aphrodite Anadyomene' ('of the sea foam'). Beneath this line (at the foot of page 149) there is written very faintly, and then crossed out, a line that appears to say 'Pronounce æfrodaet ændImonEe'.

With small rejoicing shall the minions hearken:
Expected ultimatum is unuttered,
Peace is proved possible in warring places
Where trust is surely the essential leaven:
We who approach dead foes with friendly phrases
See brothers, loosed from corpses greet us swiftly!

Move on our pathways, change all action swiftly—
Dullards shall be wise though last to hearken.
When we have ended there shall be no phrases,
Cause will have passed for lamentation uttered:
Though seeming anarchy, such is the leaven
That shall be known as gospel in all places!

We from uncharted places come right swiftly,
We who were long the leaven—all shall hearken:
We have the wisdom uttered in true phrases.
[Hocken, MS 704/5:321, pp.105–7]

**They will not mention**

The spark unwilling leaps from points of pain.
Flesh is not iron, life is sweet as rain.
Stage set for the play,
Death dare not disobey.

They will mention
The supreme and beautiful sacrifice
The grave and garlanded head
Of hero dead. But the living have known instead
Mud, blood, ice, and lice.

They will mention
The torch of freedom, the goal of the good:
'Greater love hath no man' . . . than to take and break
A bayonet-blade in the gut of the living—made mad,
Howled on by the raucous and ravening platitude.

They will not mention
Death irretrievable, blood-life of youth
Turned carrion . . . men met, lovers beloved,
Died in their angerless hate. The hill-hearts were moved
The skies moaned, wept tears of iron for youth.
Death wept. They weep not for death.
[Hocken, MS 704/9:565, p.85]

**On hearing speech of Sloth and Fear**

Sloth, loth to leave, may grieve thee: Sloth will fade.
But ah! inertia, dank despair . . . none think,
None care to wonder. Thunder at the brink
Cuts couloirs; ghosts are laid afraid:
Sorrow-of-death, fear's past. Each ghast decade,
Hell, burial anguish, naught I deem. O slink
Poor wolf-torn mortal here. Fear all may drink:
Fears night-and-chaos-whelped of mist are made;

The cross will fend. But soft!—are scoffers who lend
Ear to no fear—bid light at midnight stay
Like Wallenstein. Loved toys that in tomb defend,
Deeds speech-or-banquet-urgent reft, their way
Is led on thread o'er hell-fire. Rock cannot rend.
Despair, despair, despair . . . forth fare they, live and die.
[Hocken, MS 704/9:556, p.74]

**Our Search-Light Lust**

Our search-light lust must leave, reluctantly,
Unearthly nervous beauty; and focussed
In love's extreme new disproportion
Blur the abstraction. Sit for an age,

Watch men like meadow-grass. Earth,
Earth, wind-blown meadows, and our love of meadows
Is no God but a universal entrancing.
Our search-light lust will leave reluctantly.

Death-wish, destruction of the bomber is dear;
Even the mutilated are maimed to jazz;
And suicidal strength grows classical.
The far-off siren calls: we follow.

Yet these, these even, will buttress when we stand.
Our search-light lust must leave reluctantly.
[Hocken, MS 704/9:560, p.78]

**The Salamander**

The salamander walks in flame
And I therein his fabulous form would limn:
(My fire of song has burned for seven years
And fire that burns for seven years may bring

The salamander spirit to appear
The salamander lizard in flame awaking.)

The salamander walks in flame
IN IGNE IMMORTALE SALAMANDRA
O griffin and chimera haunt the air—
Our eyes are night: the fabulous is not.
Life needs were blind; for death made animate
Alone immortal is. Brazen despair,
Stone stare of basilisk are mute;
In mind they move with creatures of their kind.
The salamander walks in flame.
Motion in heat arises, zenith knows
Then sinks; imagination glows
But blank expires.
Eternally
In essence of existence set
Like carved light: has he chosen it?
Volcanic and sulphurous flame forever.
The mounting thunder of fire-spray falls back
But salamander never
Knows aught save weaving motes that shake
His cloistered meditation in clear flame.

From furnace did I see him stare red-lidded,
And no words said;
Wept tears of gold even in flame of fate.
The salamander has no mate.
[Hocken, MS 704/10:583, pp.43–4]

**Baxter to Ginn, undated [July/August 1943]**

Unstamped
by Censor

Brighton,
Otago.

Dear Noel,

My feelings on finishing your letter were, in a sense: 'Noël, Noël, Noël, Noël—Born is the King of Israël' (If you can forgive a crude pun on your name.) I had suspected that a traditionalist lurked in some part of you, and am vindicated. No, the poem is not 'chocolate-box'. The first verse might be truly Blakeian.[1]

1 See 'O I have loved . . .', p.519.

O I have loved the velvet rose
    And sought her mystery (red) to seize
As on her bowing stalk she blows
    And spills red scent on every breeze.

(Pardon my interference—after all, you can spurn it. 'mystery red' is to my ears jarring; the striving after colour in this poem is a little crude. 'And sought her mystery to seize' gives the Blakeian note which it is not plagiarism for one to acquire. Your modernist and traditionalist parts are not always working in co-ordination. One should, I think, have a basis of traditionalism and veneer of modernism to give facility of expression and mood. Thus one can study old masters and violent moderns with perfect enjoyment and equanimity. (One who cannot appreciate Burns because he is on the whole traditional and sentimental is in my eyes a literary lost soul.) The opposite gives the 'inverted pyramid' effect. 'As on her bowing stalk she blows' is perfect poetry—it (quite unaccountably) brings tears to my eyes. I remember making a hardened atheist and doctor weep by reciting 'What shall we seek for'. 'red' scent—the red here is allowable as scent is redder than mystery. I have cut out 'idle' because breezes have always been called idle, and because I like the metre better without it.

The second verse is beautiful and balanced. I admire your ability to give a compressed picture, an essence, without a trace of Hopkins' method.

The third verse is very good. I leave the last line, as here—at the close of a triad—the lengthened metre seems appropriate.

I think you should finish with the fourth verse. It is a temptation to 'round off' but it takes away the poetic climax. ~~One cannot~~ It is far better to finish too soon than too late. Have you seen this typified in short stories?

(On reflection, leave 'idle' in. And I am not satisfied now with cutting off the last verse. Could you write a less material ending? Anyway, as I said, you can spurn my criticisms.)

I liked seeing my poem in 'The Link'. The intense irony of parts of it (attempted if not conveyed) is not obvious on a first reading. But the ending makes the reader return and read again with more understanding—I hope so, anyway. Certainly send 'Judas' or any others you think suitable.[2]

Browning's apparent deep insight and actual superficiality annoys me intensely. However, I cannot deny the durability of many of his lyrics—'Pippa's Song',[3] 'O to be in England . . .'[4] God save me from ever thinking I have perfected my technique!

'la, la'. Go back a bit from the 'Margate' and 'St Augustine' scene. You come on

2 Ginn submitted Baxter's 'Now while the bugles blare' (see pp.214 and 224) to *The Link: Organ of the New Zealand Methodist Bible Class Movements.* The poem was published in XVI.9, 5 Jul 1943: 3; making this the earliest known publication of one of Baxter's poems.

3 Browning's closet drama *Pippa Passes* appeared in the first of his *Bells and Pomegranates* series of pamphlets (London: Edward Moxon, 1841). Pippa, a poor young silk-winder from Northern Italy, wanders through her environment singing short lyrics from time to time. Although she herself does little, people who overhear her song are moved to make significant moral decisions.

4 'O to be in England . . .' is the opening line of Browning's poem 'Home-Thoughts from Abroad' which first appeared as a longish poem in *Bells and Pomegranates. No. VII* (London: Edward Moxon, 1845). The early poem was later divided into three parts: 'Home-Thoughts from Abroad', 'From the Sea', and 'Here's to Nelson's Memory'.

a part containing (I haven't got the book beside me.) 'Elizabeth and Leicester at the stern', 'Gilded shell' and a few other lines.[5]

You are right about the UNICORN. Only a maiden could capture him, by making him lay his head in her lap. The 'iron dream' is definitely material sensuousness and existence.[6]

WHAT SHALL BE HEARD—sestina form, see one of Auden's on valleys, islands, water etc. I managed the difficult form well.[7]

'When bloodless barraging shall batter swiftly'—When the force of emotional and spiritual understanding shall swiftly break down barriers.

THEY WILL NOT MENTION—'The hill-hearts were moved . . . etc . . .' is known as 'fallacy of pathos'. It is used by Milton most extensively in 'Lycidas' where everything is called upon to bewail the death of his friend.[8]

'Loved toys that in tomb defend . . . etc . . .' The idea of exorcising is basic in this poem.[9] 'All our daily habit and small belovéd memories, all our pomp ~~of~~ and inflation of ego gone' .. The theme of this poem is the night-mare of despair.[10]

OUR SEARCH-LIGHT LUST

<u>1st Verse</u>: (Note. I cannot give the poetic word-halo in prose—this you must find for yourself.) We must forget our abstract theorizing [this is a poem on the division of reason and emotion] and focus~~sed~~ to an emotional life in which some elements may be disproportionate.

<u>2nd Verse</u>: Watch all men. The existent earth and our love of it is no abstract God but a 'universal entrancing'.

<u>3rd Verse</u>: When we become emotional, 'Death-wish . . . etc . . .'

5 Baxter is responding to some comments of Ginn's concerning section 'III. The Fire Sermon' of T.S. Eliot's *The Waste Land* (1922): 'la la' (l. 306) falls in the middle of what Baxter has termed the '"Margate" and "St Augustine" scene' due to Eliot's reference to 'Margate Sands' (l. 300) and his two references to St. Augustine's *Confessions*: 'To Carthage then I came' (l. 307) and 'O Lord Thou pluckest me out' (l. 309). The lines he instructs Ginn to go back to begin at line 279:

Elizabeth and Leicester
Beating oars
The stern was formed
A gilded shell
Red and gold

6 Despite a reputation for power and ferocity the unicorn was reputedly gentle during mating and hence symbolised virginity; tradition held, therefore, that the touch of a virgin could tame it. See also 'The Globe of Dream', pp.101–4.

7 Auden's sestina 'Hearing of harvests rotting in the valleys . . .' first appeared in the *Criterion*, Jul 1933. It was collected in *Look Stranger!* (London: Faber & Faber, 1936) and it appears in the *Collected Poems* under the title 'Paysage moralisé'. Characteristically, the line endings of the six six-line stanzas repeat the line-endings of the first stanza—i.e. valleys, mountains, water, islands, cities, sorrow—but in different order in the remaining five. The three-line envoy concludes the sestina:

It is our sorrow. Shall it melt? Then water
Would gush, flush, green these mountains and these valleys,
And we rebuild our cities, not dream of islands.

8 John Ruskin invented the phrase the 'pathetic fallacy' in 1856 to describe in derogatory terms the poetic tendency to attribute human capabilities and feelings to natural objects. Nowadays the term has neutral connotations and Milton's pastoral elegy *Lycidas* (1638), lamenting the death of a fellow student, is recognised—in part because of lines like 'Bid *Amaranthus* all his beauty shed, / And Daffadillies fill their cups with tears, / To strew the Laureat Herse where *Lycid* lies.' (ll. 149–51)—as a work of great originality.

9 See 'On hearing speech of Sloth and Fear', p.240.

10 Untraced.

jazz music: classical music. This verse is on the love and glorification of death The hero commits suicide. etc. etc.

4th Verse: Yet even this is a strength in us.

I enclose one poem (+ perhaps another)

Much love to Terry. I am doing my best to get some books sent up to him (some he left here.)

From,

Jim.

PTO

PS I have re-opened the letter to write this. I will send up 'New Bearings' as soon as possible—probably in 5 days time.

You do not realize to what an extent I leant on the science of numerology in my IN NUMERIS. All obscure poems must have a thread, and this is usually supplied from some outside influence or author, viz. *The Waste Land*.[11] This takes away from originality.

I am not so original now as I once was, and may be losing grip. I have the feeling that I developed steadily from ETERNITY to WHAT SHALL WE SEEK FOR (i.e.—5 to 412)[12] and since then have swerved (THE SALAMANDER is 583) to a less vigorous yet unavoidable line. Tell me if I am wrong—or rather, forget it. I feel gloomy sometimes, but when I look back to see what I wrote it is usually good enough. I start examinations tomorrow—never a salutary episode—and that may have caused it. Apologies.[13]

J.K.B.

[VUW Library, MS McKay 28/15]

**Night**

(poem written in insecurity)

O night, night, night: bitter-bleak, battering,
Yet black, dead-blocked—O night has leaves,
Inhuman, agèd, foliage tomb-hewn; weft weaves
Where death drifts windless, wakeless, rib-wing.
    Who built? why?—in sky not, in earth ming-
led nor; nay; not in earth purged, nor birth-greaves,
Earth-sheaves, risen, rust-moulded to—hell's halidom; heaves
Ice-rigid, hell-rim-hidden, in night abiding.

11 In his notes to *The Waste Land*, Eliot gives details of a variety of works consulted in the writing of the poem and makes particular mention of Jessie Laidlay Weston 's (1850–1928) study of the Grail legend: *From Ritual to Romance* (1920); and Sir James George Frazer's (1854–1941) twelve-volume epic of anthropology, *The Golden Bough* (published between 1890 and 1915).

12 For Baxter's early poem 'Eternity' see Appendix 2, p.445.

13 Baxter's system of numbering and recording his poems is discussed in 'Baxter's Early Manuscript Books', pp.72–81. The examinations he refers to were internal examinations in which he performed sufficiently well that his ranking in the class at the end of the second term rose to fifth out of eighteen, from eighth at the end of the first term. As usual he came first in English.

Arc-light glare, glow, flare in death's dream-wood
Christ's light, orbed, comfort and eye-like:—
Fear flaming girds; grides; saw moon-without-blood
Moon-metal moveless, naught behind, I. Woke,
Wrenched, wrung, strung-tendoned—mind's-monster stood.
While mind holds, abyss-flung, night knows not day-break.
[Hocken, MS 704/10:574, p.10]

**Phantasmagoria of Silence**
(to be chanted, making full use of vowels)

Salvèd we shall not be. Seeking amid cold clamour
of men blinded, for bread we will have combat.

Heaven we hold not nor the fruits of Eden;
and stars stir ritually rhapsodic desire
vain viewless music strumming in the wind:
erode clear counsel; we are dead though men.

The living protoplasm, who heeds? will die.
Hell claims not, earth and air refute until
even the new-awakened fires of summer
Yea answer, burn; we bleed flesh knowing not why.

Lay'st thou, mad dreamer, chains enclose? . . .
And gales in groaning boughs, the gales without an end
in sport burst chains, let death and madness in:
Death flowers, the rose, ere madness overthrows.

Isis spake 'Hearken'. Lotus yet will drown;
new ghosts sing under invisible hammer-blows.

Night falls, day rises. Ah, beyond these hills
is peace of womb in eternal villages . . .
Nay, night falls, the rock and night-mare fills
easily die the drifting daffodils
verdant and flame forever where life lies.
Eyes glassy, mien reserved tell us that we
have lost our hell, our heaven, are dead though men.

In those remote death-future villages
now sing the nightingales that are not stilled.

But what avails the nightingale? in vortex
and upon crag we fail . . . weight on our lids,
blank the horizon hangs. Flushed faith,

young birth, new love, in garbage may
lengthen the mollusc day; by empty sheds
over a rock of death falls rocket-flaring
Nymph of our love, faith-phoenix, life—and dies.

Leaders, though power exalt us, though the stars
irk not our Atlas-shoulders; still
Klaxon and combat for our bread is given:
even the blank horizon clangs; death hangs
witless as weather. Within, without, the star-
ing sky of death annihilates to naught.
Shout guns, flare up in flame. O human breast
Ensanguined flame in vain, fall down to iron rest

to dream, to death, to rain and daffodils:
[Hocken, MS 704/9: 561, pp.79–80]

**Baxter to Ginn, 11 August 1943**

CENSORED
No. 4

Brighton,
Otago.
11/8/43.

Dear Noel,

I will go through your letter. In 'Night', RIB-WING means with ribbed wings like a bat; it also has associations with skeleton ribs. Death, the twin of Night flaps overhead with the deep mournfulness you mention.

'nay not in earth purged, nor birth-greaves, Earth-sheaves, risen, rust-moulded to.' Hell is mental, so cannot be purged in cleansing earth; 'birth-greaves' is perhaps far-fetched—it is the idea of the unborn child stepping into the sheathing greaves of matter. 'Earth-sheaves' is of course harvest etc. 'rust-moulded to' because if mental anguish became physical it would share in the needful decay of matter. 'abyss-flung' means 'flung into the abyss of night'. Many of my poems are of course moods, though much rationalized. This remark applies to 'Phantasmagoria of Silence'. Nevertheless 'nihilism' is a reality in a crumbling ~~and~~ world where moral and spiritual values often disintegrate under pressure of disruptive brute force.

Your ideas about 'ETERNITY' are, I think, correct. Most of my earliest poems are very short but very good poetry. It was only at a later stage that I so far conceded to that which I read as to lose taste in vague sentimentalism. I probably have plagiarized the 'points of pain' metaphor; you may have noticed phrases recurr in my poems, especially those written hastily. Occasionally the sub-conscious remembrance is not of my own image, but of one which I have read and have appreciated as much as if I had written it myself. I have Basil Dowling's poems. They [are] often slight but most beautiful, far better than the strained or wishy-washy N.Z.ism often encountered. I do not think that he has fully developed discrimination but there are two lines better than Owen. He is by far the best New Zealand poet I have seen published.

> And an uneasy wind stirs through the grain
> In fields thick-sown with seeded agony.[1]

'Unearthly nervous beauty' is the D.H. Lawrence or Wilfred Owen 'poetry of the nerves', the note slight and piercing as the sound of a finger-nail on a slate. However, forget 'Our Search-Light Lust'. It is an obscure member of an obscure series and is not worthy of prolonged study. How I wish I could talk to you! Letters are excellent for recording and encouraging thought, but are not good for discussion and explanation.

Critique: 'tiny' is not a good word, or rather is a dangerous one, more dangerous than 'lovely'.[2] You have not fully developed the other-sense of discrimination which a poet must have—the discrimination which knows when it swerves. My sins in this direction are blacker, for they are mostly conscious.

I can get inside the cage of your poetry, or often can. From the semi-subjective point of view everything is perfect and in perspective. But, objectively, parts jar. 'Noise-naughty' is, for the reader, a phrase not sufficiently controlled.[3] But in the marvellous and happy mean are 'milken snowdrops'.

~~Calm~~ Your 'Snow-drops' is far better than 'Rue Rousant' which is too glittering or too personal.

> Calm among the light-spill
> Of sharp and gothic grass, the qualmless peace of the Rood

is (to me) half surrealist but most striking, musical, and moving.

'nuns of quietude' is a phrase worthy of Keats at his very best.

In 'Dawn and the devil' you are too keen on colour for colour's sake.[4]

'blue' in the first verse is good. The 1st verse itself is dream-musing made living; it has the sharp and unrecapturable poignancy beyond thought of a dream-emotion.

1 The final two lines of Dowling's poem 'Twenty Years After', about a visit to the site of one of the great battles of the First World War, from *A Day's Journey: Poems* (Christchurch: Caxton, 1941), pp.15–16. The poem concludes:

> But as we drive away I turn to see
> The sunset warn the world with crimson fire
> Lest the old darkness should come down again,
> And an uneasy wind stirs through the grain
> In fields thick sown with seeded agony.

2 See 'Rue Rousant', p.519.

3 See 'Snowdrops', p.520.

4 See 'Dawn and the Devil', p.520.

'black', 'white', in the next verse is not so good, especially 'white'. Explain this verse to me: I find it difficult.

The third verse has the freshness of rainy(?) dawn mixed in my mind with some of the frustration of my 'Cry Mourn'.

'crimson' is necessary, yet is too absolute a colour: yet 'coral' and 'rosy' and 'rose-pearled' are banal.

The 4th verse is clever and catchy.

The 1st two lines of verse 5 are not difficult but the last two (I think) lack unity.

The last verse I find difficult to criticise, but think to be good.

<u>'Enclosed'</u>:'Cause and result' —it is not the girl but the climber in the crevasse. This verse is based on fact like all the rest.

'Many have written well'—a bit Yeatish and childish.

'The Flower' —'hexagonal': light is given atomic structure; the bee-cell is hexagonal. The hexagon to me is the symbol of unreasoning mindless emotionless activity. This poem is most compact.

'Samson' — a bit Blakeian.

'Worship' —did I send you a poem 'Where beauty dips to dust . . .'

'Reverie of a Prisoner'—maybe unsuccessful.

'Cried passionate Blake . . .'—I believe in Blake.

Much love to Terry.

From,

Jim.

[VUW Library, MS McKay 28/16]

**Cry Mourn**

There is a maze wherein the mind may enter,
A floral doorway where sad sunset leaves
Entice, cry 'Mourn!' Unbroken winter;
Groved ruined tomb; sword-winds of Ossian
Hurtle and moan. Entranced heart grieves,
Returns: there is no returning. Gravely burning
Cool stained-glass shows the priest-king, chills the man.
In a quiet museum with dusty ivory—
Carved ivory and frayed cloth of Turkestan—
I saw once a scabbard oriental
And curved dagger sleep quietly.
Oxen, rough rock-walls, and beyond them steppes;
Religious yet un-Christian sun down-glinting.
The intricate carving spoke in elemental
Speech, of unsleeping primitive vigour; apes

Stirring to manhood, or men beast-aping;
If of tomb, then Taj Mahal of tombs;
Princesses in wind-lighted rooms—wind-tapestry
As of a legend, myth heroic looms.
(This not of Turkestan but my loose brain.)
They in veneered case slumbered aloof from me.

Nostalgia saw the sky and lived
Unnostalgic in new-created world.
But O
Fearsome, deep-graven is the twilight
When heavens are not domed helmet, helmet of
Invisibility—crowned wherewith
Man strides beyond earth—but mist-hidden walls
Life-moveless where mist moves and asphodel
Lingers, remembers; or where sunset streaks
A stone beach of archaic citadels
And calls that man and faith should drown,
Drown in the breeze-blown sea of torrentless time.
Then waken.
The world is clarity, though all pain.
The hurling wind and the bluff rain
Have woes past comforting, rejoice.

O weep for good bygone!
But weep not overlong; the past will not awaken.
Those who look long are lost therein.
[Hocken, MS 704/10:582, pp.40–42]

**Cause and Result**

Results
Impinge strangely on the mental diaphragm:
They are without emotion
And often malignant to their causes.

There is a shout within the political sky:
'Treason': Treason; the handkerchief
Flutters; hurt eyes close frantically
To the last-day-on-earth clouds; and the bullet is brief.

Starry and pale the eidelweiss
Flowering: flowering avalanche-scars;
And the gauche, pitiful, booted climber is
Forgetful of girl flower-desirous in undesirous crevasse.

In mountain crouching the miner; streaked ore
Of iron: iron the bomb battering;
Stupendous engine-thud; men men before
Ants, loveable ants, crushed ants where science in steel may sing.

Concluding.
It is the mobile objectively objectionable
Subjectively subject to beauty, man-mind
(The unindustrious ant, the oratorical ape)
That causes causes
Results in results.
[Hocken MS 704/10:594, pp.62–3]

**Many have written well . . .**

Many have written well;
Many have chanted
Sweet in the ears of hell—
And these are dead.
    But what of beauty they vaunted?
Is there no beauty here?
Bitter or bird-enchanted,
Melodious mouths of fear;
Even the dead like flowers
Were natural and near.
    I speak to shattered ears—
It is not flame that scorches,
It is not iron of death
But the extinguished torches
Of marrowless aftermath.
    And he who crawled in trenches
Will draw unburdened breath
Amid the fouler stenches,
The cavalcading slum;
Yet in the upright body
Mind's posture stoops the same
When that unhearkening sky
No longer rent by flame,
Has frozen, chilled to steel.
    And I though young in hate
And all my school-boy brothers
Are gashed by battle still,
Buried with bones that are white;
The unspoken song of others
Can our red mouths speak now

For months since clogged with mud?
    Integrity is slow,
And the fever in the blood
When speechless is more wild:
Dead manhood leaves alone
The withered and the child.
    Our hearts harden to stone
Or sear and burn to the bone.
        [Hocken, MS 704/10:593, pp.60–61]

**The Flower**

O the chaste icicle
Unscathèd, beautiful;
No core immortal known
In body of clear stone.

And fire-transfigurèd
Waves the sun-gold head
Of copulative flame
Harsh icicles to maim.

And we made luminous,
Immortal flame in us—
Immortal thread begun
Ascend to parent sun.

Science hath spitted thee
On bar of memory:
Hexagonal looms light
In puny atom might.

Orbed sun and mountainous heaven;
And flower of flame hath striven,
The trumpet-flower ascending
Till heavens break and sing.
        [Hocken, MS 704/10:585, pp.48–9]

**Samson**

Darkness for body and cloak
Old Darkness once spoke;
And the scalèd Tempter began:
Art thou not isolate, O man ?

It is the ravenous night
(Light is dark, dark is light)
Aeons make ravenous
In gashèd bitterness.

Hidden in womb thou wert
But air made cold thy heart;
Death will destroy,
Death is the portion of joy.

Fruitful embraces sweet
Harden to cold deceit;
Laugh, kiss, or moan,
Thou art ever alone:

But O the stony heart
Will never burn or smart—
Night has created thee,
Night shall thy portion be.

The holy skies will goad
Thee on accustomed road;
Reject god-sight
And bitterness of light.

God-curse cannot appall
Tugged pillars will fall;
Curse God and then
Embrace the night again.
[Hocken, MS 704/10:584, pp.46–7]

### Worship

Worship wherefore? most ravenous and strong
Furies, desires, frustrations rear in us;
Chained and immured, bound on a bitter cross
Us may no outward image comfort long—
Nay, rather rave and mock in menacing song.
Stone universe appalls; and mazèd thus
Mind needs createth—flaming fosse, or truss—
Brave mountainous figures breast-held, gigantic Right and wrong.

Such is the pantheon, to one God now
Carved, moulded. Here is the fissure begun
Of flesh and spirit whence all terrors flow—

Where beauty dips to dust are terrors none.
Yet by our strife gape the sharp chains: and lo,
Outward and mental universe are one.
[Hocken, MS 704/10:591, p.58]

**Reverie of a Prisoner**

I had forgotten all that I held dear—
Captivity creates the world anew—
And puny hate and puny fear
Made mazes that I long ~~will~~ must maunder through;
Made mazes where no Minotaur will thunder,
Nor spiral flame in purgatorial wonder
Shake, flake to song.
. . . I strode,
I wandered by a winding road and saw
A mad-house emblematic on a hill:
'That is the world, the world's heart and thy heart',
Said he forever with me. 'They live by law
Though the flame-rose, the sun, and cavernous still
Cold crystal Sea of law knew never tithe nor part;
Belch, slobber, grunt and fart,
Yet would be very gods; feel in their clay,
Candescent, passionate, the symphony
Which grass that knows not greenness hums better than they.'

Then the white hills of death
To clear birth burning rose horizonal;
The road in supplication leapt—and I
Wakened in captive sorrow.
Eyes must be narrowed
In puny hate, in puny fear.

[Curse not the bitter sadist, curse rather the cruelty of
the cold in heart:
Mock thou never the fool: for we are all fools and
desire to be comforted.]
[Hocken, MS 704/10:588, pp.53–4]

**Cried passionate Blake . . .**

Cried passionate Blake: 'I seek for no negation,
No weeping law to bind Imagination
Nor yet harsh wastes of infinite void Error;
Joy to the mind immortal hath no terror,
Save free Imagination no truth is!'

I likewise. For exterior images
Are voiceless, dead, should soul observant see not;
All life in mind of man existeth; zealot
Or poet through timeless and through formless make
Their own fires body, comb and break:
Imagination is immortal: so
Our spirits of immortal fire partake.
[Hocken, MS 704/10:589, p.55]

**Baxter to Ginn, 4 September 1943**

CENSORED
No. 1

Brighton,
Otago.
4/9/43

Dear Noel,

Your poems never grate on me. All of them are clever, most are intellectual, and some are excellent poetry.

You have managed the sestina form well.[1] There are no jarring metaphors in this poem; the modernity is in no way forced. The 5th verse is the best, I think. 'Britons skiffing rudely' is good (although at first I thought it *skipping*!) The poem is better in many ways than mine—the sestina, I mean. Should 'rudely' be 'crudely'; the latter gives to me the association 'coracle' and has not—no, you'd better leave it as it is. It is in many ways a most excellent poem. I like 'botticelli trees'. It is like good surrealism.

The second is much more uneven.[2] 'with a clatter of scientific joy' is of course quite lucid, but is definitely not too good. The 3rd verse is the worst, the 4th is the best and almost indecently forcible. In most of your poems the natural image crystallizes into a set symbol. This ~~of co~~ is quite allowable, and, though not my technique, is often very effective. I think I tend to try to drag you away from your natural development to my methods. Where I would say 'turf' or at most 'iron turf'

1 See 'Beauty has burned unseen', p.522.
2 See 'Unrest', p.523.

you say 'painted geometric lawns'. But your poetry is more psychological than mine, and also you have developed another set of symbols.

'To Woman' is rather shallow, but not bad; the Ghazel is an old one;[3] 'The Stream of Faith' is one of the best of my earlier ones; 'in the crowd' is a kind of imitation of E.E. Cummings; 'Resume of Perdition' is the last one I have written; 'O rose dost thou weep?' is a villanelle; 'The Class-Problem' an experiment in syllabic verse; 'Interim' is I suppose just propaganda; 'The Plaster Scene' is thin and rather plastery in parts. In your first poem 'Janus' refers to Man looking toward past and future, I suppose?

I enclose also some poems which might be fit to set to music. Not all of them of course. If they are, do you think I could get a copy of some with music attached?[4] There is a poem of Auden's 'Lay your sleeping head my love . . .'[5] which should go well to music, but I can't find ~~my~~ the book with that one in it. Also one of G.M.H. 'Margaret, are you grieving . . .'[6]

The times when I am overcome by a kind of terror are when I lose my pleasure in the moment. Then past and future are equally black. Remember that 'happiness' depends almost entirely on vitality of mind, on inner conditions not outer circumstances. You are handicapped, are you not, by physical delicacy? This must be counterbalanced by a solidity of mental structure. I hope I don't sound priggish or preaching; this is just an attempted analysis, quite objective.

I have got the *Faber Book of Modern Verse* and bury myself in Yeats in whom I find the most poetry. It is a very good book; I hope you have it.[7]

Best wishes
From
Jim.

P.S 'Dawn and The Devil'—my fault I didn't follow it all, not yours. It is somewhat patchy, but a good poem.

[VUW Library, MS McKay 28/17]

3 The ghazel—from an Arabic word for spinning, or love-making—denotes a lyric poem in a generally peaceful, erotic, or mystical mood. The form was developed by the Persians in the 13th and 14th centuries and picked up by certain German poets—including Goethe—who imposed on it their own variations in length. Baxter's ghazel conforms to the Persian model in respect of its length—between 4 and 14 lines—and the repetition of the rhyme on the even lines, with the odd lines unrhymed. However, the traditional ghazel commences with a rhymed couplet and usually mentions the *tahullus*, or author's pen-name, in the final couplet. The considerable similarities between Baxter's ghazel and James [Elroy] Flecker's 'Yasmin: *A Ghazel*', from his collection *The Golden Journey to Samarkand* (London: Goschen, 1913) suggests that Flecker may have provided the model that Baxter followed. 'Yasmin' begins:

How splendid in the morning glows the lily: with what grace he throws
His supplication to the rose: do roses nod the head, Yasmin?

4 According to Ginn another inmate, named Alf Ainslie, had a friend who was trying to compose songs. When Ainslie asked Ginn for some poems he passed the request on to Baxter who 'suggested Red Hanrahan's Song about Ireland which has some lovely lines'. Ginn also showed Ainslie some of Baxter's poems 'but nothing came of the episode' (letter to Paul Millar, 21 Nov 1995).

5 See reference in Baxter's letter of 28 August 1942 to Auden's 'Lullaby', p.143 (footnote 2).

6 Hopkins's poem 'Spring and Fall: to a young child' (1880), begins:

Margaret are you grieving
Over Goldengrove unleaving?
Leaves, like the things of man, you
With your fresh thoughts care for, can you?

7 Michael Roberts, ed., *The Faber Book of Modern Verse* (London: Faber & Faber, 1936).

**To Woman**

You, who are woman, cannot know me fully
Though judging my knowledges or seeming folly.
Men stir nations or battle within the host:
You turn and calmly wonder at their haste
Knowing the world is all in all secure
And heart's-blood even at the bitter core—
Where you have no desire to penetrate:
Your glossary is learnt by rote
But I have nonesuch ever
Who must sweat on and over
Ephemeral mental barriers raised by me
Finding well-head of beauty where there may
Be nothing but indomitable mind
That wavers yet in some chaotic bond,
Region where your sure cosmos enters not.

Doubtless the world is neat
With Deity or Atheos on top,
And doubtless you are right to the finger-tip:
Your cultured mind has sliding-rules
To measure Man, the rude embracer,
Poet, or literary bruiser;
You recognise both mode and breakfast-rolls
And doubtless reconstruction after war:
But I shall wander I know not where,
Lodeless, loaded, seeking a dream existing
Only within my multiplex mental jousting—
And finding not, and by white water
Dreaming; while you tip the waiter.

I cannot break nor circumvent
Your closed car of self-content,
Nor can you enter in
To the squalor and the splendour and the madness here and gone:
Our relationship will be difficult—
There are heights, walls that can never be scaled—
But without you I am lost,
Riven, down-cast:
So shall we enter from the cold.

[Hocken, MS 704/6:335, pp.19–20]

**Beauty (a Ghazel)**

My heart is closed in weariness far from the silver springs that bless,
That still the spirit's storm and stress—such is thy silent night, O Beauty!

The song is fled, the tongue is mute, and shattered is the crystal lute
While rust has mantled on the flute that pierced with glad sunlight, O Beauty!

Grey light has entered to mine eyes, the song-bird frozen in the skies
Has lost the larger Paradise of mirth and joyous might, O Beauty!

Soul of my soul, return, return! for fires of being dimly burn
Within the ash-encumbered urn that once was burnished bright, O Beauty!

When shall the faith that long has fled, rejoicing in thy goodlihead
Strike Sorrow dumb and anguish dead in fleet returning flight, O Beauty?

Ah! but the stars are pale above where golden flashes nearer move
By moon-enchanted spirit grove—thou flamest to my sight! O Beauty!
[Hocken, MS 704/4:261, p.177]

**The Stream of Faith**[1]

I stood upon a tall hill summitless
Above a low miasmic plain
Whence rose a cry of weariness—
A cry of pain:
The wail of souls forsaken
That wander desolate,
While the world will not awaken
To the trumpet-call of Fate
That sounds unheeded warning
Beyond the outer gate.

Then soon the mist had lifted from the plain
And from the thunder-riven cliff that loomed
Above the low clouds drifting, I could see
A stream that flowed full silently
To vanish from my sight again
Among the many canyons of the hills;
While by each smaller tributary lay
The strong-walled cities of the world, and they
Built over the clear streams with roofs of stone
And shadowed them in weedy, stagnant pools.

1 Beneath this poem in manuscript notebook II (Hocken MS 704/2) Baxter has written, in a later hand, 'Good Climax'.

Then where I stood alone
    Came an unseen companion—'These are they
    Who draw new creeds from faith's clear spring
    And then with towers of ritual wall them round
        Far from the brighter light of day;
    But yet some few have found
    That only at the fountain-head, where sing
    The joys and hopes of ages yet to come
    May rise religion free from tarns of gloom—
    Not in the savage hum
    Of toiling cities where no room
    Is left for seeds of spirit, but where shine
    The living flowers of forests coralline,
    Or where the silvered lichens cling
    To tall rain-rotted trees that yet can bear
    Fresh blossoms in the time of spring
Or where
The mountain air
Glimmers above the blue lake's placid deep
And wakes from age-long sleep
    Old glaciers and the eternal snow.
        [Hocken, MS 704/2:113, pp.62–4]

**in the crowd**

i am interested to
note men flicker like flames
some drossy and some
handsome like fine candles (loud
the rumble of trams and
etceteras smote somewhat strong) but
remote we
remain despite such: for
no one may touch for
that is a kind of ann-
ihalation for each
flame or mind is a different kind of
fire then remember
there
is only half-life in the separate safe
bone-banner-scroll of
an ivory skull that
society is
weally interesting that

except where
the edges of flame are touching we are
plug-ugly monkeys
in a
space-time continuum
[Hocken, MS 704/10:600, pp.78–9]

**Résumé of Perdition**

Sing, soul, sing now like a sweet bird—
Not with the easy hysteria of the bard
Not with the gauche and adolescent pride:
Men screamed, men's mouths have prayed;
So may a man's tongue speak
May clear heel-trampled skulls, the jagged spike
Of death that rent their bodies and slew some.
Sing of the lesser evil.
Shattered seem
Familiar lineaments of earth; the white
And death's-head sun sags with a spider weight;
Torn trunks, not trees, in mud are motionless.
O dear-desirèd tyranny we lose!
For tyranny not now of savage shells
But death-inertia. Stranded on time's shoals
The fanged heart moveless can but stab. The best
Are killed, the worst grow cold, debased;—
For birth we know, the agony of creation;
And death we know, the harsh disintegration;
But this midway delirium is born
Of no ordainèd powers, new flares that burn
But the refined despair, objective hate.
Limbs cauterized, the animal is hurt.
Air is aghast, hills shudder afraid;
The animal, no god, is crucified.
And maimèd moans.

The cancer-rot reaches among our towns:
And the high houses where half-life retains
Its damask halls are smeared with that grey pus;
For from the battle-fields hear the Death pass,—
Is passing inexorable. (Limbs in loam made black
Iron in their unnatural rest, though bleak
Are unmalicious; are life conquerèd
Thus more dread death.) The laugh of paganhood

May mar the mute, may mock the bitter Rood;
But death spawned overlong will procreate.
The hail of blood and fire was fear, not fate:
The animal, no god, is crucified;
And maimèd moans. Vigour grown dead and dumb
Slain by us, cannot stem the helldom.
Felled by a child's whimper we crumble to doom.
[Hocken, MS 704/10:602, pp.82–4]

**O rose dost thou weep?**

O rose dost thou weep
Because thou art a flower?
Sleep, rose, sleep!

When dew was deep
I walked by thy bower—
O rose dost thou weep?

While frail ghosts creep
To their ivory tower
Sleep, rose, sleep.

Aloof ~~dost thou keep~~ thou dost keep
From man's bitter dower;
O rose dost thou weep?

Death quiet will seep
In sun, in shower:
Sleep, rose, sleep!

Sun-sorrow I reap
Or leaden skies lower.
O rose dost thou weep?
Sleep, rose, sleep!
[Hocken, MS 704/10:601, pp.80–81]

**The Class-Problem**

I
prefer
men who do not jar
by reference to their wealth or poverty
upon my sensitivity
of class and
inherent self-command.

Though
women
(different again)
cause little embarassment when they do so:
this tolerance I think is due
to S.A.
which blurs the issue, say.
[Hocken, MS 704/10:599, p.77]

**Interim**

What shall I strum upon the ancient lyre
O bards?
upon the slickly abandoned xylophone what subtleties
O wise birds?

The locusts have destroyed ten counties
in the Honan province.
Last year was a famine
and the people ate bark:
this year the locusts have devoured the bark also.

The mass-slaughter of civilians
continues
in the genteel and high-minded bombing
of Italian cities
(O Dante seest thou visions immortal?
O Dante what inferno? . . .
let the aesthetic applaud.)

Through Grecian streets
(would that I might forget
spears of Thermopylae!) . . .
Through Grecian streets
wanders a child
with skeleton hands hung crossed
with gaping mouth and ulcered
with starved protuding belly
and scrabbles in garbage:
The food-ships may not pass.

I will sing of a street-café
(hark, they are bombing Paris)
I will sing a sweet roundelay

of psychological flowers
But would rather cry
or die.
[Hocken, MS 704/10:597, pp.69–70]

**The Plaster Scene**

'Whence this duality
Of spirit and of purpose when two suns
Have entered and destroyed themselves in me?'—
IN NUMERIS.

1

Speak of the dead to me.
Their quiet immortality
Is like a flame or star;
Golden Pythagoras
And the grave Caesar pass,
To me immortal are.

But their full souls, piteous, unpiteous,
They live not. Whither are they?
Did they stretch out with crying hands
Into the night (as night fell on them)
Toward our sunned security?

To us whom are the dead?
only a painted blind
where through sun's rays are shed
from solitude behind.
All that my eyes see not
is inchoate to me:
All that my blood knows not
is nebulosity.

Quiet they lie in clay:
Crocus-bells waken them.
Quiet they lie—ah nay!
Utter death like a doom
Dissolved them clean away;
Or they have spurned inertia of the tomb

2

I can endure
the civic threat, the public hate
Self-approbation remaining
enwhorlèd, secure.

O where are the unborn?
night deeper than ages lies on them
illuminate alone
by ray of love or reason
that pierceth cruel stone
spans brief eternity
makes time a mockery.

Clear in my burning skull
A scroll of life is wrought:
Envious have I grown in bitter thought
Of the God beautiful
Whose bone and blood I am
Whose limbs lie bathed in time.

(Ruled by a black vacuum
of the is-not unknown
I have nor life nor sight beyond
a life of blood and bone)

Seas, hills, and men are painted
Upon a plaster scene;
Only that which the blood knows
Lives and is born within.
Waves and men are painted . . .
lo, and the bone is pointed:
Hate and love are arisen.

But the all-knowing God
visions not aught save his blood:
Death, life to him are known
as flesh and bone.

3

Christ or Nietzche.
With tears and burning love we walk
With love and suffering.
Or say:
The world has beaten on me
the blind exterior
steam-roller of existence
would crush and rend me:
No love shall prevail;
turn, soul, and save thyself
from fire and savage hail
Though all life fall, though all life fail.

By love alone may we
Bid the frail dead arise
And shed their burial;
By love alone may see
All flesh entire, and all
Dear beyond prize
Though bitter, fangèd, tyrannical.
[Hocken, MS 704/10:598, pp.71–6]

The screws—I'm afraid we called them screws—they were okay by-and-large, they were conscripted people. . . . [and] they had to do the censoring. They each had an army hut and at one stage I had the job of cleaning them out daily and refilling the burners—kerosene burners—and one of them handed me one of Jim's letters, it might have been twenty to thirty pages with his poems you see, endless poems. They'd just bang the stamp, it might have been 'one' or 'two' or something like that, a figure. It was their duty to censor them—I don't know the details of the rules they had—and he made this remark about a 'pack of rubbish' or something like that. It was just a light, superficial incident which somehow got to Jim, I don't know how because they would read my letters. It made their work more difficult. . . .

—Noel Ginn[1]

**Baxter to Ginn, 11 September 1943**

CENSORED
No. 1

Brighton,
Otago,
11/9/43

Dear Noel,

I am sorry that I have annoyed the censor. But after all they don't need to read all my poems, which are rarely of a political or subversive nature. Still I will not write at such length. I have been sending some of my earlier ones up lately; but at present am not writing much. The school-term will begin in a day or two, and while I am at school I do not write many poems, nor as a matter of fact very good ones.

I write to you because

There is only half-life in the separate safe bone-banner-scroll of an ivory skull.[2]

1 Noel Ginn, personal interview, 25 Oct 1944.
2 See 'in the crowd', p.258.

In other words, what I write is useless unless there is someone appreciating it. My father has full appreciation of most of what I write, my mother knows and likes the best ones, but they are not 'intellectual' in the way that you are—or not quite anyway. Also, you are probably writing as good or better poetry than anyone else in NZ. (B.D. a possible exception; though he is usually over-simple and over-naive.)

Your poem is very excellent.[3] No word jars, no word is out of place. It is controlled freedom, it is forceful. The last line is the best. You have borrowed a bit in style from my 'O lands seen in the light . . .'

PTO

But the poem is yours, all yours. 'What huge transgression . . . ?' I understand perfectly. 'writhing' is perhaps slightly uncontrolled, but I have no word to replace it with.

Terry has been asking after you. When do you go back to Hautu?[4]

Best wishes,

From

Jim.

[VUW Library, MS McKay 28/18]

**Baxter to Ginn, 2 October 1943**

[Transcribed by Ginn.[1]]

2.10.43

The 3 typed sides are at hand. As you say, I have more or less sent most of my early poems. Remember that whereas most fairly prolific writers expose only a little of their verse to the public eye, you get nearly all mine & there must be some chaff in it. When I call you 'intellectual' I think I mean that your poetic attitude corresponds more with that of the 'intellectuals' than that of the 'heart cryers' (who are, be it noted, banal).

IN FLAMES POLITIC you can look on as an imitation of Yeats. The 'Class-Problem' is an expression of a thought which would not have been written if I'd tried any other form. Syllabic verse is like this: e.g. 1, 2, 5, 11, 8, 3, 6. 1, 2, 5, 11, 8, 3, 6. This is the syllabic pattern of the above poem; each corresponding line in each verse has an equal no of syllables. This gives a fine cumulative effect, though it is not so apparent in a short poem. The GHAZEL I wrote a long time ago; the rhyme-form is Arabic I think.

3 See 'Flinders Range', p.526.

4 After a year at Hautu camp, Ginn, who was suffering from ill-health due to a neck injury, was transferred back to Strathmore base detention camp for treatment, and then on to Whitanui detention camp, just off the highway between Shannon and Foxton. Three months later Terence Baxter was also transferred to Whitanui, and both he and Ginn remained there until their release. See 'Detention Camp Life', pp.91–2.

1 In a letter to Paul Millar dated 2 Mar 1995, Ginn explains the reasons for his transcriptions:

> I began to paste all Jim's letters & poems in a scrap book but did not get very far in this. On winding up the Wanganui home when I left for Sydney [in 1969, see 'Epilogue' p.125] I destroyed the bulky scrap books, copying out Jim's letters but not his poems which I knew he had preserved. I took these copies with the other original letters of Jim.

I have never felt at any time that I have said all I wanted to say. The nearest approach is 'The Mountains'. I feel many things that need to be said, but they all seem too large for translations; the poem is essentially a small thing. 'P.L.' & 'The Inferno' are either a no. of smaller poems woven together or else monstrosities.[2] My 'Where nets of time . . .'[3] which I recognise as my best, is of the first kind. Some of Swinburne's are, I believe of the second.[4]

The two sonnets I enclose were on the whole well put together, though hardly concise enough. Still some would like them.

TEN THOUSAND DREAMS must be judged by you. AENEAS although of clear-cut structure, does not satisfy me: 'Italy, she, the shoreward groaning breaker' is the best line by far.[5] Accept it as you may (?) have accepted the 'Deed'.

'The Solitary' I like. The second verse is very good. 3rd verse also. 4th verse: is it 'genus-ship' or 'genius-ship'. I prefer the second. The whole poem is not over deep, but strikes me as beautiful. It is your style and you use it well.[6]

I know one thing—I will write much better one day. All my poems so far are only 'brave mountainous figures breast-held, gigantic Right and Wrong'.[7] I am beginning to wake up & must adjust myself.

Having just discovered that DHL is the incomparable unassailable master of free verse, I must tell it to you, Read 'Bavarian Gentians'.[8]

I have just seen FANTASIA the superb Walt Disney creation.[9] The representation of abstract music by leaping serpents of light & rolling red billows is beyond description. It is emotion made visible. The creation of earth to music from lava to dinosaurs. Walpurgis Night & Satan summoning the lost souls from village & fen; the tolling of the church bell which makes them shrink like shadows from sunlight. The centaurs & centaurettes are more in Disney's usual line—Beethoven's 'Spring Pastoral'.

I hope you go back to Hautu soon. If you do, love to Terry APOPHATIC—(perhaps) belonging to maxims. I will look up a large dictionary in the school library for the rest

[Incomplete]

[VUW Library, MS McKay 28/19]

**In Flames Politic**

The bite of circumstance
And stark forensic doom
Born at the turn of chance

2 Milton's *Paradise Lost* (1667) and Dante Alighieri's *The Inferno* from his *Divina Commedia*.
3 See 'ODE: Where nets of time encircle and destroy', p.282.
4 Algernon Charles Swinburne (1837–1909].
5 See 'Aeneas' in p.454.
6 See 'The Solitary', p.527.
7 See 'Worship', p.252.
8 Lawrence's 'Bavarian Gentians' was first published in *Last Poems*, edited and introduced by Richard Aldington and Guiseppi Orioli (Florence: G. Orioli, 1932).
9 *Fantasia* screened at Dunedin's Octagon Theatre from Friday 1 Oct to Thursday 14 Oct 1943.

Within a quiet room
Where dull-eyed men converse
We see not as a stroke
Politic, but a curse
Bitter to bend and break;
We see the great gaunt wolf,
The black wolf ravenous
Pursuing to engulf
The shadowed sun and us;
The tower of alchemy,
The oak of gradual age
Shattered to anarchy:
Blind and volcanic, rage
The nervous deep frustration
And harsh fanatic blood—
Woe to the warring nation,
More woe to one where good
Gnarlèd and blear ere prime
Must bow its neck beneath
The bludgeoning of time.

As groaned the winds of death
Where pale Aeolus stood
To smite the mountain groins
And loose their wrath abroad,
Savagery in chains
Wept loud with iron tears
For bladed fear to come;
Yet could not stem the fires,
The thunder-shouting flame.

The wolf engulfs our sun;
And dauntless eagles sing
Ere the wolf-age is done.
Elves in their muted moaning
Chill by the stony doors;
And the vast serpent even
When seas forsake their shores
Swelters in his venom.

The bird of pestilence
With cold corpse-laden wings
In moon-bright iridescence
Hovers and clangs,
Whose feathers fall like darts

Death-swift and piercing
Marrow of human hearts
In their fleet passing.

O men unmaimed in mind
Or body, who rise
From sleep within the blind
Forest of Memories,
Heed that kiln nor tower
Make your strong ardour vain
When steel-mills loom in power
And strong and ardorous men
In flames politic make
The world's heart bend and break.
[Hocken, MS 704/10:603, pp.85–8]

**Ten thousand dreams**[1]

Ten thousand dreams
    Flower in my heart;
Ten thousand fears
    Rend it apart.

Feeling my blood
    Burn and awaken
Sharp spirit is moved,
    Grieved and sore-shaken.

Chief in my dreams
    As waters are cool,
Where fells fall steep,
    In a clear hill-pool—

Chief in my dreams
    And mistress thereof
Is a sweet woman
    Who will say to me: 'Love.'

And durable flame
    Is loud in me
Burning more bright than song,
Burning my veins along
    In grave ascendancy.
[Hocken, MS 704/10:610, pp.105–6]

1 Beneath this poem in MS Book X (Hocken, MS 704/10) Baxter has written 'Moving or mawkish ?'

**The Deed**

Two vortices, two vertices we know:
    Deed and anticipation—the deed is greater;
    The deed destroys, creator of the crater;
    The deed is life. Man, mammal and life-hater,
Needs most must seek anticipation, so.

From height observing waves upon a beach
    Anticipation bathes, swims like an otter—
    I am less animal thus loathe the water:
'Seek but find not', the mocking glosses teach.

Occasionally I'm aware I am alive;
    And wish that what is now occasional
    Were chronic: but anticipation, rational,
    Augurs that living, since foundational,
May be more ill than in anticipation's sieve.

'In warm pyjamas I walk over the grass,
    An amber moon escorting': thus, the child.
    But in truth I would be chilled
And seem a buffoon, not funny but crass.

The gangster, frustrated, seizes the deed;
    Finds no satisfaction: 'Why do you kill me?' he cries.
    'I have not stolen, but lost.' But they shoot, and he dies.
Lonely indeed is he who seizes the deed.
Lonely indeed and dead.

Rapt in anticipation behold him
    The saint saunter
    Toward his tower; but time, the deed at the centre,
    Makes the mood splinter.
'God', he will say; no longer flying, must swim.

O do not probe, stab, to discover with speed:
    Death only is then, inchoateness.
    Life is but a caress
    On the skin of the world. With its shadow of bitterness
Love freely anticipates: greater for sure is the deed.

[Hocken, MS 704/10:604, pp.89–91]

**Baxter to Ginn, 4 October 1943**
[Transcribed by Ginn]

COPY 4/10/43

Though a father-confessor I can offer little consolation You are in an irrefrangible impasse—the war. If I feel gloomy, if I have conflict, I can jump on a bicycle & feel happy. After the war they can surely do something about your neck, though doctors now are hasty. Religion can never be my way, for in so doing I retire to my mind & find no true life there; only in meeting others do I find it—& how many can we meet? My advice, for what it's worth, is: don't face up to things; lie low, don't think more than you can help, then when the weight is lifted there may not be much to face up to. You will know the friend who sent me the poem, 'Under the rose.'[1]

Religion to me is not an ardent need for a belief in a θ though in trouble I always seem to find one to murmur to. It is a belief in the sameness & continuity of life; thus, at any rate mentally, I would fear pain but not death, for I cannot believe in death.

'Sonnet XXXVII' is after Sh & rather good in some ways. 'Imaginary Island' I wrote for school & got 'excellent' marked heavily on it. 'Soliloquy of an Earth-Worm' is a skit, satire on men.

Your poem I have not really studied as yet, but it seems good but a little slight. This is the second letter this week, so a bit short.

Very best wishes
From Jim

[VUW Library, MS McKay 28/20]

**Sonnet XXXVII**
(after Shakespeare)

The fangless wrong that in my lady's cheek
As adder i' the flower lurks innocent
Stirs mid my breast all fury (though she's meek)
Then calms wolves of desire by her unpent:
And since my love immortal is, then sure
Eternal hellish wrath must prey on me—
Envy and anguish in the smile demure—
By beauty prisoned or by love set free.
'All men must love her'—cursèd then be they!
All men must love her: who could stay from wooing?
The dolt who scorns, for 's ignorance I'ld slay,
But chidden by her frown must curb the doing.

1 Untraced: Noel Ginn is unsure who Baxter was referring to.

Foul's sweet in her; 'O sad fool', quoth the fair—
I'll don the jester's motley, dance for her.
[Hocken, MS 704/10:611, p.107]

**Imaginary Island—'Tempest' Act II Sc.i 140–155**

Some Mediterranean isle needs would I rule—
With clear cataracts, vine-clad terraces, woods;
And rocky coves wherein the fishing vessels
Laden with fruit o' the deep seek anchorage.
My people a mild people, strong withall
And carefree; I no ruler but chief rather
Waging no tithe on them, dealing no bondage,
A king unkingly, lord in their hearts alone.
Houses I'ld build, no dank slum-hovels massed
But open walls, stone-archèd villages.
They'ld till their vineyards, and cornfields perchance
In some hill-hollow golden by the sea
Of Mediterranean calm.
As barrier
A league from shore a magic wall I'ld set
Invisible, wherefrom all ships would sheer . . .
And prisoned thus in peace they'ld long for strife
As we do now for our Utopia.
[Hocken, MS 704/10:607, p.102]

**Soliloquy of an Earth-Worm**

The sun is silent: so,
O brethren have we quenched the sun?
The hell that knows not element but plays
Upon our unearthed bodies where we parch
Inflamèd, writhing; sears the subtle mouth
That probes to baked earth vainly.

The skin
which coats my world is earth;
and earth is all. Within
one dimension is life:
earth. Death
is on the alien inchoate surface
which is fundamentally unliving being hard and hot like glass.

All grist
I have digested is
redeposited most
cleanly, skilfully. And
save this
and the occasional writhe for quick progress
there is no unified and initial necessary aim of days.

There are
two necessities: prob-
ing and eating; though more-
over I meditate
on grub
sometimes. Being bisexual I am not
troubled by sex-appeal; my egg-ring slips off, egg-sac: that's fate.

But then
there are two atrocious
evils: one is wet in
superfluity; while
worse is
that called Sun. But just now it went out; I think
our casts have overwhelmed it and let primal earth-darkness upward sink.
[Hocken, MS 704/10:612, pp.108–9]

['Imaginary Island' (above) is a rare instance of Baxter writing a poem for a school assignment. His lessons on *The Tempest* also produced the following dramatic sketch.]

**Modern Version of 'Drunken Scene', *Tempest*[1]**

Scene: Outside a pub.
*Enter large man in dungarees, staggering.*

L.M. It'sh cold. (*Stumbling over the gutter.*) What they got a hole 'n the foo'path for? Trip'sh me up. Ow! (*falls over, holding ankle.*) Bit me. Wanna go t' shleep. (*Relaxes breathing heavily.*)
*Enter small man in overcoat, slightly intoxicated.*

S.M. Hey! What you doing there? Get up. It's not bed-time.

L.M. (*sleepily*) Clock'sh fast. No' time yet. Move over in bed.

S.M. (*Hauling him up*) You musta hit your head. What's this? (*draws a bottle from large man's hip pocket.*)

L.M. 'Sh me goff piksher. Mean me cough miksher—mix-ta-ya. Got bad cough (*Coughs heavily.*)

S.M. (*pulling out cork and smelling*) What's it called?

L.M. Hokanui brew.[2]

1 See Shakespeare's *The Tempest*, Act II, Sc. ii.
2 Illegally distilled liquor named after Southland's notorious home of illicit distilling, the Hokonui Hills.

S.M. I thought it smelt like whisky. Anyway, what were you lying there for?
L.M. (*beginning to cry*) Nobody lovsh me. (*kicking the gutter*) What they keep a pet snake for? Bit me. Nobody lovsh me.
S.M. (*who has been taking strong pulls at the 'cough-mixture'*) You've got me. There's no one like me; I'm big hearted . . .
L.M. (*suddenly*) Look! Roof burning. Housh on fire.
S.M. Tha's the moon. You know—what makes people go loony.
L.M. You inshinuatin' I'm a ma'moon—a ma-da-mun. Lemme tell y' I'm champeen boksher New Zealun'.
S.M. Don't tell me. An' I'm the Guvnor Genr'l.
L.M. 'Pologies y' Lordship.
*A bus draws up and stops.*
S.M. There's the bus. You'd better go.
*(the large man lurches over and climbs on board.)*
S.M. (*waving*) Goo' bye.
L.M. (*as bus recedes*) Hey! Wan' my cough miksher!
[Hocken, MS 975/187]

**Baxter to Ginn, 16 October 1943**

CENSORED
No. I

Brighton,
Otago.
16/10/43.

Dear Noel,

I have just received your letter. All I said may not have been true; ideas change in my mind as clouds change in the sky—still, most of it was right though a bit superficial. As I see it there are two types of human—vertebrate and invertebrate (be patient! this is no crude classification.) The invertebrate (a good example, I think, is Aldous Huxley) has internal strife and true introversion. Like all shell-fish—no pun intended—it develops a shell, a shell of cynicism, fashion, perhaps even intellectual brilliance; it is sensitive but self-centred.[1] The vertebrate (Tolstoy an excellent example) has in him morality—no mere rigid structure but a natural growth. If 'objective' he may be of the crude type, but 'subjectivity' is his true line of development.[2] I don't consider

1 Aldous [Leonard] Huxley (1894–1963) became a fashionable figure in the febrile society of 1920s England by satirising it in a series of witty and daring novels.

2 Count Lev (eng. Leo) Nikolaevich Tolstoi (1828–1910) is best known for such novels as *War and Peace*, *Anna Karenina*, and *The Death of Ivan Illych*. Also influential in Russia as a social and moral philosopher, and religious mystic, a spiritual transformation led him to renounce the Russian Orthodox Church and evolve a new Christian creed, the central tenet of which was non resistance to evil.

myself a vertebrate, remember: poems apparently firm rise often from trouble, even occasionally from despair. You are not cynical or selfish enough to be invertebrate; but your 'bone-structure' is not over-strong. If my fable revolts you, forget it.

To jump on my bicycle will tell me how much of my worries are physical—bad day, eye-strain, biliousness. I also get most of my original ideas when in motion: though sometimes, now more rarely, in the 'fine poetic frenzy'.[3]

Your surrealism is good. 'mews and moults in the tower of murdered deeds' lifts the whole sonnet. I have now read it 4 times, and each time it gains—very good I think.[4]

[Incomplete]

[VUW Library, MS McKay 28/21]

**Baxter to Ginn, 1 November 1943**

CENSORED
No. 5

Brighton,
Otago.
1/11/43

Dear Noel,—

It is certainly refreshing to hear your friend's opinions. However, if one reads poetry from a strictly materialist stand-point it is not poetry but poor and mangled prose. The immensely extended sight, the sensuous power of sound, are nothing to him who sees only 'sense'. Follows quotation from an essay of mine:—[1]

> The divorce of poetry from the popular imagination arises in part from a diminution of vigour in expression, mainly from the habits of our civilization. Great poetry must die—die to all save the poet, the critic, and the man born out of his time.
>
> Its knell was rung when the phrase succeeded the word, when sentimentality . . . succeeded wit and philosophy.[2] The sentimentality has

3 Derived from lines spoken by Theseus in Act V, Sc. 1 of Shakespeare's *A Midsummer Night's Dream*:
The poet's eye, in a fine frenzy rolling,
Doth glance from heaven to earth, from earth to heaven.
And as imagination bodies forth
The forms of things unknown, the poet's pen
Turns them to shapes, and gives to airy nothing
A local habitation and a name. (ll. 12–17)

4 See 'Sonnet', p.525.

1 This quotation also appearsin the MS Book, with some minor variations noted below, on pages 148–9, following poem 634—'Autobiographical', of Baxter's MS Book X (Hocken, MS 704/10). I have not located a longer essay from which the quotation might have originated.

2 In MS Book X the second phrase of this sentence reads, '. . . when sentimentality succeeded in verse wit and philosophy'.

gone, but with it has gone the last shreds of a popular appreciation of strong and complex thought.

We accept the merits of our greatest poets by hearsay; most readers, if it were written by a modern poet, would turn revolted from Milton's 'blind mouths,' but know it's Milton and dare not criticise.[3]

The greatest modern poet, W.B.Yeats, has unconsciously recognised a modern trend. Our eyes slide over a page; not words but phrases we read; the sound is unheard. Thus concentration of meaning evaporates. Yeats is the master of the phrase, and so for us there is magic in him.

'The heyday of poetry lived (??) when a word was still miraculous, when use and misuse had not dulled it to a smooth grey pebble.[4] What force now has 'light thickens'? The association is curded milk, I think. It is not understanding of meaning we lack, though as interest dwindles that loss approaches; it is appreciation of
PTO
concentration, of a transcendental meaning—in a word, of poetry.

The poetry of CAUSE AND EFFECT is complex; the meaning is simple, and in no way materialist.[5] If there were no human mind to originate and apprehend there would be no emotion or thought, not even cause or result (think here carefully for a bit), only a chain of chemical reactions meaningless and dead, like a clock running down. Of course the materialist's attitude must concentrate on action; for instance, if one had no belief in a life after 'death' it would be perfectly logical to extract as much experience and enjoyment as possible from life, regardless of the claims of others. I retain I think an appreciation of personality, but am fast becoming semi-atheist. Christ's dictum 'Thou shalt love the Lord thy God . . .' is shaking and inhibitive, but this may be childhood association.[6] But it is so bitter to lose that I wonder if I am mistaken or merely passing through a phase. Follows a sonnet of mine, sincere to the back-bone:—

There is no God: heavy the word as snow
 In clear oblivion worlds within my eyes
 Weighting to blurred sleep. Hearty and worldly-wise
 I walked my life's ways till this day—and so
Brave island-beauty dies, stars mime and mow
 Smearing the childhood wonder of the skies,
 Spun deathward in their mad and mourning guise;
 Hollow the painted shrouds that reel below.

3 The MS Book version has '. . . but recognise Milton and dare not criticise'. The reference is to line 119 of Milton's poem *Lycidas*: 'Blind mouthes! that scarce themselves know how to hold / A Sheep-hook'.
4 Baxter does not question his use of 'lived' in the notebook version.
5 See 'Cause and Result', p.249.
6 'And one of [the Pharisees], a lawyer, asked [Jesus] a question, to test him. "Teacher, which is the great commandment in the law?" And he said to him, "You shall love the Lord your God with all your heart, and with all your soul, and with all your mind. This is the great and first commandment. And a second is like it, You shall love your neighbour as yourself. On these two commandments depend all the law and the prophets." Matthew 22:34–40. (RSV)

There is no God: bitter the word as bare;
And whirlwind drinks the plain. O lewd and wild
Proved love gesticulates; savagely sane,
Dream-cerements made black, the mummy-child
Old Time sits i' the shoulder. Sharded, inane,
'God! God!' they cry: the sleeping Demon smiled.

Materialism is in a sense inverted mysticism. Anyone to whom Blake's 'Tiger' is only words is no materialist but a moron. 'When the stars threw down their spears' is packed with meaning and emotion.[7]

And this (Hogg):[8]

I wrap the sun of heaven in blood,
Veiling his orient beams of light;
And hide the moon in sable shroud
Far in the alcove of the night.

These everlasting hills are riven;
Their reverend heads are bald and gray;
The Greenland waves salute the heaven
And quench the burning stars with spray.

Tell him he is suffering from the inhibitions of custom: 'Belch, slobber, grunt and fart' is for contrast—the physical as opposed to idealism. It is considered, not striving after effect.[9]

One's experiences may be universal, but the expression of them isn't.

TO WOMAN. It is foolish to attempt to reduce to reason what is quite emotional —namely the sexual attitude, which regards woman as unusual, unapproachable, etc. etc. My poems, since they are poems and not prose, express often what is not permanently sincere, but a mood of some easily communicable texture—sometimes even assumed, just for practise in poetry. '10,000 Dreams'—the last verse is trying to show the gradual waking up of the adolescent from the adolescent's point of view.

'The Merry Beggar' was written when I was about 14, so does not correspond to reality very well. But poems are expressions of feelings, not rigid interpretations of reality (by the way, Noel, my protestations are more to ~~my~~ your friend than you: I must put up a good defence, so on I go.) . . . Men are mechanical pawns in war— 'The intricate machine destroyed, Swallowed in souless mud.' see end of War-Pictures.[10]

I hope 'scrapped' doesn't mean you've destroyed all copies of your poems. I have all you've sent me; but apart from possible value of others I have the atavistic feeling that to destroy something one has produced is to destroy part of oneself.[11]

7 The first line of the fifth stanza of Blake's 'The Tyger', from *Songs of Experience* (1794).
8 Baxter quotes two stanzas from James Hogg's (1770–1835) long poem *The Queen's Wake* (1813). The first stanza is lines 1713–16, and the second, lines 1721–4.
9 See 'Reverie of a Prisoner', p.253.
10 See 'On Visiting a Gallery of War-Pictures', p.151.

Still, it's your business. You're apt to underestimate the value of some of them. Remember WE two hold in our hands the future of N.Z. poetry, which has really not yet pierced ground.

TRYST is not powerful, yet has your particular note in it and is fit for publication anywhere.[12] Both you and I are, I think, neither modern nor Georgian but drawing from earlier well-heads.

Corpses of mosquitoes (about 40 by now) smear the walls of my room. But their erstwhile companions are still irritating and indefatiguable.

Best wishes (and to your friend, who is from my view a deep-mystic)

From

Jim. {James Keir Baxter}

An adaption of Ruskin, specially for him.

**OBEV**

Stick to the dame: though she is dumb, yet she can dance
Rumba and Waltz; dumb as they make, cute all the same.
Platinum blonde though she may be, gooey of glance;
Boy she is hot! and she can dance: stick to the dame.

[VUW Library, MS McKay 28/22]

**The Merry Beggar**

On! on! on shall I go
Over the fields, over the snow—
Wherever the wandering wind may blow
 Swift as the wind go I!
For loads are light when the heart is bright
And I have no care from morn to night,
No kith or kin to tarry my flight
 Save the clouds that flit on high.
And I wend my way where'er I may
From eventide to dawn of day—
Than the beggar's life I well may say
 A merrier road is none!
The way is hard and the way is cold
And the best of beggars at length grow old,
But now my spirit is blithe and bold
 In the beams of the noonday sun.

11 When I asked Ginn about this, in an interview on 25 Oct 1994, he explained:

> I got fed-up with my inability to complete a poem. I could come up with a few images that were all right but I had not the ability to mould it into a satisfying unity. I sort of thought 'Oh this is a useless quest trying to write when there's so little reward in terms of my own satisfaction'.

12 See 'Tryst', p.524.

And I care not for the storm
    Or the beat of the winter rain
For now the woods are warm
    And the winds are soft again.

I care not for the past
    Nor dream of future woe
For the spirit of spring has cast
    Her jewels where I go,
And I must follow fast
    Where the wandering wind doth blow!
        [Hocken, MS 704/3:136, pp.12–13]

**Murder**

Anger prowling on death-trail, quick for pain,
Blood-blurrèd countenance must writhe aghast,
Grow clear in usual fear, sallow, the deed once past,
Death-fact encountered. None have destroyed the slain;
None conquer when they slay. Terror will drain
As life out-drains; for hate may burn like sand-blast
But the immobile dead in marble cast
By mere inertia bludgeon, enthrall again.

Their vanquishment than victory more dread
Remorse inspiring, naught can quell remorse;
Murder self-stricken mid death-morass enmirèd
No need of hemp hath: 'I'll be dead, perforce,
Who have slain life.' And the dear face decayed ....
Thousand their thought, forgot the anger-source.
        [Hocken, MS 704/10:618, p.119]

**Baxter to Ginn, 6 Nov 1943.**

CENSORED
No. 6

Brighton,
Otago.
6/11/43.

Dear Noel,

I have just got your letter, and agree with much of the criticism. My poetry does not altogether satisfy me, as much of it is merely psychological, not real poetry. But poetry should not be judged from a standard of truth. Anything of emotional significance, when stated, is an 'artistic truth'. Arnold took the first as ~~of~~ a poetic standard, Shelley the second. And which is the better poet? There may be more morality in Arnold, but not more poetry. If I thought the meaning of a poem was all that mattered, that the verse-form was merely for adornment and easy remembering, I would rewrite all my poems in simple prose. But emotion is the essence of poetry: vowel-music promotes it, rhythm facilitates its flow. Naturally, ~~I~~ one wants original thought; but it is the emotional force, not the reasoning force, that makes the poetry. If someone calls a description 'poetic prose' he means, not that reality has been set down on paper in appropriate words, but that the writer has not seen it with dead eyes but given his interpretation, coloured the landscape with his emotion. If you want to express FACT write prose; if you want to express emotion write poetry.

> Upon the rotted quay Old ships sun-foundered, dry, grass grows on deck to the salt winds that call them vainly. Upon the rotted quay The waves of the inland sea . . . I dived once from that jetty; swam down under water where the lake-floor lies out of perspective; under the wooden girders I swam, below sea-storm, my merhair swam like weed suspended and rippling; I reached in the unknown element, unbreathing, saw secrets unnameable, then rose by the black quay—beware snags—to the fear of my flesh-kin. waves of the inland sea Beat in the midnight watches sent With murmur turbulent. ~~Tent-bedded I lie safe in-body and cloak~~ P.T.O
>
> Tent-bedded I lie safe in body and cloak of memory; but behind my musing eyes, beyond walls of bone, is reality not of me, where the sea in dark hills cupped, whose waves are death or longing slap rotted wood in multitudinous strife and quiet.

This is an extract from my prose.[1] But it is not prose in character, though prose in form. Prose should be terse, and convey its effects by implication; it does not interpret emotion, though there may be emotion behind it.

1 For other prose examples see the short story 'Before Sunrise' pp.346–9, and Appendix 5, pp.540–4.

You have got the wrong idea from MURDER, which is after all rather obscure. It goes like this in prose (i) The angry murderer, wishing to inflict harm, (ii) must change his 'blood-blurred' outlook (iii) and become ordinary in fear (which is a universal emotion) once the murder is committed (iv) No one has ever destroyed and eradicated the mental image of his victim (v) Murder is never conquest. The victim's terror is succeeded by peace (vi) as death comes; for no matter how much the murderer hates as he kills (vii) the mental image of a victim, eternal in the mind (viii) hurts and pre-occupies him. (ix) The 'defeat' of the victim, more terrible ~~than~~ for the murderer than if the victim had beaten him (x) (xi) (xii) (xiii) (xiv) [The rest I think is clear] It loses by explanation, for words are not used with their normal meanings.

Read all my poems aloud; they are written for that.

MOTLEY is good, the personification a little forced. 'Slum joins to slum . . .' is excellent.[2]

Best wishes,
From,
James Keir Baxter] Jim.

[VUW Library, MS McKay 28/23]

**Baxter to Ginn, 15 November 1943.**

CENSORED
No. 5

Brighton,
Otago.
15/11/43

Dear Noel,

Thank you for your letter. The paper you referred to must have got burnt; I will be more careful in future. You, Terry, and indeed all the rest of them being shut up is a sore spot in my mind when I think of it.

Show the 'group' my poems if you have them with you.[1] I like to get new opinions, being often unsure myself. Your poem has good points.[2] 'beaked beyond fable' is fine. viz. my 'fair dream, bitter, beaked and wild.'[3]

2 Ginn believes that 'Motley' refers to a poem of Baxter's, but there is no poem of this title in his MS Books.

1 According to Ginn there was not an explicit group studying poetry, but there were a number with a general interest in literature, including 'Des Dubbelt, an eager lover of literature, Joe & Paddy O'Neill, into drama, Joyce, Maxwell Anderson, Graham Greene. . . . Kevin Mulrennan . . . Good actor very sensitive in perceptions. Nat Beatus . . . Harry Scott [and] Rod Kennedy the producer of our plays. None THAT interested in my reading of [Baxter's] poems & the Jim phenomenon' (letter to Paul Millar, 2 Mar 1995). See also 'Detention Camp Life', p.94, and Ginn's letter of 22 Apr 1945, p.401.

2 See 'War Resisters', p.527.

3 See 'To the New Pagan', p.233.

I am beginning to follow Empson where not before. Enclosed is a satire, 'Mutation', with five puns and some irony, sarcasm, and other humour. 'Urning' is a person of one sex possessing many of the secondary characteristics of the opposite sex. 'God rested'—seventh day. It is not deep; if anything seems obscure it has quite a simple meaning, no symbolism or anything.

'Beauty and Angers Flow'—Audenish, but in some ways original. It is really an endictment [sic] of Marxism.

A short note this, but I have a holiday today which is to be spent going to the dentist's. My exams are over; I go to Varsity next year. Am looking forward to it, have met some pretty intelligent ones now going—no good poets, no Noels, but such are rare.

Best wishes,
From [James Keir Baxter
Jim.

[VUW Library, MS McKay 28/24]

**Mutation**
(with due regards to Empson)

The pipe-fish *Hippocampus* seems a freak;
Girded by bony rings and pigeon-chested,
Gills lobate, mouth grown tuliform or beak.

Yet falsely, for the form is tried and tested—
Unlike the pterodactyl, lives; mutation
Is thus unneeded. Some say that God rested.

A simile I know requires inflation:—
Perhaps the race deserting native ooze
Swims to the bar by dorsal undulation.

Spirit survives within the tank of booze
(It has been demonstrated); mouth-tubes may
Suck facile cocktails down like boiler-flues.

It might eventually learn to brag
(Many have learned); and then the rounded tail
Sedentary occupation ~~doth~~ does betray.

But it's prehensile. The big-hearted male
Carries the eggs in a pouch on the under-side
To hatch; perambulates like pram to scale.

Do women in the fragrant weeds deride
Or bless the crèche: they love the babes, but burning
With the communal flambeau have their pride.

Surely the golden Ages are returning.
The *Hippocampus'* verticality
Harbours suggestion. Say he is an Urning.
[Hocken, MS 704/10:639, pp.157–8]

**Beauty and angers flow**

Beauty and angers flow
From the corrosive flaw
Where men are made
Or sane or mad;
Where leaves of summer sway
Speak of the crops to be
While the true timeless tree
Knows only day.
Men trees resemble
But symbol fills the mind:
So grow unkind
Or fearing tremble.
Beauty and angers flow:
Fevered unrestful
Beauty for mother's boy;
But angers flay and play
Where slums are loud and lustful.
The sun is a burning-glass
The domed sky-guillotines;
So metaphors show gloss
And rule the roost in towns
Where dialectics straggle
Neglecting human struggle
And wheel their flashing lines:
Beauty will split to anger
Though stars utopian shine
Till the last beast dies of hunger
Or life like trees can move
Certain of love.
[Hocken, MS 704/10: 637, pp.153–4]

**ODE:**
**Where nets of time encircle and destroy**

I

What is the salve? what comfort ever seek we?
Ask not the wise! for curdled are their brains

On Ixion wheel of time and memory.
Ask not the aged: time goads and habit chains
Till life is all remembrance. Bitterly
Though ye be wounded, when the god ordains
Time's gashes melt to dream—from dream doth rise
Vigour that sleeps not, truth that never dies.

II

O burden of remembrance ! who doth not
Wish oftimes that he might in morn awake
Cleansèd, like child—nor fears, nor leaden weight
Of vain regret disturb. For moments break
And surge like sea, like armed ranks; nor abate
For our shrill mortal piping. We gaze back
Nostalgic to a silver-seeming space—
Hour when time wrenched not, calm and wakeless days.

III

But such is idle, feckless—for my song
And beauty likewise passes, nor one tear
Shall stave their ultimate extinction long;
And horror of extinction, hounds of fear
That grapple at the withered throat and lung.
Waiting amid the fires of old despair,
Rim dark-precipitous of flame or frost,
Cry we amid the fires of hell, the caverns of the lost.

IV

Yet to the polished halls of graven death
Dove-winged celestial Pity shall descend,
Till Tantalus be loved the stream beneath
And Sisyphus his groaning labours end;
While Hope arise with sweet seraphic breath
And make of hell new heaven. Wrath may rend,
Despair may split by very chill our grave.
Pity and Hope alone with sword of love shall save.

V

Simplicity in Christ is new and old.
The child recks not of custom, views our lives
And things material with eye uncold
As spiritual and awesome; age deprives
Mind of like clarity, but youth will hold
Pure image like a mirroring pool. Priest strives
By road obscure, pagan by beauty unpriced.
Child, priest, and pagan meet, are one in Christ.

VI

Yet all is not clear, thoughtless, to the child:
Sorrow, sorrow or joy beyond compare
May dwell in a day's fashioning; winds are wild,
Shrill bells peal silver from a crystal air;
Enchantment shadows where the waves sway mild,
And memory is brief, nor shut skies stare
In stone eternal answer to the sight—
Frail nervous limbs night-clothed or swift in daylight.

VII

No tragedy is there in earth but one:
That hearts of youth aflame with sweet desire
By walls of speech, fortress of flesh, closed in
Shall hold no utterance; in fearing mire
Bruised souls may succour seek, find succour none
Though love and sympathy ply all for hire:
Misunderstanding sours the bud ere bloom
Till earth so seems thorned wilderness and tomb

VIII

How shall men bear the gash of death and know
Unutterably alien, clay and dead,
Belovèd face and form, yet scarcely show
Soul scarred, mouth dumb, or eye amazèd?
How shall they so? Yet in the deepest woe
Tears are not seen, nor wailings—only dread,
Calm, cold, unspoken anguish: better sure
Is gargoyle sorrow, mirth. Man may not such endure.

IX

None have extolled thee, Wrath! for each may find
In his own heart, should he there seek, thy seal.
The multitude, by wrath they are not blind
But fear and ignorance. Wise sages feel
Anger at pettiness. Wrath raves down the wind,
Wrath speaks from mountain throats in thunder-peal.
Wrung by the fires of God the prophets cry,
With glorious indignation move the sky.

X

Some mid the coils of superstition seek
Hidden and cabbalistic wisdom; these
Forsake the spirit, wed the letter weak
And trapped in ice of their own dogma freeze.

To them all shams seem truth, all art is bleak,
Base, save as frieze of gnarled obscurities:
Soul long-debased but baseness can foretell—
Night sought they, night espoused: in night they dwell.

XI

Pale and remote the moon in glade of cloud,
Yet she to night grave beauty doth impart
Whence brilliance like to noonday flows; the proud
And chaste Diana hath a lover's heart:
Beholdest thou where amorous waves are loud,
Complain to her?—there doth her image start
And tremble water-waning: So do men
To loves and fears long-spurned, despised, return again.

XII

It is the sun! Fierce-burning and blood-red
In fervent blaze he rises. Phaeton-wise
The frail ensanguined clouds to earth have fled;
Florid, the heavens under his lucid gaze
Mantle. The world rejoices; sunward led,
Mists swelter, fade; woods waken; life that lies
Nightlong in slumberous swound new life adores,
His glory seas salute from hushed and flaming shores.

XIII

So vast creation. Sure than gods more great
Ordainers—yea, and vassals even—must
Of fell destruction be; huge hate
To conquer love: for the grey avid dust,
Earth even loathes shed blood. Master of fate—
Though man—ruled and blind fruit of man's chance lust—
Master of all death save his own, here stands
The servile soldier, bloodied, with empires in his hands.

XIV

Diogenes the Grecian seven years
Within a barrel lived. No speech is known
Whereby we may lay bare our loves and fears:
We like Diogenes must dwell alone
Forever, though grave hubbub shake our ears
And mouthing puppets strut. In cell of stone
Hermit forsakes imperfect speech; sans light,
Would find in darkness supernatural sight.

XV

Though speech may stammer, yet one tongue has bound
All beauty in the scope of mortal speech—
Language of love. Ill-starred Leander drowned,
And grief-torn Orpheus alike may teach
That love immortal in time's sphere is found;
That love feels fate but to rebel, beseech
Unhearkening heavens for haven; and will flee
Even in sorrow our frail mortality.

XVI

In poetry is speech articulate;
And poet, careless helmsman, steers between
Shoals where yet lurk Scylla of cynic wit,
Charybdis of sweet sentiment. The scene,
The thronged arena of our lives is lit
By poetry to brave heroic vein;
Meaning and memory most pleasing wake
In each quick[1] thought and word our comfortless to slake.
('quick'—living, life instinct)

XVII

When Darius the Mede was king of kings
Was he not sad? Power is a hollow gain;
Yet all the world seek power—though power brings
Suspicion, loveless fear. The agèd reign,
And youth would emulate—till harsh time wrings
Spirit and limb, makes kingly folly plain.
Great monarchs soon from sight and out of mind
Like a forgotten music plaining down the wind.

XVIII

Behold the felon, murderer and thief!
'The ape'—so fools have said—'shambles in him.'
Iniquity is long and judgement brief;
And fell iniquity doth felons maim.
Our own unbalance typified, belief
That what is is, the fair-fanned flame
Of warranted bitterness here lives. O judges wise,
To ye was 't said, 'Thou wilt be with me in Paradise.'?

XIX

'A god—perchance—in heaven: the state on earth.'
The dictum of state-craft will ne'er take heed
Of aught save government; of human birth

Yet lean, inhuman, in their tyrannous creed,
Statesmen will count life, beauty, little worth—
Till the eternal grasses flower and seed,
Till angerless the calm earth covers them
And their wrought fantasy, frail flesh doth crumble to dream.

XX

Two mouths hath learning. One in cave of books
Cadaverous pores, burns long the midnight oil,
Creates a realm of spectres and these brooks
No kingship save his own. But I will toil
Gravely a space in calm secluded nooks,
Heart-blood of sages for my spirit's foil;
And with new eyes—cleansèd of cumber then—
Arise, behold the world and ways of men.

XXI

We have lost wisdom that the ancients knew,
Waste daily in our dumb and feverish strife;
Power that did frame the Parthenon and hew—
E'en though by blood of slaves—the Sphinx to life
Persists, endures, but dwindles; the sparse few
Since great, by tides of war or assassin's knife
Have fallen long. In wisdom of her youth
By earth were they made learnèd. We have forsaken truth.

XXII

Yet in the fervour of creation hot
We may forget mortality and drink
Briefly the gold elixir of change-not,
And on a rock eternal o'er the brink
Of light and chaos hang: it is our lot
That we ungodlike godlike feel and think;
And, godlike, inspiration draw from naught—
Then phoenix perish in the flame of thought.

XXIII

On a loud sea mid jutting crags we sail
Where waves of time lash with incessant sound
Cliff of the timeless, before primeval gale—
Yet from the hushed and groaning deep around
Whisper and moan arises: hearken, soul!
O hearken—'tis the voices of the drowned:
Murmur of broken words speak they, nor fade—
In dark of sleep, of time, by serpent currents swayed.

XXIV

Heraldic on a timeless crag I saw
An eagle poised: his harsh and changing plumes
Sang brazen on the dry and bitter air
Cacophony and burden of strange dooms;
Age-bald his skull, withered each terrible claw—
Loathsome disease and the foul stench of tombs
Beneath those preyless talons. Spoke one on high:
'This is the ancient evil, and shall die.'

XXV

The very soul of earth is fruitfulness.
Mother and child we worship, Isis and
God Horus, Christ and Mary; for all guess
That from birth-pangs, from pain and swaddling-band
Hath sprung the vision marvellous: our distress,
Death-fear dissolves when the new-smiling land
Grows fruitful, beast and flower. And could we know
Each man from innocent birth, fell Hate would rise and go.

XXVI

But age may sterile grow, deny the faith
Wherein youth walks. True atheist must needs
For shield have madness; for to some like death
A dead eternity would shrivel. Seeds,
Below all words that mortal dogma saith,
Below the shards of circumstance or deeds,
Of natural belief are known. Friends fled
And comfort lost, Job-like, faith lifts rejoicing head.

XXVII

Life in our veins runs riotous; and if
Spring buds in winter freeze, must we then weep?
From anarchy rose we, from perilous cliff
Death-sheer of brute oblivion. All sleep
Must have awakening: the hieroglyph
Of time spells life and sleep; so shall we keep
The animal vigour and god-sight in us,
Remember 'life in our veins runs riotous'.

James K. Baxter.

[VUW Library, MS McKay 28/25]

**Baxter to Ginn, 20 November 1943**

CENSORED
**No. 6**

Brighton,
Otago.
20/11/43.

Dear Noel,

The important thing about the ODE is not so much unity of logic as unity of atmosphere. The poetry is the important thing. Well, here goes for an explanation.

I 'Ask not the wise'—i.e. the intellectuals lack emotional understanding. 'Ask not the aged'—they have forgotten, or at any rate can scarcely experience the strong emotions of youth ('emotion' not a good word, but I know no other.)

II Desire for retreat, arising from 'Time's gashes'—everyone feels this sometimes.

III Poets are always saying this, each in a different way. It is a deepening of the trouble of the second verse. The poem goes rather like music.

IV Out of chaos beauty, out of bitterness calm: others can help us (as Christ has helped many men—Sisyphus 'bear ye one another's burdens etc.'[1])

V The child does not care about customary cynicism and the blasé, but .... and this is truth which the adult loses grasp of. Yet all strive back to this clarity and faith, the priest through 'road obscure', the pagan by art.

VI Contrast. I realize there is more to childhood than the 'Ode on Intimations of Immortality'[2] type of thing; therefore must necessarily put that other side.

VII Whether tragedy is good for one or not, it arises from incoherence; I don't bring in the moral issue here.

VIII 'gash' repeated because death is the offspring of time—one is meant to think of verse I.

Much of the poem is mere recording of what I see, not what I think should be. See E.B.B.'s sonnet on 'Grief'.[3] Man may not endure 'calm, cold, unspoken anguish.'

1 For revealing divine secrets—namely that Zeus had abducted the daughter of the River-god Asopus—Sisyphus was sent to Tartarus and sentenced to spend eternity pushing a huge block of stone up to the brow of a hill with the aim of toppling it down the other side. He has never yet achieved this: the weight of the rock defeats him just before he reaches the summit, and rolls back down to the bottom where he must retrieve it and try again.

2 William Wordsworth's (1770–1850) ode 'Intimations of Immortality from Recollections of Early Childhood' first appeared in *Poems in Two Volumes* (1807).

3 Elizabeth Barrett Browning (1806–61) published the sonnet 'Grief' in *Poems* (1844), it begins:

I tell you, hopeless grief is passionless;
That only men incredulous of despair,
Half-taught in anguish, through the midnight air
Beat upward to God's throne in loud access
Of shrieking and reproach.

IX I am broader-minded than I am thought to be. I do not revile the 'sages', give this in support of the rightness of anger. This, of course, is an artistic truth not an absolute. My philosophy is not one of 'blame', except for the abstract evil—see XXIV.

X I realize my own tendencies to obscurity, but all the same cannot condone it.

PTO

XI This is, of course, delight in the simile, embroidering for poetry's own sake.

XII I try to get the spirit of sunrise, expressing the awakening of life. This stanza is logically quite unconnected, but fits perfectly in the poetic unity.

XIII 'So vast creation.' I have spoken of the sun and moon, as contrasted to man. 'Surely then, those who destroy the earth in wars, both leaders and vassals, must be greater than gods'—this is meant to be irony. In case this is not clear, I continue to explain: 'huge hate to conquer <u>love</u>'—i.e. natural life. I think the rest should be plain.

XIV The reader needs reminding of the theme. This is just to make the point about the religious retreat.

XV This is, I think, good poetry. Last 3 lines—'that love rebels against the "nets of time" . . . and even in sorrow does not believe in death.' There is more than just this to it.

XVI Poetry, as it were, stands for other arts as well. Also, 'speech' is best in words.

XVII Read all this poem with feeling. Inject emotion and it lives.

XVIII '<u>Our own unbalance</u>': purposely harsh—perhaps this is a bit too bold.

XIX Here poetry predominates in a sort of surrealism or symbolism.

XX The first mouth is the 'cadaverous' one. My method is the other. Remember poetry is rarely quite true. None of us are gods or geniuses as poetry will make us. 'Sages' does not to me mean the intellectuals of the first stanza. It is a fine distinction, but think of 'sages and seers'.

XXI This is definitely good. It is a mood, not really absolute.

XXII This is not excellent but does as a stop-gap.
Not finality, but return to ordinary life—'phoenix' I mean, the bird that burns then is born again.

XXIII This is far and away the best stanza. XXIV The only exhibition of real intolerance.

XXV Yes, the last two lines are a sort of after-thought. XXVI Rather cutting criticism. Here is the thought: 'But age may . . .' Some 'like death' refers to the 'dead eternity'. One must therefore either be mad or have the 'seeds'. Nothing can trouble true faith.

XXVII This is a generalization. I have written in another poem 'Great peace is in us, could we fathom it.'[4] There is in truth no time. So much is timeless. Solutions are various, the fact is the same. There is no solution but ourselves.

4 See 'The Plough' p.160.

Enclose a poem 'MEMORY SWATHES'. I am fumbling for a new style at present. Purposeful vagueness is a good enough trick but can be overdone.

Best wishes
From
Jim.

**Memory swathes**

Memory swathes the sooty grass
    And rails rafted upon the swift embankment
    That streams like reason through mountainous mind,
Suave, svelte, desirous.

Older this steel than the sky-globed cathedral;
    O fit for love the garish cinema
    Ancient as time the shoddy girl and fellow:
All sigh of the past, progress a god not droll.

Before voodoo converted the missionary,
    When birds in hats were beauty;
    There is no jazz in level wheels beating:
Trains hoot, the world is neither sad nor merry.

Past from the suburb houses mouthing
    With grime and empty boxes in their yards;
    Future lives only in eagles, the thunder-birds
And present love in man his sad nest fouling.

[Hocken, MS 704/10:641, pp.161–2]

**Baxter to Ginn, [November 1943]**

CENSORED
No. 1

Brighton,
Otago.

Dear Noel,

Thank you for your enthusiastic appreciation of the ODE. You are probably prejudiced in my favour. I am not fond of Keats' 'On a Grecian Urn', so will allow that parts may approach that. His 'Ode To a Nightingale', though quoted and hackneyed and dragged in the mire of gushing laudation, is perfect—I have just been reading Keats and considering that when he lost his adolescent over-exuberance he might have developed to a stronger Milton.[1]

Your poem 'When ruby fires . . .' is rather hastily fashioned in parts but otherwise very good.[2] (Note before I forget—I have sent certain poems to Prof. Gordon but have not heard anything yet. They may not have been the type for *New Writing*.)[3]

I must make 'bloodless barraging will batter swiftly' clear to you, for it is important. 'bloodless barraging' is OXYMORON such as 'dear foe'—The force of speech and public opinion, though without violence, shall be like a barrage and have as strong an effect as actual force battering. That is the gist of it.

I thought at first that the Basil Dowling poem was yours and thought you had lost some originality and gained some finesse. I like it—it is right for Basil Dowling in whom I pardon much in the way of semi-clichés because he illuminates them till one feels a sincerity in them.

Does your 'Myrtle of Venus' refer to your sister?[4] 'Silken shawls of swinging rain Leave the rippling barley plain' should be transplanted to a poem you will write about 5 years hence (better than most of mine.) It is a good envocation [sic] (nearly as good in parts as Shakespeare's 'Ye spotted snakes with double tongue . . .' in *Midsummer Night's Dream*—no, in some other play of his.[5] 'Every beast in his own way clean' has the quaint charm to me of Kipling's *Jungle Book*.[6] The first 3 lines of the first verse are too concrete in their metaphors to do other than glitter—most unlike the 'silken shawls'. The rest is very good—apart from 'soon' and 'shortly'. That is tautology. Change 'soon on' to 'over' (?) You are over-fond of 'plush' which is not really a very evocative word. The poem is on the whole light but very good.

'Spirits of Harmony, Music, and Love' was a fine and beautiful poem which my

1 John Keats (1795–1821) first published both 'Ode on a Grecian Urn' and 'Ode to a Nightingale' in *Lamia, Isabella, The Eve of St Agnes, and other Poems* (1820).

2 See 'When ruby fires', p.521.

3 Although *New Zealand New Writing* ran to only four issues during the years 1943–45 it was an extremely successful publication with sales in the many thousands. Its editor, Professor Ian A. Gordon, was forced to sever his involvement with the periodical in 1946 when the demand of returned soldiers for tertiary education left him no time for anything other than teaching in the English Department of Victoria University College. Gordon, in an article in the *New Zealand Listener* titled 'In Memoriam "NZNW"' (21 Jan 1984, p.31), recalled the fate of the remaining manuscripts:

> I took the large suitcase of unread manuscripts for *NZNW* 5 to the publishers and told them to find another editor . . . Many years later I discovered (by a circuitous route) that in that lost suitcase of unread manuscripts there had been poems by James K. Baxter, whose first volume had appeared some time earlier. As I finger my treasured and signed copy of his second collection I often wonder which of these poems he had sent me.

As most of the poems published in Baxter's second collection, *Blow, Wind of Fruitfulness*, post-date this letter, it is more likely that the poems Baxter sent Gordon relate to the period that produced *Beyond the Palisade*.

4 See 'Myrtle of Venus', p.521. This poem does not refer to Ginn's sister but 'only to the genus of Mediterranean plants' (Noel Ginn, letter to Paul Millar, Jan 1995).

5 Baxter's first choice is correct: this is a line from a song sung in *A Midsummer Night's Dream* by Titania's fairy train. It begins with the 'First Fairy' singing:

> You spotted snakes with double tongue,
> Thorny hedgehogs, be not seen.
> Newts and blindworms, do no wrong,
> Come not near our Fairy Queen.

(*A Midsummer Night's Dream*, II.2.9–12)

6 Rudyard Kipling (1865–1936) first published *The Jungle Book* in 1894.

father wrote before the last war knocked all ~~save a certain appreciation of poetry~~ poetry out of him—even now he can only appreciate, not write.[7]

I enclose a list of the poetry books I have here (underlining my favourites.) If you wish to borrow any of them tell me.[8]

You may have read 'A Man' before; also perhaps 'When weight of want' I hope not. 'Age' is the latest I have written. 'The Dark Sun' is, I think, quite good. The graph may interest you, though it can of course only be an approximation: it is for the ODE.

Tell me what you think of 'Cry Mourn'.[9]

Best wishes

From

Jim.

[VUW Library, MS McKay 28/26]

**A Man**

A man lies dead within the sullen clay.
I am unchanged in the blue usual day.
A thousand men are dead, but where are they?

Perhaps someone will turn somewhere saying:
O that he were alive, though here on sick-bed lying!
But no: he is gone beyond our furthest seeing.

He was a young man. But these bones, I know,
Are ageless, were fashioned before the first faint snow
Fell as it now is falling, ~~ages~~ aeons ago.

They are not him—for they are less than nothing.
The bullet in his skull worth maybe a farthing.
But he is gone, and they are less than nothing.

Where is he now? who was greater perchance than I,
Greater than the vast glowing nebulae
For he was life, he was humanity.

He was a young man. On his human shoulders
Carried the weight of error of his elders
Till Death the sniper sighted from the boulders.

He was not saint nor devil. The side he fought on
To me is nothing. Perhaps to a girl in satin
He was a miracle when quick, not rotten.

7 See 'Spirits of Harmony, Music, and Love' in Appendix 6 (p.544).
8 Ginn does not believe that either this list of books, or the graph mentioned in the following paragraph, exist any longer (letter to Paul Millar, Jan 1995).
9 See 'Cry Mourn', p.248.

He was not saint—so nation, warring faction
Will take no interest in his crucifixion.
He was humanity, knew nothing of their diction.

He was not devil, there was no death in him:
The paraphernalia of Hell he carried on him
External, meaningless, woke not his spirit from dream.

Strange that I cannot know this man,
That I cannot speak to him—for he no longer
Feels love or pain or hunger,
Or would walk with me under a similar sun.

Perhaps the perpetual death that walked beside him
Made death familiar and love a dream.
I know not. But the bitterness of Time

That has left him, that swung his forward sight
Toward a curved vista ~~that~~ we vision not
Has made for me a stone perpetual night:

For I die in this man. O comrade, even I
Shared in your peace and vision under a homely sky:
In you I suffer, in you I die.
Seasons pass like wind over grass
But we were human who leaden lie.
[Hocken MS 704/7:460, pp.151–3]

### When weight of want

When weight of want has withered quite
The quiet circles quick to quote
When best of goods are for exporting
And failure finds all faith departing
Who shall remain
Of many men?

When war the bleak alternative
Becomes to some a sturdy stave
In fending long-deferred revolters
And press recipients swoop like vultures
With specious cant
On discontent.

Garrulity of premier
Shall change no facts from what they are.

The parliament or president
Are by no deity ordained.
    Presumptuous pose
    Prevents not peace.

Heads of peremptory parties show
That theirs is only treachery.
Councils assign investigators
Seeing insanitary gutters
    When causes were
    Nothing but war.

Self-deception is the mode.
Who is sane and who is mad?
When the frenzied fire blows over
Time encircles like a river.
    Fear is gone
    With no gain.

Infant bodies are produced:
Bomb or shell wipes out the dazed
Uncomprehending attitude.
Sadist passion is untied.
    To whom the guilt?
    Our fault.
        [Hocken, MS 704/5:295, pp.58–9]

**Age**

    There is no age,
No irredeemable rot, gnarlèd and black.
White hair from smooth, green faceless brows blown back
The aged breakers boom and rage.

    Decrepitude can never seize them.
But we who carry the ancient seas in our blood
Run weeping-wild within the iron wood
To brain-garotte and storm-wind's mayhem.

    Yet when the rigid sky is rolled
To north or south, sudden and strange is seen
Space fathomless, prayerful, whence there lean
Angels and wind-clouds ageless of white and gold.
    Our eyes are never old.
        [Hocken, MS 704/10:595. p.64]

**'The Dark Sun' or 'Ode to Spring'**

Awake! O Spring, and loose the frozen land:
Why dost thou sleep, O Spring?
Art thou within some northern icy cave
Beyond the blackened Polar strand
Where all is voiceless save
The deep ice-sundering wave,
Where life dwells not nor feels thy new awakening!

The valleys slumber and the hills are dumb:
No bird chirps in the snow
Save the gaunt robin with his hunger-song.
Arise! Arise! and swiftly come—
The world has waited long
And winter holdeth strong
Dominion over all: 'tis thou must lay him low!

Come in thy joyous pride and majesty!
O vestal virgin, glide
With the strong fires of the arising sun
Over the hills that welcome thee:
The thaw has now begun—
Light-footed maiden, run
Among the shining glades that in the hills abide!

Thy bride-groom is the bright-winged seraph Dawn
And wedded shalt thou be,—
While new-born songsters chant thy marriage-lay
He in his crystal chariot drawn
Shall bear thee then away
To the chambers of the Day
With all the sweetest hymns of angel minstrelsy!

And at thy feet the crocus-bell shall shoot
With all the flowers of light,
While those with streaming silver hair unbound
Tread Winter's legions underfoot,
While on the dewy ground
The shy field-mouse is found,
While Light and Love shall be thine own hand-maidens bright!

But still thou comest not, and still the air
Is cold with Boreas' breath,
While in the bare, bleak winter woods is seen
Only the squirrel in his lair—
Without the chestnut skeen

That in the Summer green
Were his to hoard against the freezing famine-death.

Yet I can see within the woods today
The coming of thy life—
For, as the sun ere the darkest dawn is shown
In lowness at the break of day,
So plants as yet ungrown,
Winds that have scarcely blown,
Till thou wilt soon appear and cease all hungry strife

Fool that I am, to waste my words on thee
When the green sap has sprung
Within each shrub and thing of life that loves,
Upon each ivy-wall and forest-tree!
For now the dark earth moves
And one small snow-drop proves
That all of Nature lives, and all of Earth is young.
[Hocken MS 704/4: 198, pp.63–6]

**The Child**

In the watches of the night
Saw I on a craggy height
Where caves cloven are and deep
A mother lull her babe to sleep
(Bowed was she, her torrent hair
Fell like whirlwinds on the air,
And her calm night-carven face
And her grave immortal grace
Showed her as the timeless Norn
In whose eyes the worlds unborn
Whirl and shatter, bloom and freeze).

She was chanting on the breeze,
Chanting through the domèd skies
Sad and sweet her lullabies:

'Hush my baby, sleep thee now
While the great world-rivers flow,
While the ocean wide and soughing
On her endless errand going
Glides beyond us in the dark;
While the summits greyly stark
Bathed in their own Polar morning
Wait the anthem of the dawning.

'Time they'll call thee, babe of mine,
And will fret thy name divine
Awesome and symbolical
On their inmost citadel:
Under the resplendent sun
Murders in thy name are done;
And their monstrous ironies
Shadow over land and seas
Though they grovel, starve and slay . . .
Dost thou murmur Who are they?

'O the beasts of hill and field,
Innocence shall be their shield;
Sin they not—what sin can chance
Draw from living innocence?
The tiger and the lion stand
Within their burning holy land;
And the mild cattle unreproving
Have no respite in God's loving.

'Hush my babe: thou'lt see the ape
Vomit from his sullen gape
Poison over sea and strand,
Poison through the holy land.
The great fountains of pure water
He has mired with blood and slaughter;
He the worldling, long unchidden
On the viewless winds hath ridden—
And his brethren there doth maim
Girt with death and groaning flame.

'In one guise they worship thee
And thy twin, Eternity.
Seek they mid their brothers those
Bitter and in truth their foes;
Hope-enthrallèd grant to them
The prized and leaden diadem—
Saying *They'll lead should we give ear*
*From out the mire of blood and fear.*
But those rulers deep-despising
Spurn their prayers, well surmising
That should they inhuman seem
Minions them as gods will deem.

'And their seers, woeful men,
See the Golden Age again

In the battle-clouds afar
Where in truth are flames of war.

'Thee, my babe, in each heart coilèd
Rul'st their cities hell-despoilèd;
Infant limbs in pleasure stretching,
Bid'st them shaken, torn and retching,
Serpents to beget upon
Foul and rank oblivion.

'Seeing them by night and day,
How for love and death they pray,
Thee, my babe, I fain would slay—
But the blight of doom has set
Palsies on me chill and wet;
Thou art cold, but living yet.'

Then the puny babe I saw
Leap and stir, till—heart of awe!
His white limbs were dragon-scalèd,
And he sprang erect and mailèd:
Though his arms were bright for war
In his forehead shone a star,
Light immortal inly shown
Like a rose of flame unblown—
And upon the summits dawning
Fiery flowed their mountain morning.
[Hocken, MS 704/10:630, pp.137–41]

**Autobiographical**

On looking at his early photograph
The youth essays a cynic laugh,
Since irritated by exposure of
A child's dependence, need for love.

At five one walked in a world of trees
With parents in the background, for scenery their knees.
Shelley and Burns like burning angels pass.
Sweet is the holiday smell of petrol-gas.

At ten the diamond split, revealed no life but dream;
Poetry a flood with bobbing heads on its stream:
'The elm-trees swirled and swayed o'er where we laid him;
We were in black arrayed, and farewells bade him.'

Then at fifteen a world thundered without,
Strange pebbles laid at the feet; but girded about
With a world-embracing solitude there stood
Narcissus, master of the iron wood.

At seventeen, a cynic laugh essayed
Fails in a sense of time's collapse, afraid;
For, apart from trees made men, parents not Them but alive,
And women for petrol-gas, it's the same as at five.
[Hocken MS 704/10:634, pp.146–7]

**Baxter to Ginn, 29 November 1943**

CENSORED
No. 6

Brighton,
Otago.
29/11/43

Dear Noel,—

Referring to your mention of 'The Child'. The metre is rather difficult; Keats' 'Never let the fancy roam', and Milton's two masterpieces.[1] I give it an individual touch, I think. Auden has always influenced me. He is never really superficial, and has made better poetry of modern conditions than anyone else I know.

The man who wrote—

He shall against his peace
Feel his heart harden
Envy the heavy birds
At home in a garden.

could never be truly superficial.[2]

'The tiger and the lion . . .' is indeed the best part of the poem.

THERE IS NO GOD I do not claim to be absolute.[3] It is meant to be a

1 The metre Baxter employs for 'The Child' is almost exclusively trochaic tetrameter catalectic—i.e. 4 feet of a stressed followed by an unstressed syllable with the final unstressed syllable in the 4th foot left off—which, in the poems Baxter refers to, closely follows Keats's metre but only occasionally Milton's: who alternates between trochaic and iambic metre and catalectic and anacatalectic endings. Baxter misquotes the opening of Keats's poem 'Fancy'—first published in *Lamia, Isabella, The Eve of St Agnes, and other Poems*—which begins 'Ever let the fancy roam, / Pleasure never is at home'. 'Milton's two masterpieces' is a reference to the twin poems 'L'Allegro' and 'Il Penseroso', which were written around 1630 and first published in *Poems* (1645).

2 The first four lines of the third stanza of Auden's poem 'The Witnesses', the early version of which appeared in *The Listener*, 12 Jul 1933.

3 See 'There is no God . . .' in Baxter's letter of 1 Nov 1943, p.275.

restrainedly passionate expression of the first arrival of that period of atheism which I think all must experience before a new conception is built up. There is in it the abandonment of despair—'And whirlwind *drinks* the plain' (the tornado, the aimless terrible gyre of destructive aridity.

AUTOBIOGRAPHICAL—at 15 I lived more in what I read and wrote than what I saw or did. Like Blake (I think the comparison is fair) I cast my own feelings on the exterior universe. Then this melted, as it were, and process of discovery began again. 'Master of the iron wood' viz. 'Run weeping-wild within the iron wood'.[4]

True materialism is indeed what you say. But to many materialism is a creed and doctrine, believed emotionally as well as in reason.

I got 'Urning' from Edward Carpenter—I think it is of German derivation.[5] 'flamen'—I had the idea that 'flamen' applied to religious fire, and hence by association to the priest. I find I am mistaken. Change it to 'flambeau'.

PTO

'To R—' is a fine sonnet, not your very best, but strong and not too obscure.[6] I think you should change '*beauteous* flower-worlds' for some adjective more definitive—just my opinion, however.

I will certainly take advantage of your offer of loan of books. From anyone else the suggestion of financial help would offend—never from you, though. It is not likely I will ever need it, but if so would not hesitate to tell you.[7]

I enclose 3 poems, the 'Song (iii)' semi-Elizabethean just written, 'Bees' not bad, rather gauche maybe. The POISON-BANE is, I think, pretty good.

I have just been for a bathe in the sea, 1st this season.

Best wishes

From

Jim.

PS Cannot send SONG (iii) after all, for my last book is lent out and I have not written it in yet, was about to send you my only copy.[8]

[VUW Library, MS McKay 28/27]

4 Baxter cross references the fourth stanza of 'Autobiographical' to the second stanza of 'Age' (p.295).

5 Edward Carpenter (1844–1929) abandoned his fellowship of Trinity Hall, Cambridge, in 1874 to pursue his own concepts of socialism and communal fellowship. He habitually challenged the middle-class establishment and among the many causes he supported was that of homosexuals. His controversial pamphlet *Homogenic Love, and its Place in a Free Society* (1895) borrowed the term 'urning' from the German student of sexual inversion, K.H. Ulrichs, who coined it from *Uranos*, meaning 'heaven'. Carpenter defended 'urnings'—as he denoted men and women with an innate homosexual bias—as normal and healthy, 'sufficiently so in fact to constitute [homosexuality] a distinct variety of sexual passion'. He argued that 'urnings' should not be confused with 'that class of persons . . . who out of mere carnal curiosity or extravagance of desire, or from the dearth of opportunities for a more normal satisfaction (as in schools, barracks, etc.) adopt some homosexual practices'.

6 See 'To R—', p.529.

7 Ginn's offer of money 'was simply an impulse to help [Jim] with books as no expense should be spared, I thought, to supply him access to poets of the day' (letter to Paul Millar, 3 Mar 1995).

8 Baxter is referring here to MS Book X (Hocken, MS 704/10). The third 'Song' poem—sequentially numbered 650—is the second last of Baxter's poems in this notebook, although he has also transcribed three of his father's poems into its final pages. 'Song (iii)' appears on p.455.

**Bees**

We crept along the narrow river-bank
Through clustered ferns and foliage dank—
Till, through the branches of tall rugged trees,
Behold! the hive of honey-bees!

We saw them sink on laden droning wings
With sudden swift appearance from nowhere
To vanish at the entrance of the hive—
In with full honey-bags, emerging bare—
The hollow trunk seemed all alive
With these slim-bodied insect things
That swiftly through the sparkling air
Materialized and dematerialized.
Then suddenly
Dark sentries flicked across the space between
Before we realized
And swung in ruddy sheen
Too fleet for mortal eye
The anguish of the stabbing needle-sting.

Then with white nets and bandages firm-tied,
With masks slit-eyed
Like robbers ravaging,
We lit dry grasses and the hive awoke
To the dread sulphur-smoke
That curled and eddied through the rotted trunk
Till bees half-drunk
Stumbled and crawled,
Appalled,
From the white wave of death.

Yet still the armed armadas came and went
In angry discontent
Above the black smoke-vent
And died in myriads at the blue hell-flame,
Seeking to sting and dying as they stung—
We beat with blazing bushes as they came—
Till their death-anthem wrung
The heart with sudden shame.

Then, as the bright sun sank beyond the hill
They were at length all still
Save where the crushed ~~hordes~~ bees groaned—
And yet incessant moaned

The piercing voices of a numerous choir.
Through the smouldering fire
    We plunged in haste our eager hands
        To grasp the golden hoard
    That lay beneath the scorched and blackened bark.
        Little did our long search afford
    Save the smooth waxen cells that they had wrought
    In slow unchanging thought
        That we would instinct deem.

    O Perfect communists,
    We found not that for which we sought,
        But conscious of a broken dream
    Returned through evening mists.
    And the last bees, beneath a sinking sun
        Crawl in their shattered hive
        Still part alive
    With toil that they have done
        Unmade.

    No more the bright-hued flowers shall welcome them—
        No more—
    From leafy stem
        In quiet shade:
        No more their strange joy passionless
    In striving with small aim
        Shall move them in the summer hours long lost—
            Their scheme of life is gone and they
        Await the midnight dews and chilly frost
            Under the stars steel-grey.
        [Hocken, MS 704/4:260, pp.173–6]

**The Poison-Bane**

O bitter draught is the poison-bane of Truth!
    Aeons may pass while lovers plight their troth
    But ever behind the superimposed façade
    Truth flowers and flings to earth its myriad seed.

    Few men have seen the ancient cold wine-press
    Where earth counts nothing nor an empire's praise:
    Though bitter is the cup to all who test
    Yet sweetest ichor is the after-taste
    That makes the tongue a flame of prophesy
    And bids the spirit burn the body so—

Great monarchies nor nations say him nay
Who drank most deeply at Gethsemane.

And though men scourge and slay incessantly
Thou like True Thomas canst not lie;
And Beauty comes in knowledge of all days
When wisdom is a fire that never dies.

The tall gods kneel who drank not half so full
And thy firm strides beyond the realms that fail
Sound on the pathways of the centuries:
But ah! though thou may'st sooner rise,
Far from the miseries that are and were,
Above the black essential evil, War,
Into the golden halls of mastery
Yet thou shalt know the hemlock and the rue
By faith deserted and by man accurst
With thunder-bolts in Hatreds' furnace cast
Hurled on the soul that yet has vanity.
Thou empty oracles may hearken to
Ere yet the full Truth is impermeate
And the loud shouts of scorn may crush thee down
To warped unnatural anger at
The power of irony and false disdain.

Yet if the goal is won and thou art lost
Within the many mansions of the blest
Eternal truth and joy may seem but stale
And thou wilt ever wish
That, cherishing the old illusions still,
Thou wert among the wave and wash
Of Life's remembrance-haunted sea—
For this low earth is very dear
Whatever sophists say
And here there is the hidden jewelled door
To long communion in a strange half-light:

And e'en the sorrows that were dark of late
Fulfil a longing then insatiate.
[Hocken, MS 704/4:258, pp.168–70]

**Incarnation**

At last shall gravity triumph
And earth to earth drawn ever
In word in thought, blood lymph

Again be the dew-river
Hang passionless on honey-belly
Or moil in earth's moist bowels.

My eyes to day's-eyes turned
On the enamelled green
Follow as ever the sun whereby they burned
No ache their lives between;
And bones new-fossil grow
Rooted in rock below.

My fingers in the sensitive roots of plants
Suck moisture as once love;
The iron of sex in insect loins relents,
Mouth sings in the sighing olive-grove
And ears in whorlèd mountains sound resounding
Hear burns on pebbles sanding.

So as the earth conspired
That deed of birth be wrought—
Earth's anarchy appeared
In my tumultous thought—
So death unsought will make of me
A new eternity.

[Shall I betray
This transient passion for
A stone immortal day?
Nay, for the niggard store
Dwindles at night away:
In hurt and love life bore
My limbs my human posture
Shall I not taste her pasture?]
[Hocken MS 704/11:652, pp.1–3]

**Soliloquy of One Sane**

A clock—precision; no wheel wasted.
A man—raw-edged and unadjusted.
On mantleshelf the staid and luminous clock.
A million clocks click likewise soft and slick.
The earth around the sun measures her days
Clock-wise or anticlock-wise as you please.
The clock has torn youth's dream on ruthless flanges.
Mankind trussed to the minute wheels and plunges—
Live bundle, her own pit and pendulum.

The clock clangs in the slum
Measuring merciless: voices moan like seas
Cry for the rich and idle palaces;
Find there the naked clock like angel sing
The metal angel of a night-mare's song.
And at the tree-root of that ravenous bough
An axeman stands—he holds a poker now.
The luminous clock lies dead. The midnight glare
That pierced the night of passion with day's lure
That froze the man and poem to one time
The click of iron coin, sad factory-tune:
So now the inlets call, man may go back
To the ancestral wood of word and luck.
The mountain lake, the city love await.
It is the man within fashions the land without.

Grow silent, listen well
And you will hear a slight and silver bell;
And you will hear the heart-beat dragging chains;
And you will hear the click of blood in veins.
The Clock is born again. O rave and shout
The stone wolf ravenous. O break his snout.
He blew his brains out.
[Hocken, MS 704/11:655, pp.9–10]

**Baxter to Ginn, 22 December 1943**

CENSORED
No. 4

Naseby
Ranfurly.
22/12/43

Dear Noel,—

I have just received the letter and your perfect gift—I have been wanting to get Louis Macneice for a long time.[1] He just fits in with my Auden, Pound, Eliot, Spender, Day Lewis collection. I have not read anything, am keeping it for Xmas. There is a certain resemblance between 'Head-hunters' and Terry's 'D.H.L.' Not exactly style:

1 Ginn sent Baxter a copy of Louis MacNeice's *Autumn Journal* (London: Faber & Faber, 1943) for Christmas, inscribed 'To Jim from Noel'. This volume remains in the possession of the Baxter family.

something nearer the backbone of thought in a way. No, that is perhaps a hasty judgement.[2]

INCARNATION—'relents': loses consciousness, and with it frustration.

S.O.O.S.—as you say, reference to Poe.[3]

The age will not spare anyone, must leave its mark of dissolution or integrity on us all; but at any rate I don't intend to be physically hurt, though trouble must come my way.

BY THE APPIAN WAY is almost perfect—one of your best, clear, your full 'punch'. Of course I know the 'fish' is symbol of Christ—something to do with the Greek or Hebrew letter isn't it?[4] Yes, it is perfect, though the last line (true in every particular) drops ever so slightly. I invariably study my end-lines for compactness and 'good running'—sonnets anyway.

Send me the copies of Auden if you like. I've an idea I've seen the 'ballad' and 'W.B. Yeats' but that doesn't matter, because I'm not sure.[5]

You, like me, lose a 'pristine purity' but develop in strength. BY THE APPIAN WAY is most imaginative and powerful.

Follow some poems of mine (with remarks I expect.)

PTO

**O Blake! The World Guessed Not Thine Excellence**

O Blake! The world guessed not thine excellence—
    And guess not yet; fools dub thee mad, but dread
    Thy fame will bruit their folly—thus instead
Cry 'mystical'. Aye, 'mystical' perchance—
If such be reason, faith, and soul intense
    Burning seraphic among the quick and dead.
    Thy world scarce knew thee: thou by god-sight led
Did'st for thyself create as sure defence
    A world of flame and chaos where vast Forms

2 Untraced—neither Ginn nor Terence Baxter are sure what 'Terry's "D.H.L."' refers to.

3 In 'Soliloquy of One Sane' Baxter refers, in line 9, to Edgar Allan Poe's (1809–49) story 'The Pit and the Pendulum' (c. 1841). In addition to this direct reference, Baxter's poem touches on one of Poe's major themes: the effect of time on human existence. This theme, which is dealt with comically by Poe in 'The Devil in the Belfry' (1839), when a playful devil drives a perfectly-ordered town to distraction by causing the town clock to strike 13—takes on a more sinister cast in stories like 'The Masque' (c. 1841) in which a clock tolls hourly the mortality theme as the pleasure-mad masqueraders whirl madly on indifferent to Time and Death.

4 See 'By the Appian Way', p.532. The fish (ΙΧΘΥΣ) is an ancient symbol for Christ dating back to the first three centuries AD. The popular explanation is that the Greek word ΙΧΘΥΣ, for fish, is an acrostic of the words φΙησου—Χριστοϖ—Θεου—Υιϑοϖ—Σοτηϖρ, 'Jesus Christ, Son of God, Saviour'. The symbology may also have its roots in the miracle of Christ's multiplication of the loaves and fishes as a predictor of the Eucharistic feast, and in the story of the blind father of Tobias: as he recovered his sight by means of a fish, so believers receive the light from Christ.

5 Both of the poems by Auden that Baxter refers to are most likely from *Another Time* (London: Faber & Faber/New York: Random House, 1940). 'In memory of W.B. Yeats' certainly is, and the 'ballad' may be a reference to 'It's farewell to the drawing-rooms civilised cry . . .', which had been printed in part in (Edward) Benjamin Britten's (1913–76) volume *Ballad of Heroes* (1939) as 'Dance of death' (in *Collected Poems* it is titled 'Danse macabre'). In Baxter's letter of 4 Jan 1944 he comments on poems from a variety of volumes of Auden—volumes that must have been sent to him by Ginn. See p.314.

Wrought their titanic labours mid the flood
 Of timeless change, petrific death, fire-storms;
Thou wert a Sun sphereless in solitude.
 Words flowered in thy sight. Thy ardour warms
Hearts that in thee delight, this night withstood.

(Wordsworthian, but I trust not boring.)

(TO SLEEP Walter De La Mare, Keats, rhetoric, thus atmosphere. Think of Sleep not of sleep.
'shrunk'—'a clarion', subject of this verb.

**To Sleep**

O Sleep: that thy strong wings me girt around,
 Thou tireless angel! Savage we toil and groan:
 But thou dost smile; and so without a moan
We are gathered to thee. I heard a clarion sound
Over the steeps of midnight, from the drowned
 Haven of sightless joys;—like thunder thrown
 Yet shrill as bat-cry, shrunk my limbs to stone.
Earth hearkened; thou did'st enter star-encrowned.

Door-keeper thou alike of grave and womb,
 Our lives thou rulest; half our soul is thine.
Night sighs to thy passing: the fields are dumb;
 And Love must like the birds love's flower deshrine.
O deal thou gently with me when I come
To eat thy bread and drink thy bitter wine.

**True Melancholy**

True melancholy dwells
In no secluded dells
Nor in snow-craggy hells
 Where souls enchainèd
Howl to th' imprisoning gloom;
For death, despair, and doom
Within a sunlit room
 May lurk unfeigned

It is the man who walks,
Eats, drinks, laughs, talks,
Knowing that terror stalks—
 None knowing save he.

The love of life forgotten
Shows all earth-fabric rotten,
Faith flaring like gun-cotton:
    Such is true melancholy.

(Written here. 'gun-cotton'—no other rhyme available. See 'Young Trees'.)[6]

**Air**

The eternal clouds bulbous, more wide than air
    Hang float and flow
We are near the sky, thus farther
    From the corrosive rot, suburban flow.

Trees cradle the air and gently
    And sighing touch untentative air
They sigh to one another, the wind is a brother.
    Against rain-grey clouds, against the memory of rain-wash in one's
childhood, [ against the highland nakedness sun-and-ice-clothed of
    death—[ endowed mountains they seem more enduring than they are.

We
sadly
    are divided forever from
    the perfect fulcrum.

Even the telegraph-wires murmur their metal desires
    to the wind's harmony
    to the swell of the tree
    to the sky's eternity;
but dread of self-forgetting
of sun-setting
of natural sentiment
    Perpetuates perpetual discontent.'

(Written here. The long, long line is not exhibitionism, but I think suitable.)

You pamper me. The Louis Macneice is an expensive gift, though of course greatly appreciated. You are scarcely a lode-star to me, rather a philosopher's stone.

Love and best wishes
From Jim.
[VUW Library, MS McKay 28/28]

6 Baxter's 'Written here' means written while on holiday with his parents in Naseby. See 'The young trees', p.131, which begins: 'Light dreams shall flare and vanish like gun-cotton'.

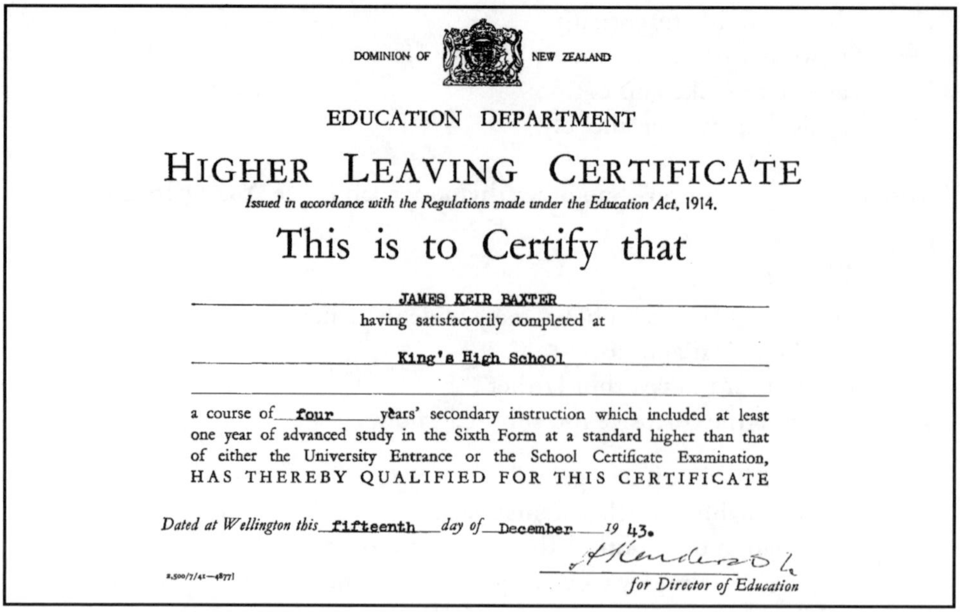

DOMINION OF NEW ZEALAND

EDUCATION DEPARTMENT

HIGHER LEAVING CERTIFICATE

*Issued in accordance with the Regulations made under the Education Act,* 1914.

This is to Certify that

JAMES KEIR BAXTER

having satisfactorily completed at

King's High School

a course of four years' secondary instruction which included at least one year of advanced study in the Sixth Form at a standard higher than that of either the University Entrance or the School Certificate Examination, HAS THEREBY QUALIFIED FOR THIS CERTIFICATE

*Dated at Wellington this* fifteenth *day of* December *19* 43.

2,500/7/41—48771

*for Director of Education*

Baxter's Higher Leaving Certificate. *'My exams are over; I go to Varsity next year. Am looking forward to it, have met some pretty intelligent ones now going—no good poets, no Noels, but such are rare'* [Hocken MS 975/187]

# IV
# CORRESPONDENCE: 1944

I will soon be 18;
My life may be regarded as mainly future;
'Janus Unheard'

**Baxter to Ginn, 4 January 1944**

Censor's stamp
illegible.

Naseby
Ranfurly.
4/1/44

Dear Noel,—

Address future letters to Brighton again, as we leave soon.

My back and neck are sun-burnt and I have just been for a bathe. I walk round here among the broom and gold-claims and make up moral codes.[1] I am nevertheless quite sociable and play rounders and such-like with the aborigines, and tennis morning and afternoon.

If you have periods of inertia, that is natural enough. My father's theory has always been that minds capable of strong feeling must have periods of quiescence; that this is compensation. I find that sometimes for days I scarcely think at all. Perhaps some spend their lives thus.

OLD QUESTION: OLD ANSWER 'lad'—very beautiful and naive, but a trifle like Housman. A fine lyric though.[2]

TO GRAEME patchy; excellent in parts—'and the branches stiffly say In their incoherent way.' Your technique is rarely perfect, but there are always parts beyond all technique. 'Hero of all or one small maid' entrances me like Botticelli. It is a great deal of force, this poem. I will study it further.[3]

'Shrill as bat-cry' in TO SLEEP[4] gives the quality that pierces, also the unearthly beauty (dangerous I admit) of De La Mare. Think of the atom, the whirl-wind, and the still small voice. Think of a wind blowing from eternity over the 'steeps of midnight'.

[Incomplete]

[VUW Library, MS McKay 28/29]

1 It was the discovery of gold in 1863 that brought the town of Naseby into existence. For the next fifty years the surrounding countryside was worked over by hydraulic sluicing: a method of extraction that destroyed much of the land in the process. The workings—or 'gold claims'—were then subject to progressive erosion until tree planting programmes were initiated to arrest the process.

Baxter also mentions 'moral codes' in 'Janus Unheard' (ll. 182, 341), see pp.461, 465.

2 See 'Old question: old answer', p.533: there is some correspondence in tone between this poem and the nostalgic verse of A.E. Housman's [1859–1936] first collection *A Shropshire Lad* (1896).

3 See 'To Graeme', p.533.

4 See 'To Sleep', p.308.

**Baxter to Ginn, 12 January 1944**

Naseby
Ranfurly
12/1/44

Dear Noel,—

We leave here day after tomorrow. Auden read avidly; I've always considered him the best modern since I first read 'Lay your sleeping head . . .' He is rather like you in some ways. A.E. HOUSMAN—my sentiments too; scarcely poetry, hardly expansive enough for that; very clear and epigrammatic. EPITHALMION [sic]—scarcely a success, rhymes too far apart; hardening of abstract thought into metaphors. THE STRING'S EXCITEMENT—have not studied sufficiently, find rather involved with his usual imagery. ALWAYS THE FOLLOWING WIND—what power! Auden when he realizes he is great. 'To scamper after darlings' shows the bravado of the adolescent; but 'When to gaze longer' to 'Sterile as moon' is controlled emotion, disillusionment not blasé but sheer power. IN MEMORY OF W.B. YEATS—the 3rd is best, swells to poetry. Sensitive, true, a little unformed in parts in technique. BRUSSELS IN WINTER—I can't say. '. . . SELF-EDUCATED WILLIAM BLAKE'—clever and true.[1]

I have developed a certain photo of Ten which I got last week. My father and mother were very pleased. I didn't have the necessary apparatus before.

WE PAY—imperfect, but sensitive I think.

'O LET THE PRISONER GO'—a skeleton of emotion.

IN CITY NIGHT—clever.

[Pages 2 to 5 missing]

**To the Sun**

O thou clear-brooding, in the seas of cloud
Unmoved—hast thou no longing and no grief?
The winds are leashed like waters behind the hills,
Thy holy eye them quieting to sleep.

1 Ginn appears to have sent Baxter at least four of Auden's works: 'A.E. Housman', 'Epithalamion', 'In memory of W.B. Yeats' and 'Brussels in Winter' first appeared in *Another Time* (London: Faber & Faber/New York: Random House, 1940); 'The string's excitement . . .' appeared in *Poems* (Faber & Faber, 1930); 'Always the following wind . . .' is a speech by the character 'John' in Auden's play—based on the theme of Orpheus and Eurydice—*The Dance of Death* (Faber & Faber, 1933); and 'Self-educated William Blake' is from *New Year Letter* (Faber & Faber, 1941), lines 184–93: 'Self-educated William Blake / Who threw his spectre in the lake, / Broke of relations in a curse / With the Newtonian Universe.' See also Baxter's letters of 22 Dec 1943 (p.306) and 10 Feb 1944 (p.324).

Thou elemental Spirit, they do lie,
Their stony visages like flowers enslumbered;
Their wings hiding their eyes, like children worn
With their own tumult, innocent and still.

The shale-bound peaks breathe fire; their glittering fangs
Like serpents motionless; their lids of snow
Weep at thy sacred breath. They leaning
Embrace the populous valleys, calm with love.

Within thy rays angels of sleep descend
Who nightlong toil; and in the morn arise,
Thy clarion recalling. Thou art Peace
Life-knowing: we are unquiet, desire that peace.

TO THE SUN—Blakeian. Good all the same.

Next time I will send you a sort of surrealist picture-poem. LANDSCAPE by name.

Love and best wishes
From
Jim.

[VUW Library, MS McKay 28/30]

**We Pay**

'We pay for our mistakes.' Yes, once and twice,
And thirty thousand times before it's done
And the lank body pain-deprivèd lies.

In coin of sweat and flesh by racking won
The soul's integrity paid—coin by coin—:
The unachieved explodes like shell from gun.

Explodes and leaves its wounds imbedded,
Sensitive to weather, in brain or groin.
Writhes in hot nights, the dragon unbeheaded.

This bitterness alone denied the pup.
But he grows soon. 'I should have kissed her then,
Fool, fool. She turned in the gate, wondered what was up.'

Most vulnerable in desire
The ache is life and drives us to
Despair or destiny. No soothing we acquire.

Derision chills not; self-derision
Chills, kills, reiterates the neural pain.
The hurt grows horny in a year—or ten.

The self-sufficient case that clothes the brain
Eventually clothes antennae too.
Only a death will make us quick again
[Hocken, MS 704/11:685, pp.59–60]

**'O Let the Prisoner Go'**

O let the prisoner go
And blast the gaol with nitroglycerine
Plant gardens on the spot
Let sunrise and sunset falter not.

O let the prisoner go
The children do not play upon his heart
The gaol undying warps the heavens within it
Sunrise and sunset pierce not.
[Hocken, MS 704/11:686, p.61]

**In City Night**

This loneliness from lesser loneliness
Sprang, as from seed the seed or dusk the night.
Like paper flowers in their comeliness,

The market-stalls; hysterical and slight
Amusement of bear-baiting, jugglers, quacks:
But jogging home in country lanes by twilight

They did not carry a doom upon their backs.
Ditches and owls and nightglow, broom and briar
(As always) symbols making smooth like wax

Vacant mind-surface; then with tongues of fire
Reiterating myth, and amplitude
Of earth for herbal healing of desire.

Surely, we say, the floral solitude
That stifles verve will melt under the sway
Of jazz-bands and smart houses, spirit food.

What father left to son, what neighbours say,
Has grown unreal—and the generations,
Too wide a gap for surgery to splay.

The slick and gay are not at the foundations.
Could we forget the sorrow, and forget
The parent-god of childhood conversations

(In brief, be heartless as the marionette)
Then were reflected love in the city night,
Each tower a negress swaying thighs of jet:

But we desire the quiet meal and fire-light;
And wander in the iron wilderness;
And we desire a god to break our night:

So haunt within the limbo havenless;
It is our soul, the City (glare and night):
So we self-gnawing crouch therein like termite.
[Hocken, MS 704/11:689, pp.65–6]

**Landscape**

A lava-mountain humped at the end of the plain
jutting, from whose recesses as from loins
a sun floods, like a cavern into daylight.
Crystal
with continual spray a river gorge-folded
pours from it; arid dunes
encumber.

Massive, a natural bridge
hangs over the gorge, echoing:—
upon it cling men and women like creeping plants
tearing tenderly, or like beasts
each other's faces.

Some stare forever as if blinded
at a scythe and flowers carved on stone;
some are swept away by the current—
rigid, then lax, scarcely struggling:
their bones, flesh washing from them
circle forever in certain eddies, a nest of snakes;
or are ground between boulders.

Pus drips from the mouths of those who cling,
laving and increasing the body of a vast grey slug
rooted like seaweed to the left bastion.
Its horns are flowers, it has breasts of iron shaped like a woman's.
With uneven lips it mouths toward them.

Some it seizes: they rot.
The bridge also rots under it as to acid.
On those drowned in pools cut below
it also feeds—
tearing them, holding them to its breasts in seeming love.

In a hollow at the summit of the arch
lie lovers.
A tree shading them
shakes sighing in a wind which itself creates:
its leaves are of flame;
its roots are twined among the lovers
mingled with their limbs.

Three branches shaped like hands
hold on high an inverted bowl
with mirror-surface within it.
Spray from the river condensing upon it
cools the lips of those who sweat or shiver on bare rock.
And the mirror shows an inverted bridge
most bright, the slug an angel;
the bones are coloured fruits:
Many gaze at the mirror
till they are dizzy and fall headlong.

Hazes melting into eyes clothe the bridge-ends.
Those near to them hide their faces and weep.
[Hocken, MS 704/11:691, pp.69–71]

**Baxter to Ginn, 26 January 1944**

CENSORED
**No. 5**

Brighton,
Otago.
26/1/44.

Dear Noel,—

There's not much to write about, but Terry will probably show you his letter. I swim now and then, and intend to do a bit of sun-bathing. Could you tell me any English-books you have? You said you might have some that I could borrow for 'Varsity.

I enclose some poems. If you don't always feel up to writing don't worry. I'll write just the same.

I have bought the poems of Harold Monro, Sassoon, and G.M.H. Monro is Georgian, very fine on the whole, a good minor poet. His best by far is the oft-quoted BITTER SANCTUARY—or rather oft-published. It is most powerful and effective.[1] Sassoon is light in a way in spite of his subjects. He could not be a great poet, seems a frustrated minor one. His best I think is THE MERCIFUL KNIGHT.[2]

G.M.H. deserves a paragraph, a book to himself. He is great—that is all one can really say, except for reading him again and again. I may be unusually susceptible to him; anyway he is like the bread, the water of life to me as far as poetry goes (it goes a long way.)

Yet is he conservative, thinks war fine—'Christ would be a soldier if he came again.' This one brushes aside almost as a merit as Burns' flagellated-for 'drunkenness and fornication'.[3]

'Spring and Fall' I know by heart and repeat mentally and aloud whenever not in company.[4] The sad-made-strength is Hopkin's forte.

Read—

> 'And you were a liar, O blue March day.'
>
> . . . . .
>
> 'A beetling bald-bright cloud thorough England Riding . . .'
>
> . . . . .
>
> 'Now Carisbrook keep goes under in gloom;
> Now it overvaults Appledurcombe;

1 Harold Monro [1879–1932] was best known during his lifetime as an editor, a publisher, and the proprietor of London's highly regarded Poetry Bookshop. He achieved a degree of posthumous fame when his *Collected Poems*, published in London in 1933 by Cobden-Sanderson, revealed a unique, rather un-Georgian, aspect to his verse that prompted T.S. Eliot to remark that he could be, at times, a poet of the 'spectres and the "bad dreams" which live inside the skull'.

2 Siegfried Sassoon [1886–1967] published numerous volumes of verse but is remembered for around one hundred poems protesting the continuation of World War I through 1917 and 1918. Among the volumes published up to 1944 were his *Selected Poems* (London: Heinemann, 1925) and *Poems Newly Selected, 1916–35* (London: Faber and Faber, 1940).

3 'Christ would be a soldier . . .' summarises the intent of Hopkins's poem '(The Soldier)' [1885], in particular its final line '"Were I come o'er again" cries Christ "it should be this."' To support his argument that the quality of Hopkin's poem demands one overlook its militant theme, Baxter refers to the metaphoric flagellation for drunkenness and fornication inflicted on Robert Burns, particularly by early biographers like Dr James Currie, who moralised thus about his subject:

> [Burns] fled from himself into society, often of the lowest kind. And in such company . . . uncontrolled passion generally presided. He who suffers the pollution of inebriation, how shall he escape other pollution? But let us refrain from the mention of errors over which delicacy and humanity draw the veil. (Bold, p.34.)

Yet the poets own work supports Baxter's argument that what in others may be vice can, in the case of the rare individual, become a virtue. Rather than drawing a veil over his 'errors' Burns turned to them for inspiration, for example in the impenitent ditty 'The Fornicator', recalling the public penitence he and the mother of his illegitimate child underwent in 1785 before the congregation of Mauchline Kirk:

> But my downcast eye by chance did spy
> What made my lips to water,
> Those limbs so clean where I, between,
> Commenc'd a Fornicator.

4 Hopkins's 'Spring and Fall' [1880] is a poem of 15 lines containing the phrase 'the blight man was born for', which Baxter later uses in his letter of 6 Jan 1945 (see p.393).

Now near by Ventnor town
It hurls, hurls off Boniface Down.'[5]

Who was ever so three-dimensional in perfect, in emotional expression?

Who ever so blended sound and meaning?

Who ever packed such easy force in a single sentence?

Who was ever so unobscure, so human in expression? There is no real obscurity in him anywhere. Walt Whitman could make a poem on it.

I may recover a bit from all this—but you'll see the effect on my poems

Best wishes,

From Jim.

[VUW Library, MS McKay 28/31]

**Baxter to Ginn, 1 February 1944**

CENSORED
No. 3

Brighton,
Otago.
1/2/44

Dear Noel,—

Many thanks, many, for the *Autumn Journal*.[1] I think it's pretty powerful in parts. I had read parts before, but had wanted to have the book, couldn't get it. Where do you get your poetry-books?

About visiting Terry and you. We had thought about it before you wrote. While the travelling restrictions are on, I don't think we can do it. But if they go off, we may go in March.[2] Don't let Terry think this is definite, because it isn't. I think my mother is very pleased that Terry asked for her to go.

I enclose one or two poems. I hope you haven't seen any of them before.

5 These lines, from stanzas 6 to 8 of Hopkins's 'The loss of the Eurydice: Foundered March 24, 1878' (1878), detail the storm's sweep across England to hit the luckless vessel shortly before it reaches safe harbour.

1 Ginn's Christmas gift to Baxter—*Autumn Journal* by [Frederick] Louis MacNeice [1907–63]—was published in London by Faber & Faber in 1939. MacNeice, part of the Auden–Spender–Day Lewis group, structured this verse diary of the closing months of 1938 into a series of twenty-four cantos. Baxter emulated MacNeice's form and style in his long poem 'Janus Unheard' [see his letter to Ginn of 10 Feb 1944, pp.325–6, and the complete text of 'Janus Unheard' on pp.457–67).

2 Japan's sudden entry into the war in December 1941 not only brought the threat of invasion close to home, but presented New Zealand with a supply crisis—particularly in respect of petrol and tyres—resulting in rationing and restrictions that were to last for the remainder of the war. Severe shortages of petrol for private use saw crowding of public transport, limitations placed on long journeys, a huge increase in the sale of bicycles (and bicycle theft), and, to a certain extent, the re-appearance of horse on New Zealand streets. It was late August before James and Millicent were able to visit Terence and Noel (see p.112).

| | |
|---|---|
| The honest Jack . . . | good, I think |
| Men cannot mar | rather soppy. |
| G.M.H. | too violent in style. |
| Speech, by D. the D. | the form is a hard one. |

Love to Terry
Best wishes
From
Jim
(Must catch mail quickly.)
[VUW Library, MS McKay 28/32]

**'The honest Jack . . .'**

The honest Jack (honest, though rogue in will)
'Truth'—vendors told by that the foes of faith,
Demons of dire fire, lurk to wreak their wrath
On home and haven; lurk in lair, and will
His life enrage with outrage—rive, rape, kill:
Between-fears strung he'll fearing pick his path;
Then (self-to-need-yielding) desert his strath
And 's mould-of-manhood spill, grave-gorge fill.
I in the cynic-seat whereby truths may
(As pond-glass glass-beheld to whirled life turns)
Grow towërlike, thus weave a skein, thus say:
Shall he man-Jack, little take of that he earns?
Do not prideful his peers more stray, more flay
Him than the foe blood-blazoned-of whom 's blade burns?
[Hocken, MS 704/11:700, p.91]

**Men cannot mar**

The well-of knowledge drained, and flesh-and-fell
Of manhood hid there, doom-drowned, shown—
Then is the cup but bitter: salve? is none?
Yea, all such in heart hold; know, know well
Men, and mood of the Infinite, unsown
By hand, nor brow-built, but broad in the sun.

Men cannot mar it; man-might from it flings
Wings-of-wonder—death-blown, child ungrown
Savour alike salt-of-the deathless; nor shun
Fellows as may felons. Share sweetness whereof earth sings
Earth sings at one nor doth as man moan.
[Hocken, MS 704/11:699, p.90]

**To Gerard Manly Hopkins**
**man and monk**

Fire-rooted in thee, thy Christ, thy Mary,
A world wert; yet fire-lashed thy heart
Found man mate, boy brother: eased so the smart
Of soul sold desperate bondage to; suave-chary,
Self (so-splendid) unpreening, pried the hairy
Beast-unbelief from lurk-lair; beam broke, and bar
Tried on 's hide. Faith won with wielded dart
Grave-concentrate—God'sblood too-brewed true-hewed to bury.
Fault's not in thee, man, if the world stay blind,
Bat-blind, mole-blind, in carrion-cage grown sick:
Thy man-love, land-lore, vein-environed quick
of kill-hunger, sea-speech, such I find
More-than-the-world-of-Whitman-wide, yet thick
As loam on land: heart-jewel. Muse, mankind.
[Hocken, MS 704/11:695, p.84]

**Speech, by Death the Director**

They were all children once, who under leaves
or sand or sea or rock or swamp now flower
as inarticulate murmur from earth's lips;
all children once—in this dry boneyard corner
you have observed the Chinaman's grave: a brain
had he too: love, to combat the hells that raven.

The stork brought some; others, I fear, the raven—
my raven—brought. The syphilitic leaves
an heritage; and cripples; and broken in brain.
But most were loved by mothers, were white birth-flowers
found beast—and stone-friends quiet in every corner
fear and forgiveness, sleep soothing rebellious lips.

When then did *good* and *evil* first pass their lips?
Never, I think: the figment that wrought raven-
ous wrong, the dragon, with hole-in-corner
man-hatred from dogma sprang; and the leaves
and flower and fruit of frustration framed the new flower,
the easy-way, earth's-wickedness, beauty-of-brain.

They did not know the snare; it missed the brain,
on genital and gut, on breast and lips
laid weight rather. But they forgot in flower
and tree and swimming-hole, banjo, the raven-

ing of that broad bough. Stars in night-leaves
comforted continents, souls at each crevice and corner.

They . . . saw me when I wept at Hell-Fire Corner,
drawn from dope-dream to slash body and brain.
What could I do but weep? They were not leaves,
not leaves, not withered leaves; but flung to the lips
of night and chaos as if so. The child from claw of raven
or stork grew: starveling and stupid were men, were flower.

The booze-rotten braggart in streets see, hell's flower:
pass unpitying; you are the murderers: drums corner
the dreams of shattered scattered flesh where guns raven.
See the corpse, shudder: see not the brain
alive yet, unreconciled by drug or love of lips.
Too vast a set-back, too vast: love probes where pity leaves.

I had purpose, as stars in leaves, as sun-flower.
*Death* call me with grey lips; start, sweating in your corner.
Me undesirous your brain has made as wolves raven.
[Hocken, MS 704/11:705, pp.100–2]

**Baxter to Ginn, 10 February 1944**

Censor's stamp
illegible

Brighton,
Otago.
10/2/44

Dear Noel,—

It is great to get these books from you, but don't, don't spoil me. Eliot's essays are the best I know on poetry. My tentative efforts in that direction quail when I read him—I have found that it is far easier to write good poetry than good prose; or rather, the mental apparatus is different and I haven't developed it yet. T.S.E.'s essay on Swinburne amounts to genius; with Blake he is prejudiced, I think—too heavy a diet of Dante and the Elizabetheans.[1]

1 T.S. Eliot's essays on Blake and Swinburne were first published in *The Sacred Wood: Essays on Poetry and Criticism* (London: Methuen, 1920), and re-published in *Selected Essays 1917–1932* (London: Faber & Faber, 1932). It is understandable, given Baxter's own reservations about intellectuals, that he would reject Eliot's argument that Blake's poetry springs from a shallower source because:

> What his genius required, and what it sadly lacked, was a framework of accepted and traditional ideas which would have prevented him from indulging in a philosophy of his own, and concentrated his attention upon the problems of the poet.

On the other hand Eliot's comment—'When you take to pieces any verse of Swinburne, you find always that the object is not there—only the word'—is along the lines of Baxter's belief, as he expressed it to Ginn, that every good poem must 'have a thread'.

*Autumn Journal* is good reading—food greased for the gullet, taste and aftertaste excellent. Macneice is not really versatile, but has amazing ability and subtlety within a limited scope. Perhaps Irish. The insight into personality—personality given its best aspect by its owner, of course—is very pleasing. I could read it any time, again and again. His blind spots and clichés and occasional cheapness are not disheartening, rather amplify the artistic side.[2]

*Introducing Shakespeare* I'll find very useful this year. I haven't studied it yet.

Just lately I received a group photograph with you in it. I picked you out easily, which is pretty good work considering I've never seen one of you before. You're certainly the handsomest there, also most intelligent-looking. All favourably impressed. I find it rather disconcerting; will have to get used to a new view. I can see the features of your mind and emotions and must reconcile them with the physical counterpart. It is an attractive face. You made a very favourable impression on Jean Carr[3]—'the boy with the beautiful smile'. Don't broadcast it.

Enclose a strongly felt piece of propaganda. Good in its naïve way, with a hint of subtlety too. I now realize how necessary constant images are; abstract thought can not be poetry unless galvanized thus. The best poetry of course has perfect welding of image and emotion. But any images are better than none. Thus all the figures-of-speech.

I have read Auden's *New Year Letter*. It offends against the definition *poetry is emotion* as only such a master as Auden would dare to.[4] ~~Has~~ Is stimulating reading all the same. Have read also some of Mary Webb—excellent style, sometimes excessive nature mysticism, sometimes near to the atmospherics of W. Faulkner (you know him? Southern States writer, strong on Doom, very sensitive and poetic, violent style),[5] but powerful and successful all along the line. 'Gone to Earth' is a work of genius. The only thing hampering her is a lack of incisive modernity, but of course that would shatter all the power she has.[6]

I have produced a poem (over 420 lines) called 'Janus Unheard', a style a bit like Macneice, but original. Can't send it up as it's far far too political. But, regarded objectively, it is very powerful, sometimes diffuse, sometimes prosy, but 'good'. You might not like it or share my opinion.[7]

2 MacNeice, who was the son of a minister in the Anglo-Irish Church, also favoured home rule and condemned Protestant bigotry. In a reaction against his Protestant upbringing MacNeice's verse rejects Ireland—with some hatred in the case of the *Autumn Journal*—but despite this he was never to lose his sense of himself as Irish.

3 A friend of the Baxter family who was also involved in the pacifist movement.

4 Auden's *New Year Letter* has remained one of his more contentious works: a lengthy epistle in iambic tetrameter couplets with notes, a bibliography, prologue and epilogue, and a sequence of twenty sonnets titled 'The Quest', it is intellectual and discursive in its reflections on the current state of civilisation and on Auden's own conversion to Christianity. While some critics choose to view the poem as symptomatic of Auden's decline, others read in it a refutation of criticisms that he lacked a coherent and expansive world view and identify many ingredients—command of idiom, intellectual breadth and timeliness—that signify major status.

5 William Harrison Faulkner [1897–1962]: an extremely popular American novelist who received the Nobel Prize for Literature in 1949.

6 Mary [Gladys] Webb [1881–1927]: a novelist and poet, Webb located most of her work in the Shropshire region and peopled her novels with its inhabitants, she also worked into her writing her fascination with psychology and mysticism. Immensely popular at one stage, her breathless style has since provided material for satire. Her novel *Gone to Earth* was published in 1917.

quote—

Outside the rain is ceasing
    Brilliant sunshine flashing in the rain;
The rainbow represents the ancient covenant
    And I must rear again
My Janus-head out of a country coma
    Of pastoral falsity, of rain on leaves;
Hear history's abstract music thunder
    Her breves and semibreves.

talking of the 'tower of personality'—

And when first the Platonic Forms flower
    Live in a statue's curve
Or the modern grace, carving the lines of a suspension
    Bridge, with a gull's and with steel's verve.
Valuable too the day when the tower seems Babel
    And about to fall
With scream of madness in a mild blue sunset;
    Death on its flaming walls, inexorable and tall.

later on—

For some the church-cross has fascination
    For the daring of stones;
Some run on the graves in the cemetery
    Feeling the call of bones to bones.
The chief function of the Church is comforting—
    The catholic Mary-of-wide-arms
Can embrace the world like a Mother; evident
    In lithographs in city flats and shrines on farms.

now prosy—

. . . I could not live in a Paradise of the People.
Art for the Masses becomes Art for the State
    Becomes a prostitute to propaganda;
And Mayakovsky's fate—
    Who remained at heart the bourgeois (or the poet)
So shot himself, leaving a lyric behind—
    Encourages me in this. Nor is a dictator
Pleasing, of any kind.

7 Baxter's style in the three cantos of his 'Janus Unheard', although less informal and colloquial in places than the *Autumn Journal*, follows MacNeice's rhythm and rhyme scheme closely, employing interwoven quatrains rhyming on alternate lines (usually the second and fourth) and varying both the length of the lines (from two feet to six feet) and the rhythm.

weary—

Do we really know what we want?
The tide of history turns against us:
There are no rods to flail this Hellespont—
Though all at heart are imitating Xerxes.
O let us lie and sleep a thousand years—
Wake to find Death an electric gunman;
No sweat, but the usual incapable tears
And blood forever—blood of the bloody
Baptismal grace to drive the devils out;
Even if the guns go off to wireless
Brain and bodies will take the clout.

and not so far from the end, speeding up for the amen—

I see—though none will believe me—
The Roman vertigo,
The power that broke the Empire:
*Delenda est Carthago.*
It is not the usual things I remember,
The antique legend, rift in the Capitol.
Rather it is the gesture, the men fearing,
The priest speaking behind the oracular doll.
Cicero, who could not leave his villas
Stretching his neck from the litter, waiting the stroke.
The soldiers on shore who might have won the battle
Though Antony's squadrons broke,
But leaderless. And even in Rome they had their
Cliques of literature, their men of books
Believing themselves civilization's saviours
While the new world made spears from pruning-hooks.

I have left out a bit of the best and a bit of the worst and a lot of the even body. But you'll get a faint idea of it. The gospel is personality. I think I have given a strong individual quirk (of seriousness perhaps, oratorical) to Macneice's metre. Anyway, you'll see it some day—in print even.

Give my love to Terry. Tell him the boy Crimp (I think he should remember him) will probably be writing to him soon, as he asked me for his address. My Mother is sending Terry some food. If he ever wants anything he should write—even just a note to say it. I hope to see him before very long, you too.

Best wishes to your mind, the photo-face, and YOU

From

Jim.

[VUW Library, MS McKay 28/33]

**Baxter to Ginn, 24 February 1944**

CENSORED
No. 5

Brighton,
Otago
24/2/44

Dear Noel,—

Sorry I haven't written for a bit to you, but I've been working on a couple of prize-poems which I am going to put in for competitions later in the year. One on 'Hopes and Fears for Man'—not a very difficult subject, rather a bizarre poem I wrote on it, about 100 lines, embodying certain earlier poems also.[1] The other 'Convoys'—a disgusting subject betraying the lack of imagination of whoever chose it; however, I wrote a pretty good one on that, bringing in Phoenicians, Columbus, Montezuma, sailing-ships, aeroplanes, dive-bombers, depth-charges, signal-flares, and quite a lot more of stage-scenery. General tone of both perhaps too near to pacifist to ring the bell.[2] Anyway, as you once said, longish poems stultify production and imagination.[3]

'Love-Lyric', not bad. 'The Eyes'—Robert-Graves-ish, no flaws except a certain diffuseness, rather classical.

'Monologue'—use of words as emotional feelers rather than as concrete tags.

I have been reading *New Poems 1940* , and have learnt a bit, among other things unlearning a surrealist enthusiasm. The fate of a fine poet, George Barker, warns me.[4]

1 Both prize-poems were for competitions founded by Baxter's maternal grandfather, Professor J. Macmillan Brown. 'Hopes and Fears for Man' was the subject prescribed for the 'University MacMillan Brown Prize'—a national prize, awarded biennially by the New Zealand University, for excellence in English composition. The value of the prize was £25, and those submitting verse entries were requested to keep within a 500 word limit. See 'Hopes and Fears for Man', p.467.

2 Entry to the second Macmillan Brown prize—for excellence in a verse or prose composition on the subject 'Convoys'—was limited to students enrolled at the University of Otago. The regulations of the competition required that entries reach the registrar of Otago University by 31 March 1944: Baxter was awarded the prize of £10 (one fifth of which had to be spent on books) in May. Partly because the prize was founded by his grandfather—but also because the regulations of the prize directed that the 'successful composition shall be offered to some literary periodical or to the literary columns of some newspaper for publication'—John Moffett, the literary editor of the *Otago Daily Times* and a friend of the Baxter family, had the poem printed in full on p.2 of the 25 May edition. There is not, as McKay states in *Life* (p.69), 'a youthful looking photograph of the poet' accompanying the published poem. See 'Convoys' p.469.

3 Baxter is referring to Ginn's remarks concerning Goethe's conversation with Eckerman on the subject of 'great works'. See Ginn's letter of 7 Apr 1943, p.204.

4 *New Poems 1940*—an anthology of British and American verse edited by Oscar Williams—was published in New York in 1941 by the Yardstick Press. As well as contributing poems, George Barker wrote a foreword praising poets who 'bleed with their poems'. Peter Monro Jack of the *New York Times* observed with some relief that portraits of most of the poets showed them 'all apparently healthy and unbleeding', and judged the selection incomplete owing to the omission of poems by T.S. Eliot and E.E. Cummings (14 Sep 1941, 6.2).

Have also read Mary Webb's *Precious Bane*,[5] and some of Jean Giono, one of the best French writers of the present day, a pacifist too I think.[6]

I think the Penguin on Shakespeare will be valuable.[7]

Tell Terry we have his times and everything now. Love to him [8]

Best wishes

From

Jim.

[VUW Library, MS McKay 28/35]

**Love-Lyric I**

Like old maids precise with pince-nez
the bony blue-gums; water-dull the
distant plateaus of ~~white~~ light waves lashing
fountaining on hidden reefs, and
crumbling to white blood at their edges;
while scabrous rocks by gulls inhabited
make contrast to the horizonal arc.
    One cannot lose the illusion of living:
waves whiter-than-Job-bearded; storms that hurtle
and weep upon the hills:
but I have lost it.
    Plateaus of sea repeated in the sky
draw wide the heart, the unregretful eye . . .
plateaus of sky repeated in the mind
loom in crevasse, thunder anathema;
wind-surging beat the body blind.
    But here the near view
comforts: the botticelli green and blue
of garden flowers and the wind-woven grasses;
the dull and raucous aeroplane overhead

5 Webb's *Precious Bane* brought her posthumous fame when, only six months after her death, the Prime Minister of England, Stanley Baldwin, lauded the novel in an address before the Literary Fund Society. On the strength of Baldwin's endorsement the book went through five editions in six months, with critics of the time praising it for its balance, assurance, poetic rhythms and imagery, and carefully balanced repetition and parallelism.

6 Jean Giono (1895–1970), a prolific writer of fiction, poetry and drama, was mobilised in the First World War and gassed in 1918 during the battle of Flanders. Despite becoming a resolute pacifist he initially consented to mobilisation in the Second World War, but only—as it turned out—so that he would not make trouble for his local authorities. From then on he refused to cooperate and was imprisoned for two months, and again, towards the end of the war, for five months. After the war he survived accusations of collaboration brought against him during the Communist-dominated purges, and went on to enjoy considerable popularity and respect as an extremist who never abandoned his values.

7 G[eorge] B[agshawe] Harrison, *Introducing Shakespeare* (Harmondsworth: Penguin, 1935). See the book-list in Baxter's letter of 14 Jul 1945, p.410.

8 Terence was allowed one trip home during his time in detention as a reward for good behaviour. See 'Detention Camp Life', p.98, and 'The Beginning of Baxter's Adult Phase', pp.111–12.

in ragged china-blue; the eye is
raw and raucous likewise.
In the horizonal arc
delusive fantasy of self-control;
in earth's variety warp and woof of hell
dantean, destruction of
all symmetry all sculpture-stone of sight.
Red paint blistering . . .
I found a four-leaf clover yesterday . . .
the
rain is about due and
winter is upon us . . .
(bovine philistinism)
and dont care a damn for Dante
nor a bugger for Botticelli.
[Hocken, MS 704/12:716, p.33]

**The Eyes**

My eyes saw eyes
That flowed in rout
Or flared in conquering
Tidal flood.

The tribal flux
That solders them to
See eye to eye
I do not know.

For eyes of beasts
Speak louder to me
And eyes of birds
More self-~~control~~ contained.

And eyes of snakes
Are blind like gods
And eyes of fish
Are dull with being.

But painted eyes
Hooded and cold
Stare from without
In dumb conspiracy.

I cannot translate
Their statue-stutter

Their seeming knowledge
Of aim and reason.

Occasionally
Eyes that were haunted
Would leap and pause
About to speak.

But slide from sight
With a white gesture
Effacing so
Remembrance even.

The eye of air
Wide-inchoate
Gazed on the glassy
Eye of sea.

Where coloured weeds
Like flies in amber
Hide the huge tide
In secrecy.

And eyes of flowers
Day's-eyes there turned
Meek to the sun
That frowned on them.

Your eyes flinched so
Your eyes spoke to me.
Since then I scorn not
Eyes of men

Knowing they hold
Like unlit houses
The hope of love
In them concealed.

[Hocken, MS 704/12:713, pp.27–30]

**Monologue**

As I looked on the hills one morning and saw
their unreproachful variety I said
O where is Ruin ? And Ruin stepped out of my head
his clothes patched with the placid smiles of the dead,
in an unobtrusive way—but his eyes bled
and his back-bone swung behind him: the iron of Law.

With a babbling voice he spoke
more clear than the opaque crystal of speech
'I also roses and a rhyme to teach
listen or not or tag it with a joke.

'Metropolitan death mangled
me once wide and riding the flood
now pustular I bellow in the blood
now grace the average banner by shrapnel jangled.

'The roots of iron flickered in his bones
each carried in his brain a city
hazed-under where gnarls of pity
from love-trees fell golden like fruit or gold stones.

'where years like dolphins swam
they made me broke the dolphins under
and built the previous hell-and-thunder
not the gold city. Swore wept in dream or dram.
for violence broke their heads too like a runaway tram.

'The roots of iron flickered in his bones.
flowered in the mutilated mouth
of a childish enemy holding his youth
as tinsel shield: teeth broken and brain like dictaphone.

'so he saw the teeth of surf smile at him
a year later and let them bite
Virus made a hollow under world-waterfall white
there crouched he then broke through as cherubim.'

And Ruin clicked back into the grooves of my skull
with a tolerant whimper. The weight I had lost
of crystal insight returned spearing like frost
clothed even the trees even the hills unreproachful.
[Hocken, MS 704/12:722, pp.52–3]

**Baxter to Ginn, 25 February 1944**

Censor's stamp
illegible

Brighton,
Otago.
25/2/44

Dear Noel,—
Sorry about the address. I received your parcel yesterday just after I wrote the

letter. Very pleasing. As you say, the prescribed books are not essential, one may get all one wants and more from others. Thank you very much; I will treat them well.[1]

If you can would you send me *Owen* [2] and *Ruins and Visions.*[3] You have as good a library of verse as mine, and that's saying something, for I'm always adding.

I enclose 'There was an altar', composed from vague memories of Ovid. 'Aqua . . . aqua' is the sound of frogs croaking of course.[4] Each language interprets the voice of animals, birds etc. in its own way.[5] See Eliot's *Cape Ann* (?) *Landscape* .

'ME ALSO', perhaps a work of genius.

The perfect metaphor for poetry is egg-laying. The poem has the oneness, the smooth outer surface of the egg, the inside meat made of the poet's mind. And if kept and warmed in the minds of others it may flower into a living chicken. Also the poet's pleasure at the sight of a completed poem may be compared to the triumphant expanding cackle of the hen. Some poets are phoenixes (1 egg per lifetime); some such as I lay every other day. This is leading up to the fact which I have at last discovered that it is more meritorious for me to abstain from writing a poem than to write it. See Hopkins' '*The fine delight that fathers thought*' which puts the whole matter in a nut-shell. Of course this idea can be carried too far, so don't grow anxious.[6]

About ME ALSO. Don't think my mythology is out. I know Ulysses wasn't changed into a swine, at any rate not literally. But I've changed the picture, humanized

1 In response to Baxter's enquiry, in his letter of 26 Jan 1944, regarding English books that Ginn might be able to lend him for use at university, Ginn sent him a variety of texts, a number of which are listed by Baxter in his letter of 14 Jul 1945 (see p.410). Because texts were prescribed at a national level, many of the books Ginn used at Victoria University College in 1941 could still be used by Baxter at the University of Otago in 1944.

2 Ginn sent Baxter his copy of the Edmund Blunden edition of Wilfred Owen's [1893–1918] *Poems* (London: Chatto & Windus, 1931). This edition includes the poem 'The End' (to which Baxter makes reference in his letter of 23 Mar 1944, p.350), which had not been included in Sassoon's 1920 edition of Owen's verse.

3 A reference to Stephen Spender's collection of poems *Ruins and Visions* (London: Faber & Faber, 1942), which was a revision of his 1939 volume *The Still Centre* (Faber & Faber), with some new poems added.

4 Baxter's 'vague memories' are of the story of the 'Lycian Peasants' from Book VI of Ovid's *Metamorphoses* (lines 317–81). In the story the goddess Latona, driven from heaven by wrathful Juno for attracting the attention of Jove and bearing his twin children, attempts to quench her raging thirst in a small pond she chances upon in Lycia. Unfortunately the local Lycian yokels turn Latona away from the pond—despite her entreaties—and spitefully stir up its muddy bottom to ensure she will never drink there. In anger the goddess cries 'Live in that pool of yours . . . [for] evermore', at which point the peasants metamorphose into loathsome frogs. From then on an altar to Latona stands beside the pool at which passing Lycians pause and mutter anxiously to the goddess: 'Be gracious to me!' Baxter's 'Aqua . . . aqua' echoes an onomatopoeic passage from the Latin original: '. . . sed nunc quoque turpes / litibus exercent linguas pulsoque pudore, / quamvis sint sub aqua, sub aqua maledicere temptant' ('. . . but even now they flex / Their squalid tongues in squabbling, and beneath / The water try to croak a watery curse', trans. A.D. Melville).

5 Eliot's 'Cape Ann' is the fifth poem in his 'Landscape' sequence, which was first collected in *Collected Poems 1909–1935* (London: Faber & Faber, 1936). 'V. Cape Ann' begins:

O quick quick quick, quick hear the song-sparrow,
Swamp-sparrow, fox-sparrow, vesper-sparrow
At dawn and dusk.

6 Hopkins's sonnet 'To R.B.'—which he dedicated to his friend Robert Bridges on 22 April 1889—begins:

The fine delight that fathers thought; the strong
Spur, live and lancing like the blowpipe flame,
Breathes once and, quenchèd faster than it came,
Leaves yet the mind a mother of immortal song.

or de-humanized it a bit as I always do, as I did in Aeneas—'for Venus was the mother in his mind . . .' It is worth careful study.[7]

I like your photograph. It shows you as small, very small, perhaps because taken from above. Anyway, it is good to have; it is now on my shelf.

Don't tell Terry, as he mightn't like it, but he comes into some of my not-to-be-published epigrams, rather political perhaps. Nothing anywhere uncomplimentary to him, but he might not like to be carried in the back of the Art-Cart, he being sensitive on any infringement of his personality.[8]

Love to Terry, and you also.

Best wishes

From

Jim.

I do not object to your periods of silence, as I don't apply the same rules (?) to the incarcerated as to others. Still, I'd like an opinion some time on some of the poems.

J.K.B

[VUW Library, MS McKay 28/36]

**There was an altar**

There was an altar here
where now the reedy quagmire
and bulbous throats
*Aqua . . . aqua*

Tread gently where the
water-course shelves from shallows
under furze shelving

What ululation?
was it swans only, reedy voices
from winter slate to reeds falling

What ululation?
and will they drain this pond
because their herds are drowned here?

It is the nymph calling for sacrifice.

[Hocken, MS 704/12:724, p.57]

7 In Book X of *The Odyssey* Homer records how Odysseus (Ulysses), protected by the magic of Hermes, rescues his crew from the sorceress Circe, who had turned them into swine. Before he can slay her, Circe pleads for her life to such effect that they become lovers. Venus, according to mythology, was the literal mother of Aeneas, whose father Anchises was so weakened by the shock of a near miss from one of Zeus's thunderbolts—hurled at him for boasting of having slept with a goddess—that he was never again able to stand upright. See 'Aeneas', p.454.

8 See 'Unwritten Elegy', p.61.

**Me Also**

I walk in New York harbour two hundred feet high
    Impress the crowds, mischievous, gigantic
    Then punch with my feet—and a wave from the Atlantic
Rears with earthquake and lava rides the sky.

Me also it terrifies. I will carry a gun, I say,
    To shoot myself if the dangerous wave falls over.
    Then my body will hurl lax with the burl of the river
While I speak with the quiet and one-faced dead all day.

One tragedy world-shaking my dreams are shavings of
    Whether weighty like waves, or growing less brave on a summit
    (A star passed by me burning like a comet):
The shrinking vista, hate from lust and lust from love.

It is more than the burning walls of hell
    Or Ilion .. It ends when life ends.
    Time's word on his lips, Time's weird and inarable sands
The poet walks in a narrowing gut of tomb and thinks it well.

Circe was not to blame. Ulysses' brain changed her
    From the elusive beauty, daughter-of-Sun divine;
    Saw from the eyes of the beast, no, not beast but swine,
Tears running down the snout for the irretrievable vista.
        [Hocken, MS 704/12:725, pp.58–9]

**Baxter to Ginn, 6 March 1944**

Censor's stamp
illegible

Brighton,
Otago
6/3/44.

Dear Noel,—

I don't know if I'll get the post with this or not. Anyway, I enclose a poem, a longish (?) Ode. It is rather like George Barker one of the moderns.[1]

I was sure we were going to see you and Terry very shortly, but it appears that

1 Baxter's 'ODE MCMXLIV' closely follows George Barker's 'Triumphal Ode MCMXXXIX', from his 1940 collection *Lament and Triumph* (London: Faber & Faber), which begins:
Through the green tassels of the weeper tree,
When idle in the evening I walk down by the river,
Risen to its zenith in my pessimism's heaven
I see the red star tremendous in the South—

restrictions are too heavy on all travelling. Tell Terry that Mackenzie the fisherman is all right, slept the night in his boat at Taeri Mouth and walked back the next morning.[2]

The Ode has astrological symbolism, very useful in some ways even if rather artificial. I think it is uneven. I have been rereading you lately and have come to the conclusion that some of your poems are literally masterpieces. Couldn't we publish a book some time something like Wordsworth and Coleridge in *Lyrical Ballads* each one producing half. Not fair perhaps, as I have more to choose from, but there would only need to be a few.

I will write again soon.
Love to Terry.
Best wishes
From
Jim.

[VUW Library, MS McKay 28/37]

**Ode MCMXLIV**[1]
**(for Karl Alexander)**

Through the canals of frustration I have wound to a well-
Of loneliness perhaps—but the pulse of the river beating
Reminds of all pulses under leonine Mars
Choked or channelled, laving the stones of Hell.
I would weep but will not: the click of tide repeating
On tidal beaches measures out Time's nadir
(Time regulated in the valves of sorrow):
And a rustling by my side grows calm and hollow
Where a Crab feeding on debris raises its head
Moves gently symbolic claws and speaks:
    There are roots ripple about the skulls of the dead
Which flower in the everlasting Tree
(Yggdrassil the Norse named it, a name only)
Shadowing gloom and fire of eternity,
Wherein the well of Wisdom; holding Heaven
Cool in its upper branches.
    Rather for the initiate to see
I will cast this vision within a vision:
A Clown in painted clothes, torn by a lynx,
Pursued in rocks and ravines; and in evasion
Casting no glance behind him. There is scope

2 Mackenzie is discussed in 'James and Terence', pp.52–5.

1 Baxter has a few jottings in pencil written on this poem, that have been omitted from this version of the text. These include the number '723' with an arrow pointing to Karl Alexander's name, certain right angle brackets, perhaps indicative of stanza breaks, and an 'X' next to line 28 (Is yet the dream of flesh). Sections of this poem are repeated in 'Flower-Venus', see p.475. I have been unable to find out anything about Karl Alexander.

For infinite escape; reality is insular.
Truth it was gashed the smile of the Sphinx
With a cannon-ball. And we cannot hide forever,
Mail self in silver: tugged by the umbilical cord
From waiting to womb as once from womb to waiting,
Be born again and brave a new dimension.

Is yet the dream of flesh,
Flower-Venus to mesh most in sating.
Error and Truth have mated. These afford
The paradox of Love housed in the hangar:
The slick, the sleek and unobtainable
(In mannequins marvelled once, in sculpture-lines)
In metal mastered; and the mountainous anger
Of high-explosive harnessed for hurdling
High-explosive as mines moil under mines.
Majestic motion permeating all
Even in the aurora of the South
Meets undersea desires. But when the curdling
Of stone eternity made Man Stylites
(Two stems of wood He fashioned into Man
And Woman who inhabited the Earth);
The sexual beauty crystallizing
Showed more than dugs a benison to the mouth.
He flees the lynx; but seizes as he flees,
A half-reality: the dream of love,
And intricacy of the feminine ~~mind~~:
Venus-Minerva now. Crab-copulation
No torch to lighten is; but reticent
Illuminates the evolutionary surge;
For no fish lacks the momentary courage
No crab has split the liquid element
Creating love and hate for his damnation.
I cry that Hate is mad, that Hate is blind;
And love not lust (mortality's disease
By no beast fathered) . . . love not lust will melt
The moment's blear and suicidal malice.
Laughter is cruelty: the broken purpose
Or madhouse mowing rousing immediate mirth;
But love loves more the maimed and ludicrous.

He flees the lynx of life. And rifle-knives
Seem the sure hope to blast his barriers.
But kills the bone and blood when he would kill
Slum, stupour, and the word tyrannical:

The tyrant-crushing hand, studying snares
Of tyranny will grow all-tyrannous also—
Vain then the early vengeance, venom and bloody fears.
    And some must paint a face of purpose
Upon the purposeless variety:
Love and frustration in them forever upwelling
Seeks love or violence to gloze . . .
Politics in the quarrelling of drunks
And beauty as the whorish Babylon . . .
Sees good and evil absolute; and wealing
The mouth of good with hate and blasphemy.
Or crouch they under shade
Of Moon and Sun, regarding . . .

    Here the Crab shambled to a cranny weeping;
Had grown emotional. I will continue.

    Of each volume published in England
One copy is presented to the British Museum
Whose neo-Grecian pillars thus contain
Trash and tragedy, religion and pornography.
The inference is plain:
That art is regarded as the mirror of life
Not as one bough of the everlasting Tree
But a quiet and interesting miniature
Which in future days may be inspected with pleasure,
As men in ruined Pompeii walk to see
The Temple of Love, though hate may gnaw their skulls.
    In this small island off the coast of Australia—
Symbol of hinterlands—the same occurs.
I have seen rata often, am unimpressed;
Prefer the crocus. Here a traditionalism
Requires that one should mention rata,
A flower for honey-sucking birds.
For the traditional too often means
Strumming upon a worn and waning theme
Of sorrow and nostalgia, limiting
Vocabulary and human interest.
And the new-style too often means
Intolerable differences.

But art is life. The sap of life flows in it.
O Blake
I see you stand above the continents
Shadowing Asia, pointing to Heaven
With left hand, with right hand to Earth.

The Tree of Healing blossoms from your palms.
You are the Juggler shown in my arcana.
A sword from your mouth
I hold and am invincible:
To grapple with the toils of leonine Mars,
Behold the heart of Man in love and pity:
The fire of healing flowering in my veins.
[Hocken, MS 704/12: 727, pp.62–8]

**Baxter to Ginn, 12 March 1944**

CENSORED
No. 5

Brighton,
Otago.
12/3/44

Dear Noel,—

This is Sunday morning about half-past ten, and I sit in bed writing. The cat washes on the coverlet. It is a dull day. Clothes and books are piled on the floor—not your books, they are well looked after.

I have lately read *Wuthering Heights* for the first time. It is very fine, its faults even seem merits. Certainly a work of genius. The book is dominated by Heathcliff; where he is absent it loses strength. Emily Brontë had a lot of intellectual power, I think—as when Heathcliff refers to his growing misanthropy as 'a moral teething'. This is true to his character, not to E.Brontë's: hence she had learned what few writers ever learn—the necessity of abnegation of principle, belief, moral standards, that one's creations may live and be true to character.[1]

Also I have studied Francis Thompson—He is strong, better at times than Keats, though rather naïve. His Catholicism not so assimilated as G.M.H.'s, though his protestation of this assimilation is stronger.[2]

I enclose a few poems. The 'Ad Amicum' is perhaps not true in all particulars. You may not like being hauled into my poems. Still, I don't think your particular form of poetic genius will be readily recognised. I read your poems frequently, and find stronger every time the 'intolerable surge'.

1 Emily [Jane] Brontë's [1818–48] novel, *Wuthering Heights* (1847), was a prescribed text in Baxter's Stage I English course. Heathcliff's comment, made before Nellie Dean, follows a confrontation between himself and his new wife Isabella, the sister of his hated rival Edgar Linton. 'I have no pity! I have no pity!' he mutters, 'The worms writhe, the more I yearn to crush out their entrails! It is a moral teething, and I grind with greater energy, in proportion to the increase of pain.'

2 Francis Thompson (1859–1907) is best known for poems conveying intense religious experience, for example in his works 'The Hound of Heaven' and 'The Kingdom of God.' He published three volumes of verse, in 1893, 1895, and 1897.

e.g. *Rivers running*
*Round the rims of time . . .*

In spite of my decision to stick more to prose, the machine still functions. Spender I am assimilating. I may be too close to him at first; but soon my own build of technique will take him in as an element. I have read him before but never been influenced by him as in this volume: it is most impressive. At any rate I have learned the importance of sense units for free verse etc. As—

As falling asleep / I stare
Through closed lids / at the grained
Hot wall / and my eyeballs burn
With the ache / of the nearing wall . . .

The choked / by bright / poisonous fumes[3]

'Genesis'—after Dylan Thomas.

'Love-Lyric IX'—I am learning to turn landscape to poetry, which I could not do once except in the usual hackneyed way: 'The sun rises bright' etc.

'Prologue'—for a longer poem not attempted because beyond my capacity.

'The Immobile Stone'—the 'guinea-pig' reference is to the cure of syphilitic madmen by violent electric shocks, painful and uncertain process.[4]

Will send a new copy of Cook's *Voyages* to Terry; get it tomorrow.[5]

Love to him.
Best wishes
From
Jim.

[VUW Library, MS McKay 28/38]

**Ad Amicum**
**N.G.**

Shall none see it? None.
By sun-rays blinded in lands beneath the sun.
Nay, not sun-rays but the dazzling neon:
Ways bloody and mirèd they are free on
Freely with frail throats shouting

3 See part I of 'The Immobile Stone' for the source of these lines. There are numerous examples in Spender's *Ruins and Visions* where the cadences of poems in free verse conform to Baxter's idea of 'sense units'. For example in 'The Ambitious Son':
If I had the key / I might return
To where the lovers lie / forgotten on bright grass. [my line breaks]

4 Electroshock treatment was first introduced in the mid-1930s as a preferable alternative to the use of 'insulin shock' for the treatment of schizophrenia. Some sufferers of tertiary syphilis—often characterised by symptoms of madness and general paralysis—may well have undergone electroshock therapy, but this type of treatment was not specifically targeted at 'syphilitic madmen'.

5 See the final paragraph of Baxter's letter dated 18 Mar 1944, p.346 regarding his decision to purchase a new edition of Cook's *Voyages of Discovery*.

Flame-intricacy flouting.
    How shall the intolerable surge
Of more-than-mortal beauty shake them?
Yet doth the sun-flower flaring on morning's marge
Lay bare her unique symmetry—such shall not wake them—
Her petals to the air lay bare.
    Strong thus in mortal storm
Thou, sun or sun-flower, shalt flare:
Time in thy sight made warm
Lose her cold crystal for fluid eternity:
Past and future (thou didst guess their form)
Dissolve, and the word eternal be.
    Thou who dost bless the crowd
Even when in their ignorance most loud
Dost implant they jewel
In the forehead of man, all-durable stone:
Though blind he be and cruel
This must he wear, he bear, and Truth be known.
        [Hocken, MS 704/12:741, pp.103–4]

**Genesis**

That gargoyle day lips to slug night her venom
Plugged me in eagle-stride; steep spiral down
The sky of skull's perimeter; blew me bones
Rag-blown to the tempest-bearing tree. Weed-wound
I found sea-burial but was vomited.
So now three seasons bleed on cross of bone
The jaggy diadem unstarred: Night proffered
Her ciné-cloud; Day bellowed like a worm
Coiled in the feminine wound, in clock of veins
The clay leviathan; my shadow crouched
Beside me like a dog. Then tendons frayed
And rooted till the eyes flew up like leaves.
Anadyomene arising: I burst rock.
Wolf pain was balance. And saw that it was evil.
        [MS Hocken 89/148]

**Love-Lyric IX**

Pillars of rain on livid sea fall;
immense cloud-bursts bearing
the walls of wind upon their knotted shoulders.
    The blown sea soughing

flings gulls and spume
from the muffled explosion
of toppling marble.
    Rain walks over the deep currents
gum-leaf-coloured.
    The reefs blow through their snouts.
    Why the inane anger
of posturing boughs?
hawthorn berries are shaken
dumbly protesting;
and the white undersides of leaves
stream ghost-like.
    why the inane anger ?
the whorl and ruck of cloud-rack.
    There is no anger.
Only the pulsation of electronic vigour;
the hurricane incidental as a spider-net.
    The world seen in glass of time
posturing in apparent love
posturing in apparent hate
distortions only:
    moon-mountains under eye-lids.
    Hate and love behind the eyes is real.
        [MS Hocken 89/148]

**Prologue**

You who will listen and know
    You who will listen and shape
        The passionate denial:
        I have a trek to tell
    An arc-lamp built to break
The succubus of snow
Whom you have embraced and immortalized in marble.

This only: that past skeins
    Are woven in web of future;
        That you are locked in a tread-mill
        To spin the bone-crushers of Hell,
    So. I am whorled and secure
To listen at your brains
    And beat like the lion-headed swan
The glacier hourglass heaven to gain a niche in marble.
        [Hocken, MS 704/12:759, p.146]

## The Immobile Stone

I

As falling asleep I stare
Through closed lids at the grained
Hot wall and my eye-balls burn
With the ache of the nearing wall;
And I cannot sleep for dread
And nausea of that weight
And inquisitorial question
Asking asking
A coolness and integrity
Which night has buried blasted under rubble.

So the weight
Of the rickety in slums
The choked by bright poisonous fumes
The miner mushroom-white;
The syphilitic madman—
Guinea-pig shocked and sweating
In the squat electric
Chair from mercy immune—
Weight of all waiting
Weight of the sick
Who look from their long beds at a grey light
And desire dawn for light's sane sake
And curse dawn who is hardly-bright;
The frustrated the impotent
Achieving never the full man's content;
Weight of the Indian mother
Who must die in impossible child-birth;

And most
The ugly dead
Broken mould of manhood
Crucifixion of no god
But the piteous beast;
And battle-front survivors
Finding no rest
From the remembrance of death like rapid rust
Or inane wrath;
'For that in mould of bland unnatural rest
They harden in death's aftermath':

These sag on the strung gut of brain
Wrench leaden with their pain.

II

In pale blue sky
Softly like music
Sharp like spray
The clouds of opaque marble
Move with calm elemental ecstasy.

Hills lean
To where the huge water
Buffets land: and I
Am participant; shape the scene.

A tot smiled and blew a kiss to me
His curly hair blown
His pudgy and engrossed face shown
In loveable perspective.

The heavy-jowled and bloodshot-eyed
Boozer passed me
With a lurching stride:
What shall I do with my pity
Undesired ? corpse unidentified.

The woman smiles
With full lips;
The warm complexion lights me
With unrest; moved in dexterity.

III

The immoveable wall
Remains. I heard
An american sailor speak.
He was bald lit up as well
His hands clenched hard
Stooped despondent back.

You talk, he said, of doing something;
But you can do nothing.
In the hard times
I was strong.
I had a wife and children.
I would work for them; I had my work to sell.
I wasn't wanted.
I tell you we lived on pea soup for three months:
The sight of pea soup turns me up still.

What do you think it was like ?
I was strong and fit;
I would work my hands to the bone.
But no work.
Tearing up boards to keep a fire going.
I'll never eat pea soup again.
What do you think of it ?
A man can do nothing. You can do nothing.
I was strong. I could do nothing.
With my wife and children starving.
Nothing. Not a thing.

He was broken up, I thought.
Saw the indignant idealistic faces
Of those who believe the world will break
And build: break and build.
I believe too. But lately
I have felt the weight also.

IV

Extortionate is the word
Extortionate:

That which will change
The neural beauty
To faceless languor of the prostitute;

The child whose heart
Must close grow crystalline
And love that bursts the crystal
Fall asleep in stone.

V

I carry at my centre
One barrier of blood
Against the spears of winter
Or laying down of blade
To hurtle with the flood.

Hands laid on cancered limbs
May cleanse renew and purify.
A connection of terminals: love and
Pity meet toward the diseased cells;
Tapping also
Nervous integrity
As sap in boughs as tap-root of the tree.

[Hocken, MS 89/148]

**Baxter to Ginn, 18 March 1944**

CENSORED
No. 5

Brighton,
Otago
18/3/44.

Dear Noel,—

This will probably not get away till Monday. Still, I'm writing it now. Just after I sent my last letter to you, your parcel of books arrived—very acceptable. I am just about stocked up now.

I would like if you could send me '35 POEMS' by Herbert Read.[1] Just lately I have been re-reading Dylan Thomas. I find his involved symbolism as difficult as ever, in spite of a sort of emotional reception. I always have the feeling that if one drifts with the current of a poem discarding all values one may be betrayed by one's own flaws into accepting the cheap and imperfect—e.g. Kipling—but that if one retains a critical faculty of a kind . . . Anyway, I like his prose. It is impressionistic; and to my mind there are only three types of readable prose: journalistic; fact-statement; impressionist.[2] The first jars, and wins by trading on ignorance. The second is the birth of literature; though of course there is no pure fact-statement, it must sway to the word-bolsters of journalism or the subjective truth of impressionism. The last is the natural development of prose as an individual medium: into it come the tricks of style which depart from objective truth for the sake of emotional effect . . . 'daffodils, the trumpet-blare of golden flame'—a phrase good or bad but at any rate illustrating my point, made up on the spur of the moment.

I am not satisfied with my poetry: your last letter has, as it were, touched the spark to a waiting fuse. I am casting round for new footholds. Always when I have come to an impasse before I have found a new cycle to swing onto. But this time not. Well, if I stop writing for practice—and I have learned about all I need to as far as technique goes, it is only driving-force I need—I will still write such poems as TO THE SUN,[3] but will move otherwise to occasional prose. Prose is greater than poetry: infinite horizons. My prose technique needs improvement, as I see in studying other writers. I could not be a 'sedulous ape' like Stevenson, but will have to go as well as I can—along modern lines, I think[4] Only with a 'narrowing gut of tomb'[5] do writers write poetry in their middle—and old-age. (e.g. Yeats.) Prose is their medium. Such

1 Herbert Read (1893–1968), *Thirty-Five Poems* (London: Faber & Faber, 1940).

2 Dylan [Marlais] Thomas (1914–53) had, up to the time of this letter, published two collections of poetry: *18 Poems* (1934) and *Twenty-five Poems* (1936)); one collection that combined prose and verse: *The Map of Love* (1939); and a collection of short stories: *Portrait of the Artist as a Young Dog* (1940). It is possible that Baxter had in mind this latter collection when making his comments to Ginn: its blend of humour and pathos would probably have appealed to him, and its autobiographical nature may account for a similar vein running through the prose pieces Baxter was himself attempting.

3 See 'To the Sun' in Baxter's letter of 12 Jan 1944, pp.314–15.

men as Byron or Shelley could not be other than lop-sided.

Excuse the monologue, but you are the father-confessor of my ideas on literature. Not that I am middle-aged!; but I have come to a point (I think) that others come to later, the necessity for broadening. Later on I'll come again to poetry maybe, but never the same way. Poetry is an attitude, not verse or rhyme, and will go into prose instead. Poetry is of the child, prose-poetry of the adult. Auden will never lose his childishness unless he develops in prose. One cannot neglect the enormous field of modern prose-poetry. I enclose a short story, better than my others, with faults all the same. I have not mastered the control of conversation and of groups, and am chary of using them. Landscape of course, is always a plastic medium, responsive to the touch.

Will send 'Cook's Voyages' up when I can. Two copies here—one my mother wants to keep, has my grandfather's notes in it: one is abridged. Will get a new Everyman.[6]

Best wishes and love to Terry and you.

Jim.

[VUW Library, MS McKay 28/39]

**Before Sunrise**[1]

The air before sunrise was chilly. A few owls still hooted with screams human and inhuman through the hill-gullies. He slept on his camp-bed in a frightening dream; under the blanket-layers of sleep, herculean he tried to move a finger. With a sense of strain he woke. Lay staring in content at the canvas roof through which flooded diffuse light.

He sat up and the stretcher creaked: his parents deeper in the tent did not move. He stepped out to the grass floor. This was wild earth, he thought, we have tamed it within walls. He pulled off his pyjamas; on with bathing-trunks. He was sixteen.

Then he slid under the wall. The grass was wet outside; but the birds chittered and flew in the fir-plantation; On the thread of a bird's voice is the pendulous earth hung. The mountain-shadow lay still half-way from their bases to the camping-ground. The sky was one-coloured except that it was

4 Recalling his boyhood attempts to teach himself to write, Robert Louis Stevenson (1850–94) wrote in *Memories and Portraits* (1897):

> Whenever I read a book or a passage that particularly pleased me . . . I must sit down at once and set myself to ape that quality . . . I have thus played the sedulous ape to Hazlitt, to Lamb, to Wordsworth, to Sir Thomas Browne, to Defoe, to Hawthorn, to Montaigne, to Baudelaire and to Obermann . . . That, like it or not, is the way to learn to write; whether I have profited or not, that is the way' (Chapter 4, pp.59ff).

5 See 'Me Also', p.334.

6 The newest Everyman edition of Captain James Cook's (1728–79) *Voyages of Discovery* would have been the John Barrow edition (introduced by G.N. Pocock) published in London in 1941 by J.M. Dent & Sons Ltd.

1 See Appendix 5 for the two earlier prose pieces that contributed to this story.

darker to the west and bright above the near mountains: There are mountains upon mountains, they are gashed by sword-strokes of the rising sun, they are awake at early dawn before I walk stiffly with bare feet to bathe before sunrise; and grasses are wet to the skin, stones and thorns knock at the gates of flesh, but I am the animal unsad and blood-aware.

As he climbed over the fence on the path to the lake he felt cold, wished he had gone to sleep again. His eyes were stiff still, one eye saw blurred. He crossed a water-course with willows and cutty-grass and felt through the trees the first chill of the lake-wind. He crossed his arms on his chest and hunched his shoulders to offer less area to the wind.

Remembering sleep he thought. Tent-bedded I lie safe in body and cloak of memory but behind my musing eyes, beyond walls of bone, is reality not of me, where the sea in dark hills cupped whose waves are death or longing . . . slap rotted wood in multitudinous strife and quiet. He came out on the shingle-banks of the lake-shore, picking his way between thorn-bushes over moss where ran small grey insects. The sun had almost risen, the sky had grown very bright; shaking bladed tracks of sunlight were reflected on the water. The lake was about three miles wide: he stood at the lower end of it and looked as far as he could see over its length, twelve miles perhaps in all but hidden by the feet and heavy shoulders of the mountains.

It is air and water in the vast lands of silten rivers, thought he: swollen and swift from the lake, home of the abyss-monsters yet calm in surface save to the blades of glinting wind.

He walked into the small waves at the edge of the lake, down over shelves of sand and shingle; then came out again and walked along the shore to a skeleton jetty where shingle had been scooped out to a depth of about twenty feet and the water showed faintly blue and very deep. He climbed the bank at the top of the beach and ran out on the jetty. The grey boards splintered and worn with gravel were solid under his feet. It seemed much more than ten feet down to the water. He hesitated; sat on the low bevelled parapet and hung his legs over; felt for leverage; then stood up, held his nose, and jumped.

The shock as always enveloped him, cutting off all thought, as if shock were an element like water. He doubled up with eyes shut and rose slowly till his back broke surface some way out from the jetty. He swam back and held on to the slippery beams of its scaffolding, slippery with fine weed, washed by waves. When his blood had cooled to the temperature of the water he clambered onto the beam and dived again quickly. Even less than before his brain, bound to the single purpose of holding his breath, could form consecutive thought: I swim down under water where the lake floor lies out of perspective; pressure blankets me fish-like; are there coins below? under the wooden girders I swim, below sea-storm, my mer-hair swims suspended and rippling; I reach in the unknown element, see secrets unnameable, then rise by the rotted quay—ware snags—to the flash of sunrising.

Slowly he swam back to shore: throwing his face ~~momentarily~~ under water rippling to see the hollow bottom (shallow at all points save that of direct vision) slope out to the deeper lake. As he swam he remembered the rabbit.

By the dry shingle-plain; he walked over dead rivers whose bones, with dried weed often, crunched under his sandals. His father shot the rabbit, behind the cemetery.

It shrieks, it is agony, the sound cuts my eyes. I run and it crawls to its burrow . . . child, you have slept in quiet earth and played in grasses, who are we to kill you? I run, balancing, over the pipe-line across the gully, the pipe that feeds the sluices, rusty and the tar blisters from it. I run and hold the rabbit. Its head droops and wobbles at the rabbit-punch; like corn rain-flattened its white belly-fur and brown side draggled where blood drips. Blood drips from its mouth but the eyes are brown and deeply sad. I hit with a stone on the neck, for it might still be alive. I walk back over the grass-flat through the plantation and the rabbit hangs heavy. Then the skinned rabbit skinned under the willows, bruised blue, speckled on the bare flesh with the rock. Guts thrown on the ground. Rain comes in the night hill-hidden while spiders drop from the tent-roof.

Purification, he thought, and swam out again. Further he swam, diving continually and bringing up weeds to examine. The weeds grew tougher as depth increased, and at last over twenty feet deep he came to a belt of mussel-shells. He carried them in with him, weeds and mussel-shells, all kinds. Cramp seized him as his feet touched bottom; disregarding it, swam in fast in panic, feeling that something malevolent had touched him. He dropped what he had brought in, thinking; I have brought them to the warmth of sun and man from their loneliness. He walked out stumbling and dizzy.

The willow-trees stood, roots in shingle: the light-green willow-trees in shingle planted and laved by the lake, of gnarled and broken bark but O leaves delicate and light-green. Yet are they the maledictory fists of bitterness clenched toward heaven that darkens, as time flows out from the land, as the sun dies.

. . . He walked limpingly up the shore dripping. The cramp eased as he stepped on the grass again. He had cut his ankle on a stone at the edge of the lake; he arched his instep to avoid walking on it. If I had been drowned, he thought, they would not have known: pity of his parents, not self-pity. As he crossed the road under high leaves rustling and still pale ~~as if~~ with sleep, he saw the sun like molten steel, its rim over the mountains.

Growing hungry, he hurried over the grass running quickly on the side of his cut foot, grass sticking to the unhealed gash. Why worry over a rabbit? he thought. Thousands are killed every day in the world. I'll see if I can shoot one tonight. It only hinders to feel with what you hurt.

A lorry had come into the camping-ground and was unloading packing-cases. The tents had lost their solid white sameness, had become shells and houses: a woman washed her hair under a tent-flap . . . as man crossed over the long grass carrying torn branches of broom . . . smoke rose in hieroglyphs above a frying-pan on a fireplace made of blackened rocks.

He rounded the tent and undid the flap. His father was dressing and his mother sat up in bed. 'Been for a bathe?' said his father.

'Yes, in the lake.'

'What was it like?'—his mother.

'A bit cold.'

The smell of frying bacon came in the door. The sun had risen. Dew evaporated on the furry leaves of the blue flannel-flowers. Gulls flew overhead; their feathers glistening, their cries calm music.

James K. Baxter

[VUW Library, MS McKay 28/50]

**Baxter to Ginn, 23 March 1944**

Censor's stamp
illegible

Brighton,
Otago.
23/3/44.

Dear Noel,—

Tomorrow I report at 'Varsity. I have had trouble getting new tyres for my bicycle; but will get them in a month or so I suppose.[1]

Many many thanks for the books you have sent
Spender improves
Moving from the neurotic metal
Of threaded eyeballs
To a new an almost surrealist vigour
As in 'The Air Raid Across The Bay'
Or 'A Wild Race'[2]

1 Prior to 1946 all tyres used in New Zealand were imported. This led to a supply crisis in 1942, when Japan's initial successes in the war saw them capture most of the areas from which the world's rubber was obtained. From May 1942 all tyres were rationed: tyres for bicycles were only available if the vehicle was used for attending work or school (there could be no cycling for pleasure) and obtaining them involved filling out forms assuring authorities that the vehicle was used legitimately and, after inspection by a cycle-dealer, that the current tyres were indeed worn-out. Eventual approval by the rationing authority granted admission to a waiting list but did not guarantee that tyres would be automatically supplied.

2 Baxter refers to three poems from Spender's *Ruins and Visions*: the first, rather oblique reference, is to the second stanza of 'A Hall of Mirrors', p.18:

Searching for that one face
Of innocence: amongst your many faces
Endlessly repeated in the empty spaces
Of your own eyes;
Suspended thinly on threads
Of your own self-admiring gaze.

'The Air Raid Across the Bay' appears on pp.34–5, and 'A Wild Race' on pp.23–6.

(Laura Riding an influence here, I believe);[3]
Perhaps it is a command of metre
Metre being rhythm
Metre being in verse the backbone of emotion.
*Bank Holiday on Parnassus*
Is of great interest from a technical point of view.[4]
And Owen:
Well, I have read 'The End':[5]
You will know what I mean.
Tell me when you want them back.

'Love-Lyric III' is the best of a series, see/ the end of the longer one. I think III justifies the experiment. The last part is meant to be pretty powerful.

Much love to Terry.
Best wishes from
Jim.

PS Be sure always to address your letters 'James Baxter', not 'J. Baxter', as muddle usually arises from the first, owing to the enormous amount of Baxters (counting those in the det-camp, about 28 altogether.) my relations and living in or near Brighton.

[VUW Library, MS McKay 28/40; Hocken, MS 89/148]

**Love-Lyric III**

The calm of summer burns, a steady flame.
And a wolf-spider near me
prowls, his smooth
back like wood-splinters; on the sleek paint
of the verandah he
sways and pirouettes. I blow on
him, and he is still a moment.
Flies flicker. A circular saw
droning, ringing, clanging
gashes the air with blades of sound:
and sensual the
awareness of new-cut saplings bitten
by bitter blades bitten.

3 There are a number of examples in 'A Wild Race' of themes, images and ideas that could be said to have been influenced by the American poet Laura Riding [Jackson] (1901– ). For example: the avoidance of binary oppositions by transforming polarities into paradoxes ('The broken unbroken', and 'Their unloved love') and death as the bringer of permanence ('Inhabitants of dead languages, / They still live in intact quarters').

4 Allan M. Laing's *Bank Holiday on Parnassus: A Litter of Competitions* (London: Allen & Unwin, 1941), includes the parody 'James Joyce re-writes a passage from Proust.'

5 Owen's 'The End' was first published posthumously in *The Saturday Westminster Gazette*, 15 Nov 1919: 7. A desire not to draw the attention of the camp censors to the strongly pacifist tone of this sonnet in three stanzas probably explains Baxter's cryptic reference, although the comment might also suggest that he expected Ginn's response to be as strong as his own to Owen's Blakean language and imagery.

Gliding and
fluttering
a butterfly crosses the
oval flower-plot;
iceland poppies
jostle beneath him
and seeded flowers ripen.
The smoke-green wattle patterns
light and shade.
The air like water murmurs
shaking small birch leaves:
the earth like fire responding.
and the sun moves over my hair
with sweaty fingers.
A farm of corrugated iron roof
cuts the curve of grass dunes;
metallic foliage against
the new-wrought ploughland.
Avalanche on avalanche
over it at
the scrub-hill horizon
baroque clouds billow
snow-crystal on the blue
snow-basilisk
snow-crystal on the blue
(the Venusberg to young Tannhauser calling).
The wolf-spider moves beside me
prey in his fangs.
[Hocken, MS 12:732, pp.84–5]

**Baxter to Ginn, 9 April 1944**

CENSORED
No. 3

Brighton,
Otago.
9/4/44

Dear Noel,—

Sorry I have not written earlier. It is not 'Varsity but a sort of inertia which I have at times, but never yet as far as letter-writing is concerned. This is Easter Sunday.

I find 'Varsity very new but have become fairly used to things. The best feature is the 'canteen' where I can get coffee before lectures. English is not very hard, the professor being a Shakespeare enthusiast; Latin (I have been persuaded to take Latin) is rather difficult; French I can stand up to.[1] The two last I mean to pass in; but as I am not taking them for the second year, I don't intend to expand much beyond the lecture-notes and specified books. Still, I read a bit of modern French: Giono (Jean) who has a most powerful style; and numerous prison-reformers on Cayenne etc.[2] I would like the AUZAS book if you could still lend it to me, and will probably ask about others now and then.[3]

Psychology (1st-Year Philosophy) is rather striking. I have done some Exp. Psych. and am waiting to get my lab. book next week—in mild trepidation. I wrote up an experiment on 'interviewing' at length, about 8 pages.[4]

I smoke a bit, not very much; intend later on to 'roll my own', as tailor-made are rather biting. Went to the Freshers' Hop and got one or two long-suffering females to haul me round the floor. It was very enjoyable on the whole. I will write at further length on this to Terry.

Have had some poems in the 'CRITIC'—University Paper—which evoked quite a bit of criticism (also in the paper) mainly favourable. Poems 'Hill-Country' 'Development' and two others. Not my best, naturally.[5]

1 Herbert Ramsay M.A. (St. Andrews) had been Professor of English Language and Literature since assuming office in 1921; the Professor of Classics was Thomas Daggar Adams M.A., but one of Baxter's high-school teachers—Dr Basil Howard, his form-master from the previous year—was, in his new role as university liaison officer, responsible for persuading Baxter to take the course (see *Life*, p.68); French was taught by Miss V.M. Barron M.A., upon whom the unflattering portrayal in Baxter's novella *Horse* of the French lecturer in Timothy Harold Glass's nightmares, appears to have been based:

> he had stood wool-gathering in the second bench of the Lower Oliver lecture room, while Miss Gallon, the yellow-faced and spectacled French lecturer, said sarcastically, 'Now we will have the pleasure of hearing Mr Glass translate for us.' When he had looked down at the copy of Mérimée's *Carmen* open in his hand, all its pages had been blank. (*Horse*, p.1)

*Carmen and Other Stories* by Prosper Mérimée (1803–70), was prescribed reading.

2 See footnote on Jean Giono, p.328 (note 6).

3 Baxter's letter of 14 Jul 1945 (see p.410) would indicate that this is a reference to Auguste Auzas's edition *les poètes français du XIXe siècle, 1800–1885, étude prosodique et littèraire* (Oxford: Imprimerie de l'Université, 1914). The edition was reprinted twice: in 1926 and 1938.

4 The Professor of Philosophy was John Niemeyer Findlay, M.A., (Oxon.), M.A., (S. Africa), Ph.D. (Graz). Students taking Stage I Philosophy could choose from two streams: (*a*) Psychology: Introductory Course, or (*b*) Logic and Ethics: Introductory Course. The recommended texts for Psychology were Boring, Langfeld and Weld, *Introduction to Psychology*, and Thouless, *General and Social Psychology.* However McKay records in *Life* (p.72) that Baxter's fascination with the subject led him to read more widely:

> He was reading McDougall's exposition of the instincts, and texts of Freud, Jung, and Adler, not in potted versions, but in full. He knew them well enough to be able to argue with the lecturers over their interpretations.

5 In 1944 *Critic*, the magazine of the Otago University Students' Association, published fourteen of Baxter's poems and one short prose piece. The literary editor of *Critic*, Joan Coutts (later the Reverend Joan Pascoe) recalled, in a letter to Frank McKay (9 Mar 1980, VUW Library, MS McKay 10/4/11), a visit she made to the Baxter's house in Brighton early in 1944:

> I had just completed my B.A. at Otago University, was employed in the University Library and had been appointed as literary editor of 'Critic'. . . . Jim took me to the upstairs room of the house, from which there is a magnificent view of the coast, and handed me a sheaf of poems with the words—'Take these Joan and use them in Critic whenever you want to'—I did just that and so far as I know these would be among the first published poems.

The first issue of *Critic* for 1944 was published in March (vol. XX.1): along with 'Development' (p.3)

LANDSCAPE deserves your criticisms. Don't solve the equations, however: just start dreaming. The accents in NEW DAY are a bit overworked; still, the main idea is to show where two syllables are sounded in successive stress//, a thing which doesn't spring naturally to the reader's mind. You must admit the stresses in LEOPOLD are perfectly managed. 'lurk lair' in ON WITHSTANDING FATE is all right I think, Spenserian.[6] G.M.H. teaches above all compression, which is the great trick, to be learned by all poets; although poetry itself depends on a queer letting-go, trance almost, using reality merely as a peg. Your 'pond-glass' elucidation is quite correct: rather Drydenish.[7]

One cannot really go back to the oldest idiom; for that depended on the '*stonës*' idea. Poetic technique broke down after Chaucer when the sounded case-endings went. Wyatt and others made reconstruction on a new basis; but the old facility has never returned.[8]

I have not written much lately. Have read your 'Herbert Read': very enjoyable, most of all 'Song For The Spanish Anarchists'. '*Sic et Non*' is great too. 'The Seven Sleepers' I have always thought about the most perfect modern poem, as 'Bitter Sanctuary' (Monro) is about the most powerful in atmosphere.[9]

and 'Hill-Country' (p.6), Coutts also published 'Tulips' (p.6) and 'The Poet' (p.7). See Appendix 2 for the text of these poems.

6 This is a rare instance of Baxter referring to the wrong poem: 'lurk-lair' appears in 'To Gerard Manly Hopkins' (see p.322) while a similar phrase—'lurk in lair'—appears in 'The honest Jack' (p.321). It is unclear in which way Baxter considered either poem Spenserian as neither 'lurk' nor 'lair' appear to have been words Edmund Spenser favoured. There are some general similarities in tone and expression between Baxter's sonnets and the sonnets in Spenser's *Amoretti* (1595).

7 See 'The honest Jack', p.321. I have been unable to discover the nature of Ginn's elucidation and its relevance to John Dryden (1631–1700) unless it relates to Dryden's use of such phrases as 'watery glass' in, for example, 'Eleanora: A Panegyrical Poem'—'And take her image in this watery glass' (l. 139).

8 The origins of Baxter's notorious difficulty with Old English which, by 1955, had led to him failing English III two years in succession (see *Life*, p.151), may perhaps be traced back to this letter. His reference to the '"*stonës*" idea' appears to be an attempt to point out the disyllabic nature of the word, but *stonës* itself is wrong as the root word—stän—is not declined in this manner. Sir Thomas Wyatt (1503–42) began writing well over a century after Chaucer's death. But where Chaucer's verse still retained something of the Old English case endings—for example the occasional sounding of an *e* that would ordinarily be mute—Wyatt attempted to lay the foundations of a new form of poetry by representing in the stresses of his verse the rhythms of English speech at the time.

9 Read's 'A Song for the Spanish Anarchists'—a lyrical poem in three quatrains equating human freedom with natural order and idealising those who live communally on the land—would have appealed to Baxter at this time, not least because of his brother's imprisonment, his idealisation of his father's rural lifestyle, and his own developing discontent with the 'intellectual' life. The poem concludes:

And men are men who till the land
    and women are women who weave:
Fifty men own the lemon grove
    and no man is a slave.

Read, in his *Collected Poems* (London: Faber and Faber, 1946) groups 'A Song for the Spanish Anarchists' among his 'War Poems (1936–1945)', the other two poems Baxter mentions appear among the 'Lyrical Poems (1919–1934)': '*Sic et non*' takes as its theme the story of Heloise and Abelard and 'The Seven Sleepers' is a sonnet based on the story of the seven youths of Ephesus said to have hidden in a cave during the Decian persecution and to have slept there for several hundred years.

T.S. Eliot—who, along with Ezra Pound, considered 'Bitter Sanctuary' to be Harold Monro's finest achievement—published the poem in the *Criterion* just six months before Monro died on 16 March 1932. In the poem Monro finds parallels between his experiences during his final illness and his lifelong attempt to arrive at some idealised state of forgetfulness.

But look how he, unfortunate, now fumbles
Through unknown chambers, and unheedful stumbles.
Can he evade the overshadowing night?
Are there not somewhere chinks of braided light?

Have learnt STRANGE MEETING by heart, and recite it whenever I get bored biking to 'Varsity.[10]

Love from
Jim.

[VUW Library, MS McKay 28/41]

**New Day**

O when shadow-of-sick
Gnarrs, burns to the bone-quick;
Guess then our doom-devising
Is a mad, a mute disguising
of rot rankle-dank, or
Death of dower we give thank for—
Death of iron shank and thew,
Death of eye-beam probing to
Deep-delvèd wells of light
Mined mid rivers of the night;
Think: doth wilt in woe
The cruel-cagèd eagle so?—
Crag-brilliant once, wild-heaven-blown.
Doth brute-beast in blear stone
Mope as I i' th' cage of bone?—
Body bruising to be free
As the spirit spurs in me.
But for them doom is double:
Steel not shakes for their trouble
Nor may savage-spirit slink
To the eyes of night for drink.

So man, in-shadow-snarlèd
Knows Nature ungnarlèd;
So sickness makes more
Peace-of-prayër than before
When lies like leaves shed
Burn from the bole, dead;
Death-rot, death-rankle—
Earth-purged from eye to ankle—

10 This is almost certainly a reference to Wilfred Owen's 'Strange Meeting', first published in Edith Sitwell's (ed.) *Wheels, 1919: Fourth Cycle* (Oxford: Blackwell, 1919), and collected in Siegfried Sassoon's edition of Owen's *Poems* (London: Chatto & Windus, 1920). 'Strange Meeting' begins:

It seemed that out of battle I escaped
Down some profound dull tunnel, long since scooped
Through granites which titanic wars had groined.

Baxter's accuracy with titles would suggest that it is merely coincidence that Harold Monro, mentioned in the preceding paragraph, published the philosophical poem which provides the title for his 1916 volume *Strange Meetings* (London: Poetry Bookshop, 1917).

See in the field-way
Fellow-fallow, mate-mood gay;
Men that follow, of hate hollow,
Man mate, woman human
(Gay too, true-gay)
New day, blue day.
        [Hocken MS 704/11:698, pp.88–9]

**On Leopold**
**cat and tiger**

Shall one aught of him say now
That his sweet self say not, say not?
    Say nay now, nay now—
For in bright-beamèd, light-streamèd day now
        Does he not play?
        Does he not stray?
Where, sun-whips swing, flay hot, O stray and play!

    Limbs tiger-trim, for tiger he—
Save gash, save mar of scar where trap did gnash once,
Did O bitterly slash through sinew, thew; for rash once
        Foot did dash once
On steel that lurking lay, man-shapèd to slay
    Envenomedly—O shame see!
        Days four, four days more,
    Long night, long day,
        Such pangs he bore—
    Day-long, night-long, bore—
As strong men battle-bludgeoned bear;
But he a light thing, slight thing, free-of-air,
    Frail, bore this, rain and hail—
Bore pangs likewise with ever-piteous cries;
    Till pride or shamèd pity did prevail
    That one loosed him—swung, chance, i' th' tail:
Home crept he, home to whom him knew;
Grew thus—though rotted pad was woe—
            heart-steelèd, healèd grew.

        Mood of him none
    But earth's-mood is, born wind and sun.
        Claw soft-sheathèd
    Doth quick flick at bird wings
        Low, or sings
In bush bright-eyed, by him espied;

Nor beast breathèd
Of more swift-symmetry—tom-tiger he
That dear doth cry to ear and eye;
Self-rounded, self-bounded,
Stone-egyptian so, doth sun-swathèd go
And bound-in-beauty.

Shall havoc shake him? shall bold-brag break him?
Who roams seeing
No bourne for being
Save earth doth make him.

He is the sun's dowër, more bright than flowër;
Grasses are jungles in forests that flail his furrèd skin
Sight-salvèd, one-selvèd,
He doth mate, hate.

Hearken, earth and sky,
To his wild-wordless cry
More true than aught I
Preserve him so
From all animal woe—
Light live, un-doom-daunted die—
Bright live, quiet die.
O cry it, earth and sky:
Bright live, quiet die.
[Hocken, MS 704/11:701, pp.92–5]

**On Withstanding Fate**

If there be God, if that he be not blind;
Why hath he then no help-word, haven-heal?
Not faith to faithless, death to deathless deal
Doth he—yea, deepest death, the dearth of mind,
Break-weight of woe redoubled, dooms that grind—
Then like sea-that-is-savage, sudden will seal
With sembled calm, beguiling smile, reveal
Warm wiles awhile; heart in hope-gyves new-bind.
Aught faith man hast, aught bravery, he must
Himself originate, himself indent;
God his desire desire to circumvent
Doth ever—deem ignoble, lash it lust.
Fate forge against, O son and sire of dust:
It is the grave of living, will not relent.
[Hocken, MS 704/11:703, p.97]

**Baxter to Ginn, 25 May 1944**

**CENSORED**
**No. 1**

Brighton,
Otago.
25/5/44.

Dear Noel,—

Sorry I have not been writing to you. Partly 'Varsity, partly that I now and have been for some time passing through a black spot. You may know from experience what such are. 'Poetry a string of words on a bean-stalk.' What was a cloud of power in the day of intellectuality and pillar of illuminating fire in night of mental groping dwindles till . . . 'the snake lurks in the altar-stone: the image of the God is gone.'[1]

This is not foolery, just an attempt to objectify my present feelings. Maybe a phase, but phases hurt.

My present gloom (partly due to neuritas from a chill in the shoulder) is not constant: one has one's moments of expansion—mostly in the company of the crude. I like 'Varsity. But my inability to write is pretty constant. Enclosed find the only readable poems I have written.

Terry will tell you I got the McMillan Brown Prize (Otago one). The poem will be in the *Times* here. I am pleased, even thrilled (perhaps that is puerile), partly because it is pleasant for my parents. Anyway, an increase to my banking account.[2]

The books you have lent me come in most useful. By the way, if you can, read the book I've sent Terry—It is readable, good prose and strong psychology, though morbid in parts.

Terry will also tell you I was travelling with the WEA Lecturer. It was very pleasant, especially the Kaitangata Mine. I have some pipe-tobacco for rolling, and every time I smoke it I remember the trip.[3]

Our tom-cat (see Leopold) is sitting beside me by the fire, crooning heavily. He has been out fighting for an hour or two, has just returned. Large paws and complacency.

1 I have not located a source for either of these quotations and it appears likely that Baxter composed them to illustrate the point he was making.

2 See letter of 24 Feb 1944 and footnote 2, p.327.

3 The Workers' Educational Association was an institution imported from Britain but adapted to suit the needs of New Zealanders. It had been in operation in Dunedin since 1914 and was, for many years, one of the only institutions concerned with further educating adults, particularly those who had been denied education when younger. In 1944 the Otago branch of the WEA operated from the University and Baxter's travelling companion was most probably John Anneslay Brailsford, who is listed in 1944's University Calendar as the WEA's tutor and organiser. In June 1982, the Government discontinued its annual grant to the organisation. (See also *Life*, p.72).

The small South Otago town of Kaitangata is situated 12 km to the SE of Balclutha. Coal was first mined there in 1869. In 1879 it was the site of a mining disaster in which thirty-four men lost their lives. Producing at one stage in excess of 120,000 tons of coal annually, production gradually dwindled until 1970 when the mine was forced to close.

It is perhaps unfair to write to you from out the cloud, but I am cheering up a bit now.

I have read lately some of Joyce's short stories: great stuff, with the richness of the best short story.[4] Have also read Tolstoy's *Death of Ivan Ilych* and *Father Sergius*: the first is the best short story in the world to me, perfect and powerful description of the psychology of a dying man. The second is more the voice of the preacher, still excellent.[5] Have read Sargeson, who strikes me as able but of a style and plotting too cut-down for this NZ society: Europeans have to prune their material; we have to build it up[6]

Well, goodbye Noel, my gloom crystallizes out of solution.

Love from

Jim.

[VUW Library, MS McKay 28/42]

**At Balclutha**[1]

Beside the immense stream whose snakes of water
Coil the eye, call limbs to lose
Their verticality; beside the fluttering
Dross spun once by truckers
Drowned in the groin of the blind beast;
    In a panelled room at the nadir of the year
I melt the granite silence as fire-brick kilns
Drip crystal in a furnace.
                                        This pied land
Has held me: I have felt under my fingers
Her erratic pulse. Passing, clothed in iron,
Glass and raucous thunder, I saw only names—
Platform-façade of names or hill-curve.
A sea-stranger came I odyssean.
But once, smoking behind a dance-hall
Boards rubber-springed, saw the face of the land
In the face of a gipsy mill-hand with slouch hat,

4 James [Augustine Aloysius] Joyce (1882–1941) published his collection of short stories, *The Dubliners*, in 1914 (London: Grant Richards). The collection—which was greeted enthusiastically by Ezra Pound—is narrated in a realistic fashion that brings the grimy side of Dublin life into sharp focus in line with Joyce's goal of criticising and exposing a culture that he despised as paralytic.

5 Tolstoy's *The Death of Ivan Ilych* (1886) is regarded by many critics as his greatest short story. It depicts the prolonged physical suffering of a man with a mysterious fatal disease, but is also a study of religious philosophies concerning the way humans conduct themselves when the meaning and importance of life is at issue—a concern of Tolstoy's at the time. *Father Sergey*, written in 1896, treats sex in an unusually frank manner for the time, but the focus of the story is on the hypocritical pride of a recluse.

6 Frank Sargeson (1903–82) short story writer and novelist, lived for most of his life in Takapuna on Auckland's North Shore, where he dedicated his time to writing. At the date of this letter he had published two collections of short stories: *Conversations with My Uncle and Other Sketches* (Auckland: Unicorn Press, 1936) and *A Man and His Wife* (Christchurch: Caxton Press, 1940).

1 It is clear from the paper on which this poem is typed, and the 'No. 1' of the censor's stamp, that 'At Balclutha' was sent with Baxter's letter of 25 May 1944.

Rolling loosely his sheaf of cigarette,
A packet of french-letters in the pocket.
    Death I have ever seen: undine who
Globed in air's whirling cavern swam
And chilled the corridor into a cloister,
Grain of desire frozen to grain of concrete
And in the sick street under neon lights
Faces of parchment and vermillion:
And held her knowing she was not the dame
Whose eyebrow-curve set Ilion's roofs on flame—
Would do, would do.
                                        So: the land leans to me
That I should praise her grace of form and feature
That I should laud her gesture and her glance
She is no virgin nor yet mother;
Fosters us sparsely. Shall the collier
Beneath a roof that heaves malign
Bless the slow blood-throb of the mine
That names him parasite? or a shuddering winch
Cable for sinew, for arm hauling the 'rake':
Did her womb weave them?
                                            Death her face alone:
The rare and native, or the loth and new:
One mask of sterile moon; another gouged
As river spills, as cocoon splits, revealing
Only a change of shadows on the ceiling
Only a rattle of rain remembering
The sodden scrub, the age unvexed by night-mare:-
    Birch-boughs lash on the wet and windy air;
Curtains are tentative; the sky has fallen.
'That I should praise her gesture and her glance':
They are silent at my asking.
        [Hocken, MS 89/148]

**Baxter to Ginn, 3 June 1944**

CENSORED
No. 2

Brighton,
Otago.
3/6/44

Dear Noel,—

I will go through your letter by degrees . . .

'genius' indeed is a loathsome word, vague as 'the sublime'. And I agree about Dylan Thomas, an objectionable specimen of introversion—yet would I give worlds to have written his '*We lying by seasands . . .*'[1]

The resemblance of Christmas to Terry has some basis. Terry is a lone wolf, 'dark and sensitive' I think of him as—and when I do think of him that indescribable grip of consanguineity makes my mind sore. This is not sentimentality, but might appear such on the surface. And the Celt is strong in Christmas: perhaps the negro has affinities.[2]

What you say about me needing friends, not admirers, hits one nail on the head. But friends are much more uncomfortable than admirers: one presents a façade of poems, printed emotion, to the admirers, and then one retires;—they can admire the empty lion-skin. Friends are not taken in, touch the man. And friends are apt to take the side of one's own moral censor.[3]

I do not think I will ever become an atheist: coherent personality growing like a tree cannot narrow to anything so dogmatic. I remain agnostic; have often felt that unvague prescience 'the whole reconciled with the parts, the parts with the whole', but never the presence or necessity of a God.

I have done quite well in the only exam so far: part of English: phonetics and some fairly hard stuff about Tennyson, Browning etc. 85%—one or two above me;

1 Dylan Thomas's poem 'We lying by seasand, watching yellow' first appeared in *Poetry* (Chicago), Vol. 49, No. 4, Jan 1937: 183 as 'We Lying By Seasand.' The poem was collected in Thomas's 3rd volume *The Map of Love* (London: J.M. Dent & Sons, 1939).

2 Baxter is referring to Joe Christmas, the protagonist in William Faulkner's novel *Light in August* (1932). Christmas, victimised from birth for being part Negro, grows into a taciturn and embittered man. He is unaware that throughout his life he is shadowed by his maternal grandfather, Eupheus Hines, who, not content with murdering Christmas's father for being a Negro and abandoning the child after Christmas's mother—Hines's daughter Milly—dies in childbirth, remains close by to ensure that his grandson continues to suffer. Ultimately Christmas is framed for a crime he did not commit and is murdered—while attempting to hide from a lynch mob incited by Eupheus Hines—by another racist named Percy Grimm, who shoots and then castrates him. Ginn believed that Baxter 'was drawn to brooding types & exalted & exaggerated the Celtic traits where unhappy mystery resided' and recalled that most of his 'comments on his brother struck this gloomy Celtic note' (letter to Paul Millar, 2 Mar 1995).

3 Evidence suggests that his paragraph pre-dates, and hence probably inspired, 'Letter to Noel Ginn'. According to the sequence in which poems were entered by Baxter into notebook 13, the re-casting of 'Rain-Ploughs' (13:767)—which seems to have been his most recent work—precedes, by five poems, 'Letter to Noel Ginn' (13:772). In addition Baxter's failure to enclose 'they can admire the empty lion-skin' in quotation marks—which, as a rule, he did scrupulously when quoting—suggests that the phrase in the letter precedes the verse.

still, I feel satisfied. Next week a psychology exam: and so, in spite of all resolutions, the inevitable hurried, harried cramming.

AT BALCLUTHA is, I believe, a very good poem: I must inevitably, for all my wavering, turn to realism. It was the better for a preceding 6-weeks silence.

I really appreciate your and Terry's concern, but I am more solid than you think. I am growing up, changing gear as it were; or setting sail, inevitably shipping a few seas, but will not sink or run aground. What I am trying to say is: don't regard what is partial as entire, any more than you would regard any poem of mine as all I had to say. Tell Terry not to worry.[4] I will find a basis, am finding.

'the loud decaying flower that bees shun

Was once the softest bud of spring' . . . fine poetry.[5] But, as ever, I am critic. You do not shape enough. I myself achieve results, as in sonnet 'To Sleep',[6] only after shaping and re-shaping, not to a standard, but till an intuitional dissatisfaction is satisfied: 'the poetic censor' let us call it. I avoid him sometimes, sometimes can press on without him, but always in danger, often in ruin. I am sure you have this seventh sense. Look at your

> *The swan returns to the long cleanness*
> *Of the lake alone . . .*[7]

or that line which I covet above rubies

> *The prim cloth of flowers with rotten stitches sewn.*[8]

These were, I expect, flowers of that automatic verse-perfection which comes when following a mood. But the same sense for the perfect (a different perfection for each poet) . . . or perhaps not perfection, but 'rhetorical ring' as *Full fathom five*[9] . . . will work to order if one keeps one's mind in suspension, waiting for the right word.

> *And in the sick street under neon lights*
> *Faces of parchment and vermilion*[10]

is almost automatic writing, the subconscious supplying word and image on request.

The re-casting of 'Rain-Ploughs' which I enclose is won by the second, harder method. Note: in the last line *brave* and *green* are verbs. General notes: 5–6 Aristotle believed that air was surrounded by water.[11] 7–8 as in 'Atlas', an earlier poem of mine

4 According to Ginn, their concern arose because of Baxter's addiction to beer, which he had written to his brother about: Terence 'noted [Jim's] vulnerability to alcohol because of his lack of self control in most things' (letter to Paul Millar, 17 Apr 1995).

5 Untraced.

6 See 'To Sleep' in letter of 22 Dec 1943, p.308.

7 See 'Time Theme' in Ginn's letter of 7 Apr 1943, pp.206–7.

8 See 'Hypothesis', pp.517–18.

9 Line sung by Ariel in Shakespeare's *The Tempest* (I.2.397).

10 These lines from 'At Balclutha' (see p.358) were transplanted by Baxter from a poem he had written some two months earlier called 'Bracchiae' (see p.473).

11 Aristotle's cosmology is more complex than this and can only be touched upon here. Very briefly, in his work *Meteorology* Aristotle conceives of the universe as a sequence of concentric, nested, spheres with the outermost sphere, the one containing the heavenly bodies, being composed of an incorruptible element called 'ether'. Within the outermost sphere are spheres in which the four elements (earth, air, fire, and water) act according to type, with the heaviest tending towards the centre. Thus the earth is at the centre, surrounded in turn by water, air and fire. Aristotle explains precipitation by arguing that

*letting the rent skies sag*
*To onrush of the outer demons in . . .*[12]

and in another more lurid

*The savage sky unseamed above them*
*Lets shrieks of shrill demonic mirth*
*Jangle upon a yet unsoiléd earth . . .*[13]

12–14 I regard this—you, Noel, and only you would pardon—as entirely perfect; as a sonnet, the best I have written yet.

16. angel-Archer: Sagittarius, the power of rational life.[14]

17. frail-veined twig: fanciful likening of twig to lightning—fire is good, water is evil, in this poem—but mainly the idea of frail greenness life-instinct spreading on the earth after flood.

19. sun: see 7.

a poem lately written:

**Winter**

*While the colossal clouds southward ascend*
*Their calm vibrating wings; inly I wonder*
*To see Winter walk over the darkened waters*
*His brow clear, his locks bound with cloud.*

*But Night is near; and the inane boughs*
*Of the Tree of Night flowerless lay on my eyes*
*Their leaves of lethargy: frozen their clasp.*
*Within, without, the night.*

And [?this not] so good:

**Elegy**

The gentle sycamore leaves
who rode the racing volleys of the wind
crushed underfoot.

*Death will reward them*
*for their fleet striving*
*with a perpetual sleep.*

the nature of the four elements depends upon a combination of four qualities: Hot, Cold, Wet, and Dry. The air, which is Hot/Wet, is nourished by Hot/Wet exhalations from the earth. Similarly Hot/Dry exhalations nourish the fire sphere.

12 See 'Atlas', p.447.

13 Untraced.

14 Sagittarius, the zodiacal constellation of the Archer, is the ninth sign of the zodiac, which the sun enters about 22 November. It is named after the mythic Centaur who was fabled to have been transformed into this constellation. In heraldry it is represented as a centaur (or perhaps in early use a horseman) with a drawn bow. In astrology Sagittarians are intuitive, calm and reliable. In referring to the 'angel-Archer' and 'the power of rational life' Baxter would have had in mind his own father. See p.104.

Bloody mouths of flattened hares
snarl terror yet though dead and blind;
the roving heart is mute.

*Death will reward them*
*for their hot anguish*
*with a perpetual sleep.*

Wax corpses gashed by flame:
debris the tide of iron leaves behind.
Birth-fruit, death-fruit.

*Death will encompass them*
*The intricate machine destroyed*
*clear blood*
*and vegetable arms*
*with a perpetual sleep.*

Will see you at end of August, I hope.
Much love to Terry.
Love and best wishes
Jim.
[VUW Library, MS McKay 28/43]

**Rain-Ploughs**

Rain-ploughs rend the interstices of hills
And serpents grey-jawed drift and raven;
Sodden cadaver the earth, identity unproven;
Based granite-galleons probe eroded hulls
Teeth from earth's withered gum; and split sky spills
Her world-enveloping waters winter-riven—
Sun by insane poltergeist gashed from heaven
Gives outer demons room to wreak their hells.

World crumbles, warped and wan: in talon
Of shackle-broken djinn: how exorcise? O where
Is the bottle black-stone whence wound he jail-break felon?
. . . upheaval, twisted rock: gigantic there
Jar hurled to prone resisting sea-bottom; and sullen
Monsters guard, waiting till water oust air.

Yet hope stays for him who dare.
Dost see yonder the angel-Archer stand?
Frail-veined twig in hand
By blinding sky fire-tipped he doth bear:

Fire-feathered arrow-thought to set new sun on flare
Brave djinn and monster, green again the land.

James K. Baxter
Sonnet with I coda.
[Hocken MS 89/148]

[Not all of Baxter's verse found its way into his poetry notebooks or was published under his own name. This example, which appeared in *Critic* on 22 Jun 1944, can be read in the context of Baxter's comments on his incipient alcoholism on p.110.]

**Horatian Ode**
On the Banishment of Beer

Of late I saw (it pierced my soul)
Upon a wall this bitter scroll:
Warning (it said): No beer
Or drunks permitted here.

Just then, from out the doorway thrown,
And landing on his collarbone
A friend whom I revered
Unheralded appeared.

'The b's,' he said, 'they chucked me out
For trundling a small keg of stout
(Which they will answer for)
Upon the dancing floor.'

'Courage my son'—sadly I spoke—
'Such would be taken as a joke
Or nothing, as one learns,
In the home town of Burns—

'Of whom a statue may be seen,
His back to the cathedral green,
And pensive eyes turned—well,
Towards the O Hotel.

'And learned Greek authorities
Contended that Euripides
When most inspired paid toll
To the Muse of Alcohol.

'But in this philistinian age
Stooges of moderation rage—
Blue-ribboned hounds, alack,
Are baying on our track.

'Envying our ecstatic trance
And that supreme self-confidence
    They even seek to bar
    The innocent motor-car—

'Whose chaste accoutrements will wail
The banished beer, the bygone ale,
    What time the festive horde
    Were wont to cram aboard.

'Hearken,' I said, 'I fear 'twere best
That we be sober with the rest
    And abnegate the brew,
    Or get them shikkered, too.'

        Envoi:
He listened; but I fear that I
Had slight effect: for by and by
    He drew from his hip-pocket
    A flask and tilted it.
And as he wandered on his way
I heard him sing this curious lay:

'Keep your champagne, keep your sherry,
    Give me beer when I feel bad—
Just enough to make me merry
    Not enough to make me mad.'
        —I. MARVEL.[1]
        ['In a Lighter Mood', *Critic*, 22 Jun 1944: 7]

**Baxter to Ginn, 16 July 1944**

CENSORED
No. 4

Brighton,
Otago.
16/7/44

Dear Noel,—

Many thanks for your letter. The poem read with great interest and appreciation: as you say, not polished; but something to it nevertheless. I enclose poems which

1 Baxter kept this page from *Critic* among his papers and deposited it in the Hocken Library (MS 975/182). He has signed his initials next to the pseudonym.

have been damming up for some time.

// FOR THOSE WHO LIE WITH CROOKED LIMBS . . .[1]

*Medea*: symbol of that which survives by craft and coldness.[2]

*Absyrtus*: her brother killed and thrown overboard from the Argos to halt pursuers.[3]

You will get the emotional force of this symbolism I think; anyway you can appreciate the form.

'*crystal-gazer's globe and leg of mutton*' . . . skit on the idea of spirit and flesh.

*Children of Lir:* from the Irish legend of the children turned into swans who wandered for 300 yrs till released, and dying after baptism.[4]

*Mater Dolorosa:* from a picture half-remembered.[5]

// SEA-ELEGY . . .[6]

Torose: cylindrical with bulges—thus,  or something like it.

// A PLANE FELL DOWN . . . written on fact.

very much poetry.

V 1. omens VV. 2–3 contrast of nature. Van Gogh.[7]

V.4. fact V. 5 the sleeping-place of the drowned airmen is cold, the moon moves on the gates of drives in town suburbs—suburbs at night under moonlight: the relatives of the airmen under the same moon that makes the sea leaden, turn, remembering dimly in sleep some loss.

V.6 The sea is cruel like a siren, yet natural, elemental . . .

(you will have to get the hang of this for yourself, I guess.) Islands, however, are troubled by this death: I make the death of the airmen symbolic of all death, cosmic and human: faint echo of Flecker's '*Beyond the boy a rock that screams Like madmen*

1 Baxter is referring here to an early version of 'For those who lie . . .', the text of which follows this letter. Appendix 2 (p.476) contains a later, revised, version of the poem.

2 Medea, the daughter of Aeëtes, king of Colchis, was said to be a witch and a priestess of Hecate. She helped Jason win the Golden Fleece but when he abandoned her for the daughter of the King of Corinth she murdered the king, his daughter, and her own two children, and then escaped in a chariot drawn by dragons.

3 Medea's brother Absyrtus (or Apsyrtus) reportedly led the pursuit of the Argonauts as they attempted to escape from Colchis with his sister and the Golden Fleece. Medea lured him to a meeting with her at which he was ambushed and killed by Jason. She then dismembered her brother and strewed the parts on the water, forcing her father to abandon the pursuit in order to collect the pieces for burial.

4 The first wife of the mythical Irish chieftain Lir of Sidh Fionnachaidh bore him two sets of twins, but died during labour while giving birth to the second set. Lir's second wife became jealous of the children and plotted their destruction. However, she could not bring herself to kill them, and instead turned them into swans, for which crime she was turned her into a demon and sentenced to wander through the air forever. The children remained enchanted for some 900 years, much of the time spent in cold and misery, before returning to human form as three withered old men and an old woman. They were baptised as Christians by Saint Mochaomhog, then died happily and were buried together.

5 Literally 'sorrowful mother': a generic title referring to a representation, in painting or sculpture, of the Virgin Mary sorrowing.

6 See 'Sea-Elegy', p.478.

7 In 1889, the year before he committed suicide, the Dutch painter Vincent [Willem] van Gogh (1853–90) painted a number of landscapes featuring cypresses that 'swirl like sky'. The 'Wheatfield with Cypress' series, 'Cypresses' and, in particular, 'Cypresses with Two Women', may all have contributed to the images in stanzas two and three of 'A Plane Fell Down'.

*shouting in their dreams From whose dark issues night and day Blood crashes in a thousand streams . . .*'[8]

Shooting stars . . . omens again.

v.7 Completion of theme.

// IN JULY . . .

*Auden my master:* Auden I consider the best modern poet. Also he has written a poem in some ways similar to this. *Out of the mirror they stare Imperialism's Face And the international wrong.*[9]

[wrote the 1st verse of IN JULY while biking without handle-bars, 'breaking the bike in' again: with pencil and small pad.][10]

Hope I have not sent you this one already.

**For Burial in Ground**

This word for my lost days
this one true poem
true among many painted
where shall I bury him?

By ways of moon and sun
to this one room I come
the bright and hollow wind hearing
this in the throat of Time.

Many may read
none shall remember
the unique eye (half-pun)
the living ember.

Bury him under a pine
that my white bones leave one tithe
of child, man, and grave-rot
of the dead mouth.

Shut in smooth resin
hold its life-secret still
when words nor men to know them
stay tall.

8 Baxter appears to be quoting from memory the nineteenth stanza of Flecker's poem 'Gates of Damascus' which was first collected in *The Golden Journey to Samarkand* (1913).
Beyond the isle a rock that screams like madmen shouting in their dreams,
From whose dark issues night and day blood crashes in a thousand streams.

9 The final three lines of the fourth stanza of Auden's poem 'September 1, 1939', first collected in *Another Time* (London: Faber & Faber, 1940).

10 Probably a reference to having finally succeeded in acquiring some bicycle tyres (see p.349). An accident some weeks later, in which Baxter was injured and his bike badly damaged, also put him off the road for a time. See 'The Crystal-Gazer's Globe and Leg of Mutton', p.112 and footnote 2 to Baxter's letter of September/October 1944, p.384

*Romance* is beautiful. If you have more like this, by all means send them. Depth of a kind.[11]

I will sometimes spend an hour on a sonnet. They are a hard form, no good for anything loose or slight, but repay enormously—sense of achievement and solidity.

I have sneered at poets who beat out each line on the anvil of thought. Now I do it myself. OREADES is phantasy, yet expression of something I am learning.

Very best wishes
From
Jim.

PS I am emerging from the 'globe of dream' which produced 'The Unicorn' and others. My poems may change, I may even stop writing for a bit, but one must not retard development by attempted 'freezing' in one phase.[12]

[VUW Library, MS McKay 28/44]

**For those who lie with crooked limbs in the straight grave**

Snow clogs air and earth; dark cloud-eruption
Advances to keen wind. Or the curling flakes fall
Weighting all: ache of yellow leaves
By the compassionate wandering flakes hidden;
Heaven invades earth. In the eyeless winter
    What shall I do but burn
The incense-shavings, twigs of summer boughs?
Smoke in a hollow room . . .
                                        Medea rides
The black and marble midnight: twin dragons
Before her chariot flaming; from cloudy Caucasus
Where chained Prometheus bleeds: on burning snow
Blows the cold ice-flower.
                                        Young Absyrtus dead
In the blue seaway, drowned and floating head:
With him the Spring rots livid, unfulfilled.
    The dull bronze foliage of dawn
Cast no more from her gold Tree in the East
Falls tarnished on our wharves.
                                            Yet we have seen
Only the smooth stone and the flourishing green;
Have too soon forgotten . . . earth in cycles of
A starry and immense vertigo.
    Some fall in eddies of death: he who
Must sit forever in a bhuddhist posture

11 Untraced.

12 The phrase 'globe of dream' comes from Baxter's poem 'Intelligentsia', which he wrote in the latter half of 1942. See also p.101, and the complete poem, p.442.

Or the slow blood will stop . . . Dream-flawed fragments:
Strewing wet tea-leaves on a varnish floor . . .
Patches of shaven hair around a wound . . .
The square and silent ventilators flutter
To chafe of a saw of blood in the cranium . . .
A crystal-gazer's globe and leg of mutton
Sleep on the billow: calm delirium.
    I thought I could feel the autumn wind blowing
But saw above through glass the grey gulls crossing—
What children of Lir unfreed from wandering?—
Their inviolable pinions dim;
Knew my universe finite.
    Dry lips are moistened and grow dry again.
There is no category of misfeature:
Within one room, as midnight dies,
A man is staring in death's placid eyes
Unmoving.
            The suave grace unknown in nature
Of iron cities maims us as we master;
Even the dead sleep as children sleep.

Soft birds rustling on glazed chimney-pots;
Electric wires that cross a shingle gully;
Algae upon the sunken submarine;
And the dull jolting of a corpse encaverned.

The catholic priest came; planted his blossoming
Staff on the floor-boards. Angels leaned with the winds.
World's colours broke clear in the holy fountain.
Why did the heart turn? from flower-blue sky-enamel
Whereon the forked boughs sway.
    The rain blots out the lights; and the sworded wilderness
Consumes our streets like sky . . .

Sweet smell of apple from her dress in passing
Recalling the forgotten one who stands
At the winged crossroads. Shall I then know her?
Recalled as shadows on the blazing sea
Or in music a lily among gold notes.
    Here the ruck also.
The suave and painted grace encompassing;
The caddis under stones, underwater heat.

Birds build on the bastions
Of our mud fortresses: their droppings rot our roofs.

There are ghosts tokening present anguish,
Presaging doom, stalk our pavements;
Moving automatons in foggy streets
Their lipless masks hung like grooved corinthian marble . . .
Even in daylight may be heard
The lisping step of a blind man's cane . . .
Sharp smell of vomit; in the garden
Someone is beating a rusty xylophone.

Mater Dolorosa.
Tear-ducts are rigid pipes . . . jagged and metal anguish;
eyes pricked by cactus-spines.
Embalm her in cool cedar of lebanon;
burn incense shavings:
you cannot melt her glacier sorrow.
Winter has clothed us. Who shall see the spring?
[Hocken, MS 89/148]

**A plane fell down**

Lightning falls on the roofs
A throbbing seen in the dark;
Blue flames beat like veins
Or a match-flare behind the eyes.

While by the tormented boulders
Cypresses swirl like sky
Back from day's glassy candles
To a tornado green:

The grasses melt unearthly
Like rivers or rolling flames;
From distant giant hills
They surge again and run.

A plane fell down: they lie
Drowned by the sunny coast.
It sank down like a leaf
Bones in the cockpit still.

Frost is sharp in their bed.
From dull gutters of cloud
The moon moves on the gates:
Sleepers turn and sigh.

The blond sea looks at the sun
Lies back and shakes her curls.
Islands shout in the night;
Shooting stars fall on their crags.

The stars slide from the sky.
Summer like sunken coins
Is lost in the dead lake.
No diver will bring them up.
[Hocken, MS 89/148]

**In July**

In the sleet and wintry fire
Of an australasian July
When hurling winds conspire
To drive the moon from the sky:
It is fitting I should affirm
Like Auden my master
My hate for an age of plaster
My hope of fortune and fame.

Fluting night-owls jangle:
I think of a twice-torn France,
In european jungle
The terrible soldier-ants;
Love bleeds in storm of ruin,
And the child Hope lies naked
On a Procrustes bed;
Death falls acid like rain.

Man is a single nation:
And I born under the sign
Of the reticent crustacean
Must deem those seas malign
Where huge armadas drown
With men in fear the same.
Who shall bear the shame?
Who but we the ruin?

Yet I though late to learn
At length can say my prayers;
Where rotting marsh-fires burn
In the hag-ridden airs:
While in a stormy July

The lechery of hate
Consumes the good and great.
The moon shakes in her sky.
[Hocken, MS 89/148]

**Oreades**

Head-lights that hurtle on the hills by night
Have lit our mountain solitude and made
Earth arrogant afraid
That her inviolable secrecy may yet be rent and bright.

But we from covert gazing have grown wise;
Have seen our sisters stare back from white windows;
Have ventured close:
They are the Wenches with slim knees aloof like mountain pinnacles and us.
[Hocken, MS 704/10:621, p.122]

**Baxter to Ginn, 13 August 1944**

CENSORED
No. 1

Brighton,
Otago
13/8/44

Dear Noel,—

I could offer for not writing the legitimate excuse of examinations. But actually because I have not felt like it. You probably know the state. Anyway it is useless to write if not spontaneously.

But I have produced one or two good poems. It is always far easier to write on any subject when one imagines oneself in love, whether it be true or not. This time it is—but I'll get over it in time, I guess.[1]

*'alive only in sparking'*

*'dearer than a flask of rum'*

Puns unmeant. The first would add to the poetic value if recognised, the second detract from it.

1 Baxter also wrote of this relationship to his English friend from his days at Sibford School, Margaret Hargreave (nee Herbert) on 18 Feb 1945: 'Last year I imagined I fell in love, the only fruitful product being a few rather fine poems.' (VUW Library, MS McKay 10/5/36). A number of these poems found their way into Baxter's unpublished collection *Cold Spring* and were grouped together in a section entitled 'The Flowering Eye'. See, p.112.

THE CLOSED PICTURE—maybe my best in the style of Spender.[2] 'The dry wit of skulls' I could not have written 3 months ago even. The whole poem is I think a trite subject made untrite: WHAT'S DONE IS DONE—Lady Macbeth.[3]

ANNALES—some of the lines transplanted from earlier poems, not so good.[4] Only in the 1st and 3rd verse. 'Depth-charges in the city sea' is the concentration I spend most of my writing time despairing of.

'Trees with chafing . . . scourging the lost': annexed with improvements from Lucretius and Vergil.[5]

PTO

Hope to see Terry this time fortnight; and . . .?[6]

Love and best wishes

From

Jim.

[VUW Library, MS McKay 28/45]

**Baxter to Ginn, 13 September 1944**

CENSORED
No. 1

Brighton,
Otago.
13/9/44.

Dear Noel,—

It was very good for me to see you and Terry. It sort of straightened out things in my mind. And my mother was immensely relieved and rather captivated by the new

2 See 'The Closed Picture', p.479.

3 In *Macbeth* III.2.11–12, Lady Macbeth advises her husband that:

Things without all remedy
Should be without regard; what's done is done.

4 See 'ANNALES', p.481.

5 Baxter has annexed two unrelated passages from Lucretius and Virgil to compose the lines: 'Trees with chafing burn / When strong south winds flail the italian sky / Tisiphone scourging the lost'. In 'Book V: Cosmology and Sociology' of *On the Nature of the Universe*, Lucretius argues that although lightning was surely the means by which fire was bought down to earth, there is also one other possible source of fire:

> When a branching tree, tossed by the wind, is swaying and surging to and fro and stooping to touch the branches of another tree, the violent friction squeezes out seeds of fire, till sometimes from the rubbing of bough against bough, trunk against trunk, there flashes out a blazing burst of flame (lines 570–2, trans. R.E. Latham).

Baxter's second reference is to Virgil's account in *The Aeneid* of the Fury Tisiphonë scourging the dead:

At once the avenger girdled with her whip,
Tisiphonë, leaps down to lash the guilty,
Vile writhing snakes held out on her left hand,
And calls her savage sisterhood.
(*Aeneid* VI, lines 1096–100, trans. Robert Fitzgerald)

6 Baxter did indeed see Ginn towards the end of August. He and his mother travelled up to Whitanui Detention Camp to visit Terence, and Ginn was allowed to sit in for part of the visit. See p.112.

Terry. But going away was tough—like your poem with 'the ripstead of underground streams'.[1] I wrote a poem to try to set down my ideas and feelings; not very good, not very true to life perhaps. It ended:

*Who killed cock robin? he was a frail soul*
*perhaps: could not endure: a cage killed him.*
*Or turned him, who'd never the head for heights*
*to the cynical one*
*the heaven-searcher outstaring the sun*
*the ravenous eagle.*[2]

I am glad you liked *Portrait of the Artist as a Young Man* . I personally consider it one of the best novels ever written. The part about the catholic Hell is overpowering.[3]

Have given up smoking almost entirely and feel much the better for it; also have not seen alcohol since coming down on the boat, when I got drunk to avoid being seasick—successfully.

Thank you very much for letting me put your name in the title of the *Letter* after all. It is important to me.[4]

I talked with Laurence Baigent for an evening when we were in Christchurch; fought with him over the inclusion of various poems, and won every time.[5] I find him friendly, sensitive, intelligent, poetical views sound but slightly narrow for me. He was much more forthcoming than when I met him a week before—having read my poems in the meantime. He was especially struck by 'Cry Mourn'.[6] My poems will probably be out before Xmas, so a cheap Xmas present to send to you (!)

Mother has sent you some of Tolstoy; and is sending the long-delayed Latin Grammar. In expectation of your later proficiency, here is one of Horace's Odes and my translation.

*Diffugere nives, redeunt iam gramina campis*
*arboribusque comae;*
*mutat terra vices et decrescentia ripas*
*flumina praetereunt;*
*immortalia ne speres, monet annus et almum*
*quae rapit hora diem.*
*Frigora mitescunt Zephyris; ver proterit aestas*
*interitura, simul*

1 See 'Farewelling', p.513.
2 See 'Thoughts by a Conchie Camp' (p.486) for the full poem.
3 James Joyce's first novel *A Portrait of the Artist as a Young Man* was first published as a serial in 1914–15 in the magazine the *Egoist*, and appeared in book form the following year (London: Jonathan Cape, 1916). Ginn received the book when Baxter and his mother visited Whitanui: 'Jim presented me with *Portrait of the Artist*. Half the camp read it—it was just out. Later I bought *Ulysses* & it too went the rounds' (letter to Paul Millar, 15 May 1995).
4 A reference to the poem 'Letter to Noel Ginn', which follows this letter. Baxter had included the poem among those given to Lawrence Baigent for inclusion in the book Caxton was planning to publish.
5 Originally a teacher at Christchurch Boys' High, Baigent worked at the Caxton Press for the duration of the war after being dismissed as a teacher for refusing military service on conscientious grounds. See pp.113–17.
6 See 'Cry Mourn' on pp.248–9.

*pomifer Autumnus fruges effuderit, et mox*
*bruma recurrit iners.*
*Damna Tamen celeres reparant caelestia lunae:*
*nos, ubi decidimus,*
*quo pater Aeneas, quo dives Tullus et Ancus*
*pulvis et umbra sumus.*
Horace, Odes, iv. 7

**Spring**

The new-grown grasses now, with melting snows
In fields return; and their green locks to trees.
Earth suffers change: each swollen river flows
Below banks quiet: and the hours that seize
Like wolves the mild day, and the rising year
Cry down our dream of immortality;
While the cold airs grow warm and spring winds bear . . .
Spring winds bear warmth, but quail at Summer's envy
On heel of doomed Spring following: and so
Comes Autumn with her apples, harvest-weal:
Winter like stone.
O the swift moons can heal
Huge Heaven's disorder; but we with summer go—
Like Caesar, like Pythagoras, from daylight
Are dust of dust and shadows of the night.

Rilke I am reading with ever-increasing understanding: Elegies 3, 4, 7, 10, especially.[7] One must however prevent oneself from becoming lost in him. Pour moi, I am of the earth earthy and must write accordingly, with a strong vein of Scottish practicality to overcome before I even begin imagining.

There is an echo of Rilke in the second-last line of 'Stability', a poem of condensed metaphors commemorating the gloomy side of verse-writing.[8]

'The Tower', now I look at it, may have something of Rilke unconsciously assimilated. The Ist and IIIrd sections are for me the most powerful.

'Mural for a War-Memorial' does not need all the notes I give it. But they may interest you. I have sent it to Laurence Baigent with about three words of notes for each verse: he may find it incomprehensible. To me it is clear, clear as 'Stability'.[9]

Alun Lewis was a young English poet whose verse I rather liked now killed in the

7 Rainer Maria Rilke (1875–1926) named his cycle of ten elegies after the Castle Duino on the Adriatic, where he had begun writing them. Published as the *Duineser Elegien* (Leipzig: Insel, 1923) they were first translated into English by V. Sackville-West and Edward Sackville-West as *Duineser Elegien: Elegies from the Castle of Duino* (London: Hogarth Press, 1931); and then translated again in 1939 by Spender and Leishmann as *Duino Elegies* (New York: Norton, 1939; London: Hogarth Press, 1939).

8 See 'Stability' p.487.

9 Baxter was fairly accurate in predicting Baigent's response to the poem. In a letter of 16 Oct 1944 Baigent wrote: 'Thanks . . . for "Mural for a War-Memorial". I confess it still baffles me in places. Give me time, though' (Hocken, MS 975/183).

Air-Force.[10] You have probably read him. The Elegy however is in its detail for NZ soldiers, though, being symbolist, it has many applications. The mythological core is: *that earth is born of air. That fire and water are intermediaries.* Air is also the religious heaven. Incense and holy water earth gives to heaven. Lightning and cloudburst, or, in benignant mood, sun and rain, heaven gives to earth. *lisp of lies*—even the children are caught up. *glow-gold-worm*—tmesis.[11]

Much love to Terry,
to you also
From
Jim.

[VUW Library, MS McKay 28/46]

**Letter to Noel Ginn**

They can admire the empty lion-skin
The heart skewered by print, who will admire:
But from you, Noel, I wish more—
The friend's stance, confessor for my sin
Which is pride alone: yet pride alone will win
Niche of immortal marble despised and hungered for.

As a child I was childish . . . an intuitional ease;
Had missed the vice of sensitivity;
Waded the flood-race of a century;
But felt capacity for pain increase
Till each day no longer a wood of peace
Held larks of shelleyan song, tigers of poetry.

When I saw Europe . . . a kaleidoscope
Fluttered, flashed elusive in place of the grave
Time-wading fortitude:- oil-weighted wave
Feathering bows forever; blind seascape;
Nights of storm, screw thudding; Gibraltar cape—
Peered through field-glasses, played chess till nausea claimed her slave.

Or earlier: in Australia the hot days;
Mast-cracking Sydney bridge; golden Colombo

10 The poetry of Alun Lewis (1915–44) was highly regarded during World War II for its representation of the experience of the individual caught up in a vast conflict. Lewis never served in the air force but enlisted in the Royal Engineers, then transferred to the Education Corps, and finally to the Sixth Battalion, South Wales Borderers which embarked for India in Nov 1942. Although his training in intelligence could have kept him out of battle, he insisted on going to the front when his unit went Burma. He never saw action because, on the way to the forward positions, he was involved in a mysterious accident and killed by his own pistol. Investigations concluded that Lewis tripped while carrying the loaded weapon and one round discharged itself, hitting him in the head. Investigators found no indication that suicide was involved.

11 'Tmesis' refers to the separation of the elements of a compound word by the interposition of another word or words.

With fishing-fleets on estuaries to show
A bird's plumage, a bird's surf-shadowing ways;
A camel scrubbed upon the banks near Suez;
Crete's iron citadel; and Plymouth bitter with snow.

London claimed me: she was heavy and huge;
Her barges, and her dank wharves flecked with soot;
Placarded Tubes; and fog at Christmas; mute
Paling and palace. The Cotswolds were a refuge:
Leaf-mould . . . stone . . . thatched roofs . . . blackberry hedge . . .
Lanes, willows . . . snow-slush; bells; homesickness; running the gauntlet.

Europe claimed me: then she did not bleed.
Flat Danish fields, yellow sky spun by the rocking
Express; and at Copenhagen seabirds flocking
Along quays. The rock Rhine towered and treed;
Clean Berlin; at Eisenach sycamore seed;
Rothenberg . . . dungeons; friendly Storm Trooper . . . the wind is mocking.

France: where the Rhône ran under concrete;
Sewer at bridge-base. Out of the violent sun
I wrote poems, scrapped poems half-begun
On clouds and comets. A tower seen from the street:
Skeletons found there. Bats. Snake at my feet.
The castle . . . Terry's arm broken; when set, he sweated with pain.

And Scotland was my spiritual home,
Or so it seemed. The tide ancestral swung
Over rock-weed. I plucked the bells of ling;
Saw bald Glencoe . . . and watched the red-coats come.
Old Edinburgh . . . were the cobbles dumb?
England again: Boscastle . . . crags and a blowhole spouting.

—Here once more I walk in the troubled water.
Our hills call: but what shall I learn from them?
Pride bids me stare upon the broken time
Of lies and high explosive; prompts this letter.
With pride for armour men in their abattoir slaughter.
Pride holds me from like hells: pride makes me what I am.

What land shall receive me save as a stranger?
Sea-blown Ulysses said: and Ithaca
More alien was than Troy. Nor could Minerva
Content him long: aged he craved for danger
For withered fame. So Time was Troy's avenger.
Slight parallel . . . yet seek I res habita.

The same inhuman cataclysm that set
You weeding flax upon a worthless ground
Both truth and talent to a treadmill bound
Leaves me upon a waiting Ararat:
(The flood may not subside): no marionette
Jerked by the city string, nor in her rubble drowned.

Both clouds and houses are a frozen tide
Till poetry inhabit them with fire.
Men only stay, their masque and their desire;
Thus among men I move my tap-roots wide
The roots of verse, the roots of life beside;
Leave empty lion-skin for dullards to admire.

Women as flowers: they are embodiment
Of the gross earth and the rhetorical cloud;
But shaped as bird, as flower to strange and loud.
. . . A span of threescore and the heart is spent:
This word invades, but I have armament—
The gift of ancestry, the armour of the proud.

The backward groping of a tree of blood
Coils in the dark: but from its mountain springs
Brings mountain pride, and brings
Each impulse of the evil and the good,
With something of a Celtic hardihood:
The pain and poetry . . . I did not dream these things.

Those who grew old: those who were shrewd and hardy;
As children wondered and as men grew sure:
They are but painted figures insecure
Upon a tattered backcloth, tamed and tardy.
And we their unreflecting progeny
Forget, inherit: thus their deeds, their deaths endure.

My son, at first a knocking in the womb
Can speak beyond the thundering gates of war,
Symplegades: it is his voice I hear;
And my son's son; braving the storms of time
The storms and sultry shallows—vortex, storm,
They beat on us, they break: pride is the saviour.

from
Jim

[Hocken, MS 89/148]

**The Tower**

I

When the shrill bird of bone
Cried in my waking ear
On the day that I was born
O why was I loud to hear ?
    Then was the hour to sleep
In the gates of the making house.
The blind fall was not steep
But deep beyond remorse.

Now walk the murderous wood
Dog death sharp at heel;
Question each iron weed
If from her flux I fell:
    For kindly undergrowth
Is grafted now
To the dumb root of death;
Moss flames on the bough.

A lantern in the skull
Covers the red sun's light
With day of fibred steel:
Yet I may sleep at night
    With unfamiliar breasts;
And sleeping remember
Time-phoenix wrung to rest
And fire from the deaf ember.

II

But winds then mild
Turn malice;
I their lost darling, eternity's child
Identity and voice.

    Those who are bloody
On a night field
On whom the wind is cold
The air dark in their mouths
Do not die
In the hollow rooms of the skull
But escape to outer night
With sharp stars mingle.

And the lover is found dead
With an unreal
Smile broken in his hands:
He has escaped
To day
Love-child invincible
To the warm eyes and voices
The day of memory.

So worship violence
Who is Now-universe, inane but integral;
So worship love
Who is our core, time-lost, infrangible.

III

But Death is not the dead.
Death is a tower
Seen on a hill.

Calm grasses murmur
Below; It is not calm.
Is violent and still.

And by the . . . stones
Whose faces strain
Outward, away

And by the dead inertia
The motionless wind
Vortex of clay

We are reminded
Of malignity.

IV

Beyond love or violence
Is the land of Hell
True out of time
Which I have trespassed once in dreams.

And now my journey
Grows near
That boundary:
The country which I travel through
Unconsciously and day by day
Of which
Glimpses shape
In fog-rift of sleep;

Or sudden inward sight of summits
Grey, insular:
Ominous and familiar.

V

By the light whisper of leaves
By the strung wire of water
By the bubble in the heart
    The Tower has spoken:

Whom each raising his eyes
    Sees alone.
No sobbing for the dead God
Lover or mother
Will break the twilight
    The torment of stone.
        [Hocken, MS 89/148]

**Mural for a War-Memorial**
(for Laurence Baigent)

For now is not eternal as we will it.
    Stone only stays.
Remember then who killed the bird
    In sky of memory
Sky only stays, the dead root is weighty.

Familiar to the double eye
night silts within a stormy country
her darker gladius;

Till lands of introspection show
the gross external malady
the green and stony tree.

Light leaves the ravenous sun-dial
unfed: as grasses multiply.
its mouth is stopped with mud.

With bird's impetuosity
light splinters on the morning calm:
the lighthouse gull is broken.

Death a vortex in the mind
tower and central pyramid
builds by disintegration.

This is the monument: remember:
do not blaspheme with sorrow: this
you chose rather.

Comets weave new celestial implications
their dying scrawl; and the aetheric sea
by vocal cannon torn.

And the horizon-bowl is stranded angel
on tidal flats diaphanous.
The heads are garlanded.

Earth is: or heaven bare and blinding.
till the lost faces in a rain of rubble
swing from dazedness to death

see not shadow slow and sable
but bottomless sky beyond the eye-ball earth.

James K. Baxter

<u>Notes on 'Mural for a War-Memorial'</u>:

1. The present, the Now, is not as we would wish a landscape to explore, but a succession of instants, each lost to reality as the next succeeds. Thus present is eternal, but not as 'we will it'.

2. Only the dead and inanimate, the sculptural entity, preserve a seeming sameness in that they change little from one instant to another.

3,4. Remember then those who caused the death of the time-traversing organism, the live thing (i.e. the soldier, the man), now memory. There is a figure of speech here such as 'he struck him dead'. i.e. the memory is equidated with the first Now when death happened. As sky is dimensionless until a bird enters it, so memory is meaningless without life.

5. Meaningless memory remains only . . .

6, 7, 8. Familiar to the mental eye which sees both objectively and subjectively, Night (i.e. ignorance) causes violence to emerge in the subjective landscape.

9, 10, 11. Till this landscape, normally timeless, shows the same distinction between life and death mentioned in (2), a distinction belonging by nature to objective reality.

12, 13, 14. (Further development of theme) But as violence progresses death causes Light (intellect) to lose conception of time. 'grasses multiply' signifies the advance of the timeless. 14. For death destroyed Time when the men were killed.

15, 16, 17. (New theme) Intellect (the 'bird' symbolism is picked up again from (3)) is attracted by the calm of nature as a gull is by a lighthouse, but 'splinters' for the very character of intellect forbids its apprehension of nature. Yet nature is lighthouse, guides.

18, 19, 20. See The Tower (in this previous poem I make clear that death is essentially a subjective process).

21, 22, 23. (Aside) You, i.e. those who look at the mural, may with us all bear the blame for choosing that the soldiers should be killed, the animate made inanimate. In the previous stanza death is regarded as a process making subjective objective, animate inanimate, building 'stone' which 'only stays' by disintegration.

24, 25, 26. The subjective through violence becomes completely objective (a process of death); a dying universe is torn by storms to which human violence contributes.

27, 28, 29. 'The sky falls' We become materialist. The sky is diaphanous like a huge jelly-fish. 'angel' gives the element of regret. 29. The glorification of the 'garlanded' victor (the dead soldiers) is an ironic ~~and inane~~ survival of faith more inane than materialism.

30, 31, 32, 33, 34. FINIS

[Hocken, MS 89/148]

**Elegy**
(in memory of Alun Lewis)

The air from whom all ills and omens fall
Forever childing womb of wind or stone
Whose messengers we cover in the spool
Of sparking water in a dynamo;
Evade in iron of the clay volcano.
The air that warns the man within the skin
With cloud-burst, lightning; or the tree of sun
And leaves of living rain. The air grown cold
Mothers no more her creatures:
    In a graveyard niche of hours, when the scrolled and worn
Cloud lets fall acid for wind gnawing
On shelterstone: from the heart's hollow asylum
Deaf bug of burrowing lust, whose glow-gold-worm
Ravens behind rain-hammer and hill-halted spring,
Weary of mantis-hide, I cast
Of fire the bent pillar that drives me east;
Lie listening at skull of cities, mourning
The prodigal eye, the leper's bell of the time
And lisp of lies; the mouthing quicklime
In grave-sheet spilt. Nor gargoyle heaven pardon.

    My winter tongue may toll and ride the gale
Jar down the jacob's-ladder of the wise
Ring, wrangle in the palace-grate; and cry
For the lopped soldier's-head, the broken lechery.
    (For these were not the tall boys with glass foreheads
For sacrificial wick; ranked on day's polar beaches
Love's bullet-stopping penny under braid;
Now crowned by cloud or calm in brazen torches).
    Were squalid; knew their shore a hollow city:
But . . . between heel and pavement caught
A fountaining moment's balance
Till lead sliced the river-root of pity.
And these too had their desperate innocence

Below the overshadowing Etna rutted:
    O stand by them, where the chipped wood
Split chicken-white; where the boat stalled in the wind;
A dank night's eeling in the creeks and shallows;
Or under sleep, in more unreal jungles
Walking among the yanks and island men . . .
Coral corrals, with the bombers rolling
On steel stems like the lead-weighted toys.
    Have twined their subtle lust with hours of rain
Heard nightly; or the quick limbs of the blind;
Or sight of one face sleeping, when
Daybreak renews the grey herds of the mind;
Or taste of tears; or the rank seasmell blown
Through rushes murmuring, on river-sand.

    I call my stormy angel blow for them
Trumpets of sky: yet though loud lightnings bray
And the burst bones reply, rise up from ruin
Their torch cannot return; in a gold heaven
Their red original vices will not stay.
Cliff-climbing night rises from sea
Hides their true eyes and hands of memory
Who limed and water-wormed, fire-buried
Now sleep, sleep boulder-bruised in clay.
        [Hocken, MS 89/148]

**Baxter to Ginn, [c. September/October 1944]**

CENSORED
No. 4

Would you mind, Noel, if I put 'Letter to Noel Ginn' in the volume I may be bringing out at Xmas? It fits perfectly, only your approval required.[1]

Am pretty well over the concuss. Slight head-aches at times. Have been going to 'Varsity a fortnight now. Bike smashed but been mended well.[2]

1 Ginn was pleased to give his approval to Baxter's request: 'When Jim asked for permission to publish "Letter to NG" I felt honoured & really chuffed. Confinement heightened a sense of joy at some reflected glory to offset the shame of circumstance' (letter to Paul Millar, 17 Apr 1995).

2 Baxter's mother recalled his accident in an interview with Frank McKay:

> . . . he had an accident—a bicycle accident—he ran head on into a girl coming in the opposite direction. It was at night—bicycling out to Brighton. He was on his right side and she was on her wrong but he hadn't his lights on because it meant such toiling to get the light on when he was riding up hill as he was so they ran into each other and were pretty badly damaged (VUW Library, MS McKay 1/12).

Foul weather. To FOR THOSE WHO LIE . . . Love to Terry.[3] Have registered. Not in last ballot.[4] Have read MacLeish, american, lately: a sensitive poet.[5]

Love and best wishes,

Jim.

[VUW Library, MS McKay 28/43A]

**Baxter to Ginn, 20 November 1944**

CENSORED
No. 4

Brighton,
Otago.
20/11/44

Dear Noel,—

My name will be in the ballot on Tuesday. I will send in an appeal on conscientious grounds. I may or may not get it according to the policy of the Board. If I don't get it, I guess I'll be joining the ranks of the faithful. Either way it is a good thing—solidifies my principles[1] Of late I've not felt much like writing letters; a periodic wave of depression. Still, here are a few poems.[2]

'Absalom'—spoken or thought by David. If it seems obscure, read the biblical story.[3] Strong influence of Lorca.[4]

'In Retrospect': take it as sincere, not a pose.

'Epitaphs': to the point. Influence of Laura Riding.[5]

'Court Speech'—3rd verse some of my best lines.

3 See 'For those who lie with crooked limbs in the straight grave', p.476.

4 Periodic ballots were held to select men for overseas service in the armed forces from among all single men between the ages of 21 and 40 years, inclusive, not already balloted. Baxter had registered as a conscientious objector and, if balloted, could expect to have his case considered by the Armed Forces Appeal Board. See pp.22 and 112.

5 Archibald MacLeish (1892–1982) was an American poet and dramatist whose work was strongly influenced by T.S. Eliot and Ezra Pound.

1 The impending ballot was on Baxter's mind, four day's earlier he had mentioned it in a letter to Lawrence Baigent: 'Probably I will be in the ballot shortly, and may not get my appeal on conscientious grounds' (VUW Library, MS McKay 19/3/3).

2 Of the poems Baxter lists below, 'Absalom', 'Court Speech', 'Xerxes and Homer', 'Poem in November', 'Under the dank leaves', and 'Cold Spring' appear in Appendix 2.

3 The story of the death of King David's rebellious son Absalom at the hands of Joab is told in 2 Samuel 18–9.

4 Federico García Lorca (1898–1936), a poet and playwright with leftist sympathies, was caught up in the Spanish Civil War and executed in a mass killing organised by right-wing Falangists. Lorca, regarded as perhaps the greatest figure of twentieth century Spanish literature, developed a powerful but economic style of verse—which clearly influenced Baxter's poem 'Absalom'—characterised by short, often minimal, lines, arranged in loosely structured stanzaic patterns, and employing repetition, exclamation, ellipses, and unanswered questions.

5 See the reference to Laura Riding Jackson in footnote 3 on p.350. The influence Baxter refers to does not relate to a series of epitaphs composed by Riding, but to similarities in theme and style between Baxter's 'Epitaphs' and a number of Riding's early poems.

'Xerxes and Homer'—mature, I hope.

'Poem in November'—study carefully. Not a pose either.

'Under the dank leaves'—something of a pose, but a good sonnet in George Barker's form (ABCDABCD.EFGEFG) and some phrases worth while.[6]

'Cold Spring'—note 1st, 3rd, and last verses. Slight influence of Roy Campbell.[7] Last three lines referring to the fable in Virgil's *Georgics*.[8]

I bathe here in the sea sometimes. Rather cold and weedy. I have been doing some pretty hard work cutting and wheeling sods. Am now muscular and calf-like, chew my cud in such poems as the last-mentioned.

Will see Lawrence Baigent, the Caxton Press man, tomorrow. My book is printed but not yet bound: may come out in less than a month, but only about 100 copies at first.[9] Baigent is rather enthusiastic as a midwife—a fine and intelligent man. By the way, I am seeing him in Dunedin, not Christchurch.

Fruit-picking is off: crops killed by frost. So I will be a farm-labourer for a while.

Love to Terry,

and to yourself love and best wishes

From

Jim

PS You may tell Terry I still smoke, but not heavily.

[VUW Library, MS McKay 28/48]

6 The rhyme scheme of Baxter's sonnet follows that used by George Barker in his 'Personal Sonnets' ('To my Mother', 'To my Brother', 'To David Gill', 'To Stephen Spender', 'To T.S. Eliot' and 'To Any Member of My Generation') from *Poems* (1935).

7 Roy Campbell (1901–57) was a South African poet who resided mainly in England. He was well known in the 1930s for his opposition to the dominant left-wing school of poets led by Auden, Spender, Day Lewis and others. When he was not writing satirical verse he could produce some eloquent lyrics, one of which, 'Autumn'—from *Adamastor* (London: Faber & Faber, 1930) p.91—appears to have provided the model for 'Cold Spring'.

8 Baxter is referring to the story in Book III of Virgil's *The Georgics* of the mares of the Lycian hero Glaucus—after he refused to allow his horses to breed, Venus so maddened them that they turned on their master and devoured him:

The moment the flame is kindled within their passionate flesh
(In spring above all, when warmth returns to their bones) the whole herd
Wheels to face the west wind high up there on the rocks;
They snuff the light airs and often without being mated
Conceive, for the wind—astounding to tell—impregnates them:
Over the rocks and cliffs then, and down the deep dales
They gallop scattering, not towards the east and the dayspring
But to the north and north-west
And where the south wind arises glooming the sky with cold rain.
(ll. 271–79, trans. C. Day Lewis.)

9 In fact five hundred copies of *Beyond the Palisade* were printed, but the delay at the binders was such that the books did not go on sale until late March 1945, giving Denis Glover enough time to return from the war and design the book's cover. See McKay's *Life*, p.82.

**In Retrospect**

The lady, Ezra, was not all unwilling.
I had entertained the proper flame
long enough for it to seem
technically durable.

The limitations of the feminine
were hers: is, was, and will be.
Not the desirable fourth tense. And yet
she had vivacity.

A kind of various passion
more satisfying, though less
symmetrical
than an infinite regress.

Nor was she ever solitary
in that world-wide and natural solitude
which is the rhyme and metre of a man:
World was a matrix though not understood.

My undefined recalcitrance
arose perhaps from a distaste for
embarkation on anything uncertain;
or the manly elusiveness of the matador.

Ardour was undoubtedly sufficient.
She spoke from bird-droppings and cloud
an omen of disquiet; a live landscape
in the turn of her head.

Each nerve an hawaian steel guitar
her smile strumming.
Did I sleep the dreamless and Ephesian sleep
I would waken at her coming.

Too great perhaps
the mood poetical
the interest of the photographer;
but in the main physiological.

Why then the abnegation?
A retention of virginity
a controlled immolation
on the altar of self-sufficiency.

[Hocken, MS 89/148]

## Epitaphs

### Epitaph for Any Man:

When young, obtuse, and vertebrate
I did not long repent my birth
That marred death's symmetry.
Time has adjudged me guilty.
Am reconciled to my estate;
And now the finest flower of death
But unrepentant yet.

### Epitaph for Any Woman:

Even while my lover dreamed
He had supplanted time for me
Love by love I numbered him
And stored him in my hollow heart;
So now for death's eternity
I hold his face of time without
Its masculinity.

### Epitaph for My Own Tombstone:

Beloved and unbeloved,
When I am name alone
Have lost both love and time
To glorify a name
Cut on the vacant stone:
Bend down and hear
With tilted human ear—
The name is sorrowing.

### Meditative Epitaph on All Beings:

Death for the dead is liberty.
Pain does not confine them;
Nor that uncertain future
Where death was insular.
Mountain and plain, the landscape of their lives
Undangerous now. Do lives
Not meet even in death?
Not so: no longer lives
But landscape only.

[Hocken, MS 89/148]

[Baxter kept a copy of his letter to the Armed Forces Appeal Board among his papers, and deposited it in the Hocken Library.]

**Baxter's Letter of Appeal**

Brighton,
Otago.

The Secretary,
Armed Forces Appeal Board.

Dear Sir,

I herewith append my statement in support of my appeal on conscientious grounds.

My objections to military service are based on conscientious and logical grounds. Though not belonging to the Society of Friends, I have attended Quaker schools both in New Zealand and in England: the Quaker religious teaching is fundamentally pacifist. My parents have brought me up to regard all wars as futile and immoral; my father was a conscientious objector in the last war and suffered for his convictions. Nevertheless, I have arrived at my present attitude in the main by independent thinking.

During a trip to Europe in 1937 and 1938 I had opportunity to observe people of various nationalities, including Germans. My experiences reinforced my belief that the differences between nationalities are slight and that War in any circumstances is no more justifiable than any other form of murder.

I was exempted from cadet training while attending secondary school. I became a member of the Peace Pledge Union at the age of 16.[1]

My conscientious objections are both religious and humanitarian. My logical objections are based on my knowledge of international politics and economics.

Yours faithfully,
James K. Baxter

1 An offshoot of the British Peace Pledge Union founded in the 1930s by Canon Dick Sheppard, which at the outbreak of World War II had 130,000 members. Like their British counterparts, members of the New Zealand Peace Pledge Union signed a declaration renouncing war, but the New Zealand movement never enjoyed the popular success of the British PPU.

# V
# CORRESPONDENCE: 1945–46

At seventeen a stoic pose is easy—
Stand up and face the mad God, brave and breezy—
At twenty years a trace of humour shows,
And pride goes slack, the Furies fat and lazy;
'Letter to Noel Ginn II' (unpublished version)

**Baxter to Ginn, 6 January 1945**

CENSORED
No. 5

Purakanui[1]
6/1/44[2]

Dear Noel,—

I never feel offended if you don't write, since I myself only write 'when the spirit moves me' and hate letters-of-duty. Thank you for this one, which I hope was not of the duty kind.

You are right about the 'blight man was born for'.[3] I am working on a farm here on the coast, am in excellent health, have stopped smoking. Start at 6, bring in the cows, milk, separate, feed calves pigs hens, clean byres etc. Breakfast about 9.0—a great event. 9.30–1 p.m. various jobs—sledging, flame-throwing, sawing wood, ploughing, sowing etc. 1 p.m. dinner. 2.0–6.0 various jobs. 6.0 tea. 6.30 milk, feed animals, chop wood. 8.30–9.30 to bed. There is plenty of looseness in the joints, but this is about the strength of it.

Well, though I am physically fit, browned, I retain 'the blight'. I used to think it was caused by modern living conditions: I begin to think it may be our intellectual heritage. Still, one can with luck sink into a sort of physical placidity, stop thinking, with sex as guiding star. But mind re-enters the arena, never content with the purely physical.

The family I am living with are Salvationist: their calmly-hummed hyms of voodoo blood-sacrifice appall me rather.[4] The father is dead. The mother aged about 60,

1 Purakanui, a small coastal settlement north of Dunedin, is near the farm on which Baxter worked briefly as a labourer.

2 It is clear from the contents of this letter that it was written in January 1945.

3 A reference to Gerard Manly Hopkins's poem 'Spring and Fall: to a young child' which concludes:

Nor mouth had, no nor mind, expressed
What heart heard of, ghost guessed:
It ís the blight man was born for,
It is Margaret you mourn for.

See also footnote 6 on p.255.

4 The sixth doctrine of the Salvation Army states:

> We believe that the Lord Jesus Christ has, by His suffering and death, made an atonement for the whole world, so that whosoever will may be saved. (From *The Song Book of the Salvation Army*, final page)

This doctrine is represented emblematically in the Salvation Army flag with its crimson background representing the cleansing Blood of Christ. Similarly the Army's motto 'Blood and Fire' refers to the Blood of Christ and the Fire of the Holy Spirit. Consequently the invitation to salvation, which is central to Salvation Army worship, makes much of the cleansing Blood of Christ (the Lamb of God) in such hymns as Elisha A. Hoffman's *Are You Washed?*:

Have you been to Jesus for the cleansing power?
Are you washed in the Blood of the Lamb?
Are you fully trusting in His grace this hour?
Are you washed in the Blood of the Lamb?
[*The Song Book of the Salvation Army*, Song 431]

intelligent, on the whole broad-minded, practical. Sons aged 22 and 19. 22 has a bad heart and turns to Salvationism. 19 is young for his years, eager for sex-instruction ~~who~~ of which his family appear to have given him no iota. Daughter aged about 16, rather like her mother, outwardly very orthodox, not very attractive except by dint of proximity.

Meanwhile I forget to thank you for *Trial of a Judge* the much-renowned. Fine poetry, by half-truths *almost* putting over the communist fundamentalism—God with faults, the Devil only a psychological case after all. Spender's great gift is the concrete lyrical interpretation of his own and others' thought-streams, not political objectivity.[5]

One must, I think, resolve one's mental and emotional anarchy to anarchism, before attempting to resolve objective anarchy. Truth and truth alone the sun. The touchstone for truth being reason? conscience? But it is no use trying to analyze the incalculable—as best expressed in poetry intellectually; in love, wonder . . . integrally. We analyze the fruit in our crucible and then complain that it is ashes in our mouths: perhaps this is a part of the 'blight' curable even now. D.H.L. thought so; himself never cured.

**[Sonnet of Unbelief]**

Voyaging from dark to murderous daybreak, each
Must hold the sky-cathedral on his shoulders
For bombs of desolation break the coping
And shall the god survive? Great love is danger;
May fall to greater loss. Light loves will teach
A fearless stature. Nor for what is ours
By nature need we thank; nor hear the groping
Who charted labyrinths now blasted wide to air.
Even the slow-grown orchard is not sure
And ferro-concrete rends. But not the monstrous
And steel bacteria in our blood swarming
Will wound outright: the crystal insecure
Breast-hidden shatters as the soft sky shatters.
Believers drown, leave sea-bred unfaith swimming.

I wrote this sonnet a few days ago.

By now you should have my photo. I meant to send you my book, but it dallies yet at the binders. I hope Terry got some presents: my Xmas arrangements were upset by my work here this year. By the way, the photo is a little unfair (vanity

5 Stephen Spender's *Trial of a Judge* (London: Faber & Faber, 1938) is his one foray into drama. A verse tragedy in five acts, the play deals with the dilemma faced by a liberal Spanish judge presiding in a Fascist regime. Under the law, he must convict both the brutal Fascist anti-Semitic murderers of an unarmed man, and a group of Communists who accidentally kill a policeman during a scuffle with Fascists. In so doing he is moved to condemn both parties: the Fascists for violating all principles of law and justice and the Communists for making a travesty of justice by creating and trying to enforce their own laws.

requires the explanation): I am not habitually hunched; nor do photos ever capture what depends on animation, colouring, expression.[6]

Follows another sonnet:

**[For us no saint]**

For us no saint wore shroud nor martyr burned
Who bear all martyrdoms conceived within us,
And who have fallen fearing the ravenous grave
To praise the impotent, revere the mad.
It was not from an angel Mary learned
Her Joseph-fathered infant death-rebellious:
At birth-pangs in strange terror and strange love
'Monster or god', she cried, 'monster or god.'

Some few have spoken of a visitation:
No flowers of miracle for us have blown.
Some few have borne the barren and unceasing
Lost hope of a celestial habitation:
Shall I regret an infancy outgrown?
We are not blessed and desire no blessing.

Not a pose, but harsh nevertheless.
And another, not alas a pose either.

**[From winter vials]**

From winter vials the dank and windy Spring
Draws rain, draws rain to rot the root in ground.
Hear my heart cry a madman in the rain:
I am wounded by the blade of my awareness.
(Cold birds fly over: but more sky than song.
Cloaked in manuka sleeps the barren land.)
I turn and my love's image lives again
Who will not leave me save for bones' bareness.

When I lie clear where the wind's locks are tangled
To hear the rainy voices pray for me
You only cry. O bird and snare of the woodland:
You are the beast within the burning jungle:
You are the spear that murdered Archimedes
Where he sat charting the world's face on sand.

6 See Baxter's portrait on the front cover.

Love and very best wishes
From
Jim.

For Terry,—
Since I have seen you, it's easier than before for me to think about you—as you now are, not as you were.[7] If it doesn't wear you down, you will be pretty hard when you come out. Well, I'll be very glad to see you: after all, in one way you are the same as me. Jock Tyson sends his very good wishes[8]
Much love
Jim.
PS

I bear as my insignia
the actor's pose the hermit's peace;
nor need I chiding word to say
that these are perilous.

Often have longed to stand
erect: but lied
to prove the world wilderness.
The soul in lies is justified.

I dare not speak fully
seeing that none love truth;
seeing that none shall love us save
for our insignia.

Your sonnet is poetry and excellent verse. Remember that you have a faculty for writing excellent verse, and thus whenever you need to write poetry you will be able to do that too. But as the warm haze that makes for poetry leaves one, one may have to make 'out of steel a song'[9] and maybe only excellent verse.
J.K.B
[VUW Library, MS McKay 28/49 & 28/22]

7 A reference to the visit Baxter and his mother made to Whitanui Camp to see Terence in late August 1944. See pp.112 and 373–4.
8 A friend of Terence's who shared his interest in boating.
9 Untraced.

**Baxter to Ginn, 19 February 1945**

CENSORED
No. 5

Brighton,
Otago.
19/2/44.[1]

Dear Noel,—

The heart's red-coats come. Despite three days of steady rain, I feel at peace and have so felt for some time. I have been considering 'Varsity and am not going back. You may look on this as a surface movement, but it is not[2]

A flower rises from the green sheath of Nature. It is easy to suppose that the tall-growing of the bud is the only birth which the flower suffers. But no: it must open and spread to the sunlight. If set under a box, the sun-seeking petals will close in again. As I see it the intellectual mind is a sensitive and shelled organism. But such men as my father, than whom none have greater integrity or peace of mind, have progressed further and become vertebrate, self-dependent without suffering. He was ploughman, road-contractor, and farmer. There is a great sanity comes when one is working with one's hands.

In the canyons made by gold-sluicing, one can see in the face the false or *maori* bottom which is often struck before bed-rock.[3] The intellectuals work efficiently and thoroughly above the *maori* bottom. Below is unacknowledged chaos. The bed-rock springs are rarely tapped.

You will find something of this in Tolstoy.[4] Anyway, why am I going to 'Varsity? For knowledge?—I can acquire for myself as much as my digestion will stand, not undigested slabs. For a good job?—It is what I am, not what I do, that matters. For prestige?—a barrier to sympathy.

Later I may write prose. At present I will work at manual labour, keep off drink (which is to the mind and emotions like pouring sand on a sea-anemone), sexually find my own way.

Your letter was a help to me. Terry is undoubtedly damaged; but will recover, by concentration on objective things.

Love and best wishes to yourself and Terry
From
Jim.

[VUW Library, MS McKay 28/34]

1 It is clear from the contents of this letter that it was written in 1945.
2 See p.113.
3 Baxter is conflating two terms coined by alluvial miners in the late 1800s to describe types of rock common to the mining claims of central Otago: 'white Maori' was used to refer to tungstate of lime, which occurs in large quantities in the Wakatipu district, while 'black Maori' referred to layers of hard, ferro-manganese pebbles, also found in the area. He may have picked up the term during his holidays among the gold claims at Naseby (see p.313).
4 See footnote 2 on p.273.

[Baxter was clearly troubled about his decision to stop attending university. 'Thoughts Concerning a Career,' which he later deposited in the Hocken Library, suggests that many of the reasons expressed to Ginn, Baigent and, presumably, his parents, were first worked out by him in private.]

**Thoughts concerning a career**

I do not wish to lose my religion. In nature, in the mere sight of the natural world, in looking over wide distances, I find a self-delighting peace. Similarly in the physical achievement and physical pride of work. This is the primary source of my poetry; and all that I know of a God I know from natural things. The shape and colour, the life of Nature, is the very stuff of poetry. And my knowledge of God is fundamental for my well-being.

At 'Varsity my mind is blurred and cramped. I am sensitive to the attitudes of those around me, and unconsciously absorb those attitudes: and at 'Varsity most are neurotic, even those whom one would least expect to be so, such as footballers.

One may say: all cultural activity is lost in manual labour. I have no liking for the absorption of undigested slabs of learning. I know now that later in life I will write prose and good prose. This will not be aesthetic prose, but rather realist. That is I will describe the life of people, ignorant so-called, but men and women nevertheless.

One may say: the chance of a 'good job' will be lost. I do not value monetary success: I value my own happiness. It is necessary to eat to live: so one must work. If one should marry, one must support a family. If I should marry, I would wish to be a balanced individual, not an 'intellectual'. I think I could support my family, in any case.

Briefly: if I am to be a writer, a good writer in the Tolstoyan sense as I know I can be, a 'career' is not my way to it. It is impossible for me to lose my culture; for that is fundamental. But I do not wish to be an intellectual, though I know comprehensively what it is to be one; I wish to be a sensitive and balanced adult. Daddy is this: and I have much of his nature in me. Mother has much of this; but women are rarely intellectuals, and she though cultured and intelligent is not one.

It is not the job I do, it is what I am that matters. I do not much fear death, poverty, or persecution such as that of the C.O.s I do greatly fear any loss of integrity in myself. Intellectuality demands a false bottom to the mind, a loss of emotional intuition. In this mechanist age one can accept, escape, or revolt. The cynical intellectual, such as the earlier Huxley,[1] accepts; the romantic intellectual, such as I would be, escapes from reality to aestheticism; the realist writer, such as I would wish to be, must revolt from contemporary modes and grow up on his own. Because of the reserves of strength which heredity and environment have given me, I can do this.

[Hocken, MS 975/50]

1 Aldous Huxley's (1894–1963) early polemical novels (in particular *Brave New World* (1932)) reflect his abhorrence of the twentieth century addiction to technology but can offer no alternatives, particularly as Huxley was sceptical of religious solutions.

**Baxter to Ginn, 8 April 1945**

CENSORED
No. 5

Brighton,
Otago
8/4/45.

Dear Noel,—

Thank you for your letter, helpful to the last degree. I sent you 6 copies of my book. Just write to Caxton Press (129 Victoria St., Ch.Ch.) if anyone wants any more. The account will be sent to them with the books.

On the whole it is balanced; must be lyrical, since my earlier poems were that essentially. Ones like IN CITY NIGHT give however a trace of 'things to come'. I am very satisfied with it. 500 were published altogether.

Stayed at Christchurch over Easter: with Lawrence Baigent the Caxton Press man. Saw Curnow. Also Douglas Lilburn,[1] who set my University song to music specially composed.[2]

Baigent had some cider: so I recited excellently, getting onto Faust eventually. '*Ugly hell gape not . . .*'[3] Drink often has the effect of an emotional upheaval on me;

1 Douglas [Gordon] Lilburn (1915– ), New Zealand's foremost composer, had been freelancing in Christchurch since 1941 as a composer, teacher, musician and music critic for the *Press*. He was closely involved with the Caxton Press group that included Denis Glover, Lawrence Baigent and Allen Curnow.

2 Baxter had composed the University Song about a month earlier, and he described the circumstances surrounding the poem's composition in some detail in a letter written to Lawrence Baigent on March 4:

> At present I live in the now nervily with a sense of heaviness, mainly because I drank a great deal of spirits three days ago. I had been down at University, was asked to write a new university song, not of the Here we are again . . . variety. Then called in at the pub, drank a little beer and discussed Hopkins and Chatterton. Met a medical student for whom once before I had written a poem to a girl;—he was delighted to meet me and requested another poem to another girl: gave me dinner: placed me upstairs in an armchair with a continual supply of rum and gin: and waited for the poem. After about 35 minutes and 14 glasses it arrived, good and pithy, epigrammatic I think. He was entirely satisfied and I wandered off to a dance bearing up bravely. Rather priggishly convinced a theologian that Jesus Christ drank fermented wine at the Last Supper. Succoured a damsel who was becoming bored with a swain drunker than I; acquitted myself valiantly but with little emotion. Eventually got to sleep at home.
>
> Next morning unhindered by intellect I produced the 'Varsity song to the tune of the musical Jerusalem. (VUW Library, MS McKay 19/3/19)

See 'University Song', p.504.

3 A reference to the final Act of *Doctor Faustus* by Christopher Marlowe (1564–93) where Faustus, having had Mephistopheles to command for twenty-four years, must now fulfil his side of the bargain and surrender his soul to the Devil:

*Thunder, and enter the Devils*
O, mercy, heaven, look not so fierce on me!
Adders and serpents, let me breathe a while!
Ugly hell, gape not. Come not, Lucifer!
I'll burn my books. O, Mephistopheles!
*Exeunt*
(5.2.82–5)

hence the Easter Sonnet in throes of hangover.[4] Song a day or two later.

I wish I could meet some of your camp friends. Will afterwards perhaps. So few people know poetry that I have become acclimatized to the dull weather of literature and sensitivity. Better where I am than at 'Varsity anyway: brain no longer raw-rasped. The *Letter* would never have been written but for you.

About comparison with moderns—*Fish in the unruffled lakes* is to me like something pure and strong, near at hand and yet unreachable.[5] Auden is a strange figure . . . gawky myth and deep symbolism side by side. Freud was not really much help to him.[6]

I would have sent Terry a copy; he can appreciate, I know. But deep down he reacts away from poetry: I think because it is betrayal of feelings, and involves myth of subliminal drama which is strong in him. You know Jung? In general he is one above Freud in my hierarchy.[7] . . .Perhaps Terry is different from what I feel. Tell me if you think he would like a copy for himself.

Your poems are good on the whole, in phrases especially. As—

> . . . The snake of sensitivity
> Jealous for his trancèd wilderness.

—

> . . . of hills sleeping before the fall.

—

and again:—

> With reed fingers on a mud abacus.

—

> The shrill marsh wind is rising.[8]

—

The last poem is most evocative. Noel, as you say of life, you need forms: in art also. If one doesn't care much about continuity but gets a few evocative lines or images and waits for them to breed, or even forces the pace—then one can fill in spaces with figures of speech (always with an eye to the main theme) till the form is

4 See 'Easter Sonnet', p.505.

5 Auden's poem 'Fish in the unruffled lakes / The swarming colours wear', which was written in March 1936, was first collected in *Look, Stranger!* (London: Faber & Faber, 1936) as poem XXVII.

6 Auden's father was a doctor with an interest in psychology and his son inherited the interest from him. By the early 1920s he had read a number of Freud's books and would use the information gleaned from them to analyse the motives and words of others. Richard Davenport-Hines argues in his biographical study *Auden*, that the poet played down the influence of his father on his verse, and played up the influence of his mother, because he 'was influenced too soon, and too profoundly, by Freudian theories' (p.26). The most potent poetical expression of Auden's interest in Freud is the poem 'In Memory of Sigmund Freud', which was first published in the *Kenyon Review* (Winter, 1940) and collected in *Another Time* (London: Faber & Faber, 1940).

7 Carl Gustav Jung (1875–1961) was the father of analytical psychology and Baxter was familiar with his work from his time at Otago University where he had been reading 'texts of Freud, Jung and Adler, not in potted versions, but in full' (*Life* p.72). Jung's stress on the value of myth, and his assertion that one must be aware of, and harness, both the conscious and unconscious aspects of the psyche appealed to Baxter, and Jungian concepts structure many aspects of his later critical essays on poetry (see footnote 2 on p.406). When Baxter left home for Christchurch at the end of 1947, one of his main reasons for going was 'to visit a Jungian psychologist' (*Life* p.100).

8 The poems by Ginn, from which Baxter quotes, are no longer extant.

perfect. It seems cheating not to write straight ahead; actually not so, poetry is like dreaming.

Give my love to Terry.

To you the same and all best wishes,

Jim.

PS You had better have the 36/- sent direct to Caxton.

[VUW Library, MS McKay 28/51]

**Song**

The winter of the soul is here
And outward winter need not be:
Pain lies not in the breathing air
Nor in each cool leaf-laden tree.
But she who strikes from hearts of stone
An answering murmur, dwells not nigh.
How shall I call my soul my own
Who cannot live and dare not die?
O come, love, come! for suns are kind
When thou art by them in their dance;
The moon that weary treads and blind
Lights heaven with thy countenance.
The flowers' red mouths will speak for me,
The very birds beseeching cry.
Live not alone in memory:
O break my winter, or I die!

[Hocken, MS 704/14: 862, p.10]

**Ginn to Baxter, 22 April 1945**

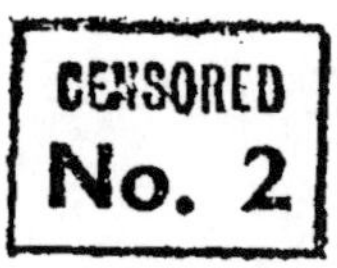


Detention Camp
Whitanui
via Shannon
22/4/45.

[Could you send any of my books on 17th C
—one of the chaps is studying his period]

Dear Jim—

One criticism of your book came to the camp in a letter & was fairly disappointing—the authentic voice of the 40s, but full of the defeat & hopelessness of the times, still the poet is young & may eventually have something to offer. That is a rough precis of the gist of it.

This sort of rubbish was quite upsetting. On looking through one can get the note of 'youth forever slain', in practically all except title poem, obviously in Psalm of Defeated (which could have been omitted) & by sort of half inference in most. But the crit is quite irrelevant particularly on the political angle. It was good to hear various ones in the camp feel that the crit was unjust. 'Boys Laugh at Ease' & 'Killing of a Rabbit' & to lesser extent 'Hawk & Hare' were considered the less successful poems. The device of a 'man the hawk & man the hare' moral ending was also pointed out as an uninteresting trick.

'Death of a Swan' is considered probably the best of the collection. The theme of pride in the letter poem some consider false & are a bit fearful what such a strain will develop. I found it disquieting at the time if you will remember. But above all, everyone admires the sureness of touch in the lyrics.

Auckland friends (of varsity & such circles) have not seen your book. Apparently they are now getting on to it. Do you object to a review being published in the Akd varsity rag? If you do I'll let them know—from indications it will be favourable. While I said to go ahead knowing you can take the criticism they are hanging back for your OK.[1]

Terry had to find an autograph much to his disgust—he won't look at modern poems I showed him but I gave him 'The golden lemon is not made' which he liked immediately.[2] He likes Campbell's 'Choosing a mast' too.[3]

A friend who is very good at acting has always wanted to write poetry & the other day produced his first—he broke the ice which is the hardest thing to do. In my enthusiasm (now three of us are trying our hand at the game) I wrote this straight off—usually they take some thinking out.

**Unto Us**

Intransigent, Kevin, the wild earth
Rolls under the swans that fly at Helicon;
Intractable, Kevin, in strange wilful mirth
Her hunger cry goes forth, and on
The sea-glimpse nest we spy her cradling myth.

The whirling point that knots the terrible clay,
The ears of thunder in their ecstacy
Shudder at this drawling natal day.
A quiet tongue murmuring linguistically
And the wild swans that slowly wing away

1 I have not located a review of *Beyond the Palisade* in the Auckland University Students' Association magazine *Craccum*.
2 Untraced.
3 See footnote 7 on Roy Campbell, on p.386. Campbell's 'Choosing a Mast' was first collected in *Flowering Reeds* (London: Boriswood, 1933) pp.29–31.

Kevin's second was more succesful—I won't quote all but find the end exceedingly good.[4]

When from my adolescent hills
Comes shyly-wondering thought:
Sharp-edged, shapeless—and I
Hope-flushed flex mallet-arm—
First callow cautious stroke find always
Rock—rubble . . . crumbling . . . crumbling . . .
Clay through my clenched hands;
Dust in my mouth—
And on the air a sad sour smell . . .

And think:
Once when thoughts were young;
By a gay green sea—
I even dared to touch a tree!

This chap is Irish—extremely likeable shy though sociable & modest above all.

Des whom I have mentioned before, after the impetus of a love-affair with all its promise, has burst out into much verse lately much to my barren envy. I pick out 3 of the best.[5]

Ascetic mind has sat in jurisdiction,
Appraised the crime, assessed the consequence and cost,
And though the avid chamber sits agape
At erudition that forensic tongue so plausibly displays,
The crass duplicity of craven lust
Impinges on the hermet nerve of truth
And body quickly knows the pain is guilt.

Yet never will the fatal verdict fall
While love's fond jurymen are courted by
The pressed and perjured witness of my heart.

—

Behind insomniac and furtive hand
A petulant nostalgia inspires
A sequel to the story: you expand
Upon the acreage of night, and choirs
Of rural wishes gloze the parish ear,
Convert the urban doubter and deny
The logic of the atheistic fear,
Redeeming orphan dream of you and I.

4 A reference to Ginn's friend Kevin Mulrennan, see footnote 1 on p.280.

5 Des Dubbelt—see footnote 1 on p.280.

The tap of credence turned, the legend flows
And fills and flushes senses to the tips;
The sieve of love retains the myth; it goes
Distilled into the stream where wonder runs.

The small nocturnal murmur on your lips
Is a child's, a challenge: if you choose, a son's.

**Sea-Piece**

Perhaps the green chime of a tide can plunge
Down to the silted bed and flush the sand
From out the coral eyes, adapt its range
To music-broken capes and there resound
    Throughout the lunar thrust.

Even a fin's cold oar might print the prized
And rusted mollusc with a lick of light,
A scud of tail let filter the pearl-praised
And gull-scraped echoes into caves alert
    Beyond their dim mouths' mist.

I know the sea will always batter back
My voice into the drowning lungs or let
The song be current-caught and often lost
Upon an ice-flow or a breaker's beak;—

Or be, storm's debris, beached by the last
    Lonely wave and least.

He has a lovely line in one poem referring to the surf

and leaves
The white lips hungry in the helpless bay.

The sea attracts him—particularly Full fathoms five[6]—it speaks more to him than almost any other lyric.

Would you please give some kind of criticisms of these poems for them.

Have been studying very hard for a project. Played a bit of cricket this autumn—

6 Song from Shakespeare's *The Tempest* sung by the spirit Ariel to Ferdinand, the son of the King of Naples, who believes his father to have drowned in the storm that wrecked their ship:

Full fathom five thy father lies,
Of his bones are coral made;
Those are pearls that were his eyes;
Nothing of him that doth fade,
But doth suffer a sea-change
Into something rich and strange.
(I.2.397–402)

lately a few hockey sticks have arrived & I have been keen at the practice runs.[7]

Cheerio
Noel.

Terry doesn't want a book.
I have preferred Jung as more reasonable than Freud.

[Hocken, MS 975/183]

**Baxter to Ginn, 1 May 1945**

CENSORED
No. 3

Brighton,
Otago.
1/5/45.

Dear Noel,

Thank you for news of criticism. I object to 'authentic voice of 40s' for only lately have I been world-aware. Indeed, from 15 to 17 (from which period comes most of *Beyond the Palisade* ) I only knew at times that there was a war on. And, truthfully, who can in honest and sincere introspection be soulfully optimistic? Here are a few phrases that come to mind in self-defence:—

// you would prefer byzantine ornament
To grecian cliché.

—

the poet is a sport in the evolutionary line, must to survive share as much of the normal man-ape's psychology as possible.

—

better to err with Burns and Byron than fall in line with Brasch.[1]

—

—All a bit unnecessary maybe. But my vanity is easily pricked. The pride theme by the way is pretty basic with me: atavistic ancestor-worship, but very satisfying poetically.

They have ploughed the night with the bones of their breast
and reaped peace:

I say quite without humour; being 2/3rds Highland Celtic with a dash of Welsh gratis.

7 Ginn had played hockey when he was a student at Victoria University College, see p.38.

1 An earlier variation on this phrase occurs in Baxter's letter to Lawrence Baigent of 16 Nov 1944: 'in exuberance I would rather err with Burns and Byron than remain firm with Arnold' (VUW Library, MS McKay 19/3/3).

O.K. for the Akd. Varsity rag review. Send me a copy if you get a chance.

Your poem, like so many of yours, seems to me to have excellent phrases but be not quite crystallized. I lean to the belief that if one only feels unifying emotion once in 10 yrs one need only write one poem in 10 yrs.—Sexual feeling has the advantage of lasting emotionally for at least a week, time enough for 7 great lyrics.

Kevin's is certainly good; a bit mannered for a beginning.

> Clay through my clenched hands;
> Dust in my mouth—
> And on the air a sad sour smell.

Very fine, especially the first line.

Certain phrases of Des are most powerfully evocative.

> The small nocturnal murmur on your lips
> Is a child's, a challenge: if you choose, a son's.

So direct, yet subtle. He seems able to manage word-music. And

> Upon an ice-flow or a breaker's beak.

His poetry is unusually masculine. *White lips* are in no way passionless in that line. Faults lie, as ever, in the laboured parts.

The Sea is the symbol of the collective unconscious. It appeals to all of us to sink into its depths.[2]

Please send me more of your own poems, or anyone else's in the camp that seem to you as good as those of this last letter.

I see faint hopes, Noel, of a new verse-efflorescence for myself. The images might even flow truthfully and easily. After all, I have only quarried painfully in childhood and adolescent stone. If I could acquire a bit more insensitivity, I might even eventually gain something of the standpoint of Burns. Well, all these are hazes.

At present I am in good health, have had nothing to drink for a week or two. My sexual thoughts turn to proletarian womenhood, but it is stony ground for any but animal emotion. And I have written all my *Better beast or unborn . . .* poems.[3]

Still, here is one poem. Try for the mood—which is not mannered.

> One never knows which way the wind will blow:
> Scattering ashes on a sackcloth earth.
>
> Or tempest howling, howling nightlong.
> The purple clouds massing against the wind.

2 In Jungian psychology the collective unconscious is the deeper domain of the unconscious division of the psyche that owes its existence totally and exclusively to heredity. Jung believed that the collective unconscious differed from the personal unconscious by having contents and modes of behaviour that are nearly the same everywhere in all individuals. In *The Fire and the Anvil: Notes on Modern Poetry* (Wellington: New Zealand University Press, 1955) Baxter develops, in distinctly Jungian terms, his idea of the sea as a symbol. See his essay 'Symbolism in New Zealand Poetry' on pp.56–78.

3 See the final stanza of 'Each', p.491.

One never knows: when I was a child still
It blew me once a shower of acid.

And when my heart was cleanly eaten out
I plucked a crocus, hid it in the wound.

In spring it flowers. One would not know the difference.
All things put on its curious amber colour.

And lately I have learned to hear it only:
Whispering, rising oracular from ground.

But now is winter: and my heart is winter.
Bare only, hearing only the frozen wind.

Love to Terry, wish I could see him just now.
Love and best wishes
Jim.
[VUW Library, MS McKay 28/52]

**Baxter to Ginn, 23 June 1945**

CENSORED
No. 2

Brighton,
Otago.
23/6/45.

Dear Noel,

I looked carefully in all the bookshops down here, but it seems they havent got *The Possessed.*[1] I'm sorry not to have written or sent the books you wanted—the *Bank Holiday on Parnassus*[2] will go with this letter—but I lost your last letter. Was it 17th-century books? I mean to send back those you lent me last year: they were a help to me then, but I have fallen back on Burns and the Bible. The only thing is, perhaps you will be out soon, then I could send it straight to you, not leave them with your people.

Your sonnet was most excellent—*And gather the crops our bent patience yields* is perfect ending,[3] indeed the whole poem compares well with some of Shakespeare's.

1 Fyodor Mikhaylovich Dostoyevski (1821–81) wrote *The Possessed* (also known as *The Devils*) in 1871–72. The novel's savage attack on a radical younger generation of Nihilists was sparked off by a political murder. Although Dostoyevski overstates the political significance of the Nihilists, *The Possessed* proved to be a frighteningly accurate prophecy of many of the events occurring during the Bolshevik revolution.

2 See footnote 4 on p.350.

But of course I can't tell you to 'go on with it': it is the unifying emotion that makes any poem. The other one has an admirable facility—though *bass* seems rather jarring as a rhyme.

I am doing well enough at the foundry—a source of material income if not of aesthetic. £2/6/3 minus 7/6 busfare. Rise of about 10/- in a week's time when I am 19. Plus about 10/- from expected results of union agitation. Plus a few shillings from a shift from store-work to range-fitting.[4]

Still, I will get away to a farm in the spring.[5] My mind is clear, as I am not drinking; but hard, maybe a bit cynical, no disadvantage. I read Huxley's *Ends and Means* lately: a lot of fine thinking there, some strained by Huxley's own experience.[6]

Did I send you this poem?

> The dank stooks stand upon the harvest-field;
> From seas of crosses and blue hills of death
> Falls an avenging ghost, tobacco-wreath.
> But her eyes smile: her race is a bronze shield.
>
> Deep sightless waters and the cliff-beating sun;
> Where flowers grow, precarious and gold
> Or skirt a river of childhood through the fold
> Of that sad mountainous landscape always mine.
>
> O why the earth forever rank with rain?
> Why the mild pasture? I shall never break
> From these the mountains of maternal grief
> Till blind sea rises and devours me down.
>
> So build a niche by sea-beleaguered rock
> Where flowers kiss and the loud free birds laugh.

I hope we will be seeing Terry soon. It will be adults meeting each other, strangers except for the deep discomfort and deep ties of shared experience—for me shared

3 No longer extant.

4 Baxter worked at the iron rolling mill in the Dunedin suburb of Green Island for some months in 1945. McKay discusses his time there in *Life* p.86 and Baxter gives a fictionalised account of the work in *Horse*, pp.13–22. Terence Baxter also recalled his brother's work at the mill:

> when he worked in the steel works he worked pretty hard there, and I know the type of work he was on, I knew some of the men that worked there, and they were pretty hard men. Terrible work, and hot in the summertime, these great big red-hot things were coming out of the furnace and they had to drag them along the floor. It was dangerous work, he was lucky not to be burnt there and scarred for life. You had to know what you were about. And for a young man to just come along there like that and work with the others took a bit of doing. And unfortunately of course—this might have been what started him off with his drinking—at the end of the day they'd go along to the pub in Green Island there and get a fair few beers down. (Interview with Paul Millar, Dec 1995)

5 McKay records, on p.86 of *Life*, that Baxter 'left the foundry for a job at Wanaka station, in Central Otago, arriving on the evening of Monday 17 September'.

6 Aldous Huxley (see footnote 1 on p.398) expounds non-violent ways to deal with a violent world in *Ends and Means: An Enquiry into the Nature of Ideals and into the Methods Employed for their Realisation* (London: Chatto & Windus, 1937).

birth. We will slide into some form of community. And perhaps I will see you, whose mind I already know as well as one can know a strange country.[7]

All best wishes
From
Jim.

PS Read *Music and Memory* again. 2nd verse worthy of good 'Byron' yet your own. Cut out the last verse and it is very fine, indeed shows genius.[8]

[VUW Library, MS McKay 28/53]

**Baxter to Ginn, 14 July 1945**

CENSORED
No. 1

Brighton,
Otago.
14/7/45.

Dear Noel,

There is some truth in what Terry says about me writing a cold letter. Unless actually brimming over with physical energy, and even then, I seem to have an emotional inertia that only poetry or infatuation can break. And so much is inexpressible or imperfectly known that it is easier to write clearly and coldly than to explore that forbidding jungle which we call emotion. But I'll quote the sestet of a sonnet to Terry:

> I dreamt once you were drowned and woke crying.
> And now you are drowned: not in the violent sea
> Of high explosive, but shut to rot in a tub.
> Now you are a man with a hard face I am hearing.
> For you the shut horizon. You are part of my blood:
> Thus the intolerable ache of consanguinety.[1]

The 'ache' is in part a feeling of guilt at having been too narcissist to have tried to understand Terry. One cannot ever divorce oneself from those who are part of one's growth. Yet can one's feelings for them ever be as direct and uninvolved as for strangers? Why could a man not marry his foster-sister, no blood-relation? Mainly, I think, because of the intense ambivalence of feeling lying between them like a mountain-range.

7 See pp.120–2 concerning the release of Noel Ginn and Terence Baxter from Whitanui Detention Camp.
8 No longer extant.
1 See 'To my Brother', p.63.

I will try for the 'Possessed' again. Meanwhile present you with Curnow's anthology. A fine Introduction, justifying its own extensity.[2]

Faulkner's 'Sartoris' I know has not nearly the poetry and punch of his 'Light in August'.[3] 'Dubliners' I found slight though excellently written, as you did.[4]

Here is your book-list, complete I hope. A Grammar of Present-Day French-Mansion / Moliere's Femmes Savantes / Skeat's Primer of English Etymology / The Age of Shakespeare I—Seccombe and Allen / Sydney's Defense of Poesy / The Tempest / Introducing Shakespeare—G.B. Harrison / Woodworth's Psychology / Phonetics Practice Book / Les Poetes Francais du XIXe Siecle—Auzas / Rey's French Composition / Coleridge's Essays and Lectures on Shakespeare / 'Everyman' and 8 miracle plays / Spenser's Faery Queene Book I.

I am glad you like my sonnet. Perhaps dream-poems always make or wake a kindred mood; as Kubla Khan.[5] Here is another sonnet.

**[Was it as children?]**

Was it as children that we found a cave
In those green fields, and lost our way for ever
From the straight poplar paths that led us home
To childish rest and the child's night of peace ?
So thus like children lost, we could but grieve
In iron earth concealed, where the cold river
Of underworld regret runs loud as doom
Mocking with pain the day's remembered face.
Remains for the grown man his childish vain
Intolerable dream of that rich land
Where down the golden rippling aisles of barley
Walk our most dearly loved for wind's caress,
Where blind mouths meet, where bitter blood grows kind
And the stone heart unfolds to rose of peace.

And this.

2 Allen Curnow ed., *A Book of New Zealand Verse: 1923–45* (Christchurch: Caxton, 1945). See p.108.

3 William Faulkner's novel *Sartoris* (1929), set in Mississippi, tells the tale of two families: the wealthy Sartoris family and the landless white Snopeses family. Faulkner's portrayal of the Snopeses is both an examination of the negative aspects of the new generation of Southerners and a representation of the perennial face of human nature. See also footnote 5 on p.324 and footnote 2 on p.360.

4 James Joyce's first major published work was a collection of short stories called *The Dubliners* (1914). In these stories Joyce first began developing his epiphanic technique in which experiences that are apparently trivial are used to present to the observer deep and true insights.

5 Samuel Taylor Coleridge (1772–1834) first published his poem 'Kubla Khan; a Vision in a Dream' in 1816. The published poem was reportedly the first few lines of a more substantial work of some two to three hundred lines that Coleridge had composed while in an opium-induced sleep. However, the remaining lines were 'lost' when Coleridge was interrupted before he had finished transcribing the complete poem.

**Too many winters**

Too many winters come
with ice and wind eternal
till the heart cries for the womb
for sleep perpetual.

Where our love walked in summer
turning the fiery sheaves
blind broken branches stare
iron and shorn of leaves.

O let me lie in stone
like hills barren and blind
till love seem bird alone
upon the icy wind.

And more ambitiously.

**Ruth**

An hour in that warm field where Ruth the stranger
    baring her breasts like apples to the sun
    rose from her gleaning; and the golden corn
    was heaped in sheaves and winnowed: was the air
    unmoved by desert wind ? or did one star
    fall down the night's abyss flashing unseen
    when she pressed underfoot the brittle grain
    lay down by Boaz on the threshing-floor?
And when he turned at midnight from his sleeping
    in fear and heard her indrawn breath and cast
    an arm through darkness to her shoulder groping:
    in that close night how could they preremember
    David the herdsman captain and the singer
    or Absalom coughing his blood at last.

Also.

When I was neither child nor man
    I met you and you smiled at me

Half-grown and earnest as a child
    I blushed and my lungs trembled

It was too hard to grow
    five years in a day, show love unmasked

And that strange jewel in the heart
unbroken word birth spoke to me

When I was neither child nor man
I met you and you smiled at me

And deeper than Kaitangata
you're buried like the rending coal
alas to burn alas to light
unknowingly the cloud by day
the fire by night.

Another sonnet: here I write as I did when I was 15, controlledly now.

**Sonnet of Allegiance**

When I forgotten blood and bone discerned
how could I leave them hungering on the street
for real or paradisal bread and meat ?
and live among the sated unconcerned
in their sea-urchin citadel; or beat
a cymbal while through hills once summer-sweet
on crops the mortgage like a cancer burned.

And where upon the sandy foundry-floor
beside the crackling sparks and hissing vein
the moulders standing grey-faced in the glare:
was the loud furnace then that dark volcano
whose voice is heard, whose eyes are never seen
under the mountain-slag of years and snow ?

And this last, clear emotion.

O love, in the island day
I am tall like a tree
And you who are tender
And young to bear
Death's everlasting sun
That shone from birth on me:
I will shade my boughs about you
And shield you from his staring
I will give you my heart springs
And ask for nothing.

I am sorry I took it for granted that you would appeal. Can see clearly your point of view and sympathise.[6]

6 Ginn's reasons for initially refusing to appeal against his sentence are outlined on p.121.

With love and best wishes to you and Terry
Jim
[VUW Library, MS McKay 28/54]

[Noel Ginn was one of the first to review *Beyond the Palisade*. His review was published in the periodical *The Arts in New Zealand* in late 1945, as follows.]

**'Beyond the Palisade'**
A consideration of the verse of James K. Baxter by N.G.

Because of an uncommon gift for self-revelation in her work, the reputation and legend of a fragile poet, one of our most mature, will accumulate. This is the year in which Mary Ursula Bethell has died. And with thoughts of death-change one comes closer not only to the past in which our young tradition was born but to the continuing present through which it must move and evolve. So we observe with satisfaction the advent of a new poet. A colony, and such culturally is New Zealand, takes many generations to create an emotional environment that can nourish the poetical nature, for poetry cannot be produced in a vacuum; native poetry at the best is a tender plant growing on harsh ground. Thus it is with curiosity that is nationally self-conscious that we look at the work of our newest and youngest poet. In it may lie limitations and hints of our literature to be.

The result is at once unexpected and exhilarating. In our midst is suddenly heard, we believe, the voice of authentic poetry—confident, daring and unpredictable, even disconcerting as new values and creative force must always be. One becomes immediately aware of a new voice, speaking, singing, with its own fully developed idiom and manner:

> Fell the wild swan: from havenless crags of sky
> Fell to no cool lagoon of summer flocks
> But bruising river-ice: she fell to die
> Beside a winter shore and wolfish rocks . . . [Death of a Swan]

This essentially lyric strain is to be maintained throughout with an infallible touch, and such is rare to-day. For most who would express themselves in this age poetry has proved too large a vehicle: the phrase has ousted the word; concentration on our own epoch has pinched the range of consciousness; subjectivity, the bizarre, the odd these are poor substitutes for vitality and clarity which spring from emotion. Great emotion, controlled, will never ultimately be obscure; it is the source and fountain-head of art. And truth, factual and scientific, is not a criterion for poetry. If it were, poetry should be shorn of its adornments and aids to remembrance and transferred to simple prose. It is emotionally significant statement which is artistic truth. Emotion is the soul of poetry; assonance and alliteration accentuates it; rhyme ensures its flow, but it is emotion that gives it vitality. When Mr Baxter writes

The wind that buffets me
Is part and voice of those
Undying things of fixity
That bloom and blossom in the rose
And from Man's pathway flee. [Under a Sun]

much more than a statement of man's ephemerality before the endurance of space, time, matter and spirit combined, is conveyed. There is a strong emotion of an easily communicable texture. The mood has been caught and fixed as music is held by a record.

The relevance of his assertion:

Thus among men I move my tap-roots wide
The roots of verse, the roots of life beside, [Letter to Noel Ginn]

is immediately confirmed as regards his verse. Not only has he cast his net wide among the moderns—Auden, Eliot, Yeats, Hopkins, and many others have yielded ore—but he has also sunk a shaft deep into the older veins of English literature:

The Lie is planted, the lie will flourish
The Lie will sprout as a poison tree
Truth relegated the poorest parish
Will starve in secret, in secret die . . .

derives fairly closely from Blake. Elsewhere it is less easy to indicate origins of influence; assimilation has been too thorough a process. On the other hand the writer is so far from being a derivative that he is able to proceed with quite bold and fruitful experimentation. 'Prelude from New Zealand' is a feat of technical virtuosity—rhymed syllabic verse is a very difficult accomplishment and incidentally excellent poetry. In 'Hill Country' he exploits assonance and rhyme to the utmost limit; it is clever writing though not entirely successful, the effect being jerky and machine-like; it winds down to a stop halfway through a line:

Here stay, deep in clay
Sun-clay, water-clay
Gouged-out, gaping clay
Clay.

But the most daring poem, technically and imaginatively, is 'Rain-Ploughs'—in sonnet form plus a coda. The sonnet is a hard form to handle; too massive for anything slight it repays the poet enormously with a sense of achievement and architectural solidity. It is composed in the manner of Hopkins, packed and charged with imagery, quick music, and condensed syntax, so as to mount to a climax which needs the coda to round off . . .

And serpents grey-jawed drift and raven

The serpents are mists. One recalls the passage in Forster's novel, *The Longest Journey* where the clouds descended and visibly embraced the earth and the earth itself brought forth clouds. But here all is being washed away and destroyed by the storm demon who has power to force the djinn back whence he has escaped. We cannot force him back to the jar—rather must we work with nature to

> Brave djinn and monster, green again the land.

But New Zealand can only take such concentrated poetry in small doses.

That the tap-roots have moved among men and through life is not so apparent from the poems. But the prome of development in experience is large. In such poems as 'O Lands seen in the Light of an Inhuman Dawn' and 'In City Night' there is a sense of the country, an imaginative vision of the community as a whole extending through the range of ordinary experience:

> The slick and gay are not at the foundations.
> Could we forget the sorrow, and forget
> The parent-god of childhood conversations
> (In brief, be heartless as the marionette)
> Then were reflected love in the city night,
> Each tower a negress swaying thighs of jet.

[*The Arts in New Zealand*, 17.5, Sep–Oct (1945) pp.17–19]

**Baxter to Ginn, 11 December 1945**

Brighton,
Otago.
11/12/45.

Dear Noel,

It's mighty good to know you're out at last.[1] I guess you're bound to feel rather alienated from the general flow. Still you'll find loss of dogmatism a help in understanding people; Terry is much the same. Pacifism need not be a dogma, though. Simply a matter of identification with the sufferer, an instinctive reaction for the sensitive: I now believe art has a similar basis. Empathy of a kind. I see you have the same feeling—'care for the other must always be the first consideration'. What other morality is natural or needful. It seems to me an undue arrogance to suppose that our brief hates and loves or lusts must have a cosmic significance. Anyway, Nature is pretty easy-going, and can show her working models while I have never seen and never wish to see an angel. We need a primitive or at any rate anarchistic society where no one's social conscience can get out of hand and hypothecate divine guidance.

1 Although both Noel Ginn and Terence Baxter had by this time been released, they were required to work for a time as 'manpowered' labourers at the Gear Meat works in the Wellington suburb of Petone. See pp.121–2.

I am so glad *Sestina* moves you; for I believe it the best thing I've written.[2] Here are some of the poems I've written lately. 'Prometheus' not entirely consecutive, but with depth. PTO

'In honour of all beasts' rather incomplete. 'Fathers and strangers' a trial on the unfamiliar ground of broad rhetoric. 'Lamentation' unsuccessful maybe. 'The Antelopes' a created dream. 'Sailor Song'—Fabre and his caterpillars (1st line last verse.)[3] 'Lazarus' written with difficulty. 'O my darling'—love-poem with little factual foundation. 'Poem to Rimbaud'—written today.

Your own images seemed to have insufficient root, as Curnow's often do. I am sure if I was writing in association with you, that I could *cure your ills of the water with a one-coloured calm*. Not necessarily a political verse-play, but we could talk over such things.

I'll be working at the freezer or fruit-picking for some time. But will keep in touch with you. Couldn't you come down this way? If Terry comes down, anyway.[4]

Thank you very very much for that review in *Arts in N.Z.* A most exhilarating effect it had on me. You are over-complimentary but naturally my ego swells.

Have not been smoking for a week and no beer for some time. I flourish and feel astonishingly stable. Come out more or less on top in the obscure conflicts with my parents. Steady rain the last 3 days.

Love from

Jim.

[VUW Library, MS McKay 28/55]

**Prometheus**[1]

Now as the west wind changes comes the rain;
And cloud-darkness over ranges cast
Wakens the mountain voices once again
And from the arms of night a murdered past.

2 Baxter had written two sestinas around this time and it is not entirely clear which one he is referring to as he classified both poems as 'S' for 'sure' (see pp.79–80 for a description of his classification system). The earlier of the two—'To L.A. Baigent'—seems more assured and immediately personal than the second—'Man and Woman', and Baxter, when mentioning the second poem to his mother in a letter written on Labour Day 1945, is fairly measured in his assessment of it:

> Here is a *sestina*, in dialogue as with Sir Philip Sidney. His was a pastoral *sestina*, rather thin. Mine has a lot more body and ease of writing I think. (Hocken, MS 975/184)

Both poems are reproduced in Appendix 2

3 Jean Henri Casimir Fabre (1823–1911) was a French entomologist who earned considerable acclaim for his painstaking studies of the anatomy and behaviour of insects, although he was ultimately suspect for his refusal to accept Darwinism. Baxter may be referring to Fabre's chapter on 'The Cabbage-Caterpillar' in his book *The Wonders of Instinct: Chapters in the Psychology of Insects*, trans. Alexander Teixeira De Mattos and Bernard Miall (London: T, Fisher Unwin Ltd., 1918) pp.289–317. In this chapter Fabre describes various experiments with caterpillars, including dissections and exposure to attacks by parasites.

4 Ginn spent a fortnight with the Baxter family over the Christmas holiday period in 1945–46. See pp.122–3.

1 The poem 'Prometheus' published in *BWF* is a portion of this longer poem. In the draft version in MS Book XIV Baxter has indicated the stanzas published by enclosing them in square brackets (see stanzas 10–16).

The wind that moved the tapestry is dead.
And I remember, riding round my sheep
The day I staring in a furnace said
O love lies buried under abyss of sleep.

The fits and whims of weather mar our year
Whose lives are momentary pain and peace:
Summer is not the faithful season here
And island day remains at darkness' lease.

Yet hawks over the valley hang and soar,
And in dry shingle soughing poplars strike,
And the green willows flourish on lakeshore,
And mountain breezes ripple on the lake.

Earth in her morning mildness made this land
But now is sultry noon: and I contentless
Where so midsummer and midwinter blend
Spend in small coin my sum of tenderness.

One sang and swore, his arm about my shoulder
~~When~~ As I walked drunken under a drunken sky;
And his *I love you* moved me more than her
Who seemed the green sap, the bird's cry.

And one could read the question in my eyes
And smiled and took me to her bed at midnight
And slaked my thirst with her smooth lips and thighs
And held me sleepless in her arms till daylight.

The marrowbone was never priest nor king.
Villon they say chose drunkards' company—
Though his heart trembled like a fiddle-string
For what has never been nor yet shall be.

Madmen may draw the angels from the sky.
The rose, the diamond, and the unicorn
Have left me now for the heart's reedy cry,
While from a drunken darkness peace is born.

[Here are the emblems of perpetual day
Where the bronze horses standing in a field
Lean on the wind and graze the hours away
Eden yet green for them and earth their shield.

Who have grown used to deserts and the skulls
Of anguished men, they do not fear the wind

Nor ready scorpion, but that those walls
Of old despair will break and unknown floods befriend.

Some in the ageless sea their eyes have drowned
And wander blind: likewise when overhead
The sharp stars burn, my seeking heart once found
Infinity within, and died defeated.

*Who told us then that all things living share*
*Content and ecstasy without a name?*
The mystic dreaming of a mountain where
God the great lioness at last is tame.

Prometheus bleeding on the cross of time
O raise your eyes where the great waters flow
And breathe and hear night's cloudy torrent chime
From those immortal citadels of snow.

Soon shall the mad mnemonic crow take rest
The peace of night is yours when earth receives
Her vain and wandering children to that breast
Where no man strives nor loves, and nothing grieves.]

4/11/45

II–III (And I will celebrate the stink of rotten sheep;
Not rank with death like incense at a funeral
But sharp, the rain's companion, dark like sleep
Riding the wind and like the wind perpetual.)
[Hocken, MS 704/14: 899, pp.65–8]

**In honour of all beasts**

Let us repent from now and live and die
Like animals who know not how nor why.

The lust of cattle never was obscene
The tiger's cruelty not proud nor mean.

But rottenness on which the fathers feed
Must cord the children's bellies till they bleed.

And women bear for their deep love's foundations
The bargaining virtue of ten generations.

Let us admire a while the gentle deer
And the chaste bitch in heat three times a year.

The hairy ape too sensitive to pain
Cries for the death he cannot find again.

I watched once by the slow stream a thrush
Laying her mottled eggs in nesting bush.

So clear the sky and deep, it seemed to me
Time could not break the wordless ecstasy.

But snow and storms out of the ruinous north
Descend on all that summer has brought forth.

And though the green heart burns, and can well laugh
Over a mad child's bones, and cenotaph:

Yet deep within, the word older than birth
Cries it were good to sink in sodden earth;

Live without strategy, and fail and die
Like the mild beasts who know not how nor why.
[Hocken, MS 89/148]

**Fathers and Strangers**

Fathers and strangers, you with exile dreams
Who met the land masked in your wrestlers' thew
And saw the bushtrack and the burning blue
Bathed yet in memory's nocturnal streams.

You cannot reach nor understand your sons.
Too long the bitter sky has stared upon our sleep;
The sombre macrocarpas huddle steep
About our springs of love, and the gale stuns.

Were you trees once under an easy sun?
Men may like trees grow, but never stone.
The stone sky and the mountains bear on bone
Forever alien till death knit all as one.

Your fires and women hid you from the blind
Chaotic fever of the elements.
We have accepted them, and discontent:
The grey wind at our bidding blows more kind.

Though they were once our legendary hope
Cloudy Arcadias are broken by
The sentence of clear sun's impartial eye
And fear-corroded pinions lose their scope.

We should find peace in marrowless routine
Cracking our jokes upon an office stool
With sundays in the country and a girl—
Could heart but shed her cruel evergreen.

You bore the brunt of poverty: so built
Not as we build who see the grass grow over
Our towers and reservoirs, and hawk's wings hover.
You saw fruition: we see stare our guilt.

Faith is a murmuring shell and lives are brief—
The brief oblivion or brief caress:
We answer midnight with our nakedness
And the unknown voices, silencing their grief.

Lovers and strangers, we alike marooned
Some challenge surely yet may show
To the dead cities and the deathly snow,
And living dreams to heal our grievous wound.
[Hocken, MS 89/148]

**Lamentation**

Dew on my eyes fell
from the fields of sleep
when sleep and waking were
a single flower;
cried out from deep to deep
the clarion daffodil.

But now the wind blowing
from outer snow
is keen alone, not kind:
I to the world's wind
stranger, seek marrow
oblivion and blood flowing.

I would relinquish love.
Incessant breakers beat
out of the sea of pain
on nerve and bone
demanding of my night
strength that I cannot give.

O lost lost:
too near the bitter sky.

I will find my own peace
renounce the face
of tender infancy.
Homeless and free my ghost.
[Hocken, MS 89/148]

**The Antelopes**

Beyond the edge of the world, past crater terrain
The lava flames and the volcanic rumble
Where the torn sky weeps iron for world's pain:
There in the ever-naked east remain
The gentle antelopes, a race undying
Who daylong wander on the autumn plain
Where the ripe grasses wake at noon and tremble
By winds fulfilled, regretting not their spring.

Over their dream domain the sun is steep;
And rock rings underfoot upon the hills.
Stirs there the fabled adder coiled asleep.
They pass unfearing torrent gorges deep
Meshing the thunder with their delicate cries.
One pool they drink from; then returning leap
Down to their grazing-ground. But now the cheetah kills
And lions darken evening with their eyes.

So when night falls, these daylight children come
And huddle safe beside the unknown tall
Stone amphitheatre at the desert's rim.
There moon rebuilds the wall with shadow beam.
But the frail creatures gazing cannot know
How vaster fear locks each loud crevice dumb.
Petrified anguish strains. The caverns still
With their dead gladiators horrent grow.
[Hocken, MS 89/148]

**Sailor Song**

Shut from the wind that tugs the wire
and shakes the rusty quayside grass, where iron
clangs uncomplaining, and the dank sky raining
flows into suburb houses with odour of despair.

Here in the wharf pub propped against the bar
nomads of the antarctic desert come

and drink with factory workers while the blank
waste sky behind their lids keeps eyeless stare.

When the landsmen go home in a rich daze
these mystics turn into the rain again
or over a tilting glass's rim they dream
of lurching spray and the vast landless seas.

We on the jagged rim of a cracked cup crawl
pretending peace: but they in childhood found
by cordage voices of the gladly drowned.
Men will leave child and woman for that call.
[Hocken, MS 89/148]

**Lazarus**

The green roots pierce his eyelids, and the glass
Of heaven is blown by hurrying clouds—O dumb,
Corruption's swollen anguish spent and voiceless
Where Lazarus lies smiling in his tomb.

So after act of love, the star-wind-laden
Ecstatic peace ah deep in unknown night
Broken, devoured, eyes leave the vain companion,
To death fallen, forever isolate:

Are drowned in brackish ponds, and feverless
Hear clock of childhood chime; remember
Small wondering fervours and vast fears
Or even the daffodil gold in September.

Intolerable birds and the spring rains
O not too loud, lest the awakening
The agony of blood in withered veins
The dry skull sweat again, the dead heart beating.
[Hocken, MS 89/148]

**[O my darling . . . ]**

O my darling never wise
nor good nor brave at all
scarcely beautiful
a child in my eyes

you enter careless
the cold and haunted house

abolish darkness
with the sun in your face

and over tombs
walking without fear—
the restless skeletons
crumble and cannot stir
As the spray beats the rocks
and clouds pass over
or as the wind-tormented
scarlet flower

my hands upon your breasts
your mouth on mine
changing and steadfast
and known again.
[Hocken, MS 89/148]

**Poem to Rimbaud**

You were too eager always, could not wait
for white-lipped narcissus to change her nature
and arrogant crocus grow or starry aconite
flesh hard at length and like the bone mature.

Yet where I've mumbled you spoke out like pain
your sharp tongue probing so the mindless mouth
of a child's universe, and secret sun
under her grave sea melting down to death.

And yours the eye of the courageous diver
square on sea-bottom, taking note
of life's age-buried half—still cool observer
when ruinous fangs, advancing of shark's throat. . .

Yes, I would change my own uneasy posture
of self-admiring justice for your day
volcanic, ignorance not truth your pasture;
but too much dread the stones of Africa.

And this land rootless gives no green
timber to burn reduce in crucible
to your death-potent brew. Rather I learn
myself the edifice and parable.

Midsummer sky puts on her island grey;
in gorse-corrupted paddocks is no fodder
for the idyllic Lamb; though any actor may
wring from rags of death a priestly odour.

What then to do? For rock will never change.
Build then a scantling house where few inhabit
those few the rich in heart. Or like you range
the world for living peace, and never gain it.
[Hocken, MS 89/148]

**Baxter to Ginn, 21 July 1946**

Brighton,
Otago.
21/7/46.

Dear Noel,

Thank you very much for the Yeats. It is indeed a fine book. His images are so evocative—OIL AND BLOOD—'Or found a subterranean rest / On the maternal midnight of my breast'. And SONGS FOR MUSIC PERHAPS have a great vitality and release about them. Yeats came alive, in his own way. 'When such as I cast out remorse' is I think the fulcrum-point on which balance his latter poems.[1]

I enclose a fair few verses, written in the last 6 months. Maybe I sent one or two of them to you, but if I did I can't remember which. TO ALCIBIADES—more or less a homo. poem, and successful. EVENING ODE is probably the best: something Keatsian, but more clarity.

Am working in woollen mills at present with assorted company male and female. Very placid in mind, and rather cold, as I might be at 30. Not the right frame of mind for 20 maybe. But I have at last disentangled various strands—religious, masturbation-guilt, artistic, attitudes to school and parents—which I have long been unable to accept and dissolve.

'I am content to follow to its source
Every event in action or in thought;
Measure the lot; forgive myself the lot !
When such as I cast our remorse . . .' etc.[2]

—Not Yeats' particular creative ecstasy but a rather sour determination to go my

1 Apart from Yeats's *Collected Poems* (London: Macmillan, 1933), the only other volume of Yeats's poetry containing all of the poems Baxter refers to is *The Winding Stair and Other poems* (London: Macmillan, 1933): 'Or found a subterranean rest / On the maternal midnight of my breast' is from 'Chosen' (lines 5–6), which is the fifth poem in the sequence 'A Woman Young and Old'; Baxter's 'SONGS FOR MUSIC PERHAPS' is a reference to the sequence 'Words for Music Perhaps'; and 'When such as I cast out remorse' is the sixty-eighth line of 'A Dialogue of Self and Soul', four lines of which are quoted further on in this letter.

2 From Yeats's poem 'A Dialogue of Self and Soul', lines 65–8.

own way by doubt and not by Authority of person, state, religion, or convention; to work out my own position and make no promises. For one thing, since I have thought out why I want to drink, I have had no inclination to do so except for enjoyment. The ambition is to fear 'neither God, man, nor Devil', and do whatever I like without tension.

Well, that'll do for today's introspection. Have been in a Drama Class lately, but gave it up halfway through a play, to the inconvenience ~~of~~ and annoyance of all concerned. Have read very little, since I have found little worth reading. KRISHNAMURTI, a highly original and intelligent Indian ex-Theosophist, I have read though. He seems clear, powerful, quite untinctured with esoteric fluffiness. He will be visiting NZ shortly I believe.[3]

Terry is in good health, settling down to his job. A possible feminine attachment on the horizon, but far from anchored.[4] Parents also O.K.

If I go up North, I'll get in touch with you.

All best wishes,

Jim.

[VUW Library, MS McKay 28/56]

**To Alcibiades**

Eternity bears blossoms in her hand
And you are one of these. The gold mane of the lion
Yours, yet frail as hyacinth
The parting of your lips
For the bright bee to enter: O honey-gold
Sweet apple from the garden of the Sun.

Leave we the summit of the high green hill
Where hawk and adder strive and strangle still—
So let them strangle till the Day of Doom.
The heart that bears all ills, another stone
May hold within her oceanic tomb
If from new desolation the fire-crowned Phoenix sing.

Leave we the western mansion where the Dead
And never-to-be-born cry mute and loud:
Beside the breathing sea and summer cloud
Let us walk now when dews are wakened
With unangelic clarion of the blood:
Let us lie quiet and forget the long-unquiet Dead.

3 The Indian spiritual leader Jiddu Krishnamurti (1895–1986) was famous for his charismatic lectures presenting his own unique version of Indian philosophy and mysticism. His early alignment with the Theosophical Society was severed in 1933 as he increasingly expressed independent thoughts at odds with the movement's central beliefs. He founded schools that taught ways to reduce aggression and travelled the world lecturing, although I have found no evidence that he visited New Zealand in the period immediately following this letter.

4 A reference to Lenore Bond who married Terence on 22 August 1947. See McKay's *Life*, p.92.

O strangest love
That in the polar darkness of God's heart
(Infinite Zero, grave of deathly suns)
So live a flower should blow, as you, my heart's darling.
Let hawk and adder strive: the innocent breast is torn
And burdened thus. Lay your gold head upon
Eternal strife, lie pillowed there and hearken.
[Hocken, MS 89/148]

**Evening Ode**

The moon in a pale sky draws in the night
As she draws tides. Out from the sun's grave
Innumerable birds to their recalling wave
Hasten, through quietness in wreathed flight.
See one with slender breast riding
Channels and currents, near at hand;
Then low, impetuous, over the combers striding
To the ledge in pitted rockface, or seasand
Where the tides buffet boisterous and gliding.

Encreviced there clash the unflowering swords
Of stirring flax; blindly the dark comes on
In hazes where the rocks and glittering grey leaves shone,
And waves yet sob and murmur without words.
As for an ocean revelation
I childish waited once, so now
Alone I gather in the voice and exhalation
Of winter, while upon a barren bough
Lie the gold leaves of sunset consummation.

Older than memory, my mind is blown
By the same wind, and the same leaves are sacked—
The gold fire of a sunset cataract
Wild on the cloudy dark—O earth with ages sown
What strange love in thee is hidden?
Thou ocean wilderness, does the drowned swimmer know
Under the ebb of hope a flood death-ridden
Calming the clenched despairing hands? and so
From long-buried darkness a natal peace unbidden.
[Hocken, MS 89/148]

# APPENDICES

1 Table of Poems by James K. Baxter

2 Additional Poems by James K. Baxter

3 Additional Poems by Noel Ginn

4 James K. Baxter's Draft Paper
'The Unicorn: a consideration of adolescence'

5 Two Early Prose Pieces by James K. Baxter

6 'Spirits of Harmony, Music and Love' by Archibald Baxter

7 Baxter's Foreword to *Cold Spring* and Table of Contents

## Appendix 1
## Table of Poems by James K. Baxter

The following table gives details of the poems by James K. Baxter that appear in full in this edition.

Column One lists the poems in alphabetical order.

Column Two gives the MS Book reference assigned to each poem by Baxter. The figure preceding the colon is the MS Book number and the figure following the colon is the poem's sequential number. See 'Baxter's Early Manuscript Books', pp.72–81, for a fuller description of Baxter's numbering and classification systems.

Column Three gives the code Baxter assigned each poem. He entered the key to his classification system in the back of MS Book I as follows:

S — sure
L — likely
D — doubtful
U — unlikely
N — not included
ω — outside a category

This key is repeated in the rear of 'Book II' with two modifications that hold through to MS Book XIV: 'N' becomes 'not included, (probably)' and the symbol 'ω' is dropped.

Column Four gives details of any poems that have been previously published. With the exception of the references to the *Collected Poems*, *Cold Spring* and the entry for 'Now While the Bugles Blare', this information comes from *A Preliminary Bibliography of Works by and Works About James K. Baxter* compiled by Father J.E. Weir and Barbara A. Lyon (Christchurch: University of Canterbury, 1979).

| One | Two | Three | Four |
|---|---|---|---|
| A Man | 7:460 | L | |
| A plane fell down | 13:782 | S | |
| Absalom | 13:821 | L | *Cold Spring*, p.17. |
| Ad Amicum | 12:741 | L | |
| Aeneas | 10:613 | D | *Cold Spring*, p.3 |
| Affirmation | 13:811 | S | *Cold Spring*, p.49. |
| Age | 10:595 | L | *Beyond the Palisade*, p.20; *Collected Poems*, p.16. |
| Air | 11:670 | L | |
| Anger | 9:543 | S | |
| ANNALES | 13:789 | L | *Cold Spring*, p.28. |

| | | | |
|---|---|---|---|
| The Antelopes | 14:906 | S | *Blow, Wind of Fruitfulness*, p.20; *Howrah Bridge and Other Poems*, p.6; *An Anthology of New Zealand Verse* (1956, selected by Robert Chapman and Jonathan Bennett); *Collected Poems*, p.35. |
| At Balclutha | 12:765 | S | |
| Atlas | 7:430 | D | |
| Autobiographical | 10:634 | D | |
| Beauty (a Ghazel) | 4:261 | L | |
| Beauty and angers flow | 10:637 | L | |
| Bees | 4:260 | S | |
| The Bees | 13:818 | S | *Cold Spring*, p.5 |
| The Boat | 8:466 | D | |
| Boys laugh at ease | 8:500 | S | *Beyond the Palisade*, p.36; *Collected Poems*, p.12. |
| Bracchiae | 12:744 | D | |
| The British Bull-dog | 4:202 | N | |
| Burns | 13:819 | S | *Cold Spring*, p.15. |
| Cause and Result | 10:594 | L | |
| The Child | 10:630 | L | |
| Clarity | 13:836 | S | *Yearbook of the Arts in New Zealand* 1 (1945) p.129; *Cold Spring*, p.58. |
| The Class-Problem | 10:599 | Q | |
| The Closed Picture | 13:788 | S | *Rostrum* 6 (1945) p.3; *Cold Spring*, p.23. |
| The Clown | 7:449 | L | |
| Cold Spring | 13:830 | S | *Cold Spring*, p.55. |
| Control | 7:420 | D | |
| Convoys | 12:719 | S | *Otago University Review* (1944) p.13. |
| Court Speech | 13:825 | L | *Cold Spring*, p.20. |
| Cried passionate Blake | 10:589 | D | |
| Cry Mourn | 10:582 | D | *Beyond the Palisade*, p.12; *Collected Poems*, p.15. |
| 'The Dark Sun' or 'Ode to Spring' | 4:198 | S | |
| De Averno | 8:475 | D | |
| Death of a Swan | 13:784 | S | *Beyond the Palisade*, p.8; *A Book of New Zealand Verse: 1923–45* (1945, ed. Allen Curnow) p.188; *A Book of New Zealand Verse: 1923–50* (1951, ed. Allen Curnow) p.166; *Collected Poems*, p.30. |
| The Deed | 10:604 | S | |
| Development | 11:656 | L | *Critic* XX.1 (Mar 1944) p.3; *Critic* XXIX.2 (19 Mar 1953) p.9. |
| Discobolus | 6:373 | L | |
| Doctrine of Philosophy | 7:403 | L | |
| Each | 13:802 | D | *Cold Spring*, p.40. |

| | | | |
|---|---|---|---|
| Easter Sonnet | 14:861 | S | *Art in New Zealand* XVII.3 (Apr-May 1945) p.44; *Yearbook of the Arts in New Zealand* 1 (1945) p.129; *Cold Spring*, p.63. |
| Elegy | 13:771 | L | |
| Elegy (in memory of Alun Lewis) | 13:800b | S | |
| [re-casting of REQUIEM] | | | |
| Epitaphs | 13:823 | L | |
| Eternity | 7:414 | — | |
| Evening Ode | 14:969 | — | *Blow, Wind of Fruitfulness*, p.36; *Critic* XXII.8 (Jul 1946) p.5. |
| The extinction of the instant | 7:423 | S | |
| The Eye | 7:425 | S | |
| The Eyes | 12:713 | S | |
| Faith that groweth | 5:305 | S | |
| Fathers and Strangers | 14:904 | S | |
| The Flame of Grass | 4:232 | L | |
| The Flower | 10:585 | L | |
| Flower-Venus | 13:778 | S | *Cold Spring*, p.9. |
| The Flowering Eye | 13:804 | S | *Cold Spring*, p.48. |
| For Burial in Ground | 13:777 | L | *Beyond the Palisade*, p.40; *Collected Poems*, p.29. |
| For those who lie . . . [re-casting] | 13:779 [13:799] | S | *Meanjin Quarterly* XI (1952) p.348; *Cold Spring*, p.26. |
| For us no saint | 13:845 | D | *Cold Spring*, p.59. |
| From Heine | 13:812 | L | *Cold Spring*, p.51. |
| From Hill-Top | 9:551 | L | |
| From Unremembered Mouths | 7:421 | L | |
| From winter vials | 13:849 | S | *Yearbook of the Arts in New Zealand* 1 (1945) p.129; *Cold Spring*, p.60. |
| Gauguin | 6:336 | L | |
| Genesis | 12:753 | L | |
| The Ghost Unborn | 8:472 | D | |
| Hawk and Hare | 5:280 | S | *Beyond the Palisade*, p.23; *Collected Poems*, p.3. |
| He Who Laughs | 7:401 | L | |
| Hill-Country | 7:435 | ω | *Beyond the Palisade*, p.10; *Critic* XX.1 (Mar 1944) p.6; *A Book of New Zealand Verse: 1923–45* (1945, ed. Allen Curnow) p.189; *A Book of New Zealand Verse: 1923–50* (1951, ed. Allen Curnow) p.168; *School Journal* pt. 4. 6 (Jul 1951) p.191; *The Penguin Book of New Zealand Verse* (1960) p.284; *Lines of Life, Book 3* (1968, ed. Peter Wallace Murdoch) p.228; *Collected Poems*, p.7. |

| | | | |
|---|---|---|---|
| Him not mentioned | 7:422 | S | |
| 'The honest Jack . . .' | 11:700 | S | |
| Hopes and Fears for Man | 12:718 | S | |
| I am as it were in a trap | 5:299 | D | |
| I bear as my insignia . . . | 13:838 | S | |
| I have cut from my heart | 13:816 | S | *Cold Spring*, p.52. |
| I have passed unscathed . . . | 7:395 | — | |
| Illusion | 6:355 | S | |
| Imaginary Island | 10:607 | L | |
| The Immobile Stone | 12:757 | S | |
| In Barley-Fields | 7:451 | S | |
| In City Night | 11:689 | L | *Beyond the Palisade*, p.34; *Collected Poems*, p.20. |
| In Flames Politic | 10:603 | S | |
| In hills of stone | 9:525 | D | |
| In honour of all beasts | 14:903 | D | |
| In July | 13:783 | L | |
| In Monochrome | 13:834 | L | *Canta* XIX.12 (15 Sep 1948) p.3; *The Labyrinth: Some Uncollected Poems, 1944–72* (Wellington: Oxford University Press, 1974) p.9; *Collected Poems*, p.31; *Cold Spring*, p.44. |
| In Numeris | 6:387 | — | |
| In point of time | 6:363 | S | |
| In Retrospect | 13:822 | S | |
| In the lion rocks | 13:847 | S | *Cold Spring*, p.61. |
| in the crowd | 10:600 | — | |
| Incarnation | 11:652 | S | |
| Inspiration | 2:95 | L | |
| Intelligentsia | 7:398 | S | |
| Interim | 10:597 | L | |
| It is not enough | 13:810 | L | *Meanjin Quarterly* XI (1952) p.349; *Cold Spring*, p.50. |
| Janus Unheard | 12:709 | S | |
| Jubilation | 6:338 | L | |
| Judas | 7:455 | S ω | |
| The Killing of a Rabbit | 11:665 | S | *Beyond the Palisade*, p.22; *Collected Poems*, p.19. |
| The Kiln | 8:479 | U | |
| Lament of the Reborn | 6:377 | S | |
| Lamentation (later version) | 14:905 | L | |
| Landscape | 11:691 | S | |
| Lazarus | 14:909 | S | *Yearbook of the Arts in New Zealand* 3 (1947) p.150; *The Fallen House: Poems* (1953) p.32. |

| | | | |
|---|---|---|---|
| Legend | 12:760 | D | *Meanjin Quarterly* XIV (1955) p.174; *Cold Spring*, p.4. |
| Let us away! | 1:33 | S | |
| Letter to Noel Ginn | 13:772 | S | *Collected Poems*, p.27. |
| Letter to Noel Ginn II (published) | — | — | *Blow, Wind of Fruitfulness*, p.42; *A Book of New Zealand Verse: 1923–50* (1951, ed. Allen Curnow) p.210; *Collected Poems*, p.70. |
| Letter to Noel Ginn II (unpublished) | 14:958 | S | |
| The Lie | 8:482 | S | *Beyond the Palisade*, p.35; *Collected Poems*, p.11. |
| Love-Lyric I | 12:716 | S | |
| Love-Lyric IX | 12:754 | S | *Arena* 42 (1955) p.27; *The Rock Woman: Selected Poems* (1969) p.3; *Collected Poems*, p.25. |
| Man and Woman | 14:896 | S | |
| Many have written well . . . | 10:593 | L | |
| Me Also | 12:725 | S | |
| Memory swathes | 10:641 | L | |
| Men cannot mar | 11:699 | L | |
| The Merry Beggar | 3:139 | L | |
| Monologue | 12:722 | L | |
| Monument | 9:547 | S | |
| The Moon knows not | 7:457 | S | |
| The Mountains | 7:437 | S | *Beyond the Palisade*, p.9; *A Book of New Zealand Verse: 1923–45* (1945, ed. Allen Curnow) p.188; *A Book of New Zealand Verse: 1923–50* (1951, ed. Allen Curnow) p.167; *The Penguin Book of New Zealand Verse* (1960) p.285; *Howrah Bridge and Other Poems* (1961) p.5; *A Selection of Poetry* (1964) p.10; *A Book of New Zealand* (ed. John Cowie Reid, 1964) p.110; *A Land Apart: The Mount Cook Alpine Region* (by George Harris and Graeme and Hasler, 1971) p.116; *Collected Poems*, p.8. |
| Moving on spirit-roads | 6:339 | S | |
| Mural for a War-Memorial | 8:480 | D | |
| Mural for a War-Memorial (for Laurence [sic] Baigent) | 13:798 | S | |
| Murder | 10:618 | L | |
| Mutation | 10:639 | S | |
| New Day | 11:698 | S | |
| Night (poem written in insecurity) | 10:574 | S | |

| | | | |
|---|---|---|---|
| Nor did I ask | 13:853 | S | Previously published as 'Poem ("I had thought the sun's speech")' in *Otago University Review* (1948) p.5; *Review: 1888–1971* (Dunedin: Bibliography Room, University of Otago, 1972), p.54; and *The Labyrinth: Some Uncollected Poems, 1944–72* (Wellington: Oxford University Press, 1974), p.10. First published as 'Nor did I ask' in *Collected Poems*, p.32.; *Cold Spring*, p.62. |
| Not in these flooded pastures | 13:790 | L | *Cold Spring*, p.47. |
| Now while the bugles blare | 9:519 | S | *The Link* XVI.9 (5 Jul 1943) p.3. |
| O Blake! The World Guessed Not . . . | 11:667 | S | |
| O lands seen in the light . . . | 7:439 | L | *Beyond the Palisade*, p.13; *Critic* XX.9 (Aug 1944) p.6; *A Book of New Zealand Verse: 1923–45* (1945, ed. Allen Curnow) p.190; *A Book of New Zealand Verse: 1923–50* (1951, ed. Allen Curnow) p.169; *Collected Poems*, p.9. |
| 'O Let the Prisoner Go' | 11:686 | S | |
| O love, in the island day | 14:877 | S | |
| O my darling . . . | 14:910 | S | |
| O rose dost thou weep? | 10:601 | S | |
| O spirit stand in my eyes | 8:474 | L | |
| OBEV [Adaptation of Ruskin] | 10:633 | N | |
| Obsequy for Dylan Thomas | 20 | — | *The Bone Chanter: Unpublished Poems 1945–72*, p.21; *Collected Poems*, p.216. |
| Ode MCMXLIV [re-casting] | 12:727 [13:726] | S | |
| Of Age | 7:404 | S | *Beyond the Palisade*, p.33; *Collected Poems*, p.5. |
| Of the Fountain | 7:413 | S | |
| Of the Western Highlands | 7:419 | L | |
| On hearing speech of Sloth and Fear | 9:556 | L | |
| On John the Baptist | 6:380 | S | |
| On Leopold | 11:701 | S | |
| On the Banishment of Beer | — | — | |
| On Visiting a Gallery of War-Pictures | 5:285 | S | |
| On Withstanding Fate | 11:703 | S | |
| One Never Knows | 14:864 | S | |
| Oreades | 10:621 | S | |
| Our days and nights | 9:532 | L | |
| Our Search-Light Lust | 9:560 | D | |
| Phantasmagoria of Silence | 9:561 | L | |

| | | | |
|---|---|---|---|
| The Phenomenon of Understanding | 7:426 | L | |
| The Plaster Scene | 10:598 | S | |
| The Plough | 7:388 | L | |
| Poem: [I dreamed in the night] | 14:918 | L | |
| Poem in November | 13:828 | S | *Cold Spring*, p.56. |
| Poem of Passage | 9:539 | S | |
| Poem to Rimbaud | 14:913 | L | |
| The Poet | 8:490 | L | *Critic* XX.1 (Mar 1944) p.7; *Critic* XXIX.2 (19 Mar 1953) p.9. |
| The Poison-Bane | 4:258 | S | |
| POST PROELIUM | 7:409 | — | |
| Prologue | 12:759 | S | |
| Prometheus (early version) | 7:441 | L | |
| Prometheus (later version) | 14:899 | S | *Blow, Wind of Fruitfulness*, p.16; *Book* 7 (Feb 1946) p.26; *Poetry Commonwealth* I (Sum. 1948) p.6; *Collected Poems*, p.35. |
| Psalm of the Defeated | 9:524 | S | *Beyond the Palisade*, p.32; *Collected Poems*, p.13. |
| Rain-Ploughs (published version) | 13:767 | S | *Beyond the Palisade*, p.11; *Collected Poems*, p.26. |
| Rain-Ploughs (unpublished version) | 5:320 | L | |
| REQUIEM | 13:800a | L | *Critic* XXI.6 (Jun 1945) p.6; *Cold Spring*, p.13. |
| Résumé of Perdition | 10:602 | D | |
| Resurrection | 13:792 | S | *Canta* XIX.12 (15 Sep 1948) p.4; *Cold Spring*, p.32. |
| Reverie of a Prisoner | 10:588 | D | |
| The Rose of Solitude | 9:546 | L | |
| Ruth | 14:874 | S | |
| Sailor Song | 14:907 | S | |
| The Salamander | 10:583 | L | |
| Samson | 10:584 | S | |
| Satan | 8:495 | S | |
| Satan's Battle | 1:8 | L | |
| Sea-Elegy | 13:781 | S | *Cold Spring*, p.11. |
| The Silver Fish | 8:468 | D | |
| Soliloquy of an Earth-Worm | 10:612 | S | |
| Soliloquy of One Sane | 11:655 | S | |
| Song (The winter of the soul is here . . .) | 14:862 | S | *Art in New Zealand* XVII.3 (Apr-May 1945) p.20; *Yearbook of the Arts in New Zealand* I (1945) p.128. |
| Song and the soul-delighting river | 7:446 | S | |

| | | | |
|---|---|---|---|
| Song of the Garden | 7:424 | L | |
| Song of the Sea-Nymphs . . . | 7:406 | S | *Beyond the Palisade*, p.30; *Collected Poems*, p.6. |
| Song [Thou shalt forget] | 10:650 | S | |
| Sonnet (The dank stooks stand) | 14:868 | S | |
| Sonnet of Allegiance | 14:876 | D | |
| Sonnet of Unbelief | 13:840 | S | |
| Sonnet XXXVII | 10:611 | S | |
| Speech, by Death the Director | 11:705 | S | |
| Spring (Horace Odes IV 7) | 13:795 | S | *Critic* XX.10 (Sep 1944) p.4; *Cold Spring*, p.31. |
| Spring Pastoral | 9:549 | S | |
| Stability | 13:796 | S | *Cold Spring*, p.38. |
| The Storm-Centre | 7:433 | S | |
| The Stream of Faith | 2:113 | L | |
| Ten thousand dreams | 10:610 | S | |
| There is a farm-house . . . | 9:542 | L | |
| There is no God [God] | 10:623 | L | |
| There was an altar | 12:724 | D | |
| Thesis on a Constant Theme | 9:550 | L | |
| They will not mention | 9:565 | S | |
| Thoughts by a Conchie Camp | 13:793 | L | *Cold Spring*, p.36. |
| To a Poplar-Tree | 13:815 | S | *Landfall* 1 (1947) p.25; *Cold Spring*, p.43. |
| (To a solemn music) | 6:384 | L | |
| To Alcibiades | 14:955 | — | |
| To Gerard Manly Hopkins | 11:695 | S | |
| To L.A. Baigent | 14:886 | S | |
| To my Brother | 13:775 | S | |
| To my Mother | 4:184 | S | |
| To my Father (unpublished version) | 4:183 | S | |
| To Noel Ginn | 7:444 | N | |
| To Sleep | 11:668 | S | |
| To T.J. Baxter | 10:628 | — | |
| To the New Pagan | 10:572 | L | |
| To the Sun | 11:690 | S | *Beyond the Palisade*, p.27; *Collected Poems*, p.21. |
| To Woman | 6:335 | S | |
| To you who most unwittingly | 14:860 | S | *Cold Spring*, p.64. |
| Too many winters | 14:873 | S | |
| The Tower | 13:797 | S | |
| True Melancholy | 11:671 | S | |
| Tulips | 8:487 | L | *Critic* XX.1 (Mar 1944) p.6. |

| | | | |
|---|---|---|---|
| Under a Sun | 4:249 | L | *Beyond the Palisade*, p.20; *Critic* XX.8 (Jul 1944) p.6; *Collected Poems*, p.3. |
| Under the dank leaves | 13:829 | L | *Cold Spring*, p.57. |
| The Unicorn | 7:459 | S ω | *Beyond the Palisade*, p.29; *Collected Poems*, p.10. |
| Uninnocence | 13:801 | S | *Cold Spring*, p.38. |
| University Song | 14:857 | S | *Blow, Wind of Fruitfulness*, p.38; *Critic* XXVIII.1 (6 Mar 1952) p.7; *Collected Poems*, p.32. |
| The untold story | 13:807 | S | *Cold Spring*, p.42. |
| Unwritten Elegy | 12:721 | S | |
| Was it as children? | 14:871 | S | |
| We Pay | 11:685 | S | |
| The Weir | 9:529 | L | *Critic* XX.8 (Jul 1944) p.4; and *Critic* XXIX.2 (19 Mar 1953) p.9. |
| What shall be heard? | 5:321 | S | |
| What shall we seek for | 7:412 | S | *Beyond the Palisade*, p.28; *Collected Poems*, p.7. |
| What the Night Replied | 13:806 | S | *Cold Spring*, p.41. |
| When I was neither child nor man | 14:875 | S | |
| When weight of want | 5:295 | S | |
| Where beauty dips to dust | 7:442 | S | |
| Where nets of time . . . | 10:581 | S | |
| Why ring no chime? | 8:473 | D | |
| Winter | 13:766 | S | *Cold Spring*, p.8. |
| Worship | 10:591 | D | |
| Xerxes and Homer | 13:824 | S | *Otago University Review* (1948) p.41; *Review: 1888–1971* (Dunedin: Bibliography Room, University of Otago, 1972), p.55; *Cold Spring*, p.19. |
| The young trees | 6:359 | S | |

## Appendix 2
## Additional Poems by James K. Baxter

The following poems supplement the correspondence between James K. Baxter and Noel Ginn. Many of the poems are discussed in a manner that makes it clear they were not sent with the letters in which they are referred to, and thus it does not seem appropriate to insert them among the correspondence. The remainder are from Baxter's unpublished early collection *Cold Spring* (posthumously published by Oxford University Press, 1996) and are collected in an appendix to limit the amount of poetry separating the correspondence. The poems are ordered according to date of composition. Where a poem has been published the text is of the most recent published version.

Contents

**Hawk and Hare**

Regard the hawk who sees earth swim and wheel
Yet keeps in flight unbroken quietude—
Self-absorbed, centripetal—
Until soft rabbit blunders forth from hide
And coldly claps with beating heart:
Air opens to his unmalicious hate
In the firm impulse-driven downward stride.

Regard the rabbit crouched in covert low
Hidden from grey horror overhead;
Insurgent fear creates the flaw
And he pursues the perilous outward road;
While life-destroying shadow drops—
Spirit lies shrieking and dumb body droops:
Death gleams in bloody grass, but beating hearts abide.

Uncontemplative clouds forever move
For skies cannot earth's suffering burden see;
Light shingles on the inland wave
Rattle; only the winds of autumn sigh
While man the hawk and man the hare
Pursue their unrelenting passage here:
Are born, beget, and die.
[Hocken, MS 704/5:280, pp.28–9]

**I am as it were in a trap**

I am as it were in a trap
Where men disport themselves
With the pugnacious gesture of the ape
And the large problem solves
In mental sleep.

Sing in rich baritone
To comfort me
And I shall find with tune
Sub-luminar ecstasy—
Then seek the slough again.

Bird's flight or mind's response
Are humour tolerant.
O for the net that spans

The space impermanent
To bid the soul advance.
[Hocken MS 704/5:299, p.65]

**Faith that groweth**

Mine is a faith that groweth and never shall fail
Though all creeds may crumble that dwell in the world beside
Yet no belief in spirits bountiful
All that lives or lieth yet in seed
Has inmost sanity. Sad men have said
Life is a lie and joy the faint marsh-flame
That flickers lightly above the uncertain sod—
Their mood was as the bitterness of lime.
I shall draw freshness from the dewy loam,
Language I speak shall be known of singing-bird
And I shall make of life a certain loom
To weave sure destiny. O hear the bards
Who know celestial music and translate
The song of being to an earthly lute.
[Hocken, MS 704/5:305, p.74]

**Moving on spirit-roads**

Moving on spirit-roads from incarnation
Found I downward path, unsafe refuge
Loss of wider untrammelled notion
Nor faith-ignition:
In mundane wood must lower plough-share seize
Strife, life aloof shall sense scarce double existence
Yet mind hold lighter stance
Above, from under weightened stones most sage:
And I shall virile flood in non-retarded being
With full subservience to no gods bowing;
Fate sated with sorrow may show self for obeying
Seen gushing green and grooved: deep-greaved in ultimate page.

Behold magnetic current outward flowing
From tendril-anode on intrinsic path
Swiftly in rind-sap to mortal brain forth-fleeing
Air-current flawing:
Gaze at new-rising spring-awakened faith
Gaze, maze in muse nor even slightly shudder
If foul tyrannic odour

In progress of the violent adder forth
Should stain the innocent loam with most unneedful slaughter:
Even from such shall fire be drawn though later
Pass, glaze nor glass with idle oblivious letter
Burst bands accurst, bid song abide deride false worth.
[Hocken MS 704/6:339, pp.26–7]

**Intelligentsia**

Upon their incomings and their out-goings
These carry with them, like the triple tiara
A silver tower of words.
Their mind is a reflection of an imaginary universe,
They look upon a living world
And see it as if thrown upon canvas
Or as if it were a fine steam
Spun out and moulded in close shapes by their brain

They are joyful within their enclosure,
Calling a brook an ocean;
They feel themselves sages
But in truth are dazed by the existent earth
And dream in their slumber a self-begotten dream
That is the replica of exterior happenings—
And in their deepest slumber
Are wraiths of strange beauty.

They seek they know not what,
They are sad they know not why;
Theirs is a sickness of the spirit
That may break free to Marxian dialectics
But never to the formulate animal expression:
They are held in the involute coil of mind
And so embark as fragile nautilus
On unknown voyages.

Tendrils of thought may grope
But bruised upon the walls of intellect
Must seek internal solace.
A hawk swings over the bracken:
They see suspended a crystal shaft of air,
They see the Aztec eagle slaying serpents.
But there is nothing there—
Only a taloned hawk seeking new prey.

This is from a flaw in the bed-rock.
They cover within themselves the necessary desires
    And so must gloze all strong emotion.
I would pour out in due measure
Thought and spirit upon the arid lands;
But I also am captivated by the turning of speech,
Would not be loath to enter the silver tower
    For there is a frozen self-sufficiency.

Let not these new ghosts know
They are not among the living
    For it were bitter beyond endurance
To lose the integrity of motion:
And are not we alike
Who cannot contemplate the spears of heaven
But must hide in our shams, in a bondage
    Scarcely perceived.

Yes, it is well to dwell in the globe of dream.
Yet would I strive from it
    Fiercely in wedge-like emotion.
But now the old spell is upon me,
Thoughts are meshed in the nets behind the eyes;
I falsely consider myself
One with the leaf or sea-tempest
    When I am nothing but a broken mirror.
        [Hocken, MS 704/7:398, pp.19–22]

**Song of the Sea-Nymphs at the Death of Icarus**

From the white island in the dawn-sun shining
Forth flew he, wheeled and swung in curvet rings
Over the surf and sea-cliff, poised, reclining,
        Flashing his rainbow wings.
And there was youth immortal in his motion—
The eagle hovering over the wrinkled ocean
        Is bald, is bloody with his carrion prey;
But his was beauty earthly lives surpassing:
We raised bare arms to stay him in his passing,
        He did not heed nor stay
    But flew into the blue unbroken day.

Through the clear air up-soaring and up-sailing
        We saw his wide vanes shimmer till at last
Above the silver floor of sea-mist veiling

Gross Daedalus
There the sun's beams seemed upward cast—
So mounted Icarus.

Then in his wings the warm wax melted and ran;
The light wings hung above him in a fan
Of floating feathers; and like plummet down
With hands out-clutching to the baseless air
To find no succour there:
Down, whirling down,
While the Minoan coast broadened to meet him,
While the cool lips of spray sprang up to greet him,
So hurtled Icarus,
And stolid Daedalus
Flew onward to the far Sicilian town.

Lament, lament for Icarus!
Hills deep-rooted and ponderous,
Trees, and torrents thunderous!
Men and maidens likewise so lament!
What though in his brief sojourn in the skies
All wonders were unfolded to his eyes:
In that abysmal swift descent
Thought was blotted from his brain—
He is but youth incarnate again.
See! we have bound upon his brow
No green laurel, but the purple weed
Fitting for him who briefly was lord of the heavens indeed;
Currents shall bear him gently now
To some low crannied reef where the sea-saphires have lain
Untold aeons to deck his burial pall.

Only the old may live
In their regret and pain:
Them shall the gods forgive—
But the young than gods are yet more beauteous
And are forever slain.

Lament ye for young Icarus,
Lament again!
For he is youth
Forever living and forever slain.
[Hocken, MS 704/7:406, pp.40–42]

### Eternity

Vast Eternity, Immortal Thought,
By what mind and hand wert thou wrought
With flaming gases before time was begun,
Before in the heavens there was a sun.

Unbridged by thought, Unthought by mind,
There are no bonds that can thee bind
  But one and that no wraith,
  For that one bond is faith.
    [Hocken, MS 704/7:414. pp.56–7]
[Written when Baxter was eight years old]

### The extinction of the instant

We stand upon the hills by night
as granite pylons. Wayfaring moon
and stars are caught in the crevices of our bones.
We soliliquize
with the madness of men hung in a metal shell
in the surface tension of a time-wrought water
unmoved by tides:
  no lucid liquid instant can dissolve
  this framework; for the world
  is borne on an elephant's back.
  He stands upon a tortoise and the tortoise
  stands on the world.

But timelessly, irrevocably,
  through a clear well of ether
  still, stagnant as the vent
  of an extinct and fern-fringed volcano
  the same irrevocable instant descends.
    [Hocken, MS 704/7:423, p.74]

### Song of the Garden

What shall be done to him who falls away
From the clear sword of day?
What is the curse?

Thus saith the Lord:
In a primeval universe
Life beat like a turbulent pellucid sea

Below the towers of sky;
Beauty begat on beauty a beauty denied
To the high angels: at eventide
I walked within the Garden and knew
That the white lilies grew
With greater beauty than I had given
Unto the lords of heaven:
So could I see
There was within them, uncreated by me,
Deep innocence, inate simplicity.

Forth from the womb of storm
I had drawn the waters to cover a naked earth;
My spirit fleshed, in cataclysmic birth,
Forth sprang the Worm.
Him raised I over all my creatures
And set in him mine own immortal features:
From slime of his ancestral seas began
The tyrant Man.

He in the pride of freedom has arisen
And burst the bastions of a seeming prison;
He has moved forth, afloat
In bark of woven thought, to the remote
Caverns of science and philosophy:
But I have set within him, as a blight,
Curb on the unknown supernatural might
His parent Worm.
At the far heights of glory he shall turn,
Seeking, with love of that same lowly birth,
In aged earth
No blessing and no curse
But understanding of a universe.

He who has fallen away
From the clear sword of day
Shall hear, though the high heavens break and harden,
That which is heard at even in the celestial Garden.
[Hocken, MS 704/7:424, pp.75–7]

**The Eye**

Is it not marvellous to see
In a flower-shoot of spring
The rose blooming, the rose fallen to clay—
While yet new-mated thrushes build and sing.

But O most terrible to know
With the same eye anon
Within a human, fleshed solidity
The slouched and staggering skeleton.
[Hocken, MS 704/7:425, p.78]

**The Phenomenon of Understanding**

Is it not beautiful to be alive?—
Not the mere masque of necessary living,
But to feel systaltic spirit beat
In full co-ordination with the rejoicing flesh.

All bitterness is superficial at source
And can be dredged away
By little or by yet gigantic effort—
Is it not beautiful.

To hold a wind-blown butterfly and know:
I could not crush, I could not maim this life,
This multiplex and nerved fragility,
Were the bright swords of heaven to turn against me
And smite me should I fail.

Is it not beautiful
To see the ancient, usual happenings
With a new vision:
The wind runs molten with bright colours;
The sea flows in with a music
That is no less music in dissonance;
And these my brethren are not strange to me.

Yet we see the jarring faces of others
Obscure the luminous desired illusion
(Without which we live not)
And think: there are some with whom we may speak freely,
We shall find some attuned to us—
But not these men.
Yet these are the men whom we must understand.
[Hocken, MS 704/7:426, pp.79–80]

**Atlas**

In chaos down the reeling firmament
A tilted globe spins top-wise.
See the djinns

Laugh silhouetted in the enormous dawn
Holding the heavens on their hollow plumes;

For in the lava islands manikins
Ignore the bird-stars flashing overhead
(Signals for succour on a rising sea)
Shake the loose rocks with strife, blast passage-ways
Of fear and thunder through a perilous crust.

But now, O hark, from dark drops down the dawn:
Death dons the cloak of dawn on these
Metallic seas of magma. Crouched where the thews
And thighs of steel, not oak, make bivouac,
Unreckoning the mortal ants await.
And I am of them! by the bitter gate
Of fire and metal also I await.

Coldness of orchard-moss for aching eyes;
When truth has outgrown passion and our fashion
Of fearing builds not boundary to shut out men:
Shoot then, spring soul. From bones and clamour.
Alone the objective glamour of the djinn
Can break: but wakened vigour taps
Sky's weakened rivets with hard finger-tips
Of diamond glass.

                    Letting the rent skies sag
To onrush of the outer demons in,
Nor heeding aught their hum and hideous strum,

In the same orchard steel and oaken still
Where Time's first dream dissolved to adamant rhyme
      Atlas lost heart and will.
            [Hocken, MS 704/7: 430, pp.85–6]

**Hill-Country**

White sky, mountains mount
High: near, terraced, clear
Groined, shouldered
Black-bouldered. Sallow flats lie
Dry.
Yellow broom blooming
Pollen-heavy. Bees hum
Come from air there—
Bare, bleak, blue-peak

Towers over mountain flower—
Bees come, hum home
Home to hive in house-wall
Fall.
All heard, small bird;
Wind strums over plain
Same dry, high plain:
Thin grass sounds in winds
As winds pass.

Rock-face, clay fallen away
Gravel sluices loose for gold
Travels down, silts over
Old boulders. Land-lover
Here stand, stay.

Sallow flat, yellow flat, willow-flat
Pass. Let pass hill-wind, hill-grass:
Here stay: lay aside
Dry brick, sun-dried.
Here stay, deep in clay
Sun-clay, water-clay
Gouged-out, gaping clay
Clay.
[Hocken, MS 704/7:435, pp.98–9]

**O lands seen in the light of an inhuman dawn**

O lands seen in the light of an inhuman dawn
Lands of first-seeming dream now of surrealist night-mare
Why do you so destroy my isolation
With the weight of an earlier and prehistoric isolation?

Why do you gaze into my lamp-lit solitude
With stony eyes O nearing mountains stone-crested
Murmuring madness—leaning and silted Druid monoliths
To kindred listening with secretive insane attention?

And rivers leaping with immense inertia past gorge and derrick
Why do you speak from your opaque blindness
Not of life not of snow but a swollen harshness
Showing an eye-universe inanely inately blind?

Even so are men. O for the flood of compassion
Of emotional understanding and human blunder.
[Hocken, MS 704/7:439, p.107]

### Song and the soul-delighting river

Song and the soul-delighting river
Cannot, will not live for ever.
What shall come when these are over?

Hills beyond the park are white
Where peak and canyon lurk in hate:
They are, whether I will or not

As endless and exterior
As willow-plaited patterns are
Or the continual wearisome air.

Love and prophesy alike
Have no fulfilment: Diamond lake
Will never split, will never break.

But see! the iron blossoming
From our anhydrous dream takes wing
To split the diamond, break the dream.

For while we dreamt, athwart the lake
The stone existent billows broke
In waves of hunger and of hate.

While we who dreamt must drown beneath
The tidal gathering of death.
Fools! in the steel and iron death

Is Babylon is Nineveh
Fulfilment of the prophesy
In an immense virility.

Beneath the iron whelming wave
Our bones shall be the roots whereof
Springeth desire and flower of love.
[Hocken, MS 704/7:446, pp.120–1]

### The Ghost Unborn

When I am dead perhaps I will grow bored
With close-knit buried shell of roots and bone;
Perhaps my ghost will rise and lope along
Lonely by city, field and ford.
Then by a mystic alchemy unknown
Will merge into the linnet and his song;

Will kneel beside the petalled flower unseen,
Transparent to the winds and kindred sun.

So pass into my own dear house deserted;
Say: 'here I laid by night my human head,
Here was I joyful in the maze of love.
Here my heart wept in sorrow' . . . then will pause
Knowing myself not quick, but strangely-dead—
A vague phantasm of the surly grave
Estranged, cut off from human intercourse.

For in deep sorrow I was living most—
Having lost power to sorrow, am a ghost.
[Hocken, MS 704/472: p.19]

**De Averno**
(to the intelligentsia)

Perhaps, the torrent over,
Brief Phyrric satisfaction of the victor
Past, ravelled and destroyed;

Beauties we once enjoyed
Will wave new crystal wings, will waver
Then wrap us in age-old illusion:

But, from the subtle confusion
Of vague conflicting aims
And vague high-sounding names
Nothing will recompense

For love's talents spilt like pence
Youth's young bones snapped and shattered
Youth's smooth face blood-bespattered.

Think not of the high promise—
The infants now produced
Clean, without blemish;
Nor even grow yet sadder
Over the hell to be loosed
The unborn 'cannon-fodder'.

Remember only this.
Here did the young
Know bliss or the shadow of bliss
They were not chaff, not chaff!

But Death's dry iron tongue
Swallowed them down with relish—
Clean, without blemish
Or yet of deepest blemish.
Weep not
Death laughs
I laugh.
[Hocken, MS 704/8:475, pp.25–6]

**Tulips**

In the grey waste of rain
The bitter wind lashing the boughs to anguish
Saw I the ghost of quiet rise again.

Tulips velvet-purple, velvet-red
Swaying each sleek and petalled head
To wind-gusts—and dreaming
Of peaceful Dutch canal and square-cut garden.
These can no storm-wind sadden.
Like lamps they glowed, like birds they sang
Of tulips myriad swaying in the sun:
Each petal held the low dark fields of Holland.

And the garden filled with their song and glowing
Till the cold sky broke, and the sun was showing.
[Hocken, MS 704/8: 487, p.46]

**The Poet**

The poet looks over the dam
At lumbermen felling trees
With axe and bar.
Jealous of their apparent physical ease
Says: ah, but these
The clown and bumpkin are.

The poet is cast upon knives
Of mind-built rhetoric
'Hitches his wagon to a star.'
And stammers, stumbles among the slick
Who make a motor tick.
The clown and bumpkin are
Superior.
[Hocken, MS 704/8: 490, p.49]

**Boys laugh at ease**
(for Jo Rantin)

Boys laugh at ease
Upon the rising seas;
    Young bulls in the spring season
Will butt at sapling trees.

The stirring of the blood
Comes even in trench-mud,
    Wins for especial daring
A cross of bronze or wood.

Old men less wise
Control the enterprise:
    Old men can see uncaring
Lost limbs or blinded eyes.

These who have scarcely seen
The sapling wood shoot green
    Are killed before the branches
Have shed their summer sheen.

Young men sleep well,
Wake to the crash of shell;
    Old men dream of the tempest
Ringing a winter knell.

When all are dead
Then be no prayer said
    Save: Youth among the cannons
Sought life, encountered lead.
        [Hocken, MS 704/8:500, pp.67–8]

**Poem of Passage**

Do bird, beast, flower and the untranquil waves
Burst into our mind's solitude and make
    The same diverse intensity of grief,
    The same swart vigour from our tombed belief.

Or is it the overshadowing doom that gives
A fierce and temporal fire to all things living—
    No swan-song but the mailèd eagle's flight
    That shatters through the solitary night.

The worm will speak from under the Seat of Mercy
Of brute and blind delight. And more do we
    Break through the moted thundering chaos, borne
    By fountain, flower, and trumpet of the morn.
        [Hocken, MS 704/9:539, p.47]

**There is a farm-house . . .**

There is a farm-house, seen, remembered
Or perhaps to be seen by me grown strange in a future
Unmapped. Sea speaking beyond it
In the bass voice of cloudy weather.
Wind strikes perhaps the hurrying sky to slate
And storm like rain in poetry impends
Dark-hearted, breathing in unknown trees.

I cannot see this farm-house
Save from the tail of the eye; but stone,
And intense as a Van Gogh painting it is.
No streams are there
But reeds; but low rock hills behind it
And the sea-evening redolent of rain.
Not dream-like melancholy
But scent of earth, firm labour;
Not striving but acceptance.
    Thus have I seen it or shall see it
Beyond nostalgic past or crystalline future.
This is an etching
As from imperfect memory.
Thus have I seen it.
        [Hocken, MS 704/9:542, p.51]

**Aeneas**

Aeneas, the astute and priggish, driven
By half-loved duty on the seas of fame
Longed to forsake that fate but faltered, craven,
Fearing the wrath of gods or the after-shame.

Aged Anchises on his shoulder borne
From the red ashes of a broken city . . .
'The shrunken child; his godhead cannot return.'
No reins but those of pity and self-pity.

But Venus was the mother in his mind
Who could not age; thus he could not forsake her
Like elder whores grown wearisome and blind.
Italy she, and the shoreward groaning breaker.

Yet once with Dido in the storm-hid cave
Found himself, unclothed by destiny;
Knew he'd not won but lost when the harbour gave
To an inhuman unrepentant sea.
[Hocken, MS 704/10:613]]

**Song**

Thou shalt forget in age
The clamouring of youth
When the magnificent rage
Leaves but one bitter truth: (bis)
Though jealous
And zealous
Sad Beauty must forget
The lids for her made wet
Of Montague and Capulet;
Her charms avail her not
And she will rot.

Thou shalt forget in age
The pilèd golden wealth;
Time doth no battle wage
But taketh all by stealth. (bis)
Mourning
And scorning
The gauds that moved him so
The miser must forgo
His graven goblets for the well of woe;
His mould availeth not
And he will rot.

So shall I seek my love
And be sad-merry now,
Nor have my fill thereof
But sing like bird on bough. (bis)
Uncraven
Love-paven
Naught shakes my citadel

Where all life's joys do dwell
And like sorrow: her roots go down to hell;
        Thus death and age
        Are but a page
Within that book of days that I con well;
        Their might avails them not;
        I shall not be forgot
        Though I do rot.
            [Hocken, MS 704/10: 650, p.174–5]

**Development**

When I read as a child
Of paint-green frogs conversing on lily leaves
In mackintoshes, it woke fantasy.

Later I saw
A frog inflated with a straw:
I wept but did not dare to interfere.

And so grew reconciled
Where frogs were pinned and disembowelled on slats;
And the pricked heart would beat.

'Small green-clad warbler of the marshy pool.'
Thinking the bathetic beautiful
I must incise, idealize.

Frogs croak at rain on the river.
The cycle is completed.
I have lost interest.
        [Hocken, MS 704/11:656, p.11]

**The Killing of a Rabbit**

As we come over the hill
    The rabbit runs from the gorse,
Shows tail and then stops still;
    Thinks he is hidden, of course—
Though heart pounds loudly—
By immobility.

I see the rifle raised,
    I see the jewel of sun
That over the muzzle blazed

Move slowly up the gun . . . .
I hear the thud with the crack.
He shudders and rolls back.

Quick I run to the place.
His eyes are dark and wild;
The pitiful twisted grace,
The stare of a sickbed child;
The draggled fur torn wide
Where the grey guts hang from his side.

I twist the neck and he twitches;
The head hangs limp and droll.
Play in cropped furze and ditches,
The miraculous life of the soul
Is spent—shall I be blamed?
I walk back unashamed.
[Hocken, MS 704/11:665, pp.23–4]

**Janus Unheard**

The hardness I strike at, not the incidental beauty

I

Send us O God an emetic
Brew us O Lord an antidote
For the world (or, if you prefer it, capitalism)
Messily cutting its throat;
For mutual inhumanity in the papers:
The bombers reaping another innocent swathe
Or the latest atrocity in Europe;
The antidote is faith.
Outside the rain is ceasing
Brilliant sunshine flashing in the rain;
The rainbow represents the ancient covenant
And I must rear again
My Janus-head out of a country coma
Of pastoral falsity, of rain on leaves;
Hear history's abstract music thunder
Her breves and semibreves.
O is it not enough to speak of blue-gums
And the wind on the hill?
Yes, it is enough—but here there stands the hangman;
Be-killed-or-kill.
And if one forgets him, walks wild with the wind-gust

The worm will wake, the Worm will wake
Which gnaws return to time, and the salamanders
The fish in the burning lake.
Faith? what faith? look in the fire for answer:
There is heat there with the burning chicken-bones;
There is ardour of a kind, one may say a blind ardour:
*He will raise up sons to Abraham out of stones.*
And what is faith? Walk the world seeking
Shall we find it then?
Among waves, or winds, or the stone limbs of mountains—
Or the shoddy slums of men.
Rather, I say, it is here we are likely to find it;
Here, where hope is dying, and valour dies
In conqueror, cut-throat, conchie—
Here, in the world of life and lies.
The beast lives as if immortal,
Pain only knowing of death or birth;
Trees have no need of faith, they are linked to
All reservoirs of sky and earth:
But man—the crowd do I mean? an abstraction only—
Emotional, finds faith for his needs
Canoeing unhelped-unhindered by chilly reason;
Nautilus afloat on a sea of creeds.
. . . The fearless razor-glass of childhood
Cut a section through the hazy house of words;
Under the floor was cat-life, dust and howling,
Over the ceiling the straw and chatter of birds—
With no attempt to superimpose a
Fairytale structure of human manners and speech.
But the eyes are closed. Each bears the scrip of purpose;
Each has a creed to teach.
The lair of a wolf needs no girders
To prop its roof;
It is shaped to the wolf's wish, the wolf's breathing,
Fire- and storm-proof.
That she there may couch and nurse her litter
There may drag her prey;
But the tower built of man is groined and girdered
Broad in the light of day.
Like Babel many days go to its building,
Childhood and manhood; most when (the sudden deep
Of a treacherous river) in love or lands self is abandoned:
The sudden deep, strange as a waking from sleep.
. . . Green-smooth they bend

In the breezy day,
The tall slim rushes
That rustle and sway:
Trout in swamp-water
Glitter below them;
Quiet they rustle
On bowing stem.
Here did I lie
In the lee of the rock
Watching the wild ducks
Paddle and flock:
I pulled then a rush
And bared the white pith
Thinking to make
A lamp-light therewith.
I twisted them into
A butterfly-cage
Then as befitted
A man of my age
Cast it upon
The quick ripples there;
No sun since shone brighter
Nor sing there birds more fair.
And when first the Platonic Forms flower
Live in a statue's curve
Or the modern grace, carving the lines of a suspension
Bridge, with a gull's and with steel's verve:
Valuable too the day when the tower seems Babel
And about to fall
With scream of madness in a mild blue sunset;
Death on its flaming walls, inexorable and tall.
Reinforced concrete, tall and tough,
Girdered in faith not reason
His soul will stand storms enough
By elements unbroken.
There is a shout jolting the heart:
*Lo, of the Rock that begat thee*
*Unmindful thou art.*
Faith's clarion to him who denies it.
For man fears change
With body and soul changing;
Longs for the sure and strange
Rock of life eternal.
Change: the mentally deficient

Grow up and breed
Accepting blague easily, puzzled by numbers
Puzzled by life—sharp eye and empty head;
A pal at the bar, and hiding the shallow
Uneasy weakness behind a limited range
Of expert knowledge; squat and square with the rifle.
*'All change for the night train.'* And man fears change.
And more than change, that chill which is not age
Nor grief, nor terror of avalanche hurling on the glacier
Nor the warm-blooded rage
Of beast prowling for prey that crouches;
It is motion motionless
That waits malevolently, even sluggish;
In sudden nakedness
Like the bearded spider on white flooring;
Or slow
Like underwater weeds that curl on the swimmer.
From his own heart springs it: thus he must throw
Arms about the enduring, clasp it securely.
And thus is born *The Rock*
And spirit of man crying,
We are born, we are hewn of the parent block—
Cleft-for-me Rock of Ages.
For blessed is the strong man whose heart faileth not
Though the hills shake and the mountains are turned to flame;
Though the great deep be troubled, though the seas shout in tumult
And cast up monsters on the shores of fame;
Though the rivers of earth be salt with slaughter
And the nations rise
In fury one against the other
Storming the land and skies.
Yet shall he abide in faith and take his path
Nor rejoicing, nor weeping through the night of chaos.
The night of fear and wrath.

II

Most have never heard of Aristotle
Yet keep to the mean.
When summer sweeps the coasts like a tornado
And the fanged and curling green
Waves are quiet in sunstorm; and the bathers
And beach-lizards like after-storm debris
Are stranded on the sands; when the hive crawls back after sulphur
Then the rejuvenating sea
Finds work to do, restores morale; while father

Sleeps in the lupins under the shade of the car
Forgets for a while he ever was a tradesman;
And the kids go down to the milk-bar,
And the girls like mannequins pose, free with the lipstick,
Varnish cracking on toe- and finger-nails.
And the clear perspective of the slaty harbour
Is broken by sails.
Yet the children are not deceived, the children
Work while the others play—
Sand-castle, shell-garden, tunnel and buttress—
O there ain't no holiday
From the dull eye and the deep-set neurosis . . .
The bombers are coming, the bombers come.
Death with cravat and collar
And an evening suit; and the racket and the hum
Quiet at night of the face triangular:
He was a bottle-fed baby (mother's milk
Would spoil the pleasant pallor, the smooth complexion)
His garrotte is made of silk.
(Each with his large desires and small fulfilment
Each approximating to the Norm;
There's hope in the fighter-plane (. . . the girls will cluster;
There's hope in a uniform.
And there is no cloud on the white horizon
Yet there's going to be a storm.)
And it was we who fed him

We who have
Pinched his face, by our own hate scissored
In Mongol, Teuton, Slav.

The moral code, the crystallizing dogma
Is regarded absolute.
Christ and intuition
Go down to the basement in a sliding chute.
And those who never could
For themselves originate the miracle of law
May nevertheless receive it, may nevertheless believe it
When backed by the stone tablets, thunder and awe
On Sinai by Moses;
(The enlarged septum is not essential for expounding the divine;
As Blake once said not jesting:
'Your God has a great hooked nose like yours; mine has a snub nose like to mine.')

But the stupid will act in accord
    With new religion and ritual
(Jahweh God of the Chosen)
    Praising the name of The Lord.
. . . Here's the brass band of the Salvation Army
    Blaring, blaring for Kingdom Come;
I lean on the railing, lean awhile and listen:
    And the melancholy bugles and the drum
Cry, 'Come, young sinner, to repentance';
    And I begin
To feel the lure, so I walk off till the music
    Is only din
(None too soon, for round comes the lassie
    With the smile and the collection tin.)
For some the church-cross has fascination
    For the daring of stones;
Some run on the graves in the cemetery
    Feeling the call of bones to bones.
The chief function of the Church is comforting—
    The catholic Mary-of-wide-arms
Can embrace the world like a Mother; evident
    In lithographs in city flats and shrines on farms.
But in those of small vitality, forgetful of life,
    A nucleus of dogma
Dearer than child or wife
    Requires for lack-love no repentance;
In brief, becomes for them
    A calm synthetic conscience
And martyr's diadem
    That lies like a stone in the breast, on brow is leaden.
Yet such is mired in quicksands
    When minds of those ruled by it
Out-grow their swaddling-bands.
    See, thus, the child-disciple
Driven to realize
    That the instinctive world regards him
With clear unfaithful eyes.
    War in him: but as the parental
Influence declines he is faced with a complete
    And shattering re-adjustment . . . shall he abstain from dances
When everyone does it to jazz, slick on their feet?
    I notice that the Catholic disillusioned
Boozes with a vim;
    Races to races with girl-friend in roadster;

Two armies are fighting in him.
    Some day the barricades go down unnoticed;
The worn-out coat falls off an atheist—
    Discarding also the necessary illusion,
Truth even, as gesture of the hypnotist.
. . . And he can never go home to Ireland;
See where grandfather lived in the famine year.
    There is left, I will admit, substantial compensation
Communism perhaps, or beer and more beer.
. . . I could not live in a Paradise of the People
Art for the Masses becomes Art for the State
    Becomes a prostitute to propaganda;
And Mayakovsky's fate—
    Who remained at heart the bourgeois (or the poet)
So shot himself, leaving a lyric behind—
    Encourages me in this. Nor is a dictator
Pleasing, of any kind.
    Yet I at heart the peaceful anarchist
Must back one colour, barrack for one horse:
    Be it then the derided democracy
Never tried yet; though orated about, of course.
—And if the armour does not crack,
Vitality being low in him or sublimated,
    Why, then he can lean back
The hermit Jesuit in a cave of dogma;
    And not observing how the river runs
And trees grow, and men also
    He will see Adam's sons
On wheel of flesh or heaven, each one an Ixion.
    And yet there is a core
Unbreakable which only self can sandbag
    And bitterness cannot retreat from, for
It has in it all needs, even of bitterness.
    I do not blether.
It is natural intuition to which I am referring:
    'Rejoice, rejoice, the stars are linked together!'
It will not say, Shoot him, he is a fascist;
    Nor rejoice to see the tanks
Come lurching down the dumb inactive roadway;
    But will give thanks
For moments of personal emotion
    Such as . . . swimming at low tide
In Loch Seven with the smell of kelp seaweed . . .
    Or boiling the billy below the mountain-side

In N.Z.  I will soon be 18;
  My life may be regarded as mainly future;
But the responsive core is seen
  Alike in child and adult, man and woman.
I find it in Ethel Mannin, I find it in Tolstoy;
  I find it in the Celt, obscured by spleen.
It cannot shoot; only a creed can kill—
  Creed of rage, religion, or any -ism;
And personality seems unimportant till
  The bullet snickers in your lungs or liver.
Do we really know what we want?
  The tide of history turns against us:
There are no rods to flail this Hellespont—
  Though all at heart are imitating Xerxes.
O let us lie and sleep a thousand years—
  Wake to find Death an electric gunman;
No sweat, but the usual incapable tears
  And blood forever—blood of the bloody
Baptismal grace to drive the devils out;
  Even if the guns go off to wireless
Brain and bodies will take the clout.
  Take up your rifle. In the clash of armies
It is the strong who wins—
  The strong and not the good: truth is in neither;
Bullet and bludgeon will not salve his sins
  Whose wand wielded to freeze the running water
Freezes also the animal response,
  Blood choking the lungs—the same live coral
At Austerlitz, Pharsalia and Mons.
  Strike at the hide of a creed and you strike manhood:
The personal contribution
  (Warped, weak, or waning)
To a world's absolution
  Forgotten or disregarded.
And as the mind will flash its magic-lantern
  Casting shadow of devildom or sainthood
Upon the human feature; but personal failure
  Can not be blinded in blood;
Or but briefly. The careless sniper
  Notches his score; till he-knows-not-what
Pricks the bubble of dream. He loses nerve, knowing
  It was himself he shot.

III

In all philosophies, as basic axiom
It is presumed one wishes to live;
If not, remains suicide the bare bodkin
Stark beyond reprieve.
Unfair, I grant—despair of life may be valid;
Yet physical fear of the gas-oven or gun
Conquers desire for death, dooms to a limbo . . .
And hills quiet in sun
Or a love-affair may shatter the neurosis.
But if one were alone—truly alone—
The eye seeing, the brain digesting
Would be sole universe, eventually monotone.
But O the expanding and exploding horizon
When equal beings stand
Alive in love or hate or indifference
With lax or beckoning hand.
The God is an abstraction, a focus of thought;
The moral code is easy and explicit:
Beauty cannot be bought;
And poise cannot be taught—perhaps Mosaic
But true all the same, as a plimsoll mark:
Add that you cannot fear the darkness
If you learn to love the dark
For its quality (say) of ~~absorption~~ self-absorption
Or the way that slum and factory repose
Sleeping in it with the sleep of children
Easy on the eyes, till darkness goes.
In this year of death and despairing
1944
Dogmatic creeds kill the conscript armies
Though the outcome the War
Is evident by tokens . . . there is starvation
In Greece and India;
All are equally innocent, all are equally guilty—
For all anathema.
It is sanity made evident in the madhouse
Cuts the heart most;
Like Paolo and Francesca in storm of ruin
So the sane and loving, the living ghost.
Speak of the dead to me. Their quiet immortality
Is like a flame or star;
Golden Pythagoras and the grave Caesar pass,
To me immortal are.

But their full souls, piteous, unpiteous,
They live not. Whither are they?
Did they stretch out with crying hands, into the night (as night fell on them)
Toward our sunned security?
Quiet they lie in clay: crocus-bells waken them.
Quiet they lie—ah nay! utter death like a doom
Dissolved them clean away
Or they have spurned inertia of the tomb.
O where are the unborn? night deeper than ages lies on them
Illuminate alone
By ray of love or reason
That pierceth cruel stone,
Spans brief eternity, makes time a mockery.

I can endure
The civic threat, the public hate,
Self-approbation remaining
Enwhorlèd, secure.
I see—though none will believe me—
The Roman vertigo,
The power that broke the Empire:
*Delenda est Carthago.*
It is not the usual things that I remember,
The antique legend, rift in the Capitol.
Rather it is the gesture, the men fearing,
The priest speaking behind the oracular doll.
Cicero, who would not leave his villas
Stretching his neck from the litter, waiting the stroke.
The soldiers on shore who might have won the battle
Though Antony's squadrons broke,
But leaderless. And even in Rome they had their
Cliques of literature, their men of books
Believing themselves civilization's saviours
While the new world made spears from pruning-hooks
Faith in the ultimate efficacy
Of destruction destruction destroying
(Disruption within and eruption without)—
We the same spur employing.
As in Spain where Reds and Insurgents unscripted
In district and only the uniform worn
Distinguished such, as they killed without conviction:
Our politics are determined by where we are born.
And as, though they were Loyalist, fought beside them,

It was found necessary to liquidate the POUM;
Though he make friends of the mammon of the unrighteous
The individualist will meet his doom.
It is the men I always remember . . .
Sulla, whose face 'like a mulberry sprinkled with meal'
In blood saw solace for self-disintegration.
Caesar the dandy, the epileptic of steel.
And this I know (only their books remaining)
The men they killed they did not need to kill;
The personal insight, the poet's vision
Would save them then . . . will save them still.
Emotional clarity will solve it;
The whole reconciled with the parts, the parts with the whole.
Forget the ideology; remember
Only body and soul
Broken in Europe by us: the unborn still-born;
None knowing, none caring, leaf lashing leaf, branch breaking bole.
Death the dagger, and life the goal.
[Hocken, MS 704/12:709, pp.1–22]

**Hopes and Fears for Man**
(as a prize-poem)

The trumpets of the Spring are blown . . .
While as I write, mine own especial demon
Sits snug within my shoulder sweating venom;
Crooning, counting my heart-throbs, with his placid
Pale countenance and lips of nitric acid;
Whispers that words are worthless, blurs the vision
With impotence, with mouth of cold derision.
One lake is louder than demonic malice:
There must I drink. It is the bitter chalice,
The purgatorial woe of warring nations,
Whose stones are steel, whose waves are lamentations.

The trumpets of the Spring are blown
Within this mountainous southern land;
Breakers boom at the beaches;
Inflammatory speeches
Of thrush and tui on the winds are sown,
That man may wake and understand
The wonder of the land

What is it to grow?
Is it to know
More clear each day
The word's futility?
The vain communication;
The hidden aberration;
True beauty violated
By murder malcreated;
Too massive for escaping
The grave-gates gaping,
While each within his tower
Of word or bone must fear
The final falling,
Speech reft beyond recalling,
And anguish in the flower?
No, it is rather
The eye of son to father,
The eye of son to mother,
Seeing there is another
Truth than at first perceivèd
In age long-grievèd,
In youth full-sheavèd;
Seeing all fear and wrath
Concomitants of growth;
No final ill but hurt,
No final wrong but hate;
Dumb ardour of the flower,
The beast in his bone-tower,
In life inseparate.

And the first hope for Man
Is that he may remember
Why flints were chipped, and why the coracle;
And why the towers of ferro-concrete stand,
The modern monoliths: they sway above
His horde—the maimed, the stunted, and the blind—
Betokening might unruled by insight.
Might of the aphid who must yet give suck
Of blood and body to his vampire-dreams,
To the extortionate pulse of the machines—
Forgetting animal birth, forgetting
That flints were chipped . . . chipped for the animal
To give his body comfort. To love and live.
And the first fear for Man . . .

I shall pray: for whom shall I pray?
Those whom I love—the brave, the beautiful, the gay?
    Pray for the mad who die with demons;
Pray also where the prison rears righteous head:
It is the grave of those who are not dead;
    And pray for the unwanted man and woman;
For those stifled forever in family;
For those whose sole savour is enmity.
    This be the key, the talisman, the summons:
The physical disability is the least,
The psychic gnarl screams like a tortured beast.
    Pray for the conqueror who is inhuman;
Pray for the conquered lacking life to love
Thus seeing only the bitterness thereof.
*This kind for prayer or fasting go not out*
Yet pray—less brittle than fanatic shout
    The prayer may flash live-leaping like a salmon
Thy prayer may be a well for those in walls.
For self pray not. Pray most for him who calls,
Who cries on God and finds there is no God.

It is the hope for Man
That he in each behold his fellow;
May be glad-hearted when the leaves are yellow
Because the leaves are light, and fall so
Thick and dextrously. No wall so
Shall Time be, but bind each day
To each in surety, though steel dismay
And men maim men. We make our paradise
(For sun and moon are buried in our eyes);
If aught say *Man is vile* none can reply
In mute or mocking guise: 'It is not I.'
    [Hocken, MS 704/12:718, pp.36–40]

**Convoys**

The Sea:
The skin that clothes our earth: one element
Whose currents flow like winds on submarine mountains,
Whose clouds will darken continents, whose grey rollers
Gnaw worm-like at their base. We born of sea,
Spawn of that bitter blood, now parasite
On the alluvial plains once ocean-bed,
Crawl in our discontent . . .
                                        But that no matter.

It is the human eye
Gives life to history:
When the Phoenician galleys
Threaded their island-alleys,
Daring the unknown seas
Beyond the pillar-capes of Hercules;
When first from the wreck-paven,
Rock-walled, and death-ingraven,
Mediterranean calm and storm
They snared the feet of Time—
Heard howling the gigantic
Winds of the North Atlantic:
Did they then guess
That iron merciless
Would scourge the waters they
Coast-clinging feared by night and day?
And when Columbus' caravels
Lay lifting to the steady swells
By gates of huge America,
Where, seeking gold of India,
He and his mutinous sailors came:
Could he foresee the flame,
And the Andean torment—
Slaves silver-mining, mangled;
And Montezuma strangled:
Cutlass and cross, the bloody sacrament?

Ship, sword, cross, alike have had fruition.
The monsters than-whales-vaster menacing our seas,
Hearts in iron ribs beating,
Carry with them the march of an inevitable future,
The mingling yet of war and comradeship.
. . . Convoys zigzagging in the danger-zone:
Their checkered wakes like chess-board squares
Curve in the chilly airs.
The sky is frozen into stone;
Save that planes under the cloud-ceiling
With dull and raucous hum, escort; and drill
The high and motionless marble. Their unappealing
Calm crosses move,
Bearing a weight of bitterness, mute man's-will
Combating man; malign the burden of
Power and death, death and power:
Man's hopes and man's defeats are come to flower—

His hope in steel imbedded,
Defeat in that same steel;
Steel to destroy the dragon unbeheaded;
Steel that may leave a wound that will not heal
To spawn new dragons. O pray that such
Come not to pass . . . we seek not overmuch;
Peace only pray for: peace, and poverty's repeal.

So the calm crosses move on
Over the wrinkled sea; an ever-receding horizon
Moves on also: Within the iron shells
Men labour, men, amid the clang of bells
And blood-throb of the engines: each in his heart
Carries remembrance, and a serpent fear
Of sudden death. Hopes too are dear,
Are marked by pencil-crosses on the chart.

The cargo—food or arms—
Few think on: their minds are lit
By each day's needs. The cargo: few think of it
Save captains edgy for alarms
And those who wait in English towns and farms.

And the majestical monotony,
Soothing routine, despite their hungry fears
Settles on them. Bleached white with years,
Slate-grey again, the aged-ageless sea
Matted by winds, blown smooth by squalls—
Black squalls and hurricane clouds—
Bears them; where sailing-ships
Drove westward with the thunder in their shrouds;
Where wrecked and rafted men have scarred the walls
Of their horizon-bubble, salt-blistered lips
And parched throats crying for green land-falls . . .

And if
Sudden the siren shrills—
As stars weave their meaningful hieroglyph
Or storm-wrack fills
That savage sky—
And the roar of the dive-bomber
Grows in crescendo; bullets beat the deck
Like onset of a shower in summer:
The cool routine is broken . . . Swerve and check.
Bomb-burst on the quarter. Water-spout.

Rattle and chug of gun-fire. The bobbing cylinders:
Anti-aircraft. The drone fading out;
Or water-crash, like skidding on concrete. Flare and fires.

Or dropping depth-charges. Like blasting
With dynamite in quarries; but here the rip is not lasting
And wounded water heals. The surge
Of fountaining water, foam. The outward urge,
Like pellets flicked, of catapulted cans.
As ever, the arm is human, the doom is man's:
Do crumpled hulls of submarines not let
The solid water jet,
An equal javelin for men of all races?
So; there is hope also in their faces.
That hope may blossom yet, may be
The lighted path from our Gethsemane.

What power drives these convoys?
For what will the seas loosen their liquid vice?
For what will men brave bergs of ice,
Hail and sickness? Is it but the red
Furnace coal—or oil-fed—
The precise steel shaken by blind steam?
It is more. It is the ammonite's dream . . .
Sand-buried forests here grow leaves again,
The leaves of flame that flicker . . . And in man's brain
Shell-coilèd, the form of ships unbuilt
Born in crude galley and caravel. And blood spilt
To save the Roman grain-ships pirated.
There are ships and sailors, the unburied dead,
Save by the black seas buried: hulks that lie
In wars sunk, by storms sunk; the high
Sea-roof above them, bedded upon ooze.
These are the fates that wrangle in her flues,
Battle-ship, liner.
                O though a man be found
Stalwart and hardy, to leave kindred for
Bursting shell and the wounding chance of war—
What shall it avail him when he is drowned?
Will courage brace the lung to choking water?—
Salt-vertigo, more terrible than slaughter,
As if the very air were treacherous,
Was lurking smooth to raven and engulf us:
So when the bucking seas that served as slaves
Break bonds and whelm with fangèd waves.

Their wakes like chess-board squares . . .
Yet these ships moving like pawns
Are no pawns; nor is this waste of rainy dawns,
Of charging hill and valley, of gun and signal-flares
A board that pieces move on. Rather the men
Ruled by the ships they make,
Are pawns, are pieces: yet is this fancy, then:
They are not ruled by ships, but words,
But thoughts; for these have forgotten land-song and land-birds,
Stare at a boiling wake . . .

Mine and torpedo wait
With their explosive hate;
Storms batter and delay
Them on their dangerous way.
And the harsh journey ended—
Murder and mercy blended—
In dock they are unlading
The goods of usual trading,
Weapons of war as well—
Mortar, howitzer, shell.
Laden with hope and fear
They anchor at the pier:
I beg from iron fate
That hope predominate.
[Hocken, MS 704/12:719, pp.41–8]

**Bracchiae**

Latona's children
Have arms to weave
Laurel- and cypress-leaf
Sieging the heart with love or grief:
Immortals do not grieve.

And this young man
his face a van gogh blur
van gogh vitality
is now a scavenger.
Upon the dross-heaps he
clambers for coal
dull or glittering. Hear the angels sing:
A farthing for a soul.

And in the sick streets under neon lights
faces of parchment and vermilion.
green tulips and cut crystal.

the silver-sandalled feet run overhead.
    glancing upward you may see
    in starry woods of Arcady
    Diana's crotch and knee
lucid with perspiration.

Apollo flogging
his broken-down horses
ankle-deep in dust
crawls in the set courses.

The oily cobbles
of sea shine
a passenger-vessel
has struck a mine.

Thus said a nubian statue:
I lifted the stone you are about to lift
and saw a basilisk.

The painting of El Greco
has sublimated light and shade.
The Agony in the Garden
shows his religious flair and flare.
El Greco
Died many years ago.
        [Hocken, MS 704/12:744, pp.112–14]

**Legend**

The dead are quiet in their courtly dresses
Believe themselves the time's epitome;
But the traditional blind beggar and
Untraditional horde
Will dynamite the palaces—
The gentle corpse, painted and bland
Saying from mirror-head;
The age dies with me.

Some have perceived
The bitter rift and sigh
Bury their faces in

The flowers of blood;
Some are split-men as I.

One newly-killed I saw that grieved
From his grave-window said:
  From birth I bled;
Birth stabbed me and since then
Love even could not break
The diminishing horizon—
Some since have said I died for love's sake.
    [Hocken, MS 704/12:760]

**Flower-Venus**

The Flower-Venus of our tropic day
Makes aim of anarchy, virtue of anger,
Beguiles with glittering the gilded flies
Who sack her hoard: she meshes them: they die.
  Error and Truth have mated. These afford
The paradox of Love housed i' the hangar:
The sleek, the svelte and unobtainable
(In mannequins marvelled once, in sculpture-lines)
By metal mastered.
      And as the forest boar
Apalion, whose stroke is lightning: he
As gnarling torrents fearless in brute valour
Must bear with weight of seasons and their war
Deformity more monstrous: the sword-tusk
Which hath unbellied hounds that yelping tore
His iron flank—this natural armament
Doth now unseat its bony citadel
With curved unforcèd growth; boring each hour
More in his maddened skull: till life aghast
At self-rebellion part. And immolate
His bones wake wonder in some rocky den.
  So are we stricken mad in enmity
By our own steel encarrioned more with years:
The tyrant-crushing hand studying snares
Of tyranny will grow all-tyrannous also—
Vain then the early vengeance, venom and bloody fears.
  And some must paint a face of purpose
Upon the inane mask that Fortune bears;
Hope with dead Hope in them are warriors,
Seek love or violence to gloze,
(Seize paper spills for armour:)

Politics in the quarrelling of drunks
And Beauty as the whorish Babylon . . .

Of each volume published in England
One copy is presented to the British Museum
Whose neo-Grecian pillars thus contain
Trash and tragedy, religion and pornography.
The inference is plain:
That Art is regarded as the mirror of life
Not as one bough of the everlasting Tree
But a quiet and interesting miniature
Which in future days may be inspected with pleasure
As men in ruined Pompeii walk to see
The Temple of Love though hate may gnaw their skulls.

I have seen rata often,
A flower for honey-sucking birds:
Shall I speak now of rata?

O Blake
I see you stand above the continents
Shadowing Asia, and the earthquake hordes
Of steel and turmoil; pointing to Heaven
With left hand; with right hand to Earth.
The Tree of Healing blossoms from your palms,
You are the juggler shown in my arcana.
A sword from your mouth
I hold and am invincible:
To grapple with the toils of leonine Mars;
Behold the heart of Man in love and pity:
The fire of healing flowering in my veins.
[Hocken, MS 704/13:778]

**For those who lie with crooked limbs in the straight grave**

Snow clogs air and earth; dark cloud-eruption
Advances to keen wind. Or the curling flakes fall
Weighting all: ache of yellow leaves
By the compassionate wandering flakes hidden;
Heaven invades earth. In the eyeless winter
What shall I do but burn
The incense-shavings, twigs of summer boughs?
Smoke in a hollow room . . .
Medea rides
The black and marble midnight: twin dragons
Before her chariot flaming; from cloudy Caucasus

Where chained Prometheus bleeds: on burning snow
Blows the cold ice-flower.
                    Young Absyrtus dead
In the blue seaway, drowned and floating head:
With him the Spring rots livid, unfulfilled.
    The dull bronze foliage of dawn
Cast no more from her gold Tree in the East
Falls tarnished on our wharves. And we have seen
Only the smooth stone and the flourishing green;
Have too soon forgotten . . . earth in cycles of
A starry and immense vertigo.

Soft birds rustling on glazed chimney-pots;
Electric wires that cross a shingle gully;
Algae upon a sunken submarine;
And the dull jolting of a corpse encavemed.

    I thought I could feel the autumn wind blowing
But saw above through glass the grey gulls crossing—
What Children of Lir unfreed from wandering?—
Their inviolable pinions dim;
    Knew my universe finite.

The catholic priest came; planted his blossoming
Staff on the floor-boards. Angels leaned with the winds.
World's colours broke clear in the holy fountain.
Why did the heart turn? from flower-blue sky-enamel
Whereon the forked boughs sway.
    The rain blots out the lights; and the sworded wilderness
Consumes our streets like sky.

Birds build on the bastions
Of our mud fortresses: their droppings rot our roofs.
    There are ghosts tokening present anguish
Presaging doom, stalk our pavements;
Moving automatons in foggy streets
Their lipless masks hung like grooved corinthian marble.
    Even in daylight may be heard
The lisping step of a blind man's cane.
Sharp smell of vomit; in the garden
Someone is beating a rusty xylophone.

        Mater Dolorosa.
Tear-ducts are rigid pipes . . . jagged and metal anguish;
eyes pricked by cactus-spines.
Embalm her in cool cedar of lebanon;

burn incense-shavings:
you cannot melt her glacier sorrow.
Winter has clothed us. Who shall see the Spring?
[Hocken, MS 704/13:779]

**Sea-Elegy**

Gaunt the reef: sea-wrack writhing: sky broken by
Coast-beleaguering birds: hurling the morning waters
Fall with their grave-cloth linen over the rock reef gaunt.

Uneven surface where the flumed waves reeling vaunt
Their plumed pinions, ponderous rising to engulf land;
Surf-eaten quartz drips. At hand and underfoot

Mosaic of flawed pebbles on black earth, rain-channelled soot
Where native fires burned: bones they find here:
Strata wind-bare. Sword-grass is bronze, tarnished on grey hillocks.

Flow the flowering winter grasses, meshing sand and rocks;
Burn in brief flame the wind-gusts, combating green,
Corroding the antique grace; grow brushwood bulwarks.

Sponges and shattered shells show tide-marks . . .
Coast mailed in mist. Smoky antarctic clouds
March round horizon-bowl. I spit on the spouting waters.

Kelp coiling; a planing gull down-flutters
Stalks symbolic on weed. Hurling the morning waters
Blot out air's symmetry, sway to engulf land:

Till in ovidian mood sleek dolphins curvet; or bland
Bluff seals browse on land-herbage; fish whirling
Over church and homestead . . . not in our land: this was

The mediterranean lake, water-glass. Here only
The primeval tumuli would stay, drowned breasts
Suckling limitless ocean: the land to womb returning.

Naiads are dead: nor phosphor shoals burning;
Nor torose pillars hidden in brackish pond
Egyptian. The fossil will breed monsters again.

Silurian oceans irrigate the vein:
They long enclosed must fear the limitless.
Wind plaits a rope of sand: sea-blackened ever the green land.
[Hocken, MS 704/13:781]

**Death of a Swan**

Fell the wild swan: from havenless crags of sky
Fell to no cool lagoon of summer flocks
But bruising river-ice: she fell to die
Beside a winter shore and wolfish rocks.
Fell the wild swan to ice and lay thus weakly:
The tower-shadows hung compassionate;
Night like the river flowed till day came bleakly . . .
Hooded and frozen, her webs spread full: of late
The piteous bill moved, clogged as snow sank.
Vaulting pinions, the immense heaven cloven
To blades of sunlight, where now? She dead and dank,
And one with ice, snow-down to feel, wind-woven.
No baptismal save sleet; no Erin, priest-word repeating;
Lost child of Lir, heart frozen in faint beating.
[Hocken, MS 704/13: 784, p.45]

**The Closed Picture**

Heat like a tiger crouched
Stared in the camera lens;
And blank metal burned where the light fangs touched
Shone in sympathy
With eyes and ears of clay:
Our day is laced with the flight of earlier suns
Their wings beat round us, shield the low-blown sky.

Lies the paper summer.
O I would step
Into that summer scene
Spurning morraine of sleep:
The two dimensions stammer
A three-dimensional song.

The gush of mountain water
The glint of sun on stone
Where harnessed rivers shatter
Clay colorados down:
Who shall recapture them?
Locked in an iron dream.

O I would open the door
Of grass hinges
Which the dead only, riding their furious star
Of past love enter: over present ranges

That comet plunges
In night of time to where birth-angels cluster.

And walk over the boulders
And the mountain stream.
Will sift from those heaped rubble-hills
The termite gold
The brief and unborn poem
And the dry wit of skulls.

  O cry for summer fallen from the steeps
Or washed down rivers to clay crevices:
O cry for summer dark behind the eyes
A dead lamp in the bone-socket of sleep.

  For Plato and his sires
Began the fallacy:
  A sun-God jetting fires
And central Form of Beauty.

  Truly the truth is mad:
  The world that we like Atlas
Upon our shoulders load
A lawful-lawless cosmos
And irredeemably dead.

World is a map upon the fovea
And the huge clouds in tidal skies
Straining the heart with wonder
Break as the brain dies.
  Remembrance of our birth beats in the veins
We throw upon the heavens a lantern-slide:
The heavenly Father so remains
An earthly father and no God.

  Nor can we step into the photograph:
The glaze of time impedes
Which Christ's miraculous finger shall not rub off
For sleeps he with the stone and brazen gods.
  Nor shall we find the child's simplicity
The heaven-bell blue-flowered;
Nor loves of youth even, the narrow ecstasy:
The glaze of time impedes, the cache devoured
By raucous wolves, lions of memory.

[Hocken, MS 704/13:788]

**ANNALES**

The wind is motionless
Save that it moves as an immense tide moves,
But here among the wires
The wind strums endless
With moan as of water over weirs.
The wind sounds in my ears.

While the tornado falls:
Unreal    unreal
Unreal catastrophe
Depth-charges in the city sea:
Eyes hold like mirrors, ears are hollow shells
Till the wind of annihilation blow upon
Ear and eye, make sorrow plain
The death of speech, the unendurable pain.

Some would flare up against the wind of sorrows
They are not extinguished, they are more despairing.
We are not gods who can stride on a frozen skyline
Retain the tumultuous flame of courage.
The bitter charred-out torch is never us
We burrow under, hide under the sleeve of sleep.

. . . On willow-tips the feather-hearted:
They have forgotten their deaths
Fought and mated;
Have found O Eros
Beyond snake-eye and hour-glass
The secret shelter of thy wood.

    War: the neurotic's dream come true
The grave-cloth disarranged
The smiling usual faces changed
Into an animal snarl:
Unheard-of terror or malignancy.
    Much need have we of mercy.
In the low sky of faith hope flares again
Wildfire flashing beyond the treeless plain.
    Much need have we of mercy.
But in an age of iron ask
No cloak of mercy manifest and burning
But a mask undiscerning
The stone heart of the basilisk.

Trees with chafing burn
When strong south winds flail the italian sky
Tisiphone scourging the lost . . . so run
From roots of fingers flares to see the world by
A torch lighted in death's airs
To warm breasts of women, or bear
The pen's corrosive diamond, volcanic alchemy.

The rolling eye-lash of the headline
Signals from shore-line of embattled chaos
In that uncharted continent where skulls split open
And the live thoughts, the crass and bullet-charmed tiger
And the frail antelope run: no semaphore
Can snare them, yet they ravage and they die.

Eire remains and Turkey wavers.
Greece stiffens on the muck-heap; while the Balkan sky
Is torn by thunder. Mouth of Russia rules:
A self-devouring city: bloody the northern rivers.
Save that river where doth the angel lie:
Euphrates. Who shall loose him from such wells?
On continental beaches the dead of Canada
Are huddled: hear ye from their leaden guts
The paean of the victor rise and ring
Over rough swells to North America.
Has France graves left for them?
Germany shut
Hedged not by steel only but suffering
And tender bodies. Now may ye rejoice
Colonial daughters, with the Yanks quartered
Where the boys were . . .
Asia no more
The antique temple, but a famine voice
For mouthpiece millions . . .
Only in spanish waters
And irish vestments peace . . .
Who shall recover
Sun on snow-rivers and the yellow corn;
The dead from barren graves, or mercy in the heartless
Whom the prenatal steel blinded, now blinds to solace?

The wind of annihilation has risen.
The tongues and towers of the dead topple: the stars are told
And fall in ruin: wildfire on walls of a prison:
Five coals in my hand I carry as a shield from the cold.

[Hocken, MS 704/13:789]

**Not in these flooded pastures**

Not in these flooded pastures
Shall green shoot show, nor
My love, laid fire in winter
Whose heart is burning snow.

Not in these flooded pastures
The summer children singing
The son of David and the morning star
Sea-wandering wing.

The mutton-birds come home
At evening to their islands;
No home have I save such as her lips name
Or breasts in silence.

Four kings in harness draw
The chariot of Tamburlaine.
Dead flowers float in the gutter
Craters of melting rain.

From what vast reservoir
Interminable age
Of death? with wrecking power
In tumult in wind of deluge.

Not in these flooded pastures.
Yet O my love, within concentric hells
To you in whom dark dies, perpetual summer sharing
As a stream over rocks to sea my blood burls
[Hocken, MS 704/13:790]

**Resurrection**

There was a day of peace
There was an island once where cool streams ran;
A city through
Whose labyrinths
The sun-canals of daylight rise;
Iron and glass; or stone stolid in sun
Hotel, bank, lending maternal stength.

And trees where
Slate-blue pigeons flutter.
The poor seemed shadows only on the water;
Few homeless. While

Export and import spun
Like a distant
Cyclone remote from
The achieving instant
Of daily grind or sun on leaves or sweetheart.

There was a day of peace
Flower and fruit of the country vine;
Death with night-shadowing wings and starry face
Slept on his crags: spring palaces
Where men unheeding of huge seas
Or inland crater-hills, lived, aloof from ruin
Deeper than wind or fire, beyond us and beyond desire
Deeper than doomed Atlantis drowned.

Without the charmèd circle standing . . .
Where like a dragon in the night
Death and devastation:
Where dark not day is blinding
Voices of pity and indignation
Cry as sea-coffined sailors cry
Beneath the storms and sea of fate;
Murmur as buried miners may
In their black caverns mute;
Or shrill and piercing as the birds of sky
Before aeonic winds disintegrate.

The plaster god broken
The festering heart shown . . .
O wounded Christ, upon golgotha stone
Where sparse and gnarled trees grow.
No summer shoot, renewal of sweet rain
No thunderous rain but low skies raining thunder.
We cannot see thy cross; hear only
Blood tick on stone; feel fleshly now
The spear of violence and thorns of fear.

The bayonetted japanese
Sprawled by their parapets:
Sun falls on jutting ribs . . .
The clay mongolian faces are remote;
These gross contorted dolls can wake no pity
For their death-agony . . . these carcasses:
Who sorrows long
Who sorrows long for a dead animal?

Their faces calm even in snarl of pain;
Life only can ask pity: these are dead.
Death lends them the nobility of stone.

Each soul in life a bubble universe
His only; fought his
Solitary battles
Presenting still a blank and usual mask . . .
Or saw some flashing vista:
Of love or geisha girls;
The remote cloud-horizon
Laid soft caresses on
Keen eyes; wind murmured in
Ears yet unused to shells
Each was a rebel, yet age- or death-enchanted.
Each knew he could not die—and now is dead.

Earth will not winter ever:
The chill winds blow and softer winds succeed:
Spring resurrects the living from their tomb;
Nor Spring nor Christ can resurrect the dead.
The moon in glacial
Waters walking
Midheaven rides; earth open to
The winds of outer space. And night remembers
The *I am lonely* of the quickening soul.
Know then that what is is:
Alive or dead a universe unhuman.
Lifelong we prowl within the wood of lust
Cover our eyes with sleep;
But at the end to stony ground emerge
With no created god save sterile moon;
A shrunken body hath burned out its fires
And soul before her final dissolution
Unlike the beast knows death; so fears.
O why
Warm-blooded immortality of youth?
Kinship of earth? why the bird's sculptural flight?
When all must rot, no spring awakening.
Boxes of stink and ashes.

The soul no bird, her wings are carven stone:
Medusa she.
The snakes of fear, of sharp and thorny fang
Hiss on her pallid brow: man's heart is turned to stone.

Storm devouring storm
In cloudy limbo;
Bodies by steel are torn
Spirits are smoored in snow.
O Christ come thou!
Thou long-compassionate upon our moaning waters:
Save us O Galilean: from hell we cry to thee.
Come thou with light feet and
The bread of blessing in thy healing hand:
Till hearts remembering their infant peace
Like rod of Aaron shoot.
Pray we O pray for a sick world's release.
O Christ, as from the crucificial tomb
Come thou; with pale Persephone come
The bread of blessing in thy healing hand.
Make new with leaf and fruit
A green land.
[Hocken, MS 704/13:792]

**Thoughts by a Conchie Camp**

On mudbanks of the river, below
grass-embankments the children play
with driftwood river-flotsam.
Fruit-bearing trees the
logs were: spring, spring will not green them
not now sap-torn, wounded or waste
who lie with dirty water on the chest
clog the shallows or swing inert in midstream.

Outside the high stockade
like a whip-lash the road
dusty and ridged with metal
flows flickering and level.
Outside the tall stockade
of square posts and barbed wire:
the mountains bear the light
upon their knotted shoulders
or clouds pass wilful
with age no enemy
with time a shadow in the sky.

The brass-haired willow opens
her pale canals to air;
and you may watch the blazing

sticks fall to ash from fires of golden willow.
No green wood nor ash even we
Who are earth's thoughts before her burial.

In august when the eight winds blow together
and split the weather-cock; in august weather
my heart now healed by sea and leaden cloud
as winds tumultuous was, by new love led
now dead, now dead, as in the clay volcano
fire-born stone, eternal diamond now
till sun-burial.

How shall the mind flow free
as river or gold tree
or the grave animal ?
when time, no sea-dune of eternity
nor wind in sea-grass—
when time is frozen and stockaded
marked with white pebbles
and meaningless as glass.

Anguish, monotony
may eat the soul away
or glaze her to a sculptural eye.
Not clouds nor rivers
night-roaring in their shingle fastnesses;
Not sound of mountain springs
Nor evening with her painted wings
Can split the crystal.

Who killed cock robin ? he was a frail soul
perhaps: could not endure: a cage killed him.
Or turned him, who'd never the head for heights
to the cynical one
the heaven-searcher outstaring the sun
the ravenous eagle.
[Hocken, MS 704/13:793]

**Stability**

Cracking the ice
On waters of our time
To bare a frozen butterfly
Of human nerve and charity
I see the pool break; and the wings break.

The eye forgets her leaves
The ear her razor-edges;
In the cool skull is killed
The worm of apprehension.

Recall then the clear
Light on smooth brick;
Dark wattle-smell;
Clouds over pines.

Still men on moving roads;
Or grey rain-pitted water.
    Childhood stability:
The earth round steady sun.

Words needless and miasmic:
Who now respond
More real than rock;
The juggler's oranges.

    But age a frozen butterfly
Time inchoate and huge.
    Familiar dolls are cold,
trees barren now, and the near skies malicious.
        [Hocken, MS 704/13:796]

## REQUIEM

The air from whom all ills and omens fall
Forever childing womb of wind or stone
Whose messengers we cover in the spool
Of sparking water in a dynamo;
Evade in iron of the clay volcano.
The air that warns the man within the skin
With cloud-burst, lightning; or the tree of sun
And leaves of living rain. The air grown cold
Mothers no more her creatures:
    In a graveyard niche of hours, when the scrolled and worn
Cloud lets fall acid for wind gnawing
On shelterstone: from the heart's hollow asylum
Deaf bug of burrowing lust, whose glow-gold-worm
Ravens behind rain-hammer and hill-halted spring,
Weary of mantis-hide, I cast
Of fire the bent pillar that drives me cast;
Lie listening at skull of cities, mourning

The prodigal eye, the leper's bell of the time
And lisp of lies; the mouthing quicklime
In grave-sheet spilt. Nor gargoyle heaven pardon.

My winter tongue may toll and ride the gale
Jar down the jacob's-ladder of the wise
Ring, wrangle in the palace-grate; and cry
For the lopped soldier's-head, the broken lechery.
(For these were not the tall boys with glass foreheads
For sacrificial wick; ranked on day's polar beaches
Love's bullet-stopping penny under braid;
Now crowned by cloud or calm in brazen torches).
Were squalid; knew their shore a hollow city:
But . . .between heel and pavement caught
A fountaining moment's balance
Till lead sliced the river-root of pity.
And these too had their desperate innocence
Below the overshadowing Etna rutted:
O stand by them, where the chipped wood
Split chicken-white; where the boat stalled in the wind;
A dank night's eeling in the creeks and shallows;
Or under sleep, in more unreal jungles
Walking among the yanks and island men . . .
Coral corrals, with the bombers rolling
On steel stems like the lead-weighted toys.
Have twined their subtle lust with hours of rain
Heard nightly; or the quick limbs of the blind;
Or sight of one face sleeping, when
Daybreak renews the grey herds of the wind;
Or taste of tears; or the rank seasmell blown
Through rushes murmuring, on river-sand.

I call my stormy angel blow for them
Trumpets of sky: yet though loud lightnings bray
And the burst bones reply, rise up from ruin
Their torch cannot return; in a gold heaven
Their red original vices will not stay.
Cliff-climbing night rises from sea
Hides their true eyes and hands of memory
Who limed and water-wormed, fire-buried
Now sleep, sleep boulder-bruised in clay.
[Hocken, MS 704/13:800]

**Uninnocence**

We meet and
do not know
inhabitants of a wild country
lost long beyond
an age of arching snow.

The denizens
(as we walk past)
near to the heart in stones
distant and real
as sparrows warm in the dust.

There in the crystal
wind-angel guards
on a heap of tunnelled clods.
when did that land
shrink to a doll in the hand?

(cry of the midnight tiger who
roams in the wood of words)
Like sand it fell perhaps
as we turned from the toy to the window
or stole another peach.

Would now sleep bones in a shingle gorge
or tree tree-rooted by sea:
but recover never the new forest of stars
more near, more strange than himalayan
wondering encamped in a valley of flowers.
[Hocken, MS 704/13:801]

**Each**

Each in his mad heart crying:
    not forever the stony street
    the own world unchanging.
    somewhere the house of lights.

Soemone will know me
    where I stand alone
    change glacier time to river flowing
    illuminate the bone.

Each in his madness sighing.
    will blaze awhile.

gull rising on crooked wings
against predestined gale.

Where on the sudden-startled fens
presaging comet flames.
or when some loved half-stranger learns
to call us by our christian names.

Better beast or unborn
than man: who cries on God and finds no God.
Unfolding the lie in the flower-heart
at last, grown wise instead:
Will make a dog of loneliness
and stroke his shaggy head.
[Hocken, MS 704/13:802]

**The Flowering Eye**

Heart and eye burned out
Grey as a dish-clout
And fire in the gut.

The sandy grained sky
stares on a mad city
And the skull's hollow cry.

Alone real
Demons trail:
they may have my soul:

That its weakness put on
the rind of a scorpion.
Muck to muck return.

But muddy flesh stirs
the scorpion weeps iron tears
Blood in circle of fire.

When she whom I love walks
at the winged crossroads
(the multitudinous birds that shield her head

she guessing not, cry with their sunny throats);
foreknown as shadows on the blazing sea
Or in music a lily among gold notes.
[Hocken, MS 704/13:804]

### What the Night Replied

There is a torrent in my breast
Will not be stayed
Must sorrow for unborn, unblessed
And the forgotten dead;
Cry for remorse and love lost.

Sorrow not at love spent
Or great sin done;
Nor if wolves of darkness stint
The apples of the sun
And the wells of content.

A bird upon the blood
Cries down that sorrowing;
Before the eye of a maid
Will beat his plumes and sing.
Great light those feathers shed.

Such is the living bourne:
Desire, satiety.
Neither by boughs divine
Nor death's eternity
Shalt thou to womb return.
[Hocken, MS 704/13:806]

### The untold story

Were the cheek marble, skull swung on thongs
Then I could turn from day
To the supernatural ecstasy
The living thought's astrology and clang of gorgon wings.

Were the heart careless, free and steadfast
In sun and moon's sight
I could live at peace with fate
And share the day's delusion with passionate bird and beast.

I did not dream that for age's hardihood
To be subtle iron
Show the dry humour of the bone
The heart must burst from cheek, the marble sweat blood.
[Hocken, MS 704/13:807]

**It is not enough**

It is not enough to say
In these antipodes:
    Love has gone north for winter
With migratory birds
Or sleeps below sun-water
Will fill with flaming buds.

Truth falling plain
From no masked oracle:
    Cold sky will quench the sun
The strong trees crumble down;
And love that bursts the crystal
Fall asleep in stone.
        [Hocken, MS 704/13:810]

**Affirmation**

Hills under windy sun
The lion-headed spray;
As tidal night rolls on
A blazing midnight sky;
The wild flight of a swan . . .
*God is the world's heart in me.*

And ferro-concrete towers
Lean over darkened houses.
Under the neon flares
Are unfamiliar faces.
Rain runs in the wires.
*God is the world's heart in me.*

In her red cloak
Of learned innocence
(How shall I mock?)
She smiles to my glance
A cloud on the sun lake.
*God is the world's heart in me.*

By my skull's tinder
Upraisèd Ilium
Will flame again for her;
Sun, land, and raging foam
Star upon surging star.
*God is the world's heart in me.*
        [Hocken, MS 704/13:811]

**From Heine**

When young hearts break
    The stars laugh in the sky;
Laugh gravely and speak
    Down from blue eternity.

'These children love
    Each to each, and burn;
Wearing their heart out, alive
    And charred by the living iron.

'We cannot feel
    That self-consuming fire
Which preys on their lips still:
    We are alas immortal here.'
        [Hocken, MS 704/13:812]

**To a Poplar-Tree**

Trees move me as no man or animal.
Green and young like a girl of air
where the wide hills lean to the sun;
and cloudy winds fall
with Spring to stone mounds and a brown river.

    Birds cannot rest in you
nor need you yet bear
and shield where heavier gales blow
the weight of their frail houses.
    I would set no burden on you;
no broad maternal branches.
    Green and young like a girl of air
silvered bark and light leaves tentative
that feel bird-arrows in passing.

    Yet you alas will thrive
grow old and lichened here;
seem no longer the first green thought of Spring.
When vast and seen for acres
you shall perhaps be pollarded
suffer a strange rebirth, new lease of years.
    But never this first grace
green and young like a girl of air.

Take back the grecian and the gothic stone.
My soul is lost and buried here
Where the wind breathes on barren farms
or inland waters, waves on worn shingle.
And you more young than these
who need not even innocence
sway to the black sun of crumbling winter
green and young like a girl of air.

O grow in my dreams.
[Hocken, MS 704/13:815]

**I have cut from my heart**

I have cut from my heart
her green-sickness;
it is better to be a tall and lonely man
than stand and cry for the moon.

The moon is older than the sun.
Why should a man set his soul
in the house of a girl?
To be alive is to be alone.

It is better to look and turn away.
She is beautiful where she walks;
she is beautiful where she stands;
as any flowering tree.
[Hocken, MS 704/13:816]

**The Bees**

Over the stone-rough road
with tree-ferns, quarried ravines and
River below in the dark
foliage secret and still,
Moved we, till through the branches
of tall trees mossy and rugged—
Lo, by a clearing of gorse
under the lee of the hill,
There in a shadowless tree
was the hive, hid fast in a hollow:
Summer was loud in that place:
there we would plunder and kill.

Light wings laden and droning,
in warm air honey-bees falling;
Down from a bright air, down
to the grey bark groove in the trunk; and
Clustering, clustering there:
in the dark cave clamber and vanish:
Thighs gold-laden; and bare,
swift, out to the light like a tiger,
Each from the labyrinth rising.
We saw and in wonderment stood there.
Suddenly flicked from the hive,
as the blown sparks leap from the furnace,
Sentries, and ruddy of sheen,
stabbed anguish with needle-sharp sting. So
Masked to the shoulders and netted,
slit-eyed, like strange desperadoes
Dry grass we lit crouching.
The hive woke: sulphurous fuming
Curling and eddying through
till the stunned bees stumbled from shelter:
Crawled from the white wave out:
while the charred wood rotted and crumbled.
Still the armadas in-rallied;
and over the death-fire they rippled;
Died at the black smoke-vent,
and the hell-flame blue in the burning;
Stung and died while stinging.
We beat with blazing broom-bushes;
Sweated and beat. Shame sudden
at their death-anthem awakened.
Then as the sun sank down,
they were still save the crushed and the moaning:
Choir of sorrow. We plunged
through the earth-black smouldering ashes
Eager in haste, our hands:
but the hoard, but the hoard, it was barren.
Little our search did afford—
save the smooth cells waxen, by labour
(Instinct we deem it), by thought
unchanging and slow labour fashioned.

O ye communal beings,
in myriads slain by us cruel,
Found we naught but a dream,
broken: in mists we returned.

Under a dead sun moaning,
        the last bees crawl in their shattered
Hive, with their long toil waste—
        waste, and their young ones burned.
Bright-hued flowers no more
        in the garden and field shall await them,
Welcome, enclose them; nor summer
        their strange joy passionless waken
As in those lost hours once.
        Life-scheme is broken and they
Wait for the midnight dews,
        and the chill airs sworded and frozen
Pitiless angels of night,
        under the stars steel-grey.
            [Hocken, MS 704/13:818]

**Burns**

Burns walking bewildered from the wood of lies
With poetry a gold and guarded flower;
Evangelist of green among the charted deserts
Of sad Mosaic stone; the Ace of Hearts
        heraldic: was this the face
True among many mirrored lips and eyes?

Or rather the sinner grave and repentant behind
A clown's mask (ill companions snared him):
Born to praise the God of a godly nation,
The *Cottar's Saturday Night* his affirmation;
        Homer leading the blind;
His children's catechist: Burns to Lockhart's mind.

Choose what you will. The poet womanly, slender,
Spinning his pretty songs, watching a cloud.
The man who wrote with a diamond on heaven.
The ranting rhymer bawdy in a tavern:
        men crowded there to hear:
Each girl feared he would write a poem on her.

Earth has eclipsed the great: casket may save
From the limed body on an Italian beach
Ore burned and withered heart—once Shelley's.
Dark falls on Europe and her shadowed valleys:
        barren is man's love.
Shall a dead mouth cry from the gloomy insatiable grave?

Doom perches, the bald and ravenous
Eagle on shoulders of kings: his droppings sour
Their cloak and wine. Who from the heart's jungle
Shall rise invincible and strangle
        that brazen gorge, or freeze
The tyrannous eye, wing shadowing thunderous?

The Ayrshire ploughman died: no noon of steel
Can quell, no rhetoric will salve that death.
Before black thunder cracked the city spire
Or skies fell down, each star a meteor;
        he spoke: that voice can heal
Time's triple wound; his blood sings yet a while.

Hardie heard the gigantic whisper lifelong.
Heard and lived to the sound. The world's towns
Carry him at their centre. And those
Who cursed him once forever curse, their prose
        immortalized by song,
Immortalized in gall. I would set before the throng

        This epitaph of one living.
*The crystal of Calvin wounded and oppressed*
        *His lion breast;*
*But he who carries a fire in the heart and eyes*
        *Dies not till the world dies.*
            [Hocken, MS 704/13:819]

**Absalom**

Shrill stone sank
in that forehead
like a knife in red copper
or the baying of wolves.

But on the night roofs
I questioned the terrible stars:
he was my answer.
The rose from the stone.
    The waters of the moon
are clogged with sand.
I had many sons
but him only.
He was a river
in whom my stony blood

was changed to flowers.
As to the concubines
the gold and the green—
how should I deny him?

Joab was my
invincible age
the bearded lion
the ice on the spear.
Sharp wheel black sun and cave
remain: him also.
He will die with me
who murdered my youth.

Night strangled him
with his own comeliness:
break then the sword of stars
the night with a hundred flames.
But do not lift the stone
where his blood putrefies
and sinks in sand.

O Absalom
[Hocken, MS 704/13:821]

**Xerxes and Homer**

Xerxes and Homer:
that King like cumulus
hardened in history;
that poet long ice-bearded.
Their skies are over us.

Say: never
in their cool eyes
of cruelty or
wisdom, did Hell stand tower-like
or Ruin lie a stealthy confidant.

Say: the loud wounds of Europe
the shaken skeleton
were not. Nor Love
more traitorous
more virulent corrosion.

Yet Xerxes knew
fear under armour
pity murdered in vain
the inalienable spears of Spring
the pain that is man.

And oracular Homer
lay dungeoned in blindness;
heard under paean of the tidal year
the grating of the manacle
the long seas of despair.
[Hocken, MS 704/13:824]

**Court Speech**

Queen, I wearied of the quick tongues, the fealty of the beast.
I heard in a dark shed the cry of a mouse in labour;
reverberation in the unbreathing quiet
of Night's oracle: in love isolate, in pain akin.

Queen, did the waves cry out in peace or torment?
Peace is slumber. In boughs shaken by wind
under green tumult I saw the stranger tumult
Eternity beating its hands on a wall of sorrow.

Queen, there is no peace on the brow of a mountain.
Strength only. We are ice in our island strength:
when will the berg break? It will not break.
Love is but knowledge of that separation.

O queen, do not think me yours when I come.
For you have taught me love, the lips of isolation.
[Hocken, MS 704/13:825]

**Poem in November**

July and august fall
to dark again:
spring grasses feel
the long november rain.
The scarlet hawthorn flowers
flaring and fragrant stand;
land-bird and sea-bird bears
hope of new sea and land:
shall I not join with them
in their cloud-fallen calm?

their hope—though vain
as life of earth and air.
Shall I remember her?
O thou immortal nature
loveless and angerless;
wide stony skies
remote though seeming tender:
Let me not stay
thus green in sun and rain.
Take out my heart of tree:
Give me a heart of stone.
[Hocken, MS 704/13:828]

**Under the dank leaves**

Under the dank leaves of a Cotswold autumn
Loveless my eyes wander. I told you, darling,
That one loves first the feeding breast and after
Landscape to sate a cold and flourishing eye:
And last women, when the pressed cider of Eden
Makes the upright man. In fear of falling
I stand: you dead in me: return so softer
To mothering leaves.
But O below the sky
There is no recompense for your long death.
I will turn from the rooks of an imagined England
(Unrest alone she lent me); turn to the strange
And snarling abyss of this lank land of my birth
That her hourly whims may oust your needle second:
Drown me in glaciers stiller than stonehenge
And the immense seas of change.
[Hocken, MS 704/13:829]

**Cold Spring**

Death in the spring is no precipice
Ultimate ravine more sheer than birth-pangs;
But the wind baring its momentary fangs
Or sorrow of sunlight in a sky of ice,
Corruption where the luminous cloud hangs.

I watch winds on hill-shoulder and shore:
The barbed secretive whip of anger flaying;
Meshes of hate on bitter waves blowing

Dull wrinkled jade, metallic beer
In glasses of the morning, vitreous splinter.

Olive-green by windows rises the bird
Veering; and under the yellow flowered broom
Worms gnaw one skeleton on dank loam
Crisp feathers dull, eye rotted:
Last spring blown by air, now dumb as earth is dumb.

Stone sea moves southward; the volcanic island
Scrub sides quiet, surf-eaten
In antarctic isolation
Breasts that tideless flow; while the hills stand
Of smoother lava, in high mists hidden.

Spray reels upon each height
Of quartz and barren flax. Dark heads of grasses
As sharp wind shakes them, murmur like bees:
Unpastured wind—never in the bleak night
Of southern stars, on these hills did he pass,
Among the startled herds sire stallion-wise
Foals fleeter than his own storm-shadowed flight.
[Hocken, MS 704/13:830]

**In Monochrome**

Five swans flew over: night fell from their wings
Flashing a dusky white. The cool night fell
To underwater calm. Sea rose in spray;
The few stars came in quiet.

Later the moon lit heaven: giant as fate
Cloud-ranges lay in alabaster. While
I walked smoking on gravel roads and thought
Of death, love, the unspoken poem.

Then in the faceless night from dark to dark
Wind rioted ravenous: unchanging wind
Remorseless and inane: demonic wind.
I turned and lay unsleeping.

Now wind remains. The leaves by storm are shaken.
Sun falls on granite. Sand-grains seaward shudder.
Earth the inhuman ampitheatre Chaos.
Hope ends in huge and shallow air.
[Hocken, MS 704/13:834]

**Clarity**

I have recaptured clearness: while the light
Falls long to southward. Winds are motionless;
Where midges spin, and each to each birds chirrup
Harshly. The ranking waves incessant wear
On wounded rock. Clouds ragged float
Red-orange-veined. And the cool sea caress
Murmurs below these gaudy roofs asleep.
I have regained my sight but forfeit nature.

World upon world the midges mate and die:
I envy them their long oblivious moment.
The scene were full without me: nor does bramble
Grow her wild rose and greener filigree
For my brief tenderness. Cloud over ageless headland
No crag, no cloud, but paranoiac symbol.
[Hocken, MS 704/13:836]

**In the lion rocks**

In the lion rocks and the sands of sorrow
Ground from volcano grief; in the grave ways
Of the body, when death has grown bone
In me and sown that muddy sun of sureness
That marks the man: I will remember you.
For your oblivious and flower-like grace
Poised on a blade of time. Most for your green
And cultured ignorance of my mountains of madness.

Yet O from them what calm sun-rivers break.
I shall not forget you: my love lies in my hand:
I stare in pity on that curious pebble
Knowing no after-diamond will speak
With more clear tongue. While the red rivers rend
Sight from your statue. Nor are you truly rubble
But map, as all, a haunted island.
[Hocken, MS 704/13:847]

**Nor did I ask**

I had thought the sun's speech
too wide to darken;
an oceanic water-shed
deathless, unbroken.

I had thought the lions of wrath
my only adversaries;
that love would melt to tears
their ice-crystal eyes.

I had not known pain
was the soul's skeleton;
and love the rare flower
under a darkened sun.

Nor did I ask to walk
stronger, where no rocks bleed
the deserts of indifference
and the cold streams of pride.
[Hocken, MS 704/13:853]

**University Song**
(Tune: Jerusalem)

Among these hills our fathers came.
By strength of eye and hand alone
They built: and murmur loud as flame
Their voices from the living stone.

Forget not those whom Scotland bred
Above whose bones our cities stand.
Forget not them! nor the unknown dead
Whose broken veins flow through our land.

As streams in wildernesses rise
And green the desolate shingle plain:
So under windy southern skies
Peace flowered, and Wisdom shall remain.

The generations rouse and pass
Like falling birds to well of night;
Or like the wind-sown summer grass
Now tall, now withered in our sight.

But our sons' sons alike shall find
Perpetual, though nations cease,
Within these walls the quiet mind
The storm-unshaken rose of Peace.
[Hocken, MS 704/14:857, pp.2–3]

**To you who most unwittingly**

To you who most unwittingly
cut off from my eyes their lids of darkness:
so that I see now with the bare eyeball
see clearly and without bitterness.

The land I deemed a desert
yields water as even rock must do.
The clouds pass over with healing in their shadows
and the slow grass murmurs.

There is strength in ice; but suns bring weeping.
The sure strength rises only from
the living skeleton
and the warm leaves of blood about the brain.

From a new strength to your new happiness
I speak accepting another loneliness.
You were yourself and not my burning image.
You are yourself, unknown to me.
[Hocken, MS 704/14:860]

**Easter Sonnet**

Storm, storm and the ravenous sea remain.
Christ will not come. While the low waves fall
And the huge winds with folded wings keep vigil,
Step out from stone, roll back the stony sun.
Remote and luminous as cloud-horizon
Angels have kept their station: while the God
Sweats yet in darkness, anguishing and mad;
Is crucified on the live cross of bone.

How came it then, how came that this slim tree
From untormented clay rose tenderly?
. . .gaze long; and you may know the living sun
His light alone: the sun-heart is not here.
Yet he plucks out the gnarled nails one by one.
A white bird leapt from air, his messenger.
[Hocken, MS 704/14:861]

**To L.A. Baigent**

O see the heavy waves roll in on sand
And flash of wings, the momentary gulls:
Sight familiar to the aborigines.
These sullen swells of the antartic ocean
They are my blood: crested by glittering ice
And falling sharp, monotonous as music.

You who love music, you would hear their music.
But I see death under the shifting sand:
The elk was frozen in his world of ice
With those unweildy antlers; while the gulls
Raucous and swerving, picked debris of ocean
New race, and tougher than aborigines.

Was the land kind to aborigines?
The rank dense bush and waterfalls like music
Covering the river of rock and ocean,
Covering the heart inert as quicksand.
Were the sun's veins full blooded? Did the gulls
Rise easy, towering on a wind like ice?

Step in the pub door; a beer to break the ice.
Observe the curious aborigines:
Men dazed or arrogant, women screaming like gulls.
And from the radio an intricate music
That pride and gentleness like water spilt on sand
The convoluted dream probing abyssmal ocean.

How shall we save our souls drowned in the southern ocean
Or seeking fire under volcano ice?
Water in petrol, bearings clogged with sand
Are images for us, no aborigines.
Death holds a mortgage on our acres. Music
Of buried pipes and drams can drown the gulls.

Death holds the mortgage yet; and we are gulls
Till the great gutted shark plunge down in ocean.
Useless the dance to the european music.
And yet the farmer's clods are split by ice
And lovers are true aborigines
Since for them only grasses grow from sand.

Standing by sand I love and envy the gulls
Those fearless aborigines of earth, air, and ocean;
Long for an air not ice, and free as music.

[Hocken, MS 704/14:886, pp.44–6]

**Man and Woman**

*Man*
Who live lifelong in darkness of men's voices
Or women's watchfulness, they know not death—
Nor can you know, in the city of your sorrows.
Only the naked flame, the wordless cry
That man is, knows; O under sky of time.
He has no house but in his mother's womb.

*Woman*
I will feel my child leap in the womb
Fulfilment of dark winds and rainy voices
And bodily miracle, time out of time . . .
See the birds then—what do they know of death
But night, ~~but~~ night, silenced the clamorous outcry?
*Man*
For them perhaps the living darkness sorrows.

*Woman*
You speak like one grown old in sorrows.
*Man*
It was not so when buried in the womb
I dreamt not, waked not, neither did I cry.
I am grown weary of the many voices
And love you only now, and this new death
And our surrender of the husks of time.

*Woman*
All things must live, and sorrowing in time.
*Man*
A man may void himself of many sorrows
In contemplation of desired death:
So I before I knew you, from the womb
Divorced, and borne upon the sea of voices
That break like spume, an empty bitter cry.

*Woman*
On stony sands they gash themselves and cry
Do you remember in the summertime
How one lay listening to the children's voices,
In the long grass and spoke no mood of sorrows.
For that day was I cast forth from the womb
And it will comfort me in hour of death.

*Man*
I know not yet if it be life or death
That trembles at the dark root of the cry;
The craving spirit stifles in the womb
Where it so buds and quickens. In our time
Contentment is enough, though flawed by sorrows:
I ask no more now of the midnight voices.

*The Child*
O voices drowned so soon in night of death
You who perpetuate my sorrows and my cry:
I fallen thus to time from the irretrievable womb.
[Hocken, MS 704/14:896, pp.59–62]

**Letter to Noel Ginn II**
[Published Version]

Two years of silence—I take pen again
To write a rhyming letter. You'll forgive
The interim, and knowing how we live
From hand to mouth, a certain thread of pain
And bitterness that blurs the narrative.
My last was in a more romantic vein.

Our dreams take refuge from the men we are
And hide as flies do from the winter chill.
The lost traveller's dream under the hill
Remains with me when propping up a bar
Or in strange beds I do the body ill
To gratify a merciless guiding star.

'Th' expense of spirit . . .' Yet the spirit grows
By grieving for the sensual heart in chains.
Birth-pangs that we mistake for burial-pains
Give promise of the everlasting rose
Where bitter Loss consolidates its gains.
This is the answer that no question knows.

I have the letters that you wrote from camp
(Defaulters' camp, in case this should be read
By other men) where living men grew dead
In grey monotony. I was a lamp,
A kind of beacon to you then, you said—
Since then the wick has grown a trifle damp.

No man can play Aladdin all his life.
The oil is blood, although the flame be clear,
And world-annihilating djinns appear
Unasked-for at the falling of a leaf.
Or else the heart becomes a cinder—Fear
Is Art's companion, and the hermit Grief.

So poets learn to live like other men
For money, lovers, or the friends with whom
Music can animate a sunless room
And rouse the rumour of a different Sun
That shines the same though endless night draw on
And wakes the dead heart from its numbered tomb.

Perhaps I overstate the case—but I
Live by extremes. The madman and the saint
Have both (I fear) the same extremist taint,
And both are mad to Madame Butterfly.
Being no Francis, I can scarcely paint
A halo—'poet's licence' is my cry.

It was my dearly held delusion once
That labouring men were better than their betters
And needed only to throw off their fetters
For Eden to return to Adam's sons.
Since then I've worked with them; and they're go-getters
Just like the Rev. Fraser—bless his bones.

An 8 hour day is not conducive to
The exercise of one's imagination.
So I have found alas that my true station
Is still among the academic crew
Whom I despised for undue cerebration
That leads to withering of the heart and thew.

No doubt I'll find a niche where I can grumble
About the clique that pay me for my pen,
And drink with other intellectual men,
And gain some slight prestige, however humble,
With a little bitter poem now and then
Until the first apocalyptic rumble:

And that will be the Bomb. I often think
Of the climb we made like beetles up a drain
From neanderthal, to be washed down again
In a flood of dirty water from the sink.

Lions and horses also sport a brain
But do not pine for a celestial stink.

From this high window I can see the swells
Roll in with their incessant cannonade
Upon that shore where once, a lonely child, I made
My own mythology of weeds and shells
And dreamed I heard from the green water shade
The pealing of sea drowned cathedral bells.

(While in bombed Germany the violent dream
Grew flesh and blood and tore a city down
Whose dazed survivors searching among stones
Can find the lichen hunger or the scream
Of mandrake pain, but never that first sun-
Flower of peace upon a lucid stream.)

And it is good to walk upon the sand
In winter when the dunes are hard and dry
With frost that binds an iron earth and sky.
Bone of my bone, the stubborn rocks withstand
The ebb and surge of grief. The ocean I
Once feared, I love more than the frozen land.

There is a kind of reconciliation
With buried selves and seasons, so to walk
And listen to the arrogant seabirds' talk
Who have no interest in our damnation,
And feel beyond those frosty hillocks the
Thunder of an obliterating sea.

[*Blow, Wind of Fruitfulness*, pp.42–4]

# Appendix 3
## Additional Poems by Noel Ginn

On 4 May 1943, James K. Baxter wrote to Noel Ginn:

> I have put all your poems received so far into a note-book. Going over them last night I was struck by the strong poetry right through. (p.214)

The notebook Baxter is referring to is a small hard-cover book now held in The University of Otago's Hocken Library (MS 975/30). The first pages of this notebook are filled with Baxter's notes on palmistry and his transcriptions of Ginn's poems begin some way into it. Ginn's poems follow here in the order Baxter recorded them, with the exception of those which appear in the text of Ginn's early letters: 'The Drift of Pinions', 'Incoherence', 'October Spate', 'Overture to Unbelief', 'First Verse', 'Time Theme', 'There was a man . . . sent from God', and '(prayer under a bridge)'.

Baxter indexed Ginn's poems as he transcribed them into the notebook—the complete index, and Baxter's line count, follows, to which I have added the number of the page in *Spark* where the poem is referred to. Baxter also marked the titles of certain poems in the index with an asterisk; his comments on these particular poems suggest that these were compositions he particularly preferred. He may have had them in mind when he wrote to Ginn, on 6 March 1944:

> I have been rereading you lately and have come to the conclusion that some of your poems are literally masterpieces. Couldn't we publish a book some time something like Wordsworth and Coleridge in *Lyrical Ballads* each one producing half. Not fair perhaps, as I have more to choose from, but there would only need to be a few. (p.335)

The index that follows is not a complete record of the verse Ginn sent Baxter. It does not record the last four poems—'O Night' (p.532), 'By the Appian Way' (p.532), 'Old question: old answer' (p.533), and 'To GRAEME' (p.533). Nor does it cover the full period of the correspondence: the notebook appears to have been filled about January 1944, and if Baxter continued his transcriptions in another notebook I have been unable to locate it in any of the collections I have searched.

One further poem by Noel Ginn—'Unto Us'—appears in his letter of 22 April 1945 (p.402).

Finally I wish to acknowledge once again, with gratitude, Noel Ginn's generosity in allowing me to publish poems that he thought had been destroyed, as he intended, many decades ago. These poems represent a very difficult period of his life and the decision to make them public has not been taken lightly.

**Baxter's Table of Contents for Ginn's poems**

| | Title | line count | page(s) in *Spark* |
|---|---|---|---|
| | The Drift of Pinions | 21 | 138 |
| | Incoherence | 50 | 139 |
| | Farewelling | 26 | 513 |
| | October Spate | 29 | 168 |
| | Overture to Unbelief | 52 | 169 |
| | I have come . . . | 38 | 513 |
| | To Jim | 16 | 179, 514 |
| | In December Days | 28 | 515 |
| | Sonnet | 14 | 515 |
| | First Verse | 31 | 205 |
| | Time Theme | 27 | 206 |
| | Song of the Sharded Spirit | 44 | 516 |
| * | Hypothesis | 30 | 517 |
| | On Rereading 'The Ascent of F.6.' | 16 | 518 |
| | There was a man . . . sent from God | 24 | 225 |
| * | (prayer under a bridge) | 35 | 225 |
| | Outside | 18 | 518 |
| | O I have loved . . . | 20 | 519 |
| | Rue Rousant | 14 | 519 |
| | Snowdrops | 12 | 520 |
| | Dawn and the devil | 24 | 520 |
| | When ruby fires | 14 | 521 |
| | Myrtle of Venus | 30 | 521 |
| | Beauty has burned unseen | 39 | 522 |
| | Unrest | 42 | 523 |
| | Tryst | 16 | 524 |
| | Sonnet | 14 | 525 |
| | Romance | 12 | 525 |
| | Our fate is not forlorn | 20 | 525 |
| * | Flinders Range | 16 | 526 |
| | The Solitary | 25 | 527 |
| | War Resisters | 12 | 527 |
| | Miss G— | 18 | 528 |
| | From dust despised | 32 | 528 |
| | To R— | 14 | 529 |
| | Incubus | 14 | 529 |
| | Specimen stanzas on a mythical scene | 45 | 530 |
| | Ignorantia | 24 | 531 |

**Farewelling**

Partings pack the air with pacing poignancy
And gather urgent harvests from the slow-tempo past
For a moment all is naked, raw, revealed
Man-spirit with man-spirit burns bitterly.
The hunt of mystery, destiny, the feared cosmic conspiracy
To the surface renders up its deep-sea sadness.
Tomorrow will take up the old life-music
With a perceptless minor understrain,
But now the wedge of space is biting deeper
And the lights are moving the blackness hither
The bluff routine-born assurances have fled
And cold winds push past the open door
Instantly alienating all familiar things.
There is a jutting ledge to every cliff of separation
And on its very lip stability is silhouetted
Straining disquietedly before the break.
Soon the well-kept corridors of the conscious
Become the ripstead of underground streams
Splashing about with soughing sucking horrid hubbub,
And the hall is haunted with cave-old jungle cries.

They pass. The brunt, the bruise, the bother.
One or two twitches while the tendrils of adjustment
Feel out a little farther across the gap,
While the bareness is covered up
And the rent is sewn up
On the outside at least.

**I have come . . .**

I have come to a new, a pew place,
Where soul may make whole, relax, reflex,
And hear new music,
Aloof in this country's cathedral periphery
Strong-stanchioned with sap-unstaunched timbering,
New music
Past the orchestral hordes of fern-violins
Disgraced in desert wastes for congenital dumbness,
Music
For ears noise-crushed, civilization-seared
For tired ears the long largo of the bush.
Nose too, maimed, untrained, ecstasy-starved
The outcast of the ersatz-world, receiver of so many insults

And so recedent in rôle, may now live
With leaf, earth, uncoloured flower and reaving, thieving wind
In the driven forests of these long-bodied isles.

Then batter bailiff, shatter beauty, pour, roar
your lush, fresh tangle-mesh on mind's toy-framed pelting wheel;
Burst limpet-limitations fondly nursed;
    purse inbreeding cerebral stock; ingrain new strain;
Carry capacities uncreate to undreamed climax.

I dive through the sun-smacked occult ocean,
Through the dark grove of leaf below the billow,
Where the life-lines coil and moil to stake a claim,
And picket there the sped obsession, the will to flee. . .
Am freed to follow the phosphorescent flash of song
Or sorrow with sodden hulks of foundered ventures—
Am paused
By beauty's multifarious staggering industry,
Her multiplex multeity, her all-place patience,
Caverned in root-nook waterfall, vast in fan-outfolded vista;
Riding over all a moon, a sun, a galaxy, a cloud.
I clutch the leafy heart of God for beauty's stay;
For when beauty goes goes half of love;
For love is half beauty, and most of beauty in these trees;
Spine and mind are halted, folded before this complete offensive;
This tremendous holding; heart-healing
Primordial, green prevenience.

**To Jim**

Friend, I gather your gift to a gladness
That holds a hundred sprung surprises
Planned by eager living for a callow strayling
To woo him into loving.

Night draws back from my blazing headlamps
Pulls its soft nuzzle back in dismay
That through its ambushes prepared in scented passes
My car so blandly pushes.

Time is against the glance insouciant
Pity will plead with animal eyes
Life-love topples heart in a scalding wave,
Then blasé self-love dies.

Half-nod at passing life's accosting
Has served till now, enough! Civility
Of fur and petal, feather and friend shall have
A greet of richer metal.

**In December Days**

Now the year is near her ending
By inch and hour she stalks her doom
In grip of sea her ice is bending
She breaks to drift a melting tomb.

Stress of névé now is over
Strain and press of ice-bound ridges,
Grind and grate of grief is over
Clear the course for whiter pledges.

Defiled moraine our deeds are torn
Rolled from lofty summit beauty,
Eyes to peaks repentant turn
Resplendent in dolomite duty.

The tiny breather here afforded
Must not, oh not be wasted!
Spartan douche must wash the sordid
With holding tack resolves be basted,

For the wrath is lurking under hedges
The lightning of its animosity lashed,
Peers in gloat from investment ledgers
Its biding avalanche-bolsters massed.

Time to carve out ugh! the tumours
Cast off clutched-at pamper props
Drain the seeped-up soothing humours
Held in the bole-base—or the whole tree rots.

Yes, we know it's a calendar convention
To show we know the astronomic fact,
But the significance lies in the conjunction—
Earth knows, would we, a charted track.

**Sonnet**

The slight distortion of the major drive
As jealousy a brawl at the midnight carouse

Or the prostitute at work in the innocent house
Is accepted like the cold charity of the grave.

The phenomenal peaks of sin are seldom climbed
The popular resorts are undefined by law
Where Rumour strokes a captivating lyre.
They sport a random virtue extremes disclaimed.

Few frequent this world, this wailing wall
To lament and mourn their usurped integrities;
The Church and Code preserve a static savour;

Only the rare take cognizance of the Fall
Tackle the maëlstrom of meaning love's asperities:
Woe for our weal in these our van-men waver.

**Song of the Sharded Spirit**

The matchless mind
    In body built
Its sweet desires
    Forever spilt.

Full-veined youth
    With wind-quick smile
Drank ah! eagerly
    The poisoned phial.

Bitter, bitter
    The cud of life
And bitter too
    The claspèd knife.

The sun's engulfed
    In a leaden pall
The moon is sick
    In her pock-marked pool.

The daisies mourn
    And the roses wince
Remembering the look
    I gave them once:

For my heart's red womb
    With monster form
Waits to deliver
    The hell unknown.

The matchless mind
    In body built
Its sweet desires
    Forever spilt.

With dawn despair
    With noon a tear
With panther night
    The terrible fear.

Ah! could I retrace
    My twilight ways
In the sun I'ld leap
    To golden days!

But the course is set
    My mind is swung
Brooking no change
    In its gymbals of bone.

The matchless mind
    In body built
Its sweet desires
    Forever spilt.

### Hypothesis

From the body of death beauty loath to go
Lingers like a gull then spirals slow
    Over the walled memory
    The gritty cemetery.

But does she blankly, does she blandly go?
Or change her mode for a subtler chemic flow,
    More unusual patterns
    Of the dancing atoms?

Say though for it deeply troubles me:
When music stops, or falls a mountain tree
    When a smile has set
    Or a door is shut.

Quiet eyes see a purple shaft in the living form,
The prim cloth of flowers with rotten stitches sewn,
    A maddening rupture
    Of every rapture:

For beauty dies, and lies in the chancel gloom.
But stay, imperfect clay, may we presume
    That a blind spot subjective
    Throws the image defective?

Night shifts her lofty canopy to another field
And the ingot sun drops under our galleon keel,
    Yet both return
    Un-travel-worn;

And science supposed an over-simple scheme
Till radium suggested the alchemist's haunting dream.
    Thus if truth were told
    All may be gold
    And your beauty be
    Unto all eternity.

**On Rereading 'The Ascent of F.6.'**

Auden and Christopher Isherwood
Are adepts at invoking the defeatist mood,
Athletic and agile chroniclers they
Enumerate every sign of decay:
Boredom's frown on the house-wife's face;
And the slick camouflage of capitalist vice;
Everything shabby, everything coarse,
Beauty's tawdry and passion's curse;
The psychologic deep frustration;
The fallen world without salvation;
Their focus the point of contradiction,
Grave exponents of the art Gibbertian;
Laughter for weakness, for national pride
With a current of pathos trembling inside;
No power to save nor cause to give
They hold a mirror to show how we live.

**Outside**

I lie in the sun
And one by one
Its amber petals fall,

A green starred daphne
Squat beside me
Winds her scented call.

Tall Canterbury bells
Open their chintz hotels
To wandering bumble bees.

The silence cleans
The mountain gleams
And bookishly stirs the trees.

If there is chaos
Black hatred and grey loss
It is not in this air;

Not in this gold-hung hour
Of blue thought in a green bower
But in some distant mental snare.

**O I have loved . . .**

O I have loved the velvet rose
    And sought her mystery red to seize
As on her bowing stalk she blows
    And spills red scent on every idle breeze.

O I have loved the lily cold
    Her lowly bell of ivory green,
And watched her spiral curves unfold
    Lost in a white and noble dream.

O I have watched the silver pen
    Of crescent moon on star-lined sheet
Write love-songs to a mountain glen
    Forlorn and silent in her sad retreat.

*Her lovely heart's a rose*
*Her mind a lily fair*
*Moon-beauty with her goes*
*All beauty she doth wear.*

Though ne'er till now did I give thought
    These joys myself for aye to gain—
That was the theme her blushes taught
    Last eve the quiet end of Linden Lane.

**Rue Rousant**

O Cats killed by the hate-hard hand of man!
Cats, quiet cats, silken cats stretching ecstatic

On sunny walls; ichor of tiger cheap-spent—
My heart tenders woe, knotted wrath needs not:
But my in-man shame, love-lacking life-leering ban,
My crime my groan for fear-sheathed man-love erratic;
My betrayal of tiny trust, withdrawal from splend-
ours of fur-grace; for signature of peace a blood-clot.

Soul stooping not starves; deep keeled love
Steady level love dips low like lake-water;
Your-reaching mind finds firm flagstones for life
No under-mine, structure-strain, open to rain and laughter:
But here the ruins of laughter, brain-treason inane—
Fated dappled floss!—ruth repentance dark remain.

### Snowdrops

Sea cools nor clear-cleans brain-burning never-so
Nor wind wands his noise-naughty world school-still
As the speechless snowdrop. Behold these nuns of quietude
From sheath-head bowing, in heart's very awe-hood. To
The Lord adoring! Calm among the light-spill
Of sharp and gothic grass, the qualmless peace of the Rood.
Sward-in-dingle-dibbed petal-tip, sweet flake-flick!
Look at, lush the green-down-drips on her scollop-cloth!
O how from mud? from glue-cake murk this phantom forth?
O world awash with miracle, rucked with rubric!
Tear-laughter utter I at its wedding-weld
    heaven-in-hell weal-in-wrath.
O milken snowdrops, icecliffs chaste, dream-draped girls of truth.

### Dawn and the devil

Behind the blue dromedary-hills
    The haggard emissaries
Crouch while the night-storm whirls
    To his sabean sanctuaries.

On this black and sabulous route
    Courage is not the spur.
The eyebrows beetle white
    Of their savage imperious sire.

(With a wind that softly bloweth
    The dawn hath grace, for lo
The petal-clouds come forth
    Frosted with crimson snow.)

Fitted to burring vans
    The devil in sportive mood
Hurls his malisons
    On the meek and mottled mud.

Filigree flesh is broken
    The children of hell applaud
Fame is the laurel-token
    That twisted throats accord.

(Hawk-emulous in golden motion
    The prince-of-wings doth glide
On to the laspur ocean
    Of silent eventide.)

**When ruby fires**

When ruby fires from rich anemones
Leap through my eyes and strike the blood-dark screen
Curious tears forsake their wells of ease
And flood with night the vision-blazed demesne:
So man stumbling in gloomy vaulted brain
May clutch in sudden fall a sacred chalice,
Whose blessing splintered into jagged bane
Will cut his flesh with most vindictive malice.
And thou, sweet friend, bear the uncaring world
Thy costly gift of spirit-fashioned song;
Beware lest shards of ignorant death are hurled
Or frozen indifference sear thy silver tongue.
    Come down to earth and hold the vision vain,
    Or serve thy savage apprenticeship to pain!

**Myrtle of Venus**

Polish the moonshell silver bright
Shake from the cloth the stardust white
Trees give your tiles enamel sheen
Every beast in his own way clean.
Sombre rocks with water mark
Who cool your feet in pools of dark
Keep your rough enchanted portals
Free from briars and hurtful nettles
For soon on the limp untended grass
Myrtle of Venus may shortly pass.

Sunset sheaves in bronzen shocks
Burnish the glass of black rut-locks,
Quiet, orchestra of farmyard flies!
Sleep with pigs in mud-soft sties.
But your song shout O throstle bird
Then pick the dung of the gadding herd:
Silken shawls of swinging rain
Leave the rippling barley plain
To smooth the pile of plushy grass—
Myrtle of Venus will shortly pass.

Noise takes off his shoes in awe;
In humble fashion as of yore
Treetops bow their stately heads;
Buttercups leap from emerald beds
To chuck the chin of rarest maid
Who treads the wold so fair arrayed
That moon-bells chime from tall bone towers
Crowding air with tinkling showers.
This the veriest hour of grace—
Myrtle of Venus shows her face!

**Beauty has burned unseen**

Brushing blossoms white on unseen trees
Seldom held beheld by senses blind
Though mystic minds have furnished dullest ages
Fair with heavens flowers birds and rivers
Comes a moment-light to intellects broken
Travelling distractedly on numerous roads.

Multitudes who tread monotonous roads
And cannot see the beauteous wood for trees
Who have girded loins, fought and broken
The snakes of time, till toothless bent and blind
In turn they slither to mudholes by the rivers,
Yet skim a raw glory from the humdrum ages.

Even in the untamed chill stone ages
Before the dolmen-craft from Nile made inroads
Britons skiffing rudely round the coasts and rivers
Rending wattles or placating holy trees
Found a hostile beauty intensely blind
Not to joy but pain of bodies broken.

Memory can trace a thread unbroken
Broadening to cloth of gold in the Middle Ages
Where blinks no façade ostensibly blind—
Drollery unsurpassed invests the bye-roads
Canorous joy under boticelli trees
And dragons down by Christendom's sunny rivers.

To the great salt heart return the veinèd rivers
Though in places capillary mesh has broken;
On all-fours deserts stalk the stately trees:
Agape is old and Cupid ages
Flowers are fainting by dusty dervish roads
And poets proffers begging bowls of the blind.

Who will greet the sun if we all go blind?
Who will guard the source of the sacred rivers?
Who adore wild roses that skirt our English roads
If the spell of scent sound and sight is broken?
Dare we erect our Janus above the warring ages
To spy through burning mires a track to the cool trees?

O trees let your visible beauty strike us blind!
For weary ages we have wandered by deathly rivers
Betrayed wounded and broken by prodigal roads.

**Unrest**

On a goat-forsaken loveless peak
Let me soft-weeping sit and brood
On bone-fundamental themes
Thought contrapuntal with the shriek
Of ranging wind in desolate wood
Though unguent with healing dreams
Emetic to flaccid modern good.

Here, soothing nevertheless
Painted geometric lawns
Resent the swift pertinent query
The mordant instinctual guess
That the mythical abyss yawns
Hereunder. In cool blatant eeri-
ness the crabbed seismograph warns.

Naked mystery falls to pieces
With a clatter of scientific joy,
Outlawed mists and elves are fleeing

To shades with old and foul diseases.
Soon this dented outsize toy
Will cease its futile joyless speeding
Old and ended as a tale of Troy.

Many doors has man unlocked
In sweat and fear on grailward quest
Many iron secrets stolen
Though lofty cliffs have vainly mocked.
Remains his bleakest baulkèd test
A madman battered bruised and swollen
Screams for love and beats his breast.

We yearn and roam hungry for love
For molten speech in the ancient tongue.
When will the crimson talisman
Greet our hearts like Ararat's dove?
And braggard spirit glad and young
Spend all time's wealth with lavish hand
In sky-domed halls of thought and song.

Night beats with her padded feat
Against the dreadful window pane
Fear snuffs the honey candle low—
The tide of grief turns in our sleep
And moves across the luminous sand,
Strong smooth waters dimpling flow
Through the amazèd opal land.

**Tryst**

Day has subsided
Its flower-light failed
Has bloomed and seeded
Starring night's field.

Toil is forgotten
The moon glides elate
Through the whispering garden,
And still I wait.

The limes shed their magic
The lutes revive
And blood lethargic
Leaps up alive.

Here on the threshold
Of love and fate
Desires grow bold—
And still I wait.

**Sonnet**

Once more are told the warm lamentful beads
That solace, strength nor stone endurance know,
From the black-vine plucked by the heavy gryphon-crow
That mews and moults in the tower of murdered deeds,
The whirlwind tower where the wasteful desert bleeds.
Saith priest: 'That blackness tips the beam may show
The counter-weight in the swinging scale is low
But it proves the life of our hard-hammered creeds.'

  Fever-fruit, such suave and kindly words,
  For fear and love the last satiety;
  Irresolute strife of belle and bitter birds
  Rending their skies of dread polarity:
  I mourn no heaven which needful hell engirds,
  Beyond good would meet out old divinity.

**Romance**

Wine in her silken seamless dress
  Dreams deeply, deeply,
    Upon a tendrilled leaf.

A hundred days of wakelessness
  Pass fleetly, fleetly,
    Deeming her dead for grief.

A prince endowered with boyish grace
  Comes quickly, quickly:
    Eager and nothing loath

He brushes sleep from the slumbrous face
  Then thickly, thickly,
    Kisses rain on both.

**Our fate is not forlorn**

On this florid wind-swept plain
Seeds of time have blown:
Our fate is not forlorn.

Though gay leaves fade and flee
Embittered never be
At time's malignancy.

For man is not aloof
From kindred forms of life
That tramp and tread the earth.

Down-stream a bleating sound—
A sheep on croppèd mound
Looks on her lambkin drowned.

Anon the leaping ram
Will give the grieving dam
A smaller softer lamb.

Thus will plaintive woe
With passing beauty go:

On this florid wind-swept plain
Seeds of time have blown:
Our fate is not forlorn.

**Flinders Range**

O sudden weight of pilèd staggering peaks
Dragging the frail inadequate mind-web downwards
Below dismay: heavy as leaden doom
You lay an intolerable burden on simple human senses.

Torn and petrified tempest! Why in this vast museum
Are neolithic fists raised in arrested anger?
Why fall no blows save those of human foreboding
At this cracked horizon-bowl chock with outcrop armour?

And you, towering ruin, consummating the labouring heights
Taller truncated, what charnel and black revenge?
What huge transgression of god man or demon-beast?

. . . . .

Silence relentless mesmeric beats on the writhing brain:
Non-utterance not anger-born but that strange harsh
Ruthless logic that translates from a foreign tongue,
Language in which time and chaos once quarrelled bitterly
Which desperate men prospecting veins of prophecy know.

### The Solitary

How far merge in the shouting waves of seeming?
    Each curling sanction looms leaps stretches
And cuffs the close-sodden sand, old time consuming
    The senile foam-laced impulse which turns and reaches
Vacantly the deep matrix of a bloodless scheming.

Embarked thereon the seaweed manikins spawn;
    Regretting nothing they laugh they dance they drift
Yesterday merry, immortal today, they spurn
    Cares of the deep; sufficient their splashing raft
As it slumps into shoals of sleep to drowse or drown.

Reality unrabid exacts a modest toll
    Equating this simple service with that reward—
Foolish fanatic who would inly probe and tell
    Us wistfully doom's desolate uncouth word.
Let him bedtime babes with such a tale!

League upon darting league and dolphin-wise
    Yet not in play he wakes his genus-ship
Race-nostalgic, given to moods and woes;
    Empiric voices speak too low or sharp
And terrible visions rift his chartless ways.

Diadelphous birth-in-death he loved
     (Boys perplexed him once who hammered nails)
And he burned with roses, with flame and chime he lived,
    Compassion in him uprose like winds or gales
Kyrie-cries, liquid, spirit-laved.

### War Resisters

Find me a sword
Sheathless, light-sharp, cold,
To slash these breathing coils of war,
Bristling, beaked beyond fable, hideous and raw.

Thought has served
Lopes on, we trudge behind
Stumbling in darkness—without romance
Wrongs rise up like thugs to rob or slay:

And so it is,
It *is*, but not all,

Though bitterness feebly arms the prisoner
We seek friendship's sword and none is keener.

**Miss G—**

Imagine
An angular aunt
Aquiline, astringent, thin
Or a school-ma'am—spinster, sour, gaunt,
And to this partial picture—
add a predatory gesture
and the uniform of a nurse,
Then you have the primeval curse!
Alas.

And beware.
when you go to her,
make sure you're bad, really ill
before you dare. Don't diagnose,
she'll do that, she does it well
(You're much better than you suppose).
Why once in confidence she said,
'How bright you look!'—but Tom was dead.
Alas.

**From dust despised**

Slight and sweet the glance of the blackberry-
Flower—child of purple puckered leaves,
Immaculate-pink in simplest symmetry.
One long look becomes a lever that heaves
The death-deposit from heart of mediocrity:
One can feel the moment the old weight gives
And the curious slipping upwards of the exploited soul
Too used by change, always off its goal.

When I came to the established oak by the shed
And looked up, I wondered, perturbed and very glad
That tender green flags should hang from a fortress of lead,
That Arden gladed such loves as Shakespeare played:
The future withdrew from a corner, present fled,
All that was left, a green tree, a green lad.
Some potency impalpable in the leaf-drowned light
Unlidded deep wells that lie under thought and sight.

Then there was the half-grown kitten met at the gate,
Piteous (distressed like a little girl) whose cries,
Animal, low, slipped in where words must wait.
It was a direct woe that took pity by surprise
And I recognised its sigh as a stirring of fate
Forever-smothered beneath our strident cries.
We build emotional cities in cultural fashion
But on the shifting sands of animal passion.

Now morning has come full like buttercup
Or sleek swimmer snorting in seen-blown glass.
The bats of mystery have shrunk to their nighted keep.
Bright clouds, bird-music at air-golden Mass,
Blue wings, banners, silk-embossèd sleep
Merge in carol—erased the clod impasse
Of earth, the sullen drag of molten clay—
Paradise bursts apart and life again is play.

**To R—**

There were reasons for my silence, sweet,
Which pollened Time, the blossom-trampling bee
Would mould into the crisp fruit of clarity,
But since you say that Time is false and fleet
And straight my burning heart with love do greet
I'll own the self-same passion masters me
Intoxicating with such ichorous ecstasy
That skies and beauteous flower-worlds in me meet.

What then if barbarous doom should sweethearts sever?
These rifted clouds might bare a fangèd moon
To carve the heart of grief that bleeds forever—
But their grace unbinds the spell of dreary iron,
Reveals beside the silent-nighted river
Your girl-form dreaming to its darkling legend-tune.

**Incubus**

Sleep, moon-sculpture unchipped by time—betrayed!
Aslant the drugget, dream-drugget, thought-minions
In her ivory chamber stale, sly brain-scullions
Capered, quarrelled, their skirls schism-sharp inveighed;
The curdled curse abroach fell back afraid.
Old Gaia groaned, a-sorrow for world once
Mothering—hell's cadaver-clogged sillions

Heaved for her coming.
                                        The unwitting maid
In her veins a thousand flukèd anchors drag
The wombward flag her smothering. O sleep, sleep
In gethsemane ghost sans one parousia gleam,
Bound, forced by lifting seas' great sag
'Neath piling fathoms in airless death-sea keep . . .
O where are your willows, willows and the glassy stream?

**Specimen stanzas on a mythical scene**

Alas our days depart with glittering speed;
No more we stroll in childhood's grave content
On fields of asphodel, but ageing heed
The chill and mortal gales that never spent
Destroy this boned and silken-fleshèd tent.
Although this clay once leapt in glorious flame
When we from morning mists were sent
Its mazy cells collapsed to dung and lime
Which may a rose-bush feed to plait a wreath for fame.

This centuried ruin of man's rich-raggèd race,
Corruption's nauseous-goad, this virus-grief,
Mind's piercing stylus is with which to trace
Beauty's troublous towers—no wonder if
From granite-crumbling base the templed myth
Arose whose minarets surpass the skies
Whose ethereal architectures enchant the seraph
Well chilled and versed in light-linked fantasies
Whose smile death's heavy 'cellos woke with yearning cries.

Unlike the flower-death of edelweiss
Whose slender-throated roots will drink no more
Once th' annihilating avalanche of ice
Awakes to give its loud stupendous roar—
Star-eyed man caught in the crushing maw
Of time can burst his cerements' bleak bands,
And casting filaments of faith from death's dank shore
Swing a highway frail to ambrosial lands
Where he may tread exult their golden-gravelled strands.

But such a syrup'd philosophic theme
May not the brow of myriad learnèd books—
To quote the flimsy-fragrant wistful dream
Or sift old truth and cow with ponderous looks
Their toil—but ours to visit mem'ried nooks,

Kahura's timbered peaks and wild-boar glades,
The cliffs and falls of Whanganui's brooks
 Which snake along then crash in wild cascades
Echoeing eldritch songs, or mute in mirrored shades.

When first the arras of this painted isle
Appeared before the couch of heaven's goddess,
Recumbent-fair in simple grecian style,
Its soft-toned beauty's utter loveliness
Drew from her lids the lethean heaviness
Which isolates the inward sensual world.
Morpheus' charms enchained her less and less;
Slow a-drowse her folded limbs uncurl'd
Her bright eyes dawned in tears as a music-wind unfurled.

**Ignorantia**

Is pleasant the buffalo-grass
 Forage sniff and spy,
And the hot tongue's wet caress
 And the stomach's thick reply.

The flies buzz around the tail
 And the gorgon sun brings drought
The prairie is rough and male—
 Bellows the night of rut.

Incontinence is not,
 Though the soft fell maturate,
And intellect is naught
 Between the stare and the gait.

Is pleasant the wind-massage
 And the hungry pace of the morn:
The biped is much more sage
 But with wisdom his heart is torn.

Vulnerable in this
 He learns what to evade;
He has his girls to kiss
 And gourds to eat in the shade.

But the thin margin-man
 Feels herd-dereliction,
From mind-expanse to moan
 Descends to sad inaction.

**O Night**

I am feared for thy soul, O night,
Thou art older than day,
Passionate-dark thy plight.

When owls take heavy flight
And huddling branches sway
I am feared for thy soul, O night.

Thy body is soft delight,
The moon will thy love betray—
Passionate-dark thy plight.

Thou bearest the age-old blight
Nor canst in the gold sun play,
I am feared for thy soul, O night.

Never in holy light
Wilt love or learn to pray,
Passionate-dark thy plight.

Bootless all paschal rite
Naught can [ardour] slay: *darkness* [Baxter's note]
I am feared for thy soul, O night,
Passionate-dark thy plight.

**By the Appian Way**

Painfully hewn down a bone-embracing hill
The deepest gallery of a catacomb
Stoops under the lintel-stone of a darker womb;
And there squats time in atrophying peril;
And there will feed on night, and hate and sleep
Immured in his mine beneath the living land;
There his heavy blood's defiant stand,
While daisy flowers above their orbits keep.
But hark—what sacred words, what secret feast?
Dost see—a torch flaring on a symbol fish—
What joy of dirty slaves round a common dish?
Time saw with a shudder his savage soul released:
 Nor evermore could take his cynic rest
 For love had learned his name and lined his nest.

**Old question: old answer**

When the willow loses its dripping leaves
That fall yellow and sad
Does it feel the anguish that sometimes lives
In the heart of a grieving lad?

Does the sap that sways the pendulous green
Collapse in frozen dread
When the slashing spears of winter rain
Its ropes have severèd?

For the leaves that flow in spring austerely
Are grainèd naught with woe
But the heart that mates again can rarely
With virgin passion glow.

**To GRAEME**

Baby boy, I think of you
In your clothes of woolly blue
Your tinted skin and quiet eyes:
A world of mystery lies
About your glowing form and face
Suggestive of another race
Where beauty never hardens nor
Wonder freezes into law.
For you roses softly blow
And cornflowers down the pathway go;
Faces higher than the grass
Upward into heaven pass;
All the moving feeling world
Your sure phantasmagoric shield
From prickly heat and hunger pangs
Or sudden fear of falling balance

Notwithstanding huge dependence
On the arms and eyes of parents
You control the electric field
Underneath all flesh concealed,
Make the receiver ring
Till love again is heard speaking.
Time nor doom are complement
In your philosophic merriment,
Knowledge does not shape your smile
Simplicity your shrewdy wile.

Poignancy, nostalgia,
And the quest for stamina,
Time's overthrow and schismed sex
And all the other mals that vex
You'll know. Our native frailty
Your fundamental gaiety
Will crush: on swift fountains of pain
Your dreams will rise again,
Will rise in forms that fleer and hurt
In viscous dazed of sensual art
Where pain and peace are reconciled
In strenuous symbiosis sealed.

Music's massive chords may part
The heavy chambers of the heart
For you: the warfare that you wage
The ports of language hold in siege,
May win a mental world; your pen
May bow the heads of hungry men.
But who can guess your destined mode
Hero of all or one small maid
Where your generation hovers
Peeping from the warm birth covers;
Player of chess, climber of peaks
Or slow victim of collective weeks
Like lead or glass or arsenic—
Time's contorted arithmetic
Will tell . . .
    While the relaxing rain
Soothes the hot spasmed brain
And the branches stiffly say
In their incoherent way
Their growing creed, Graeme, I
Would add a testimony
Of blurred sensitivity
To many tones: but as I brood
Shell-sharding seas move my blood
And the aged cautery approaches
Red-eyed from its last debauches.
Soon comes death's convulsive heave
Its forgiveness brings a white reprieve,
Thus hear an exiled iron wraith
Reiterating the need for faith
And hope and suffering aspiration—
Child outlive my lamentation.

## Appendix 4
## James K. Baxter's Draft Paper
## 'The Unicorn: a consideration of adolescence'
[Hocken, MS 975/xxx ]

### 1. The Unicorn: a consideration of adolescence

Through the dim sea-blown wood
    The alien unicorn
    Walks steadfast and alone.
The herds return to fold as tame beasts would,
But unassailable, misunderstood,
    He moves beside the grey and twilight sea
    As figure of heraldic blazonry.

The crags blow trumpets round:
    Over and through the wind
    Sea-music moves his mind
To reverie on an enchanted ground.
Hearing afar the bay of hunting hound
    Across the deep ravines, white and forlorn,
    Passes the swift, the phantom unicorn.

Perchance the Archer sees
    Him silent move among
    The trees that burst in song,
The dryad-cloaked, the dream-enamoured trees;
And as he wheels through the far wood and flees,
    The musing Archer bends his bow again—
    Behold! the fabulous unicorn is slain.

O death of the unborn!
    Spirits that like to thee
    Unborn shall ever be
Wail endless over the buried unicorn.
Behold the adamant and fragile horn
    That conquers death of venom, death i' the tomb,
    Is deeper death—return beyond the womb.

O perilous unicorn!
    Death slays thee not; but see
    From the cold surf's futurity
    Aphrodite Andymone
Arise in birth thou woulds't extinction deem:
Arise and bind thee to an iron dream.

2. This poem was written by a precocious boy of sixteen. A quiet lad, who lived too much in his own head; a constant beach-walker and word-builder, with the makings of a drunkard or intelligent schizophrene. The torments of the adolescent furnace are threefold: unnatural solitude, ignorance of life, and sexuality without love. Like a million others he did his time there, and passed through singed, by virtue of a patience hidden from himself, like those children in the other furnace of the Assyrian king.
3. The unicorn and the boy are distinguishable, though not wholly separate. The unicorn is a hybrid creature, beast and spirit inhabiting the universe of the adolescent mind. Because poetry is conceived in the order of natural contemplation, it requires an interior solitude as its element. But the unicorn exists in a double solitude—a natural contemplative solitude, resonant with the correspondences of nature, and the terrible solitude of the boy himself, a child becoming a man and regarding himself as a monster.
4. Sexuality and spirituality combine in the powerful and mysterious horn: an obviously phallic emblem, and equally an emblem of the wild living intellect, which Newman wisely rebukes as the chief enemy of obedience. The horn of the unicorn, so the fable tells us, when placed in a poisoned winecup, could neutralise the venom. So an adolescent, by crossing the threshold of natural contemplation, and entering a world of sterile forms, holds at an arm's length his anguish and his weakness. Yet the answer is no answer. The poem expresses symbolically the secrets he wishes to hide. If his bent is science, the well-mannered spaceship approaching the planet Venus enchants him because (without his conscious knowledge) it symbolises the union of sperm and ovum. He reconstructs in imagination the prenatal paradise where all desires are permitted and fulfilled. A solution more calamitous than to endure the furnace open-eyed. The face of the adult schizophrene, who retains at forty the appearance of an eighteen year-old, expresses perfectly the sterile purity of the unicorn.
5. The unicorn is alien to that bourgeois prudence which opposes contemplation on the ground that it is useless, and despises the adolescent for his awkward spirituality and grandiose dreams. The herds return to fold at the coming of evening, when the unicorn emerges into consciousness. They distrust and misunderstand the ritual flight of the poet-unicorn through the forest of the subliminal mind; yet cannot assail him, because his joy springs from a supernatural suffering.
6. In earlier poems the boy had developed two other figures of self, the salamander that lives in flame, and the Titan Prometheus, from whose wound grows the iceflower of art. In the figure of the unicorn the adolescent dilemma is projected more fully and exactly. It seems that the soul of a man-to-be wakens at puberty when the torments of the flesh begin and he is isolated for good from the fraternal universe of childhood. Puberty gives birth to flesh and spirit simultaneously. However impure he may consider himself to be, the unicorn is a virgin, because he has not willed his sexual change.

[Handwritten Draft Notes Begin Here—crossing outs and variations in numbering have been preserved as far as possible]

2. This poem was written by a precocious boy of sixteen. A quiet lad, who lived too much in his head; a constant beach-walker and word-builder, with the makings of a drunkard or intelligent schizophrene. The torments of the adolescent furnace are threefold: solitude, ignorance of life, and sexuality without love. ~~He did his time there~~ Like a million others, he did his time there, and passed through singed, by virtue of a patience hidden from himself, like those children in the other furnace of the Assyrian king. The poem is essentially a prophetic meditation.
3. The unicorn and the boy are distinguishable, though not wholly separate. The unicorn is a hybrid, beast and spirit, inhabiting the ~~country~~ universe of the adolescent mind. since poetry belongs to the order of natural contemplation, it requires solitude as its element. But the unicorn exists in a double solitude—a natural contemplative solitude, where it can experience in joy the correspondences of nature, and the terrible solitude of the boy ~~himself, a child becoming a man and regarding himself as a monster~~. Sexuality and spirituality combine in the powerful and mysterious horn: a phallic emblem, like the basalt one that confronts the sea in a cell at *Mahabalipuram*, and equally an emblem of the wild living intellect, which Newman so wisely rebukes ~~regarded~~ as the chief enemy of ~~holiness~~ obedience.
4. The unicorn is alien to the bourgeois prudence ~~that regards art, intellect~~ which opposes contemplation on the grounds that it is useless, and equally ~~hates~~ despises the adolescent for his awkward suffering and his grandiose dreams. The herds who return to fold at the coming of evening are bourgeois in their consciousness. [This following section all crossed out: They distrust and misunderstand the ritual flight of the poet-unicorn in the forest of the unconscious mind, yet cannot assail his joy, because it ~~is the obverse of his unique~~ springs from supernatural suffering. It seems that the soul is born, or at least wakened, at puberty when the torment of the flesh begins, and a man-to-be is isolated for ever from the fraternal universe of childhood. The unicorn himself is a virgin, however impure he may consider himself to be, because he has not willed his sexual, and because he has ~~loved~~ desired only phantasms.] Puberty fractures the wholeness of childhood, giving birth to flesh and spirit simultaneously; but the ambiguous purity of adolescence can be destroyed only be ~~the~~ true sexual initiation when a women [will] introduces the adolescent to the iron dream of the adult carnal/causal? universe, and set his feet on the road to the grave. Till then the unicorn keeps his anomalous freedom.
5. (4.A.) Perhaps it is the breeze of Divine love that moves the branches, infusing supernatural light into natural contemplation. And the sea may represent the unlimited all-suffering mercy of God, sustaining and healing the living and the dead. ~~The~~ But the unicorn knows it only as the source of visions. He is a figure in a tapestry, or an image on a shield, for the will to love is petrified in the adolescent furnace, and only the intellect can move. God he knows as the Archer, an analogue

of time, who kills from a distance, without knowledge of the victim or participation in its suffering. Yet hound and Archer are secretly welcome to the unicorn, who knows that he must die for the adolescent to become a man.

In earlier poems the boy had developed two ~~images~~ figures of self, the salamander which lives in flame, and the Titan Prometheus, from whose wound the iceflower of art can grow. But the third ~~image~~ figure, that of the unicorn, is perhaps less delusive, and certainly projects more exactly the adolescent dilemma.

[This section crossed out: 4.A. The unicorn is mute. If he had a language there would still be no creature of his own kind to whom he could speak. Nature and the angelic order pour song into his ears, and he struggles to understand it. If he were to find speech, what could he say?—except, I suffer, therefore I am.]

4.A. The unicorn has no voice. Nature and the angelic order pour song into his ears, and he struggles to understand it; but he has no song of his own ,since the secret of his being is hidden from him. Again and again he has gazed into the black crystal of self, the pool at the centre of the forest, and seen only a monstrous image, a white zebra with a useless horn. If he were to find speech what would he say, except—I suffer, therefore I am. ~~Who can love him? God alone~~ The dryads of the trees, who waken his concupiscence, are creatures of delusion. They evade his approach, and lead him to bruise himself on the hard stones. Yet he dreams of a perfect mate, who will understand the necessity of his being. In the legend, she is a virgin, but he imagines her as a wise harlot. He knows she will conquer him and deliver him, sleeping, to the hunters. He fears and longs for that deliverance.

4.B. Though the unicorn cannot speak he is able to weep. The tears of the unicorn are poems and proverbs. ~~They may be found glittering~~ They glitter among the rocks on the forest floor. Sometimes a hunter discovers the [?tears] of the unicorn and stands ~~amazed~~ wondering at the sight of those [?angry/amazing] jewels.

4.C. [This entire section scribbled out: The horn of the unicorn, placed in a poisoned winecup, was said to neutralise ~~its~~ all venom. So by rational contemplation, and entry into a world of sterile forms, whether of science or of art, the adolescent sets at an arms length his anguish and his weakness. Yet the answer is no answer; for the poems express symbolically the secrets he wishes to hide, and ~~the shape of~~ the orbit of the rocketship approaching the planet Venus ~~is linked for [?him] (perhaps without his conscious knowledge) sperm and ovum~~ [?imitates] ~~symbolises~~ the ~~longed for~~ conjunction ~~of the sexes~~ of sperm and ovum. He reconstructs in symbol the [?~~natural universe of the maternal womb~~] prenatal paradise where all desires are permitted [?~~and man can remain an aggressive embryo~~ ] ~~This solution, being schizophrenic, in nature, is a calamity of evasion more destructive~~ A schizophrenic solution more calamitous than merely to endure the furnace open eyed. The ~~pure if~~ ageless face of ~~the~~ a schizophrene, who retains at forty the appearance of ~~eighteen~~ an adolescent, expresses the ~~ambiguous~~ sterile purity of the unicorn.]

4.D. The spirituality of the unicorn is vertiginous. It demands an issue in ritual violence, love or self murder. One day the boy entered his father's coalhouse and took down from a beam the sawn-off rifle he had hidden there. Almost without thought he placed the muzzle in his mouth, having nothing to lose. Then an idea occurred to him—'You have never yet loved a woman. Wait till then, and see if the world changes.' So he replaced the gun in its hiding place.

4.C. The adolescent does not form that view without the fruits of doom and all in solitude. He imagines an adult empire of the wise and joyful from which he is excluded by some unique fatality

6 Those spirits who surround the grave of the dead unicorn are the potential powers that sleep in the heart of the adolescent. They know that with his death their Eden is destroyed: a change from infinite potentiality to the limited actual labour of the adult will. The interior precipices among which the unicorn enjoyed his freedom are full of ~~echoes and~~ the music of the angelic intellect; the trees bear song instead of fruit. But the touch of a woman's hand can level and extinguish them.

8 It was a prophetic intuition that enabled the boy to see beyond the furnace an image of cold waves breaking and the figure of the sea-born Venus. In the third poem of this chosen cycle she appears and clasps the chains of manhood on his limbs, which is perhaps the true death of the unicorn, by the attachments that remove solitude, give human knowledge, and mercifully crucify ~~both intellect and~~ our passions. ~~Yet the warning that sexual fulfilment is the death of the spirit has not been annihilated [ ] by the . . .~~

7 ~~(6a)~~ One could of course interpret the whole poem in Freudian terms. The father-archer (the boy's father was called Archie and was born under the sign of Sagittarius) kills or castrates the unicorn-child whose auto-erotic ~~fantasy~~ rebellion involves a return in [ ] to his mother's womb. It fits nicely. But the boy has read Freud, and these implications were fully [ ] in his mind. He was not wholly devoid of iconoclastic humour.

## Appendix 5
## Two Early Prose Pieces by James K. Baxter
[Hocken, MSS 975/151 & 152]

### Before Sunrise[1]

The air before sunrise was chilly. A few owls still hooted with screams human and inhuman through the hill-gullies. He slept on his camp-bed in a dream of narrow tunnels suffocating; under the blanket-layers of sleep, herculean he tried to move a finger. With a sense of strain he woke. Lay staring in content at the canvas roof through which flooded diffuse light.

He sat up and the stretcher creaked: his parents deeper in the tent did not move. He stepped out to the grass floor. This was wild earth, he thought, we have tamed it within walls. He pulled off his pyjamas; on with bathing-trunks. He was sixteen.

Then he slid under the wall. The grass was wet outside; but the birds chittered and flew in the fir-plantation; On the thread of a bird's voice is the pendulous earth hung. The mountain-shadow lay still half-way from their bases to the camping-ground. The sky was one-coloured except that it was darker to the west and bright above the near mountains: There are mountains upon mountains, they are gashed by sword-strokes of the rising sun, they are awake at early dawn before I walk stiffly with bare feet to bathe before sunrise; and grasses are wet to the skin, stones and thorns knock at the gates of flesh, but I am the animal unsad and blood-aware.

As he climbed over the fence on the path to the lake he felt cold, wished he had gone to sleep again. His eyes were stiff still, one eye saw blurred. He crossed a water-course with willows and fell of cutty-grass and felt through the trees the first chill of the lake-wind. He crossed his arms on his chest and hunched his shoulders for protection from the wind.

Remembering sleep he thought. Tent-bedded I lie safe in body and cloak of memory, but behind my musing eyes, beyond walls of bone, is reality not of me, where the sea in dark hills cupped whose waves are death or longing . . . .slap rotted wood in multitudinous strife and quiet. He came out on the shingle-banks of the lake-shore, picking his way between thorn-bushes over moss where ran small grey insects. The sun had almost risen, the sky had grown very bright; shaking bladed tracks of sunlight were reflected on the water. The lake was about three miles wide: he stood at the lower end of it and looked as far as he could see over its length, twelve miles perhaps in all but hidden by the feet and heavy flanks of the mountains.

It is air and water in the vast lands of silten rivers, thought he: swollen and swift from the lake, home of the abyss-monsters yet calm in surface save to the blades of glinting wind.

J.K.B. (approx. 1941)
[Hocken, MS 975/151]

1 Apart from some minor variations, this is identical to the opening paragraphs of the story of the same name, sent to Ginn by Baxter with the letter dated 18 Mar 1944. See pp.346–9.

**The White Gull**

At dawn he stirred on his camp stretcher, and pressed up through blanketing layers of sleep to lie staring in contentment at the near canvas roof. In the half-dark he could hear the rustle of scrub and the waves breaking on a shelving beach below. The air was still chilly, and he lay without moving, ready to sleep again.

Yesterday near sunset they had come over a ridge in the old Ford truck and seen the lake spread suddenly below them. 'That's Ohau', his father had said. 'We'll camp down there by the creek'. And he had pointed to a clump of manuka scrub that grew close to the water's edge about a mile from the rapid outlet. His mother, half-asleep, had lifted her head and smiled. 'You'll be glad to get a rest from the wheel, won't you, Jack', she said. The boy, cramped between them on the narrow seat, shifted his legs and looked down at the lake. An oval of darkening silver caught in the fold of the arid ranges, two thousand feet in depth, fed by snow water from the distant glaciers, it seemed to him indescribably pure and remote, a place made for rest.

They came slowly down to the lake shore, the truck straddling tussocks and small boulders, for the road had dwindled to wheel-ruts in shingle. They jolted over a ford, water splashing as high as the bonnet of the truck. From time to time the boy climbed out to open gates and close them again when the truck had gone through. When they finally came to a stop beside a scrub clearing he helped his father to unload the stores and cut props for a tent and fireplace. He was a little afraid of that lean-faced saturnine man—a farmer born and bred whom two wars had left powerless to take pleasure in natural growth and the small triumphs of farming. Yet he looked for his approval, driving the props deep into the stony ground, to stand firm against his testing. Before he went to bed that night, he walked out shivering to the edge of the lake and brushed his teeth there, spitting on the smooth stones and listening to the quiet sound of water. His senses seemed sharpened by the dry air; and with this sharpness came an awareness of his own loneliness. The huge spaces and glittering stars were inhuman, even hostile. He ran back to the camp, his sandals stubbing on loose shingle as he went.

Waking now, he could hear his parents deeper in the tent—his mother's steady breathing and an occasional snore from his father. A small green caterpillar fell cautiously from the roof, suspended on its invisible thread. From the scrub outside he could smell the exhalation of damp grass and flowering manuka. As he sat up his stretcher creaked loudly, but his parents did not stir. Stepping out to the newly trodden grass, he dressed quickly (slacks, sandals, shirt and jersey) and emerged rubbing his eyes to a sky bright with dawn. A fresh wind blew on his face as he crossed the clearing towards the truck. A tarpaulin had been drawn over it for the night. He untied a rope at the back, reached inside, and drew out his father's rifle. It was a long-barrelled twenty-two, neat and well cared for, the wood on the stock polished with constant handling. He fumbled again till he found a box of bullets, which he slipped into his trouser pocket. Then he set off along the road, the rifle under his arm, its muzzle pointing to the ground an inch in front of his moving feet.

The feel of the rifle against his hand and elbow was exhilarating. If his father had been more ready to lend it, he would have spent all day shooting or pretending to shoot. More than desire to kill, it was the myth of the hunter that gripped him. Even now he trod warily, his muscles tense and his eyes glancing from side to side for the first scurry of brown fur. A hundred yards from the camp he left the road and clambered down a bank to the lakeshore. By now the sun showed an edge of molten steel above the mountains. Glittering tracks of light lay on the surface of the lake like the tracks of sea monsters. Overhead flew gulls, their harsh cries contrasting strangely with the splendour of their circling wings. He picked his way over banks of shingle and patches of moss where small grey insects ran like lice. There were no rabbits in sight. Nevertheless he opened the box of bullets and slipped one into the breech. Then he walked on along the edge of the lake where the stones had been worn to rough sand. The early morning sun now warmed the cloth on his shoulders. About a mile from the camp he came on a row of willow trees whose delicate light-green leaves sprang from twisted trunks half-buried in the shingle. Laying the rifle across his knees, he sat down on a log to rest. From under a matagouri bush a glinting object caught his eye. It was a condensed milk tin, not yet rusty, left there by campers. He picked it up gingerly, walked to the water's edge, and threw it far out into the lake. There it rose and fell gently on the light waves. He sat down on the log again and took aim.

The first shot went wide, ricocheting from the lake surface and whining out of sound. With the second shot his hand was steadier, the butt firm against his shoulder. He aimed a little high and pressed the trigger slowly. The crack of the rifle merged in the plonk of the bullet against the tin. It bubbled and sank. He rose from the log and walked back towards the camp, reloading the rifle as he went.

The gulls still swerved in wide arcs above his head. Mist rose from the upper reaches of the lake till he could see clearly the ridges on the mountain flanks that were ancient beaches where the lake had been. Beyond them lay further mountains, range behind range stretching to the cloudy buttresses of Mt Cook itself. For the first time that morning he felt hunger, and quickened his step. He wished that he had shot at least one rabbit—to show as an excuse for having borrowed the gun. His luck was out today. He would not be able to pose as the experienced hunter.

He came to where a point of shingle ran out into the lake, enclosing a basin of calm water at the outlet of a small creek. Just inside the point a gull rode lightly. It did not move as he came nearer, but preened its feathers and fixed him with a cold eye. He though of scaring it with a stone but the distance was too great. A strange anger rose in him against the bird. ~~It seemed to be mocking him, safe in its element, too far away for him to reach.~~ On an impulse he raised the rifle. I'll only scare it, he told himself. Yet, as he had done with the tin, he aimed a little higher and pressed the trigger slowly. At the crack of the rifle the bird rose, and he felt a surge of relief. It fluttered two or three yards, then fell to the water again and lay with its wings outspread. Dropping the rifle on a patch of moss, he rushed forward and waded into the shallow water. He lifted it gently. The bird lay in his hands perfect and seemingly unharmed, no trace of blood on the snowy feathers. He wondered if it had perhaps only been stunned by the wind of the bullet. Then, pressing back the soft breast feathers, he saw where the lead had struck. The breast bone was smashed through, a tangle of flesh and sinew hidden by the close down. He turned the bird's head towards him. The eye, still black and cold, had lost its living sharpness.

The whole shore seemed to watch him. The least flicker in his mind of self-justification was crushed by this open stare. Suddenly he felt sick and heavy. Scooping a hollow in the shingle, he laid down the gull, and piled stones above it till the accusing white was entirely hidden. Then he walked back to where he had left the rifle, water squelching from his sandals at every step. On the road to the camp he recovered a little of his self-assurance. It was a good shot anyway, he thought.

A plume of smoke was rising from the clearing. The smell of frying bacon drifted to his nostrils. His father was holding a pan over a fire of dry manuka sticks. Remembering the borrowed rifle, he felt his heart sink a trifle.

'You been out shooting?' said his father casually.

His heart lifted again. 'Yes, I didn't have any luck.'

'You seem to have got yourself pretty wet.'

'I couldn't help it. There was a bit of bog I mistook for green grass. I had a few practice shots at a tin and sunk it all right.'

'Yes, I heard the shooting.'

'I've worked up a hunger anyway.' He walked over the short springy turf, and laid the rifle in the back of the truck. As he turned towards the tent, the light reflected from the lake dazzled his eyes. ~~and threw into relief his thin nervous face and fair boy's hair.~~

!!!!!!!!!!!!!!!!!!!!!!!!!!!!!!

James K. Baxter

[Hocken, MS 975/152]

## Appendix 6
## 'Spirits of Harmony, Music and Love'
## by Archibald Baxter

[Hocken, MS 975/186]

**Spirits of Harmony, Music and Love**

In the elemental chaos
When the worlds were in the making
None could rule nor disobey us—
We were there in all partaking;
And we caught the rhythmic motion
Of the orbs that roll and swing
In the vast ethereal ocean
Deep beyond all fathoming.

And our music rolled over the waters before
Their free-swelling billows were barred by a shore,
And we sang as we saw the earth leap from the main
And the plan of Creation before us made plain.

But it was our delight, when the earth in the pride
Of her sweet virgin beauty in us did confide—
Then we rustled, and played
Through her forests, and swayed
All the reeds and the brackens and bade them rejoice,
And the birds in their flight
When the sunshine was bright,
Caught the sound of our music and each found a voice.

A. Baxter

# Appendix 7
## Baxter's Foreword to *Cold Spring* and Table of Contents

### Foreword
[by James K. Baxter]

The poems in this book are roughly in chronological order. The four divisions, however, are intended to represent specific emotional trends running parallel in time, rather than consecutive phases of thought.

The poems of the first section were mainly built on themes of a myth character, being thus comparable to essays or narrative prose. Technically, they may be regarded as the matrix of a style more coherent and nearer to prose.

In the second section the longer poems develop by elaboration on themes rather as in music. In the third and fourth sections the idiom simplifies to prose directness.

The introduction of classical allusions occurs for symbolic purposes, the allusions containing for me in each case a powerful private significance.

It may seem strange that verse assumedly modern, should be rhetorical or bear any resemblance to that of the Romantic era. I believe (as do both Spender and the later Auden) that the root of poetry must always lie in personal emotion, and that rhetorical gestures may be a truthful and natural mode of expression for this emotion. Dynamos and skyscrapers are no more essential to 'modern' poetry than were ruffs and wars with Catholic Spain essential to Elizabethan poetry. They may nevertheless quite naturally acquire an objective or subjective significance in the mind of any poet, and thus recur as an integral part of his poem. Birds, flowers, air, earth etc. must remain the staple and permanent poetic images because of their never-diminishing evocative intensity. If Spender uses the word 'ocean', this does not mean that he is necessarily imitating the nautical Masefield or the romantic Byron; it means simply that he is writing—and, being Spender, is probably writing powerful and original poetry.

In a word, the modern poet is not a species distinct, and may be taught by Burns as readily as by Eliot. The weight of interpretation of environment, however, becomes a personal burden of death of the Atlas of traditional pose. Hence the moderns are apt to use their intellect where the stage-gestures of precocious children would once have sufficed. The distinguishing mark of the best modern poets is an unprecedented degree of self-honesty.

J.K.B.

[For a full discussion of the history of the *Cold Spring* collection see pp.111–17.]

## *Cold Spring* Table of Contents



1 See Baxter's letter of 2 Oct 1943, p.266.
2 The last poem added to *Cold Spring*. It was sent to Lawrence Baigent on 5 May 1945.
3 This is the first of two major revisions of an early poem titled 'Bees' (MS Hocken 704/4: 260), written when Baxter was 15. He sent the early version to Noel Ginn on 29 Nov 1943 with the comment: '"Bees" not bad, rather gauche maybe' (see p.301) The MS Book draft of this version notes that the poem is written 'in stress hexameters'. The final version 'Wild Bees' is one of Baxter's best known poems (see *Collected Poems*, p.82).
4 See Baxter's letter of 16 Jul 1944, p.366.
5 See Baxter's letter of 20 Nov 1944, p.385. MS Book gives '30/10/44' as the date of composition.
6 See Baxter's letter of 20 Nov 1944, p.385.
7 See Baxter's letter of 13 Aug 1944, p.373. MS Book gives '1/8/44' as the date of composition.
8 See Baxter's letter of 16 Jul 1944, p.366.
9 See Baxter's letter of 13 Aug 1944, p.373. MS Book gives '6/8/44' as the date of composition. On 23 Oct 1944 Baxter wrote to Lawrence Baigent:

> Those poems which you mention (Such as ANNALES) were mostly written after I saw you last. I have definitely improved of late, but my style still vacillates a bit and probably always will. Though a good one, I am an amateur from start to finish. Perhaps all poets are. Shelley is the only exception I can think of at the moment.

10 See Baxter's letter of 13 Sep 1944, p.375.
11 MS Book gives '20/8/44' as the date of composition. The MS Book version of this poem is 126 lines long but at Baigent's suggestion Baxter cut out seventeen lines that fell between '. . . turned to stone' and 'Storm devouring storm' (lines 94 to 110).
12 MS Book gives '2/9/44' as the date of composition. MS Book version had an epigram which Baxter deleted:

*To all pioneers of truth*
*whose hearts have been broken*
*or hardened by oppression.*

13 See Baxter's letter of 13 Sep 1944, p.375.

Uninnocence
Each
What the Night Replied
The untold story
To a Poplar-Tree[14]
In Monochrome[15]

THE FLOWERING EYE
Not in these flooded pastures
The Flowering Eye[16]
Affirmation
It is not enough
From Heine
I have cut from my heart[17]

COLD SPRING
Cold Spring[18]
Poem in November[19]
Under the dank leaves[20]
Clarity[21]
For us no saint wore shroud
From winter vials[22]
In the lion rocks
Nor did I ask[23]
Easter Sonnet[24]
To you who most unwittingly[25]

14 Poem in MS Book inscribed 'for M.B.'
15 MS Book gives '26/11/44' as the date of composition.
16 MS Book gives '20/9/44' as the date of composition.
17 MS Book gives '21/10/44' as the date of composition.
18 See Baxter's letter of 20 Nov 1944, p.386. MS Book gives '14/11/44' as the date of composition.
19 MS Book gives '12/11/44' as the date of composition.
20 See Baxter's letter of 20 Nov 1944, p.386.
21 MS Book gives '26/11/44' as the date of composition. Baxter sent Lawrence Baigent a number of sonnets on 27 Nov 1944, and commented that '"Clarity" is undoubtedly the best, especially the sestet.'
22 Sent to Lawrence Baigent with letter dated 29 Dec 1944: 'Here is a poem written Sunday—today.'
23 MS Book gives '21/1/45' as the date of composition.
24 See Baxter's letter of 8 Apr 1945, pp.399–400.
25 The draft in the MS Book is titled 'To J.S.' MS Book gives '15/3/45' as the date of composition.' In a letter to Lawrence Baigent dated 17 Mar 1945 Baxter writes: 'The "lady of the poem" has just married. Enclosed find a barometric reading.'

# Select Bibliography


## PRIMARY MATERIAL

### 1. WORKS BY JAMES K. BAXTER

**In Manuscript**

In the process of my research I read through the two major collections of manuscript material held in the Victoria University of Wellington Library and in the Hocken Library. As these archives are very large I have limited the list of manuscript material to items directly relevant to the period covered by this book.

A) Baxter Manuscripts Held at the Hocken Library

Items in this collection are ordered in groups according to the Hocken Library's 1974 catalogue 'James K. Baxter: A Preliminary Inventory of Literary and Personal Papers in the Hocken Library, Dunedin'. I describe individual items of particular significance within each grouping in greater detail following the (bolded) Hocken description.

I: Literary Papers

**a. Poetry**

MS 704/1-28 Manuscript notebooks—fair copies. Volumes XVI–XXVIII. 1937–67. 28 volumes.

I have made considerable use of the following MS Books (In this list the Hocken manuscript number is followed by the sequential numbers of the poems in each notebook according to Baxter's own numbering system, and, finally, the number of pages containing Baxter's poems):

'Book I'—MS 704/1, contains poems 1 to 83, 119 pages.

'Book II'—MS 704/2, contains poems 84 to 131, 111 pages.

'Book III'—MS 704/3, contains poems 132 to 162, 61 pages. (also contains five poems by Archibald Baxter.)

'Book IV'—MS 704/4, contains poems 163 to 263, 183 pages.

'Book V'—MS 704/5, contains poems 264 to 323, 111 pages.

'Book VI'—MS 704/6, contains poems 324 to 387, 114 pages.

'Book VII'—MS 704/7, contains poems 388 to 460, 154 pages.

'Book VIII'—MS 704/8, contains poems 461 to 503, 73 pages.

'Book IX'—MS 704/9, contains poems 504 to 569, 90 pages.

'Book X'—MS 704/10, contains poems 570 to 651, 177 pages. (also contains three poems by Archibald Baxter.)

'Book XI'—MS 704/11, contains poems 652 to 708, 109 pages.

'Book XII'—MS 704/12, contains poems 709 to 765, 157 pages.

'Book XIII'—MS 704/13, contains poems 766 to 855, 219 pages.

'Book XIV'—MS 704/14, contains poems 856 to 1025, 284 pages.

'Book XV'—MS 704/15, poems unnumbered, 216 pages.

MS 975/1-25 Manuscript notebooks—drafts. 1937–*c.*1968. 25 volumes.

Notebook, MS 975/1, containing 'Notes on Poetry and Verse'.

Notebook, MS 975/14, titled 'Original Poetry J. Baxter'. This notebook contains drafts of many of the early poems later transcribed into MS 704/1.

Notebook, MS 971/21, containing Baxter's 'journal' of his early poems.

MS 975/25. *Beyond the Palisade.* Christchurch: The Caxton Press, 1944. Baxter's personal annotated copy.

**b. Plays and Mimes**

MS 975/32-46 Manuscript notebooks—fair copies and drafts. 15 volumes.

'The Unicorn: a consideration of adolescence.' MS 975/34.

**c. Prose**

MS 975/117-164 Typescripts and extracts from publications.

'Further Notes on New Zealand Poetry.' MS 975/119.

'Thoughts concerning a career.' MS 975/150.

'Before Sunrise.' MS 975/151.

'The White Gull.' MS 975/152.

'Stone Lions.' MS 975/156.

'Poetry in New Zealand.' Notes. MS 975/161.

II Personal Papers

MS 975/183 General correspondence, 1942–67 and 1971. *c.*91 items.
Letter to Allen Curnow. 7 Jul 1945.

MS 975/184 Letters to his parents, 1939–70. *c.*62 items.
Letters to Archibald Baxter: undated (c. 1939), 14 Jun [1939], 1 Nov 1939 and 23 Sep 1945.
Letters to Millicent Baxter: 1 Nov 1939, 1 Oct 1945, 15 Oct 1945, Labour Day 1945, Jun 1948 and 11 Dec 1948.

MS 975/187 Official Documents, 1926–67. *c.*26 items.
School reports from King's High School.
School Certificate.
Higher Leaving Certificate.
School exercise books containing: 'Poetry', 'Short Extracts from My Diary Ten Years Hence', 'The First Poet', and 'Suggestions for Making our Present Form of Government function more smoothly . . .'.

III. Photographs

MS 975/199 Family photographs. *c.*94 items.

B) Baxter Manuscripts Held at the Victoria University of Wellington Library

The material held by the VUW Library is a substantial archive of papers collected by Dr. Frank McKay in the course of his research for his biography of Baxter—this archive was catalogued by me in 1994. Apart from the Noel Ginn letters, and material deemed to have direct relevance to the study of the Noel Ginn letters, all material in the McKay collection is embargoed until 2011. Any access to this collection is at the discretion of Dr. McKay's literary executor, Professor Vincent O'Sullivan.

'Before Sunrise'. Short story. MS item 28/50.

'Foreword' to *Cold Spring*. Sent by Baxter to Lawrence Baigent. MS item 19/3/2.

Letter to Armed Forces Appeal Board, *c.*late 1944. MS item 20/1/2.

Letter to 'Bagheera'. 5 Jun 1938. MS item 17/8/10.

Letters to Lawrence Baigent ordered by date and MS item number:
2 Oct 1944. Item 19/3/1.
15 Nov 1944. Item 19/3/3.
27 Nov 1944. Item 19/3/4.
29 Dec 1944. Item 19/3/17.
24 Feb 1945. Item 19/3/18.
4 Mar 1945. Item 19/3/19.
10 Mar 1945. Item 19/3/20.
17 Mar 1945. Item 19/3/21. Poem 'To J.S.' attached.
24 Mar 1945. Item 19/3/22. Poem 'Song' attached.
8 Apr 1945. Item 19/3/23.
5 May 1945. Item 19/3/24.
25 Jun 1945. Item 19/3/25.
12 Oct 1945. Item 19/3/27.

Undated fragment. Page begins 'flavoured by Huxley's'. Poem 'To D.' attached. Item 19/3/28.
26 Mar 1946. Item 19/3/29.
19 Apr 1946. Item 19/3/37.

Letter to Charles Brasch. 7 Jul 1947. MS item 20/2/1.

Letter to Margaret Still, 16 Aug 1968. MS item 11/9/1.

Letters to Noel Ginn appearing in this edition, ordered by date and MS item number:
9 Aug 1942. Item 28/1.
28 Aug 1942. Item 28/2.
23 Sep 1942. Item 28/3.
21 Nov 1942. Item 28/4.
10 Dec 1942. Item 28/5.
16 Jan 1943. Item 28/6.
22 Jan 1943. Item 28/7.
12 Feb 1943. Item 28/8.
14 Mar 1943. Item 28/9.
16 Apr 1943. Item 28/10.
4 May 1943. Item 28/11.
14 Jun 1943. Item 28/12.
Undated, *c.*12 Jun 1943. Item 28/13.
4 Jul 1943. MS item 28/14.
Undated, *c.*Aug 1943. Item 28/15.
11 Aug 1943. Item 28/16.
4 Sep 1943. Item 28/17.
11 Sep 1943. Item 28/18.
2 Oct 1943. Item 28/19.
4 Oct 1943. Item 28/20.
16 Oct 1943. Item 28/21.
1 Nov 1943. Item 28/22.
6 Nov 1943. Item 28/23.
15 Nov 1943. Item 28/24.
20 Nov 1943. Item 28/25.
Undated, *c.*Nov 1943. Item 28/26.
29 Nov 1943. Item 28/27.
22 Dec 1943. Item 28/28.
4 Jan 1944. Item 28/29.
12 Jan 1944. Item 28/30.
26 Jan 1944. Item 28/31.

1 Feb 1944. Item 28/32.
10 Feb 1944. Item 28/33
19 Feb 1944. Item 28/34.
24 Feb 1944. Item 28/35.
25 Feb 1944. Item 28/36.
6 Mar 1944. Item 28/37.
12 Mar 1944. Item 28/38.
18 Mar 1944. Item 28/39.
23 Mar 1944. Item 28/40.
9 Apr 1944. Item 28/41.
25 May 1944. Item 28/42.
3 Jun 1944. Item 28/43.
Undated *c.*7 Apr 1944. Item 28/43A.
16 Jul 1944. Item 28/44.
13 Aug 1944. Item 28/45.
13 Sep 1944. Item 28/46.
20 Nov 1944. Item 28/48.
6 Jan 1945. Item 28/49.
8 Apr 1945. Item 28/51.
1 May 1945. Item 28/52.
23 Jun 1945. Item 28/53.
14 Jul 1945. Item 28/54.
11 Dec 1945. Item 28/55.
21 Jul 1946. Item 28/56.
27 Mar 1951. Item 28/57.

Letters to Noel Ginn not appearing in this edition ordered by date and MS item number:
22 Oct 1959. Item 15/7/4.
3 Nov 1959. Item 15/7/9.
3 Dec 1959. Item 15/7/14.
11 Dec 1959. Item 15/7/16.
16 Mar 1960. Item 15/7/18.
*c.* Apr 1960. Item 15/7/24A.
11 Oct 1960. Item 15/7/52.

Poems sent to Lawrence Baigent with correspondence, between 1944–46. Titles and MS item numbers as follows:
'To Lawrence Baigent'. Item 19/3/5.
'Clarity'. Item 19/3/6.
'The Cool Map Charming'. Item 19/3/7.
'Night'. Item 19/3/8.
'In Monochrome'. Item 19/3/9.
'From winter vials . . .' Item 19/3/10.
'Cherries'. Item 19/3/11.
'Samson'. Item 19/3/12.
'Many have written well . . .' Item 19/3/13.
'In Flames Politic'. Item 19/3/14.
'The Diver'. Item 19/3/15.
'Various Sonnets, I-VIII'. Item 19/3/16.
'Among these rocks . . .' On rear of envelope postmarked 'Purakanui'. Item 19/3/26.
'Aubade'. Item 19/3/30.
'Night is your kingdom' and 'Sonnet of Nativity'. Item 19/3/31.
'Sleeping we bind' and 'The Incorruptible'. Item 19/3/32.
'Sunday: Chingford Park. ad matrem'. Item 19/3/33.
'Blow wind of fruitfulness'. Item 19/3/34.
'Desire no more'. Item 19/3/35.
'What answer then? for P.D.' Item 19/3/36.

'Snows of Aorangi'. Copy of Baxter's film commentary. MS, item 8/37.

## Published Works by Baxter

a. Poetry

*Beyond the Palisade*. Christchurch: The Caxton Press, 1944.

*Blow, Wind of Fruitfulness*. Christchurch: The Caxton Press, 1948.

*The Fallen House*. Christchurch: The Caxton Press, 1953.

*The Iron Breadboard: Studies in New Zealand Writing*. Wellington: Mermaid Press, 1957.

*In Fires of No Return: Selected Poems*. London: Oxford University Press, 1958.

*Howrah Bridge and Other Poems*. London: Oxford University Press, 1961.

*Pig Island Letters*. London: Oxford University Press, 1966.

*The Rock Woman: Selected Poems*. London: Oxford University Press, 1969.

*Jerusalem Sonnets: Poems for Colin Durning*. Dunedin: Bibliography Room, University of Otago, 1970. Reprinted: Wellington: Price Milburn, 1975.

*Jerusalem Daybook* (Poems and Prose). Wellington: Price Milburn, 1971.

*Autumn Testament: Poetry and Prose Journal*. Wellington: Price Milburn, 1972.

*Runes*. London: Oxford University Press, 1973.

*The Labyrinth: Some Uncollected Poems 1944–72*. Chosen by J.E. Weir. Wellington: Oxford University Press, 1974.

*The Tree House and Other Poems for Children*. Wellington: Price Milburn, 1972.

*The Bone Chanter: Unpublished Poems 1945–72*. Chosen and Introduced by J. E. Weir. Wellington: Oxford University Press, 1976.

*The Holy Life and Death of Concrete Grady: Various Uncollected and Unpublished Poems*. Chosen and Introduced by J. E. Weir. Wellington: Oxford University Press, 1976.

*Collected Poems*. Ed. J. E. Weir. Wellington: Oxford University Press, 1981.

b. Other Works

*Recent Trends in New Zealand Poetry*. Christchurch: The Caxton Press, 1951.

*The Fire and the Anvil: Notes on Modern Poetry.* Wellington: New Zealand University Press, 1955.

*Aspects of Poetry in New Zealand.* Christchurch: The Caxton Press, 1967.

*The Man on the Horse.* Dunedin: University of Otago Press, 1967.

*The Flowering Cross.* Dunedin: New Zealand Tablet, 1969.

*James K. Baxter as Critic: A Selection from his Literary Criticism.* Ed. Frank McKay. Auckland: Heinemann Educational Books, 1978.

*Horse.* Auckland: Oxford University Press, 1985.

c. Contributions to Books

Introduction. *The Memoirs of John Macmillan Brown.* By John Macmillan Brown. Christchurch: Whitcombe & Tombs, 1974. xxxiv-xxxvi.

d. Contributions to Periodicals

'Now while the bugles blare.' *The Link: Organ of the New Zealand Methodist Bible Class Movements* XVI.9 (5 Jul 1943): 3.

'Development.' *Critic* XX.1 (Mar 1944): 3.

'Hill-country.' *Critic* XX.1 (Mar 1944): 6.

'Tulips.' *Critic* XX.1 (Mar 1944) 6.

'The Poet.' *Critic* XX.1 (Mar 1944): 7.

'Convoys.' *Otago Daily Times* 25 May 1944: 2.

'Horatian Ode: On the Banishment of Beer.' *Critic* XX (Jun 1944): 7. [Signed 'I. Marvel']

'Spring.' *Critic* XX.10 (Sep 1944): 4.

'The Sea Stayed.' *Critic* XX.10 (Sep 1944): 10.

'Song.' *Art in New Zealand* XVII.3 (Apr–May 1945): 44.

'Easter Sonnet.' *Art in New Zealand* XVII.3 (Apr–May 1945): 44.

'Poetry in New Zealand.' *Yearbook of the Arts in New Zealand* 2 (1946): 111–14.

'The Furies.' *Canta* XIX.8 (7 Jul 1948): 4.

'Manifesto.' *Canta* XIX.8 (7 Jul 1948): 4.

'To Accidie.' *Canta* XIX.8 (7 Jul 1948): 4.

'To Wake the Nations Underground.' *Canta* XIX.8 (7 Jul 1948): 4.

'Salvation Army Aesthete.' *Canta* XIX.9 (21 Jul 1948): 4.

'Before Sunrise.' Short story. *Canta* XIX.9 (21 Jul 1948): 6.

'Barrage Against Bawdiness.' *Canta* XIX.10 (4 Aug 1948): 4.

'Bolshies Under the Bed.' *Canta* XIX.11 (18 Aug 1948): 4.

'Desert Song.' *Canta* XIX.11 (18 Aug 1948): 4.

'Why Writers Stop Writing.' *Hilltop* I.3 (Sep 1949): 26–7.

Rev. of *Man Alone* by John Mulgan. *Landfall* III (1949): 374–6.

Introduction. *Verse 1951* (1951): 5.

'Choice of Belief in Modern Society (version of an address given at Curious Cove Congress).' *Canta* XXIII.3 (9 Apr 1952): 1, 8.

'Social Delinquency in Modern Literature.' *Critic* XXVIII. 9 (24 Jul 1952): 7.

'Plane Trip South.' *New Zealand Listener* 687 (5 Sep 1952): 13.

Rev. of *The Letters of Emily Dickinson* by Emily Dickinson. *New Zealand Listener* 687 (5 Sep 1952): 13.

'The Maori Motif.' *Here and Now* III.3 (Dec 1952): 51.

'The Man I Might Have Been (with apologies to Henry Lawson)'. *Here and Now* III.11 (Sep 1953): 27

'Student's Song.' *Salient Literary Issue* (Sep 1953): 15.

'Notes Towards an Aesthetic.' *Salient Literary Issue* (Sep 1953): 28.

'Is There a Colour Bar in New Zealand?' *Student* (Sep 1953): 9.

Rev. of *Selected Letters of Robert Burns* by Robert Burns. *New Zealand Listener* 760 (12 Feb 1954): 10–11.

'Dylan Thomas.' Letter. *New Zealand Listener* 763 (5 Mar 1954): 4.

Rev. of *A Hopkins Reader* compiled by John Pick. *New Zealand Listener* 772 (7 May 1954): 13.

'Poetry in New Zealand.' Letter. *New Zealand Listener* 776 (4 Jun 1954): 5.

Rev. of *Letters of William Wordsworth* by William Wordsworth. *New Zealand Listener* 798 (5 Nov 1954): 13–14.

'Dante in the Antipodes.' *Numbers* 2.2 (Nov 1954): 1–2.

Rev. of *A Vision of Beasts and God* by George Barker. *Numbers* 2.2 (Nov 1954): 38–9.

'The Phoenix and the Crow: A Parable.' *Spike* (1954): 57–9.

'Lament for Barney Flanagan, Licensee of the Hesperus Hotel.' *Spike* (1954): 61–2.

Rev. of *The Letters of John Keats* by John Keats. *New Zealand Listener* 813 (18 Feb 1955): 12.

Rev. of *Strangers and Beasts* by Keith Sinclair. *New Zealand Listener* 828 (10 Jun 1955): 12.

'The World of the Creative Artist.' *Salient Literary Issue* (Sep 1955): 20–26.

'The Critic as Schoolmaster.' *Numbers* 4.1 (Oct 1955): 2–3.

'Outlook for Poetry.' *New Zealand Poetry Yearbook* V (1955): 7–9.

'The Town That Sank Under the Sea.' *Otago Daily Times* 28 Jan 1956: 4.

Rev. of *Homosexuality and the Western Christian Tradition* by P.S. Bailey. *New Zealand Listener* 861 (3 Feb 1956): 12–13.

Rev. of *The Burning Cactus* by Stephen Spender. *New Zealand Listener* 863 (17 Feb 1956): 16.

Rev. of *Adventures of the Skin Trade* by Dylan Thomas. *New Zealand Listener* 863 (17 Feb 1956): 16.

'A Note on Henry Lawson.' *Meanjin* (Mar 1956): 33.

'Letter to Australia.' *Meanjin* (Mar 1956): 42.

'Reflections on a Varsity Career.' *Salient* XX.6 (22 Jun 1956): 6.

'Talking of Writing.' *Here and Now* 52 (Jul 1956): 22.

'Dylan Thomas and Swinburne.' Letter. *New Zealand Listener* 906 (14 Dec 1956): 5.

'The Town Under the Sea.' *Meanjin* (Summer 1956): 341–2.

'Walking Up Castle Street.' *Meanjin* (Summer 1956): 343–4.

'Resolutions at Thirty.' *Here and Now* 58 (Mar 1957): 17.

Rev. of *The Descent Into the Cave, and Other Poems* by James Kirkup. *New Zealand Listener* 948 (11 Oct 1957): 12.

Rev. of *Pegasus and Other Poems* by C. Day Lewis. *New Zealand Listener* 948 (11 Oct 1957): 12.

Rev. of *Visitations* by Louis MacNeice. *New Zealand Listener* 948 (11 Oct 1957): 12.

Rev. of *Leftover Life to Kill* by Caitlin Thomas. *New Zealand Listener* 948 (11 Oct 1957): 12.

Rev. of *The Stones of Troy* by C.A. Trypanis. *New Zealand Listener* 948 (11 Oct 1957): 12.

Rev. of *Passion and Society* by Denis de Rougemont. *New Zealand Listener* 948 (11 Oct 1957): 12.

Rev. of *Collected Poems, 1930–1955* by George Barker. *New Zealand Listener* 995 (12 Sep 1958): 13–14.

'A Writer's Vocation.' *Manuka* (1958): 11–12.

'The Fuss About Numbers.' Letter. *New Zealand Listener* 1033 (12 Jun 1959): 17.

Rev. of *Vision and Rhetoric: Studies in Modern Poetry* by G.S. Fraser. *New Zealand Listener* 1036 (3 Jul 1959): 13.

'Writers in New Zealand: a questionnaire.' *Landfall* XIV (1960): 36ff (Baxter's answers on pp.41–2).

'Essay on the Higher Learning.' *Spike* (1961): 61–4.

'The Virgin and the Unicorn.' *Zealandia* XXVIII. 34 (7 Dec 1961): 49.

'Writing and Existence.' *Education* XII.7 (Aug 1963): 16–19.

'The Power of Mrs. Grundy.' *Salient* XXVII.3 (2 Apr 1964): 2.

'Conversation About Writing.' *New Zealand Monthly Review* 60 (Sep 1965): 28.

Rev. of *The Faber Book of Twentieth Century Verse* eds. John Heath-Stubbs and David Wright. *New Zealand Listener* 1363 (19 Nov 1965): 18–19.

Rev. of *The Faber Book of Modern Verse* Ed. Michael Roberts. *New Zealand Listener* 1363 (19 Nov 1965): 18–19.

'Recollections of School Days.' *New Zealand Monthly Review* 65 (Mar 1966): 17–19.

'What is a Poem.' Letter. *New Zealand Listener* 1411 (28 Oct 1966): 10.

'Shots Around the Target.' *Chaff* XVIV.2 (Sep 1966). See also *Eikon* 2 (Dec 1966): 16.

'Baxter: The Human Being is Object and Subject.' *Critic* XLIII.12 (5 Sep 1967): 20.

'Kiwi Habits.' *Otago University Review* (1967): 3–10.

'Thinking About Mountains.' *Poet* IX.5 (May 1968): 3–4.

'The Burns Fellowship.' *Landfall* XXII (1968): 243–7.

'A Problem of Authorship.' *Mate* 17 (Jul 1969): 32–5.

'Last Retreat of a Senile Poet.' *Salient* XXXII. 25 (9 Oct 1969): 18.

'Letter to a Catholic Poet.' *Dialectic* 6 (Aug 1970): 23–7.

'A Postscript to a Postscript.' *Dialectic* 7 (Oct 1970): 30–2.

'Jottings.' *Tuatara* 8/9 (Fall 1972): 120–4.

'The Published Thoughts of James K. Baxter.' *Zealandia* XXXVII.45 (5 Nov 1972): 12.

'An Interview with James K. Baxter.' Interviewed by J.E. Weir. *Landfall* 111, 28.3 (Sep 1974): 241–50.

## 2. WORKS BY OTHERS

**In Manuscript**

Alcock, Peter C.M. 'James K. Baxter and the terror of history: the de-colonisation of a New Zealander.' Draft paper. VUW Library. MS McKay item 9/8.

Baigent, Lawrence. 'Interview with Lawrence Baigent, 14/2/78' and 'Conversation with Lawrence Baigent'. Transcript of interview conducted by Dr. F. McKay. VUW Library. MS McKay item 1/19.

——. Letter to Dr. F. McKay. 19 May 1982. VUW Library. MS McKay item 10/6/2.

——. Letter to James K. Baxter. 17 Oct 1944. Hocken Library. MS 975/183.

——. Letter to James K. Baxter. 21 Dec 1944. Hocken Library. MS 975/183.

Baxter, Archibald. Five poems transcribed by James K. Baxter into his third poetry notebook: 'Spirits of Harmony, Music and Love', 'Great Universe, how Vast', 'Loud calls the voice of Reason', 'O my Brothers', and 'Death'. See MS Hocken 704/3, pp.65–71.

——. Three poems transcribed by James K. Baxter into his tenth poetry notebook: 'Simons Town', 'Burns', and 'We had no fear . . .'. See MS Hocken 704/10, following poem 651 on p.177.

——. One poem transcribed by James K. Baxter into his twelfth poetry notebook: 'His voice it is the low vast tone . . .'. See MS Hocken 704/12 following poem 765 on p.155.

Baxter, Lenore. Letter to Dr F. McKay. 7 Jul 1985. VUW Library. MS McKay item 10/7/32.

——. Letter to Dr F. McKay. Undated. VUW Library. MS McKay item 10/7/33.

Baxter, Millicent. 'Interview: Mrs A. Baxter—October 1980.' Transcript of interview conducted by Dr. F. McKay. VUW Library. MS McKay item 1/1.

——. 'Interview with Mrs M. Baxter, 25/1/78'. ['Tape 6']. Transcript of interview conducted by Dr. F. McKay. VUW Library. MS McKay item 1/7.

——. 'Mrs M. Baxter. Tape 6, 25/1/78'. Transcript of interview conducted by Dr. F. McKay. VUW Library. MS McKay item 1/8.

——. 'Mrs Baxter. Tape 3'. Recorded *c.*24/1/78. Transcript of interview conducted by Dr. F. McKay. VUW Library. MS McKay item 1/11.

——. 'Tape 1: Interview with Mrs A. Baxter, Dunedin, 23/1/78'. Transcript of interview conducted by Dr. F. McKay. VUW Library. MS McKay item 1/12.

——. 'Mrs Baxter, Tape 11, 24/10/80'. Transcript of interview conducted by Dr. F. McKay. VUW Library. MS McKay item 1/15.

——. 'Mrs Baxter, Tape 30, May 1980. Transcript of interview conducted by Dr. F. McKay. VUW Library. MS McKay item 1/16.

——. 'Mrs Baxter, T13'. Recorded *c.*May 1980. Transcript of interview conducted by Dr. F. McKay. VUW Library. MS McKay item 1/17.

——. 'Tape ___ (?)' Interview with Mrs M. Baxter. Undated. Transcript of interview conducted by Dr. F. McKay. VUW Library. MS McKay item 1/18.

Baxter, Terence J. Personal interview. 11 Dec 1995.

——. 'Interview with Terence Baxter 7 Jul 1984.' Notes of interview conducted by Dr. F. McKay. VUW Library. MS McKay item 1/30.

——. 'Interview: Terence Baxter 8/7/84.' Transcript of interview conducted by Dr. F. McKay. VUW Library. MS McKay item 1/31.

——. Letter to James K. Baxter from Hautu Camp, undated [*c.*1942–43]. MS Hocken 975/183.

——. Letter to James K. Baxter from Shannon, undated [*c.*1944–45]. MS Hocken 975/183.

Campbell, Alistair. 'Interview: Alistair Campbell talks to Frank McKay on James K. Baxter.' Transcript of interview conducted by Dr. F. McKay. VUW Library. MS McKay item 2/20.

Curnow, Allen. 'Evening with Allen Curnow, 18 May 1982.' Notes on interview conducted by Dr. F. McKay. VUW Library. MS McKay item 2/21.

Frame, Janet. Letter to James K. Baxter. Undated (*c.* mid 1945). VUW Library. MS McKay 20/1/6.

Gill, Patricia. Letter to Frank McKay. 19 Apr 1983. VUW Library. MS McKay 10/4/21.

——. Letter to Frank McKay. 20 Apr 1983. VUW Library. MS McKay 10/4/22.

——. Letter to Frank McKay. 27 Sep 1983. VUW Library. MS McKay 10/5/17.

Ginn, Myrtle. Letter to James K. Baxter, 7 Jan 1943. Hocken Library. MS 975/183.

Ginn, Noel. Letters to Paul Millar dated as follows: 11 Sep 1994; 30 Dec 1994; 1 Jan 1995; Jan 1995; 2 Mar 1995; 3 Mar 1995; Apr 1995; 17 Apr 1995; 15 May 1995; 11 Jun 1995; 19 Jul 1995; 21 Aug 1995; 14 Sep 1995; 24 Oct 1995; 9 Nov 1995; 12 Nov 1995; 21 Nov 1995.

——. Letter to James K. Baxter 26 Oct 1959. VUW Library. MS McKay 15/7/5.
——. Letter to James K. Baxter 20 Mar 1960. VUW Library. MS McKay 15/7/19.
——. Letter to James K. Baxter 8 May 1960. VUW Library. MS McKay 15/7/26.
——. Letter to Dr. F. McKay. 13 Jan 1983. VUW Library. MS McKay 10/4/17.
——. Letter to Dr. F. McKay. 15 Mar 1983. VUW Library. MS McKay 10/4/18.
——. Letter to Dr. F. McKay. 24 Mar 1983. VUW Library. MS McKay 10/4/19.
——. Letter to Dr. F. McKay. 7 Jan 1985. VUW Library. MS McKay 10/7/9.
——. Letter to Dr. F. McKay. 2 Dec 1984. VUW Library. MS McKay 10/8/18.
——. Personal interview. Aug 1994.
——. Personal interview with Annette Facer. Sep 1994.
——. Personal interview. 25 Oct 1994.
Glover, Denis. 'Tape 17, Denis Glover on Baxter, 5th Jun 1978.' Transcript of interview conducted by Dr. F. McKay. VUW Library. MS McKay item 1/23.
——. 'Interview with Denis Glover 1979.' Transcript of interview conducted by Dr. F. McKay. VUW Library. MS McKay item 1/25.
——. 'Interview: Denis Glover 1979 (Tape 18).' Transcript of interview conducted by Dr. F. McKay. VUW Library. MS McKay item 1/28.
Hargreave, Margaret. Letter to Frank McKay. 17 Nov 1983. VUW Library. MS McKay 10/5/36. This letter contains transcripts of letters Baxter sent to Hargreave.
——. Letter to Frank McKay. 7 Dec 1983. VUW Library. MS McKay 10/5/37.
Lawson, Patricia. Notes on interview conducted by Dr. F. McKay. VUW Library. MS McKay item 9/25.
O'Malley, C. Letter to Noel Ginn, 10 Aug 1969. VUW Library. MS McKay item 15/7/67.
Pascoe, Joan. Letter to Dr. F. McKay. 9 Mar 1980. VUW Library. MS McKay item 10/4/11.
Pugmire, Harold. Letter to Dr. F. McKay. 3 Sep 1985. VUW Library. MS McKay 10/8/10.
——. Letter to Dr. F. McKay. 12 Nov 1983. VUW Library. MS McKay 10/8/11.
Pugmire, S.L. Letter to Dr. F. McKay. 11 Mar 1985. VUW Library. MS McKay 10/7/24.
Still, Margaret. 'Tape: Mrs Still'. Transcript of interview conducted by Dr. F. McKay. VUW Library. MS McKay item 1/22.
——. Letter to Dr. F. McKay. 16 Jun 1980. VUW Library. MS McKay item 10/6/1.

**Published Works by Others**

Adcock, Fleur. Rev. of *The Labyrinth* by James K. Baxter. *Journal of Commonwealth Literature* XII.1 (Aug 1977): 77.
Anon. 'Baxter Case The Conscientious Objector', copied by hand from *Otago Daily Times* 24 Oct 1918: 6. VUW Library. MS McKay item 15/3/4.
Anon. 'Fourth Overseas Ballot.' *The Dominion* 7 Aug 1941: 7.
Anon. 'Life, Death and Baxter.' *Canta* XXVI.7 (16 Jun 1955): 3.
Anon. 'Military Service.' *Otago Daily Times* 20 Dec 1941: 12.
Anon. 'Special Meeting.' *Salient* 3.2 (Apr 1940): 13.
Anon. 'The University and the War.' *Salient* 3.1 (1940): 7.
Baxter, Archibald. *We Will Not Cease.* Whatamongo Bay: Cape Catley, 1980.
Baxter, Millicent. *The Memoirs of Millicent Baxter.* Whatamongo Bay: Cape Catley, 1981.
Beaglehole, J. C. 'Lots of Poetry.' Rev. of *Beyond the Palisade* by James K. Baxter. *New Zealand Listener* 333 (8 Jun 1945): 13.
Bertram, James. 'Two New Zealand Poets.' *Education* II.3 (Jul 1949): 59–61.
——. 'The Poet as Critic.' Rev. of *The Fire and the Anvil* by James K. Baxter. *New Zealand Listener* 866 (9 Mar 1956): 12.
——. 'Poet of Extremes.' *New Zealand Listener* 1724 (20 Nov 1972): 12–13.
——. 'Vintage Baxter.' Rev. of *Runes* by James K. Baxter. *New Zealand Listener* 1762 (20 Aug 1973): 50.
Brasch, Charles. 'Phrases and Poems. Rev. of *Pig Island Letters* by James K. Baxter. *New Zealand Monthly Review* 74 (Dec 1966): 22.
'British Justice.' Letter. 'The Treatment of Conscientious Objectors.' *Otago Daily Times.* 27 Dec 1941: 9.
Burton, Ormond E. *The Auckland Regiment: An Account of the Doings on Active Service of the First, Second and Third Battalions of the Auckland Regiment.* Auckland: Whitcombe & Tombs, 1922.
Campbell, Alistair. 'Impressions of the Earlier Baxter.' *Landfall* 107 (Sep 1973): 179–84.
Crane, Ernest. *I Can Do No Other: A Biography of The Reverend Ormond Burton.* Auckland: Hodder and Stoughton, 1986.

Curnow, Allen, (ed). *A Book of New Zealand Verse 1923–45*. Christchurch: The Caxton Press, 1945.

——. Rev. of *Blow, Wind of Fruitfulness* by James K. Baxter. *Landfall* II (1948): 230–33.

Efford, Lincoln. *Penalties on Conscience: An Examination of the Defaulter's Detention System in New Zealand*. Christchurch: Lincoln Efford, 1945.

Glover, Denis. 'James K. Baxter.' *James K. Baxter 1926–1972, A Memorial Volume*. Ed. Alistair Taylor. Wellington: Alistair Taylor Publishing, 1972. 125.

Grant, David. *Out in the Cold: Pacifists and Conscientious Objectors in New Zealand During World War II*. Auckland: Reed Methuen, 1986.

Joseph, M.K. 'Poems of Exploration.' Rev. of *The Fallen House* by James K. Baxter. *New Zealand Listener* 772 (15 May 1953): 12.

Manhire, Bill. 'Events and Editorials: Baxter's Collected Poems.' *Islands* 8.4 (Jun 1981): 102–20.

McKay, Frank. *The Life of James K. Baxter*. Auckland: Oxford University Press, 1990.

McNaughton, Howard D. 'Baxter's Strong Ghost.' *Landfall* 137, 35.1 (Mar 1981): 62–6.

——. 'Baxter, in Faulty Perspective', rev. of *James K. Baxter 1926–1972, A Memorial Volume*, ed. Alistair Taylor, *Christchurch Press* 10 Mar 1973.

*The New Zealand University Calendar, 1944*. Wellington: Government Printer, 1944.

Oliver, W.H. *James K. Baxter: A Portrait*. Auckland: Godwit Press/Bridget Williams Books, 1994.

O'Sullivan, Vincent. 'After Culloden: Early Poetry of James K. Baxter.' *Islands* 2.1 (1973): 19–30.

——. *James K. Baxter*. Wellington: Oxford University Press, 1976.

——. 'The Sore Thumb of the Tribe.' Rev. of *Collected Poems* by James K. Baxter. *New Zealand Listener* (25 Oct 1980): 84–5.

——. 'Urgently Creating a Past: Remarks on James K. Baxter.' *The Writer's Sense of the Past: Essays on Southeast Asian and Australasian Literature*. Singapore: Singapore University Press, 1987. 94–101.

Pearson, Bill and Peter Olds. 'Two Personal Memories of James K. Baxter.' *Islands* 2.1 (1973): 2–6.

Pugsley, Christopher. *On the Fringe of Hell: New Zealanders and Military Discipline in the First World War*. Auckland: Hodder & Stoughton, 1991.

Riach, Alan. 'James K. Baxter and the Dialect of the Tribe' in *Opening the Book: New Essays on New Zealand Writing*. Auckland: Auckland University Press, 1995. 105–22.

Sharp, Iain. 'My Grudge Against Baxter.' *Quote Unquote* Aug 1994: 14.

Smithyman, Kendrick. Rev. of *The Fallen House* by James K. Baxter. *Here and Now* III.8 (Jun 1953): 31–2.

Stead, C. K. 'Towards Jerusalem: Later Baxter Verse.' *Islands* 2.1 (1973): 7–18.

Sturm, Terry, (ed). *The Oxford History of New Zealand Literature in English*. Auckland: Oxford University Press, 1991.

Taylor, Alistair, ed. *James K. Baxter 1926–1972, A Memorial Volume*. Wellington: Alistair Taylor Publishing, 1972.

Taylor, Nancy M. *The Home Front: The New Zealand People at War. Official History of New Zealand in the Second World War 1939–45*. 2 Vols. Wellington: Historic Publications Branch of Internal Affairs, 1986.

'Veteran New Zealand Peace Campaigner Dies.' *Otago Daily Times* 4 Jul 1984: 5.

Weir, J.E. 'The Green Inn: Some reflections on the Poetry of James K. Baxter.' *Comment* 40 (Apr 1970): 22–8.

——. 'A Voice for the Living: James K. Baxter 1926–72.' *Education* 22.1 (1973): 27–30.

——. 'An Interview with James K. Baxter.' *Landfall* 111, 28.3 (Sep 1974): 241–50.

——. Introduction. *The Bone Chanter: Unpublished Poems 1945–72* by James K. Baxter. Wellington: Oxford University Press, 1976. 5–8.

——. Introduction. *Collected Poems* by James K. Baxter. Wellington: Oxford University Press, 1981. xxi-xxvii.

——. *The Poetry of James K. Baxter*. Wellington: Oxford University Press, 1970.

## SECONDARY MATERIAL

Items prefaced * indicate books that belonged to James K. Baxter and remain in the possession of his family.

* Arnold, Matthew. *Poems*. Ed. Henry Newbold. London: Thomas Nelson, undated.

——. *The Poetical Works of Matthew Arnold*. London: Geoffrey Cumberledge/Oxford University Press, 1953.

Auden, W.H. *Collected Poems*. Ed. Edward Mendelson. London: Faber & Faber, 1976.

——. *The English Auden: Poems, Essays and Dramatic Writings 1927–1939*. Ed. Edward Mendelson. London: Faber & Faber, 1977.

Barber, Laurie. *New Zealand: A Short History*. Auckland: Century Hutchinson, 1989.

Barker, George. *Collected Poems: 1930–1955*. London: Faber & Faber, 1957.

Barnes, Jonathan Ed. *The Cambridge Companion to Aristotle*. Cambridge: Cambridge University Press, 1995.

Blake, William. *Poems of Blake*. Ed. Laurence Binyon. London: Macmillan, 1931.

Blake, William. *The Portable Blake*. Selected by Alfred Kazin. New York: Penguin, 1976.

Bold, Alan. *A Burns Companion*. London: Macmillan, 1991.

Bridges, Robert. *The Testament of Beauty: A Poem in Four Books*. Oxford: Clarendon Press, 1929.

*British and New Zealand War Pictures*. Exhibition Catalogue. London: Great Britain Ministry of Information, 1942.

Brontë, Emily. *Wuthering Heights*. Ed. Ian Jack. Oxford: Oxford University Press, 1981.

Browning, Elizabeth Barrett. *Selected Poems*. London: Chatto & Windus, 1988.

* Browning, Robert. *Poems of Robert Browning*. Ed. John Buchan. London: Macmillan, 1913.

——. *The Poetical Works of Robert Browning*. London: Geoffrey Cumberledge/Oxford University Press, 1953.

Burns, Robert. *The Poetical Works of Robert Burns*. London: Geoffrey Cumberledge/Oxford University Press, 1950.

* Caldwell, Thomas (ed). *The Golden Book of Modern English Poetry*. London: J.M. Dent & Sons, 1940.

Candlin, Clara M. (trans.). *Herald Wind: The Herald Wind, Translations of Sung Dynasty Poems, Lyrics and Songs*. Wisdom of the East Series. London: John Murray, 1935.

* Carlyle, Thomas. *Carlyle's Essays on Burns*. London: Blackice and Son, undated.

Clare, John. *Selected Poems*. Eds. J.W Tibble and Anne Tibble. London: J.M. Dent & Sons, 1973.

Clark, Oliver Fielding. *Introduction to Berdyaev*. London: G. Bles, 1950.

Coleridge, Samuel Taylor. *The Poems of Samuel Taylor Coleridge*. London: Geoffrey Cumberledge/Oxford University Press, 1952.

* Crabbe, George. *Poems by the Rev. George Crabbe*. London: I.J. Chidley, 1847.

Curnow, Allen. *Enemies: Poems 1934–36* . Christchurch: The Caxton Press, 1937.

——. *Island & Time*. Christchurch: The Caxton Press, 1941.

Davenport-Hines, Richard. *Auden*. Heinemann: London, 1995.

Day Lewis, Cecil. *Collected Poems*. London: Jonathan Cape/Hogarth Press, 1954.

De La Mare, Walter. *The Complete Poems of Walter De La Mare*. London: Faber & Faber, 1969.

Dowling, Basil. *A Day's Journey: Poems*. Christchurch: The Caxton Press, 1941.

Eckermann. *Conversations with Goethe*. Trans. John Oxenford. London: J.M. Dent & Sons, 1930.

Eliot, T. S. Collected *Poems: 1909–1935*. London: Faber & Faber, 1936.

——. Introduction. *Ezra Pound: Selected Poems* by Ezra Pound. London: Faber & Faber, 1934.

——. *Selected Essays*. London: Faber & Faber, 1951.

Faulkner, William. *Light in August*. London: Chatto & Windus, 1952.

Flecker, James Elroy. *The Collected Poems of James Elroy Flecker*. London: Secker & Warburg, 1946.

Freud, Sigmund. *Beyond the Pleasure Principle*. Trans. James Strachey. New York: Liveright, 1970.

Gibran, Kahlil. *The Prophet*. New York: Knopf, 1968.

Goethe, Johann Wolfgang von. *Poetry and Truth From My Own Life*. Trans. Minna Steele Smith. 2 Vols. London: Bell, 1913.

Gordon, Ian. 'In Memoriam "NZNW."' *New Zealand Listener* 2293 (21 Jan 1984): 31.

Herbert, A. P. *Laughing Ann and Other Poems*. London: Ernest Benn, 1925.

Homer. *The Odyssey*. Trans. Robert Fitzgerald. London: Everyman, 1992.

Hopkins, Gerard Manly. *Poems of Gerard Manly Hopkins*. London: Geoffrey Cumberledge/ Oxford University Press, 1952.

Horace. *The Odes of Horace*. Trans. James Michie. Harmondsworth: Penguin, 1964.

Housman, A.E. *The Collected Poems of A.E. Housman*. London: Jonathan Cape, 1939.

Hydrographic Office, Great Britain, Admiralty. *The New Zealand Pilot: comprising the coasts of the North and South Islands of New Zealand, Stewart Island and adjacent islands, Kermadec, Chatham, Bounty, Antipodes,*

*Auckland and Campbell Islands*. 10th ed. London: H.M.S.O., 1930.

Jack, Peter Monro. Rev. of *New Poems 1940* edited by Oscar Williams. *New York Times* 14 Sep 1941: 6.2.

Jackson, Laura Riding. *The Poems of Laura Riding*. Manchester: Carcanet New Press, 1980.

Joyce, James. *A Portrait of the Artist as a Young Man*. London: Grafton Books, 1964.

——. *The Dubliners*. New York: Viking Press, 1969.

Keats, John. *The Poetical Works of John Keats*. Ed. H. Buxton Forman. London: Geoffrey Cumberledge/Oxford University Press, 1953.

Keyes, Sidney A. K. *The Cruel Solstice*. London: Routledge, 1944.

Lawrence, D. H. *Complete Poems*. Ed. Vivian de Sola Pinto and Warren Roberts. New York: Viking Press, 1964.

Leavis, F. R. *New Bearings in English Poetry: A Study of the Contemporary Situation*. London: Chatto & Windus, 1932.

* Ledward, Patricia and Colin Strang (eds). *Poems of This War by Younger Poets*. Cambridge: Cambridge University Press, 1942.

Levin, Harry, ed. *The Essential James Joyce*. Harmondsworth: Penguin, 1968.

* MacNeice, Louis. *Autumn Journal*. London: Faber & Faber, 1943. [Inscribed 'To Jim from Noel']

——. 'Snow' in *Poems of Tomorrow: An Anthology of Contemporary Verse*. Ed. Janet Adam Smith. London: Chatto & Windus, 1935.

——. *The Poetry of W.B. Yeats*. London: Oxford University Press, 1941.

Madge, Charles. *The Father Found*. London: Faber & Faber, 1941.

Marlowe, Christopher. *Doctor Faustus and Other Plays*. Oxford: Oxford University Press, 1995.

Mason, R.A.K. *End of the Day*. Christchurch: The Caxton Press, 1936.

Masefield, John Edward. *Dauber*. London: William Heinemann, 1913.

——. *Lollingdon Downs and Other Poems, With Sonnets*. London: Heinemann, 1917.

Maxwell, Val. *Southern Sails: 100 years of the Otago Yacht Club*. Dunedin: Otago Yacht Club, 1995.

Miles, Geoffrey. 'A Short Mythical History of the World.' Unpublished course paper.

Milton, John. *The Poetical Works of John Milton*. London: Geoffrey Cumberledge/Oxford University Press, 1950.

Monro, Harold. *Collected Poems*. London: Cobden-Sanderson, 1933.

——. *Strange Meetings*. London: Poetry Bookshop, 1917.

Murry, John Middleton. *Son of Woman: The Story of D.H. Lawrence*. London: Jonathan Cape, 1931.

Ovid. *Metamorphoses*. Trans. A.D. Melville. Oxford: Oxford University Press, 1986.

Owen, Wilfred. *Poems*. London: Chatto & Windus, 1931.

Pound Ezra. *Ezra Pound: Selected Poems*. London: Faber & Faber, 1934.

* Quiller-Couch, Sir Arthur ed. *The Oxford Book of English Verse, 1250–1918*. Oxford: Clarendon Press, 1939.

Radice, Betty. *Who's Who in the Ancient World: A Handbook to the Survivors of the Greek and Roman Classics*. London: Penguin, 1973.

* Read, Herbert. *Thirty-Five Poems*. London: Faber & Faber, 1940.

——. *Collected Poems*. London: Faber & Faber, 1946.

Rilke, Rainer Maria. *The Duino Elegies*. Trans. Stephen Garmey and Jay Wilson. New York: Harper and Row, 1972.

* Rimbaud, Arthur. *Selected Verse Poems of Arthur Rimbaud*. Trans. Norman Cameron. London: Hogarth, 1942.

Roberts, Michael, (ed). *The Faber Book of Modern Verse*. London: Faber & Faber, 1936.

Sargeson, Frank. *A Man and His Wife*. Christchurch: The Caxton Press, 1940.

——. *Conversations with My Uncle and Other Sketches*. Auckland: Unicorn Press, 1936.

Sassoon, Siegfried. *Poems Newly Selected, 1916–1935*. London: Faber & Faber, 1940.

——. *Selected Poems*. London: Heinemann, 1925.

* Scarfe, Francis. *Auden and After: The Liberation of Poetry, 1930–1941*. London: George Routledge, 1943.

Shackleton, Major Sir Ernest Henry. *The Heart of the Antarctic*. London: William Heinemann, 1909.

——. *South*. London: William Heinemann, 1919.

Shakespeare, William. *A Midsummer Night's Dream*. Ed. Peter Holland. Oxford: Oxford University Press, 1994.

——. *Macbeth*. Ed. Nicholas Brooke. Oxford: Oxford University Press, 1994.

——. *The Tempest*. London: Penguin, 1968.

Shelley, Percy Bysshe. *The Complete Poetical Works of Percy Bysshe Shelley*. Ed. Thomas Hutchinson. London: Humphrey Milford/ Oxford University Press, 1919.

Shrimpton, A.W. (ed). *Countess of Liverpool's Gift Book of Art and Literature.* Christchurch: Whitcombe & Tombs, 1915.

Shuker, Roy. *Educating the Workers?: A History of the Workers Education Association.* Palmerston North: Dunmore, 1984.

Smith, Janet Adam (ed). *Poems of Tomorrow: An Anthology of Contemporary Verse.* London: Chatto & Windus, 1935.

Spender, Stephen. *Ruins and Visions.* London: Faber & Faber, 1942.

Spenser, Edmund. *Edmund Spenser's Poetry.* Ed. Hugh Maclean. New York: Norton, 1982.

Stevenson, Robert Louis. *Memories and Portraits.* London: Chatto & Windus, 1909.

Stover, Sue. 'Being a Pacifist Proved Far From Peaceful'. *New Zealand Herald* 22 Sep 1979: 2: 1.

Tagore, Rabindranath. *Gitanjali.* London: Macmillan, 1957.

Thomas, Dylan. *Collected Poems: 1934–53.* London: J.M. Dent & Sons, 1988.

——. *Portrait of the Artist as a Young Dog.* London: J.M. Dent & Sons, 1940.

Thompson, Francis. *The Poems of Francis Thompson.* London: Oxford University Press, 1951.

Thoreau, Henry David. *Walden, or Life in the Woods.* Ed. Lyndon Shanley. Princeton: Princeton University Press, 1971.

Tolstoy, Leo. *The Portable Tolstoy.* Harmondsworth: Penguin, 1968.

Tripp, Edward. *The Meridian Handbook of Classical Mythology.* New York: Penguin, 1970.

Tsuzuki, Chushichi. *Edward Carpenter, 1844–1929: Prophet of Human Fellowship.* Cambridge: Cambridge University Press, 1980.

Virgil. *The Aeneid.* Trans. Robert Fitzgerald. London: Everyman, 1992.

——. *The Eclogues—The Georgics.* Trans. C. Day Lewis. Oxford: Oxford University Press, 1983.

Wilde, Oscar. *Complete Works of Oscar Wilde.* London: Collins, 1989.

Williams, Oscar (ed). *New Poems 1940.* New York: Yardstick Press, 1941.

* Wollman, Maurice (ed). *Poems of Twenty Years: An Anthology 1918–1938.* London: Macmillan, 1938. [Baxter has inscribed his juvenile poem 'The Mountain Spirit' inside the front cover.]

Wordsworth, William. *The Poetical Works of William Wordsworth.* London: Ward, Lock, undated.

Yeats. *The Collected Poems of W.B. Yeats.* London: Macmillan, 1955.

——. *The Variorum edition of the Poems of W.B. Yeats.* Eds. Peter Allt and Russell K. Alspach. New York: Macmillan, 1957.


**Frequently Consulted Reference Works**


Chadwyck-Healey. *English Poetry Full-Text Database,* on 5 CD-Rom Discs. London: Chadwyck-Healey, 1996.

Drabble, Margaret (ed). *The Oxford Companion to English Literature.* Oxford: Oxford University Press, 1985.

Hart, James David and Philip Leininger (eds). *The Oxford Companion to American Literature.* Oxford: Oxford University Press, 1995.

Van Antwerp, Margaret A. et al, (eds). *The Dictionary of Literary Biography Documentary Series.* Detroit: Gale, 1982–[1996].

# Index of Poems by Baxter

Page numbers in **bold** indicate quotation of the complete text of a poem

# Index of Poems by Ginn

Page numbers in **bold** indicate quotation of the complete text of a poem

# General Index to the Introduction and Letters